Lecture Notes in Computer Scie T0238595

Commenced Publication in 1973
Founding and Former Series Editors:
Gerhard Goos, Juris Hartmanis, and Jan van Leeuwen

Editorial Board

Bob Coecke   Luke Ong
Prakash Panangaden (Eds.)

Computation, Logic, Games, and Quantum Foundations

The Many Facets of Samson Abramsky

Essays Dedicated to Samson Abramsky
on the Occasion of His 60th Birthday

 Springer

Volume Editors

Bob Coecke
Luke Ong
University of Oxford, Department of Computer Science
Parks Road, Wolfson Building, Oxford OX1 3QD, UK
E-mail: {bob.coecke, luke.ong}@cs.ox.ac.uk

Prakash Panangaden
McGill University, Department of Computer Science
3480 Rue University, Montréal, QC, H3A 0E9, Canada
E-mail: prakash@cs.mcgill.ca

ISSN 0302-9743　　　　　　　　　　　e-ISSN 1611-3349
ISBN 978-3-642-38163-8　　　　　　　e-ISBN 978-3-642-38164-5
DOI 10.1007/978-3-642-38164-5
Springer Heidelberg Dordrecht London New York

Library of Congress Control Number: 2013936943

CR Subject Classification (1998): F.3, F.1, F.4, D.2.4, D.2-3, I.2.2-4, D.1, E.1

LNCS Sublibrary: SL 1 – Theoretical Computer Science and General Issues

Typesetting: Camera-ready by author, data conversion by Scientific Publishing Services, Chennai, India

Printed on acid-free paper

Springer is part of Springer Science+Business Media (www.springer.com)

Samson Abramsky

Preface

When one encounters Samson Abramsky it is hard to believe that he is 60, but when one attempts to survey his work it is equally hard to believe that he is only 60! The three editors of this volume have known Samson for a long time, the last two since the mid-1980s and the first since the early years of this century. In that period Samson's interests have undergone a number of striking changes. The papers in this volume reflect this variety and give some indication of the depth of his contributions in these areas.

His first publication in 1982 was on programming distributed systems; a surprise perhaps for all those who know him as an outstanding theoretician but a good indication of why his theoretical work has been grounded in computational practice. The third editor was struggling to understand the semantics of nondeterministic dataflow networks in 1983 when he encountered a paper called "Semantic Foundations of Applicative Multiprogramming." His reaction at the time was, "this guy thinks he has solved all the hard problems in this area," but a closer look led him to exclaim, "he has solved all the hard problems!" This paper was an inspiration to him and led to his subsequent work on concurrency. They met shortly thereafter and have enjoyed a fruitful scientific relationship as well as a warm friendship ever since.

The second editor was Samson Abramsky's first PhD student and wrote a thesis on the semantics of the lazy λ-calculus. This led to an interest in the full abstraction problem, which they solved in spectacular fashion in two independent but closely related approaches based on games. Subsequently Samson and his students studied many different language features and showed how the games paradigm allows a unified view of many programming language features.

The first editor, while still in the process of making some suicidal career moves within the then hibernating field of quantum foundations, came across Samson's work with Vickers on quantales as algebras of processes in the late 1990s. He was saved by Samson from the academic gutter in 2001 (on the advice of the third editor!) and began his collaboration with Samson on categorical quantum mechanics. This began with a famous paper in the *Proceedings of IEEE Symposium on Logic in Computer Science 2004*, the first on quantum computing ever accepted to LiCS, and this activity has grown into a large group at Oxford with close to 40 members today. It is fair to say that the categorical approach and the still growing group have been instrumental both in establishing quantum computing as a thriving field within the computer science community, as well as in the revival of the field of quantum foundations as a whole, an area in which Samson has been primarily involved in the last few years. It has even had successes in database analysis, computational linguistics, and relativistic aspects of quantum mechanics.

Samson's work in the 1980s was largely in the area of programming language semantics. He made key contributions to concurrency theory, domain theory, and abstract interpretation. Perhaps his most famous paper from this era was "Domain Theory in Logical Form," which connected many different threads in semantics: modal logic, domain theory, Stone-type duality.

In the early 1990s he began to think deeply about linear logic, which had been introduced by Girard in 1987. He produced his influential unpublished work on linear realizability algebra, which allowed one to think of linear logic as a programming language. In 1991 Radha Jagadeesan completed his PhD under the supervision of the third editor and went on to be Samson's post-doc at Imperial College and joined in the linear logic enterprise. They produced another classic influential paper, "Games and Full Completeness for Multiplicative Linear Logic," which built on an earlier paper "New Foundations for the Geometry of Interaction" in the *Proceedings of IEEE Symposium on Logic in Computer Science 1992*.

The game approach led to the resolution of the long-standing PCF full abstraction problem by Abramsky, Jagadeesan, and Malacaria, and by Hyland and Ong, and by Nickau. These papers laid the foundations of game semantics and have led to several PhD theses and a revolution in the understanding of programming language semantics.

In 2004, Samson was elected a Fellow of the Royal Society. In 2007 he received the LiCS "Test of Time" award for his paper on "Domain Theory in Logical Form."

The papers in this volume represent his manifold contributions to semantics, logic, games, and quantum mechanics. The papers of Hoare, Plotkin, Mislove, Jung, Honsell and Lenisa, Martin, and Vickers represent the programming languages and domain theory phase of Samson's interests. His interest in category theory is represented by the papers of Fiore and Devesas Campos, Melies, and Pavlovic. His interest in games both for logic and for computation is well represented by the papers of Hankin and Malacaria, van Benthem, Clairambault, Gutierrez and Winskel, Murawski and Tzevelekos, Väänänen, and Ghica who even applies these ideas to hardware design.

The remaining papers are all from the "quantum phase" of Samson's interests and include papers from physicists (Hardy), former physicists (Panangaden), economists (Brandenburger), category theorists (Malherbe, Scott and Selinger, and Yanofsky), computer scientists (Nagarajan and Gay) and logicians (Keisler), as well as current and former members of the Oxford group (Coecke, Kissinger and Heunen, and Hines). We hope that Samson enjoys reading these papers as much as we enjoyed putting this collection together.

March 2013

Bob Coecke
Luke Ong
Prakash Panangaden

Organization

Program Committee

Bob Coecke	University of Oxford, UK
Ross Duncan	Université Libre Bruxelles, Belgium
Dan Ghica	University of Birmingham, UK
Chris Heunen	University of Oxford, UK
Peter Hines	University of York, UK
Radha Jagadeesan	DePaul University, USA
Achim Jung	University of Birmingham, UK
Aleks Kissinger	University of Oxford, UK
Luke Ong	University of Oxford, UK
Prakash Panangaden	McGill University, Canada
Noson Yanofsky	Brooklyn College, USA

Samson Abramsky's Doctoral Students

Former Students and Their Theses

- Luke Ong: *The Lazy Lambda Calculus: an Investigation into the Foundations of Functional Programming*, Imperial College London, 1988.
- David Fuller: *Partial Evaluation and Logic Programming*, Imperial College London, 1989.
- Bent Thomsen: *Calculi for Higher Order Communicating Systems*, Imperial College London, 1991.
- Ian Mackie: *The Geometry of Implementation: Applications of the Geometry of Interaction to Language Implementation*, Imperial College London, 1994.
- Simon Gay: *Linear Types for Communicating Processes*, Imperial College London, 1995.
- Guy McCusker: *Games and Full Abstraction for a Functional Metalanguage with Recursive Types*, Imperial College London, 1996.
- Rajagopal Nagarajan: *Typed Concurrent Programs: Specification & Verification*, Imperial College London, 1998.
- Jim Laird: *A Semantic Analysis of Control*, University of Edinburgh, 1999.
- José Espírito Santo: *Conservative Extensions of the Lambda-Calculus for the Computational Interpretation of Sequent Calculus*, University of Edinburgh, 2002.
- Juliusz Chroboczek: *Game Semantics and Subtyping*, University of Edinburgh, 2003.
- Jan Jurjens: *Principles for Secure Systems Design*, University of Edinburgh, 2004.
- Ross Duncan: *Types for Quantum Computing*, University of Oxford, 2007.
- Nikos Tzevelekos: *Nominal Game Semantics*, University of Oxford, 2008.
- William Edwards: *Non-locality in Categorical Quantum Mechanics*, University of Oxford, 2009.
- Jacob Biamonte: *Categorical Models of Quantum Information in Many-Body Systems*, University of Oxford, 2010.
- Alexander Kissinger: *Pictures of Processes: Automated Graph Rewriting for Monoidal Categories and Applications to Quantum Computing*, University of Oxford, 2011.
- Andrei Akhvlediani: *Relating Types in Categorical Universal Algebra*, University of Oxford, 2012.

Current Students at the University of Oxford

- Philip Atzemoglou: *Higher-Order Semantics for Quantum Programming Languages with Classical Control.*
- Miriam Backens: *Classical vs. Quantum in Graphical Models.*
- Carmen Constantin: *Aspects of the Topos Approach to Quantum Theory.*
- Abhishek Dasgupta: *Frameworks for Parallelising Machine Learning Using Generic Inference.*
- Nadish de Silva: *Geometric Aspects of Quantum Phase Space.*
- Raymond Lal: *Causal Structure in Categorical Quantum Mechanics.*
- Shane Mansfield: *Approaches to Non-locality and Contextuality in Possibilistic Theories, and Extensions to Probabilistic Theories.*
- Daniel Marsden: *Parameterized Logics and Applications to Quantum Systems.*
- Yoshihiro Maruyama: *Duality, Categorical Logic, and Quantum Symmetry .*
- Alexander Merry: *Foundations for an Interactive Theorem Prover for Graphical Calculi.*
- Hugo Nava Kopp: *Abstract Approach to Entropy.*
- Johan Paulsson: *Between Probabilities and Categories; A Diagrammatic Approach to Foundations of Quantum Theory.*
- Roman Priebe: *The Regular Histories Formulation of Quantum Theory.*
- Rui Soares Barbosa: *Contextuality in Quantum Mechanics.*
- Colin Stephen: *Categories for Tropical Quantum Computing.*
- Norihiro Yamada: *Constructive Mathematics and Proofs as Programs.*
- Vladimir Zamdzhiev: *Graph Grammars and Their Applications to Quantum Computing.*

Tabula Gratulatori

Tony Hoare: Best wishes for your birthday and for long continuation of your inspiring research career: from your precursor at Oxford, Tony.

Alexandru Baltag
Jon Barrett
Johan van Benthem
Richard Blute
Richard Bornat
Adam Brandenburger
Stephen Brookes
Peter Buneman
Bob Coecke
Robert Constable
Ross Duncan
Martin Escardo
Marcelo Fiore
Simon Gay
Dan Ghica
Jeremy Gibbons
Georg Gottlob
Chris Hankin
Lucien Hardy
Chris Heunen
Jane Hillston
Peter Hines
Furio Honsell

Ian Horrocks
Martin Hyland
Radha Jagadeesan
Achim Jung
Elham Kashefi
Juliette Kennedy
Aleks Kissinger
Dexter Kozen
Daniel Kroening
Marta Kwiatkowska
Marina Lenisa
Paul Levy
Ian Mackie
Pasquale Malacaria
Keye Martin
Paul-Andre Mellies
Albert Meyer
Michael Mislove
John Mitchell
Andrzej Murawski
Rajagopal
    Nagarajan
Peter O'Hearn

Luke Ong
Joel Ouaknine
Prakash Panangaden
Dusko Pavlovic
Gordon Plotkin
John Reynolds
Bill Roscoe
Mehrnoosh Sadrzadeh
Dana Scott
Philip Scott
Robert Seely
Peter Selinger
Alex Simpson
Sonja Smets
Nikos Tzevelekos
Jouko Vannanen
Jamie Vicary
Glynn Winskel
Ben Worrell
Noson Yanofsky
Mingsheng Ying

Samson and His Research Group

Samson and His Friends

Table of Contents

Use of a Canonical Hidden-Variable Space in Quantum Mechanics[*]

Adam Brandenburger[1] and H. Jerome Keisler[2]

[1] NYU Stern School of Business, New York University, New York, NY 10012
adam.brandenburger@stern.nyu.edu, www.stern.nyu.edu/~abranden
[2] Department of Mathematics, University of Wisconsin-Madison, Madison, WI 53706
keisler@math.wisc.edu, www.math.wisc.edu/~keisler

Abstract. In Brandenburger and Keisler ([2012b]) we showed that, provided only that the measurement and outcome spaces in an experimental system are measure-theoretically separable, then there is a canonical hidden-variable space, namely the unit interval equipped with Lebesgue measure. Here, we use this result to establish a general relationship between two kinds of conditions on correlations in quantum systems: Bell locality ([1964]) and λ-independence on the one hand, and no signaling (Ghirardi, Rimini, and Weber ([1980]), Jordan ([1983])) on the other hand.

"I rose the next morning, with Objective-Subjective and Subjective-Objective inextricably entangled together in my mind"[1]

1 Introduction

Among the most striking properties of quantum systems is that of **entanglement** — i.e., stronger-than-classical correlations — between particles that may be situated a large distance apart from each other. Bell ([1964]) famously proved that these correlations are indeed stronger-than-classical, but left open the question of just how strong they can be. A natural candidate for the answer to this question is that the correlations can be arbitrarily strong, provided they do not violate relativistic causality. Popescu and Rohrlich ([1994]) showed that this is false. There are correlations that respect relativistic causality and yet are stronger than can arise in any quantum system — they are **superquantum**.

The formal statements of these propositions rely on giving mathematical content to the concepts of classicality and relativistic causality. The first is captured via the condition of **Bell locality** ([1964]) combined with λ-**independence**,

---

[*] This chapter was prepared for the symposium in honor of the 60th birthday of Samson Abramsky. Work with Samson Abramsky, Lucy Brandenburger, Andrei Savochkin, and Noson Yanofsky was an important input into the current work. The authors are grateful to two referees and the volume editor for valuable feedback, and to the NYU Stern School of Business for financial support.
[1] *The Moonstone*, by Wilkie Collins, 1868.

B. Coecke, L. Ong, and P. Panangaden (Eds.): Abramsky Festschrift, LNCS 7860, pp. 1–6, 2013.
© Springer-Verlag Berlin Heidelberg 2013

while the second is captured via the condition of **no signaling** (Ghirardi, Rim-ini, and Weber ([1980]), Jordan ([1983])). In these terms, quantum correlations are a strict superset of correlations satisfying locality and λ-independence, and are a strict subset of correlations satisfying no signaling.

In particular, then, we know that the conjunction of locality and λ-independence is a strictly stronger condition on correlations than is no signal-ing. But, can we say more about the relationship? Locality itself is known to be equivalent to the conjunction of two conditions, namely **parameter inde-pendence** and **outcome independence** (Jarrett ([1984]), Shimony ([1986])). In this chapter we give a result that relates no signaling to the conjunction of parameter independence and λ-independence.

Our result relates to work being done by the first author with Samson Abram-sky and Andrei Savochkin, the purpose of which is to provide a justification for the no-signaling condition that does not involve an appeal to a different branch of physics (special relativity). The present result is technical in nature. It extends a result from Brandenburger and Yanofsky ([2008]), which is used in Abram-sky, Brandenburger, and Savochkin ([2013]), from finite to infinite measurement spaces. It also relates to recent work by Colbeck and Renner ([2011]), ([2012]) on the issue of whether a subjective (or epistemic) vs. objective (or ontic) view of quantum states is tenable; see, especially p.4 in their 2011 paper.

2   Preliminaries

Alice has a space of possible measurements, which is a measurable space $(Y_a, \mathcal{Y}_a)$, and a space of possible outcomes, which is a finite set X_a equipped with its power set, denoted $\mathcal{X}_a$. Likewise, Bob has a space of possible measurements, which is a measurable space $(Y_b, \mathcal{Y}_b)$, and a space of possible outcomes, which is a finite set X_b equipped with its power set, denoted $\mathcal{X}_b$. There is also a hidden-variable space, which is an unspecified measurable space $(\Lambda, \mathcal{L})$. We restrict attention to bipartite systems, but our result extends to multipartite systems. Write

$$(X, \mathcal{X}) = (X_a, \mathcal{X}_a) \otimes (X_b, \mathcal{X}_b), \tag{1}$$
$$(Y, \mathcal{Y}) = (Y_a, \mathcal{Y}_a) \otimes (Y_b, \mathcal{Y}_b). \tag{2}$$

Definition 1. *An **empirical model** is a probability measure e on $(X, \mathcal{X}) \otimes (Y, \mathcal{Y})$.*

Definition 2. *A **hidden-variable model** is a probability measure p on $(X, \mathcal{X}) \otimes (Y, \mathcal{Y}) \otimes (\Lambda, \mathcal{L})$.*

Definition 3. *We say that a hidden-variable model p **realizes** an empirical model e if $e = \text{marg}_{X \times Y} p$. Two hidden-variable models, possibly with different hidden-variable spaces, are (**realization-) equivalent** if they realize the same empirical model.*

All definitions and notation parallel those in Section 3 of our 2012a paper. The reader should consult that paper for details and, in particular, for the notation for **conditional probability**, the definition of the **extension** of a probability measure, and the definition of the **fiber product** $p \otimes_Z q$ of two probability measures p and q over Z.

The key technique we use in proving our main result in the next section is the replacement of an arbitrary hidden-variable model with one where the hidden-variable space $(\Lambda, \mathcal{L})$ is the unit interval with the Borel subsets and $\mathrm{marg}_\Lambda p$ is Lebesgue measure. Theorem 5.1 in our 2012b paper shows if the measurement and outcome spaces are countably generated, then this can always be done — in such a way that the two hidden-variable models are realization-equivalent and that various properties (parameter independence and λ-independence included) satisfied by the first model are again satisfied by the second model.

The next two definitions are taken from Section 4 of our 2012a paper.

Definition 4. *The hidden-variable model p satisfies **parameter independence** if for every $x_a \in X_a$ and $x_b \in X_b$ we have*

$$p[x_a||\mathcal{Y} \otimes \mathcal{L}] = p[x_a||\mathcal{Y}_a \otimes \mathcal{L}], \quad p[x_b||\mathcal{Y} \otimes \mathcal{L}] = p[x_b||\mathcal{Y}_b \otimes \mathcal{L}]. \qquad (3)$$

In words, the probability of a particular outcome for Alice, if conditioned on Alice's choice of measurement and the value of the hidden variable, does not depend on Bob's choice of measurement; and vice versa, with Alice and Bob interchanged.

Definition 5. *The hidden-variable model p satisfies λ-**independence** if for every event $L \in \mathcal{L}$,*

$$p[L||\mathcal{Y}]_y = p(L). \qquad (4)$$

This is an independence requirement between the hidden variable on the one hand, and the measurements chosen by Alice and Bob on the other hand. Whatever process determines the value of the hidden variable, this process does not influence the measurements Alice and Bob choose.

Next is the property of empirical models which we study.

Definition 6. *An empirical model e satisfies **no signaling** if for every $x_a \in X_a$ and $x_b \in X_b$ we have*

$$e[x_a||\mathcal{Y}] = e[x_a||\mathcal{Y}_a], \quad e[x_b||\mathcal{Y}] = e[x_b||\mathcal{Y}_b]. \qquad (5)$$

In words, the probability of a particular outcome for Alice, if conditioned on Alice's choice of measurement, does not depend on Bob's choice of measurement; and vice versa, with Alice and Bob interchanged.

We will make use of the following notation:

$$e_a = \mathrm{marg}_{X_a \times Y_a} e, \quad e_b = \mathrm{marg}_{X_b \times Y_b} e, \qquad (6)$$

$$s = \mathrm{marg}_Y e, \qquad (7)$$

$$p_a = \mathrm{marg}_{X_a \times Y \times \Lambda} p, \quad p_b = \mathrm{marg}_{X_b \times Y \times \Lambda} p, \tag{8}$$

$$q_a = \mathrm{marg}_{X_a \times Y_a \times \Lambda} p, \quad q_b = \mathrm{marg}_{X_b \times Y_b \times \Lambda} p, \tag{9}$$

$$r = \mathrm{marg}_{Y \times \Lambda} p. \tag{10}$$

Lemma 1. *An empirical model e satisfies no signaling if and only if e is a common extension of the fiber products $e_a \otimes_{Y_a} s$ and $e_b \otimes_{Y_b} s$.*

Proof. By Lemma 3.6 in our 2012a paper.

3 The Result

Theorem 1. *Assume that the σ-algebra $\mathcal{Y}$ is countably generated. Then an empirical model e satisfies no signaling if and only if there is a hidden-variable model p which realizes e and satisfies parameter independence and λ-independence.*

Proof. First suppose e satisfies no signaling. We build the (trivial) hidden-variable model where Λ is a singleton. It is immediate that this model realizes e and satisfies parameter independence and λ-independence.

Now suppose that there is a hidden-variable model p which realizes e and satisfies parameter independence and λ-independence. By Lemma 1, we must show that e is an extension of the fiber product $e_a \otimes_{Y_a} s$.

By Theorem 5.1 in our 2012b paper, e is realized by a hidden-variable model p where $(\Lambda, \mathcal{L})$ is the unit interval with the Borel subsets, $\mathrm{marg}_\Lambda p$ is Lebesgue measure, and p satisfies parameter independence and λ-independence. Let $\mathcal{L}^1, \mathcal{L}^2, \ldots$ be an increasing chain of finite algebras of sets whose union generates $\mathcal{L}$. By parameter independence, p_a is the fiber product $p_a = q_a \otimes_{Y_a \times \Lambda} r$.

For each n, let q_a^n and r^n be the restrictions of q_a and r to $\mathcal{X}_a \otimes \mathcal{Y}_a \otimes \mathcal{L}^n$ and $\mathcal{Y} \otimes \mathcal{L}^n$ respectively. In general, p will not be an extension of the fiber product $q_a^n \otimes_{Y_a \times \Lambda} r^n$. Our plan is to show that $q_a^n \otimes_{Y_a \times \Lambda} r^n$ is an extension of $e_a \otimes_{Y_a} s$, and converges to p_a as $n \to \infty$.

We first prove convergence. Fix an integer $k > 0$, and element $x_a \in X_a$, and sets $U \in \mathcal{Y}_a \otimes \mathcal{L}^k$ and $K_b \in \mathcal{Y}_b$. Then $q_a^n[x_a || \mathcal{Y}_a \otimes \mathcal{L}^n]$ is a uniformly bounded martingale with respect to the sequence of σ-algebras $\mathcal{Y}_a \otimes \mathcal{L}^n$, $n \geq k$. By the Martingale Convergence Theorem (Billingsley ([1995, Theorem 35.5])), $q_a^n[x_a || \mathcal{Y}_a \otimes \mathcal{L}^n]$ converges to $q_a[x_a || \mathcal{Y}_a \otimes \mathcal{L}]$ p-almost everywhere. Similarly, for each $K_b \in \mathcal{Y}_b$, $r^n[K_b || \mathcal{Y}_a \otimes \mathcal{L}^n]$ converges to $r[K_b || \mathcal{Y}_a \otimes \mathcal{L}]$ p-almost everywhere. We have

$$(q_a^n \otimes_{Y_a \times \Lambda} r^n)(\{x_a\} \times U \times K_b) = \int_U q_a^n[x_a || \mathcal{Y}_a \otimes \mathcal{L}^n] \times r^n[K_b || \mathcal{Y}_a \otimes \mathcal{L}^n] \, dp \tag{11}$$

and

$$p_a(\{x_a\} \times U \times K_b) = \int_U q_a[x_a || \mathcal{Y}_a \otimes \mathcal{L}] \times r[K_b || \mathcal{Y}_a \otimes \mathcal{L}] \, dp. \tag{12}$$

Moreover, as $n \to \infty$,

$$q_a^n[x_a||\mathcal{Y}_a \otimes \mathcal{L}^n] \times r^n[K_b||\mathcal{Y}_a \otimes \mathcal{L}^n] \to q_a[x_a||\mathcal{Y}_a \otimes \mathcal{L}] \times r[K_b||\mathcal{Y}_a \otimes \mathcal{L}] \quad (13)$$

p-almost everywhere. By Fatou's Lemma (Billingsley ([1995, Theorem 16.3])),

$$\int_U q_a^n[x_a||\mathcal{Y}_a \otimes \mathcal{L}^n] \times r^n[K_b||\mathcal{Y}_a \otimes \mathcal{L}^n] \, dp \to \int_U q_a[x_a||\mathcal{Y}_a \otimes \mathcal{L}] \times r[K_b||\mathcal{Y}_a \otimes \mathcal{L}] \, dp. \quad (14)$$

Therefore

$$(q_a^n \otimes_{Y_a \times \Lambda} r^n)(\{x_a\} \times U \times K_b) \to p_a(\{x_a\} \times U \times K_b). \quad (15)$$

It follows that for each $x^a \in X_a, K_a \in \mathcal{Y}_a$, and $K_b \in \mathcal{Y}_b$,

$$(q_a^n \otimes_{Y_a \times \Lambda} r^n)(\{x_a\} \times K_a \times K_b) \to p_a(\{x_a\} \times K_a \times K_b) = e(\{x_a\} \times K_a \times K_b). \quad (16)$$

We next prove that for each n, $q_a^n \otimes_{Y_a \times \Lambda} r^n$ is an extension of $e_a \otimes_{Y_a} s$. Let $\mathcal{A}^n$ be the set of all atoms of $\mathcal{L}^n$ of positive Lebesgue measure. Then $\mathcal{A}^n$ is a finite collection of pairwise disjoint subsets of Λ whose union has Lebesgue measure 1. Let $u = q_a^n \otimes_{Y_a \times \Lambda} r^n$. By Lemma 3.6 in our 2012a paper,

$$u[x_a||\mathcal{Y} \otimes \mathcal{L}^n] = u[x_a||\mathcal{Y}_a \otimes \mathcal{L}^n]. \quad (17)$$

The conditional probability $u[x_a||\mathcal{Y} \otimes \mathcal{L}^n]_{(y,\lambda)}$ depends only on y and the atom $A \in \mathcal{A}^n$ that contains λ, so we may write

$$u[x_a||\mathcal{Y} \otimes \mathcal{L}^n]_{(y,\lambda)} = u[x_a||\mathcal{Y} \otimes \mathcal{L}^n]_{(y,A)} \quad (18)$$

whenever $\lambda \in A \in \mathcal{A}^n$. We have

$$u[x_a||\mathcal{Y}]_y = \sum_{A \in \mathcal{A}^n} u[x_a||\mathcal{Y} \otimes \mathcal{L}^n]_{(y,A)} \times p[A||\mathcal{Y}]_y. \quad (19)$$

A similar computation holds with $\mathcal{Y}_a$ in place of $\mathcal{Y}$. Since p satisfies λ-independence,

$$p[A||\mathcal{Y}]_y = p(A) = p[A||\mathcal{Y}_a]_y \quad (20)$$

for each $A \in \mathcal{A}^n$ and $y \in Y$. Therefore

$$u[x_a||\mathcal{Y}] = u[x_a||\mathcal{Y}_a]. \quad (21)$$

Since q_a^n is an extension of e_a, and r^n is an extension of s, we have from Lemma 3.6 in our 2012a paper that $u = q_a^n \otimes_{Y_a \times \Lambda} r^n$ is an extension of $e_a \otimes_{Y_a} s$. Thus

$$(e_a \otimes_{Y_a} s)(\{x_a\} \times K_a \times K_b) \quad (22)$$

is a constant sequence that converges to $e(\{x_a\} \times K_a \times K_b)$, and hence

$$(e_a \otimes_{Y_a} s)(\{x_a\} \times K_a \times K_b) = e(\{x_a\} \times K_a \times K_b) \quad (23)$$

for all $x_a \in X_a, K_a \in \mathcal{Y}_a$, and $K_b \in \mathcal{Y}_b$. This shows that e is an extension of $e_a \otimes_{Y_a} s$. A similar argument holds for b in place of a, so e satisfies no signaling by Lemma 1 above.

References

[2013]   Abramsky, S., Brandenburger, A., Savochkin, A.: No-Signalling is Equivalent to Free Choice of Measurements (2013)
[1964]   Bell, J.: On the Einstein-Podolsky-Rosen Paradox. Physics 1, 195–200 (1964)
[1995]   Billingsley, P.: Probability and Measure, 3rd edn. Wiley (1995)
[2012a]   Brandenburger, A., Keisler, H.J.: Fiber Products of Measures and Quantum Foundations. In: Chubb, J., Eskandarian, A., Harizanov, V. (eds.) Logic & Algebraic Structures in Quantum Computing & Information. Association for Symbolic Logic/Cambridge University Press (2012) (forthcoming)
[2012b]   Brandenburger, A., Keisler, H.J.: A Canonical Hidden-Variable Space (2012), http://www.stern.nyu.edu/~abranden, http://www.math.wisc.edu/~keisler
[2008]   Brandenburger, A., Yanofsky, N.: A Classification of Hidden-Variable Properties. Journal of Physics A: Mathematical and Theoretical 41, 425302 (2008)
[2011]   Colbeck, R., Renner, R.: No Extension of Quantum Theory Can Have Improved Predictive Power. Nature Communications 2, 411 (2011)
[2012]   Colbeck, R., Renner, R.: Is a System's Wave Function in One-to-One Correspondence with Its Elements of Reality. Physical Review Letters 108, 150402 (2012)
[1980]   Ghirardi, G., Rimini, A., Weber, T.: A General Argument Against Superluminal Transmission Through the Quantum Mechanical Measurement Process. Lettere Al Nuovo Cimento (1971-1985) 27, 293–298 (1980)
[1984]   Jarrett, J.: On the Physical Significance of the Locality Conditions in the Bell Arguments. Noûs 18, 569–589 (1984)
[1983]   Jordan, T.: Quantum Correlations Do Not Transmit Signals. Physics Letters A 94, 264 (1983)
[1994]   Popescu, S., Rohrlich, D.: Quantum Nonlocality as an Axiom. Foundations of Physics 24, 379–385 (1994)
[1986]   Shimony, A.: Events and Processes in the Quantum World. In: Penrose, R., Isham, C. (eds.) Quantum Concepts in Space and Time, pp. 182–203. Oxford University Press (1986)

Imperfect Information
in Logic and Concurrent Games

Pierre Clairambault[1], Julian Gutierrez[2], and Glynn Winskel[1]

[1] Computer Laboratory, University of Cambridge
[2] Dept. of Computer Science, University of Oxford

Abstract. This paper builds on a recent definition of concurrent games as event structures and an application giving a concurrent-game model for predicate calculus. An extension to concurrent games with imperfect information, through the introduction of 'access levels' to restrict the allowable strategies, leads to a concurrent-game semantics for a variant of Hintikka and Sandu's Independence-Friendly (IF) logic.

Keywords: Concurrent games, Event structures, IF logic.

1 Introduction

Traditional games and strategies, in which one move is made at a time, have most often been represented by trees. If we are to develop a theory of concurrent, or distributed, games it seems sensible to investigate games and strategies formulated in terms of the concurrent analogue of trees, *viz.* event structures. (Just as transition systems unfold to trees so models such as Petri nets, which give an explicit account of concurrency, unfold to event structures [13]).

Concurrent games as event structures were introduced in [14] as a tentative new basis for the formal semantics of concurrent systems and programming languages. Such games carry an explicit representation of causal dependencies between moves. The concurrent-games model was extended in [5] by winning conditions in order to specify objectives for the players of the game. Games with winning conditions are a useful tool for expressing and solving problems in logic and verification.

The games studied in [5] are of perfect information. They are determined (*i.e.* there is a winning strategy for one of the two players) whenever they are well-founded and satisfy a structural property, called race-freedom, that prevents one player from interfering with the moves available to the other. The paper [5] provides a concurrent-game semantics for the predicate calculus, where nondeterministic winning strategies can be effectively built and deconstructed in a compositional manner.

This paper illustrates how by allowing imperfect information within concurrent games we obtain a compositional game semantics for a variant of Hintikka and Sandu's Independence-Friendly (IF) logic [7]; the concurrent-game semantics in this paper generalises that for the predicate calculus in [5]. A striking mathematical feature of the concurrent-game semantics is the facility with which event

B. Coecke, L. Ong, and P. Panangaden (Eds.): Abramsky Festschrift, LNCS 7860, pp. 7–20, 2013.

structures lend themselves to the form of dependence and independence central to IF logic and its variants.

The extension to concurrent games with imperfect information is achieved by adjoining 'access levels.' It was guided originally by the wish to handle games with imperfect information in a way that respects the existing bicategorical structure of concurrent games. There are strong similarities with work by Samson Abramsky and Radha Jagadeesan on an extension of AJM games to handle access control [1].

Related Work. Perhaps the first encounter of logic with imperfect information was in Henkin's generalisation of first-order quantifiers to free up the dependencies between quantified variables [6]. His idea led to other revisions of first-order logic: Hintikka and Sandu's Independence-Friendly (IF) logic [7]; Väänänen's Dependence logic [15] and its 'team semantics;' the latter being a variant of Hodges' compositional semantics of IF logic [8]. Semantics for such logics are often given in terms of games with imperfect information, in which players only have access to a limited, 'visible' part of the history of the games they play. Imperfect information is often captured by requiring that strategies behave in a uniform manner across plays with the same visible history. With concurrent games as event structures we can express imperfect information by specifying the permitted causal dependencies directly.

Within the theory of concurrent computation we see the modal and fixed-point variants of IF logic developed by Bradfield *et al* [4,3] and the alternating-time temporal logic (ATL) of Alur, Henzinger and Kupferman [2]. In modal IF logic a direct link is made between the independence of IF logic and the independence of actions seen in concurrent computation, a correspondence echoed in the semantics of IF logic presented here. The semantics of ATL is given in terms of 'concurrent game structures,' which are essentially Blackwell games [11]. The two players in a Blackwell game play in a series of rounds in which they choose their moves independently. We shall see how to express such rounds via access levels within the broader framework of concurrent games as event structures—see Example 2.

2   Event Structures and Concurrent Games

An *event structure* comprises $(E, \leq, \mathrm{Con})$, consisting of a set E, of *events* which are partially ordered by $\leq$, the *causal dependency relation*, and a nonempty *consistency relation* Con consisting of finite subsets of E, which satisfy four axioms:

$$\{e' \mid e' \leq e\} \text{ is finite for all } e \in E,$$
$$\{e\} \in \mathrm{Con} \text{ for all } e \in E,$$
$$Y \subseteq X \in \mathrm{Con} \implies Y \in \mathrm{Con}, \text{ and}$$
$$X \in \mathrm{Con} \ \& \ e \leq e' \in X \implies X \cup \{e\} \in \mathrm{Con}.$$

The *configurations*, $\mathcal{C}^\infty(E)$, of an event structure E consist of those subsets $x \subseteq E$ which are

Consistent: $\forall X \subseteq x.\ X$ is finite $\Rightarrow X \in \mathrm{Con}$, and
Down-closed: $\forall e, e'.\ e' \leq e \in x \implies e' \in x$.

Often we are concerned with just the finite configurations of E. We write $\mathcal{C}(E)$ for the *finite* configurations of E.

We say an event structure is *elementary* when the consistency relation consists of all finite subsets of events. Two events which are both consistent and incomparable w.r.t. causal dependency in an event structure are regarded as *concurrent*. In games the relation of *immediate* dependency $e \rightarrow e'$, meaning e and e' are distinct with $e \leq e'$ and no event in between plays an important role. For $X \subseteq E$ we write $[X]$ for $\{e \in E \mid \exists e' \in X.\ e \leq e'\}$, the down-closure of X ; note if $X \in \mathrm{Con}$ then $[X] \in \mathrm{Con}$. We use $x\text{-}\subset y$ to mean y covers x in $\mathcal{C}^\infty(E)$, *i.e.* $x \subset y$ with nothing in between, and $x \xrightarrow{\ e\ }\subset y$ to mean $x \cup \{e\} = y$ for $x, y \in \mathcal{C}^\infty(E)$ and event $e \notin x$. We use $x \xrightarrow{\ e\ }\subset$, expressing that event e is enabled at configuration x, when $x \xrightarrow{\ e\ }\subset y$ for some y.

Let E and E' be event structures. A *(partial) map* of event structures $f : E \rightarrow E'$ is a partial function on events $f : E \rightarrow E'$ such that for all $x \in \mathcal{C}(E)$ its direct image $fx \in \mathcal{C}(E')$ and if $e_1, e_2 \in x$ and $f(e_1) = f(e_2)$ (with both defined) then $e_1 = e_2$. The map expresses how the occurrence of an event e in E induces the coincident occurrence of the event $f(e)$ in E' whenever it is defined. Partial maps of event structures compose as partial functions, with identity maps given by identity functions. We say that the map is *total* if the function f is total. A total map of event structures which preserves causal dependency is called *rigid*.

The category of event structures is rich in useful constructions on processes. In particular, it has products and pullbacks (both forms of synchronised composition) and coproducts (nondeterministic sums). Event structures support a simple form of hiding associated with a factorization system. Let $(E, \leq, \mathrm{Con})$ be an event structure. Let $V \subseteq E$ be a subset of 'visible' events. Define the *projection* of E on V, to be $E{\downarrow}V =_{\mathrm{def}} (V, \leq_V, \mathrm{Con}_V)$, where $v \leq_V v'$ iff $v \leq v'$ & $v, v' \in V$ and $X \in \mathrm{Con}_V$ iff $X \in \mathrm{Con}$ & $X \subseteq V$. Consider a partial map of event structures $f : E \rightarrow E'$. Let $V =_{\mathrm{def}} \{e \in E \mid f(e) \text{ is defined}\}$. Then f clearly factors into the composition $E \xrightarrow{\ f_0\ } E{\downarrow}V \xrightarrow{\ f_1\ } E'$ of f_0, a partial map of event structures taking $e \in E$ to itself if $e \in V$ and undefined otherwise, and f_1, a total map of event structures acting like f on V.

Event Structures with Polarities. Both a game and a strategy in a game are represented in terms of an event structure with polarity, comprising an event structure E together with a polarity function $pol : E \rightarrow \{+, -\}$ ascribing a polarity + (Player) or − (Opponent) to its events; the events correspond to moves. Maps of event structures with polarity are maps of event structures which preserve polarities.

Event structures with polarities support two key operations. The *dual*, $E^\perp$, of an event structure with polarity E comprises the same underlying event structure E but with a reversal of polarities. The *simple parallel composition* $E \| E'$ forms the disjoint juxtaposition of E and E', two event structures with polarity; a finite subset of events is consistent if its intersection with each component is consistent.

2.1   Concurrent Games and Strategies

Pre-strategies. Let A be an event structure with polarity, thought of as a game; its events stand for the possible occurrences of moves of Player and Opponent and its causal dependency and consistency relations the constraints imposed by the game. A pre-strategy represents a nondeterministic play of the game—all its moves are moves allowed by the game and obey the constraints of the game; the concept will later be refined to that of *strategy* and *winning strategy*. Formally, a *pre-strategy* in A is a total map $\sigma : S \to A$ from an event structure with polarity S. A map between pre-strategies $\sigma : S \to A$ and $\tau : T \to A$ in A will be a map $\theta : S \to T$ such that $\sigma = \tau\theta$. When θ is an isomorphism we write $\sigma \cong \tau$.

Let A, B be event structures with polarity. Following Joyal [9], a pre-strategy from A to B is a pre-strategy in $A^\perp \| B$, so a total map $\sigma : S \to A^\perp \| B$. We write $\sigma : A \rightarrowtail B$ to express that σ is a pre-strategy from A to B. Note that a pre-strategy σ in A coincides with a pre-strategy from the empty game $\sigma : \varnothing \rightarrowtail A$.

Composing Pre-strategies. We can present the composition of pre-strategies via pullbacks. Given two pre-strategies $\sigma : S \to A^\perp \| B$ and $\tau : T \to B^\perp \| C$, ignoring polarities we can consider the maps on the underlying event structures, *viz.* $\sigma : S \to A \| B$ and $\tau : T \to B \| C$. Viewed this way we can form the pullback in the category of event structures as shown below

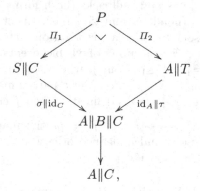

where the map of event structures $A \| B \| C \to A \| C$ is undefined on B and acts as identity on A and C. The partial map from P to $A \| C$ given by the diagram above (either way round the pullback square) factors as the composition of the partial map $P \to P \downarrow V$, where V is the set of events of P at which the map $P \to A \| C$ is defined, and a total map $P \downarrow V \to A \| C$. The resulting total map gives us the composition $\tau \odot \sigma : P \downarrow V \to A^\perp \| C$ once we reinstate polarities.

Concurrent Copy-Cat. Identities w.r.t. composition are copy-cat strategies. Let A be an event structure with polarity. The copy-cat strategy from A to A is an instance of a pre-strategy, so a total map $\gamma_A : \mathbb{C}\mathbb{C}_A \to A^\perp \| A$. For $c \in A^\perp \| A$ we use $\bar{c}$ to mean the corresponding copy of c, of opposite polarity, in the alternative component. Define $\mathbb{C}\mathbb{C}_A$ to comprise the event structure with polarity $A^\perp \| A$ together with the extra causal dependencies generated by $\bar{c} \leq_{\mathbb{C}\mathbb{C}_A} c$ for all events c with $pol_{A^\perp \| A}(c) = +$. The *copy-cat* pre-strategy $\gamma_A : A \dashrightarrow A$ is defined to be the map $\gamma_A : \mathbb{C}\mathbb{C}_A \to A^\perp \| A$ where γ_A is the identity on the common set of events.

Strategies. The main result of [14] is that two conditions on pre-strategies, called *receptivity* and *innocence*, are necessary and sufficient for copy-cat to behave as identity w.r.t. the composition of pre-strategies. Receptivity ensures an openness to all possible moves of Opponent. Innocence, on the other hand, restricts the behaviour of Player; Player may only introduce new relations of immediate causality of the form $\ominus \rightarrowtail \oplus$ beyond those imposed by the game. Formally:

Receptivity: A pre-strategy σ is *receptive* iff
$\sigma x \xrightarrow{a} c \ \& \ pol_A(a) = - \implies \exists! s \in S. \ x \xrightarrow{s} c \ \& \ \sigma(s) = a$.
Innocence: A pre-strategy σ is *innocent* when it is both
+-innocent: if $s \rightarrowtail s' \ \& \ pol(s) = +$ then $\sigma(s) \rightarrowtail \sigma(s')$, and
--innocent: if $s \rightarrowtail s' \ \& \ pol(s') = -$ then $\sigma(s) \rightarrowtail \sigma(s')$.

Theorem 1 (from [14]). *Let $\sigma : A \dashrightarrow B$ be pre-strategy. Copy-cat behaves as identity w.r.t. composition, i.e. $\sigma \circ \gamma_A \cong \sigma$ and $\gamma_B \circ \sigma \cong \sigma$, iff σ is receptive and innocent. Copy-cat pre-strategies $\gamma_A : A \dashrightarrow A$ are receptive and innocent.*

Then, a *strategy* is a pre-strategy which is receptive and innocent. In fact, we obtain a bicategory, in which the objects are event structures with polarity—the games, the arrows from A to B are strategies $\sigma : A \dashrightarrow B$ and the 2-cells are maps of (pre-)strategies, defined above. A strategy $\sigma : A \dashrightarrow B$ corresponds to a dual strategy $\sigma^\perp : B^\perp \dashrightarrow A^\perp$. This duality arises from the correspondence between pre-strategies $\sigma : S \to A^\perp \| B$ and $\sigma^\perp : S \to (B^\perp)^\perp \| A^\perp$.

Deterministic Games and Strategies. There is the important subcategory of *deterministic* strategies. An event structure with polarity S is deterministic iff

$$\forall X \subseteq_{\text{fin}} S. \ Neg[X] \in Con_S \implies X \in Con_S,$$

where $Neg[X] =_{\text{def}} \{s' \in S \mid pol(s') = - \ \& \ \exists s \in X. \ s' \leq s\}$. Say a strategy $\sigma : S \to A$ is deterministic if S is deterministic. Deterministic strategies are necessarily mono, and so can be identified with certain subfamilies of configurations of the game, and in fact coincide with the receptive ingenuous strategies of Mimram and Melliès [12]. While deterministic strategies do compose, a copy-cat strategy γ_A can fail to be deterministic. However, γ_A is deterministic iff there is no immediate conflict between +ve and −ve events, a condition we call 'race-free:'

$$x \xrightarrow{a} c \ \& \ x \xrightarrow{a'} c \ \& \ pol(a) \neq pol(a') \implies x \cup \{a, a'\} \in \mathcal{C}(A). \quad \textbf{(Race - free)}$$

We obtain a sub-bicategory by restricting objects to race-free games and strategies to deterministic ones. Via the presentation of deterministic strategies as subfamilies of configurations, the sub-bicategory of deterministic games and strategies is equivalent to a mathematically simpler order-enriched category.

3   Winning Strategies and Determinacy

A *concurrent game with winning conditions* [5] comprises $G = (A, W)$ where A is an event structure with polarity and $W \subseteq C^\infty(A)$ consists of the *winning configurations* for Player. We define the *losing conditions* to be $C^\infty(A) \smallsetminus W$.

A strategy in G is a strategy in A. A strategy in G is regarded as *winning* if it always prescribes Player moves to end up in a winning configuration, no matter what the activity or inactivity of Opponent. Formally, a strategy $\sigma : S \to A$ in G is *winning (for Player)* if $\sigma x \in W$ for all +-maximal configurations $x \in C^\infty(S)$—a configuration x is +-maximal if whenever $x \overset{s}{-\!\!\!-\!\subset} c$ then the event s has −ve polarity.

Equivalently, a strategy for Player is winning if when played against any counter-strategy of Opponent, the final result is a win for Player. Suppose that $\sigma : S \to A$ is a strategy in a game (A, W). A counter-strategy is a strategy of Opponent, so a strategy $\tau : T \to A^\perp$ in the dual game. We can view σ as a strategy $\sigma : \varnothing \dashrightarrow A$ and τ as a strategy $\tau : A \dashrightarrow \varnothing$. Their composition $\tau \odot \sigma : \varnothing \dashrightarrow \varnothing$ is not very informative; rather it is the set of configurations in $C^\infty(A)$ their full interaction induces what decides which player wins. Ignoring polarities, we have total maps of event structures $\sigma : S \to A$ and $\tau : T \to A$. Form their pullback,

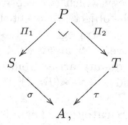

to obtain the event structure P resulting from the interaction of σ and τ. Because σ or τ may be nondeterministic there can be more than one maximal configuration z in $C^\infty(P)$. A maximal configuration z images to a configuration $\sigma \Pi_1 z = \tau \Pi_2 z$ in $C^\infty(A)$. Define the set of *results* of playing σ against τ to be

$$\langle \sigma, \tau \rangle =_{\text{def}} \{\sigma \Pi_1 z \mid z \text{ is maximal in } C^\infty(P)\}.$$

It can be shown [5], that a strategy σ is a winning for Player iff all the results of the interaction $\langle \sigma, \tau \rangle$ lie within the winning configurations W, for any (deterministic) counter-strategy $\tau : T \to A^\perp$ of Opponent.

Operations. There is a *dual*, $G^\perp$, of a game with winning conditions $G = (A, W_G)$, defined as $G^\perp = (A^\perp, C^\infty(A) \smallsetminus W_G)$, which reverses the role of Player and Opponent, and consequently that of winning and losing conditions. Moreover, the *parallel composition* of two games with winning conditions $G = (A, W_G)$, $H = (B, W_H)$ is $G \,⅋\, H =_{\text{def}} (A \| B, W_{G⅋H})$ where, for $x \in \mathcal{C}^\infty(A \| B)$, $x \in W_{G⅋H}$ iff $x_1 \in W_G$ or $x_2 \in W_H$ —a configuration x of $A \| B$ comprises the disjoint union of a configuration x_1 of A and a configuration x_2 of B. To win in $G⅋H$ is to win in either game. The unit of $⅋$ is $(\varnothing, \varnothing)$. Defining $G \otimes H =_{\text{def}} (G^\perp \| H^\perp)^\perp$ we obtain a game where to win is to win in both games G and H. The unit of $\otimes$ is $(\varnothing, \{\varnothing\})$. Defining $G \multimap H =_{\text{def}} G^\perp ⅋ H$, a win in $G \multimap H$ is a win in H conditional on a win in G: For $x \in \mathcal{C}^\infty(A^\perp \| B)$, $x \in W_{G \multimap H}$ iff $x_1 \in W_G \implies x_2 \in W_H$.

Again following Joyal, a (winning) strategy from G to H, two games with winning conditions, is a (winning) strategy in $G \multimap H$. We compose strategies as before. The composition of winning strategies is winning. However, for a general game (A, W) the copy-cat strategy need not be winning. A necessary and sufficient condition for copy-cat to be winning is given in [5]—see **(Cwins)** of Section 4 for its precise statement. The condition is assured for games which are race-free. We can refine the bicategories studied in [14] to bicategories of concurrent games with winning conditions [5].

Determinacy for Well-Founded, Race-Free Concurrent Games. A game with winning conditions is said to be *determined* when either Player or Opponent has a winning strategy. Not all games are determined.

Example 1. Consider the event structure A with two inconsistent events $\oplus$ and $\ominus$ with the obvious polarities and winning conditions $W = \{\{\oplus\}\}$. In the game (A, W) no strategy for either player wins against all other counter-strategies of the other player. In particular, let σ be the unique map of event structures that contains $\oplus$ and τ a particular counter-strategy for Opponent:

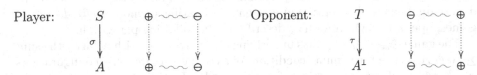

Then, neither $\langle \sigma, \tau \rangle \subseteq W$ nor $\langle \sigma, \tau \rangle \subseteq L$ since $\{\{\oplus\}, \{\ominus\}\} \subseteq \langle \sigma, \tau \rangle$.   ∎

Note that G is not *race-free*. Being race-free is not in itself sufficient to ensure a game is determined. However, with respect to the class of well-founded games, *i.e.* games where all configurations in $\mathcal{C}^\infty(A)$ are finite, we have the following:

Theorem 2 (from [5]). *Let A be a well-founded event structure with polarity. The game (A, W) determined for all winning conditions W iff A is race-free.*

It is tempting to believe that a nondeterministic winning strategy always has a winning deterministic sub-strategy. This is not so and determinacy does not hold for well-founded race-free games if we restrict to deterministic strategies.

Nondeterministic (winning) strategies are also useful if one wants to define a partial-order concurrent-game semantics for classical logics—as shown next.

3.1 Application: Concurrent Games for the Predicate Calculus

The syntax for predicate calculus: formulae are given by

$$\phi, \psi, \cdots ::= R(x_1, \cdots, x_k) \mid \phi \wedge \psi \mid \phi \vee \psi \mid \neg\phi \mid \exists x.\ \phi \mid \forall x.\ \phi$$

where R ranges over basic relation symbols and $x, x_1, x_2, \cdots, x_k$ over variables.

A model M for the predicate calculus comprises a non-empty universe of values V_M and an interpretation for each of the relation symbols as a relation of appropriate arity on V_M. We can then define, by structural induction, the truth of a formula of predicate logic w.r.t. an assignment of values in V_M to the variables of the formula. We write $\rho \vDash_M \phi$ iff formula ϕ is true in M w.r.t. environment ρ; we take an environment to be a function from variables to values.

W.r.t. a model M and an environment ρ, we can denote a formula ϕ by $[\![\phi]\!]_M \rho$, a concurrent game with winning conditions, so that $\rho \vDash_M \phi$ iff there is a winning strategy in $[\![\phi]\!]_M \rho$ (for Player). The denotation as a game is defined as:

$$[\![R(x_1, \cdots, x_k)]\!]_M \rho = \begin{cases} (\varnothing, \{\varnothing\}) & \text{if } \rho \vDash_M R(x_1, \cdots, x_k), \\ (\varnothing, \varnothing) & \text{otherwise.} \end{cases}$$

$$[\![\phi \wedge \psi]\!]_M \rho = [\![\phi]\!]_M \rho \otimes [\![\psi]\!]_M \rho \quad [\![\phi \vee \psi]\!]_M \rho = [\![\phi]\!]_M \rho \,\invamp\, [\![\psi]\!]_M \rho \quad [\![\neg\phi]\!]_M \rho = ([\![\phi]\!]_M \rho)^\perp$$

$$[\![\exists x.\ \phi]\!]_M \rho = \bigoplus_{v \in V_M} [\![\phi]\!]_M \rho[v/x] \qquad [\![\forall x.\ \phi]\!]_M \rho = \ominus_{v \in V_M} [\![\phi]\!]_M \rho[v/x].$$

We use $\rho[v/x]$ to mean the environment ρ updated to assign value v to variable x. The game $(\varnothing, \{\varnothing\})$, the unit w.r.t. $\otimes$, is the game used to denote true and the game $(\varnothing, \varnothing)$, the unit w.r.t. $\invamp$, to denote false. Denotations of conjunctions and disjunctions are denoted by the operations of $\otimes$ and $\invamp$ on games, while negations denote dual games. Universal and existential quantifiers denote *prefixed sums* of games, operations which we now describe in the following paragraph.

The game $\bigoplus_{v \in V}(A_v, W_v)$ has underlying event structure with polarity the sum $\sum_{v \in V} \oplus.A_v$ where the winning conditions of a component are those configurations $x \in \mathcal{C}^\infty(\oplus.A)$ of the form $\{\oplus\} \cup y$ for some $y \in W$. In $\sum_{v \in V} \oplus.A_v$ a configuration is winning iff it is the image of a winning configuration in a component under the injection to the sum. Note in particular that the empty configuration of $\bigoplus_{v \in V} G_v$ is not winning—Player must make a move in order to win. The game $\ominus_{v \in V} G_v$ is defined dually, as $(\bigoplus_{v \in V} G_v^\perp)^\perp$. In this game the empty configuration is winning but Opponent gets to make the first move. Writing $G_v = (A_v, W_v)$, the underlying event structure of $\ominus_{v \in V} G_v$ is the sum $\sum_{v \in V} \ominus.A_v$ with a configuration winning iff it is empty or the image under the injection of a winning configuration in a prefixed component.

It is easy to check by structural induction that for any formula ϕ the game $[\![\phi]\!]_M \rho$ is well-founded and race-free, so determined by Theorem 2. With the help of techniques to build and deconstruct strategies we can establish:

Theorem 3 (from [5]). *For all formulae ϕ and environments ρ, we have that $\rho \vDash_M \phi$ iff the game $[\![\phi]\!]_M \rho$ has a winning strategy, for Player.*

4 Concurrent Games with Imperfect Information

We show how to extend concurrent games by imperfect information to form a bicategory, which in the case of deterministic strategies specializes to an order-enriched bicategory.

We first introduce the framework of games with imperfect information through a simple example.

Consider the game "rock, scissors, paper" in which the two participants Player and Opponent independently sign one of r ("rock"), s ("scissors"), or p ("paper"). The participant with the dominant sign w.r.t. the relation

$$r \; beats \; s, \;\; s \; beats \; p \text{ and } p \; beats \; r$$

wins. We could represent this game by RSP, the event structure with polarity

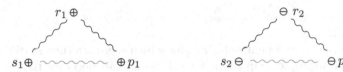

with the three mutually inconsistent signings of Player in parallel with the three mutually inconsistent signings of Opponent. Without neutral configurations, a reasonable choice is to take the *losing* configurations (for Player) to be

$$\{s_1, r_2\}, \; \{p_1, s_2\}, \; \{r_1, p_2\}$$

and all other configurations as winning for Player. In this case there is a winning strategy for Player, *viz.* await the move of Opponent and then beat it with a dominant move. But this strategy cheats. In "rock, scissors, paper" participants are intended to make their moves *independently*. The problem with the game RSP as it stands is that it is a game of *perfect information* in the sense that all moves are visible to both participants. This permits the winning strategy above with its unwanted dependencies on moves which should be unseen by Player. In order to model "rock, scissors, paper" more adequately we can use a concurrent game with *imperfect information* where some moves are masked, or inaccessible, and strategies with dependencies on unseen moves are ruled out.

To extend concurrent games with imperfect information while respecting the bicategorical structure of games we assume a fixed preorder of *levels* $(\Lambda, \leq)$. The levels are to be thought of as levels of access, or permission [1]. Moves in games and strategies are to respect levels: moves will be assigned levels in such a way that a move is only permitted to causally depend on moves at equal or lower levels; it is as if from a level only moves of equal or lower level can be seen.

A Λ-game (G, l_G) comprises a game $G = (A, W)$ with winning conditions together with a *level function* $l_G : A \to \Lambda$ such that $a \leq_A a' \implies l_G(a) \leq l_G(a')$ for all events $a, a' \in A$. A Λ-strategy in the Λ-game (G, l_G) is a winning strategy $\sigma : S \to A$ for which $s \leq_S s' \implies l_G\sigma(s) \leq l_G\sigma(s')$ for all $s, s' \in S$. For example, for "rock, scissors, paper" we can take Λ to be the discrete preorder consisting of levels 1 and 2 unrelated to each other under $\leq$. To make RSP into a suitable Λ-game the level function l_G takes +ve events in RSP to level 1 and −ve events to level 2. The (winning) strategy above, where Player awaits the move of Opponent then beats it with a dominant move, is now disallowed as it is not a Λ-strategy— it introduces causal dependencies which do not respect levels. If instead we took Λ to be the unique preorder on a single level the Λ-strategies would coincide with all the strategies.

Example 2. Through levels we can restrict play to a series of rounds in the way of *Blackwell games* [11] and *concurrent game structures* [2]. An appropriate choice of Λ is the infinite elementary event structure:

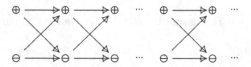

Consider A, a race-free concurrent game, for which there is a (necessarily unique) polarity-preserving rigid map from A to Λ—this map becomes the level function. The existence of such a map ensures moves in A occur in rounds comprising a choice of move for Opponent and a choice of move for Player made concurrently. ∎

The introduction of levels meshes smoothly with the bicategorical structure of concurrent games. For a Λ-game (G, l_G), define its dual $(G, l_G)^{\perp}$ to be $(G^{\perp}, l_{G^{\perp}})$ where $l_{G^{\perp}}(\overline{a}) = l_G(a)$, for a an event of G. Similarly, for Λ-games (G, l_G) and (H, l_H), define their parallel composition $(G, l_G) \,\mathfrak{N}\, (H, l_H)$ to comprise $G \,\mathfrak{N}\, H$ with levels those inherited from the components. A strategy between Λ-games from (G, l_G) to (H, l_H) is a strategy in $(G, l_G)^{\perp} \,\mathfrak{N}\, (H, l_H)$.

As mentioned earlier, in general a copycat strategy is not necessarily winning. Each event structure with polarity A possesses a 'Scott order' on its configurations $\mathcal{C}^{\infty}(A)$: $x' \sqsubseteq x$ iff $x' \supseteq^{-} x \cap x' \subseteq^{+} x$, where we use the inclusions $x \subseteq^{-} y$ iff $x \subseteq y$ & $pol_A(y \setminus x) \subseteq \{-\}$ and $x \subseteq^{+} y$ iff $x \subseteq y$ & $pol_A(y \setminus x) \subseteq \{+\}$, for $x, y \in \mathcal{C}^{\infty}(A)$. The 'Scott-order' is in fact a partial order. It is helpful in expressing a necessary and sufficient condition for copy-cat to be winning w.r.t. a game (G, l_G):

if $x' \sqsubseteq x$ & x' is +-maximal & x is −−maximal,

then $x \in W \implies x' \in W$, for all $x, x' \in \mathcal{C}^{\infty}(A)$. **(Cwins)**

The condition **(Cwins)** is automatically satisfied when A is race-free. We can now state:

Theorem 4. *Let (G, l_G) be a Λ-game.*
(i) If G satisfies **(Cwins)**, *then the copy-cat strategy on G is a Λ-strategy.*
(ii) The composition of Λ-strategies is a Λ-strategy.

5 Λ-IF: A Parametrized Logic of Independence

We present a variant of Hintikka and Sandu's Independence-Friendly (IF) logic and propose a semantics in terms of concurrent games with imperfect information. Our logic is parametrized by a preorder that states the possible dependencies between variables. Assume a preorder $(\Lambda, \leq)$. The syntax for our logic, denoted by Λ-IF, is essentially that of the predicate calculus, but with levels in Λ associated with quantifiers: formulae, where $\lambda \in \Lambda$, are given by

$$\phi, \psi, \cdots ::= R(x_1, \cdots, x_k) \mid \phi \wedge \psi \mid \phi \vee \psi \mid \neg \phi \mid \exists^\lambda x.\ \phi \mid \forall^\lambda x.\ \phi$$

where R ranges over basic relation symbols and $x, x_1, x_2, \cdots, x_k$ over variables.

Assume M, a non-empty universe of values V_M and an interpretation for each of the relation symbols as a relation of appropriate arity on V_M. W.r.t. a model M and an environment ρ, we denote each closed formula ϕ of Λ-IF logic by a Λ-game, following very closely the definitions for predicate calculus. The differences are the assignment of levels to events and that the order on Λ has to be respected by the (modified) prefixed sums which quantified formulae denote.

The prefixed game $\oplus^\lambda.(A, W, l)$ comprises the event structure with polarity $\oplus.A$ in which all the events of $a \in A$ where $\lambda \leq l(a)$ are made to causally depend on a fresh +ve event $\oplus$, itself assigned level λ. Its winning conditions are those configurations $x \in \mathcal{C}^\infty(\oplus.A)$ of the form $\{\oplus\} \cup y$ for some $y \in W$. The game $\oplus_{v\in V}^\lambda (A_v, W_v, l_v)$ has underlying event structure with polarity the sum $\Sigma_{v\in V} \oplus^\lambda.A_v$, maintains the same levels as its components, with a configuration winning iff it is the image of a winning configuration in a component under the injection to the sum. The game $\ominus_{v\in V}^\lambda G_v$ is defined dually, as $(\oplus_{v\in V}^\lambda G_v^\perp)^\perp$.

True denotes the Λ-game the unit w.r.t. $\otimes$ and false denotes the unit w.r.t. $\invamp$. Denotations of conjunctions and disjunctions are given by the operations of $\otimes$ and $\invamp$ on Λ-games, while negations denote dual games. W.r.t. an environment ρ and a model M, quantifiers are denoted by *prefixed sums* of Λ-games:

$$[\![\exists^\lambda x.\ \phi]\!]_M^\Lambda \rho = \bigoplus_{v\in V_M}^\lambda [\![\phi]\!]_M^\Lambda \rho[v/x] \qquad [\![\forall^\lambda x.\ \phi]\!]_M^\Lambda \rho = \bigominus_{v\in V_M}^\lambda [\![\phi]\!]_M^\Lambda \rho[v/x].$$

Definition 1. *For all Λ-IF formulae ϕ, environments ρ, and models M, we say that: (i) ϕ is true in M w.r.t. ρ, written $\rho \vDash_M^\Lambda \phi$, iff Player has a winning strategy in the Λ-game $[\![\phi]\!]_M^\Lambda \rho$; (ii) ϕ is false in M w.r.t. ρ, written $\rho \overline{\vDash}_M^\Lambda \phi$, iff Opponent has a winning strategy in $[\![\phi]\!]_M^\Lambda \rho$ (note that $\rho \overline{\vDash}_M^\Lambda \phi$ is equivalent to $\rho \vDash_M^\Lambda \neg\phi$ but different from $\rho \nvDash_M^\Lambda \phi$); and (iii) ϕ is* undetermined *in M w.r.t. ρ, otherwise.*

6 Λ-IF Logic vs. IF Logic

The language of Λ-IF formulae is, essentially, that of IF logic where two Λ-IF variables are incomparable w.r.t. $(\Lambda, \leq)$ if they are independent within IF logic. Some similarities and differences between IF logic and Λ-IF logic are illustrated in the following examples.

Example 3. Let Λ be the poset with two incomparable elements 1 and 2 , *i.e.* neither $1 \leq 2$ nor $2 \leq 1$, and consider the formula: $\phi = \forall^1 x.\ \exists^2 y.\ x = y$, whose semantics gives rise to a Λ-game (G, l_G) played on an event structure A whose set of events is (isomorphic to) $V_M + V_M$, with the discrete partial order as causal dependency, consistency $X \in \text{Con}$ if the restriction of X to either copy of V_M is a singleton set of events, and polarity $pol((1, v)) = -$ and $pol((2, v)) = +$. The winning conditions are $W = \{\varnothing, \{\{(2, v)\} \mid v \in V_M\}, \{\{(1, v), (2, v)\} \mid v \in V_M\}\}$. Finally, the level function l_G sends $(1, v)$ to 1 and $(2, v)$ to 2, for all $v \in V_M$. It can be checked that whenever V_M has at least two distinct elements neither player has a winning strategy. Then, ϕ is *undetermined* in the model M. ∎

Example 4. Now, consider the same formula as in Example 3 but with the partial order Λ' containing two elements $1, 2$ with $1 \leq 2$. Its interpretation yields a Λ'-game (G', l'_G) played on the event structure with polarity A' which differs from A in that we now have $(1, v) \leq (2, v)$ for all $v \in V_M$. The winning condition and the level function are unchanged, but this game now has a winning strategy: the identity map of event structures $\text{id}_A : A \to A$ is receptive, innocent, and winning. Therefore, ϕ is true as a Λ'-formula, but undetermined as a Λ-formula. ∎

In the previous two examples the two Λ-IF specifications are semantically equivalent to their corresponding IF logic counterparts. However:

Example 5. Take the Λ-IF formula $\phi = (\forall^1 x.\ \exists^2 y.\ x = y) \vee (\exists^1 x.\ \forall^2 y.\ x \neq y)$, where neither $1 \leq 2$ nor $2 \leq 1$. Even though the two sub-games under $\vee$ are undetermined in the general case, the concurrent game induced by ϕ has a winning strategy (for Player): the copy-cat strategy for $[\![\forall^1 x.\ \exists^2 y.\ x = y]\!]_M^\Lambda \rho$. ∎

6.1   On the Expressivity of Λ-IF

Although IF and Λ-IF are semantically different logics, a translation from IF logic to Λ-IF logic is possible provided the dependencies of variables in IF logic can be described as a partial order (or even as a preorder), as is the case for IF-formulae without signaling [10]. In this case a translation from such IF-formulae to Λ-IF-formulae can be given directly. It also follows from a (fairly direct) translation of Henkin logic to Λ-IF. Henkin logic is propositional logic extended with Henkin quantifiers [6]; a Henkin (or branching) quantifier comprises a finite partial order of quantified variables—the partial order assigning the dependency between variables, in the same manner as levels $(\Lambda, \leq)$. For example, in the Henkin formula

$$\left(\begin{smallmatrix} \forall x_1 \exists y_1 \\ \forall x_2 \exists y_2 \end{smallmatrix} \right) \phi(x_1, x_2, y_1, y_2).$$

the variable y_1 may depend on x_1, but not on x_2, or y_2. This formula has meaning given in terms of Skolem functions by

$$\exists f. \exists g. \forall x_1. \forall x_2.\ \phi(x_1, x_2, f(x_1), g(x_2))$$

and has semantics given by the following game with imperfect information: in a Henkin quantifier $\left(\begin{smallmatrix} \forall x_1 \exists y_1 \\ \forall x_2 \exists y_2 \end{smallmatrix} \right) \phi(x_1, x_2, y_1, y_2)$ Player chooses y_2 independently of the choice of x_1 by Opponent, who chooses x_2 independently of the choice of y_1 by Player. This behaviour is the same as given by the Λ-IF formula

$$\forall^a x_1.\exists^b y_1.\forall^c x_2 \exists^d y_2.\ \phi(x_1, x_2, y_1, y_2)$$

with $a \leq b$, $c \leq d$, $a\ co\ d$, and $b\ co\ c$ (where $\lambda\ co\ \lambda'$ iff neither $\lambda \nleq \lambda'$ nor $\lambda' \nleq \lambda$).

Being able to encode the Henkin quantifier has two consequences. Firstly, the ability to encode IF logic from the interpretation of IF-logic in Henkin logic. Secondly, that Λ-IF inherits from Henkin logic the expressive power of the existential fragment of second-order logic.

Example 6. We illustrate the translation from IF formulae to Henkin formulae to Λ-IF formulae. Take the IF formula $\forall x.\exists y/x.\ x = y$. Its translation to Henkin logic is

$$\left(\begin{smallmatrix}\forall x \exists y_1 \\ \forall x_2 \exists y\end{smallmatrix}\right) x = y$$

and to Λ-IF logic is (given the translation above)

$$\forall^a x.\exists^b y_1.\forall^c x_2.\exists^d y.\ x = y$$

with $a \leq b$, $c \leq d$, $a\ co\ d$, and $b\ co\ c$; and eliminating unnecessary quantifiers into

$$\forall^a x.\exists^d y.\ x = y$$

with $a\ co\ d$. As described in Example 3 such a formula is undetermined in any model M with more than two distinct elements. ∎

Remark. Note that, in fact, a formula with a Henkin quantifier

$$\left(\begin{smallmatrix}\forall x_1 \exists y_1 \\ \forall x_2 \exists y_2\end{smallmatrix}\right) \phi(x_1, x_2, y_1, y_2)$$

can be translated to the Λ-IF formula

$$\forall^a x_1.\exists^a y_1.\forall^d x_2 \exists^d y_2.\ \phi(x_1, x_2, y_1, y_2)$$

with $a\ co\ d$, which has *only two* incomparable levels.

7 Conclusion

Although strongly related to IF, the logic Λ-IF has a different evaluation game: as illustrated by Example 5, the formula $\psi \vee \neg\psi$ is always a tautology within Λ-IF (as copy-cat is winning there), whereas it is not in IF when ψ is undetermined. There is the possibility of giving a proof theory for Λ-IF since it satisfies the axiom rule, which is not the case for IF logic.

Acknowledgments. This paper is dedicated to Samson Abramsky on the occasion of his 60th birthday. The authors acknowledge the financial support of the ERC Research Grants ECSYM (at Cambridge) and RACE (at Oxford).

References

1. Abramsky, S., Jagadeesan, R.: Game semantics for access control. Electronic Notes in Theoretical Computer Science 249 (2009)
2. Alur, R., Henzinger, T.A., Kupferman, O.: Alternating-time temporal logic. J. ACM 49(5) (2002)
3. Bradfield, J.C.: Independence: logics and concurrency. Acta Philosophica Fennica 78 (2006)
4. Bradfield, J.C., Fröschle, S.B.: Independence-friendly modal logic and true concurrency. Nord. J. Comput. 9(1) (2002)
5. Clairambault, P., Gutierrez, J., Winskel, G.: The winning ways of concurrent games. In: LICS. IEEE Comp. Soc. (2012)
6. Henkin, L.: Some remarks on infinitely long formulas. Infinitistic Methods (1961)
7. Hintikka, J., Sandu, G.: A revolution in logic? Nordic J. of Phil. Logic 1(2) (1996)
8. Hodges, W.: Compositional semantics for a language of imperfect information. Logic Journal of the IGPL 5(4) (1997)
9. Joyal, A.: Remarques sur la théorie des jeux à deux personnes. Gazette des sciences mathématiques du Québec 1(4) (1997)
10. Mann, A.L., Sandu, G., Sevenster, M.: Independence-Friendly Logic: A Game-Theoretic Approach. London Mathematical Society Lecture Note Series, vol. 386. Cambridge University Press (2011)
11. Martin, D.A.: The determinacy of blackwell games. The Journal of Symbolic Logic 63(4), 1565–1581 (1998)
12. Melliès, P.-A., Mimram, S.: Asynchronous games: innocence without alternation. In: Caires, L., Vasconcelos, V.T. (eds.) CONCUR 2007. LNCS, vol. 4703, pp. 395–411. Springer, Heidelberg (2007)
13. Nielsen, M., Plotkin, G., Winskel, G.: Petri nets, event structures and domains. Theoretical Computer Science 13, 85–108 (1981)
14. Rideau, S., Winskel, G.: Concurrent strategies. In: LICS. IEEE Comp. Soc. (2011)
15. Väänänen, J.A.: Dependence Logic - A New Approach to Independence Friendly Logic. London Mathematical Society Student Texts, vol. 70. Cambridge University Press (2007)

Compositional Quantum Logic

Bob Coecke, Chris Heunen, and Aleks Kissinger

Department of Computer Science, University of Oxford
{coecke,heunen,alek}@cs.ox.ac.uk

Abstract. Quantum logic aims to capture essential quantum mechanical structure in order-theoretic terms. The Achilles' heel of quantum logic is the absence of a canonical description of composite systems, given descriptions of their components. We introduce a framework in which order-theoretic structure comes with a primitive composition operation. The order is extracted from a generalisation of C*-algebra that applies to arbitrary dagger symmetric monoidal categories, which also provide the composition operation. In fact, our construction is entirely compositional, without any additional assumptions on limits or enrichment. Interpreted in the category of finite-dimensional Hilbert spaces, it yields the projection lattices of arbitrary finite-dimensional C*-algebras. Interestingly, there are models that falsify standardly assumed correspondences, most notably the correspondence between noncommutativity of the algebra and nondistributivity of the order.

It is our great pleasure to dedicate this paper to Samson, who has been a key architect of the current multidisciplinary climate, encompassing conceptual mathematics and fundamental physics, that now flourishes in many computer science departments. His contributions to the field over the past three decades have not only been striking in their own right, but have created a wide spectrum of opportunities for young scientists from a variety of backgrounds who have a passion for conceptual depth and true mathematical beauty. We in particular appreciate his appetite for hiring weirdos, high-maintenance drama queens, and outlaws–including some of us who were hereby saved from the academic gutter. If only he wasn't a ManU fan...

1 Introduction

In 1936, Birkhoff and von Neumann questioned whether the full Hilbert space structure was needed to capture the essence of quantum mechanics [3]. They argued that the order-theoretic structure of the closed subspaces of state space, or equivalently, of the projections of the operator algebra of observables, may already tell the entire story. To be more precise, we need to consider an order together with an order-reversing involution on it, a so-called *orthocomplementation*, which can also be cast as an *orthogonality relation*. Support along those lines comes from Gleason's theorem [21], which characterises the Born rule in

B. Coecke, L. Ong, and P. Panangaden (Eds.): Abramsky Festschrift, LNCS 7860, pp. 21–36, 2013.

terms of order-theoretic structure. In turn, via Wigner's theorem [43], this fixes unitarity of the dynamics.

These developments prompted Mackey to formulate his programme for the mathematical foundations of quantum mechanics: the reconstruction of Hilbert space from operationally meaningful axioms on an order-theoretic structure [31]. In 1964, Piron "almost" completed that programme for the infinite-dimensional case [34,35]. Full completion was achieved much more recently, by Solèr in 1995 [40].[1]

Birkhoff and von Neumann coined the term 'quantum logic', in light of the developments in algebraic logic which were also subject to an order-theoretic paradigm. In particular they observed that the distributive law for meets and joins, which is key to the deduction theorem in classical logic, fails to hold for the lattice of closed subspaces for a Hilbert space [3].

This failure of distributivity and hence the absence of a deduction theorem resulted in rejection of the quantum 'logic' idea by a majority of logicians. However, while the name quantum logic was retained, many of its researchers also rejected the direct link to logic, and simply saw quantum logic as the study of the order-theoretic structure associated to quantum phenomena, as well as other structural paradigms that were proposed thereafter [20,30].

The Quantum Logic Paradigm

In the Mackey-Piron-Solèr reconstruction, the elements of the partially ordered set become the projections on the resulting Hilbert space, that is, the self-adjoint idempotents of the algebra of operators on the Hilbert space:

$$p \circ p = p, \qquad p^\dagger = p. \tag{1}$$

Conversely, the ordering can be recovered from the composition structure on these projections:

$$p \leq q \iff p \circ q = p, \tag{2}$$

and the orthogonality relation can be recovered from it, too:

$$p \perp q \iff p \circ q = 0. \tag{3}$$

In fact, the reconstruction does not produce Hilbert space, but Hilbert space with superselection rules. That is, depending on the particular nature of the ordering that we start with, it either produces quantum theory or classical theory, or combinations thereof.

---

[1] See also the survey [41], which provides a comprehensive overview of the entire reconstruction, drawing from the fundamental theorem of projective geometry. Reconstructions of quantum theory have recently seen a great revival [24,6]. In contrast to the Piron-Solèr theorem, this more recent work is mainly restricted to the finite-dimensional case, and focuses on operational axioms concerning how (multiple) quantum and classical systems interact.

The presence of "quantumness" is famously heralded in order-theoretic terms by the failure of the distributive law, giving rise to the following comparison.

$$\frac{\text{classical}}{\text{quantum}} \simeq \frac{\text{distributive}}{\text{nondistributive}}$$

This translates as follows to the level of operator algebra.

$$\frac{\text{classical}}{\text{quantum}} \simeq \frac{\text{commutative}}{\text{noncommutative}}$$

Thus, the combination yields the following slogan.

$$\frac{\text{distributive}}{\text{nondistributive}} \simeq \frac{\text{commutative}}{\text{noncommutative}} \tag{4}$$

This is indeed the case for the projection lattices of arbitrary von Neumann algebras: the projection lattice is distributive if and only if the algebra is commutative [36, Proposition 4.16], and has been a guiding thought within the quantum structures research community.

Categorical Quantum Mechanics

More recently, drawing on modern developments in logic and computer science, and mainly a branch called type-theory, Abramsky and Coecke introduced a radically different approach to quantum structures that has gained prominence, which takes *compositional structure* as the starting point [1]. Proof-of-concept was provided by the fact that many quantum information protocols which crucially rely on the description of compound quantum systems could be very succinctly derived at a high level of abstraction.

In what is now known as categorical quantum mechanics, composition of systems is treated as a primitive connective, typically as a so-called *dagger symmetric monoidal category*. Additional axioms may then be imposed on such categories to capture the particular nature of quantum compoundness. In other words, a set of equations that axiomatise the Hilbert space tensor products is generalised to a broad range of theories. Importantly, at no point is an underlying vector-space like structure assumed.

In contrast to quantum logic, this approach led to an abstract language with high expressive power, that enabled one to address concretely posed problems in the area of quantum computing (see e.g. [4,12,18,27]) and quantum foundations (see e.g. [9]), and that has even led to interesting connections between quantum structures and the structure of natural language [16,8].

One of the key insights of this approach is the fact that many notions that are primitive in Hilbert space theory, and hence quantum theory, can actually be recovered in compositional terms. For example, given the pure operations of a theory, one can define mixed operations in purely compositional terms, which together give rise to a new dagger symmetric monoidal category [37]. We will refer to this construction, as (Selinger's) *CPM–construction*. While this construction applies to arbitrary dagger symmetric monoidal categories (as shown in [7,10]), Selinger also assumed *compactness* [29], something that we will also do in this paper. These structures are called *dagger compact categories*.

Another example, also crucial to this paper, is the fact that orthonormal bases can be expressed purely in terms of certain so-called *dagger Frobenius algebras*, which only rely on dagger symmetric monoidal structure [15,2]. In turn, these dagger Frobenius algebras enable one to define derived concepts such as stochastic maps. All of this still occurs within the language of dagger symmetric monoidal categories [14]. We will refer to this construction as the *Stoch–construction*. Similarly, finite-dimensional C*-algebras can also be realised as certain dagger Frobenius algebras, internal to the dagger compact category of finite-dimensional Hilbert spaces and linear maps, the tensor product, and the linear algebraic adjoint [42].

Recently [11], the authors have proposed a construction, called the *CP*–construction*, that generalises this correspondence to certain dagger Frobenius algebras in arbitrary dagger compact caterories. At the same time, this construction unifies the CPM–construction and the Stoch-construction, starting from a given dagger compact category. The resulting structure is an abstract approach to classical-quantum interaction, with Selinger's CPM–fragment playing the role of the "purely quantum", and the abstract stochastic maps fragment playing the role of the "purely classical".[2]

Overview of this Paper

In this paper, we take this framework of "generalised C*-algebras" as a starting point, and investigate the structure of the dagger idempotents. We will refer to these as in short as projections too, since these dagger idempotents provide the abstract counterpart to projections of concrete C*-algebras.

We show that, just as in the concrete case, one always obtains a partially ordered set with an orthogonality relation. However, equation (4) breaks down in general. More specifically, in the dagger compact category of sets and relations with the Cartesian product as tensor and the relational converse as the dagger, there are commutative algebras with nondistributive projection lattices.

As mentioned above, the upshot of our approach is that it resolves a problem that rendered quantum logic useless for modern purposes: providing an order structure representing compound systems at an abstract level, given the ones describing the component systems. Since we start with a category with monoidal structure, of course composition for objects is built in from the start, and it canonically lifts to algebras thereon. Let us emphasise that our framework relies solely on dagger categorical and compositional structure: the (sequential) composition of morphisms, and the (parallel) tensor product of morphisms. This is a

---

[2] There is an earlier unification of the CPM–construction and the Stoch-construction [38], into which our construction faithfully embeds, see [11]. However, this construction does not support the interpretation of "generalised C*-algebras" [11].

key improvement over previous work [22,26,23,28] that combines order-theoretic and compositional structure.[3]

2   Background

For background on symmetric monoidal categories we refer to the existing literature on the subject [13]. In particular we will rely on their graphical representations, which are surveyed in [39].

Diagrams will be read from bottom to top. Wires represent the objects of the category, while boxes or dots or any other entity with incoming and outcoming wires – possibly none – represents a morphism, and their type is determined by the respective number of incoming and outgoing wires. The directions of arrows on wires represent *duals* of the compact structure.

Our main objects of study are symmetric Frobenius algebras, defined as follows. Let us emphasise that this is a larger class of Frobenius algebra than just the commutative ones, which previous works on categorical quantum mechanics have mainly considered.

Definition 1. *Let $(\mathbf{C}, \otimes, I)$ be a symmetric monoidal category which carries a dagger structure, that is, an identity-on-objects contravariant involutive endofunctor $\dagger : \mathbf{C}^{op} \to \mathbf{C}$. A Frobenius algebra in $\mathbf{C}$ is an object A of $\mathbf{C}$ together with morphisms*

$$\text{\Large A} : A \otimes A \to A \qquad \text{\Large \^{}} : I \to A \qquad \text{\Large V} : A \to A \otimes A \qquad \text{\Large V} : A \to I$$

satisfying the following equations, called associativity (top), coassociativity (bottom), (co)unitality, and the Frobenius condition:

A Frobenius algebra is symmetric when the following equations hold:

A dagger Frobenius algebra is a Frobenius algebra that additionally satisfies the following equation:

$$\text{\Large V} = (\text{\Large A})^{\dagger} \qquad\qquad \text{\Large Q} = (\text{\Large \^{}})^{\dagger}$$

---

[3] The construction in [22] needs the rather strong extra assumption of dagger biproducts, while the construction in [26] requires the weaker assumption of dagger kernels. The intersection of both constructions can be made to work, provided one additionally assumes a weak form of additive enrichment [23].

Symbolically, we denote the *multiplication of two points* $p, q \colon I \to A$, that is,

$$\wedge \circ (p \otimes q) \colon I \to A \ ,$$

as $p \cdot q$. Also, since the multiplication fixes its unit, and the dagger fixes the comultiplication given the multiplication, we will usually represent our algebras as $(A, \wedge)$.

Remark 2. In [11], rather than symmetry, the stronger condition of *normalisability* is used. As this condition implies symmetry for dagger Frobenius algebras [11, Theorem 2.6], the results in this paper apply unchanged to normalisable Frobenius algebras.

We write **FHilb** for the category of finite-dimensional Hilbert spaces and linear maps, with the tensor product as the monoidal structure, and linear adjoint as the dagger.

Theorem 3 ([42]). *Symmetric dagger Frobenius algebras in* **FHilb** *are in 1-to-1 correspondence with finite-dimensional C*-algebras.* $\qquad\square$

Recall that **FHilb** is a *compact category* [29], that is, we can coherently pick a *compact structure* on each object as follows. If $\mathcal{H}$ is a Hilbert space and $\mathcal{H}^*$ is its conjugate space, the triple

$$\left(\mathcal{H}, \quad \begin{matrix} \epsilon_{\mathcal{H}} \colon \mathbb{C} \to \mathcal{H}^* \otimes \mathcal{H} \\ 1 \mapsto \sum_i |i\rangle \otimes |i\rangle \end{matrix} , \quad \begin{matrix} \eta_{\mathcal{H}} \colon \mathcal{H} \otimes \mathcal{H}^* \to \mathbb{C} \\ |\psi\rangle \otimes |\phi\rangle \mapsto \langle\psi|\phi\rangle \end{matrix} \right)$$

is a compact structure which can be shown to be independent of the choice of basis–see [13] for more details. We depict the maps $\epsilon_{\mathcal{H}}$ and $\eta_{\mathcal{H}}$ respectively as:

and compactness means that they satisfy:

Each symmetric dagger Fobenius algebra also canonically induces a 'self-dual' compact structure. The cups and caps of this compact structure are given by:

and one easily verifies that it follows from the axioms of a symmetric Frobenius algebra that the required 'yanking' conditions hold:

3 Abstract Projections

A *projection* of a C*-algebra is a *-idempotent. In this section we will recast this definition in light of Theorem 3, that is, we will identify what these projections are when a C*-algebra is presented as a symmetric dagger Frobenius algebra in **FHilb**, as in [42].

We claim that the projections of a C*-algebra arise as points $p: I \to \mathcal{H}$ satisfying:

$$\text{(5)}$$

where the symmetric dagger Frobenius algebra is the one induced by Theorem 3. Note that the first condition is simply idempotence of $\overset{\curvearrowright}{\wedge}$-multiplication of points, and the second one is *self-conjugateness* with respect to the compact structure induced by the symmetric dagger Frobenius algebra. Symbolically, we denote this conjugate of p as p^*.

A C*-algebra is realised as a symmetric dagger Frobenius algebra as follows. Each finite dimensional C*-algebra decomposes as a direct sum of matrix algebras. These can then be represented as *endomorphism monoids* End($\mathcal{H}$) in **FHilb**, which are triples of the following form:

$$\left(\mathcal{H}^* \otimes \mathcal{H} , \ 1_{\mathcal{H}^*} \otimes \eta_{\mathcal{H}} \otimes 1_{\mathcal{H}} : (\mathcal{H}^* \otimes \mathcal{H}) \otimes (\mathcal{H}^* \otimes \mathcal{H}) \to \mathcal{H}^* \otimes \mathcal{H} , \ \epsilon_{\mathcal{H}} : \mathbb{C} \to \mathcal{H}^* \otimes \mathcal{H} \right) ,$$

Diagrammatically, for an endomorphism monoid the multiplication and its unit respectively are:

The elements $\rho : \mathbb{C}^n \to \mathbb{C}^n$ of the matrix algebra are then represented by underlying points:

$$p_\rho := \qquad \boxed{\rho} \quad : \ \mathbb{C} \to (\mathbb{C}^n)^* \otimes \mathbb{C}^n$$

By compactness, each point of type $\mathbb{C} \to (\mathbb{C}^n)^* \otimes \mathbb{C}^n$ is of this form. By Theorem 3 we know that all symmetric dagger Frobenius algebras in **FHilb** arise in this manner.

We can now verify the above stated claim on how the projections of a C*-algebra arise in this representation. For these points p_ρ the conditions of equation (5) respectively become:

that is, using again compactness, $\rho \circ \rho = \rho = \rho^\dagger$, i.e. *idempotence* and *self-adjointness*.

We can now generalise the definition of projection to points $p : I \to A$ to arbitrary symmetric dagger Frobenius algebras $(A, \text{⋔})$ in any dagger symmetric monoidal category.

Definition 4. *A projection of a symmetric dagger Frobenius algebra $(A, \text{⋔})$ in a dagger symmetric monoidal category $\mathbf{C}$ is a morphism $p \colon I \to A$ satisfying equations (5).*

The next section studies the structure of these generalised projections of abstract C*-algebras.

Before that, we compare abstract projections to *copyable points*. These played a key role for commutative abstract C*-algebras, because they correspond to the elements of an orthonormal basis that determines the algebra [15]. However, as we will now see, in the noncommutative case, there simply do not exist enough copyable points (whereas the projections do have interesting structure, as the next section shows). Recall that a point $x \colon I \to A$ is *copyable* when the following equation is satisfied.

$$\underset{x}{\curlyvee} = \underset{x \quad x}{\mid \mid} \tag{6}$$

Lemma 5. *Copyable points of symmetric dagger Frobenius algebras are central.*

Proof. Graphically:

The middle equation follows from symmetry of $(A, \text{⋔})$.   □

Let us examine what this implies for the example of $A = (\mathbb{C}^n)^* \otimes \mathbb{C}^n$ in **FHilb** above. Equivalently, we may speak about n-by-n matrices, so that ⋔ becomes actual matrix multiplication. Because it is well known that the central elements of matrix algebras are precisely the scalars, any copyable point is simply a scalar by the previous lemma. But substituting back into (6) shows that the only scalar satisfying this equation is 0 (unless $n = 1$). That is, no noncommutative symmetric dagger Frobenius algebra in **FHilb** can have nontrivial copyable points. This explains why we prefer to work with (abstract) projections.

4   Quantum Logics for Abstract C*-Algebras

Definition 6. *A zero projection of $(A, \text{⋔})$ is a projection $0 \colon I \to A$ satisfying*

$$0 \cdot p = 0$$

for all other projections $p \colon I \to A$ of $(A, \text{⋔})$.

We will assume that an algebra always has a zero projection.

Definition 7. *An* orthogonality relation *is a binary relation satisfying the following axioms:*

- symmetry: $a \perp b \iff b \perp a$;
- antireflexivity above zero: $a \perp a \implies a = 0$;
- downward closure: $a \leq a'$, $b \leq b'$, $a' \perp b' \implies a \perp b$.

Lemma 8. *We have*

Proof. First, note the following stardard equation for Frobenius algebras:

Then, the result follows from associativity:

□

Lemma 9. *For projections we have:*

(i) $(p \cdot q)^* = q^* \cdot p^*$;
(ii) *If $p \cdot q$ is a projection, then $p \cdot q = q \cdot p$.*

Proof. (i) We have

where the middle equation follows from Lemma 8. (ii) If $p \cdot q = r$ then, by self-conjugateness of projections and (i), $q \cdot p = q^* \cdot p^* = (p \cdot q)^* = r^* = r = p \cdot q$. □

Theorem 10. *In a dagger symmetric monoidal category, projections on a symmetric dagger Frobenius algebra with a zero projection are partially ordered and come with an orthogonality relation.*

Proof. The order is defined as $p \leq q \iff p \cdot q = p$. Reflexivity follows by the idempotence of projections. If $p \cdot q = p$ and $q \cdot p = q$ then by Lemma 9 (ii) we have $p = q$, so the order is anti-symmetric. If $p \cdot q = p$ and $q \cdot r = q$ then $p \cdot r = p \cdot q \cdot r = p \cdot q = p$, so the order is transitive.

Orthogonality is defined as $p \perp q \iff p \cdot q = 0$. Symmetry follows by Lemma 9 (ii) and anti-reflexivity above 0 by idempotence of projections. If $p \cdot p' = p$, $q \cdot q' = q$ and $p' \cdot q' = 0$ then $p \cdot q = p \cdot p' \cdot q' \cdot q = p \cdot 0 \cdot q = p \cdot 0 = 0$ where we twice relied on Lemma 9 (ii). $\qquad\qquad\qquad\qquad\qquad\qquad\qquad\qquad\qquad\qquad\qquad$ □

Remark 11. The zero projection guarantees that the partially ordered set has a bottom element.

Given a symmetric dagger Frobenius algebra $(A, \overset{\wedge}{\underset{\wedge}{Q}})$, we will denote the partial order and orthogonality of the previous theorem as $\mathrm{Proj}(A, \overset{\wedge}{\underset{\wedge}{Q}})$. The following two examples correspond to the "pure classical" and the "pure quantum" in the "concrete" case of **FHilb**.

Example 12. Commutative dagger special Frobenius algebras $(H, \overset{\wedge}{\underset{\wedge}{Q}})$ in **FHilb** correspond to orthonormal bases of H [15]. For $\mathrm{Proj}(H, \overset{\wedge}{\underset{\wedge}{Q}})$, we obtain the atomistic Boolean algebra whose atoms are the 1-dimensional projections on the basis vectors.

Example 13. If H is a finite-dimensional Hilbert space with any chosen compact structure on it, then $L(H) = (H^* \otimes H, \diagup\!\!\diagdown)$ is a symmetric dagger Frobenius algebra in **FHilb**. For $\mathrm{Proj}(L(H))$ we obtain the usual projection lattice of projections $H \to H$, the paradigmatic example in [3].

Remark 14. In [11], it is shown that algebras of the form $(A^* \otimes A, \diagup\!\!\diagdown)$ are those that realise Selinger's CPM–construction as a fragment of the encompassing CP*–construction. The commutative dagger special Frobenius algebras were the ones used to underpin abstract categories of stochastic maps in [14].

Proposition 15. *Let* $(A, \overset{\wedge}{\underset{\wedge}{Q}})$ *be any symmetric dagger Frobenius algebra in any dagger symmetric monoidal category. For* $p, q \in \mathrm{Proj}(A, \overset{\wedge}{\underset{\wedge}{Q}})$, *the following are equivalent:*

(a) p and q commute;

(b) $p \cdot q \in \mathrm{Proj}(A, \overset{\wedge}{\underset{\wedge}{Q}})$;

(c) $p \cdot q$ is the greatest lower bound of p and q in the partial order $\mathrm{Proj}(A, \overset{\wedge}{\underset{\wedge}{Q}})$.

Proof. Unfold the definitions of Theorem 10. $\qquad\qquad\qquad\qquad\qquad\qquad\qquad$ □

In general, every commutative monoid of idempotents is a meet-semilattice with respect to the order $p \leq q \iff p \cdot q = p$, and if it is furthermore finite, then it is even a (complete) lattice. As shown in [14], in this case the notion of an idempotent can be generalised to arbitrary types $A \to B$. Considered together for all algebras, this always yields a cartesian bicategory of relations in the sense of Carboni-Walters [5]. The conclusion we draw from the previous proposition is the following: considering noncommutative algebras obstructs the construction of the categorical operation of composition.

5 Composing Quantum Logics

Given two symmetric dagger Frobenius algebras we can define their *tensor* as follows.

$$(A, \text{⚶}) \otimes (B, \text{⚶}) := (A \otimes B, \text{⚶⚶})$$

It is easily seen to inherit the entire algebraic structure. So we can define a compositional structure on the corresponding partial orders with orthogonality as follows.

$$\text{Proj}(A, \text{⚶}) \otimes \text{Proj}(B, \text{⚶}) := \text{Proj}(A \otimes B, \text{⚶⚶}) \,.$$

By a *bi-order map* we mean a function of two variables that preserves the order in each argument separately when the other one is fixed (*cf.* bilinearity of the tensor product).

Theorem 16. *The following is a bi-order map.*

$$- \otimes - : \text{Proj}(A, \text{⚶}) \times \text{Proj}(B, \text{⚶}) \to \text{Proj}(A, \text{⚶}) \otimes \text{Proj}(B, \text{⚶})$$
$$(p, q) \mapsto p \otimes q$$

If the monoidal structure moreover preserves zeros, that is, if 0_A is a (necessarily unique) zero with respect to A then for all $q : I \to B$ we have that $0_A \otimes q$ is a zero with respect to $A \otimes B$, then the map $- \otimes -$ also preserves orthogonality in each component.

Proof. If $p \cdot p' = p$ then:

$$(p \otimes q) \cdot (p' \otimes q) = \quad\text{[diagram]}\quad = \quad\text{[diagram]}\quad = (p \cdot p') \otimes (q \cdot q) = p \otimes q \,.$$

If $p \cdot p' = 0$ then $(p \otimes q) \cdot (p' \otimes q) = (p \cdot p') \otimes (q \cdot q) = 0_A \otimes q = 0_{A \otimes B}$. $\square$

Remark 17. The assumption of the existence of zero projections as well as the assumption of monoidal structure preserving zeros, are both comprehended by the single assumption of the existence of a "zero scalar", that is, a morphism $0_I : I \to I$ such that for any other morphisms $f, g : A \to B$ we have that $0_I \otimes f = 0_I \otimes g$. We can then define zero projections $0_A := \lambda_A \circ (0_I \otimes 1_A) \circ \lambda_A^{-1}$ where $\lambda_A : A \simeq I \otimes A$.

6 Commutativity versus Distributivity

Having abstracted projection lattices to the setting of arbitrary dagger symmetric monoidal categories, we can now consider other models than Hilbert spaces.

We will be interested in the category **Rel** of sets and relations, where the monoidal structure is taken to be Cartesian product, and the dagger is given by relational converse. This setting will provide a counterexample to equation (4). Here, symmetric dagger Frobenius algebras were identified by Pavlovic (in the commutative case) and Heunen–Contreras–Cattaneo (in general) in [33] and [25], respectively. They are in 1-to-1 correspondence with small groupoids. As it turns out, even in the commutative case, groupoids may yield nondistributive projection lattices.

Proposition 18. *Let* **G** *be a groupoid, and* $(G, \text{\AA})$ *the corresponding symmetric dagger Frobenius algebra in* **Rel**. *Elements of* $\mathrm{Proj}(G, \text{\AA})$ *are in 1-to-1 correspondence with subgroupoids of* **G**, *i.e. subcategories of* **G** *that are groupoids themselves.*

Proof. This follows directly from [25, Theorem 16]. □

It immediately follows that in **Rel**, like in **FHilb**, the abstract projection lattice is a complete lattice, even though we are not dealing with finite sets.

Corollary 19. *If* $(G, \text{\AA})$ *is a symmetric dagger Frobenius algebra in* **Rel**, *then* $\mathrm{Proj}(G, \text{\AA})$ *forms a complete lattice.*

Proof. The collection of subgroupoids is closed under arbitrary intersections. □

In fact, for our counterexample to equation (4), it suffices to consider groups (*i.e.* single-object groupoids). In this case abstract projections correspond to subgroups, and it is known precisely under which conditions the lattice of subgroupoids is distributive, thanks to the following classical theorem due to Ore. A group is *locally cyclic* when any finite subset of its elements generates a cyclic group.

Theorem 20. *The lattice of subgroups of a group G is distributive if and only if G is abelian and locally cyclic.*

Proof. See [32, Theorem 4]. □

Perhaps the simplest example of an abelian group that is not locally cyclic is $\mathbb{Z}_2 \times \mathbb{Z}_2$. It has three nontrivial subgroups, namely:

$$a := \mathbb{Z}_2 \times \{0\};$$
$$b := \{(0,0), (1,1)\};$$
$$c := \{0\} \times \mathbb{Z}_2.$$

But evidently distributivity breaks down: $a \wedge (b \vee c) = a \neq 0 = (a \wedge b) \vee (a \wedge c)$.

By Theorem 20, we know that the converse (distributive $\implies$ commutative) holds for groups, but what about for arbitrary groupoids. Consider the groupoid with two objects x, y and the only non-identity arrows $f : x \to y$ and $f^{-1} : y \to x$. The lattice of subgroupoids has the following Hasse diagram:

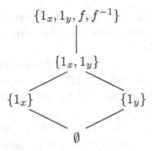

which is indeed distributive, but $f \circ f^{-1} \neq f^{-1} \circ f$. Thus we have proven the following corollary.

Corollary 21. *For symmetric dagger Frobenius algebras* $(G, \text{Å})$ *in* **Rel***:*

$$(G, \text{Å}) \text{ is commutative} \rightleftharpoons \text{Proj}(G, \text{Å}) \text{ is distributive.}$$

$\square$

Let us finish by remarking on the copyable points in **Rel**. As in **FHilb**, they differ from the projections. But unlike in **FHilb**, where there are only trivial copyable points, copyable points in **Rel** are more interesting, for similar reasons as the above corollary.

Lemma 22. *If* $(G, \text{Å})$ *is a symmetric dagger Frobenius algebra in* **Rel** *corresponding to a groupoid* **G***, then its copyable points correspond to the connected components of* **G***.*

Proof. A point x of G in **Rel** corresponds to a subset $X \subseteq \text{Mor}(\mathbf{G})$. Copyability now means precisely that

$$X^2 = \{(g, fg^{-1}) \mid f \in X, g \in \text{Mor}(\mathbf{G}), \text{dom}(f) = \text{dom}(g)\}.$$

Hence if $f \in X$, and $g \in \text{Mor}(\mathbf{G})$ has $\text{dom}(f) = \text{dom}(g)$, then also $g \in X$. Because **G** is a groupoid, this means that X is precisely (the set of morphisms of a) connected component of **G**. $\square$

7   Further Work

From the point of view of traditional quantum logic, a number of questions arise, in particular about which categorical structure yields which order structure:

– when is the orthogonality relation an orthocomplementation?
– when do we obtain an orthoposet?
– when do we obtain an orthomodular poset?
– when is the partial order a (complete) lattice?
– when is this lattice Boolean, modular or orthomodular?

Conversely, what does the lattice structure say about the category? An important first step is the characterisation of dagger Frobenius algebras in more example categories besides **FHilb** and **Rel**.

There is a clear intuition of the comultiplication of the algebra being a "logical broadcasting operation" in the sense of [17]. A more general question then arises on the general operational significance of the partial ordering and orthogonality relation constructed in this paper.

One of the more recent compelling results which emerged from quantum logic is the Faure-Moore-Piron theorem [19] on the reconstruction of dynamics from the lattice structure together with the its operational interpretation. A key ingredient is the reliance on Galois adjoints. Does this construction have a counterpart within our framework, and its (to still be understood) operational significance?

References

1. Abramsky, S., Coecke, B.: A categorical semantics of quantum protocols. In: Proceedings of the 19th Annual IEEE Symposium on Logic in Computer Science (LICS), pp. 415–425. IEEE Computer Society (2004), Extended version: arXiv:quant-ph/0402130

2. Abramsky, S., Heunen, C.: H*-algebras and nonunital Frobenius algebras: first steps in infinite-dimensional categorical quantum mechanics. In: Abramsky, S., Mislove, M. (eds.) Clifford Lectures. Proceedings of Symposia in Applied Mathematics, vol. 71, pp. 1–24. American Mathematical Society (2012)

3. Birkhoff, G., von Neumann, J.: The logic of quantum mechanics. Annals of Mathematics 37, 823–843 (1936)

4. Boixo, S., Heunen, C.: Entangled and sequential quantum protocols with dephasing. Physical Review Letters 108, 120402 (2012)

5. Carboni, A., Walters, R.F.C.: Cartesian bicategories I. Journal of Pure and Applied Algebra 49, 11–32 (1987)

6. Chiribella, G., D'Ariano, G.M., Perinotti, P.: Informational derivation of quantum theory. Physical Review A 84(1), 012311 (2011)

7. Coecke, B.: Axiomatic description of mixed states from Selinger's CPM-construction. Electronic Notes in Theoretical Computer Science 210, 3–13 (2008)

8. Coecke, B.: The logic of quantum mechanics – take II (2012), arXiv:1204.3458

9. Coecke, B., Edwards, B., Spekkens, R.W.: Phase groups and the origin of non-locality for qubits. Electronic Notes in Theoretical Computer Science 270(2), 15–36 (2011), arXiv:1003.5005

10. Coecke, B., Heunen, C.: Pictures of complete positivity in arbitrary dimension. Quantum Phsyics and Logic, Electronic Proceedings in Theoretical Computer Science 95, 27–35 (2011)

11. Coecke, B., Heunen, C., Kissinger, A.: A category of classical and quantum channels. In: QPL 2012 (2012)

12. Coecke, B., Kissinger, A.: The compositional structure of multipartite quantum entanglement. In: Abramsky, S., Gavoille, C., Kirchner, C., Meyer auf der Heide, F., Spirakis, P.G. (eds.) ICALP 2010. LNCS, vol. 6199, pp. 297–308. Springer, Heidelberg (2010), Extended version: arXiv:1002.2540

13. Coecke, B., Paquette, É.O.: Categories for the practicing physicist. In: Coecke, B. (ed.) New Structures for Physics. Lecture Notes in Physics, pp. 167–271. Springer (2011), arXiv:0905.3010

14. Coecke, B., Paquette, É.O., Pavlović, D.: Classical and quantum structuralism. In: Gay, S., Mackie, I. (eds.) Semantic Techniques in Quantum Computation, pp. 29–69. Cambridge University Press (2010), arXiv:0904.1997
15. Coecke, B., Pavlović, D., Vicary, J.: A new description of orthogonal bases. Mathematical Structures in Computer Science (2011) (to appear), arXiv:quant-ph/0810.1037
16. Coecke, B., Sadrzadeh, M., Clark, S.: Mathematical foundations for a compositional distributional model of meaning. Linguistic Analysis (2010)
17. Coecke, B., Spekkens, R.W.: Picturing classical and quantum Bayesian inference. Synthese 186, 651–696 (2012), arXiv:1102.2368.
18. Duncan, R., Perdrix, S.: Rewriting measurement-based quantum computations with generalised flow. In: Abramsky, S., Gavoille, C., Kirchner, C., Meyer auf der Heide, F., Spirakis, P.G. (eds.) ICALP 2010. LNCS, vol. 6199, pp. 285–296. Springer, Heidelberg (2010)
19. Faure, C.-A., Moore, D.J., Piron, C.: Deterministic evolutions and Schrödinger flows. Helvetica Physica Acta 68(2), 150–157 (1995)
20. Foulis, D.J., Randall, C.H.: Operational statistics. I. Basic concepts. Journal of Mathematical Physics 13(11), 1667–1675 (1972)
21. Gleason, A.M.: Measures on the closed subspaces of a Hilbert space. Journal of Mathematics and Mechanics 6, 885–893 (1957)
22. Harding, J.: A link between quantum logic and categorical quantum mechanics. International Journal of Theoretical Physics 48(3), 769–802 (2009)
23. Harding, J.: Daggers, kernels, Baer *-semigroups, and orthomodularity. To appear in Journal of Philosophical Logic (2010)
24. Hardy, L.: Quantum theory from five reasonable axioms. arXiv:quant-ph/0101012 (2001)
25. Heunen, C., Contreras, I., Cattaneo, A.S.: Relative frobenius algebras are groupoids. Journal of Pure and Applied Algebra 217, 114–124 (2012)
26. Heunen, C., Jacobs, B.: Quantum logic in dagger kernel categories. Order 27(2), 177–212 (2010)
27. Horsman, C.: Quantum picturalism for topological cluster-state computing. New Journal of Physics 13, 095011 (2011), arXiv:1101.4722
28. Jacobs, B.: Orthomodular lattices, foulis semigroups and dagger kernel categories. Logical Methods in Computer Science 6(2), 1 (2010)
29. Kelly, G.M., Laplaza, M.L.: Coherence for compact closed categories. Journal of Pure and Applied Algebra 19, 193–213 (1980)
30. Ludwig, G.: An Axiomatic Basis of Quantum Mechanics. 1. Derivation of Hilbert Space. Springer (1985)
31. Mackey, G.W.: The mathematical foundations of quantum mechanics. W. A. Benjamin, New York (1963)
32. Ore, O.: Structures and group theory II. Duke Mathematical Journal 4(2), 247–269 (1938)
33. Pavlovic, D.: Quantum and classical structures in nondeterminstic computation. In: Bruza, P., Sofge, D., Lawless, W., van Rijsbergen, K., Klusch, M. (eds.) QI 2009. LNCS, vol. 5494, pp. 143–157. Springer, Heidelberg (2009)
34. Piron, C.: Axiomatique quantique. Helvetia Physica Acta 37, 439–468 (1964)
35. Piron, C.: Foundations of quantum physics. W. A. Benjamin (1976)
36. Rédei, M.: Quantum Logic in Algebraic Approach. Kluwer (1998)
37. Selinger, P.: Dagger compact closed categories and completely positive maps. Electronic Notes in Theoretical Computer Science 170, 139–163 (2007)

38. Selinger, P.: Idempotents in dagger categories (extended abstract). Electronic Notes in Theoretical Computer Science 210, 107–122 (2008)
39. Selinger, P.: A survey of graphical languages for monoidal categories. In: Coecke, B. (ed.) New Structures for Physics. Lecture Notes in Physics, pp. 275–337. Springer (2011), arXiv:0908.3347
40. Solèr, M.P.: Characterization of Hilbert spaces by orthomodular spaces. Communications in Algebra 23(1), 219–243 (1995)
41. Stubbe, I., van Steirteghem, B.: Propositional systems, Hilbert lattices and generalized Hilbert spaces. In: Lehmann, D., Gabbay, D., Engesser, K. (eds.) Handbook Quantum Logic, pp. 477–524. Elsevier Publ. (2007),
http://www.mat.uc.pt/~isar/PDF/HilbertLatticesELSEVIER.pdf
42. Vicary, J.: Categorical formulation of finite-dimensional quantum algebras. Communications in Mathematical Physics 304(3), 765–796 (2011)
43. Wigner, E.P.: Gruppentheorie. Friedrich Vieweg und Sohn (1931)

The Algebra of Directed Acyclic Graphs

Marcelo Fiore and Marco Devesas Campos

Computer Laboratory
University of Cambridge

Abstract. We give an algebraic presentation of directed acyclic graph structure, introducing a symmetric monoidal equational theory whose free PROP we characterise as that of finite abstract dags with input/output interfaces. Our development provides an initial-algebra semantics for dag structure.

Keywords: dag, PROP, symmetric monoidal equational theory, bialgebra, Hopf algebra, topological sorting, initial-algebra and categorical semantics.

Dedicated to Samson Abramsky on the occasion of his 60th birthday

1 Introduction

This work originated in a question of Robin Milner in connection to explorations he was pursuing on possible extensions to his theory of bigraphs [7]. The particular direction that concerns us here is the generalisation of the spatial dimension of bigraphs from a tree hierarchy to a directed acyclic graph (dag) structure.

In [6], Milner provided axioms for bigraphical structure, axiomatising tree-branching structure by means of the equational theory of commutative monoids. As for the axiomatisation of dag structure, he foresaw that it would also involve the dual theory of commutative comonoids and, in conversation with the first author, raised the question on how these two structures should interact. In considering the problem, it soon became clear that the axioms in question were those of commutative bialgebras (where the monoid structure is a comonoid homomorphism and, equivalently, the comonoid structure is a monoid homomorphism) that are degenerate in that the composition of the comultiplication followed by the multiplication collapses to the identity. This gives the axiomatics of wiring for dag structure.

The natural setting for presenting our work is the categorical language of PROPs; specifically relying on the concept of free PROP, which roughly corresponds to the symmetric strict monoidal category freely generated by a symmetric monoidal equational theory. Indeed, our main result characterises the free PROP on the theory D of degenerate commutative bialgebras with a node (endomap) as that of finite abstract dags with input/output interfaces, see Section 5. Let us give an idea of why this is so.

B. Coecke, L. Ong, and P. Panangaden (Eds.): Abramsky Festschrift, LNCS 7860, pp. 37–51, 2013.

It is important to note that the theory D is the sum of two sub-theories: the theory R of degenerate commutative bialgebras and the theory N_1 of a node (endomap). Each of these theories captures a different aspect of dag structure. The free PROP on R provides relational edge structure; while the free PROP on N_1 introduces node structure. Thus, the free PROP on their sum, which is essentially obtained by interleaving both structures, results in dag structure. A main aim of the paper is to give a simple technical development that formalises these intuitions.

This work falls within a central theme of Samson Abramsky's research: the mathematical study of syntactic structure, an example of which in the context of PROs is his characterisation of Temperley-Lieb structure [1].

2   Directed Acyclic Graphs

2.1   Dags

A *directed acyclic graph (dag)* is a graph with directed edges in which there are no cycles. Formally, a directed graph is a pair $(N, R \subseteq N \times N)$ consisting of a set of nodes N and a binary relation R on it that specifies a directed edge from a node n to another one m whenever $(n, m) \in R$. The acyclicity condition of a dag (N, R) is ensured by requiring that the transitive closure R^+ of the relation R is irreflexive; *i.e.* $(n, n) \notin R^+$ for all $n \in N$.

2.2   Idags

We will deal here with a slight generalisation of the notion of dag. An *interfaced dag (idag)* is a tuple of sets I, O, N and a binary relation $R \subseteq (I + N) \times (O + N)$, for $+$ the sum of sets, subject to the acyclicity condition $(n, n) \notin (p \circ R \circ \imath)^+$ for all $n \in N$, where the relations $i \subseteq N \times (I + N)$ and $p \subseteq (O + N) \times N$ respectively denote the injection of N into $I + N$ and the projection of $O + N$ onto N.

Informally, idags are dags extended with interfaces. An idag (I, O, N, R), also referred to as an (I, O)-dag, is said to have input interface I and output interface O; N is its set of internal nodes. Fig. 1 depicts two examples with input and output sets of ordinals, where for $n \in \mathbb{N}$ we adopt the notation $\underline{n}$ for the ordinal $\{0, \ldots, n - 1\}$.

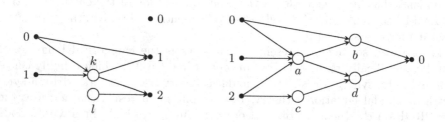

Fig. 1. A $(\underline{2}, \underline{3})$-dag and a $(\underline{3}, \underline{1})$-dag

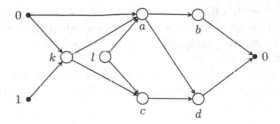

Fig. 2. The concatenation of the idags of Fig. 1

The notion of dag is recovered as that of idag with empty sets of input and output nodes. Idags also generalise binary relations, as these are in bijective correspondence with idags without internal nodes.

2.3   Operations on Idags

The extension of dags with interfaces allows for two basic operations on them.

The *concatenation* operation $D' \circ D$ of an (I, M)-dag $D = (N, R)$ and an (M, O)-dag $D' = (N', R')$ is the (I, O)-dag that retains the hierarchy information of both idags except that edges in R from input and internal nodes in D to intermediate nodes in M become redirected to target internal and output nodes in D' as specified by R'. Formally, $D' \circ D = (N + N', R'')$ where R'' is the composite

$$I+N+N' \xrightarrow{R+\mathrm{id}} M+N+N' \cong M+N'+N \xrightarrow{R'+\mathrm{id}} O+N'+N \cong O+N+N' \ .$$

The *juxtaposition* operation $D \oplus D'$ of an (I, O)-dag $D = (N, R)$ and an (I', O')-dag $D' = (N', R')$ is the $(I + I', O + O')$-dag $D \oplus D' = (N + N', R'')$ where R'' is the composite

$$I+I'+N+N' \cong I+N+I'+N' \xrightarrow{R+R'} O+N+O'+N' \cong O+O'+N+N' \ .$$

Thus, juxtaposition puts two idags side by side, without modifying their hierarchies.

2.4   The Category of Finite Abstract Idags

As we are to look at idags abstractly, we need a notion that identifies those that are essentially the same. Accordingly, we set two (I, O)-dags (N, R) and (N', R') to be isomorphic whenever there exists a bijection $\sigma : N \cong N'$ such that $(\mathrm{id} + \sigma) \circ R = R' \circ (\mathrm{id} + \sigma)$.

Abstract (I, O)-dags are then defined to be equivalence classes of isomorphic (I, O)-dags. The operations of concatenation and juxtaposition respect isomorphism and one can use them to endow abstract idags with the structure of a symmetric monoidal category. We will restrict attention to the finite case: The category **Dag** has objects given by finite sets and homs **Dag**(I, O) given by abstract (I, O)-dags with a finite set of internal nodes. These are equipped with composition operation given by concatenation and identities given by identity relations. Furthermore, the juxtaposition operation provides a symmetric tensor product with unit the empty set.

The aim of the paper is to give an algebraic presentation characterising **Dag**. The appropriate setting for establishing our result is that of PROPs, to which we now turn.

3　Product and Permutation Categories

3.1　PROPs

A *PROduct and Permutation category (PROP)*, see [5], is a symmetric strict monoidal category with objects the natural numbers and tensor product given by addition. This definition is often relaxed in practice, allowing symmetric strict monoidal categories with underlying commutative monoid structure on objects isomorphic to the commutative monoid of natural numbers. A typical example is the additive monoid of finite ordinals $(\{\underline{n} \mid n \in \mathbb{N}\}, \underline{0}, \oplus)$, for which $\underline{n} \oplus \underline{m} = \underline{n+m}$.

The main example of PROP to be studied in the paper follows.

Example. The category **Dag** is equivalent to the PROP **D** consisting of its full subcategory determined by the finite ordinals.

PROPs describe algebraic structure, with the category $\mathsf{Mod_P}(\mathscr{C})$ of *functorial models* of a PROP **P** in a symmetric monoidal category $\mathscr{C}$ given by symmetric monoidal functors $\mathbf{P} \to \mathscr{C}$ and symmetric monoidal natural transformations between them.

3.2　Free PROPs

As remarked by Mac Lane in [5], "[a] useful construction yields the free PROP [...] with given generators and relations"; the usefulness residing in it being "adapted to the study of universal algebra". We briefly recall the construction and its universal characterisation.

A *signature* consists of a set of operators O together with an assignment $O \to \mathbb{N} \times \mathbb{N}$ of arity/coarity pairs to operators. In this context, it is usual to use the notation $o : n \to m$ to indicate that the operator o is assigned the arity/coarity pair (n, m). For a signature Σ, we let $\mathrm{E}(\Sigma)$ consist of the expressions with arity/coarity pairs generated by the language of symmetric strict monoidal categories with underlying commutative monoid the additive natural numbers together with the operators in Σ (*cf.* [3]). A *symmetric monoidal presentation* on a signature Σ is then a set of pairs of expressions in $\mathrm{E}(\Sigma)$ with the same arity/coarity pair. A *symmetric monoidal equational theory* consists of a signature together with a symmetric monoidal presentation on it. An *algebra* for a symmetric monoidal equational theory $(\Sigma, \mathcal{T})$ in a symmetric monoidal category is an object A equipped with morphisms $A^{\otimes n} \to A^{\otimes m}$ for every operator of arity/coarity pair (n, m) in Σ such that the interpretation of every equation in $\mathcal{T}$ is satisfied. We write $\mathsf{Alg}_{(\Sigma, \mathcal{T})}(\mathscr{C})$ for the category of $(\Sigma, \mathcal{T})$-algebras and homomorphisms in $\mathscr{C}$.

The free PROP $\mathbf{P}[\Sigma, \mathcal{T}]$ on a symmetric monoidal theory $(\Sigma, \mathcal{T})$ has homs $\mathbf{P}[\Sigma, \mathcal{T}](n, m)$ given by the quotient of the set of expressions $\mathrm{E}(\Sigma)$, with arity n and coarity m, under the laws of symmetric strict monoidal categories and the presentation $\mathcal{T}$. It is universally characterised by a natural equivalence

$$\mathsf{Mod}_{\mathbf{P}[\Sigma, \mathcal{T}]}(\mathscr{C}) \simeq \mathsf{Alg}_{(\Sigma, \mathcal{T})}(\mathscr{C})$$

for $\mathscr{C}$ ranging over symmetric monoidal categories.

4   Examples of Free PROPs

We give examples of symmetric monoidal equational theories together with abstract characterisations of their induced free PROPs.

4.1   Empty Theory

The free PROP $\mathbf{P}$ on the *empty symmetric monoidal theory* (with no operators and no equations) is the initial symmetric strict monoidal category, *i.e.* the groupoid of finite ordinals and bijections.

4.2   Nodes

For a set L, the free PROP $\mathbf{N}_L$ on the symmetric monoidal theory of *nodes* $\mathsf{N}_L = \big(\{ \lambda : 1 \to 1 \}_{\lambda \in L}, \emptyset \big)$ is the free symmetric strict monoidal category on the free monoid $(L^\star, \varepsilon, \cdot)$. Explicitly, $\mathbf{N}_L$ has finite ordinals as objects and homs $\mathbf{N}_L(\underline{n}, \underline{m}) = \mathbf{P}(\underline{n}, \underline{m}) \times (L^\star)^n$ with identities $(\mathrm{id}_n, \varepsilon)$ and composition $(\tau, w) \circ (\sigma, v) = \big(\tau \circ \sigma, (w_{\sigma(i)} \cdot v_i)_{0 \le i < n} \big)$.

4.3   Idempotent Objects

The symmetric monoidal theory of an *idempotent object* has signature with operators $\Delta : 1 \to 2$ and $\nabla : 2 \to 1$ subject to the presentation

$$\nabla \circ \Delta = \mathrm{id}_1 \; : 1 \to 1 \; , \quad \Delta \circ \nabla = \mathrm{id}_2 \; : 2 \to 2 \; .$$

The free PROP $\mathbf{V}$ on it is a groupoid, with hom $\mathbf{V}(1, 1)$ given by Thompson's group V, see [2].

4.4   Commutative Monoids and Commutative Comonoids

The symmetric monoidal theory of *commutative monoids* has signature with operators $\eta : 0 \to 1$ and $\nabla : 2 \to 1$ subject to the presentation

$$\nabla \circ (\eta \otimes \mathrm{id}_1) = \mathrm{id}_1 = \nabla \circ (\mathrm{id}_1 \otimes \eta) \; : 1 \to 1 \; ,$$
$$\nabla \circ (\nabla \otimes \mathrm{id}_1) = \nabla \circ (\mathrm{id}_1 \otimes \nabla) \; : 3 \to 1 \; ,$$
$$\nabla \circ \gamma_{1,1} = \nabla \; : 2 \to 2$$

where γ denotes the symmetry. The free PROP on it is the category of finite ordinals and functions.

The dual symmetric monoidal theory is that of *commutative comonoids*. It has signature with operators $\epsilon : 1 \to 0$ and $\Delta : 1 \to 2$ subject to the presentation

$$(\epsilon \otimes \mathrm{id}_1) \circ \Delta = \mathrm{id}_1 = (\mathrm{id}_1 \otimes \epsilon) \circ \Delta \ : 1 \to 1 \ ,$$
$$(\Delta \otimes \mathrm{id}_1) \circ \Delta = (\mathrm{id}_1 \otimes \Delta) \circ \Delta \ : 1 \to 3 \ ,$$
$$\gamma_{1,1} \circ \Delta = \Delta \ : 2 \to 2 \ .$$

The free PROP on it is of course the opposite of the category of finite ordinals and functions.

4.5   Commutative Bialgebras

The symmetric monoidal theory B of *commutative bialgebras* has signature with operators $\eta : 0 \to 1$, $\nabla : 2 \to 1$, $\epsilon : 1 \to 0$, and $\Delta : 1 \to 2$ subject to the presentation consisting of that of commutative monoids, commutative comonoids, and the following

$$\epsilon \circ \eta = \mathrm{id}_0 \ : 0 \to 0 \ ,$$
$$\epsilon \circ \nabla = \epsilon \otimes \epsilon \ : 2 \to 0 \ , \quad \Delta \circ \eta = \eta \otimes \eta \ : 0 \to 2 \ ,$$
$$\Delta \circ \nabla = (\nabla \otimes \nabla) \circ (\mathrm{id}_1 \otimes \gamma_{1,1} \otimes \mathrm{id}_1) \circ (\Delta \otimes \Delta) \ : 2 \to 2 \ .$$

The symmetric monoidal theory of *degenerate commutative bialgebras* extends the above with the equation

$$\nabla \circ \Delta = \mathrm{id}_1 \ : 1 \to 1 \ .$$

The free PROP **B** on the symmetric monoidal theory of commutative bialgebras has homs $\mathbf{B}(n, m) = \mathbb{N}^{n \times m}$ under matrix composition. Accordingly, the free PROP **R** on the symmetric monoidal theory of degenerate commutative bialgebras is the category of finite ordinals and relations. See *e.g.* [5, §10], [8], and [4].

4.6   Commutative Hopf Algebras

The symmetric monoidal theory of *commutative Hopf algebras* extends that of commutative bialgebras with an *antipode* operator $s : 1 \to 1$ subject to the laws:

$$s \circ \eta = \eta \ : 0 \to 1 \ , \nabla \circ (s \oplus s) = s \circ \nabla \ : 2 \to 1 \ ,$$
$$\epsilon \circ s = \epsilon \ : 1 \to 0 \ , (s \oplus s) \circ \Delta = \Delta \circ s \ : 1 \to 2 \ ,$$
$$\nabla \circ (s \oplus \mathrm{id}_1) \circ \Delta = \eta \circ \epsilon = \nabla \circ (\mathrm{id}_1 \oplus s) \circ \Delta \ : 1 \to 1 \ .$$

Its free PROP **H** has homs $\mathbf{H}(n, m) = \mathbb{Z}^{n \times m}$ under matrix composition.[1]

---

[1] We are grateful to Ross Duncan and Aleks Kissinger for bringing this example to our attention.

4.7   Commutative Monoids with a Node

The symmetric monoidal theory of *commutative monoids with a node* is the sum of the theory of commutative monoids and the theory of a single node. Its free PROP **F** has homs consisting of interfaced forests. Precisely, **F** is the sub-PROP of **D** determined by the interfaced dags (N, R) with R a total function, see [6].

5   The Algebra of Idags

5.1   Algebraic structure

The generator $\underline{1}$ of the PROP **D** carries two important algebraic structures:

1. the degenerate commutative bialgebra

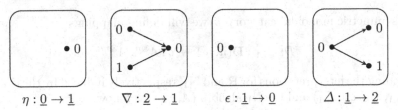

$$\eta : \underline{0} \to \underline{1} \qquad \nabla : \underline{2} \to \underline{1} \qquad \epsilon : \underline{1} \to \underline{0} \qquad \Delta : \underline{1} \to \underline{2}$$

and
2. the node

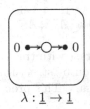

$$\lambda : \underline{1} \to \underline{1}$$

These respectively induce universal injections of PROPs as follows

$$(1)$$

The main result of the paper is that together the PROPs **R** and $\mathbf{N_1}$ characterise the PROP **D**.

Theorem 1. *The PROP* **D** *is free on the symmetric monoidal theory* D *of degenerate commutative bialgebras with a node (i.e. the sum of the theory* R *of degenerate commutative bialgebras and the theory* N_1 *of a node).*

The theorem is proved by establishing the universal property of the free PROP by means of the following lemma, whose proof occupies the rest of the section.

Lemma 1. *The cospan (1) is a pushout of symmetric monoidal categories for the following span of universal PROP injections*

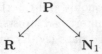

5.2   Categorical Interpretation

We start by giving an interpretation of finite idags on degenerate commutative bialgebras with a node in arbitrary symmetric monoidal categories. Specifically, for every D-algebra

$$(A, \eta_A : I \to A, \nabla_A : A \otimes A \to A, \epsilon_A : A \to I, \Delta_A : A \to A \otimes A, \lambda_A : A \to A)$$

in a symmetric monoidal category $\mathscr{C}$ we will define mappings

$$\mathcal{D}\llbracket - \rrbracket_A : \mathbf{D}(\underline{n}, \underline{m}) \to \mathscr{C}(A^{\otimes n}, A^{\otimes m})$$

extending the interpretations for $\mathbf{R}$ and $\mathbf{N}_1$, respectively induced by the R-algebra $(A, \eta_A, \nabla_A, \epsilon_A, \Delta_A)$ and the N_1-algebra (A, λ_A), as follows

$$\mathbf{R}(\underline{n}, \underline{m}) \longrightarrow \mathbf{D}(\underline{n}, \underline{m}) \longleftarrow \mathbf{N}_1(\underline{n}, \underline{m})$$

For dag structure, in stark contrast with tree structure, there is no direct definition of the interpretation function by structural induction, and a more involved approach to defining it is necessary. This proceeds in two steps as follows.

1. We give an interpretation $\mathcal{D}_\sigma\llbracket D \rrbracket_A$ parameterised by topological sortings σ of D.
2. We show that the interpretation is independent of the topological sorting, in that $\mathcal{D}_\sigma\llbracket D \rrbracket_A = \mathcal{D}_{\sigma'}\llbracket D \rrbracket_A$ for all topological sortings σ and σ' of D.

A *topological sorting* of a finite $(\underline{n}, \underline{m})$-dag $D = (N, R)$ is a bijection

$$\sigma : [N] \to N \ , \quad \text{for } [N] = \{ 0, \ldots, |N| - 1 \}$$

such that

$$\forall 0 \leq i, j < |N|. \ \big(\imath_2(\sigma_i), \imath_2(\sigma_j) \big) \in R \implies i < j$$

where $\imath_2$ denotes the second sum injection. Every such topological sorting induces a canonical decomposition in $\mathbf{D}$ as follows:

$$D = D^\sigma_{|N|} \circ (\mathrm{id}_{n+|N|-1} \oplus \lambda) \circ D^\sigma_{|N|-1} \circ \cdots \circ (\mathrm{id}_n \oplus \lambda) \circ D^\sigma_0 \tag{2}$$

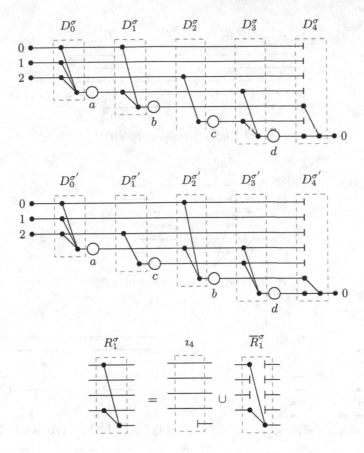

Fig. 3. Decompositions of the $(\underline{3},\underline{1})$-dag of Fig. 1 for the topological sortings $\sigma = (a, b, c, d)$ and $\sigma' = (a, c, b, d)$; and the decomposition of an auxiliary relation

where, for $0 \leq k < |N|$, each $D_k^\sigma \in \mathbf{D}(\underline{n} \oplus \underline{k}, \underline{n} \oplus \underline{k} \oplus \underline{1})$ corresponds to the relation $R_k^\sigma = (\imath_{n+k} \cup \overline{R}_k^\sigma) \in \mathbf{R}(\underline{n} \oplus \underline{k}, \underline{n} \oplus \underline{k} \oplus \underline{1})$ with $\imath_{n+k}$ the inclusion relation and $\overline{R}_k^\sigma$ encoding the edges from the input nodes $0 \leq i < n$ and the internal nodes σ_ℓ for $0 \leq \ell < k$ to the internal node σ_k; while $D_{|N|}^\sigma \in \mathbf{D}(\underline{n} \oplus [N], \underline{m})$ corresponds to the relation $R_{|N|}^\sigma \in \mathbf{R}(\underline{n} \oplus [N], \underline{m})$ encoding the edges from the input and the internal nodes to the output nodes. Explicitly, for $0 \leq k < |N|$ and $0 \leq j < m$,

- $\forall 0 \leq i < n.\, (i, n + k) \in \overline{R}_k^\sigma \iff (\imath_1(i), \imath_2(\sigma_k)) \in R$
- $\forall 0 \leq \ell < k.\, (n + \ell, n + k) \in \overline{R}_k^\sigma \iff (\imath_2(\sigma_\ell), \imath_2(\sigma_k)) \in R$
- $\forall 0 \leq i < n.\, (i, j) \in R_{|N|}^\sigma \iff (\imath_1(i), \imath_1(j)) \in R$
- $\forall 0 \leq \ell < |N|.\, (n + \ell, j) \in R_{|N|}^\sigma \iff (\imath_2(\sigma_\ell), \imath_1(j)) \in R$

where $\imath_1$ and $\imath_2$ respectively denote the first and second sum injections. See Fig. 3 for two sample decompositions.

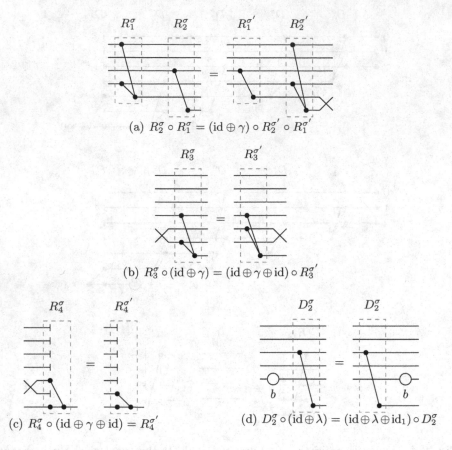

Fig. 4. Graphical demonstration of the identities in Lemma 2 for the $(\underline{3},\underline{1})$-dag of Fig. 1

For a finite $(\underline{n},\underline{m})$-dag D, we are led to define $\mathcal{D}_\sigma[\![D]\!]_A : A^{\otimes n} \to A^{\otimes m}$ as the composite

$$\mathcal{R}[\![R^\sigma_{|N|}]\!]_A \circ (\mathrm{id}_{n+|N|-1} \otimes \lambda_A) \circ \mathcal{R}[\![R^\sigma_{|N|-1}]\!]_A \circ \cdots \circ (\mathrm{id}_n \otimes \lambda_A) \circ \mathcal{R}[\![R^\sigma_0]\!]_A .$$

The above definitions have been specifically chosen so that the properties to follow are readily established.

A first remark is that the interpretation is invariant under isomorphism.

Proposition 1. *Let $D = (N, R)$ and $D' = (N', R')$ be two finite $(\underline{n},\underline{m})$-dags isomorphic by means of a bijection $\beta : N \cong N'$. If σ is a topological sorting of D, then $\sigma' = \beta \circ \sigma$ is a topological sorting of D' and $\mathcal{D}_\sigma[\![D]\!]_A = \mathcal{D}_{\sigma'}[\![D']\!]_A$.*

Proof. Because one has by construction that $R^\sigma_i = R'^{\sigma'}_i$ for all $0 \le i \le |N|$.

More fundamental is the independence of the interpretation under topological sorting.

Lemma 2. *Let σ and σ' be two topological sortings of a finite $(\underline{n}, \underline{m})$-dag $D = (N, R)$ with $|N| \geq 2$. If σ and σ' differ only by the transposition of two adjacent indices, say $\sigma'_i = \sigma_{i+1}$ and $\sigma'_{i+1} = \sigma_i$ for $0 \leq i < |N| - 1$, then the following identities hold:*

1. *$R_j^{\sigma} = R_j^{\sigma'}$ for all $0 \leq j < i$,*

2. *$R_{i+1}^{\sigma} \circ R_i^{\sigma} = (\mathrm{id}_{n+i} \oplus \gamma) \circ R_{i+1}^{\sigma'} \circ R_i^{\sigma'}$,*

3. *$R_j^{\sigma} \circ (\mathrm{id}_{n+i} \oplus \gamma \oplus \mathrm{id}_{j-i-2}) = (\mathrm{id}_{n+i} \oplus \gamma \oplus \mathrm{id}_{j-i-1}) \circ R_j^{\sigma'}$ for all $i+1 < j < |N|$,*

4. *$R_{|N|}^{\sigma} \circ (\mathrm{id}_{n+i} \oplus \tilde{\gamma} \oplus \mathrm{id}_{|N|-i-2}) = R_{|N|}^{\sigma'}$,*

5. *$\mathcal{R}\llbracket R_{i+1}^{\tau} \rrbracket \circ (\mathrm{id}_{A^{\otimes n+i}} \otimes \lambda_A) = (\mathrm{id}_{A^{\otimes n+i}} \otimes \lambda_A \otimes \mathrm{id}_A) \circ \mathcal{R}\llbracket R_{i+1}^{\tau} \rrbracket$ for $\tau = \sigma, \sigma'$.*

Proof. The identities (1–4) follow by construction. Identity (5) is a consequence of the following general fact: for every $R \in \mathbf{R}(k+1, k+2)$ such that, for all $j \in \underline{k+2}$, $(k, j) \in R$ iff $j = k$ one has $R = (\mathrm{id}_k \oplus \gamma) \circ (R' \oplus \mathrm{id}_1)$ for $R' \in \mathbf{R}(\underline{k}, \underline{k+1})$; so that, for all $f : A \to A$,

$$\mathcal{R}\llbracket R \rrbracket_A \circ (\mathrm{id}_{A^{\otimes k}} \otimes f) = (\mathrm{id}_{A^{\otimes k}} \otimes \gamma) \circ (\mathcal{R}\llbracket R' \rrbracket_A \otimes \mathrm{id}_A) \circ (\mathrm{id}_{A^{\otimes k}} \otimes f)$$

$$= (\mathrm{id}_{A^{\otimes k}} \otimes \gamma) \circ (\mathrm{id}_{A^{\otimes k+1}} \otimes f) \circ (\mathcal{R}\llbracket R' \rrbracket_A \otimes \mathrm{id}_A)$$

$$= (\mathrm{id}_{A^{\otimes k}} \otimes f \otimes \mathrm{id}_A) \circ (\mathrm{id}_{A^{\otimes k}} \otimes \gamma) \circ (\mathcal{R}\llbracket R' \rrbracket_A \otimes \mathrm{id}_A)$$

$$= (\mathrm{id}_{A^{\otimes k}} \otimes f \otimes \mathrm{id}_A) \circ \mathcal{R}\llbracket R \rrbracket_A$$

Proposition 2. *For any two topological sortings σ, σ' of a finite $(\underline{n}, \underline{m})$-dag D,*

$$\mathcal{D}_\sigma\llbracket D \rrbracket_A = \mathcal{D}_{\sigma'}\llbracket D \rrbracket_A : A^{\otimes n} \to A^{\otimes m} .$$

Proof. It is enough to establish the equality for σ and σ' as in the hypothesis of Lemma 2. Let us then assume this situation.

By Lemma 2 (1), we have

$$(\mathrm{id} \otimes \lambda_A) \circ \mathcal{R}\llbracket R_{i-1}^{\sigma} \rrbracket_A \circ \cdots \circ (\mathrm{id} \otimes \lambda_A) \circ \mathcal{R}\llbracket R_0^{\sigma} \rrbracket_A$$

$$= (\mathrm{id} \otimes \lambda_A) \circ \mathcal{R}\llbracket R_{i-1}^{\sigma'} \rrbracket_A \circ \cdots \circ (\mathrm{id} \otimes \lambda_A) \circ \mathcal{R}\llbracket R_0^{\sigma'} \rrbracket_A$$

so that we need only show

$$\mathcal{R}\llbracket R_{|N|}^{\sigma} \rrbracket_A \circ (\mathrm{id} \otimes \lambda_A) \circ \mathcal{R}\llbracket R_{|N|-1}^{\sigma} \rrbracket_A \circ \cdots \circ (\mathrm{id} \otimes \lambda_A) \circ \mathcal{R}\llbracket R_i^{\sigma} \rrbracket_A$$

$$= \mathcal{R}\llbracket R_{|N|}^{\sigma'} \rrbracket_A \circ (\mathrm{id} \otimes \lambda_A) \circ \mathcal{R}\llbracket R_{|N|-1}^{\sigma'} \rrbracket_A \circ \cdots \circ (\mathrm{id} \otimes \lambda_A) \circ \mathcal{R}\llbracket R_i^{\sigma'} \rrbracket_A$$

For this we calculate in three steps as follows:

1. $(\mathrm{id} \otimes \lambda_A) \circ \mathcal{R}[\![R^\sigma_{i+1}]\!]_A \circ (\mathrm{id} \otimes \lambda_A) \circ \mathcal{R}[\![R^\sigma_i]\!]_A$

    $= (\mathrm{id} \otimes \lambda_A) \circ (\mathrm{id} \otimes \lambda_A \otimes \mathrm{id}_A) \circ \mathcal{R}[\![R^\sigma_{i+1}]\!]_A \circ \mathcal{R}[\![R^\sigma_i]\!]_A$

      , by Lemma 2 (5)

    $= (\mathrm{id} \otimes \lambda_A) \circ (\mathrm{id} \otimes \lambda_A \otimes \mathrm{id}_A) \circ (\mathrm{id} \otimes \gamma) \circ \mathcal{R}[\![R^{\sigma'}_{i+1}]\!]_A \circ \mathcal{R}[\![R^{\sigma'}_i]\!]_A$

      , by Lemma 2 (2)

    $= (\mathrm{id} \otimes \gamma) \circ (\mathrm{id} \otimes \lambda_A) \circ (\mathrm{id} \otimes \lambda_A \otimes \mathrm{id}_A) \circ \mathcal{R}[\![R^{\sigma'}_{i+1}]\!]_A \circ \mathcal{R}[\![R^{\sigma'}_i]\!]_A$

    $= (\mathrm{id} \otimes \gamma) \circ (\mathrm{id} \otimes \lambda_A) \circ \mathcal{R}[\![R^{\sigma'}_{i+1}]\!]_A \circ (\mathrm{id} \otimes \lambda_A) \circ \mathcal{R}[\![R^{\sigma'}_i]\!]_A$

      , by Lemma 2 (5)

2. $(\mathrm{id}_{A^{\otimes n+|N|-1}} \otimes \lambda_A) \circ \mathcal{R}[\![R^\sigma_{|N|-1}]\!]_A \circ \cdots$

    $\cdots \circ (\mathrm{id}_{A^{\otimes n+i+2}} \otimes \lambda_A) \circ \mathcal{R}[\![R^\sigma_{i+2}]\!]_A \circ (\mathrm{id}_{A^{\otimes n+i}} \otimes \gamma)$

    $= (\mathrm{id}_{A^{\otimes n+|N|-1}} \otimes \lambda_A) \circ \mathcal{R}[\![R^\sigma_{|N|-1}]\!]_A \circ \cdots$

      $\cdots \circ (\mathrm{id}_{A^{\otimes n+i+2}} \otimes \lambda_A) \circ (\mathrm{id}_{A^{\otimes n+i}} \otimes \gamma \otimes \mathrm{id}_A) \circ \mathcal{R}[\![R^{\sigma'}_{i+2}]\!]_A$

      , by Lemma 2 (3)

    $= (\mathrm{id}_{A^{\otimes n+|N|-1}} \otimes \lambda_A) \circ \mathcal{R}[\![R^\sigma_{|N|-1}]\!]_A \circ \cdots$

      $\cdots \circ (\mathrm{id}_{A^{\otimes n+i}} \otimes \gamma \otimes \mathrm{id}_A) \circ (\mathrm{id}_{A^{\otimes n+i+2}} \otimes \lambda_A) \circ \mathcal{R}[\![R^{\sigma'}_{i+2}]\!]_A$

    $\vdots$

    $= (\mathrm{id}_{A^{\otimes n+i}} \otimes \gamma \otimes \mathrm{id}_{A^{\otimes |N|-i-2}}) \circ (\mathrm{id}_{A^{\otimes n+|N|-1}} \otimes \lambda_A) \circ \mathcal{R}[\![R^{\sigma'}_{|N|-1}]\!]_A \circ \cdots$

      $\cdots \circ (\mathrm{id}_{A^{\otimes n+i+2}} \otimes \lambda_A) \circ \mathcal{R}[\![R^{\sigma'}_{i+2}]\!]_A$

3. $\mathcal{R}[\![R^\sigma_{|N|}]\!]_A \circ (\mathrm{id}_{A^{\otimes n+i}} \otimes \gamma \otimes \mathrm{id}_{A^{\otimes |N|-i-2}}) = \mathcal{R}[\![R^{\sigma'}_{|N|}]\!]_A$, by Lemma 2 (4)

5.3   Compositionality

We show that the interpretation of finite idags is compositional for the operations of concatenation and juxtaposition.

Proposition 3. *Let $D = (N, R)$ be a finite $(\underline{n}, \underline{m})$-dag topologically sorted by σ and $D' = (N', R')$ a finite $(\underline{m}, \underline{\ell})$-dag topologically sorted by σ'. Write σ'/σ for the topological sorting of the concatenation $(\underline{n}, \underline{\ell})$-dag $D' \circ D = (N + N', R'')$ according to σ and then σ' (that is, with $(\sigma'/\sigma)_i = \sigma_i$ for $0 \le i < |N|$ and $(\sigma'/\sigma)_{|N|+j} = \sigma'_j$ for $0 \le j < |N'|$). Then,*

$$\mathcal{D}_{\sigma'}[\![D']\!]_A \circ \mathcal{D}_\sigma[\![D]\!]_A = \mathcal{D}_{\sigma'/\sigma}[\![D' \circ D]\!]_A .$$

Proof. The result follows from the definition of the interpretation function and the following identities:

1. $R^\sigma_i = R''^{(\sigma'/\sigma)}_i$ for all $0 \le i < |N|$,

2. $R'^{\sigma'}_j \circ \left(R^{\sigma}_{|N|} \oplus \mathrm{id}_j\right) = \left(R^{\sigma}_{|N|} \oplus \mathrm{id}_{j+1}\right) \circ R''^{(\sigma'/\sigma)}_{|N|+j}$ for all $0 \le j < |N'|$,

3. $R'^{\sigma'}_{|N'|} \circ \left(R^{\sigma}_{|N|} \oplus \mathrm{id}_{|N'|}\right) = R''^{(\sigma'/\sigma)}_{|N+N'|}$.

Proposition 4. *Let $D = (N, R)$ be a finite $(\underline{n}, \underline{m})$-dag topologically sorted by σ and let $D' = (N', R')$ be a finite $(\underline{n'}, \underline{m'})$-dag topologically sorted by σ'. The $(\underline{n + n'}, \underline{m + m'})$-dag $D \oplus D' = (N + N', R'')$ obtained by juxtaposition is topologically sorted by σ'/σ and*

$$\mathcal{D}_\sigma[\![D]\!]_A \otimes \mathcal{D}_{\sigma'}[\![D']\!]_A = \mathcal{D}_{\sigma'/\sigma}[\![D \oplus D']\!]_A .$$

Proof. The result follows from the definition of the interpretation function and the following identities:

1. $R''^{(\sigma'/\sigma)}_i = R^{\sigma}_i$ for all $0 \le i < |N|$,

2. $R''^{(\sigma'/\sigma)}_{|N|+j} = \mathrm{id}_{n+|N|} \oplus R'^{\sigma'}_j$ for all $0 \le j < |N'|$,

3. $R''^{(\sigma'/\sigma)}_{|N+N'|} = R^{\sigma}_{|N|} \oplus R'^{\sigma'}_{|N'|}$.

Proof (of Lemma 1). For a cone

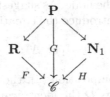

of symmetric monoidal categories, consider the D-algebra

$$A = G1$$

$$\eta_A = (I \cong F0 \xrightarrow{F\eta} A) , \quad \nabla_A = (A \otimes A \cong F(2) \xrightarrow{F\nabla} A)$$

$$\epsilon_A = (A \xrightarrow{F\epsilon} F0 \cong I) , \quad \Delta_A = (A \xrightarrow{F\Delta} F(2) \cong A \otimes A)$$

$$\lambda_A = (A \xrightarrow{H\lambda} A)$$

and define the unique mediating functor $\mathbf{D} \to \mathscr{C}$ to map $D \in \mathbf{D}(\underline{n}, \underline{m})$ to the composite

$$\mathcal{D}[\![D]\!]_A = \left(G(n) \cong A^{\otimes n} \xrightarrow{\mathcal{D}_\sigma[\![(N,R)]\!]_A} A^{\otimes m} \cong G(m) \right)$$

for a topological sorting σ of a representation (N, R) of the abstract idag D. (The symmetric monoidal structure of this functor is inherited from that of G.)

6 Conclusion

We have given an algebraic presentation of dag structure in the categorical language of PROPs, establishing that the PROP of finite abstract interfaced dags is universally characterised as being free on the symmetric monoidal equational theory of degenerate commutative bialgebras with a node. A main contribution in this respect has been a simple proof that provides an initial-algebra semantics for dag structure.

The technique introduced in the paper is robust and can be adapted to a variety of similar results. Firstly, one may drop the degeneracy condition on bialgebras. In this case, the free PROP on the sum of the symmetric monoidal equational theories B and N_1 consists of idags with edges weighted by positive natural numbers. These can be formalised as structures $(I, O, N, R \in \mathbb{N}^{(I+N) \times (O+N)})$ such that $(I, O, N, \{(x, y) \mid R(x, y) \neq 0\})$ is an idag. Secondly, one may introduce an antipode operator. In this case, the free PROP on the sum of the symmetric monoidal equational theories H and N_1 consists of idags with edges weighted by non-zero integers. Analogously, these can be formalised as structures $(I, O, N, R \in \mathbb{Z}^{(I+N) \times (O+N)})$ such that $(I, O, N, \{(x, y) \mid R(x, y) \neq 0\})$ is an idag. Of course, these two weightings respectively come from the structure of **B** and **H**, see §§ 4.5 and 4.6. Finally, one may generalise from N_1 to N_L for a set of labels L. The resulting free PROPs consist of the appropriate versions of L-labelled idags.

In another direction, one may consider extending the symmetric monoidal theory D with equations involving the node. As suggested to us by Samuel Mimram, an interesting possibility is to introduce the equation

$$\lambda = \nabla \circ (\lambda \oplus \mathrm{id}_1) \circ \Delta \; : 1 \to 1 \; .$$

According to the canonical decomposition (2), the effect of this equation on the free PROP **D** is to force on idags D the identification

$$D = D^\sigma_{|N|} \circ (\mathrm{id}_{n+|N|-1} \oplus \lambda) \circ D^\sigma_{|N|-1} \circ \cdots \circ (\mathrm{id}_n \oplus \lambda) \circ D^\sigma_0$$

$$= D^\sigma_{|N|} \circ (\mathrm{id}_{n+|N|-1} \oplus (\nabla \circ (\lambda \oplus \mathrm{id}_1) \circ \Delta)) \circ D^\sigma_{|N|-1} \circ \cdots$$

$$\cdots \circ (\mathrm{id}_n \oplus (\nabla \circ (\lambda \oplus \mathrm{id}_1) \circ \Delta)) \circ D^\sigma_0$$

$$= D^+$$

for D^+ the transitive closure of D. The free PROP consists then of transitive idags. For another example, one may consider introducing the equations

$$\lambda \circ \eta = \eta \; : 0 \to 1 \; , \quad \epsilon \circ \lambda = \epsilon \; : 1 \to 0 \; .$$

The resulting free PROP is that of idags with no dangling internal nodes.

References

[1] Abramsky, S.: Temperley-Lieb algebra: from knot theory to logic and computation via quantum mechanics. In: Mathematics of Quantum Computing and Technology, pp. 515–558 (2007)

[2] Fiore, M., Leinster, T.: An abstract characterization of Thompson's group F. Semigroup Forum 80, 325–340 (2010)

[3] Jay, C.B.: Languages for monoidal categories. Journal of Pure and Applied Algebra 59, 61–85 (1989)

[4] Lack, S.: Composing PROPs. Theory and Applications of Categories 13(9), 147–163 (2004)

[5] Mac Lane, S.: Categorical algebra. Bulletin of the American Mathematical Society 71(1), 40–106 (1965)

[6] Milner, R.: Axioms for bigraphical structure. Mathematical Structures in Computer Science 15(6), 1005–1032 (2005)

[7] Milner, R.: The Space and Motion of Communicating Agents. Cambridge University Press (2009)

[8] Pirashvili, T.: On the PROP corresponding to bialgebras. Cahiers de Topologie et Géométrie Différentielle Catégoriques 43(3), 221–239 (2002)

Diagrammatic Reasoning
for Delay-Insensitive Asynchronous Circuits

Dan R. Ghica

University of Birmimingham

Abstract. In this paper we construct a new trace model of delay-insensitive asynchronous circuits inspired by Ebergen's model in such a way that it satisfies the compositional properties of a category, with additional monoidal structure and further algebraic properties. These properties taken together lay a solid mathematical foundation for a diagrammatic approach to reasoning about asynchronous circuits, which represents a formalisation of common intuitions about asynchronous circuits and their properties.

1 Asynchronous Circuits

In the last few decades interest in asynchronous digital design ebbed and flowed. On the one hand, many studies have identified a great promise in asynchronous circuits, in particular low power consumption and modularity. On the other hand problems such as large silicone footprint and difficulties of fabrication hampered the adoption of asynchronous technology into the mainstream. These are just some of the well known advantages and disadvantages of the technology [1].

Another challenge raised by asynchronous design is that of reasoning about the correctness of circuits, and it has attracted a great deal of research interest. Several models of asynchronous circuits exists, such as Huffman [2] and burst-mode circuits [3], which fall in the broader category of *bounded-delay circuits*, and *delay-insensitive circuits*, of which a notable version are the so-called *micropipelines* [4].

The bounded-delay model takes explicitly into account the precise propagation delays of signals along circuit paths, or at least bounds on these delays. This is a fairly obvious model, but it has serious disadvantages. The first one is that computing delays is complicated, as propagation delays in a circuit can be data-dependent. The second one is that reasoning needs to be "geometric" rather than "topological", as wire lengths are highly relevant. This means that accurate reasoning can only be made after a circuit is placed and routed. Because one logical design can have a large number of concrete instantiations (*layouts*) this low-level way of reasoning is highly undersirable.

Far more attractive is the delay-insensitive model, which aims to design circuits that behave well no matter what the delays in the circuit. This is the model we will focus on. Typically, delay insensitive circuits are constructed out of a fixed set of primitive gates. Some of the most common are:

B. Coecke, L. Ong, and P. Panangaden (Eds.): Abramsky Festschrift, LNCS 7860, pp. 52–68, 2013.

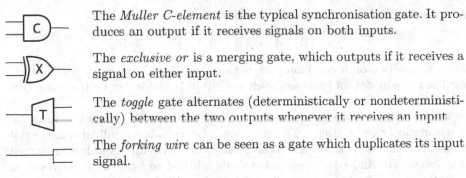

The *Muller C-element* is the typical synchronisation gate. It produces an output if it receives signals on both inputs.

The *exclusive or* is a merging gate, which outputs if it receives a signal on either input.

The *toggle* gate alternates (deterministically or nondeterministically) between the two outputs whenever it receives an input.

The *forking wire* can be seen as a gate which duplicates its input signal.

By *signal* we understand either a high-to-low or a low-to-high change in voltage on a pin. Other more complex gates can be introduced either as primitives or constructed out of these.

The main correctness challenge of the design of asynchronous circuits is to avoid so called "glitches": two signals which travel along the same wire can, if too close to each other, cancel each other out:

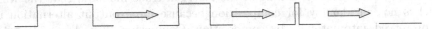

The reason is that the wires in a circuit are not ideal conductors but have capacitance, which acts like an inertial delay. If the signals are too close, they are "absorbed" by the capacitive inertia. A typical glitchy circuit is the one below:

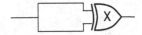

If the two wires going into the XOR gate have different enough delays the circuit will output two signals, otherwise it will produce no output.

1.1 Ebergen's Trace Model

Glitchy circuits are obviously undersirable. In order to assess the absence of glitches a circuit must be modeled. The most widely used is a trace model due to Ebergen [5]. We will present it briefly below. By $K : A_1 \otimes \cdots \otimes A_m \to A'_1 \otimes \cdots \otimes A'_n$ let us denote a circuit K with inputs $A_1, \ldots, A_m$ and outputs $A'_1, \ldots, A'_n$ and let us denote by $[\![K]\!]$ the set of traces modelling that circuit, where each event represents an input/output on the port as identified by the label in the signature. Using the notation of regular expressions extended with interleaving $(- \,|\, -)$ and prefix closure $([-])$, the basic gates given above are modelled as:

$$[\![C : A_1 \otimes A_2 \to A']\!] = \big[((A_1 \,|\, A_2) \cdot A')^*\big]$$
$$[\![X : A_1 \otimes A_2 \to A']\!] = \big[(A_1 A' + A_2 A')^*\big]$$
$$[\![T : A \to A'_1 \otimes A'_2]\!] = \big[(AA'_1 + AA'_2)^*\big]$$
$$[\![F : A \to A'_1 \otimes A'_2]\!] = \big[(A \cdot (A'_1 \,|\, A'_2))^*\big].$$

A trace model is also given for the wire:

$$[\![W : A \to A']\!] = [(AA')^*].$$

The composition on a common port is the usual "synchronisation and hiding" used in trace models of processes such as CSP [6,7] and it can be used to model larger circuits.

Although the Ebergen trace model is useful and useable, it has practical and mathematical disadvantages. The behaviour of circuits is not fully defined, e.g. it is assumed that a Fork will not receive two consecutive inputs unless an output intervenes. This indeed corresponds to safe, glitch-free behaviour. However, in order to verify whether a circuit is safe, the formula for (de)composition needs to be elaborated and we must verify that, indeed, the outputs from one circuit do not violate the input assumptions on the other. Technically this is done by showing that there exists a correct projection of the composite traces onto the components. This is an awkward semantic condition of correctness, very difficult to check either by hand or automatically.

Another technical shortcoming of the Ebergen trace model is that the wire model is not an identity for composition because input-output alternation is not preserved automatically by composition. Composing $W : A_1 \to A_2$ with $W' : A_2 \to A_3$ allows the production of traces such as $A_1 A_1 A_3 A_3$, which project correctly on the components but are not themselves wire-like in behaviour. This means that Wire is not even idempotent. This technical problem becomes an issue if we aim to structure asynchronous circuits into a category which, as discussed below, is highly desirable.

2   Preliminaries

Let $in : A \to A + B$ be the usual injection and $out : A + B \rightharpoonup A$ be its section (a partial function). If $f : A \rightharpoonup B$ is a (partial) function let $f^* : A^* \to B^*$ be the (total) function defined as its *point-wise lifting* to the corresponding free monoids.

$$f^*(\epsilon) = \epsilon$$
$$f^*(a \cdot w) = f(a) \cdot f^*(w) \qquad \text{if } f \text{ is defined at } a \in A$$
$$f^*(a \cdot w) = f^*(w) \qquad \text{if } f \text{ is not defined at } a.$$

Let $\iota : A^* \to (A + B)^*$ be the retraction of the point-wise lifting of $out : A + B \rightharpoonup A$ and let $\omega = out^* : (A + B)^* \to A^*$. If $f \subseteq (X + Y)^*$ and $g \subseteq (Y + Z)^*$ we define $f \|_Y g = \omega(\iota_1(f) \cap \iota_2(g)) = (f; \iota_1 \cap g; \iota_2); \omega$ where $\iota_1 : (X + Y)^* \to (X + Y + Z)^*, \iota_2 : (Y + Z)^* \to (X + Y + Z)^*, \omega : (X + Y + Z)^* \to (X + Z)^*$. Note above that it is often convenient to write function application in *diagrammatic order*, i.e. $f(g(a)) = a; g; f$.

We call $\iota : A^* \to (A + B)^*$ the *injection* of A into $A + B$, $\omega : (A + B)^* \to A^*$ the *projection* of $A + B$ onto A, and $f \|_Y g$ the *composition* of f and g on Y. In general we will use the following notations:

$$\omega_{XY}^X = \omega : (X+Y)^* \to X^* \qquad \iota_X^{XY} = \iota : X^* \to (X+Y)^*.$$

The following properties are immediate.

Lemma 2.01. *1. $\omega_{XY}^X; \iota_X^{XZ} = \iota_{XY}^{XYZ}; \omega_{XYZ}^{XZ}$.*
2. for any $f, g \subseteq X^*$, $(f \cap g); \iota_X^{XY} = f; \iota_X^{XY} \cap g; \iota_X^{XY}$.
3. for any $f \subseteq (X+Y)^*, g \subseteq Y^*$, $(f; \omega_{XY}^X \cap g) = (f \cap g; \iota_X^{XY}); \omega_{XY}^X$.

Lemma 2.02. *Composition is associative, i.e. for any $f \subseteq (X+Y)^*, g \subseteq (Y+Z)^*, h \subseteq (Z+U)^*$ we have that $f \|_Y g \|_Z h = f \|_Y (g \|_Z h)$.*

Proof.

$$
\begin{aligned}
LHS &= ((f; \iota_{XY}^{XYZ} \cap g; \iota_{YZ}^{XYZ}); \omega_{XYZ}^{XZ}; \iota_{XZ}^{XZU} \cap h; \iota_{ZU}^{XZU}); \omega_{XZU}^{XU} \\
&= ((f; \iota_{XY}^{XYZ} \cap g; \iota_{YZ}^{XYZ}); \iota_{XYZ}^{XYZU}; \omega_{XYZU}^{XZU} \cap h; \iota_{ZU}^{XZU}); \omega_{XZU}^{XU} && \text{from Lem. 2.01(1)} \\
&= ((f; \iota_{XY}^{XYZ}; \iota_{XYZ}^{XYZU} \cap g; \iota_{YZ}^{XYZ}; \iota_{XYZ}^{XYZU}); \omega_{XYZU}^{XZU} \cap h; \iota_{ZU}^{XZU}); \omega_{XZU}^{XU} && \text{from Lem. 2.01(2)} \\
&= (f; \iota_{XY}^{XYZ}; \iota_{XYZ}^{XYZU} \cap g; \iota_{YZ}^{XYZ}; \iota_{XYZ}^{XYZU} \cap h; \iota_{ZU}^{XZU}); \omega_{XYZU}^{XZU}; \omega_{XZU}^{ZU} && \text{from Lem. 2.01(3)} \\
&= (f; \iota_{XY}^{XYZU} \cap g; \iota_{YZ}^{XYZU} \cap h; \iota_{ZU}^{XU}); \omega_{XYZU}^{XU} && \text{from Lem. 2.01(2)} \\
&= RHS,
\end{aligned}
$$

which can be brought to the same "ternary composition" form following similar algebraic manipulations.

The interleaving of two strings is a language which we define inductively on the length of the two strings. For sets it is applied pointwise to all pairs of strings.

$$\epsilon \mid \epsilon = \epsilon$$
$$XW \mid X'W' = X \cdot (W \mid X'W') + X' \cdot (XW \mid W')$$
$$f \mid g = \bigcup_{W \in f, W' \in g} W \mid W'.$$

Note that:

Proposition 2.03. *If $f : X \to Y$ and $f' : X' \to Y'$ with X, X', Y, Y' all mutually disjoint then $f \mid f' = f \|_\emptyset f'$.*

3 An Affine Model

In this section we will develop a simple, idealised model of asynchronous circuits in which there exists an idealised wire component behaving like a genuine identity. The model is developed in two stages. First we examine an *affine use* model in which every input is received at most once. This model is a simplified version of Ebergen's trace model. In subsequent sections we *lift* the model to a setting in which inputs can be received an arbitrary number of times. Unlike Ebergen's model, there will be no assumption of *seriality*, i.e. several inputs can be processed before the output is issued. The idealised wire model is the key component that allows the structuring of the model in a category. However, as explained in the previous section, this model is physically unrealisable, a weakness which we remedy separately.

The basic gates given above are modelled as before, except that Kleene and prefix closure are not required:

$$[\![C : A_1 \otimes A_2 \to A']\!] = (A_1 \mid A_2) \cdot A'$$
$$[\![X : A_1 \otimes A_2 \to A']\!] = A_1 A' + A_2 A'$$
$$[\![T : A \to A_1' \otimes A_2']\!] = AA_1' + AA_2'$$
$$[\![F : A \to A_1' \otimes A_2']\!] = A \cdot (A_1' \mid A_2')$$
$$[\![W : A \to A']\!] = AA'$$
$$[\![U : \emptyset \to A]\!] = \epsilon$$
$$[\![E : A \to \emptyset]\!] = A$$
$$[\![P : \emptyset \to A]\!] = A.$$

In addition to the conventional gates we also have an open connector (W), a "dangling-input" connector (U) and a "dangling-output" connector (E). Finally, we have a one-pulse generator component P.

We introduce the following notations. If $f \subseteq (X + Y)^*$ we write $f : X \to Y$. If $f : X \to Y, g : Y \to Z$, with X, Y, Z mutually disjoint, then $f; g \stackrel{\text{def}}{=} f \parallel_Y g$. For any $f : X \to Y, f' : X' \to Y'$, with X, X', Y, Y' mutually disjoint, then $f \otimes g \stackrel{\text{def}}{=} (f; inl^*) \parallel_{\emptyset} (g; inr^*)$. It is immediate that in this case $f; g : X \to Z$ and $f \otimes g : X + X' \to Y + Y'$.

The definition of wire can be extended in the obvious way to that of a *bus*.

$$W^0 : \emptyset \to \emptyset, \qquad\qquad W^0 \stackrel{\text{def}}{=} id_{\emptyset}$$
$$W^k : A_1 \otimes \cdots \otimes A_k \to A_1' \otimes \cdots \otimes A_k', \qquad W^k \stackrel{\text{def}}{=} W^{k-1} \otimes W.$$

Theorem 3.04. *Affinely-used asynchronous circuits form category, which we shall call* **AffAsy***, where*

1. *Objects are ports of shape $A_1 \otimes \cdots \otimes A_n$.*
2. *Morphisms $f : X \to Y$ are sets of traces $f \subseteq (X + Y)^*$.*
3. *Composition of morphisms $f : X \to Y, g : Y \to Z$ is defined as $f; g = f \parallel_Y g$.*
4. *The identity morphism on X is W^n if $X = A_1 \otimes \cdots \otimes A_n$.*

Proof. The associativity of composition is Lem. 2.02. The fact that W^n is an identity is immediate.

Theorem 3.05. **AffAsy** *is a symmetric monoidal category where*

1. *The tensor of two objects is $X \otimes Y = X + Y$.*
2. *The tensor of two morphisms $f : X \to Y, g : Y \to Z$ is $f \otimes g : X \otimes X' \to Y \otimes Y'$.*
3. *The unit object is $\emptyset$.*

4. *The associator, left identity, right identity and symmetry are the corresponding isomorphisms for disjoint sum, lifted pointwise to sequences.*

Proof. We show that $\otimes$ is functorial for composition, i.e. if $f : X \to Y, g : Y \to Z, f' : X' \to Y', g' : Y' \to Z'$, then $(f \otimes f'); (g \otimes g') = f; f' \otimes g; g'$. Lets write $U = X + X' + Y + Y' + Z + Z'$. Expanding the definitions, the LHS is

$$((f; inl; \iota_{XY}^{XX'YY'} \sqcap f'; inr; \iota_{X'Y'}^{XX'YY'}); \iota_{XX'YY'}^{U}$$
$$\sqcap (g; inl; \iota_{YZ}^{YY'ZZ'} \sqcap g'; inr; \iota_{Y'Z'}^{YY'ZZ'}); \iota_{YY'ZZ'}^{U}); \omega_{U}^{XX'ZZ'}$$

We use Lem. 2.01(2) and we combine consecutive injections to rewrite LHS as

$$LHS = (f; inl; \iota_{XY}^{U} \sqcap f'; inr; \iota_{X'Y'}^{U} \sqcap g; inl; \iota_{YZ}^{U} \sqcap g'; inr; \iota_{Y'Z'}^{U}); \omega_{U}^{XX'ZZ'}$$

Using similar algebraic manipulations the RHS can be brought to the same form.

The functoriality of $\otimes$ on identity is by definition. The coherence properties are the same as for disjoint sum and are preserved by point-wise lifting.

This model is, of course, limited in that it gives the wrong result for glitchy circuits, which do not behave in an affine way. For example $F; X = \emptyset$, which can be interpreted as the fact that this composition has no "safe" traces. An additional serious limitation is that linearity cannot model circuits where the output is fed back into an input port.

However, this model is a stepping stone which we shall elaborate towards more realistic behaviours in a way in which basic algebraic properties are preserved. Here are some of the main such properties.

Theorem 3.06. *In* AffAsy

1. (A, X, U) *is a commutative monoid, with T a retract of X.*

Associativity $(W \otimes X); X = (X \otimes W); X.$

Unit $(U \otimes W); X = (W \otimes U); X = W.$

Commutativity $\gamma_A; X = X.$

Retract $T; X = W.$

2. (A, C, P) *is a commutative monoid with* U *an absorbing element.*

Associativity $(W \otimes C); C = (C \otimes W); C.$

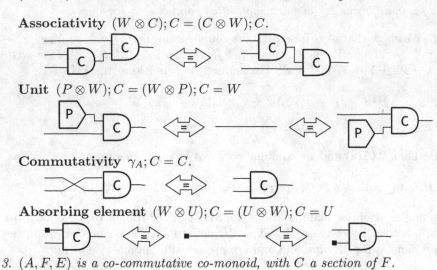

Unit $(P \otimes W); C = (W \otimes P); C = W$

Commutativity $\gamma_A; C = C.$

Absorbing element $(W \otimes U); C = (U \otimes W); C = U$

3. (A, F, E) *is a co-commutative co-monoid, with* C *a section of* $F.$

Co-associativity $F; (F \otimes W) = F; (W \otimes F).$

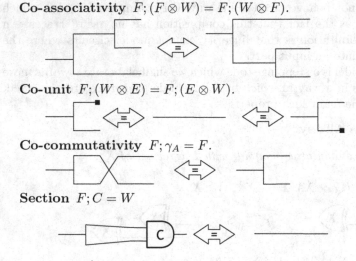

Co-unit $F; (W \otimes E) = F; (E \otimes W).$

Co-commutativity $F; \gamma_A = F.$

Section $F; C = W$

The non-trivial interplay of the basic gates gives rise to a richer algebraic structure:

Theorem 3.07. *1.* (A, X, E, F, U) *is a bialgebra.*
Distributivity $X; F = (F \otimes F); (W \otimes \gamma_A \otimes W); (X \otimes X).$

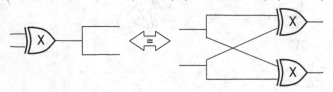

Unit $E; F = E \otimes E.$

Co-unit $X; U = U \otimes U.$

2. (A, C, F, X) *is a Laplace pairing (in the sense of Rota, as per [9]).*

$$(X \otimes W); C = (W \otimes W \otimes F); (W \otimes \gamma_A \otimes W); (C \otimes C); X.$$

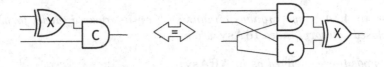

Proof. The proof is immediate from definitions.

The notion of *Laplace pairing* above is "categorified" in the obvious way from the conventional algebraic formulation: $(x \oplus y) \otimes z = (x \otimes z) \oplus (y \otimes z)$.

The proofs of Thm. 3.06 and Thm. 3.07 are immediate from definitions and only involve simple calculations. Note that all the compositions above are "safe" in the sense that "no traces are lost in the composition". In Ebergen's terminology, the interaction between components has no *computation interference*. Exploiting equality in the presence of "interference" would allow us to introduce more equations (e.g. $\bullet T; C = \emptyset = F; X$), but we will see in the following section why such equations are not interesting.

4   An Interleaved Model

4.1   An Idealised Wire Model

The next step is to "lift" the model from the previous affine use to unrestricted use. Given a set of traces f we define $!f$ as the smallest set of traces containing f, closed under self-interleaving. We define closure under self-interleaving as: $f^0 = \emptyset, f^k = f \mid f^{k-1}, !f = \bigcup_{i \geq 0} f^i$. Note that if $f : X \to Y$ then $!f : X \to Y$. We define $\mathsf{C} = !C, \mathsf{X} = !X, \mathsf{T} = !T, \mathsf{F} = !F, \mathsf{W} = !W, \mathsf{U} = !U, \mathsf{E} = !E,$ $\mathsf{P} = !P$, the models of basic components, closed under self-interleaving. This is a crucial difference between this model and Ebergen's, we do not assume serial use. However, the consequence is that the wire W has the physically unrealistic behaviour of an infinite-bounded buffer which can receive (and store) any n signals as inputs before issuing them as outputs.

Definition 4.11. *We say that $f : X \to Y, g : Y \to Z$ compose safely if and only if $!(f; g) = !f; !g$.*

Our notion of safety corresponds to Ebergen's computational noninterference. We can see that $T; C = !(T; C) = \emptyset$, whereas $\mathsf{T}; \mathsf{C}$ includes traces such as AAA', with A the input and A' the output of the composition.

Lemma 4.12. *All the compositions in Thms. 3.06 and 3.07 are safe in the sense of Def. 4.11.*

Proof. Immediate, by inspection.

Lemma 4.13. *If $f : X \to Y, f' : X' \to Y'$ then $!(f \otimes g) = !f \otimes !g$.*

Proof. Immediate from Prop. 2.03.

Theorem 4.14. *Asynchronous circuits with an interleaved model form a compact closed category, called* **IdAsy** *where*

- *composition is defined as in* **AffAsy***;*
- *identity is* W*;*
- *the structural monoidal morphisms (associator, left identity, right identity, symmetry, unit, co-unit) are obtained by applying $!-$ to the corresponding structural morphisms in* **AffAsy***;*
- *objects are self-dual $A^* = A$;*
- *the unit $\eta_A : I \to A_1^* \otimes A_2$ and the co-unit $\epsilon_A : A_1^* \otimes A_2 \to I$ have the same sets of traces as the identity $W : A_1 \to A_2$.*

In the compact-closed category it is convenient to define the dual of a morphism $f : A \to B$ as $f^* : B^* \to A^*$, $f^* = (\eta_A \otimes id_{B^*}); (id_{A^*} \otimes f \otimes id_{B^*}); (id_{A^*} \otimes \epsilon_{B^*})$. This construct has an intuitive diagrammatic representation:

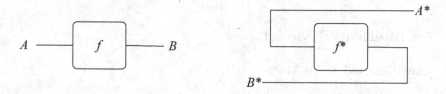

Note that:

Lemma 4.15. $\mathsf{U}^* = \mathsf{E}$.

Theorem 4.16. *The algebraic structure of* **AffAsy** *is preserved by interleaving ($!-$) in* **IdAsy***:*

- *$(A, \mathsf{X}, \mathsf{U})$ is a commutative monoid with T a retract of X.*
- *$(A, \mathsf{C}, \mathsf{P})$ is a commutative monoid with U an absorbing element.*
- *$(A, \mathsf{F}, \mathsf{E})$ is a co-commutative co-monoid with C a section of F*
- *$(A, \mathsf{X}, \mathsf{E}, \mathsf{F}, \mathsf{U})$ is a bialgebra.*
- *$(A, \mathsf{C}, \mathsf{F}, \mathsf{X})$ is a Laplace pairing.*

Proof. Composition in **IdAsy** is defined like in **AffAsy** and it is associative. W is an identity immediately from Lem. 4.14(1) because composition with W is safe for any morphism. Similarly, all the equations defining the symmetric compact closed structure involve only safe compositions, so are preserved by self-interleaving. The equations involved in Thms. 3.06 and 3.07 are also constructed out of safe compositions (Lem. 4.12).

Tho oafoty roquiromont in Lom. 4.12 io ooontial oinoo oolf intorloaving may introduce new traces in unsafe compositions. For example $F; X = \emptyset$ but $F; X^2 = AA'A'$, and in fact $F; X = !(AA'A')$ where $F; X : A \to A'$. This example also illustrates the physically unrealistic nature of this model, because consecutive signals $A'A'$ are never absorbed by the wire capacitance. A realistic model should give $F; X = !(A \cdot (A'A' + \epsilon))$, reflecting the fact that in this composition consecutive A' signals may, non-deterministically, disappear.

To prepare the ground for a more realistic model we introduce a new component $K : A \to A'$ defined as $[\![K]\!] = !(AA' + AA)$. We call this component a

capacitive wire and we represent it as $\boxed{\text{K}}$. Not accidentally, this is reminiscent of the symbol conventionally used for unknown bounded delay; this is an unknown bounded capacitance. Its behaviour is to either propagate a signal correctly or to absorb consecutive inputs, non-deterministically.

Let $|t|$ be the length of a sequence. Let $t \sqsubseteq t'$ denote a prefix t of a sequence t'. It is easy to see that all sequences in K have more inputs than outputs in any prefix and, overall, an even number of outputs can be lost.

Lemma 4.17. *Let $\iota_k : (A_1 + A_2)^* \to A_i$ for $k = 1, 2$. $t \in [\![K : A_1 \to A_2]\!]$ if and only if both these conditions hold:*

- *there exsists $k \in \mathbb{N}$ such that $|t; \iota_1| - |t; \iota_2| = 2k$*
- *for any prefix $p \sqsubseteq t$, $|p; \iota_1| \geq |p; \iota_2|$.*

The capacitive wire has the following important property:

Lemma 4.18. *1. $K : A \to A$ is idempotent, i.e. $K; K = K$.*
2. $K^n : A^n \to A^n$ is idempotent, i.e. $K^n; K^n = K^n$.

Proof. The idempotence of K is proved showing that the two conditions of Lem. 4.17 are preserved by composition. If the first capacitive wire loses $2k$ signals and the second capacitive wire loses $2k'$ signals then their composition loses $2(k + k')$ signals, which is also a valid trace in a capacitive wire.

The second property follows immediately from the naturality of $\otimes$.

4.2 A Capacitive Wire Model

We are now in a position to give a more physically accurate account of asynchronous circuits by removing the idealised wire W from the set of basic components. However, this raises a technical problem because W plays a structural role in the category as the identity. Also, the traces of the compact-closed unit (η_A) and co-unit (ϵ_A) behave like idealised wires. In order to restore the categorical structure we use the following standard construction.

Definition 4.21. *The* Karoubi *envelope of category* **C**, *sometimes written* **Split(C)**, *is the category whose objects are pairs of the form* (A, e) *where* A *is an object of* **C** *and* $e : A \to A$ *is an idempotent of* **C**, *and whose morphisms are triples of the form* $(e, f, e') : (A, e) \to (A, e')$ *where* $f : A \to A'$ *is a morphism of* **C** *satisfying* $f = e; f; e'$.

Definition 4.22. *The category of* delay-insensitive asynchronous circuits *is defined as* **DIAsy = Split(IdAsy)**.

The basic morphisms of the **DIAsy** category are

1. $\mathsf{c} = (\mathsf{K} \otimes \mathsf{K}); \mathsf{C}; \mathsf{K}$
2. $\mathsf{x} = (\mathsf{K} \otimes \mathsf{K}); \mathsf{X}; \mathsf{K}$
3. $\mathsf{t} = \mathsf{K}; \mathsf{T}; (\mathsf{K} \otimes \mathsf{K})$
4. $\mathsf{f} = \mathsf{K}; \mathsf{F}; (\mathsf{K} \otimes \mathsf{K})$.

The physical and diagrammatic representation of this construction is that all basic gates have capacitive wires as connectors:

Lemma 4.23. *1.* $\mathsf{c} = \mathsf{C}; \mathsf{K} = (\mathsf{K} \otimes \mathsf{K}); \mathsf{C}$
2. $\mathsf{x} = \mathsf{X}; \mathsf{K} = (\mathsf{K} \otimes \mathsf{K}); \mathsf{X}$
3. $\mathsf{t} = \mathsf{T}; (\mathsf{K} \otimes \mathsf{K}) = \mathsf{K}; \mathsf{T}$
4. $\mathsf{f} = \mathsf{F}; (\mathsf{K} \otimes \mathsf{K}) = \mathsf{K}; \mathsf{F}$.

Proof. From Lem. 4.17. For example, in the case of c if m respectively m' signals arrive as input, $m - 2k$ respectively $m' - 2k'$ reach the C-gate and $min(m - 2k, m' - 2k')$ are output. For post-composition with K, $min(m, m') - 2k'' = min(m - 2k'', m' - 2k'')$ signals are output. For any choice of k, k' we take $k'' = max(k, k')$.

We also have

Proposition 4.24. *1.* $e = K; E = E$
2. $u = U; K = U$
3. $p = P; K = P$.

Diagrammatically:

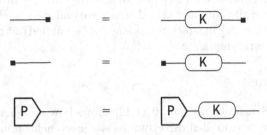

The first two equalities are obvious. For the last one, since P generates an *arbitrary* number of signals it does not matter than some of them are lost.

Theorem 4.25. *The category of delay-insensitive asynchronous circuits* **DIAsy** *is compact closed with*

1. *dual objects* $(A, K)^* = (A^*, K^*)$
2. *unit* $\overline{\eta}_A : I \to A^* \otimes A$ *defined as* $\overline{\eta}_A = \eta_A; (K^* \otimes K)$;
3. *co-unit* $\overline{\epsilon}_A : A^* \otimes A \to I$ *defined as* $\overline{\epsilon}_A = (K^* \otimes K); \epsilon_A$.

Diagrammatically, the unit and co-unit of the closed structure are:

Moreover, the fact that K is an idempotent means that the existing algebraic structure is preserved by the construction.

Theorem 4.26. *The algebraic structure of* **AffAsy** *and* **IdAsy** *is preserved in* **DIAsy***:*

- (A, x, u) *is a commutative monoid with* t *a retract of* x.
- (A, c, p) *is a commutative monoid with* u *an absorbing element.*
- (A, f, e) *is a co-commutative co-monoid with* c *a section of* f
- (A, x, e, f, u) *is a bialgebra.*
- (A, c, f, x) *is a Laplace pairing.*

Proof. Immediate. For example distributivity in the bialgebra $((A, x, e, f, u)$ is:

$$(f \otimes f); (K \otimes ((K \otimes K); \gamma_A) \otimes K); (x \otimes x)$$
$$= K^2; (F \otimes F); (W \otimes \gamma \otimes W); X^2; K^2 \qquad \text{(Lem. 4.23)}$$
$$= K^2; X; F; K^2 \qquad \text{(Thm. 4.16)}$$
$$= x; f. \qquad \text{(Lem. 4.23)}$$

Note that the proposition above involves circuits in a realistic model of glitchy circuits. The fact that we use the idealised connector W in proofs does not detract from the realism of the model.

To conclude, the category we have constructed has a complex trace model, which incorporates circuits with glitches. Reasoning directly in the trace model is awkward. However, its compact closed structure and rich algebraic properties provide a useful framework in which reasoning can be carried out more abstractly, algebraically or diagrammatically.

5   Applications

The Geometry of Synthesis project [10,11,12] shows how a higher-level programming language can be compiled directly into static asynchronous circuits, more specifically Event Logic, starting from its game semantic model [13]. The model of asynchronous circuits used there is based on the category **DIAsy** of delay-insensitive circuits but reasoning is carried out at the level of traces, and is tedious. As an application, we will show just one of the equivalences that needs to be proved in order to prove the soundness of the technique, and we do it in a purely algebraic or diagrammatic fashion [11].

We first introduce the Event Logic component $\mathsf{CALL} : A^* \otimes A \to (A^* \otimes A) \otimes (A^* \otimes A)$. It works as a stateful multiplexer-demultiplexer circuit between one occurrence of $A^* \otimes A$ on the left and two on the right. In [11] it is used to implement the *diagonal morphism* in a Cartesian category of circuits of particular shape. One of the required equations of the Cartesian product, mapped into circuits, amounts to showing that $\overline{\eta}_A; \mathsf{CALL}; (u^* \otimes e \otimes \overrightarrow{id}^2) = \overline{\eta}_A$. Diagrammatically, this is:

Lemma 5.07.

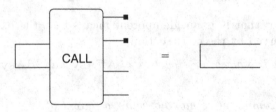

The implementation of CALL, not a basic circuit, is given below.

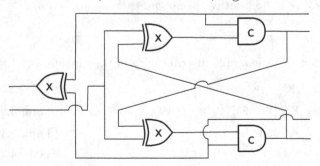

In the category, the construction is:

$$\mathsf{CALL} = (\mathsf{x}^* \otimes \overline{id}); (\overline{id}^* \otimes \overline{\gamma}); (\overline{id}^* \otimes \overline{\eta} \otimes \overline{id} \otimes \overline{\eta} \otimes \overline{id}^*);$$
$$(\mathsf{f}^* \otimes \overline{id} \otimes \overline{id}^* \otimes \overline{id} \otimes \mathsf{f}^*); (\overline{id}^* \otimes \mathsf{DW} \otimes \overline{id}^*),$$

where

$$\mathsf{DW} = (\overline{id} \otimes \mathsf{f} \otimes \overline{id}); (\overline{id}^2 \otimes \overline{\eta}^2 \otimes \overline{id}^2); (\overline{id} \otimes \mathsf{x} \otimes \overline{\gamma} \otimes \mathsf{x} \otimes \overline{id}),$$
$$(\mathsf{c} \otimes \overline{id}^2 \otimes \mathsf{c}); (\mathsf{f} \otimes \overline{id}^2 \otimes \mathsf{f}); (\overline{id} \otimes \overline{\epsilon}^2 \otimes \overline{id})$$

In the structural morphisms, if the index is not specified, it is by default A, so $\overline{\eta} = \overline{\eta}_A$, and so on. It is quite clear that trace-level reasoning about such circuits is extremely difficult! On the other hand, the algebraic proof of Lem. 5.07 is a sequence of straightforward calculations using categorical and algebraic properties. The diagrammatic representation of the proof, as a rewriting of the circuit is given in Fig. 1.

The key circuit simplifications come out the fact that e and x are either unit or co-unit or absorbing element for x, c, f taken as (co)monoids. This process of reduction results in the circuit $\overline{\eta}; \overline{\gamma}; (\overline{id} \otimes \overline{\eta} \otimes \overline{id}); (\mathsf{c} \otimes \mathsf{f}^*)$. Standard diagrammatic reasoning using the compact-closed structure allows bringing the circuit to the simpler form $\overline{\eta}; ((\mathsf{f}; \mathsf{c}) \otimes \overline{id})$ where using the fact that c is a section of f completes the proof.

6   Conclusion

In this paper we have constructed a trace model for delay-insensitive asynchronous circuits similar to Ebergen's, but generalised to handle glitchy behaviour. We showed that even in the absence of an idealised connector, which would behave naturally as an identity for compositions, such circuits can be structured in a category by taking advantage of the Karoubi envelope construction where the idempotent is a realistic connector of unknown capacitance. We further show that even though the trace model is complicated and very awkward as a basis for reasoning about such circuits, they enjoy many algebraic properties which allow diagrammatic reasoning consistent with common intuitions about such circuits. Such properties seem promising as a starting point for mechanised reasoning via, for example, circuit rewriting.

The most severe limitation of this model is its handling of circuits where feedback leads to non-terminating behavior. It is only a model of terminating computations, represented as complete traces. Technically, this is due to the fact that, unlike Ebergen, we do not adopt prefix closure. Prefix-closure cannot be naively introduced because causality loops created by feedback can lead to unrealistic solutions. For example this circuit

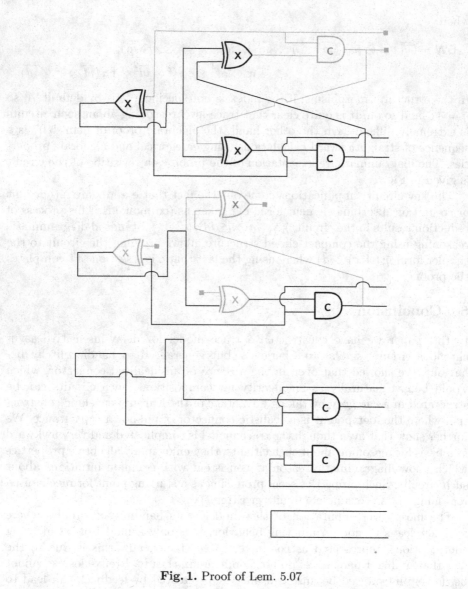

Fig. 1. Proof of Lem. 5.07

would be trace-equivalent to p (pulse), when in fact it is equivalent to u (dangling input). Our model instead equates

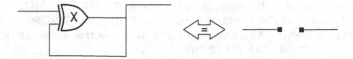

with u; e (an unresponsive circuit) which is sound but incomplete. To fix this problem causality, which we currently ignore, needs to be introduced in the model.

In a more theoretical direction it would be interesting to examine how the specific algebraic structures arising in asynchronous circuits interact with the generic framework introduced by Burroni [14] and further developed by Lafont [15], in which boolean circuits can be reduced to unique canonical forms. These notions are essential if we aim to automate reasoning about asynchronous circuits.

Acknowledgments. This paper is inspired in goals and methodology by Abramsky, Coecke and their collaborators work on categorical, algebraic and diagrammatic foundations for quantum computing [8]. This work greatly benefitted from conversations with Peter Selinger, John Baez, Bob Coecke, Samson Abramsky, Prakash Panangaden, Bertrfried Fauser, Alex Smith, Paul B. Levy, Claudio Hermida and Paul-André Melliès.

References

1. Hauck, S.: Asynchronous design methodologies: An overview. Proceedings of the IEEE 83(1), 69–93 (1995)
2. Huffman, D.: The synthesis of sequential switching circuits. Journal of the Franklin Institute 257(3), 161–190 (1954)
3. Yun, K., Dill, D.: Automatic synthesis of extended burst-mode circuits I (specification and hazard-free implementations). IEEE Transactions on Computer-Aided Design of Integrated Circuits and Systems 18(2), 101–117 (1999)
4. Sutherland, I.: Micropipelines. Communications of the ACM 32(6), 720–738 (1989)
5. Ebergen, J.: A formal approach to designing delay-insensitive circuits. Distributed Computing 5(3), 107–119 (1991)
6. Hoare, C.A.R.: Communicating Sequential Processes. Prentice-Hall (1985)
7. Josephs, M.B., Udding, J.T.: Delay-insensitive circuits: An algebraic approach to their design. In: Baeten, J.C.M., Klop, J.W. (eds.) CONCUR 1990. LNCS, vol. 458, pp. 342–366. Springer, Heidelberg (1990)
8. Abramsky, S., Coecke, B.: Categorical quantum mechanics. In: Handbook of Quantum Logic and Quantum Structures: Quantum Logic, pp. 261–324 (2008)
9. Fauser, B.: On the Hopf-algebraic origin of Wick normal-ordering. Journal of Physics A: Mathematical and General 34(105) (2001)
10. Ghica, D.R.: Geometry of Synthesis: A structured approach to VLSI design. In: Hofmann, M., Felleisen, M. (eds.) The ACM SIGPLAN-SIGACT Symposium on Principles of Programming Languages (POPL), pp. 363–375. ACM (2007)

11. Ghica, D.R., Smith, A.: Geometry of Synthesis II: From games to delay-insensitive circuits. Electr. Notes Theor. Comput. Sci. 265, 301–324 (2010)
12. Ghica, D.R., Smith, A.: Geometry of Synthesis III: Resource management through type inference. In: Ball, T., Sagiv, M. (eds.) The ACM SIGPLAN-SIGACT Symposium on Principles of Programming Languages (POPL), pp. 345–356. ACM (2011)
13. Ghica, D.R., Murawski, A.S., Ong, C.H.L.: Syntactic control of concurrency. Theor. Comput. Sci. 350(2-3), 234–251 (2006)
14. Burroni, A.: Higher-dimensional word problems with applications to equational logic. Theoretical Computer Science 115(1), 43–62 (1993)
15. Lafont, Y.: Towards an algebraic theory of boolean circuits. Journal of Pure and Applied Algebra 184(2), 257–310 (2003)

Payoffs, Intensionality and Abstraction in Games

Chris Hankin[1] and Pasquale Malacaria[2]

[1] Institute for Security Science and Technology, Imperial College London
[2] School of Electrical Engineering and Computer Science,
Queen Mary University of London

Abstract. We discuss some fundamental concepts in Game Theory: the concept of payoffs and the relation between rational solutions to games like Nash equilibrium and real world behaviour. We sketch some connections between Game Theory and Game Semantics by exploring some possible uses of Game Semantics strategies enriched with payoffs. Finally we discuss potential contributions of Abstract Interpretation to Game Theory in addressing the state explosion problem of game models of real world systems.

1 Introduction

1.1 An Historical Note

Samson Abramsky joined the Department of Computing at Imperial College London in 1983 and Hankin joined him there in 1984. They had previously collaborated on the launch of an informal inter-collegiate PhD course on Theoretical Computer Science. Their scientific collaboration with Geoffrey Burn led to work on higher-order strictness analysis of functional programs [7] and ultimately to an edited volume on abstract interpretation of declarative languages [1]. Whilst Samson's main focus was on domain logics at this time, he also made important contributions to the theory of program analysis through his invention of the notion of *polymorphic invariance* [2] and a deep study of the role of logical relations in establishing the correctness of program analyses [3]. Even his work on domain logics found an application in program analysis through Jensen's development of strictness logics [14].

Malacaria came to Imperial College London in 1993. He worked with Samson and Radha Jagadeesan on Game Semantics, solving the long standing open problem of providing a fully abstract semantics for PCF [5].

The authors of this paper subsequently worked together on using Game Semantics as a basis for program analyses that were correct by construction. This work culminated in [15] which uses Game Semantics as a basis for an Information Flow analysis. More recently, we have been studying the use of Game Theory in decision support for cyber security.

1.2 This Paper

Textbook presentations of Game Theory are often extensional: game solutions are found on normal form games. We are interested in a more intensional

B. Coecke, L. Ong, and P. Panangaden (Eds.): Abramsky Festschrift, LNCS 7860, pp. 69–82, 2013.

approach and look to Game Semantics to provide a framework for approaching this problem. In the next section we address some of the criticisms that have recently been addressed at Game Theory. We then present a common framework based on [8]. We next discuss some of the potential uses of payoffs in Game Semantics. We conclude by considering the role of abstraction in making the problem of finding game solutions more tractable.

2   The Problem with Payoffs

Game Theory is sometimes criticised for providing solutions that are unrealistic. Classical examples enlightening this criticism are provided by the centipede game or the game of ultimatum bargaining, both extensively studied by economists and social scientists. More recently what we believe to be a similar criticism has also arisen in a cyber-security context. In this section we will discuss these criticisms.

2.1   The Centipede Example

The centipede game [18] is a well known example in the Game Theory literature illustrating a variety of features and issues about Nash equilibrium solutions in games. The centipede is a multi-stage alternating game where at each stage the player whose turn is to move can either decide to end the game with some payoffs or continue. Crucially the payoffs are arranged so that if one player were to decide to continue to the next stage but at the next stage the other player were to decide to stop, the first player would get an inferior payoff than if he had decided to stop at the previous round. Figure 1 illustrates a simple centipede game. If the red player were to stop at the first stage he would get 3.20, if the blue player were to stop at stage 2, the red player would however get an inferior payoff of 1.60. However if both players were to continue playing until the end they would end up with much higher payoffs than if they were to stop at any earlier stage.

One interesting aspect of this game is that the equilibrium solution says that players should stop at the very beginning, thus ending up with payoff 3.20 for

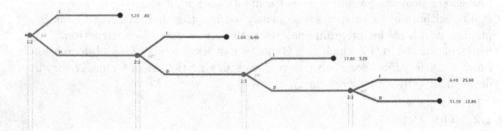

Fig. 1. The Centipede game

red and .80 for blue. This solution is explained as follows: at the very last move, which is a blue move, the blue player has interest in choosing the move giving him payoff 25.6 which would be bad for the red player who would get 6.40. Hence the red player should have stopped at the previous round as he would have gotten the higher payoff 12.8; but in that case the blue player would have gotten 3.20, which is inferior to 6.40 the reward he would have gotten had he stopped at the previous round; and so on...

The problem is that when this game is played "in reality" the outcome is different. Experimental studies show that people tend not to stop at the early stages, a notable exception being chess grand masters who when playing the game tend to stop at the beginning and so behave consistently with the equilibrium solution.

So what is wrong with Nash equilibrium? Are ordinary people irrational? Is Game Theory unrealistic?

These are fundamental questions that arise over and over in one form or another in any context where Game Theory is applied.

A classic game theoretical answer to these questions is that there is not much wrong with Nash equilibrium itself: the point is that the game with the payoffs described above is not the game ordinary people play when they are asked to play it.... In real life, e.g. when the payoffs are money, people will reason that the other player may have interest to go ahead too and not stop at the next round. Hence as long as the red player thinks that his expected future payoff, given the probability that the blue player stops at the next round, exceeds the payoff he would get by stopping at the current round then he will carry on. Therefore to match reality the payoffs of the game should be adjusted to match the real payoffs. This matching is tricky and depends on very specific circumstances, e.g. the amount involved compared with the wealth and greediness of the individual, the suspicion about the other player motives and trustworthiness, etc. Somehow the payoffs need to be tailor-made for each player.

Without taking into account all these factors in the payoffs, comparing the formal game with the game played in the real world is just comparing apples and pears.

2.2 The Prime Factorization Game

Halpern and Pass [17] consider the following game. A player is given a random odd n-bit number x and he is supposed to decide whether x is prime or composite. Guessing correctly will give him $2, however an incorrect guess will give him $-\$1000$, i.e. he will have to pay a penalty of $1000. The player can however choose the "playing safe" strategy by giving up, in which case he receives $1.

The game theoretical solution is to play, i.e. not to give up: game theoretical players have mathematical unbounded power so they never make wrong guesses and so they will always get $2. However clearly in reality people wouldn't choose the equilibrium solution: we don't need experiments to see that.

So what is wrong with Nash equilibrium? Are ordinary people irrational? Is Game Theory unrealistic?

We have already seen these questions above and the game theoretical answer is the same as we saw above: people are not playing the game those rules describe. In order to model reality we need to take into account the cost of computation and so the crucial point in matching the above payoffs to the real game is that guessing correctly will give the player payoff $2 - F(x)$, where $F(x)$ is a function representing the cost of determining whether x is prime. Again this $F(x)$ ought to be tailor-made for specific players, e.g. players having available thousands of powerful machines will tend to play for larger x as long as other factors like the electricity required by the factorisation will make it profitable still. Even if general guidelines from computability and complexity may be helpful they still miss factors that may be important to the model, e.g. the cost of electricity: for example in real world, crypto contexts like Bitcoin mining, electricity and the cost of GPUs are the key criteria in deciding whether to play the game. Once the right $F(x)$ is used the game theorist would claim that the solution matches reality.

This game is interesting because $F(x)$ depends heavily on intensional aspects like the computational resources available and limits of computational devices. These factors are external to classical Game Theory: an attempt to develop a Game Theory where computational limitations are taken into account is developed in [17]. We will suggest in section 4.1 that the intensional aspect of Game Semantics can be used for similar purposes.

3   A Common Framework

To get further in the discussion and relate Game Theory and Game Semantics it is necessary to have a formalism common to both. This has been developed by Chatterjee, Jagadeesan and Pitcher in [8]. We present some definitions based on that paper that will help in the following discussion.

3.1   Turn-Based Probabilistic Games

We consider two person games with alternating moves. At each state, exactly one player can make a move, following which the system may evolve into a new state with some probability. At this point, the other player can make a move. Hence, a typical evolution has the form:

> The system with players A and B is in state s. In this state A can move with action a resulting in the system moving to state t from which it evolves to state t_i with probability p_i. In this state B can move with action b and so on.

In [8] this is formalized by a structure $((S, E), (S_1, S_2, S_{1\bullet}, S_{2\bullet}), \delta)$ where (S, E) is a graph with nodes S and labelled edges E, $(S_1, S_2, S_{1\bullet}, S_{2\bullet})$ is a partition of S s.t. $E \subseteq \cup_i (S_i \times L \times S_{i\bullet})$ (with L the label set) and $\delta : S_{i\bullet} \to \mathcal{D}(S_{(i+1)\%2})$ associates a distribution over the states to each target state of a player move, from which the other player can move.

We use player A as a synonym for player 1 and player B as a synonym for player 2. We will consider finite games, i.e. all plays have a finite length.

As argued in [8] this is a general framework for stochastic games, e.g. non strictly alternating games can be interpreted using *dummy* moves. To recover Game Semantics of sequential languages we can use point mass distributions, in effect eliminating probabilities.

Edges (in E) have rewards associated to them, these are encoded by two maps r_1, r_2 with $r_i : E_i \to \mathbb{R}$ where E_i is the set of transition whose source is a state where player i can move.

As is usual in the literature, a strategy for a player is a method to extend a play. Given the history of the play where player A can move, a strategy for A chooses a successor state and an action to extend the play. A pure strategy is one where this choice is given by a function. A mixed strategy is a choice of several pure strategies according to some probabilities. Notice however that in a play, once a strategy is chosen by a player, that player will stick to it along that particular play, i.e. the same function is used to decide what move to make at each stage.

Since we can encode histories into states it will be enough to consider history-free or Markovian strategies, i.e. maps from states to transitions having that state as origin. Hence by pure strategies in this paper we refer to maps $\sigma, \tau : s \mapsto e$ where $e = s \to^l t$ for some l, t, with σ associated to player 1 and τ to player 2, and ρ a generic strategy. We will often write transitions as triples (s, l, t).

Given a path in the game tree, i.e. a sequence of transitions $P = e_1, ..., e_n$ we consider the mean value of this sequence to each player, so

$$\text{val}_i(P) = \frac{\sum_j r_i(e_j)}{m}$$

where the transitions e_j have source states where player i can move and m is the number of such transitions in the path P. As usual the probability of the path P is the product of the probabilities of the edges in P.

A *path* in a strategy ρ for player i is a path in the game tree where whenever it is the turn of player i to move, it will use ρ to choose the move. The set of all paths for ρ is denoted by Π^ρ.

Given a pair of strategies (σ, τ) the payoff v_ρ for player i is the expected values of the mean values of the sequences possible according to (σ, τ), i.e. the payoff (v_σ, v_τ) is defined as

$$v_\sigma = E\{\text{val}_\sigma(P) \mid P \in \Pi^\sigma \cap \Pi^\tau\}, v_\tau = E\{\text{val}_\tau(P) \mid P \in \Pi^\sigma \cap \Pi^\tau\}$$

A Nash equilibrium (N.E.) is a strategy pair (σ^*, τ^*) from which no player has advantage in deviating unilaterally, i.e.:

$$\forall \sigma, \tau. \ (v_\sigma, v_\tau^*) \leq (v_{\sigma^*}, v_\tau^*) \wedge (v_{\sigma^*}, v_\tau) \leq (v_{\sigma^*}, v_\tau^*),$$

3.2   Game Algebras

An interesting contribution of [8] is to consider how to build up composite games and in particular how equilibrium solutions are preserved by such constructions.

The authors present a rich algebra of games which includes operators for synchronous product, restriction, sequencing, iteration, player choice, probabilistic choice and tensor. Here, we just consider binary player choice – player i is able to choose between games with player i start states.

We consider rooted game graphs:

$$G^A = ((S^A, E^A), (S_1^A, S_2^A, S_{1\bullet}^A, S_{2\bullet}^A), \delta^A)$$

and

$$G^B = ((S^B, E^B), (S_1^B, S_2^B, S_{1\bullet}^B, S_{2\bullet}^B), \delta^B)$$

with start states $s^A \in S_i^A$ and $s^B \in S_i^B$. Then the player choice between these two games, written $G^A \oplus_i G^B$, is a game graph $((S, E), (S_1, S_2, S_{1\bullet}, S_{2\bullet}), \delta)$ such that:

$$S_i = S_i^A \uplus S_i^B \uplus \{\langle s^A, s^B \rangle\}$$

$$S_{(i+1)\%2} = S_{(i+1)\%2}^A \uplus S_{(i+1)\%2}^B$$

$$E = E^A \uplus E^B \uplus \{(\langle s^A, s^B \rangle, l, t) \mid (s^A, l, t) \in E^A \vee (s^B, l, t) \in E^B\}$$

$$\delta = \delta^A \uplus \delta^B$$

The reward functions are also modified in the following way (for $j = 1, 2$):

$$r_j(e) = \begin{cases} r_j^A(e), \text{if } e \in E^A \\ r_j^A((s^A, l, t)), \text{if } e = (\langle s^A, s^B \rangle, l, t) \wedge (s^A, l, t) \in E^A \\ r_j^B(e), \text{if } e \in E^B \\ r_j^B((s^B, l, t)), \text{if } e = (\langle s^A, s^B \rangle, l, t) \wedge (s^B, l, t) \in E^B \end{cases}$$

Following [8] we then have that any equilibrium payoff of a component game is an equilibrium payoff of the choice game if and only if there is no other equilibrium payoff in the other component with a higher value for player i. The cited paper discusses similar results for the other games constructions.

4   Payoffs in General Game Semantics

4.1   Some General Remarks

The games algebra from [8] is closely related to game constructions in Game Semantics, but while that work shows some interactions between equilibria and constructions on Game Semantics, it doesn't demonstrate their relevance for game theoretical problems.

We now consider more general relationships between these theories.

Game Semantics were first introduced in [5,13]. Games are "types" i.e. for example the game $N \to N$ represents the space of programs taking a natural number as input and returning a natural number. The basic types are simple one stage games where the player named Opponent starts by asking a question (he has only one move available, i.e. a single question) and the player named Proponent answers the question with a value of that basic type, for example the boolean game B can be described by the game graph on the left of Figure 2: Hence each basic value corresponds to a strategy for Proponent. The game graph

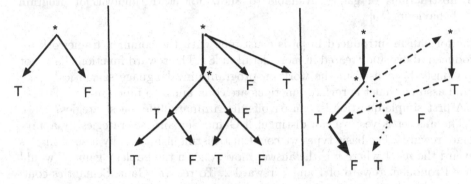

Fig. 2. Boolean Game

for $B \multimap B$ is in the centre of Figure 2. The affine implication $B \multimap B$ is a weaker form of $B \to B$ and represents the type of all algorithms from B to B using their argument at most once. Notice that the role of Proponent and Opponent change at each level in the game graph: * is a move for Opponent at the first level of the game graph but becomes a Proponent move at the second level: this is the program asking for its input. At the third level Opponent plays data values: this corresponds to the environment providing values for the program. Next the program plays a data value which, in the $B \multimap B$ example, is the final value returned by the program.

Programs are interpreted as strategies for Proponent; for example in the game $B \multimap B$ the program that performs the negation of a boolean input is interpreted by the strategy whose paths in the game graph are $**TF, **FT$. The constant programs that do not inspect their argument are: $\lambda x.T$ with path $*T$ and $\lambda x.F$ with path $*F$.

An essential aspect of Game Semantics is composition; composing two strategies corresponds to synchronizing them and hiding their interaction. For example to compose the strategy for the boolean negation with the constant T-function results in the following interaction: start by playing the strategy negation, so to the initial Opponent question play the following question asking for the argument, now see this question as the initial question for the strategy constant, hence the strategy constant will answer T, this will be seen as the Opponent answer to the Proponent question and so Proponent will now play the negation i.e. F. The crucial point here is that these interactions where Proponent moves are transferred to the other game as the Opponent moves is then hidden, so the composition results in the simple strategy in $B \multimap B$ that to the initial Opponent question answers T. This is illustrated in the right hand side of Figure 2 where only the first and last move are left once the interaction (dotted arrows) are factored out.

The important features of Game Semantics include:

1. compositionality
2. trace level description of computational processes
3. abstractions of games available to allow for static analysis of program behaviours [15]

The formalism introduced in [5] is consistent with the common framework introduced above and treated in more detail in [8]. The reward functions have not previously been used in the work on programming language semantics[1] – we could assume that the reward functions are constant zero functions.

A first simple question is: can payoffs discriminate different strategies?

The answer is yes: we can distinguish Game Semantics strategies by appropriate rewards. For basic types we could just distinguish them by associating as reward the $n + 1$ where n is the answer move, e.g. in the boolean game F would have Proponent reward of 1 and T reward 2. To recover Game Semantics composition we can think of assigning zero rewards to moves in the hidden part. In this interpretation hence two programs representing the same function become indistinguishable in a game theoretical sense.

This simple rewards structure can be elaborated to make finer distinctions, for example we can make the rewards in the hidden interaction count. e.g. by "accumulating the rewards in the hidden part" we can get a cost for the length of computation, so two strategies answering the same number but doing so with different computational cost will differ. Also complexity distinctions would appear at this stage, e.g. polynomial vs non-polynomial strategies. A step in this direction is already taken in [11]. This line of investigation may provide a way to find the "right payoffs" in a computational setting in the spirit of [17].

5   Game Theory in Game Semantics

We now explore a novel way to think of Game Semantics where Nash equilibrium becomes a tool for deciding which strategy the system and the environment should choose, given a particular objective quantified by payoffs. Notice how we now move the focus, from the classical single strategy game semantics view, to a space of candidate strategies in a game type.

In the following two examples we play classical Game Theory games in the context of Game Semantics. This is specially interesting in that these games enlighten deep issues about social interaction, competition and cooperation.

We interpret these issues in computer science terms of trustworthiness, usability and security.

---

[1] There is however some recent interesting work by Clairambault and Winskel [9] on payoffs for concurrent games.

5.1   The Centipede PCF Game

We revisit the centipede game within Game Semantics as follows. Consider the game

$$(((B \multimap B) \multimap B) \multimap B)$$

In this game there is a strategy for Proponent answering immediately the initial Opponent question and one following the initial Opponent question with another question about the second rightmost B and so on. By assigning the appropriate rewards to the answer moves we recover the centipede game. The rewards are as follows: questions have 0 rewards for both players, the answer T at level 0 has rewards 3.20 for Proponent and 0.8 for Opponent, the answer F has reward 0 for both players (at any level), the answer T at level $i+1$ has Proponent reward $2n$ where n is the Opponent reward for the Opponent T answer at level i and symmetrically the answer T at level $i+1$ has Opponent reward $2m$ where m is the Proponent reward for the Proponent T answer at level i.

We now consider Opponent and Proponent strategies whose first answer is T and all the following answers are F. This models the centipede game. Hence the equilibrium would tell us that in this game the rational thing to do is to play the constant program $\lambda x.T$. What is the meaning of the equilibrium in this context? It expresses a mistrust by the system that the environment has any reliability, e.g. the system fears that the environment will not perform correctly, if at all, the required computation.

It is easy to see, consistently with the previous discussion about the original centipede game, how degrees of trust of the system with respect to the environment could be reflected in the payoffs and so how to make the choices about what the best thing the system should do given a specific degree of trust.

5.2   The System Administrator Dilemma

In a similar vein we can consider the famous prisoner dilemma game and we look for a simple interpretation in Game Semantics. In the prisoner dilemma both players have two options: to cooperate or to not cooperate (defect). Each player receives his maximum payoff if he defects and the other cooperates, his minimum if he cooperates and the other player defects, mutual cooperation provides second best payoff and mutual defection second worst payoff; so for each player payoffs have the property $c > a > d > b$ where c is defect-cooperate, a mutual cooperation, d mutual defection and b is cooperate-defect.

Again we can see this as a system and environment game where the system may want to guarantee security and the environment usability. So the system may have the highest security by denying all access requests; in fact this is the only secure strategy in an authentication system. The environment on the other hand may have interest, from a usability point of view, in bypassing any authentication by providing access to any request.

We can model this in the space

$$((N \multimap B) \multimap B)$$

Here Proponent can choose the answer false to the initial opponent question (defect) or may instead decide to cooperate by choosing the strategy that engages with the environment by asking the initial question in the authentication module of type $(N \multimap B)$. Here Opponent can choose to answer true and so provide access to any user or he can act with due diligence and ask for the user credentials at type N which the system provides, following which Opponent checks the user credentials and provides an authentication response (true/false, accept/reject) and based on this answer Proponent can now decide whether to allow user access.

The game theoretical solution is that in the one shot prisoner dilemma the only Nash equilibrium is for both players to defect: so the system and opponent are better off not engaging with each other: the system is secure and usable, because both operate in a vacuum. A major point of debate in the Game Theory community is that the payoff the players get from both defecting may be much below the payoff they would get by both cooperating: it would make much more sense for the system to have its resource used instead of being paralysed under the fear of unauthorized intrusion.

An interesting twist is in considering the iterated prisoner dilemma. Here we are hence thinking of something like an operating system where authentication and resource access are available an unbounded number of times. In this case the solution favours cooperation and a richer panorama of equilibria with higher payoff than defection is obtained, e.g. when each player plays cooperation until the other player defects at which point the player will defect too (this is the Grim trigger strategy). This strategy well reflects the idea of a good compromise between usability and security: play nice until the other player plays dirty.

6   Games and Abstraction

Many classic examples in Game Theory like the prisoner dilemma, the centipede game and prey-predator games can be seen as illustrating the richness and conceptual complexity of rational interaction. However when applying Game Theory to the real world a state explosion problem often occurs. A large set of actions or states usually makes equilibrium non-computable; also the conceptual aspect is obfuscated by such complexity. Some form of ad-hoc abstraction is then introduced for these computational and conceptual reasons.

Our longer term objective is to replace this ad-hoc approach to abstraction by a more rigorous framework akin to Abstract Interpretation. In [15] we developed an Abstract Interpretation for Game Semantics; the most salient features of this abstraction were

1. replacing all data values by a single abstract data value
2. replacing the potentially infinite depth tree game by cyclic graphs

One application of this abstraction was in security, by tracking information flow along paths in the graphs and, for example, disallowing paths where a "high" move was followed by an observable "low" move. Similar ideas have been developed, in the context of access control, by Abramsky and Jagadeesan in [4]. We should mention also related work on abstract game semantics which has been developed by Ghica [12] and Ong [16].

Following our earlier discussion a natural development of this line of work would be to add payoffs. This would pose two important questions:

1. what are the appropriate payoffs to use in such abstract games?
2. how should we interpret Nash equilibria in the abstract game – what do they tell us about Nash equilibria in the concrete game?

Most recently, the authors of this paper have been studying the use of Game Theory in cyber security. In the last decade Game Theory has been increasingly applied in this area. Examples of applications are in the field of intrusion detection systems, anonymity and privacy, economics of network security and cryptography: for a survey of these applications we refer to [6].

The basic idea is that many cyber security situations can be modelled in terms of an Attacker attempting to breach security of the system and/or damaging its services and a Defender aiming to enhance the system security both in terms of design and response. The Attacker and the Defender clearly have conflicting goals that can be quantified in terms of economic gain/loss or disruption time; even more serious criminal threats like cyber terrorism can, with some effort, be quantified in a reasonable way. The Attacker and the Defender will, in general, interact with some knowledge of each others possible actions: to be effective both players need to be clever or, in Game Theoretical terms, rational. Because of this the notion of Nash equilibrium, discussed above, is important; an equilibrium describes a possible outcome of decision makers trying to optimize their gain while being aware of each others possible actions. Often this will result in mixing possible actions according to some probability.

Attacker and the Defender are already an abstraction whose appropriateness is often questionable e.g. when multiple players and coalitions are more appropriate. More crucially we tend to abstract on possible behaviours, i.e. while in the real world a very large number of choices may be possible we abstract them to few, for example in a cyber-security scenario there could be thousands of different types of malware leading to botnets but we may find it convenient, or even indispensable, to reduce them to a small set of "Attacker's choices". The underlying argument is that if they are "similar enough" then the reasoning on the reduced set is applicable to the original set.

6.1 A Simple Example

If we restrict ourselves for simplicity to the case of games in normal form we can think of the following scenario: Attacker A can choose between strategies $A_1, A_2, \ldots A_n$ with A_1 being "no attack" and $A_2, \ldots A_n$ being similar potential malware attacks. Suppose defender D can choose between three strategies, D_1, D_2, D_3 e.g. D_1 could be do nothing, D_2 to alert the user, D_3 to stop the service. Suppose moreover that $A_2, \ldots A_n$ result in very close payoffs. In most cases then we would be inclined to translate this into a simpler game where

A has two strategies $A_1, A_{2,...,n}$ with the $A_{2,...,n}$ payoff being a function of the original payoffs e.g. the average, or the minimum or maximum of the original payoffs. A stable Nash equilibrium in the simpler game (2×3) matrix would then suggest the following strategy for D in the original $n \times 3$ matrix: Play D_k. with $A_{i,\ i>1}$ with the same probability of playing D_k with $A_{2,...,n}$ in the reduced game. Intuitively if the $A_2, \ldots A_n$ are almost indistinguishable play the same way with each of them individually.

A concrete example is given in Figure 3 where the Attacker has three choices (columns) the last two having very similar payoffs and Figure 4 where the two last choices are reduced to one by averaging. The meaning of the payoff values should be clear e.g. $(10, -22)$ indicates that blocking malware 2 is very good for the Defender (value 10) and very bad for the Attacker (value -22). Both games have a unique and very close Nash equilibrium: in the original Defender plays 1 (resp 3) with probability $\frac{3}{7}$ (resp $\frac{4}{7}$) and Attacker plays 1 (resp 3) with probability $\frac{15}{22}$ (resp $\frac{7}{22}$) . In the reduced game equilibrium Defender plays 1 (resp 3) with probability $\frac{16}{35}$ (resp $\frac{19}{35}$) and Attacker plays 1 (resp 2) with probability $\frac{15}{22}$ (resp $\frac{7}{22}$).

A formal way to build this abstraction is to consider the matrices α, γ defined in Table 1.

The abstraction is given by α and the concretisation by γ. The abstract game in Figure 4 is obtained by the original game from Figure 3 by multiplying it with the matrix α.

	1		2		3	
1	2	2	-5	20	-5	22
2	-2	-1	0	-5	1	-7
3	-5	-5	10	-22	10	-20

Fig. 3. The original malware game

	1		2	
1	2	2	-5	21
2	-2	-1	0.5	-6
3	-5	-5	10	-21

Fig. 4. The abstract malware game

Table 1. Matrices α and γ

$$\begin{pmatrix} 1 & 0 \\ 0 & \frac{1}{2} \\ 0 & \frac{1}{2} \end{pmatrix} \qquad \begin{pmatrix} 1 & 0 & 0 \\ 0 & 1 & 1 \end{pmatrix}$$

The general form of α, γ for a general normal form game is given by γ being the normalized transpose of α and α is the matrix whose columns are buckets of columns of the original matrix and coefficients are: $\alpha_{i,j} = 0$ if i, j are not in the same bucket, $\alpha_{i,j} = \frac{1}{n}$ if i, j are in the same bucket and n is the size of the bucket.

Then γ is the Moore-Penrose pseudo-inverse of α i.e. it satisfies the following properties:

1. $\alpha\gamma\alpha = \alpha$
2. $\gamma\alpha\gamma = \gamma$
3. $(\alpha\gamma)^* = \alpha\gamma$
4. $(\gamma\alpha)^* = \gamma\alpha$

An important consequence of γ being the Moore-Penrose pseudo-inverse of α is that γ provides the least square approximation [10]. In other terms whilst $\gamma\alpha = 1$ which, consistently with the classical theory of Abstract Interpretation, means that the abstraction α is surjective, the other composition $\alpha\gamma$ provides a "best fit" (least square) approximation.

The Abstract Interpretation ideas we have sketched here are applicable beyond normal form games, e.g. when considering stochastic games, and can be integrated with Abstract Interpretation of Game Semantics and approximate bisimulation.

7 Final Remarks

The paper should be seen as an initial roadmap rather than a completed piece of work. In particular, the role of abstraction in making the approximate solution of games a tractable problem needs considerably more study.

Some of the seeds of the ideas presented in this paper were sown twenty to thirty years ago through our joint and separate work with Samson. We wish Samson many years of continued scientific work and hope, one day, to be able to discuss our results with him.

Aknowledgments. We thank Dusko Pavlovic and Fabrizio Smeraldi for helpful discussions on this work. Both authors are partially supported by the "Games and Abstraction: the Science of Cyber Security" project (EPSRC projects EP/K005790/1 and EP/K005820/1).

References

1. Abramsky, S., Hankin, C. (eds.): Abstract Interpretation of Declarative Languages. Ellis Horwood (1987)
2. Abramsky, S.: Strictness analysis and polymorphic invariance. In: Ganzinger, H., Jones, N.D. (eds.) Programs as Data Objects. LNCS, vol. 217, pp. 1–23. Springer, Heidelberg (1986)

3. Abramsky, S.: Abstract Interpretation, Logical Relations and Kan Extensions. J. Log. Comput. 1(1), 5–40 (1990)
4. Abramsky, S., Jagadeesan, R.: Game Semantics for Access Control. Electr. Notes Theor. Comput. Sci. 249, 135–156 (2009)
5. Abramsky, S., Jagadeesan, R., Malacaria, P.: Full Abstraction for PCF. Inf. and Comput. 163(2), 409–470 (2000)
6. Alpcan, T., Basar, T.: Network Security: A Decision and Game Theoretic Approach. Cambridge University Press (2011)
7. Burn, G.L., Hankin, C., Abramsky, S.: Strictness Analysis for Higher-Order Functions. Sci. Comput. Program. 7(3), 249–278 (1986)
8. Chatterjee, K., Jagadeesan, R., Pitcher, C.: Games for Controls. In: CSFW 2006, pp. 70–84 (2006)
9. Clairambault, P., Winskel, G.: On concurrent games with payoff, http://www.cl.cam.ac.uk/~cdt25/ecsym/Publications/
10. Di Pierro, A., Hankin, C., Wiklicky, H.: Measuring the confinement of probabilistic systems. Theor. Comput. Sci. 340(1), 3–56 (2005)
11. Ghica, D.R.: Slot games: a quantitative model of computation. In: Proc. POPL 2005, pp. 85–97 (2005)
12. Ghica, D.R.: Applications of Game Semantics: From Program Analysis to Hardware Synthesis. In: LICS 2009, pp. 17–26. IEEE Computer Society (2009)
13. Hyland, M., Ong, L.: On Full Abstraction for PCF: I, II, and III. Inf. and Comput. 163(2), 285–408 (2000)
14. Jensen, T.P.: Strictness Analysis in Logical Form. In: Hughes, J. (ed.) FPCA 1991. LNCS, vol. 523, pp. 352–366. Springer, Heidelberg (1991)
15. Malacaria, P., Hankin, C.: Non-Deterministic Games and Program Analysis: An Application to Security. In: LICS 1999, pp. 443–452. IEEE Computer Society (1999)
16. Ong, C.-H.L.: Some Results on a Game-Semantic Approach to Verifying Finitely-Presentable Infinite Structures (Extended Abstract). In: Ésik, Z. (ed.) CSL 2006. LNCS, vol. 4207, pp. 31–40. Springer, Heidelberg (2006)
17. Pass, R., Halpern, J.: Game theory with costly computation: formulation and application to protocol security. In: Proceedings of the Behavioral and Quantitative Game Theory: Conference on Future Directions. ACM (2010)
18. Rosenthal, R.: Games of Perfect Information, Predatory Pricing, and the Chain Store. Journal of Economic Theory 25(1), 92–100 (1981), doi:10.1016/0022-0531(81)90018-1
19. von Neumann, J., Morgenstern, O.: Theory of Games and Economic Behavior. Princeton University Press, Princeton (1944)

On the Theory of Composition in Physics

Lucien Hardy

Perimeter Institute, 31 Caroline Street North,
Waterloo, Ontario N2L 2Y5, Canada

Abstract. We develop a theory for describing composite objects in
physics. These can be static objects, such as tables, or things that happen in spacetime (such as a region of spacetime with fields on it regarded
as being composed of smaller such regions joined together). We propose
certain fundamental axioms which, it seems, should be satisfied in any
theory of composition. A key axiom is the order independence axiom
which says we can describe the composition of a composite object in any
order. Then we provide a notation for describing composite objects that
naturally leads to these axioms being satisfied. In any given physical context we are interested in the value of certain properties for the objects
(such as whether the object is possible, what probability it has, how wide
it is, and so on). We associate a *generalized state* with an object. This
can be used to calculate the value of those properties we are interested
in for for this object. We then propose a certain principle, *the composition principle*, which says that we can determine the generalized state
of a composite object from the generalized states for the components by
means of a calculation having the same structure as the description of
the generalized state. The composition principle provides a link between
description and prediction.

1 Introduction

It is a great pleasure to contribute to this festschrift for Samson Abramsky. Over
the last twenty years the worlds of quantum theory and computer science have
collided giving rise to quantum information and quantum computing. What has
singled out Samson's approach has been the emphasis on fundamental structure.
Physicists tend to rely on partial differential equations and simple circuit models.
Computer science, on the other hand, investigates a much richer and deeper set
of paradigms for dynamics. Samson has been the leading force in bringing these
deeper structural insights to bear on quantum theory through his work on the use
of category theory in quantum information [7, 8], his work on investigating the
sheaf-theoretic structure of various no-go theorems in quantum foundations [6, 9],
and much more (for example [5, 10, 3, 4, 1, 2]). The present contribution is in the
same spirit, and Samson's influence will be clear to all readers of this volume.

Science proceeds by analyzing big things in terms of smaller things while
keeping note of how these smaller things are joined together. In other words,
it concerns composite objects. The composite objects we wish to analyze may
be static objects to be specified at a given time or they may be something that

B. Coecke, L. Ong, and P. Panangaden (Eds.): Abramsky Festschrift, LNCS 7860, pp. 83–106, 2013.

happens in spacetime. Thus, a table is made out of pieces of wood joined together appropriately. A region of spacetime with fields on it can be thought of as being composed of many smaller regions of spacetime joined at their boundaries. A quantum optical experiment can be thought of as consisting of many apparatus uses (or operations) joined together so that apertures on these apparatuses are aligned. And so on. In many different branches of physics (and indeed science generally) we see ideas of composition. Indeed, it is difficult to imagine scientific explanation that does not correspond to some kind of compositional analysis. The usual approach is to reinvent basic ideas about how these smaller parts are composed to make bigger things every time we set up a new physical theory. It makes sense to think about composition of this sort in the abstract. Having obtained general notions about the theory of composition, we can see how these work for particular applications. In this way we may gain useful insight about how science works in general. This is the subject of this paper.

In the example of a table we can describe how different parts are actually joined (by somebody) to make the table. However, we do not need to imagine that somebody is actually putting the composite object together for a theory of composition to be useful. Rather, we may merely be analyzing an object in terms of its parts. This is the case in the example of a region of spacetime with fields on it. Given some larger region we can divide it up into smaller regions (in many different ways). Nobody is actually building the larger region out of smaller regions. There may, indeed, be many ways of regarding a bigger object as being made out of smaller parts.

Initially we will be interested in the *description* of composite objects irrespective of whether some particular laws of physics actually allow any given object to exist. Indeed, an interesting example of a composite object that we can describe, yet is impossible, is the Penrose (or impossible) triangle.

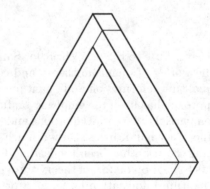

This well known example consists of three straight beams each having square cross section and each legally joined to the other two at the ends at right angles (as shown). The resulting object, however, is clearly impossible. In our theory of composition we would be able to describe this object simply by specifying the three objects and the way they are joined.

Having discussed the description of composite objects, we will then go on to discuss what *predictions* different physical theories might make about such objects. The sort of statements a physical theory will make depends on what type of physical theory we have. Deterministic theories can give us a yes or no answer to whether a particular object can exist. Probabilistic theories might give us a probability. We will propose a principle that may be of some use in setting up new physical theories. This is the *composition principle*. This principle says that we can establish the generalized state for a composite object by means of a calculation having the same structure as the description of the composition of that object.

In this paper we will be concerned with some preliminary ideas concerning composition. We will set up some further notation and introduce some axioms for composition which may, or may not, be satisfied in certain situations. Our original motivation for these considerations comes from quantum theory. However, the claim is a stronger one. Namely that all physical theories can be understood in these terms and that the composition principle can always be made to hold. The hope is that these ideas can play a role in the construction of a theory of quantum gravity. With regard to quantum theory it is possible that, by thinking about composition in an abstract and structural way, we may be able to provide deeper motivation for the kind of axioms that have recently been used in operational reconstructions of quantum theory [21, 15, 27, 13, 29, 23]. In particular, we will see that there is a link between the axiom of tomographic locality and the composition principle proposed here.

2 Examples and the Tensorial Notation

2.1 Tables

To get us warmed up let us consider an example. A piece of furniture is composed out of many separate parts joined together in different ways. For example, the following (two-dimensional) table

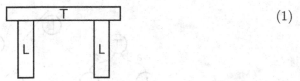

(1)

is made by joining legs, L, to a top T. We can illustrate how the table is put together by showing the joins as follows

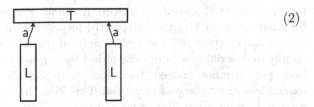

(2)

Here we join the leg to the table by a join of a type we describe as a. We have an arrow because joins are typically asymmetric. For example, we may join the leg to the table by putting glue on the leg then fixing it in place on the table (a stronger join may involve screws as well). In this illustration we retain the shapes of the objects. We can use more abstract notation

$$\Leftrightarrow \quad L^{a_1} L^{a_2} T_{a_1 a_2} \tag{3}$$

We will call this abstract notation *the tensorial notation* because of its similarity with tensor notation (though, of course, here it is being used to describe composite objects). The advantage of more abstract notation is that we may use the same notation across different branches of physics (not just furniture). In the diagrammatic notation (on the left) we represent each object by a circle. The table has two different positions one can join legs and these are represented by the arrow entering the circle in different places. In the symbolic notation the two different positions are represented by whether we consider the first or second subscript respectively on $T_{a_1 a_2}$. In the symbolic notation we need to introduce integers, 1 and 2, to label the different joins. These integers have no significance beyond that they label the joins. We can relabel them with different integers (or permute the integers used) and have the same object.

The tensorial notation carries no particular order on the objects. For example, we can write

$$L^{a_1} L^{a_2} T_{a_1 a_2} = L^{a_2} T_{a_1 a_2} L^{a_1} = T_{a_1 a_2} L^{a_1} L^{a_2} = L^{a_2} L^{a_1} T_{a_1 a_2} \tag{4}$$

This lack of order is even clearer in the diagrammatic notation. There we do not care where the circles are placed on the page so long as we preserve the exit and entry positions on the circles for the joins as well as preserving the graphical information. For example

$$\tag{5}$$

This lack of order is important. Often we are tempted to think in terms of there being a particular order in particular physical situations. For example, when we buy a piece of self-assembly furniture it usually comes with detailed instructions for what order one is advised to put the pieces together in. This is useful advice to have if one is trying to build a piece of furniture. However, here we are interested simply in describing a composite object, not in accounting for how it might have been put together. Indeed, there may be many alternative orders in which to assemble a given piece of furniture. This idea that one should not think of the objects in some particular order will play an important role in what follows.

2.2   Circuits

A common type of situation in physics is a circuit (such as in quantum theory). A circuit consists of operations wired together. Here is an illustration of a circuit:

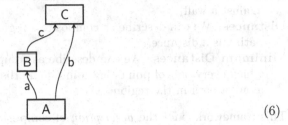

$$(6)$$

which can be described by the notation

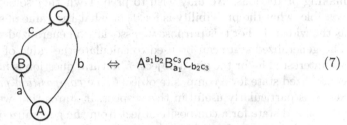

$$\Leftrightarrow \quad A^{a_1 b_2} B^{c_3}_{a_1} C_{b_2 c_3} \tag{7}$$

An operation corresponds to one use of an apparatus. The apparatus has apertures that are aligned with each other so that systems of various types, denoted
by a, b, etc can pass between the operations. A system of type a passing from
one operation to another corresponds to a join which we will say is of type a.
The apparatus has on it outcomes (such as lights that flash, a meter whose nee-
dle points to a particular number, a LED display indicating an outcome, etc).
The operation has a subset of all the possible outcomes associated with it (this
is implicit in the symbol A). We will say that the operation "happens" if the
outcome recorded is in the set of outcomes associated with the given operation.
In a deterministic theory a given circuit is either possible or impossible. In a
probabilistic theory a given circuit will have a probability for happening (the
probability that the outcome at each circuit is in the set of outcomes for that
operation). A general operational theory for circuits (with particular application
to quantum theory) using the notation in this paper is given in [22–24].

2.3   Other Examples

We can use the same notation to describe many different kinds of situations.
Here are some examples:

Penrose Objects. This is the class of objects described in the following way.
  We take a number of square cross-section beams of a certain length. Then
  each beam can be joined to others at right angles at its ends. Most objects so
  formed will be impossible. In particular, we can describe Penrose triangles
  and generalizations thereof (such as Penrose squares, Penrose pentagons,
  ...) in this notation. Some objects described in this way will be possible.

Spacetime with Fields. We can describe a region of spacetime with fields defined on it that is being regarded as composed of many joined smaller regions.

Statics Problems. We can describe statics problems (such as a ladder leaning against a wall).

Distances. We can describe as composite a region of spacetime in which every path has a distance.

Minimum Distances. We can describe as composite a region of spacetime in which every pair of points has a minimum distance measured between them along a path in the region

This framework is for the *description* of composite objects without saying anything about whether these objects are possible. In physics we are interested in making predictions. We may wish to predict whether some particular object is possible, what the probability is for it, or what the value of some property (such as the width) is. For this purpose we associate a generalized state with an object. The generalized state can be used to calculate the value of those properties we are interested in for the given object. A natural question is how do we obtain the generalized state for a composite object? The *composition principle* discussed in Sec. 5 is particularly useful in this respect. It states that we can determine the generalized state for a composite object from the generalized states for the components by means of a calculation that has the same form as the description of the given composite object. For example,

$$\mathsf{A}^{a_1 b_2}\mathsf{B}_{a_1}\mathsf{C}_{b_2} \quad \text{has generalized state} \quad A^{a_1 b_2} B_{a_1} C_{b_2} \tag{8}$$

where $A^{a_1 b_2}$, B_{a_1}, and C_{b_2} are the generalized states associated with the components. In the case of probabilistic circuits, for example, these mathematical objects are tensors. The placement of subscripts and superscripts indicates some particular mathematical procedure for completing the calculation (it need not be a tensor calculation). If we can always write down our calculations in this way then the composition principle may turn out to be a very powerful way of obtaining new physical theories.

3   Background

A decade or so ago, Abramsky and Coecke initiated a hugely influential approach to quantum theory based on category theory [7]. This emphasizes the compositional structure of quantum circuits and the connection between this compositional structure and the structure of quantum calculations. One aspect of this work is the use of diagrammatic notation. This is taken to heart here. Another tradition in quantum foundations has been the convex probabilities approach (in which states are represented by lists of probabilities). This approach goes back to Mackey [26] and has been worked on by many people over the years including Ludwig [25], Davies and Lewis [16], Gunson [20], Mielnik [28], Araki [11], Gudder *et al.* [19], Foulis and Randall [18], Fivel [17] as well as more recent incarnations [21, 12]. More recently there has been some work combining the diagrammatic approach of Abramsky and Coecke with the the convex probabilities approach (for example, see the papers of Chiribella, D'Ariano, and Perinotti [14, 13] and the duotensor formulation due to the present author [22–24]). In this paper, the approach developed in [22–24] which concerns probabilistic circuits is taken as a springboard to a more general theory of composition. The notation used there (though in a more restricted context) is the same as the tensorial notation for describing composite object used here. Thus, rather than writing $(A \otimes B) \circ (C \otimes D)$ or $(A \circ C) \otimes (B \circ D)$ for

$$
\begin{array}{cc}
\boxed{C} & \boxed{D} \\
a \uparrow & \uparrow b \\
\boxed{A} & \boxed{B}
\end{array}
\tag{9}
$$

we write

$$A^{a_1} B_{a_1} C^{b_2} D_{b_2} \tag{10}$$

This change of notation signals a change of attitude. The tensor product $\otimes$ is replaced by the notion of a *null join* and is treated as yet another type of join, albeit with special properties (as will be discussed in Sec. 4.1 and Sec. 4.3). The superscript/subscript structure now tells us where the components are joined. This is a more versatile notation than the $\circ$ symbol which plays the same role in the example given. This notation is such that we can mix up the order and still denote the same circuit. For example, $C^{b_2} B_{a_1} D_{b_2} A^{a_1}$ corresponds to the same circuit. This notation is also good for describing other kinds of composite object (such as tables) where we are not concerned with process or the passage of systems between boxes.

Although the ideas in this paper are categorical in spirit, no attempt will be made to bring the formal apparatus of category theory to bear on theory of composition proposed here. However, given unifying power of categorical approaches, it is to be expected that much good would come of such an endeavor.

4   The Description of Composite Objects

In Sec. 2 we provided a particular notation (which we dubbed the tensorial notation) for describing composite objects. This notation has, built into it, various assumptions about the nature of composition. In this Sec. 4.1 we wish to take a step back and analyze some of these basic assumptions. We will do this by suggesting some fundamental axioms. We do not claim that these constitute a complete set of axioms. They are simply proposed to help us to gain some insight into the notion of composition. The first, and most fundamental, of these is the *composition axiom*. This will allow us to use a more primitive form of notation (than the tensorial notation) which we will call *the bipartite notation*. Once we have the bipartite notation we propose two more fundamental axioms. These are the *order independence axiom* and the *null joins axiom* (actually a set of axioms concerning null joins). These axioms take us much, but not all of the way to being able to use the tensorial notation. In Sec. 4.2 we will state the composition locality axiom which, basically, is an axiom saying that we can use the tensorial notation for describing composite objects. We will also state the *R-enablement axiom* which enables us to regard joins in either direction. The remainder of this section will deal with joins. We will discuss sufficient sets of joins, and a certain *boundary axiom*.

All these axioms are motivated by thinking about composite objects such as a piece of furniture or a region of spacetime broken up into smaller regions. None of these axioms need be true and some are more basic than others. In this section we are interested in the description of composite objects irrespective of whether the laws of physics say the given object is possible. We will address what the laws of physics say is possible in latter sections.

4.1   The Bipartite Notation and Fundamental Axioms

We assume we have various types of object, A, B, C, ... We could have more than one object of a given type. An object is fully specified if we provide a specification such that no other object has the same specification. Objects whose full specifications are the same are of the same type and should be represented by the same letter. Objects whose full specifications are different are different object types and should be represented by a different letter. We now state the most basic of axioms.

Composition Axiom: Any object composed of two objects is fully specified if one is provided with a full specification of the two component objects and a description of the way in which they are joined.

This axiom corresponds to a kind of reductionism. Were it not true it would be difficult to develop a theory of composition. We will denote the ways in which one object can be joined to another by α, β, γ, ... If we join B to A by means of join α, according to the composition axiom, we fully specify the resulting object by

$$(A, B)_\alpha. \tag{11}$$

We call this *the bipartite notation*. Note that the α indicates not only the method of joining but also the join positions on the two objects. For example, A may represent a wooden die, B a metal die. Then α may represent the join in which we attach the six side of a wood die to the five side of the metal die by putting glue on the six of the wooden die and pressing it into place on the five side of the metal die. Note that there are two aspects of the join. First, there is the type of join (involving a certain area and glue) and then there is the position of the join on the two objects. We will denote the type of join by a, b, ... and the position of the join by x, y, ... Thus, we have $\alpha = (a, x, y)$ where a is the type of join (applying glue over a certain area) and x is the position of the join on the first object (the six side of the wooden die) and y is the position of the join on the second object (the five side of the medal die). Another example is in a circuit.

Then a join $\alpha = (\mathsf{a}, x, y)$ would correspond to aligning the aperture at position x on the first operation with the aperture at position y on the second operation so that a system of type a can pass between the two operations.

Joins are, in general, asymmetric. For example, we put glue on the first object then press it into place on the second object. We define α^R through

$$(\mathsf{A}, \mathsf{B})_\alpha = (\mathsf{B}, \mathsf{A})_{\alpha^R}. \tag{12}$$

Hence, if $\alpha = (\mathsf{a}, x, y)$ then $\alpha^R = (\mathsf{a}^R, y, x)$. Here a^R is the same join type as a but described in the reverse direction (for example, we put glue on the second object then press it into place on the first object).

Here are some examples of composite objects.

$$((\mathsf{A}, \mathsf{B})_\alpha, \mathsf{C})_\beta \quad ((\mathsf{A}, \mathsf{B})_\alpha, \mathsf{C})_\beta, \quad ((\mathsf{A}, \mathsf{B})_\alpha, ((\mathsf{C}, \mathsf{A})_\beta, \mathsf{A})_\gamma)_\delta, \quad (((\mathsf{A}, \mathsf{B})_\alpha, \mathsf{C})_\beta, \mathsf{D})_\delta \tag{13}$$

We get quite complicated bracketting structure here indicating a particular order of composition.

The second most fundamental axiom we propose is the following

Order Independence Axiom: A given composite object with three components can be regarded as being composed in any order. Thus, if

$$D = (\mathsf{A}, (\mathsf{B}, \mathsf{C})_\beta)_\alpha$$

then there exists some γ, δ, μ, ν such that

$$D = ((\mathsf{A}, \mathsf{B})_\gamma, \mathsf{C})_\delta \quad \text{and} \quad D = ((\mathsf{A}, \mathsf{C})_\mu, \mathsf{B})_\nu$$

This is a very basic axiom since, were it not true, it would matter what order we chose to describe the way in which the composite object is built up from its components. However, if we take this axiom to heart it has potentially far reaching consequences since, in fact, we do typically choose a special order when analyzing composite objects for some physical situations. The most pertinent example is objects composed in time. For example, we may evolve a state through a number of discrete time steps. Typically we consider the corresponding patches of space time in sequence. The point of the order independence axiom in this case is that one can consider the components of such physical objects in any order, not just the order suggested by the sequence in time.

Whichever way we choose to divide a composite object into two parts, these two parts are, by definition, joined. However, one way of joining is where we do not directly join two things but merely consider them both to be "part of the picture" (and specify no further relationship between them). We represent this by $(A, B)_0$ and call 0 the null join. We will say that two objects joined by the null joint are *disjoint*. It is reasonable to assume this particular way of joining objects will have special properties since otherwise it would not be distinguished from other types of join. We assume, then, that

Null Joins Axioms: Null joins have the following properties:

Universality: any pair of objects, A and B, can be joined by a null join.

Uniqueness: If $(A, B)_\alpha = (A, B)_0$ then $\alpha = 0$.

Symmetry: We have $(A, B)_0 = (B, A)_0$ for any pair of objects, A and B.

Refinement: if an object is joined to a composite object by the null join then it is appended to each component of the composite object by the null join. This means that if we have an object $((A, B)_\alpha, C)_0$ and we write $((A, B)_\alpha, C)_0 = ((A, C)_\beta, B)_\gamma$ (by the order independence axiom) then we must have $\beta = 0$.

Although we give the null join a special name and propose a certain axioms for it, we do not otherwise treat it on a different footing to other joins. It is just another type of join. If we are going to compose the space time regions associated with three sequential time steps in an order that is not that of the sequence then we might use the null join. Thus, if these three time steps are A, B, and C to be taken in that sequence then we could write $((A, B)_\alpha, C)_\gamma$ where the join α is that between the first and second time step and the join γ is that of attaching the third time step. But we might write $((A, C)_0, B)_\delta$ where δ is the join of inserting the time step B in between A and C. It is reasonable to expect that physical properties for objects connected by the null join will behave in certain ways. For example, in the duotensor framework [22–24], the probability for a circuit composed of two disjoint parts factorizes.

4.2   Tensorial Notation and Composition Locality

We will now take steps taking us from the bipartite notation, $(A, B)_\alpha$, to the tensorial notation in the light of the two fundamental axioms just introduced. The bipartite notation is good for describing a bipartite composite object. However, when we consider an object consisting of more than two parts it becomes cumbersome. A tripartite object is represented by $((A, B)_\alpha, C)_\gamma$. The problem with this notation is that it does not represent the spirit of the order independence axiom. If it does not matter what order three or more parts are joined in, then it would be convenient if notation treated all the parts on an equal footing. The tensorial notation accomplishes this though at the cost of assuming something about the nature of composition. This is the assumption of composition locality given below.

Let us write

$$(A, B)_\alpha = A^{\mathsf{a}_1}[x] B_{\mathsf{a}_1}[y] \tag{14}$$

where $\alpha = (\mathsf{a}, x, y)$ and a is the type of join, x is the "position" of the join to object A, and y is the "position" of the join to object B. Here we are just creating the possibility that joins, such as α, can be separated into type information and position information (since this is the case in the examples we will consider). However, we don't have to do this. We could simply have a new type for every pair of positions. Hence, this is just notation (we are not assuming anything extra quite yet). The integer label, 1, on the right is not strictly necessary here but is essential when we have more than one join in the tensorial notation. Now, if we have three objects joined together, we have

$$((A, B)_\alpha, C)_\beta = (A^{a_1}[x]B_{a_2}[y])^{d_2}[u] \ C_{d_2}[v] \tag{15}$$

where $\alpha = (a, x, y)$ and $\beta = (d, u, v)$. The bracketing means that we do not, strictly, need the integer labels. However, we include them as we are taking steps to the tensorial notation where we will need them. Recall that the particular integers used are of no significance - they are just labels. The example in (15) can be read as first joining A at x to B at y by join a and then joining the composite object $(A, B)_\alpha$ at u to C at v to by join d. It seems reasonable that when we join C in this way we can understand the join d to be composed of a join to A and a join to B. Indeed, consider the object

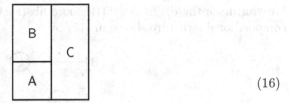

$$\tag{16}$$

Here a bigger rectangle is composed from a square and two smaller rectangles. We can explode this to illustrate where the joins are

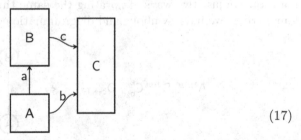

$$\tag{17}$$

In this example C is joined separately to A and B. We can think of the join, (d, u, v) in (15) as being equal to (bc, qr, st) where A at q is joined to C at s by a join of type b and B at r is joined to C at t by a join of type c. We would like our notation to reflect this structure. We will first simplify our notation by absorbing the positions of the joins into the specification of the object. Thus, rather than writing $A^{a_1 b_2}[xq]$ we will write $A^{a_1 b_2}$ where the positions x and q have been absorbed into the definition of A. Similarly, we write $B^{c_3}_{a_1}$ and $C_{b_2 c_3}$ absorbing the relevant positions into the definitions of B and C respectively. It may, sometimes, be useful to go back to the more cumbersome notation where we explicitly give the positions.

With this notation in place we can provide a new axiom that is motivated by the above discussion.

Composition Locality. We can represent a multipartite composite object as follows:

$$A^{a_1 b_2} B^{c_3}_{a_1} C_{b_2 c_3} \tag{18}$$

for a tripartite object, and

$$A^{a_1b_2c_3}B^{d_4e_5}_{a_1}C^{f_6}_{b_2d_4}D_{c_3e_5f_6} \tag{19}$$

for an object with four components, and so on. In such expressions the order of the objects and the particular choice of integer labels are unimportant. For example,

$$A^{a_1c_3}B^{d_4}_{a_1}C_{c_3d_4} = A^{a_7c_3}C_{c_3d_1}B^{d_1}_{a_7} = B^{d_4}_{a_1}A^{a_1c_5}C_{c_5d_4} = \dots \tag{20}$$

In each of these equivalent expressions we maintain the same types of joins between objects.

The notation in (18) exactly captures the structure of the diagram in (17). We can make the diagram a little more abstract. Thus, we can represent the compositional structure shown in (17) by

$$\tag{21}$$

Indeed, since one can use diagrammatic notation, this diagram and this symbolic notation are just two ways of notating the same thing. Likewise, when we have four parties, we have symbolic and diagrammatic notation:

$$A^{a_1b_2c_3}B^{d_4e_5}_{a_1}C^{f_6}_{b_2d_4}D_{c_3e_5f_6} \quad \Leftrightarrow \tag{22}$$

The composition locality axiom enables us to represent composite objects in this way. It is worth commenting on what is ruled out by this axiom. It could be the case that when we join two objects, A and B, some new joins become possible that cannot be understood in terms of joins to A and B separately. It could be the case that some kinds of join can only be regarded as being between more than two objects. It could matter what order we understand the composition of the objects to be taken in. These things are ruled out if we assume composition locality. In the symbolic notation this is illustrated by the fact that we can write the objects in any order (as illustrated in (20)). In the diagrammatic notation it is illustrated by the fact that we can place the objects anywhere on the page (so long as we maintain the joins between the objects).

In general joins are asymmetric. This is why we use asymmetric notation. For example, we place glue on the object with raised superscript before pushing it into place on the object with lowered superscript. Any asymmetrically described join can be described in the other direction. Thus, we may apply glue on the object with lowered superscript object then press it into place on the object with raised superscript. We denote this reverse description of a join by using a R superscript. So, if a is some join type, then a^R is the same join described in the reverse direction. This means that

$$A^{a_1}B_{a_1} = A_{a_1^R}B^{a_1^R} \tag{23}$$

Hence, definitionally, we can raise and lower superscripts and subscripts in this case if we append the R superscript. If we have more subscripts and superscripts we would like to be able to do the same. Hence we assume

R-Enablement. In any description of a composite object in tensorial notation we can reverse the direction of any particular join by changing a subscript to a superscript, changing the corresponding superscript to a subscript and appending a R to each. For example,

$$A^{a_1 b_2}C_{a_1}^{a_3}B_{b_2 a_3} = A_{a_1^R}^{b_2}C^{a_1^R a_3}B_{b_2 a_3}$$

We note that, when subscripts are raised or lowered we should maintain a record of the positions of the joins. We can do this by appropriate indentation of the labels (though, for the most part, we will not worry about this in this paper). The assumption of R-enablement is very natural. In diagrammatic notation this simply corresponds to reversing the direction of the arrows. In diagrammatic notation we reverse the direction of the join simply by reversing the direction of the arrows. For example,

$$\tag{24}$$

It is natural to lump together the last two axioms. If we have R-enablement and composition locality then we will say that we have R-enabled composition locality. In this case we can use the tensorial notation and reverse the direction of any join.

We will now show that R-enabled composition locality implies the order independence axiom. We can write

$$A^{a_1 b_2}B_{a_1}^{c_3}C_{b_2 c_3} = (A, B^{c_3}C_{c_3})_\alpha \tag{25}$$

where $\alpha = (ab, xy, uz)$ corresponds to joining A at xy to $B^{c_3}C_{c_3}$ at uz by a join of type ab (where u is a position at B and z is a position at C). It is then clear that

$$R\text{-enabled composition locality} \Rightarrow \text{the order independence axiom} \tag{26}$$

To see this we write

$$A^{a_1 b_2}B_{a_1}^{c_3}C_{b_2 c_3} = A_{a_1^R}^{b_2}B^{a_1^R c_3}C_{b_2 c_3} = (B, A^{b_2}C_{b_2})_\beta \tag{27}$$

where $\beta = (\mathsf{a}^R \mathsf{c}, uv, xw)$ corresponds to joining B at uv to A at x and C at w by a join of type $\mathsf{a}^R \mathsf{c}$.

We have not proven that the order independence axiom implies the composition locality axiom. It would be interesting to find examples of composite objects that satisfy the very fundamental order independence axiom while violating composition locality. In this case we could not use the tensorial notation.

4.3 Composition Locality and Null Joins

Some properties follow from the uniqueness axiom for null joins. Thus, consider two joins, $\alpha = (\mathsf{a}, x, y)$ and $\beta = (\mathsf{b}, u, v)$ where both of these joins are, actually, the null join. By uniqueness, $\alpha = \beta = 0$. Hence, we have $\mathsf{a} = \mathsf{b}$. What this means is that the join type is the same for any null join between a given pair of objects. We will denote the null join type by the symbol 0. Thus, in this case we have $\mathsf{a} = \mathsf{b} = 0$. We also have $x = u$ and $y = v$. This means that the null join does not really have a position at either object. It is also worth noting that $0^R = 0$ by the symmetry axiom for null joins. All these properties are consistent with the idea that the null join just corresponds to taking two objects to be part of the picture without specifying any relationship beyond this.

Consider the composite object $(\mathsf{A}, \mathsf{B}^{\mathsf{a}_1} \mathsf{C}_{\mathsf{a}_1})_0$. This consists of two disjoint parts (that is parts connected by the null join). According to the R-enabled composition locality axiom we can write

$$(\mathsf{A}, \mathsf{B}^{\mathsf{a}_1} \mathsf{C}_{\mathsf{a}_1})_0 = \mathsf{A}^{\mathsf{b}_2 \mathsf{c}_3} \mathsf{B}^{\mathsf{a}_1}_{\mathsf{b}_2} \mathsf{C}_{\mathsf{a}_1 \mathsf{c}_3} = \mathsf{B}^{\mathsf{a}_1 \mathsf{b}_2^R} \mathsf{A}^{\mathsf{c}_3}_{\mathsf{b}_2^R} \mathsf{C}_{\mathsf{a}_1 \mathsf{c}_3} = (\mathsf{B}, \mathsf{A}^{\mathsf{c}_3} \mathsf{C}_{\mathsf{c}_3})_\alpha = ((\mathsf{A}, \mathsf{C})_\beta, \mathsf{B})_{\alpha^R}$$

(28)

for some b, c, β and α. Now, according to the refinement axiom for null joins, we must have $\beta = 0$ and hence $\mathsf{c} = 0$. By a similar argument, we must have $\mathsf{b} = 0$. Hence,

$$(\mathsf{A}, \mathsf{B}^{\mathsf{a}_1} \mathsf{C}_{\mathsf{a}_1})_0 = \mathsf{A}^{0_2 0_3} \mathsf{B}^{\mathsf{a}_1}_{0_2} \mathsf{C}_{\mathsf{a}_1 0_3}$$

(29)

We can notate this this simply by omitting the null joins. Thus, we can write

$$(\mathsf{A}, \mathsf{B}^{\mathsf{a}_1} \mathsf{C}_{\mathsf{a}_1})_0 = \mathsf{A} \mathsf{B}^{\mathsf{a}_1} \mathsf{C}_{\mathsf{a}_1}$$

(30)

where the null joins are taken to be implicit. Another example is the following

$$(\mathsf{A}^{\mathsf{a}_1} \mathsf{B}_{\mathsf{a}_1}, \mathsf{C}^{\mathsf{b}_2} \mathsf{D}_{\mathsf{b}_2})_0 = \mathsf{A}^{\mathsf{a}_1} \mathsf{B}_{\mathsf{a}_1} \mathsf{C}^{\mathsf{b}_2} \mathsf{D}_{\mathsf{b}_2}$$

(31)

Again, the null joins are taken to be implicit. We can show that the right of (31) follows from composition locality and the refinement axiom for null joins. This is true in general. Every pair of objects that are not joined by some non-null join are joined by a null join. Hence, when we adopt these axioms, we are effectively forced to notate null joins this way in the tensorial notation (there is no point in explicitly including the null joins as it is clear where must be). We can also see, immediately, that if we do notate null joins in this way then all the null join axioms are satisfied. Diagrammatically we have

$$A^{a_1}B_{a_1}C^{b_2}D_{b_2} \quad \Leftrightarrow \quad \text{(diagram)} \tag{32}$$

Thus, disjoint parts of a composite object are naturally represented by disjoint parts of the graph.

4.4 Pruning

We now wish to address the possibility that we may have more joins listed in specifying an object than necessary. We may be able to prune the graph while still describing the composite object as fully as we require for our purposes. It is worth setting up this discussion with an example.

The notion of a join is really an abstraction. It does not have to correspond to two objects actually being in contact. For example, we may have a join type, b, between two squares (with unit length edges) that corresponds to "joining" the second square one unit of distance to the right of the first square. Thus our object looks like

$$\boxed{A} \xrightarrow{\text{1unit}} \boxed{C} \tag{33}$$

which we can write as

$$A^{b_1}C_{b_1} \quad \Leftrightarrow \quad \text{(A)} \xrightarrow{b} \text{(C)} \tag{34}$$

This join does not correspond to placing the two squares exactly next to each other but letting them have a given displacement from one another. Now, if we place a third square directly between the two objects then we have the following object:

$$\boxed{A \mid B \mid C} \tag{35}$$

If the join type corresponding to placing the second square immediately to the right of the first square is denoted a then we can denote this composite object as

$$A^{a_1 b_3}B_{a_1}^{a_2}C_{a_2 b_3} \quad \Leftrightarrow \quad \text{(A)} \xrightarrow{a} \text{(B)} \xrightarrow{a} \text{(C)} \tag{36}$$

If we had also to include joins where the squares had relative displacements of two units, three units, and so on, then as the number of squares increase the number of joins would increase faster ($N(N-1)$ joins are possible for N objects). Fortunately, we note that the fact that A and C are joined by a join of type c is implied by the other joins (the fact that A is joined to B and then B is joined to C by joins of type a). Hence, we do not lose any information by pruning the description to the form

$$A^{a_1}B^{a_2}_{a_1}C_{a_2} \quad \Leftrightarrow \quad \text{(A)} \xrightarrow{a} \text{(B)} \xrightarrow{a} \text{(C)} \tag{37}$$

However, this is a little unsatisfactory. If a third object (B) is present then we can prune join c. Otherwise we cannot. In this example, we can avoid this problem by enlargening our set of objects to include "empty space" objects. Thus, we denote by E an empty unit square. For definiteness, we can imagine that the squares are made out of sheet aluminium. Then an empty square means that we have a one unit area with no sheet aluminium in it. Then we can denote the object illustrated in (33) by the "pruned" notation

$$A^{d_1}E^{e_2}_{d_1}C_{e_2} \quad \Leftrightarrow \quad \text{(A)} \xrightarrow{d} \text{(E)} \xrightarrow{e} \text{(C)} \tag{38}$$

where d and e denote the appropriate join types here. If we proceed in this way then the number of joins need not grow as fast with the number of objects. Further more, we can specify the object using only joins that correspond to the components being in contact.

This particular example motivates the following definition for the general case.

> *A sufficient set of join types* for some given set of objects is a set of join types such that any composite object formed from the given set of objects is fully specified (in the tensorial notation) if all joins of the type in the sufficient set are given where they exist between the components.

This, in turn, motivates the following definition

> *A minimal set of join types* for some given set of objects is a sufficient set of join types having the property that, if any element is removed, we no longer have a sufficient set.

The key idea behind sufficient (and minimal) sets of join types is that some joins, while they may exist, need not be specified in the context of a given set of objects. If we have a sufficient or, better, a minimal set of join types then we can proceed more efficiently.

4.5   Boundaries

Typically objects are joined to each other at boundaries of those objects. These boundaries live in space, time, or space-time. An object will have a boundary that delimits what else it can be joined to. This motivates the following axiom:

Boundary Axiom: given some sufficient set of joins, $\mathcal{J}_{\text{suff}}$, then for any object A and any join a $\in \mathcal{J}_{\text{suff}}$ admitted by A there exists a unique join b in $\mathcal{J}_{\text{suff}}$ such that if A is joined to some object by ab then no further joins in $\mathcal{J}_{\text{suff}}$ at A are possible other than the null join.

Let us call the unique join, b, in this definition the *complement to* a *for* A. We can write it as $\bar{a}_A$. By $\bar{0}_A$ we denote the complement to the null join. This deserves a special name so we call it the complete join for A. If A is joined to any other object by its complete join then it does not admit further joins (other than the null join). Thus, the complete join can be thought of as representing the boundary of A.

Once we have the boundary axiom, we can introduce a final refinement to the tensorial notation for composition. We can denote an object by $A^{a_1}_{b_2}$ where we demand that $ab^R = \bar{0}_A$. The subscripts and superscripts may be composite. For example, we may have $A^{a_1 b_2}_{c_3 d_4}$ where $abc^R d^R = \bar{0}_A$. The advantage of this notation is that if there are joins left open we can read it off. For example, we may have a composite object

$$A^{a_1 b_2} B^{c_3}_{a_1} C_{c_3 d_4} \tag{39}$$

This has open joins b at A and d^R at C. This is even clearer if we represent this diagrammatically

$$\tag{40}$$

5 The Composition Principle

Up to now we have discussed the *description* of composite objects and we have developed the tensorial notation for this description. In physics we are also interested in predicting the values of properties pertaining to the given physical object. Here are a few examples of properties we might try to predict.

Possible or Impossible. We may be interested in whether some particular object is actually possible. If it is possible we can return the value 1 and if not, we can return the value 0. An example of this are what we might call "Penrose objects" consisting of beams with square cross section that are joined at right angles at their ends. The Penrose triangle is an example of an impossible object and so we should return the value 0. The possible/impossible approach is a way of understanding deterministic theories (such as Newtonian dynamics). Processes that violate the predictions of the theory are, within the context of this theory, impossible.

Probability. We may ask what the probability of a particular set of outcomes is. An example where we do this is for probabilistic circuits.

Dimensions. We may be interested in what the dimensions of some object is (its height, width, length).

Minimum Distances. We may be interested in the minimum distance between points in the object (as measured within the object).

In a typical situation in physics we are only interested in some subset of properties (for example, in thermodynamics, we are interested in the values of certain macroscopic variables but we are not interested in the velocity of individual atoms). We define the following notion

> **The generalized state** is a mathematical object, A, associated with an object, A, which can be used to calculate the value of those properties we are interested for this object.

Typically in physics a state pertains to a given time and is used to make predictions for later times. The generalized state is a more general notion than this since we may be making predictions of a more general type (such as in the examples given above).

A key question is how do we calculate the generalized state for a composite object? We propose the following principle.

> **THE COMPOSITION PRINCIPLE:** The generalized state for a composite object can be calculated from the generalized states for the components by means of a calculation having the same structure as the description of the composition of that object.

For example, we can write

$$\mathsf{A}^{a_1 b_2} \mathsf{B}^{c_3}_{a_1} \mathsf{C}_{b_2 c_3} \quad \text{has generalized state} \quad A^{a_1 b_2} B^{c_3}_{a_1} C_{b_2 c_3}$$

where $A^{a_1 b_2}$, $B^{c_3}_{a_1}$, and $C_{b_2 c_3}$ are the generalized states associated with $\mathsf{A}^{a_1 b_2}$, $\mathsf{B}^{c_3}_{a_1}$, and $\mathsf{C}_{b_2 c_3}$ respectively. The subscript/superscript placement corresponds to some mathematical operations respecting the composite structure. We will not show that the composition principle holds for all physical situations (such as those given). There may be counterexamples. However, we will illustrate the principle with a few simple examples.

5.1   Circuits

Here is an example of the composition principle in action. We consider circuits as described in Sec. 2.2 where we are interested in calculating the probability of seeing outcomes at the operations that are in the associated outcome sets. A much discussed assumption for probabilistic circuit models is *tomographic locality* (see [23] and references therein). This property has many equivalent formulations. The most common is that the state associated with a bipartite system can be determined by local measurements on each of the systems. In the case where we have *tomographic locality* the composition principle holds for calculating probabilities. To calculate the probability of the circuit

$$\Leftrightarrow \quad A^{a_1 b_2} B^{c_3}_{a_1} C_{b_2 c_3} \tag{41}$$

we can write

$$\text{Prob}(\mathsf{A}^{a_1 b_2} \mathsf{B}^{c_3}_{a_1} \mathsf{C}_{b_2 c_3}) = A^{a_1 b_2} B^{c_3}_{a_1} C_{b_2 c_3}$$

where $A^{a_1 b_2}$, $B^{c_3}_{a_1}$, and $C_{b_2 c_3}$ are tensors. The subscript/superscript placement now corresponds to Einstein summation. In this example $A^{a_1 b_2} B^{c_3}_{a_4}$ corresponds to *multiplying* two numbers (the elements of the tensors with these particular values of the subscripts and superscripts) and then the repeated index corresponds to summation. Thus, we have two operations, multiplication and summation. This means that something like $C^{a_1} D_{a_1}$ is a sum of products. These two operations guarantee that we can do the calculation in any order. Thus, we can write

$$A^{a_1 b_2} B^{c_3}_{a_1} C_{b_2 c_3} = C_{b_2 c_3} A^{a_1 b_2} B^{c_3}_{a_1} = B^{c_3}_{a_1} A^{a_1 b_2} C_{b_2 c_3} = \cdots$$

by the associativity property of multiplication and we can perform the three different summations in any order by the associativity property of summation. The composition principle is satisfied since, for the purpose of calculating probabilities, we have generalized states (the tensors) and the are determined by means of a calculation having the same structure as compositional structure.

Quantum theory satisfies the principle of tomographic locality and it can be formulated in such a way that the generalized state is given by tensors as just described. However, for quantum theory, there exists a more tailor-made way of representing the generalized state in such a way that the composition principle is satisfied. This is to represent the generalized state of the operation $\mathsf{B}^{c_3}_{a_1}$, for example, by an hermitian operator $\hat{B}^{c_3}_{a_1}$ satisfying certain properties (see [23, 24] for more details). Then we can write

$$\text{Prob}(\mathsf{A}^{a_1 b_2} \mathsf{B}^{c_3}_{a_1} \mathsf{C}_{b_2 c_3}) = \hat{A}^{a_1 b_2} \hat{B}^{c_3}_{a_1} \hat{C}_{b_2 c_3}$$

In the notation on the right, the repeated label indicates partial trace over the appropriate part of the operator space (as outlined in [23, 24]).

Tomographic locality has been used as a postulate in many of the recent reconstructions of quantum theory. It is intriguing that it is connected to the even deeper idea of the composition principle. In the context of probabilistic circuit theories, the composition principle follows from tomographic locality. It is possible that the converse is true. This raises the intriguing possibility of using the composition principle as a basis for reconstructing quantum theory. The composition principle is a deeper principle than tomographic locality and it may play a role in formulating physics that goes beyond the circuit setting of quantum theory (such as a theory of quantum gravity).

5.2 Labeled Tiles

We consider square tiles of unit length that are labeled $n = 1, 2, \ldots$. Let the nth such tile be $\mathsf{T}[n]$. A complete set of join types is $\{x, y, 0\}$. The join type x corresponds to placing one immediately to the right of the other as follows

$$\mathsf{T}^{x_1}[m] \mathsf{T}_{x_2}[n] \quad \Leftrightarrow \quad \boxed{m \mid n} \tag{42}$$

The join type y corresponds to placing one tile immediately above the other

$$T^{y_1}[m]T_{y_2}[n] \quad \Leftrightarrow \quad \boxed{\begin{array}{c} n \\ \hline m \end{array}} \tag{43}$$

The third join type is the null join where we simply consider the two tiles as part of the same picture without specifying their relationship any further.

$$T[m]T[n] \quad \Leftrightarrow \quad \boxed{n} \quad \boxed{m} \tag{44}$$

We can define x^R and y^R to correspond to joins in the opposite direction. For example,

$$T^{x_1^R}[m]T_{x_2^R}[n] \quad \Leftrightarrow \quad \boxed{\begin{array}{c|c} n & m \end{array}} \tag{45}$$

We can build up highly composite objects by joining many tiles. For example,

$$D = T^{x_2}_{y_1}[1]\ T^{y_1 x_3}[2]\ T^{y_4}_{x_3}[3]\ T^{y_5}_{y_3 x_2}[4]\ T_{y_5}[5]\ T^{x_6}[6]\ T_{x_6}[7] \quad \Leftrightarrow \quad \boxed{\begin{array}{cc} & 5 \\ \hline 1 & 4 \\ \hline 2 & 3 \end{array}} \quad \boxed{\begin{array}{c|c} 6 & 7 \end{array}} \tag{46}$$

This particular composite object is disjoint (it consists of two disjoint parts).

We are interested in calculating geometric properties having to do with the relative displacement of tiles (where defined). Hence, we define the following generalized state for objects that have no disjoint parts

$$A = \{((m,n),(\Delta x, \Delta y)) : \text{for all tile labels } m,n \text{ in A}\} \tag{47}$$

where Δx is the horizontal displacement from tile m to tile n and Δy is the vertical displacement between these tiles (so $(\Delta x, \Delta y)$ is the displacement between these two tiles). We can obtain the generalized state for objects that do have disjoint parts by using the null join. Corresponding to the object, AB we have

$$AB := A \cup B \tag{48}$$

(recall that we suppress the 0 but we could write $A^{0_1}B_{0_1}$ for this object). For the composite object D in (46) we would get all the displacements in each of the two disjoint parts. However, no displacements would be specified between the two disjoint parts since these are not defined.

We can join two composite objects by an x join by specifying the tiles in each object where this join is to occur. So,

$$C = A^{x_1}[u]B_{x_1}[v] \tag{49}$$

means that we join A at tile u to B at tile v by an x type join. The associated generalized state is given by

$$C = A^{x_1}[u]B_{x_1}[v] = A \cup B \cup \mathcal{X}(A[u], B[v]) \tag{50}$$

where

$$\mathcal{X}(A[u], B[v]) =$$
$$\{((m,n), \boldsymbol{\Delta}_{(m,u)} + (1,0) + \boldsymbol{\Delta}_{(v,n)}) : \forall (m,u) \in \mathsf{A} \text{ and } (v,n) \in \mathsf{B}\} \quad (51)$$

and $\boldsymbol{\Delta}_{(m,u)}$ is the displacement between tile m and tile u. This is the set of displacements between A and B that are established by this new join. For this join to be consistent no two tiles should end up at the same position. Clearly, one can determine this by taking an appropriate function of C. The effect of a y join is given by

$$E = A^{y_1}[u] B_{y_1}[v] = A \cup B \cup \mathcal{Y}(A[u], B[v]) \quad (52)$$

where

$$\mathcal{Y}(A[u], B[v]) =$$
$$\{((m,n), \boldsymbol{\Delta}_{(m,u)} + (0,1) + \boldsymbol{\Delta}_{(v,n)}) : \forall (m,u) \in \mathsf{A} \text{ and } (v,n) \in \mathsf{B}\} \quad (53)$$

If we just have a single tile, $\mathsf{T}[n]$, then the corresponding generalized state is

$$T[n] = \{((n,n),(0,0))\} \quad (54)$$

It is now easy to see that, in building up the generalized state corresponding to any composite object (such as D in (46)), we get the same answer no matter what order we do the calculation. Further, it is clear that geometric properties are all given by appropriate functions of the resulting generalized state. The composition principle clearly holds since we obtain generalized states by means of a calculation having the same structure as that of the description of the composite object.

When we have more than one join we have an additional consistency condition. Namely, the displacement between any pair of tiles should be the same. If the joins are inconsistent then we will get more than one displacement for any given pair of tiles. This consistency condition is easily checked by taking an appropriate function of the mathematical object corresponding to the constructed composite object.

It is worth adding that we could have a more compact specification of the generalized state. Thus, rather than specifying the relative displacement of every pair of tiles in each disjoint part, we could simply specify the relative displacement of every tile from a given *fiducial* tile in each disjoint part. We could expand this compressed information simply by subtraction to get the displacement between any two tiles. A similar compression appears in the circuit framework above where we effectively specify a state by listing the probabilities for a fiducial set of measurement outcomes from which all others can be calculated.

5.3   Other Examples

It is a simple matter to set up the theory for other examples but lack of space prohibits us from doing so here. For example, Penrose objects can be specified by calculating the displacement between the two ends in the coordinate system that is given by the average of coordinate systems for each beam. Arbitrary regions of spacetime with fields can be joined by requiring that the fields match and a certain number of derivatives match at the boundaries. Given a new example it requires a certain amount of ingenuity to set up the appropriate mathematical objects along with appropriate joining conditions. However, it seems likely that this can be done for any physical example. This raises the question of whether assuming the composition principle actually amounts to assuming something of the world, or whether it can always be made to be true. Even if the latter is the case, the composition principle could be a useful tool in constructing new physical theories. In particular, in a theory of quantum gravity we must, presumably, build up a picture of bigger things by joining smaller things. However, we can expect to have indefinite causal structure and consequently boundaries between such smaller things can be expected to be causally fuzzy. In this case, the new tools developed in this paper could be very useful for the process of theory construction.

6   Conclusions

We have developed the tensorial notation for describing composite objects and explored the assumptions going into this notation using the more primitive bipartite notation. In describing objects we are not making any predictions for them. The composition principle suggests that there is a correspondence between objects and certain mathematical objects (generalized states) that allow us to make predictions of properties of the objects by means of equations that have the same structure as the description of the composition of those objects. We have given a few simple examples where the composition principle can be seen to hold. We make the stronger claim that any reasonable physical theory can be formulated in a way that this principle holds. Further, we claim that all physical theories *ought* to be formulated in a way that makes it clear that the composition principle holds. This is a potentially very useful principle in constructing new physical theories, such as a theory of quantum gravity.

References

1. Abramsky, S.: Petri nets, discrete physics, and distributed quantum computation. In: Kleijn, J., Yakovlev, A. (eds.) ICATPN 2007. LNCS, vol. 4546, pp. 1–2. Springer, Heidelberg (2007)
2. Abramsky, S.: Temperley-lieb algebra: From knot theory to logic and computation via quantum mechanics. In: Mathematics of Quantum Computing and Technology, pp. 415–458. Taylor and Francis (2007)
3. Abramsky, S.: Relational hidden variables and non-locality. Arxiv preprint arXiv:1007.2754 (2010)

4. Abramsky, S.: Big toy models: representing physical systems as chu spaces. Syntheso, 1–22 (2011)
5. Abramsky, S.: Relational databases and bell's theorem. arXiv preprint arXiv:1208.6416 (2012)
6. Abramsky, S., Brandenburger, A.: The sheaf-theoretic structure of non-locality and contextuality. New Journal of Physics 13(11), 113036 (2011)
7. Abramsky, S., Coecke, B.: A categorical semantics of quantum protocols. In: Proceedings of the 19th Annual IEEE Symposium on Logic in Computer, pp. 415–425 (2004)
8. Abramsky, S., Coecke, B.: Physics from computer science: a position statement. International Journal of Unconventional Computing 3(3), 179 (2007)
9. Abramsky, S., Hardy, L.: Logical bell inequalities. Physical Review A 85(6), 062114 (2012)
10. Abramsky, S., Heunen, C.: Operational theories and categorical quantum mechanics. arXiv preprint arXiv:1206.0921 (2012)
11. Araki, H.: On a characterization of the state space of quantum mechanics. Communications in Mathematical Physics 75(1), 1–24 (1980)
12. Barrett, J.: Information processing in generalized probabilistic theories. Physical Review A 75(3), 032304 (2007)
13. Chiribella, G., D'Ariano, G.M., Perinotti, P.: Informational derivation of Quantum Theory. ArXiv:1011.6451 and Physical Review A 84, 012111 (2011)
14. Chiribella, G., D'Ariano, G.M., Perinotti, P.: Probabilistic theories with purification. ArXiv:0908.1583 and Physical Review A 81(6), 062348 (2010)
15. Dakic, B., Brukner, C.: Quantum theory and beyond: is entanglement special? Arxiv preprint arXiv:0911.0695 (2009) and Halvorson, H. (ed.): Deep Beauty: Understanding the Quantum World Through Mathematical Innovation, pp. 365–392. Cambridge University Press (2011)
16. Davies, E.B., Lewis, J.T.: An operational approach to quantum probability. Communications in Mathematical Physics 17(3), 239–260 (1970)
17. Fivel, D.I.: How interference effects in mixtures determine the rules of quantum mechanics. Physical Review A 50(3), 2108 (1994)
18. Foulis, D.J., Randall, C.H.: Empirical logic and tensor products. Interpretations and Foundations of Quantum Theory 5, 9–20 (1979)
19. Gudder, S., Pulmannová, S., Bugajski, S., Beltrametti, E.: Convex and linear effect algebras. Reports on Mathematical Physics 44(3), 359–379 (1999)
20. Gunson, J.: On the algebraic structure of quantum mechanics. Communications in Mathematical Physics 6(4), 262–285 (1967)
21. Hardy, L.: Quantum theory from five reasonable axioms. Arxiv preprint quant-ph/0101012 (2001)
22. Hardy, L.: A formalism-local framework for general probabilistic theories including quantum theory. Arxiv preprint arXiv:1005.5164 (2010)
23. Hardy, L.: Reformulating and reconstructing quantum theory. Arxiv preprint arxiv:1104.2066 (2011)
24. Hardy, L.: The operator tensor formulation of quantum theory. Arxiv:1201.4390 and Philosophical Transactions of the Royal Society A: Mathematical, Physical and Engineering Sciences 370, 3385–3417 (1971)
25. Ludwig, G.: An axiomatic basis of quantum mechanics, vols. I, II. Springer, Berlin (1985, 1987)

26. Mackey, G.W.: The mathematical foundations of quantum mechanics: a lecture-note volume. Addison-Wesley (1963)
27. Masanes, L., Müller, M.P.: A derivation of quantum theory from physical requirements. ArXiv:1004.1483 and New Journal of Physics 13(6), 063001 (2011)
28. Mielnik, B.: Theory of filters. Communications in Mathematical Physics 15(1), 1–46 (1969)
29. Zaopo, M.: Information theoretic axioms for quantum theory. arXiv preprint arxiv:1205.2306 (2011)

On the Functor ℓ^2

Chris Heunen

Department of Computer Science, University of Oxford*
heunen@cs.ox.ac.uk

Abstract. We study the functor ℓ^2 from the category of partial injections to the category of Hilbert spaces. The former category is finitely accessible, and in both categories homsets are algebraic domains. The functor preserves daggers, monoidal structures, enrichment, and various (co)limits, but has no adjoints. Up to unitaries, its direct image consists precisely of the partial isometries, but its essential image consists of all continuous linear maps between Hilbert spaces.

I am delighted to dedicate this paper to Samson Abramsky, on the occasion of his 60th birthday. Among all the wisdom he has imparted on me is this contradictory gem: "Never solve a problem completely, or noone will have a reason to cite you". My better nature gladly took some time off to let this paper follow his advice.

1 Introduction

The rich theory of Hilbert spaces underpins much of modern functional analysis and therefore quantum physics [24,20], yet important parts of it have resisted categorical treatment. In any categorical analysis of a species of mathematical objects, free objects of that kind play a significant role. The important ℓ^2-construction is in many ways the closest thing there is to a free Hilbert space: if X is a set, then

$$\ell^2(X) = \left\{ \varphi \colon X \to \mathbb{C} \;\middle|\; \sum_{x \in X} |\varphi(x)|^2 < \infty \right\}$$

is a Hilbert space, in fact the only one of its dimension up to isomorphism. The ℓ^2-construction can be made into a functor, if we take partial injections as morphisms between the sets X, as first observed by Barr [6]. Outside functional analysis, it also plays a historically important role in the geometry of interaction (which has been noticed by many authors; an incomplete list of references includes [9,1,12,13,17]).

* The author was supported by U.S. Office of Naval Research Grant Number N000141010357, and would like to thank Jiří Rosicky, Bart Jacobs, Peter Hines, Samson Abramsky, Prakash Panangaden, John Bourke, Norbert Schuch, and Jamie Vicary for encouragement and pointers.

B. Coecke, L. Ong, and P. Panangaden (Eds.): Abramsky Festschrift, LNCS 7860, pp. 107–121, 2013.

Explicit categorical properties of the ℓ^2–construction are few and far between in the literature. These notes gather and augment them in a systematic study. Section 2 starts with the category of Hilbert spaces: it is self-dual, has two monoidal structures, and its homsets are algebraic domains, but its enrichment and limit behaviour is wanting. Section 3 discusses the category of partial injections, which is more well-behaved: it is also self-dual, has two monoidal structures, and is enriched over algebraic domains; moreover, it is finitely accessible. Section 4 introduces and studies the functor ℓ^2 itself. It preserves the self-dualities, monoidal structures, and enrichment. It also preserves (co)kernels and finite (co)products, but not general (co)limits. Therefore it has no adjoints, and in that sense does not provide free Hilbert spaces. It is faithful and essentially surjective on objects. Section 5 studies the image of the functor ℓ^2. Up to unitaries, its direct image consists precisely of partial isometries. Remarkably, it is essentially full, that is, its essential image is the whole category of Hilbert spaces.

Choice issues are lurking closely beneath the surface of these results. In fact, $\ell^2(X)$ is not just a Hilbert space; it carries a priviledged orthonormal basis. The functor ℓ^2 is an equivalence between the category of partial injections, and the category of Hilbert spaces with a chosen orthonormal basis and morphisms preserving it. But the latter class of morphisms is too restrictive: all interesting applications of Hilbert spaces require a change of basis. Following the guiding thought "a gentleman does not choose a basis", Section 6 suggests directions for further research.

2   The Codomain

Definition 2.1. We are interested in the category **Hilb**, whose objects are complex Hilbert spaces, and whose morphisms are continuous linear functions.

2.2. The category **Hilb** has a *dagger*, that is, a contravariant involutive functor $\dagger\colon \mathbf{Hilb}^{\mathrm{op}} \to \mathbf{Hilb}$ that acts as the identity on objects. On a morphism $f\colon H \to K$ it is given by the unique adjoint $f^\dagger\colon K \to H$ satisfying $\langle f(x)\,|\,y\rangle = \langle x\,|\,f^\dagger(y)\rangle$. For example, an isomorphism u is unitary when $u^{-1} = u^\dagger$.

2.3. Furthermore, the usual tensor product of Hilbert spaces provides the category **Hilb** with symmetric monoidal structure. The monoidal unit is the 1-dimensional Hilbert space $\mathbb{C}$. In fact, **Hilb** has *dagger symmetric monoidal* structure, *i.e.* $(f \otimes g)^\dagger = f^\dagger \otimes g^\dagger$, and all coherence isomorphisms are unitaries.

2.4. Direct sums of Hilbert spaces provide the category **Hilb** with (finite) *dagger biproducts*. That is, $H \oplus K$ is simultaneously a product and a coproduct, the projections are the daggers of the corresponding coprojections, and $(f \oplus g)^\dagger = f^\dagger \oplus g^\dagger$. Similarly, the 0-dimensional Hilbert space is a *zero object*, *i.e.* simultaneously initial and terminal.

2.5. Let us emphasize that we take continuous linear maps as morphisms between Hilbert spaces, rather than linear contractions. The category of Hilbert spaces with the latter morphisms is rather well-behaved, see *e.g.* [5]. However, it is the former choice of morphisms that is of interest in functional analysis and quantum physics. Unfortunately it also reduces the limit behaviour of the category **Hilb**, as the following lemma shows.

Lemma 2.6. *The category* **Hilb**:

(i) *has (co)equalizers,*
(ii) *does not have infinite (co)products;*
(iii) *does not have directed (co)limits.*

Proof. Part (i) holds because **Hilb** is enriched over abelian groups and has kernels [16]. For (ii), consider the following counterexample. Define an $\mathbb{N}$-indexed family $H_n = \mathbb{C}$ of objects of **Hilb**. Suppose the family (H_n) had a coproduct H with coprojections $\kappa_n \colon H_n \to H$. Define $f_n \colon H_n \to \mathbb{C}$ by $f_n(z) = n \cdot \|\kappa_n\| \cdot z$. These are bounded maps, since $\|f_n\| = n \cdot \|\kappa_n\|$. Then for all $n \in \mathbb{N}$ the norm of the cotuple $f \colon H \to \mathbb{C}$ of (f_n) must satisfy

$$ n \cdot \|\kappa_n\| = \|f_n\| = \|f \circ \kappa_n\| \leq \|f\| \cdot \|\kappa_n\|, $$

so that $n \leq \|f\|$. This contradicts the boundedness and hence continuity of f. Finally, part (iii) follows from (ii) and [23, IX.1.1] □

2.7. Despite the previous lemma, **Hilb** is *conditionally (co)complete*, in the sense that it does have objects that partially obey the universal property of infinite (co)products: for a family H_i of Hilbert spaces,

$$ H = \big\{ (x_i) \in \prod_i H_i \mid \sum_i \|x_i\|^2 < \infty \big\}. $$

is a well-defined Hilbert space under the inner product $\langle (x_i) \mid (y_i) \rangle = \sum_i \langle x_i \mid y_i \rangle$ [20]. The evident morphisms $\pi_i \colon H \to H_i$ satisfy $\pi_i \circ \pi_i^\dagger = \mathrm{id}$ and $\pi_i \circ \pi_j^\dagger = 0$ when $i \neq j$. A cone $f_i \colon K \to H_i$ allows a unique well-defined morphism $f \colon K \to H$ satisfying $\pi_i \circ f = f_i$ if and only if $\sum_i \|f_i\|^2 < \infty$. Note, however, that the cone (π_i) itself does not satisfy this condition. In this sense, $\ell^2(X)$ is the conditional coproduct of X many copies of $\mathbb{C}$.

2.8. A similar phenomenon occurs for simpler types of (co)limits. Monomorphisms in **Hilb** are precisely the injective morphisms, and epimorphisms are precisely those morphisms with dense range [15, A.3]. Not every monic epimorphism is an isomorphism. For example, the morphism $f \colon \ell^2(\mathbb{N}) \to \ell^2(\mathbb{N})$ defined by $f(\varphi)(n) = \frac{1}{n}\varphi(n)$ is injective, self-adjoint, and hence also has dense image. But it is not surjective, as the vector $\varphi \in \ell^2(\mathbb{N})$ determined by $\varphi(n) = \frac{1}{n}$ is not in its range.

2.9. If $f, g \colon H \to K$ are morphisms in **Hilb**, then so are $f + g$ and zf for $z \in \mathbb{C}$. Because composition respects these operations, **Hilb** is enriched over complex vector spaces. In general, the homsets are not Hilbert spaces themselves [2], so

Hilb is not enriched over itself, and hence not Cartesian closed. At any rate, there is another way to structure the homsets of **Hilb**, which is of more interest here. Say $f \leq g$ when $\ker(f)^\perp \subseteq \ker(g)^\perp$ and $f(x) = g(x)$ for $x \in \ker(f)^\perp$. The following proposition shows that this makes all homsets into *algebraic domains* [4], but that this is not respected by composition. This is closely related to [8, 2.1.4], but **Hilb** is not a restriction category in the sense of that paper: setting $\overline{f}$ to be the projection onto $\ker(f)^\perp$ does not satisfy $\overline{fg} = \overline{g}\overline{f}$.

Proposition 2.10. *All homsets in the category **Hilb** are algebraic domains, but composition is not monotone.*

Proof. The least upper bound of a directed family f_i is given by continuous extension to the closure of $\bigcup_i \ker(f_i)^\perp$; this makes all homsets into directed-complete partially ordered sets. If $f \leq \bigvee_i f_i$ always implies $f \leq f_i$ for some i, then $\ker(f)^\perp$ must have been finite-dimensional; thus morphisms f satisfying $\dim(\ker(f)^\perp) < \infty$ are the compact elements. It is now easy to see that any morphism is the directed supremum of compact ones below it, making all homsets into algebraic domains.

Now consider composition. First suppose that $f \leq f'$ and $g \leq g'$. If $x \in \ker(f)$, then clearly $gf(x) = 0$. If $x \in \ker(f)^\perp$, then $f(x) = f'(x)$, so $g'f'(x) = 0$ implies $f(x) \in \ker(g') \subseteq \ker(g)$. Because we may write $\mathrm{dom}(gf) = \ker(f) \oplus \ker(f)^\perp$, we conclude $\ker(gf)^\perp \subseteq \ker(g'f')^\perp$. But unless $f(\ker(gf)^\perp) \subseteq \ker(g)^\perp$, it need not be the case that gf equals $g'f'$ on $\ker(gf)^\perp$. For an explicit counterexample, let

$$f = f' = \begin{pmatrix} 1 & 1 \\ 0 & 1 \end{pmatrix}, \qquad g = \begin{pmatrix} 1 & 0 \\ 0 & 0 \end{pmatrix}, \qquad g' = \begin{pmatrix} 1 & 0 \\ 0 & 1 \end{pmatrix}.$$

Then $f \leq f'$ and $g \leq g'$. But $\ker(gf)^\perp = \{(\begin{smallmatrix} x \\ -x \end{smallmatrix}) \mid x \in \mathbb{C}\}^\perp = \{(\begin{smallmatrix} x \\ x \end{smallmatrix}) \mid x \in \mathbb{C}\}$, and $gf(\begin{smallmatrix} x \\ x \end{smallmatrix}) = (\begin{smallmatrix} 2x \\ 0 \end{smallmatrix}) \neq (\begin{smallmatrix} 2x \\ x \end{smallmatrix}) = g'f'(\begin{smallmatrix} x \\ x \end{smallmatrix})$, so $gf \nleq g'f'$. □

3   The Domain

Definition 3.1. A *partial injection* is a partial function that is injective, wherever it is defined. More precisely, it(s graph) is a relation $R \subseteq X \times Y$ such that for each x there is at most one y with $(x, y) \in R$, and for each y there is at most one x with $(y, x) \in R$. Sets and partial injections form a category **PInj** under composition of relations $S \circ R = \{(x, z) \mid \exists y \colon (x, y) \in R, (y, z) \in S\}$.

3.2. Notationally, a partial injection $f \colon X \to Y$ can be conveniently represented as a span $(X \leftarrow_{f_1} \!\prec\! F \!\succ\!_{f_2} \to Y)$ of monics in **Set**. Here, f_1 is (the inclusion of) the domain of definition of f, and f_2 is its (injective) action on that domain. Composition in this representation is by pullback. We will also write $\mathrm{Dom}(f) = f_1(F)$ for the domain of definition, and $\mathrm{Im}(f) = f_2(F)$ for the range of f.

If it wasn't already, the span notation immediately makes it clear that **PInj** is a *dagger* category: $(X \leftarrow_{f_1} \!\prec\! F \!\succ\!_{f_2} \to Y)^\dagger = (Y \leftarrow_{f_2} \!\prec\! F \!\succ\!_{f_1} \to X)$.

3.3. The category **PInj** has two dagger *symmetric monoidal* structures. The first one, that we denote by $\otimes$, acts as the Cartesian product on objects. Because the Cartesian product of injections is again injective, $\otimes$ is well-defined on morphisms of **PInj** as well. The monoidal unit is a singleton set **1**. Notice that $\otimes$ is not a product, and hence not a coproduct either.

The second dagger symmetric monoidal structure on **PInj**, denoted by $\oplus$, is given by disjoint union on objects. It is easy to see that a disjoint union of injections is again injective, making $\oplus$ well-defined on morphisms of **PInj**. The monoidal unit is the empty set. Notice that $\oplus$ is not a coproduct, and hence not a product either.

Lemma 3.4. *The category* **PInj**:

(i) has (co)equalizers;
(ii) has a zero object;
(iii) does not have finite (co)products;

Proof. The equalizer of $f, g \colon X \to Y$ is the inclusion of

$$\{x \in X \mid x \notin (\mathrm{Dom}(f) \cup \mathrm{Dom}(g)) \vee (x \in (\mathrm{Dom}(f) \cap \mathrm{Dom}(g)) \wedge f(x) = g(x))\}$$

into X. The empty set is a zero object in **PInj**.

Towards (iii), notice that if $(X \overset{\kappa_X}{-}{\to} X + Y \overset{\kappa_Y}{\leftarrow} Y)$ were a coproduct in **PInj**, then one must have $\mathrm{Dom}(\kappa_X) = X$, $\mathrm{Dom}(\kappa_Y) = Y$ and $\mathrm{Im}(\kappa_X) \cap \mathrm{Im}(\kappa_Y) = \emptyset$, because otherwise unique existence of mediating morphisms is violated. Hence any coproduct must contain the disjoint union of X and Y. Let $f \colon X \to Z$ and $g \colon Y \to Z$ be any morphisms. Then a mediating morphism $m \colon X + Y \to Z$ has to satisfy $m(x) = f(x)$ for $x \in \mathrm{Dom}(f)$ and $m(y) = g(y)$ for $y \in \mathrm{Dom}(g)$. But such an m is not unique, unless $\mathrm{Dom}(f) = X$ and $\mathrm{Dom}(g) = Y$. In fact, it is not even a partial injection unless $\mathrm{Im}(f) \cap \mathrm{Im}(g) = \emptyset$. We conclude that **PInj** does not have binary (co)products. $\qquad\square$

3.5. In fact, part (ii) of the previous lemma follows from the existence of directed colimits, which we now work towards. Recall that a category has directed colimits if and only if it has colimits of chains, *i.e.* colimits of well-ordered diagrams [5, Corollary 1.7]. Observe that for a chain $D \colon I \to$ **PInj**, if $c_i \colon D(i) \to X$ is a cocone on D, then $\mathrm{Dom}(c_i) \subseteq \mathrm{Dom}(D(i \leq j))$ for all $j \geq i$. To see this, notice that $c_i = c_j \circ D(i \leq j)$ since c_i is a cocone, and therefore

$$\mathrm{Dom}(c_i) = \mathrm{Dom}(c_j \circ D(i \leq j)) \subseteq \mathrm{Dom}(D(i \leq j)).$$

This observation suggests that the colimit of a well-ordered diagram in **PInj** should consist of all 'infinite paths'. The following proposition shows that this is indeed a colimit.

Proposition 3.6. *The category* **PInj** *has directed colimits.*

Proof. Let $D\colon I \to \mathbf{PInj}$ be a chain. Define

$$X = \{x \in \coprod_i D(i) \mid \forall_{j \geq i}[x \in \mathrm{Dom}(D(i \leq j))]\}/ \sim,$$

where the coproduct is taken in $\mathbf{Set}$, and the equivalence relation $\sim$ is generated by $x \sim D(i \leq j)(x)$ for all $i \leq j$ in I and $x \in \mathrm{Dom}(D(i \leq j))$. For $i \in I$, define $c_i\colon D(i) \to X$ by

$$\mathrm{Dom}(c_i) = \{x \in D(i) \mid \forall_{j \geq i}[x \in \mathrm{Dom}(D(i \leq j))]\},$$

and $c_i(x) = [x]$.

First of all, let us show that the c_i form a cocone. One has:

$$\mathrm{Dom}(c_j \circ D(i \leq j))$$
$$= \{x \in D(i) \mid x \in \mathrm{Dom}(D(i \leq j)) \wedge D(i \leq j)(x) \in \mathrm{Dom}(c_j)\}$$
$$= \{x \in D(i) \mid x \in \mathrm{Dom}(D(i \leq j)) \wedge \forall_{k \geq j}[D(i \leq j)(x) \in \mathrm{Dom}(D(j \leq k))]\}.$$

The well-orderedness of I implies that

$$\forall_{k \geq i}[P(k)] \Leftrightarrow \forall_{k \geq j}[P(k)] \wedge P(j)$$

for any property P on the objects of I, whence

$$\mathrm{Dom}(c_j \circ D(i \leq j)) = \{x \in D(i) \mid \forall_{k \geq i}[x \in \mathrm{Dom}(D(i \leq k))]\} = \mathrm{Dom}(c_i).$$

Moreover $c_j \circ D(i \leq j)(x) = [D(i \leq j)(x)] = [x] = c_i(x)$ for $x \in \mathrm{Dom}(c_i)$, by definition of the equivalence relation.

Next, we show that c_i is universal. Let $d_i\colon D(i) \to Y$ be any cocone, and define $m\colon X \to Y$ by

$$\mathrm{Dom}(m) = \{[x] \mid x \in \mathrm{Dom}(d_i)\}$$

and $m([x]) = d_i(x)$ for $x \in D(i)$; this is well-defined since d_i is a cocone. Then

$$\mathrm{dom}(m \circ c_i) = \{x \in D(i) \mid x \in \mathrm{Dom}(c_i) \wedge m_i(x) \in \mathrm{Dom}(m)\}$$
$$= \{x \in D(i) \mid \forall_{j \geq i}[x \in \mathrm{Dom}(D(i \leq j))] \wedge x \in \mathrm{Dom}(d_i)\}$$
$$= \mathrm{Dom}(d_i)$$

by 3.5, and $m \circ c_i(x) = m([x]) = d_i(x)$ for $x \in D(i)$. Thus $m \circ c_i = d_i$, so m is indeed a mediating morphism.

Finally, if $m'\colon X \to Y$ satisfies $m \circ c_i = d_i$, then it follows from the above considerations that $\mathrm{Dom}(m') = \mathrm{Dom}(m)$ and $m'(x) = m(x)$ for $x \in \mathrm{Dom}(m)$. Hence m is the unique mediating morphism. □

3.7. Recall that an object X in a category $\mathbf{C}$ is called *finitely presentable* when the hom-functor $\mathbf{C}(X, -)\colon \mathbf{C} \to \mathbf{Set}$ preserves directed colimits. Explicitly, this means that for any directed poset $D\colon I \to \mathbf{C}$, any colimit cocone $d_i\colon D(i) \to Y$

and any morphism $f\colon X \to Y$, there are $j \in I$ and a morphism $g\colon X \to D(j)$ such that $f = d_j \circ g$. Moreover, this morphism g is essentially unique, in the sense that if $f = d_i \circ g = d_i \circ g'$, then $D(i \to i') \circ g = D(i \to i') \circ g'$ for some $i' \in I$.

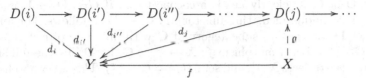

A category is called *finitely accessible* [5] when it has directed colimits and every object is a directed colimit of finitely presentable objects.

Lemma 3.8. *A set is finitely presentable in* **PInj** *if and only if it is finite.*

Proof. The only thing, in the situation of 3.7 with X finite, is to notice that if a partial injection g is to exist, we must have $\mathrm{Dom}(g) = \mathrm{Dom}(f)$. The rest follows from [5, 1.2.1]. □

Theorem 3.9. *The category* **PInj** *is finitely accessible.*

Proof. It suffices to prove that every set in **PInj** is a directed colimit of finite ones. But that is easy: X is the colimit of the directed diagram consisting of its finite subsets. □

Definition 3.10. An *inverse category* is a category **C** in which every morphism $f\colon X \to Y$ allows a unique morphism $f^\dagger\colon Y \to X$ satisfying $f = ff^\dagger f$ and $f^\dagger = f^\dagger f f^\dagger$. Equivalently, it is a dagger category satisfying $f = ff^\dagger f$ and $pq = qp$ for idempotents $p, q\colon X \to X$. The proof of equivalence of these two statements is the same as for inverse semigroups (see [22, Theorem 1.1.3] or [8, Theorem 2.20]). Inverse categories are a special case of *restriction categories* [8].

The category **PInj** is an inverse category under its dagger (see 3.2). The following categorification of the Wagner–Preston theorem [22, Theorem 1.5.1] shows that it is in fact a representative one. See also [8, 3.4].

Proposition 3.11. *Any locally small inverse category* **C** *allows a faithful embedding* $F\colon \mathbf{C} \to \mathbf{PInj}$ *that preserves daggers.*

Proof. First suppose that **C** is small. Then we may set $F(X) = \coprod_{Z \in \mathbf{C}} \mathbf{C}(X, Z)$. For $f\colon X \to Y$ define $F(f)\colon F(X) \to F(Y)$ by $F(f) = (\_) \circ f^\dagger$ on the domain $\{g \in \mathbf{C}(X, Z) \mid Z \in \mathbf{C}, g = gf^\dagger f\}$; this gives a well-defined partial injection. It is functorial, since clearly $F(\mathrm{id}) = \mathrm{id}$, and

$$\mathrm{Dom}(F(gf)) = \{h\colon X \to Z \mid h = hf^\dagger g^\dagger gf\}$$
$$= \{h\colon X \to Z \mid h = hf^\dagger f, hf^\dagger = hf^\dagger g^\dagger g\} = \mathrm{Dom}(F(g) \circ F(f)).$$

It preserves daggers, because $F(f^\dagger) = (\_) \circ f = F(f)^\dagger$, and

$$\mathrm{Dom}(F(f^\dagger)) = \{h\colon Y \to Z \mid h = hff^\dagger\}$$
$$= \{gf^\dagger\colon Y \to Z \mid g = gf^\dagger f\colon X \to Z\} = \mathrm{Im}(F(f)) = \mathrm{Dom}(F(f)^\dagger).$$

Finally, F is clearly injective on objects. It is also faithful: if $F(f) = F(g)$, then $ff^\dagger = Ff(f) = Fg(f) = fg^\dagger$ and $gf^\dagger = Ff(g) = Fg(g) = gg^\dagger$, whence $fg^\dagger f = f$ and $gf^\dagger g = g$, and so $f = g$.

Now suppose $\mathbf{C}$ is locally small. Consider the diagram of small inverse subcategories $\mathbf{D}$ of $\mathbf{C}$. It clearly has is a cocone to $\mathbf{C}$. If $G_\mathbf{D} : \mathbf{D} \to \mathbf{E}$ is another one, there is a unique mediating functor $M : \mathbf{C} \to \mathbf{E}$ as follows. For an object X of $\mathbf{C}$, let $\mathbf{D}'$ be the full subcategory of $\mathbf{C}$ with only one object X, and set $M(X) = G_{\mathbf{D}'}(X)$. For a morphism $f : X \to Y$ of $\mathbf{C}$, let $\mathbf{D}''$ be the full subcategory of $\mathbf{C}$ on the objects X, Y, and set $M(f) = G_{\mathbf{D}''}(f)$. This gives a well-defined functor. So $\mathbf{C}$ is the colimit in $\mathbf{Cat}$ of its small inverse subcategories. By the above, any small inverse subcategory $\mathbf{C}$ embeds into $\mathbf{PInj}$. It follows that $\mathbf{C}$ itself embeds into $\mathbf{PInj}$.   □

3.12. Like any inverse category, the homsets of $\mathbf{PInj}$ carry a natural partial order: $f \leq g$ when $f = gf^\dagger f$. Concretely, $f \leq g$ means $\mathrm{Dom}(f) \subseteq \mathrm{Dom}(g)$ and $f(x) = g(x)$ for $x \in \mathrm{Dom}(f)$. It is easy to see that this makes homsets into directed-complete partially ordered sets, with $\mathrm{Dom}(\bigvee_i f_i) = \bigcup_i \mathrm{Dom}(f_i)$ for a directed family of morphisms $f_i : X \to Y$. In fact, as in Proposition 2.10, homsets are algebraic domains: any partial injection is the supremum of compact ones below it, which are those partial injections with finite domain. Moreover, composition respects these operations. Thus $\mathbf{PInj}$ is enriched in algebraic domains. This is a satisfying reflection of Theorem 3.9 on the level of homsets.

4   The Functor

Definition 4.1. There is a functor $\ell^2 : \mathbf{PInj} \to \mathbf{Hilb}$, acting on a set X as

$$\ell^2(X) = \{\varphi : X \to \mathbb{C} \mid \sum_{x \in X} |\varphi(x)|^2 < \infty\}.$$

This vector space becomes a well-defined Hilbert space under the inner product $\langle \varphi \mid \psi \rangle = \sum_{x \in X} \overline{\varphi(x)} \psi(x)$. The action on morphisms sends a partial injection $(X \leftarrow_{f_1} \prec F \succ_{f_2} \to Y)$ to the linear function $\ell^2 f : \ell^2(X) \to \ell^2(Y)$ determined informally by $\ell^2 f = (\_) \circ f^\dagger$. Explicitly,

$$(\ell^2 f)(\varphi)(y) = \sum_{x \in f_2^{-1}(y)} \varphi(f_1(x)).$$

4.2. In verifying that $\ell^2 f$ is indeed a well-defined morphism of $\mathbf{Hilb}$, it is essential that f is a (partial) injection.

$$\sum_{y \in Y} |(\ell^2 f)(\varphi)(y)|^2 = \sum_{y \in Y} \Big| \sum_{x \in f_2^{-1}(y)} \varphi(f_1(x)) \Big|^2 \leq \sum_{y \in Y} \sum_{x \in f_2^{-1}(y)} |\varphi(f_1(x))|^2$$

$$= \sum_{x \in F} |\varphi(f_1(x))|^2 \leq \sum_{x \in X} |\varphi(x)|^2 < \infty.$$

That this breaks down for functions f in general, instead of (partial) injections, was first noticed in [6], and further studied in [13]. That is, ℓ^2 is well-defined on the category of sets and partial injections; on the category of finite sets and functions; but not on the category of sets and functions; nor on the category of finite sets and relations. Functoriality of ℓ^2 is easy to verify.

4.3. The following calculation shows that the ℓ^2 functor preserves daggers. For a partial injection $(X \twoheadleftarrow f_1 \rightarrowtail F \rightarrowtail f_2 \rightarrow Y)$, $\varphi \in \ell^2(X)$ and $\psi \in \ell^2(Y)$:

$$\langle (\ell^2 f)(\varphi) \mid \psi \rangle_{\ell^2(Y)} = \sum_{y \in Y} \overline{(\ell^2 f)(\varphi)(y)} \cdot \psi(y) = \sum_{y \in Y} \sum_{x \in f_2^{-1}(y)} \overline{\varphi(f_1(x))} \cdot \psi(y)$$

$$= \sum_{x \in F} \overline{\varphi(f_1(x))} \cdot \psi(f_2(x)) = \sum_{x \in X} \sum_{x' \in f_1^{-1}(x)} \overline{\varphi(x)} \cdot \psi(f_2(x'))$$

$$= \sum_{x \in X} \overline{\varphi(x)} \cdot \left(\sum_{x' \in f_1^{-1}(x)} \psi(f_2(x')) \right) = \langle \varphi \mid \ell^2(f^\dagger)(\psi) \rangle_{\ell^2(X)}.$$

4.4. The functor ℓ^2 preserves the tensor product $\otimes$, *i.e.* it is symmetric (strong) monoidal. There is a canonical isomorphism $\mathbb{C} \cong \ell^2(\mathbf{1})$. The required natural morphisms $\ell^2(X) \otimes \ell^2(Y) \to \ell^2(X \otimes Y)$ are given by mapping (φ, ψ) to the function $(x, y) \mapsto \varphi(x)\psi(y)$. That there are inverses is seen when one realizes that $\ell^2(X \otimes Y)$ is the Cauchy-completion of the set of functions $X \times Y \to \mathbb{C}$ with finite support. The required coherence diagrams follow easily.

4.5. Also, the ℓ^2 functor is symmetric (strong) monoidal with respect to $\oplus$. There is a canonical isomorphism between the 0-dimensional Hilbert space and the set $\ell^2(\emptyset)$ consisting only of the empty function. The natural morphisms $\ell^2(X) \oplus \ell^2(Y) \to \ell^2(X \oplus Y)$ map (φ, ψ) to the cotuple $[\varphi, \psi]: X \oplus Y \to \mathbb{C}$. One sees that these are isomorphisms by recalling that $\ell^2(X \oplus Y)$ is the closure of the span of the Kronecker functions δ_x and δ_y for $x \in X$ and $y \in Y$, on which the inverse acts as the appropriate coprojection. Coherence properties readily follow.

4.6. From the description of the structure of homsets in **PInj** and **Hilb** as algebraic domains in 3.12 and 2.9, respectively, it is clear that the functor ℓ^2 preserves this enrichment: $\ell^2(\bigvee_i f_i) = \bigvee_i \ell^2 f_i$ if $f_i: X \to Y$ is a directed family of morphisms in **PInj**. See also [18, Theorem 13].

4.7. The functor ℓ^2 preserves (co)kernels and finite (co)products (because **PInj** has very few of the latter). But it follows from Lemma 2.6(iii) and Proposition 3.6 that ℓ^2 cannot preserve arbitrary (co)limits. For an explicit counterexample to preservation of equalizers, take $X = \{0, 1\}$, $Y = \{a\}$, and let $f, g: X \to Y$ be the partial injections $f = \{(0, a)\}$ and $g = \{(1, a)\}$. Their equaliser in **PInj** is $\emptyset$.

But

$$eq(\ell^2(f), \ell^2(g)) = \{\varphi \in \ell^2(X) \mid \ell^2(f)(\varphi) = \ell^2(g)(\varphi)\}$$

$$= \Big\{\varphi \in \ell^2(X) \mid \forall_{y \in Y}. \sum_{u \in f_2^{-1}(y)} \varphi(f_1(u)) = \sum_{v \in g_2^{-1}(y)} \varphi(g_1(v))\Big\}$$

$$= \{\varphi \colon \{0, 1\} \to \mathbb{C} \mid \varphi(0) = \varphi(1)\} \cong \mathbb{C}.$$

Hence $eq(\ell^2(f), \ell^2(g)) \cong \mathbb{C} \ncong \{\emptyset\} = \ell^2(eq(f, g))$.

Corollary 4.8. *The functor $\ell^2 \colon \mathbf{PInj} \to \mathbf{Hilb}$ has no adjoints.*

Proof. If ℓ^2 had an adjoint, it would preserve (co)limits, contradicting 4.7. $\square$

4.9. The functor ℓ^2 is clearly faithful. It is also essentially surjective on objects: every Hilbert space H has an orthonormal basis X, so $H \cong \ell^2(X)$. It cannot be full because of 4.8, but it does reflect isomorphisms: if $\ell^2 f$ is invertible, so is f.

4.10. If X is a set, $\ell^2(X)$ is not just a Hilbert space; it comes equipped with a chosen orthonormal basis (given by the Kronecker functions $\delta_x \in \ell^2(X)$ for $x \in X$). Hence we could think of ℓ^2 as a functor to a category of Hilbert spaces H with a priviledged orthonormal basis $X \subseteq H$. If we choose as morphisms $(H, X) \to (K, Y)$ those continuous linear $f \colon H \to K$ satisfying $f(X) \subseteq Y$ and $f f^\dagger f = f$, then the functor ℓ^2 in fact becomes (half of) an equivalence of categories [3, 4.3].

4.11. Lemma 4.8 showed that $\ell^2(X)$ is not the free Hilbert space on X, at least not in the categorically accepted meaning. It also makes precise the intuition that 'choosing bases is unnatural': the functor $\ell^2 \colon \mathbf{PInj} \to \mathbf{Hilb}$ cannot have a (functorial) converse, even though one can choose an orthonormal basis for every Hilbert space.

It is perhaps also worth mentioning that ℓ^2 is not a fibration in the technical sense of the word, not even a nonsplit or noncloven one, as the reader might perhaps think; Cartesian liftings in general do not exist because 'choosing bases is unnatural'.

5   The Image

5.1. The choice of morphisms in 4.10 is quite strong, and does not capture all morphisms of interest to quantum physics. From that point of view, one would at least like to relax to *partial isometries*: morphisms i of Hilbert spaces that satisfy $i i^\dagger i = i$. Equivalently, the restriction of i to the orthogonal complement of its kernel is an isometry. The following proposition proves that, up to isomorphisms, the direct image of the functor ℓ^2 consists precisely of partial isometries.

Definition 5.2. For a category $\mathbf{C}$, denote by $\mathbf{C}_\cong$ the groupoid with the same objects as $\mathbf{C}$ whose morphisms are the isomorphisms of $\mathbf{C}$.

The category **Hilb**$_\cong$ is a groupoid, and hence has a dagger. It carries two dagger symmetric monoidal structures: $\uplus$ and $\otimes$. Because having (co)limits only depends on a skeleton of the specifying diagram, **Hilb**$_\cong$ does not have (co)equalizers, nor (finite) (co)products, but does have directed (co)limits.

Proposition 5.3. *A morphism in* **Hilb** *is a partial isometry if and only if it is of the form* $v \circ \ell^2 f \circ u$ *for morphisms* f *in* **PInj** *and unitaries* u, v *in* **Hilb**$_\cong$.

Proof. Clearly a map of the form $v \circ \ell^2 f \circ u$ is a partial isometry. Conversely, suppose that $i \colon H \to K$ is a partial isometry. Choose an orthonormal basis $X \subseteq H$ for its initial space $\ker(i)^\perp$, and choose an orthonormal basis $X' \subseteq H$ for $\ker(i)$, giving a unitary morphism $u \colon H \to \ell^2(X \oplus X')$. Let $Y = i(X) \subseteq K$. Then Y will be an orthonormal basis for the final space $\ker(i^\dagger)^\perp$ because i acts isometrically on X. Choose an orthonormal basis $Y' \subseteq K$ for $\ker(i^\dagger)$, giving a unitary $v \colon \ell^2(Y \oplus Y') \to K$. Now, if we define $f = (X \oplus X' \longleftarrow X \xrightarrow{i} Y \oplus Y')$, then $i = v \circ \ell^2 f \circ u$. $\qquad\square$

5.4. However, partial isometries are not closed under composition. To see this, consider the partial isometries $\left(\begin{smallmatrix}1\\0\end{smallmatrix}\right) \colon \mathbb{C} \to \mathbb{C}^2$ and $(\,\sin(\theta)\ \cos(\theta)\,) \colon \mathbb{C}^2 \to \mathbb{C}$ for a fixed real number θ. Their composition is $(\,\sin(\theta)\,) \colon \mathbb{C} \to \mathbb{C}$, which is not a partial isometry unless θ is a multiple of $\pi/2$. There are other compositions that do make partial isometries into a category [19], but these are not of interest here. Instead, we shall extend the previous proposition to highlight one of the most remarkable features of the functor ℓ^2.

5.5. The example in 5.4 shows that any linear function $\mathbb{C} \to \mathbb{C}$ between -1 and 1 is a composition of partial isometries. Note that the projections $\pi_i \colon \mathbb{C}^m \to \mathbb{C}$ and coprojections $\pi_i^\dagger \colon \mathbb{C} \to \mathbb{C}^n$ are partial isometries, as are the weighted diagonal $\Delta/\sqrt{n} \colon \mathbb{C} \to \mathbb{C}^n$ given by $\Delta(x) = (x, \ldots, x)$ and the weighted codiagonal $\Delta^\dagger/\sqrt{m} \colon \mathbb{C}^m \to \mathbb{C}$ given by $\Delta^\dagger(x_1, \ldots, x_m) = \sum_i x_i$. Moreover, it is easy to see that if f and g are (compositions of) partial isometries, then so is $f \oplus g$. Finally, any linear map $f \colon \mathbb{C}^m \to \mathbb{C}^n$ has a matrix expansion, and can hence be written in terms of biproduct structure as $f = \Delta^\dagger \circ (\bigoplus_{i=1}^m \bigoplus_{j=1}^n \pi_j^\dagger \circ \pi_j \circ f \circ \pi_i^\dagger \circ \pi_i) \circ \Delta$. Thus any $f \colon \mathbb{C}^m \to \mathbb{C}^n$ with $\|f\| \le 1/\sqrt{mn}$ is a composition of partial isometries.

5.6. The *essential image* of a functor $F \colon \mathbf{C} \to \mathbf{D}$ is the smallest subcategory of $\mathbf{D}$ that contains all morphisms $F(f)$ for f in $\mathbf{C}$, and that is closed under composition with isomorphisms of $\mathbf{D}$.

It follows from 5.5 that the essential image of the functor ℓ^2 contains at least all morphisms of **Hilb** of finite rank. For infinite rank that strategy fails because Δ is then no longer a valid morphism (see 2.7). Nevertheless, Theorem 5.11 below will prove that the essential image of ℓ^2 is all of **Hilb**. In preparation we accommodate an intermezzo on *polar decomposition*.

A morphism $p \colon H \to H$ in **Hilb** is *nonnegative* when $\langle px \,|\, x \rangle \ge 0$ for all $x \in H$, and *positive* when $\langle px \,|\, x \rangle > 0$. Nonnegative maps are precisely those of the form $p = f^\dagger f$ for some morphism f.

Proposition 5.7. *For every morphism* $f\colon H \to K$ *between Hilbert spaces, there exist a unique nonnegative map* $p\colon H \to H$ *and partial isometry* $i\colon H \to K$ *satisfying* $f = ip$ *and* $\ker(p) = \ker(i)$.

Proof. See [14, problem 134].   □

5.8. The previous proposition stated the usual formulation of polar decomposition, but the unicity condition $\ker(p) = \ker(i)$ is something of a red herring. It should be understood as saying that both i and p are uniquely determined on the orthogonal complement of $\ker(f) = \ker(p) = \ker(i)$. On each point of $\ker(f)$, one of i and p must be zero, but the other's behaviour has no restrictions apart from being a partial isometry or positive map, respectively. Dropping the unicity condition, we may take p to be a positive map, by altering i to be zero on $\ker(f)$, and p to be nonzero on $\ker(f)$. More precisely, define $p' = p$ on $\ker(f)^\perp$ and $p' = \mathrm{id}$ on $\ker(f)$; since $\ker(f)$ is a closed subspace, $H \cong \ker(f) \oplus \ker(f)^\perp$, and this gives a well-defined positive operator $p'\colon H \to H$. Similarly, setting $i' = i$ on $\ker(f)^\perp$ and $i' = 0$ on $\ker(f)$ gives a well-defined partial isometry $i'\colon H \to K$, satisfying $f = i'p'$.

Lemma 5.9. *Positive operators on Hilbert spaces are isomorphisms.*

Proof. Let $p\colon H \to H$ be a positive operator in **Hilb**. Since p is self-adjoint, the spectral theorem [24] guarantees the existence of a measure space (S, Σ, μ), a unitary $u\colon H \to L^2(S, \Sigma, \mu)$, and a measurable function $f\colon S \to \mathbb{C}$ whose range is the spectrum $\sigma(p)$ of p, such that $p = u^\dagger \circ m \circ u$, where m is the multiplication operator induced by f. Because p is positive, f must take values in $\mathbb{R}^{>0}$. This makes the function $f^{-1}\colon S \to \mathbb{C}$ given by $s \mapsto f(s)^{-1}$ a well-defined measurable function. Let m^{-1} be the multiplication operator induced by f^{-1}. Then $u^\dagger \circ m^{-1} \circ u$ is the inverse of p.   □

Definition 5.10. A functor $F\colon \mathbf{C} \to \mathbf{D}$ is *essentially full* when for each morphism g in $\mathbf{D}$ there exist f in $\mathbf{C}$ and u, v in $\mathbf{C}_\cong$ such that $g = v \circ Ff \circ u$.

It follows that the essential image of such a functor is all of $\mathbf{D}$.

Theorem 5.11. *The functor* $\ell^2\colon \mathbf{PInj} \to \mathbf{Hilb}$ *is essentially full.*

Proof. Let g be a morphism in **Hilb**. By Proposition 5.7 and 5.8, we can write $g = pi$ for a positive morphism p and a partial isometry i. Use Proposition 5.3 to decompose $i = v' \circ \ell^2 f \circ u$ for f in **PInj** and unitaries v', u. Finally, Lemma 5.9 shows that $v = p \circ v'$ in $\mathbf{Hilb}_\cong$ satisfies $g = v \circ \ell^2 f \circ u$.   □

5.12. Writing **2** for the ordinal $2 = (0 \leq 1)$ regarded as a category, the category $\mathbf{C}^2$ is the *arrow category* of $\mathbf{C}$: its objects are morphisms of $\mathbf{C}$, and its morphisms are pairs of morphisms of $\mathbf{C}$ making the square commute. A functor $F\colon \mathbf{C} \to \mathbf{D}$ is essentially full if and only if $F^2\colon \mathbf{C}^2 \to \mathbf{D}^2$ is essentially surjective on objects. From this point of view Definition 5.10 is quite natural. Nonetheless we might consider weakening it to take $u = \mathrm{id}$ or $v = \mathrm{id}$. But this would break the previous theorem. For example, if $g\colon \ell^2(X) \to \ell^2(Y)$ is a morphism in **Hilb**, there need not be $f\colon X \to Y$ in **PInj** and v in **Hilb$_\cong$** with $g = v \circ \ell^2 f$. For a counterexample, take $X = Y = \{a, b\}$, and $g(a) = g(b) = a$; if $g = v \circ \ell^2 f$, then $(v \circ \ell^2 f)(a) = (v \circ \ell^2 f)(b)$, so $(\ell^2 f)(a) = (\ell^2 f)(b)$, so $f(a) = f(b)$, whence f cannot be a partial injection. Similarly, because of the dagger, if $g\colon \ell^2(X) \to \ell^2(Z)$ is a morphism in **Hilb**, there need not be $f\colon Y \to Z$ in **PInj** and u in **Hilb$_\cong$** with $g = \ell^2 f \circ u$.

6 The Future

6.1. Theorem 5.11 naturally raises a coherence question: is there any regularity to the isomorphisms u and v that enable us to write an arbitrary morphism of **Hilb** in the form $v \circ \ell^2 f \circ u$? How do they behave under composition? Curiously enough, essentially full functors do not seem to have been studied in the categorical literature at all. The results in this article suggest such a study.

It would be very interesting to reconstruct **Hilb** (up to equivalence) from **Hilb$_\cong$** and **PInj** via the ℓ^2 functor. The objects are easily recovered, because they are the same as those of **Hilb$_\cong$**. Theorem 5.11 also lets us recover the homsets and identities, as soon as we can identify when two morphisms in **Hilb** of the form $v \circ \ell^2 f \circ u$ are equal. The main problem is how to recover composition, which requires a way to turn $\ell^2 g \circ v \circ \ell^2 f$ into $w \circ \ell^2 h \circ u$. (Note that turning $\ell^2 g \circ v$ into $w \circ \ell^2 h$ would be sufficient, because we could then use functoriality of ℓ^2 and composition in **PInj**. But 5.12 obstructs this; the isomorphism v in the middle is crucial.) This will likely lead into bicategorical territory.

6.2. The ℓ^2–construction has a continuous counterpart, that turns a measure space (X, μ) into a Hilbert space $L^2(X, \mu)$ of square integrable complex functions on X. The L^2–construction is quite fundamental and well-studied, but surprisingly enough functorial aspects seem not to have been considered before. One possibility is to mimic Definition 4.1, and endow the category of measure spaces with essential injections $(X, \mu) \to (Y, \nu)$ as morphisms, *i.e.* subsets $R \subseteq X \times Y$ such that $\nu(\{y \mid xRy\}) = 0$ for all $x \in X$ and $\mu(\{x \mid xRy\}) = 0$ for all $y \in Y$.

The importance of L^2–spaces lies in the following formulation of the spectral theorem: every normal operator $f\colon H \to H$ is of the form $f = u^{-1} \circ g \circ u$ for a unitary $u\colon H \to L^2(X, \mu)$ and an operator g induced by multiplication with a measurable function $X \to \mathbb{C}$. This perspective warrants choosing complex measurable functions as (endo)morphisms on measure spaces, with multiplication for composition. With 5.8 in mind, we could even restrict to a groupoid of positive maps. A solution to 6.1 could then be regarded as reconstructing quantum mechanics (as embodied by **Hilb**) from its continuous, quantitative aspects (encoded by the L^2 functor), and its discrete, qualitative aspects (encoded by the ℓ^2 functor).

At any rate, the continuous cousin L^2 of ℓ^2 poses an interesting research topic.

6.3. Letting $\mathcal{L}$ be the class of positive morphisms, and $\mathcal{R}$ the class of partial isometries in **Hilb**:

1. every morphism f can be factored as $f = rl$ with $l \in \mathcal{L}$ and $r \in \mathcal{R}$;

2. every commutative square as below with $l \in \mathcal{L}$ and $r \in \mathcal{R}$ allows a unique diagonal fill-in d making both triangles commute.

The second property follows immediately from Lemma 5.9. The established notion of *orthogonal factorization system* additionally demands that (3) both $\mathcal{L}$ and $\mathcal{R}$ are closed under composition, and (4) all isomorphisms are in both $\mathcal{L}$ and $\mathcal{R}$. But (3) is not satisfied by 5.4, and the map $-1: H \to H$ is a counterexample to (4).

Write **3** for the ordinal $3 = (0 \leq 1 \leq 2)$, regarded as a category. Then objects of $\mathbf{C}^3$ are composable pairs of morphisms. Recall that a *functorial factorization* is a functor $F: \mathbf{C}^2 \to \mathbf{C}^3$ that splits the composition functor. Lemma 5.9 ensures that polar decomposition at least provides a functorial factorization system. It is usual to require extra conditions on top of a functorial factorization, such as in a *natural weak factorization system*. For details we refer to [11]. It leads too far afield here, but polar decomposition does not satisfy the axioms of a natural weak factorization system.

In short, polar decomposition unquestionably provides a notion of factorization. But it does not fit existing categorical notions, despite the fact that factorization has been a topic of quite intense study in category theory [10,7,11,21,25]. This is an interesting topic for further investigation.

References

1. Abramsky, S.: Retracing some paths in process algebra. In: Sassone, V., Montanari, U. (eds.) CONCUR 1996. LNCS, vol. 1119, pp. 1–17. Springer, Heidelberg (1996)
2. Abramsky, S., Blute, R., Panangaden, P.: Nuclear and trace ideals in tensored *-categories. Journal of Pure and Applied Algebra 143, 3–47 (1999)
3. Abramsky, S., Heunen, C.: H*-algebras and nonunital Frobenius algebras: first steps in infinite-dimensional categorical quantum mechanics. In: Abramsky, S., Mislove, M. (eds.) Clifford Lectures. Proceedings of Symposia in Applied Mathematics, vol. 71, pp. 1–24. American Mathematical Society (2012)
4. Abramsky, S., Jung, A.: Domain theory. In: Handbook of Logic in Computer Science, vol. 3, pp. 1–168. Oxford University Press (1994)
5. Adámek, J., Rosicky, J.: Locally Presentable and Accessible Categories. London Mathematical Society Lecture Note Series, vol. 189. Cambridge University Press (1994)
6. Barr, M.: Algebraically compact functors. Journal of Pure and Applied Algebra 82, 211–231 (1992)
7. Bousfield, A.K.: Constructions of factorization systems in categories. Journal of Pure and Applied Algebra 9(2-3), 207–220 (1977)
8. Robin, J., Cockett, B., Lack, S.: Restriction categories I: categories of partial maps. Theoretical Computer Science 270(1-2), 223–259 (2002)

9. Danos, V., Regnier, L.: Proof-nets and the Hilbert space. In: Advances in Linear Logic, pp. 307–328. Cambridge University Press (1995)
10. Freyd, P., Kelly, M.: Categories of continuous functors I. Journal of Pure and Applied Algebra 2 (1972)
11. Grandis, M., Tholen, W.: Natural weak factorization systems. Archivum Mathematicum 42, 397–408 (2006)
12. Haghverdi, E.: A categorical approach to linear logic, geometry of proofs and full completeness. PhD thesis, University of Ottawa (2000)
13. Haghverdi, E., Scott, P.: A categorical model for the geometry of interaction. Theoretical Computer Science 350, 252–274 (2006)
14. Halmos, P.: A Hilbert space problem book, 2nd edn. Springer (1982)
15. Heunen, C.: An embedding theorem for Hilbert categories. Theory and Applications of Categories 22(13), 321–344 (2009)
16. Heunen, C., Jacobs, B.: Quantum logic in dagger kernel categories. Order 27(2), 177–212 (2010)
17. Hines, P.: The algebra of self-similarity and its applications. PhD thesis, University of Wales (1997)
18. Hines, P.: Quantum circuit oracles for abstract machine computations. Theoretical Computer Science 411(11-13), 1501–1520 (2010)
19. Hines, P., Braunstein, S.L.: The structure of partial isometries. In: Semantic Techniques in Quantum Computation, pp. 361–389. Cambridge University Press (2009)
20. Kadison, R.V., Ringrose, J.R.: Fundamentals of the theory of operator algebras. Academic Press (1983)
21. Korostenski, M., Tholen, W.: Factorization systems as Eilenberg-Moore algebras. Journal of Pure and Applied Algebra 85(1), 57–72 (1993)
22. Lawson, M.V.: Inverse semigroups: the theory of partial symmetries. World Scientific (1998)
23. Lane, S.M.: Categories for the Working Mathematician, 2nd edn. Springer (1971)
24. Reed, M., Simon, B.: Methods of Modern Mathematical Physics. Functional Analysis, vol. 1. Academic Press (1972)
25. Rosicky, J., Tholen, W.: Lax factorization algebras. Journal of Pure and Applied Algebra 175, 355–382 (2002)

Quantum Speedup
and Categorical Distributivity

Peter Hines

University of York
peter.hines@york.ac.uk

Abstract. This paper studies one of the best-known quantum algorithms — Shor's factorisation algorithm — via categorical distributivity. A key aim of the paper is to provide a minimal set of categorical requirements for key parts of the algorithm, in order to establish the most general setting in which the required operations may be performed efficiently.

We demonstrate that Laplaza's theory of coherence for distributivity [13,14] provides a purely categorical proof of the operational equivalence of two quantum circuits, with the notable property that one is exponentially more efficient than the other. This equivalence also exists in a wide range of categories.

When applied to the category of finite-dimensional Hilbert spaces, we recover the usual efficient implementation of the quantum oracles at the heart of both Shor's algorithm and quantum period-finding generally; however, it is also applicable in a much wider range of settings.

Keywords: Category Theory, Quantum Computing, Shor's Algorithm, Monoidal Tensors, Distributivity, Coherence.

**This work is dedicated to Samson Abramsky,
on the occasion of a birthday with prime factors 2, 3, and 5.**

1 Introduction

1.1 Shor's Algorithm: Oracles and Quantum Fourier Transforms

The structure of Shor's algorithm is deceptively simple: an oracle which acts classically on the computational basis computes modular exponentials; this oracle is conjugated by the circuit for the quantum Fourier transform. Up to some relatively simple classical post-processing (computing continued fraction expansions), this is enough to find the prime factors of a number in an exponentially fast time – at least, as compared with the *best known* classical algorithm.

The traditional view of Shor's algorithm and other quantum period-finding algorithms is that their power arises from the quantum Fourier transform; [17] lists Shor's algorithm in the section "Applications of the Fourier transform". This was challenged in [3], where it was demonstrated that the quantum Fourier

B. Coecke, L. Ong, and P. Panangaden (Eds.): Abramsky Festschrift, LNCS 7860, pp. 122–138, 2013.

transform has a *low bubble width* circuit — and any quantum algorithm that is built entirely from low bubble-width circuits has an efficient classical simulation. Thus, it appears that the obstacle to an efficient classical simulation of Shor's algorithm is the oracle for modular exponentiation, rather than the conjugating quantum Fourier transform.

The conclusions drawn in [3] (the claim that the quantum power of Shor's algorithm arises from the central oracle) were, and remain, controversial. However, further evidence to support this claim was provided in [21], where it was demonstrated that modular exponentiation, in of itself, is sufficient. From [21]: *Any classical algorithm that can efficiently simulate the circuit implementing modular exponentiation for general product input states and product state measurements on the output, allows for an efficient simulation of the entire Shor algorithm on a classical computer.* A special case of this, as noted in [21], would be any tensor contraction scheme for the modular exponentiation circuit.

1.2   The Aims of this Paper

This paper describes the circuit for modular exponentiation used in [19] in purely categorical terms. The motivation is to find the most general structures in which this precise form of the oracle may be implemented. We therefore avoid, where possible, categorical machinery that is closely or uniquely associated with the theory of finite-dimensional Hilbert spaces.[1] Instead, we will simply require a category with two monoidal tensors related by a notion of distributivity. As this is established for abstract categories, any concrete category satisfying this simple requirement is sufficient.

1.3   The Structure of the Paper

This paper is divided into two sections: pure category theory, and concrete realisations of this abstract theory.

1. We first use the abstract theory of categories with two monoidal tensors related by distributivity to define endofunctors and further categorical operations on such categories. We use these to define an 'iterator' operation $!^N(\ )$ on endomorphism monoids of such categories, and use Laplaza's theory of coherence for distributivity to give an exponentially efficient factorisation of this operation.

2. The second half of the paper gives a concrete realisation of this operation, and its efficient factorisation, within the quantum circuit paradigm. The $!^N(\ )$ operation has a concrete realisation as the oracle required for quantum period-finding, and its efficient factorisation is exactly Shor's implementation of modular exponentiation oracle.

---

[1] In particular, the constructions we will present are significantly simpler in the presence of compact closure and biproducts – two categorical properties closely associated with quantum mechanics. However, neither of these categorical properties are necessary, so we work in the more general setting.

2   Basic Definitions

Our abstract setting is that of categories with distributivity, defined in [13,14]:

Definition 1. *A* **category with distributivity** *is a category $\mathcal{C}$ with two distinct symmetric monoidal tensors: the* **multiplicative tensor** *($\otimes$) : $\mathcal{C} \times \mathcal{C} \to \mathcal{C}$ and the* **additive tensor** *($\oplus$) : $\mathcal{C} \times \mathcal{C} \to \mathcal{C}$ that are related by natural distributivity monomorphisms*

$$dl_{ABC} : A \otimes (B \oplus C) \to (A \otimes B) \oplus (A \otimes C) \tag{1}$$
$$dr_{XYZ} : (X \oplus Y) \otimes Z \to (X \otimes Z) \oplus (Y \otimes Z) \tag{2}$$

satisfying coherence conditions laid out in [13,14].

The required coherence conditions are decidedly non-trivial and form an infinite family of diagrams that are required to commute, although these may be significantly simplified (from [13], *"we are reduced to a finite number of types of diagrams if we drop unnecessary commutativity conditions"*).

Notation 1. *We adopt the convention of using the Greek alphabet for the structural isomorphisms related to the multiplicative tensor, and the Roman alphabet for the additive tensor. We denote the multiplicative associativity and symmetry isomorphisms by $\tau_{XYZ} : X \otimes (Y \otimes Z) \to (X \otimes Y) \otimes Z$ and $\sigma_{X,Y} : X \otimes Y \to Y \otimes X$, and the additive associativity and symmetry by $t_{XYZ} : X \oplus (Y \oplus Z) \to (X \oplus Y) \oplus Z$ and $s_{XY} : X \oplus Y \to Y \oplus X$. We will frequently appeal to MacLane's coherence theorem for associativity, and treat both the multiplicative and additive tensors as strict.*

We will also denote the multiplicative unit object by I, and the additive unit object by 0.

A special case that is often considered (e.g. [6,7]) is where the distributivity monomorphisms are in fact isomorphisms.

Definition 2. *Let $(\mathcal{C}, \otimes, \oplus)$ be a category with distributivity. We say that is is* **strongly distributive** *when the natural distributivity monomorphisms have global inverses,*

$$dl_{ABC}^{-1} : (A \otimes B) \oplus (A \otimes C) \to A \otimes (B \oplus C) \tag{3}$$
$$dr_{XYZ}^{-1} : (X \otimes Z) \oplus (Y \otimes Z) \to (X \oplus Y) \otimes Z \tag{4}$$

Strongly distributive categories are a special case of Definition 1, so we may still appeal to Laplaza's coherence theorems. Appropriate care will be taken when using commutative diagrams containing inverses of these canonical isomorphisms to ensure that an equivalent result may be derived without the use of inverses. See the proof of Lemma 1 for an example of this.

2.1   Distinguished Objects, and Copying Functors

Strongly distributive categories have two distinguished objects: the additive and multiplicative unit objects $0, I \in Ob(\mathcal{C})$. Their interaction with the two monoidal tensors is given (up to straightforward canonical isomorphism) by the following tables:

$\otimes$	0	I
0	0	0
I	0	I

$\oplus$	0	I
0	0	I
I	I	$I \oplus I$

Observe that $I \oplus I$ is neither 0 nor I; thus in the absence of any further identities, strongly distributive categories have additional distinguished objects.

Definition 3. *We define* $2 \in Ob(\mathcal{C})$ *to be the additive tensor of two multiplicative units, so* $2 = (I \oplus I)$.

Such objects are considered in [7], where – in the special case that $\otimes$ and $\oplus$ are a product and coproduct respectively – they generate Boolean algebras. The classical logical interpretation is well-established. As noted in [5] the form of distributivity introduced in [13] is entirely unsuitable for linear logic, since distributivity implies a form of 'copying' operation that we now describe:

Lemma 1. *Let* $(\mathcal{C}, \otimes, \oplus)$ *be a strongly distributive category. Then*

1. $2 \otimes X \cong X \oplus X$
2. *for all* $f \in \mathcal{C}(X, Y)$, *the following diagram commutes:*

$$
\begin{array}{ccc}
2 \otimes X & \xrightarrow{\;1_2 \otimes f\;} & 2 \otimes Y \\[4pt]
{\scriptstyle dr^{-1}_{I,I,X}}\big\uparrow & & \big\downarrow{\scriptstyle dr_{I,I,Y}} \\[4pt]
X \oplus X & \xrightarrow{\;f \oplus f\;} & Y \oplus Y
\end{array}
$$

Proof.

1. By distributivity, and the fact that I is the unit object for the multiplicative tensor, $2 \otimes A = (I \oplus I) \otimes A \cong (I \otimes A) \oplus (I \otimes A) \cong A \oplus A$.
2. By naturality, the following diagram commutes:

$$
\begin{array}{ccc}
(I \oplus I) \otimes X & \xrightarrow{\;1_{I \oplus I} \otimes f\;} & (I \oplus I) \otimes Y \\[4pt]
{\scriptstyle dr_{I,I,X}}\big\downarrow & & \big\downarrow{\scriptstyle dr_{I,I,Y}} \\[4pt]
X \oplus X & \xrightarrow[\;f \oplus f\;]{} & Y \oplus Y
\end{array}
$$

As $(\mathcal{C}, \otimes, \oplus)$ is strongly distributive, we may replace dr_{IIX} in the above diagram by dr_{IIX}^{-1}, and reverse the corresponding arrow:

$$
\begin{array}{ccc}
(I \oplus I) \otimes X & \xrightarrow{1_{I \oplus I} \otimes f} & (I \oplus I) \otimes Y \\
\Big\uparrow dr_{I,I,X}^{-1} & & \Big\downarrow dr_{I,I,Y} \\
X \oplus X & \xrightarrow[f \oplus f]{} & Y \oplus Y
\end{array}
$$

$\square$

Definition 4. *Let $(\mathcal{C}, \otimes, \oplus)$ be strongly distributive. We define the* **copying endofunctor** *to be $\delta = (2 \otimes \_) : \mathcal{C} \to \mathcal{C}$.*

This terminology is motivated by the following result:

Proposition 1. *Let $\Delta : \mathcal{C} \to \mathcal{C} \times \mathcal{C}$ be the diagonal functor given by*

- **(Objects)** $\Delta(A) = (A, A)$.
- **(Arrows)** $\Delta(f) = (f, f)$

Then there exists a natural isomorphism (i.e. a natural transformation whose components are isomorphisms) from the composite functor $(\_ \oplus \_)\Delta : \mathcal{C} \to \mathcal{C}$ to the functor $(2 \otimes \_) : \mathcal{C} \to \mathcal{C}$.

We draw this diagrammatically, as follows:

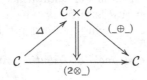

Proof. For arbitrary $X \in Ob(\mathcal{C})$, the components of this natural transformation are given by the distributivity isomorphisms $dl_{I,I,X} : 2 \otimes X \to X \oplus X$ (treating units arrows as strict). The required identity then follows from Lemma 1. $\square$

Remark 1. At first sight, this 'copying' behaviour appears to be at odds with the 'no-cloning' and 'no-deleting' theorems [20,18] of quantum information. However, these are based on tensor products ('multiplicative' tensors), whereas the functor of Definition 4 acts as a form of copying for the additive structure – it is related to the fanout operation [10] rather than the forbidden quantum cloning.

Iterating a copying operation gives a form of exponential growth, as we demonstrate:

Corollary 1. *For all $f \in \mathcal{C}(X, Y)$ and $n \geq 1 \in \mathbb{N}$, there exists canonical isomorphisms $\lambda_X^{(n)} : 2^{\otimes n} \otimes X \to \bigoplus_{j=0}^{2^n - 1} X$ making the following diagram commute:*

$$
\begin{array}{ccc}
2^{\otimes n} \otimes X & \xrightarrow{\delta^n(f)} & 2^{\otimes n} \otimes Y \\
\Big\downarrow \lambda_X & & \Big\uparrow \lambda_Y^{-1} \\
\bigoplus_{j=0}^{2^n-1} X & \xrightarrow[\bigoplus_{n=0}^{2^n-1} f]{} & \bigoplus_{j=0}^{2^n-1} Y
\end{array}
$$

Proof. We give the canonical isomorphisms $\lambda_X^{(n)} : 2^{\otimes n} \otimes X \to \bigoplus_{j=0}^{2^n-1} X$ by induction: we take $\lambda_X^{(1)} = dr_{I,I,X} : 2 \otimes X \to X \oplus X$, and

$$\lambda_X^{(n)} = dr_{I,I,\bigoplus_{j=0}^{2^{n-1}-1} X} \left(1_2 \otimes \lambda_X^{(n-1)} \right).$$

The above diagram then commutes by naturality. $\qquad\qquad\qquad\qquad\qquad$ $\square$

We now demonstrate that $\delta : \mathcal{C} \to \mathcal{C}$ is a (weak) *monoidal* endofunctor, for the additive, but not multiplicative, structure.

Proposition 2. *The functor* $\delta = (2 \otimes \_) : \mathcal{C} \to \mathcal{C}$ *does not preserve the multiplicative monoidal structure, even up to isomorphism; however the additive structure is preserved up to a simple distributivity isomorphism.*

Proof. To see that δ does not preserve the multiplicative tensor, observe that note that

$$\delta(A) \otimes \delta(B) = (1_2 \otimes \sigma_{A,2} \otimes 1_B) \delta^2(A \otimes B)$$

Thus, unless $\delta(X) \cong \delta^2(X)$ for all $X \in Ob(\mathcal{C})$, the copying functor does not preserve the multiplicative tensor, even up to isomorphism.

However, $\delta(0) \cong 0$, and the following diagram also commutes:

$$
\begin{array}{ccc}
\delta(A \oplus B) & \xrightarrow{\ \cong\ } & \delta(A) \oplus \delta(B) \\
{\scriptstyle =}\Big| & & \Big|{\scriptstyle =} \\
2 \otimes (A \oplus B) & \xrightarrow[dl_{(I \oplus I),A,B}]{} & 2 \otimes A \oplus 2 \otimes B
\end{array}
$$

Since the required isomorphisms are canonical coherence isomorphisms in both cases, $\delta : (\mathcal{C}, \oplus) \to (\mathcal{C}, \oplus)$ is a (weak) monoidal functor. $\qquad$ $\square$

2.2   Copying and the Iterator

We now study an operation on endomorphism monoids closely related to the copying functor $\delta : (\mathcal{C}, \oplus) \to (\mathcal{C}, \oplus)$.

Definition 5. *Let* $(\mathcal{C}, \otimes, \oplus)$ *be a strongly distributive category. For all* $f \in \mathcal{C}(A, A)$, *we define the* **N^{th} iterator** *of* f *to be*

$$!^N(f) = \bigoplus_{j=0}^{N-1} f^j \in \mathcal{C}\left(A^{\oplus N}, A^{\oplus N}\right)$$

We will give an efficient factorisation of $!^{2^n}(f)$. This will rely on the following interaction of the functor $\delta = (2 \otimes \_) : \mathcal{C} \to \mathcal{C}$, and the multiplicative and additive symmetries $\sigma_{X,Y} : X \otimes Y \to Y \otimes X$ and $s_{A,B} : A \oplus B \to B \oplus A$.

Lemma 2. *Let A, B, C be objects of a strongly distributive category $(\mathcal{C}, \otimes, \oplus)$. Then the following diagram commutes:*

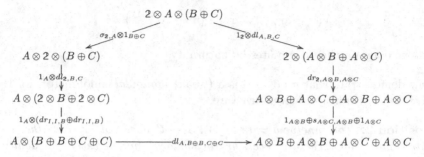

Proof. The commutativity of this diagram follows immediately from the coherence theorems of [13,14] (note that we have elided associativity isomorphisms, for clarity). □

Theorem 2. *For arbitrary $n \geq 1$ and $f \in \mathcal{C}(X, X)$, the arrow $!^{2^{n+1}}(f)$ can be defined in terms of $!^{2^n}(f)$, the functor $(2 \otimes \_)$, and canonical isomorphisms, with the exact relationship expressed by the commutativity of the following diagram:*

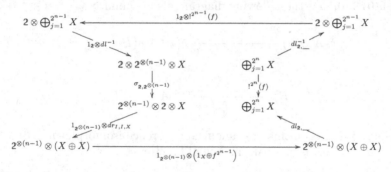

Proof. Consider the left hand path in the coherent diagram of Lemma 2 above, from $2 \otimes A \otimes (B \oplus C)$ to $A \otimes B \oplus A \otimes B \oplus A \otimes C \oplus A \otimes C$, along with arrows $f \in \mathcal{C}(B, Y)$ and $g \in \mathcal{C}(C, Z)$. Then naturality of canonical coherence isomorphisms implies the commutativity of the diagram in Figure 1. The required result is then the special case where $X = Y$ and $A = 2^{\otimes n}$. □

2.3   String Diagrams for Categories with Distributivity

Results such as Theorem 2 above may be given as string diagrams, using the conventions formalised in [11,12]. When we have two distinct monoidal tensors,

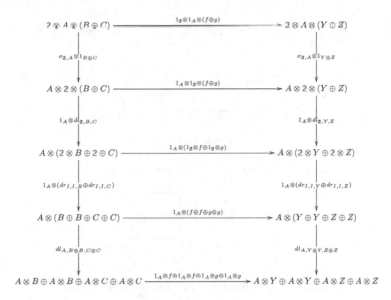

Fig. 1. A technical result implied by naturality

we adopt various conventions to ensure that such a diagrammatic reasoning is still valid:

1. Lines are separated by an implicit *multiplicative* rather than an *additive* monoidal tensor.
2. Operations involving *additive* monoidal tensors are enclosed in a double box.
3. Entering / leaving a double box requires an (implicit) distributivity isomorphism / its inverse. Provided care is taken with labelling of objects, the required canonical isomorphism may be deduced from the type of the operation.

We may then use diagrammatic manipulations on either the diagram as a whole (treating each additive box as a single operation), or on the contents of an individual double box (treating it as an entire diagram in of itself). These conventions ensure that the diagrammatic manipulations of [11,12] are valid, simply by restricting the permitted manipulations.

Using the above, an illustration of Theorem 2 is given in Figure 2.

Corollary 2. *There exists an efficient construction of $!^{2^n}(f)$ in $O(n)$ steps, based on canonical coherence isomorphisms.*

Proof. This follows by iterating the construction of Theorem 2. A diagrammatic illustration is given in Figure 3. □

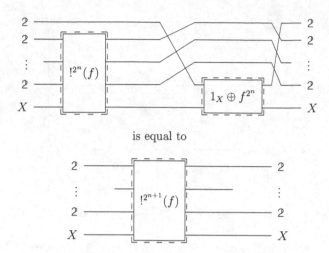

is equal to

Fig. 2. A 'string diagram' illustration of Theorem 2

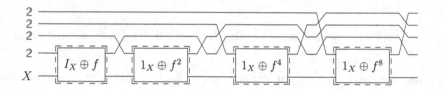

Fig. 3. The efficient construction of $!^{16}(f) = 1_X \oplus f \oplus \ldots \oplus f^{15} \oplus f^{16}$

Table 1. Translating abstract theory into a concrete setting

Abstract category C	Concrete category $\mathbf{Hilb_{FD}}$
Multiplicative tensor $H = H_1 \otimes H_2$	**Tensor product** *(Treating two systems as a single compound system).*
Additive tensor $(U \oplus 1)$ $(1 \oplus V)$	**Direct sum** *(U controlled on $\vert 0\rangle$)* *(V controlled on $\vert 1\rangle$)*
Multiplicative unit I	**Complex plane** $\mathbb{C}$
Additive unit 0	**Zero-dim. space** $\{0\}$
Distinguished object $2 = I \oplus I$	**Qubit space** Q, with orthonormal basis $\{\vert 0\rangle, \vert 1\rangle\}$

3   Concrete Realisation in Hilbert Space

The following sections assume a small degree of familiarity with quantum circuits and Hilbert spaces. More details may be found in in [17] or any other text on quantum computing and information.

We now consider the constructions of the previous section in the concrete setting of finite-dimensional complex Hilbert spaces. The two monoidal tensors are the familiar tensor product and direct sum — the distributivity isomorphisms relating the these are well-established.

The translation of the basic concepts is given in Table 1. A subtlety of this is the interpretation of the distinguished object 2. The direct sum of two 1-dimensional spaces is of course a two-dimensional space. However, since $\mathcal{Q}$ is built up in this way, we should think of it as having a fixed orthonormal basis specified by the canonical inclusions[2] – this will allow us to use matrix representations for arrows in this category.

Remark 2. A key point of this paper is that the structures required for the central oracle of Shor's algorithm are *not* dependent on the machinery of either traditional quantum mechanics (such as a matrix calculus, or notions of linearity and convergence), or categorical reinterpretations (compact closure, biproduct structures, &c.). However, the existence of matrix representations certainly makes the concrete instantiation simpler, as the following sections will demonstrate.

3.1   Interpreting the Direct Sum in the Circuit Model

In the translation from an abstract to a concrete setting provided in Table 1, the interpretation of the tensor, the multiplicative unit, and the distinguished object 2 are standard. Furthermore, as we are forced by the category theory to specify an orthonormal basis for the two-dimensional qubit space, we are now, for all practical purposes, working within the quantum circuit paradigm. The final connection arises from the interpretation of the direct sum in terms of 'quantum conditionals', or 'controlled operations' [9].

Definition 6. *Let U, V be unitary operations on a finite-dimensional Hilbert space H. The* **controlled operations** *$Ctrl_0 U$ and $Ctrl_1 V$ are the operations on $\mathcal{Q} \otimes H$ defined by:*

$$Ctrl_0 U \,|0\rangle \,|\psi\rangle = |0\rangle \, U \,|\psi\rangle \quad and \quad Ctrl_0 U \,|1\rangle \,|\psi\rangle = |1\rangle \,|\psi\rangle$$

$$Ctrl_1 V \,|0\rangle \,|\psi\rangle = |0\rangle \,|\psi\rangle \quad and \, Ctrl_1 V \,|1\rangle \,|\psi\rangle = |1\rangle \, V \,|\psi\rangle$$

with standard circuit representations shown in figure 4.

---

[2] This is, of course, related to the 'classical structures' of [8] — these are a special form of Frobenius algebra that play the role of orthonormal bases in categorical quantum mechanics. They are based on a 'copying' operation; the connection between these, and the $2 \otimes \_$ copying functor of Definition 4, is straightforward.

Denoting the n-qubit identity operation by I_n, these operations have matrix representations given by $C_0U = \begin{pmatrix} U & 0 \\ 0 & I_n \end{pmatrix}$ and $C_1V = \begin{pmatrix} I_n & 0 \\ 0 & V \end{pmatrix}$. The direct sum $U \oplus V$ is then simply the composite $U \oplus V = Ctrl_0U.Ctrl_1V = Ctrl_1V.Ctrl_0U$.

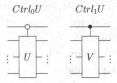

Fig. 4. Quantum circuits for 'Control on 0' and 'Control on 1'

Controlled operations can themselves be controlled. Given 2^n unitary maps $\{U_a\}_{a=0}^{2^n-1}$, the construction of $\bigoplus_{a=0}^{2^n-1} U_a$ is immediate via an n-qubit ancilla. This is illustrated in Figure 5 for the direct sum of 2^3 unitaries, and the 'binary counting' pattern on controls is immediate.

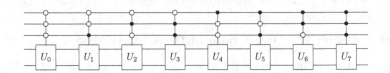

Fig. 5. A circuit for the direct sum $\bigoplus_{a=0}^{7} U_a$

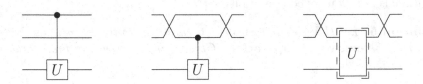

Fig. 6. Three equivalent diagrams

3.2   Controlled Operations and Categorical Swap Maps

In the standard quantum circuit formalism, controlled operations are not necessarily controlled by the qubit directly above them (i.e. the more significant qubit). We treat this as simply a diagrammatic convention, so a circuit where

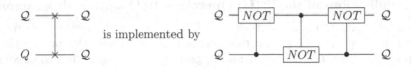

Fig. 7. The multiplicative symmetry via controlled additive symmetries

the control qubit is not adjacent to the controlled operation is implemented using multiplicative symmetries (i.e. qubit swap maps) in the obvious way. Thus, the three circuits of Figure 6 are equivalent, with the first being the usual quantum circuit notation, and the third conforming to the categorical conventions of Section 2.3.

The qubit swap map (i.e. multiplicative symmetry) itself has an interesting categorical interpretation via the standard decomposition shown in Figure 7. The single qubit NOT gate ($NOT\,|0\rangle = |1\rangle$, $NOT\,|1\rangle = |0\rangle$) is the additive symmetry $s_{\mathsf{C},\mathsf{C}}$ of two multiplicative unit objects. Figure 7 expresses an abstract categorical identity relating the multiplicative symmetry $\sigma_{2,2}$, the additive symmetry $s_{I,I}$, and distributivity. Details are left as an interesting exercise.

3.3   Interpreting the Iterator in the Quantum Circuit Paradigm

The interpretation of $!^{2^n}(U) = 1_H \oplus U \oplus U^2 \oplus \ldots \oplus U^{2^n-1}$ for some some unitary operation $U : H \to H$ is immediate; it is simply the sequence of multiply-controlled operations shown in Figure 8. The operational interpretation is immediate:

Proposition 3. *Given an arbitrary quantum state $|\psi\rangle \in H$ and a computational basis ancilla state $|a\rangle$, the circuit of Figure 8 acts on their tensor product as $|a\rangle\,|\psi\rangle \mapsto |a\rangle\,U^a\,|\psi\rangle$.*

Proof. This follows by definition of the action of controlled operations in the quantum circuit model. ☐

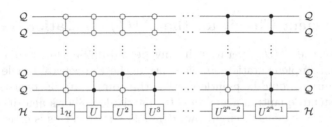

Fig. 8. A circuit for $!^{2^n}(U)$

3.4   Applications of the $!^N(U)$ Operation in Quantum Programming

Quantum circuits acting as $|a\rangle\,|\psi\rangle\,\mapsto\,|a\rangle\,U^a\,|\psi\rangle$ have an important role to play in quantum period-finding algorithms (although, of course, the precise circuit of Figure 9 is *not* used). The best-known period-finding algorithm is, of course, Shor's factorisation algorithm, based on period-finding for modular exponential functions.

Period-finding algorithms rely on a central oracle that acts classically on some subset of the computational basis (we refer to [17] for a formal definition, and [9] for a categorical interpretation in terms of Barr's l_2 functor [4]). Given a classical reversible function f, they require a unitary that acts as $|a\rangle\,|x\rangle\,\mapsto\,|a\rangle\,|f^a(x)\rangle$. Given an oracle U_f for the classical computation f, we may instead write this as $|a\rangle\,|x\rangle\,\mapsto\,|a\rangle\,U_f^a\,|x\rangle$ and observe that the required oracle for quantum period-finding is in fact $!^N(U_f)$, for some suitably large integer $N = 2^n$.

The complete quantum period-finding algorithm (up to some straightforward classical pre- and post- processing) is then simply given by conjugating such an oracle by a quantum Fourier transform, applied to the first register only. For example, in Shor's algorithm the central oracle is required to implement modular exponentials, via the action $|x\rangle\,|1\rangle\,\mapsto\,|x\rangle\,|r^x\ (mod\ K)\rangle$ and hence, by linearity,

$$\left(\sum_{x=0}^{N}|x\rangle\right)|1\rangle\,\mapsto\,\sum_{x=0}^{N}|x\rangle\,|r^x\ (mod\ K)\rangle$$

Given a (readily constructed) quantum oracle U that acts on the computational basis as $U\,|p\rangle\,=\,|rp\ (mod\ K)\rangle$, then, by Proposition 3, the required oracle for Shor's algorithm is $!^N(U)$. Thus the (quantum part of) Shor's algorithm is as shown in Figure 9.

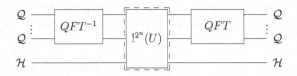

Fig. 9. The quantum circuit in Shor's algorithm

4   An Efficient Circuit for the $!^N(U)$ Operation

The utility of the $!^N(U)$ operation in any period-finding algorithm must rely on an efficient implementation. Implementing the the central oracle using the circuit of Figure 8 would be pointless, given the complexity of constructing such a circuit. Instead, quantum algorithms (in particular, Shor's algorithm) use an exponentially more efficient circuit; we demonstrate that this is exactly the implementation given by Corollary 2.

Proposition 4. *The circuits A and B shown in Figure 10 are equivalent.*

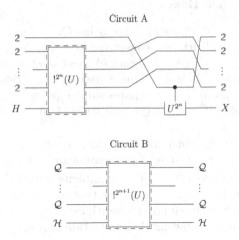

Fig. 10. Two equivalent quantum circuits

Proof. This follows directly from the Theorem 2 – in particular, the diagrammatic illustration given in Figure 2 makes it immediate. Note that the canonical multiplicative symmetry for qubits is drawn as a category-theoretic symmetry, rather than the traditional quantum circuit equivalent shown in Figure 7.   □

A simple corollary of Proposition 4 above, and the notational simplifications of Section 3.2, is that we may give a quantum circuit for $!^{2^n}(U)$ using $O(n)$ controlled quantum logic gates as follows:

Corollary 3. *The circuit of Figure 11 implements the* $!^{2^n}(U)$ *operation.*

Proof. This follows by induction on Proposition 4 above.   □

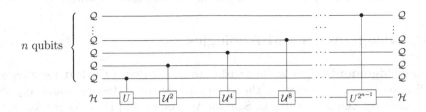

Fig. 11. An efficient implementation of $!^{2^n}(U)$

Remark 3. The efficient circuit of Figure 11 is exactly the circuit used by P. Shor to implement modular exponentiation [19]. From a purely quantum circuit point of view, it is straightforward to demonstrate the equivalence of the circuits of Figure 8 and Figure 11. The interest, from our point of view, is that this equivalence of circuits is an expression of a canonical coherence identity, and thus holds in any strongly distributive category.

4.1   Oracles and Black Boxes

In referring to the circuit of Figure 11 as requiring $O(n)$ primitive gates to implement $!^{2^n}(U)$, we have explicitly *not* considered the complexity of implementing $U, U^2, U^3, \ldots$. Rather, we have treated each of these operations as a 'black box'. For concrete algorithms, this is a serious omission; in particular, any practical realisation of Shor's algorithm also requires some efficient way of implementing (controlled versions of) U^{2^k}, where the operation $U |p\rangle = |rp \ (mod \ K)\rangle$ is as described in Section 3.4.

Fortunately, such an efficient implementation also exists — an oracle for the squaring operation $c \mapsto c^2 \ (mod \ K)$ (up to some suitable ancilla, and garbage collection) provides a simple, efficient way of implementing U^{2^k}, for $k = 1, \ldots, n$. This is described in detail in [19]. Note that this technique is not available for arbitrary functions; rather, modular exponentiation is one of the few arithmetic functions for which such an efficient decomposition exists.

5   Conclusions and Future Directions

We have demonstrated that the structural isomorphisms for strongly distributive categories have a role to play in understanding quantum algorithms – or at least that perhaps familiar operations in quantum circuits can be given an abstract interpretation in terms of categorical coherence.

Classically, equivalence up to canonical isomorphism is often used in program transformation, and it is pleasing, although not entirely unexpected, to see it in the quantum setting as well. Of more interest is how little of the machinery of categorical quantum mechanics we have used in establishing these transformations — the only assumption required is that of two monoidal tensors related by distributivity up to isomorphism, and thus the constructions of this paper are valid in a wide range of different categorical and algebraic settings.

Acknowledgements and Apologies

Acknowledgements. The author wishes to thank Robin Cockett for interesting discussions on the category theory of distributive categories, and applications. Similarly, thanks are due to Samson Abramsky and Bob Coecke for many discussions on the interpretation of distributivity and the direct sum, and on categorical quantum mechanics generally. Thanks are also due to Philip Scott, for discussions and references on categorical models of linear logic, with particular reference to the treatment of both distributivity and models of Girard's bang $!(\ )$ operation.

An Apology. The work in this paper was first presented at a QICS quantum computing conference (Oxford 2010), under the title *'The role of coherence in quantum algorithms'* (*http://www.comlab.ox.ac.uk/quantum/content/1005021/*).

After the talk, the speaker was approached by a delegation of experimental physicists, who explained that they had attended the talk because of the mention of 'coherence' in the title, in the hope that it would be a break from the hardcore category theory presented in other talks. The author wishes to apologise for the (intentionally) misleading title, but hopes that they enjoyed the talk nevertheless.

References

1. Abramsky, S., Coecke, B.: A categorical semantics of quantum protocols. In: Proc. 19th Annual IEEE Symp. on Logic in Computer Science (LICS 2004), pp. 415–425. IEEE Computer Soc. Press (2005)
2. Abramsky, S.: Abstract Scalars, Loops, and Free Traced and Strongly Compact Closed Categories. In: Fiadeiro, J.L., Harman, N.A., Roggenbach, M., Rutten, J. (eds.) CALCO 2005. LNCS, vol. 3629, pp. 1–29. Springer, Heidelberg (2005)
3. Aharanov, D., Landau, Z., Makowsky, J.: The quantum FFT can be classically simulated, arXiv:quant-ph/0611156 v1 (2006)
4. Barr, M.: Algebraically Compact Functors. Journal of Pure and Applied Algebra 82, 211–231 (1992)
5. Blute, R.F., Cockett, J.R.B., Seely, R.A.G., Trimble, T.H.: Natural deduction and coherence for weakly distributive categories. Mathematical Structures in Computer Science 113, 229–296 (1991)
6. Carboni, A., Lack, S., Walters, R.: Introduction to Extensive and Distributive Categories. Journal of Pure and Applied Algebra 84, 145–158 (1993)
7. Cockett, J.R.B.: Introduction to Distributive Categories. Mathematical Structures in Computer Science 3, 277–307 (1993)
8. Coecke, B., Pavlovic, D.: Quantum measurements without sums. In: Chen, G., Kauffman, L., Lamonaco, S. (eds.) Mathematics of Quantum Computing and Technology. Taylor and Francis (arxiv.org/quant-ph/0608035) (2007)
9. Hines, P.: Quantum circuit oracles for abstract machine computations. Theoretical Computer Science 411, 1501–1520 (2010)
10. Høyer, P., Špalek, R.: Quantum Fan-out is Powerful. Theory of Computing 1(5), 81–103 (2005)
11. Joyal, A., Street, R.: The geometry of tensor calculus. Advances in Mathematics (102), 20–78 (1993)
12. Joyal, A., Street, R.: The geometry of tensor calculus II (manuscript)
13. Laplaza, M.: Coherence for categories with associativity, commutativity, and distributivity. Bulletin of the American Mathematical Society 72(2), 220–222 (1972)
14. Laplaza, M.: Coherence for distributivity. In: MacLane, S. (ed.) Coherence in Categories. Springer Lecture Notes in Mathematics, vol. 281, pp. 29–65 (1972)
15. MacLane, S.: Duality for groups. Bulletin of the American Mathematical Society 56(6), 485–516 (1950)
16. MacLane, S.: Categories for the working mathematician, 2nd edn. Springer, New York (1998)

17. Nielsen, M., Chuang, I.: Quantum Computation and Quantum Information. Cambridge University Press (2000)
18. Pati, A., Braunstein, S.: Impossibility of deleting an unknown quantum state. Nature 404, 164–165 (2000)
19. Shor, P.: Algorithms for quantum computation: discrete log and factoring. In: Proceedings of IEEE FOCS, pp. 124–134 (1994)
20. Wootters, W., Zurek, W.: A Single Quantum Cannot be Cloned. Nature 299, 802–803 (1982)
21. Yoran, N., Short, A.: Classical simulability and the significance of modular exponentiation in Shor's algorithm, arXiv:quant-ph/0706.0872 v1 (2007)

Unifying Semantics
for Concurrent Programming

Tony Hoare

Microsoft Research
Cambridge
United Kingdom

Abstract. Four well-known methods for presenting semantics of a programming language are: denotational, deductive, operational, and algebraic. This essay presents algebraic laws for the structural features of a class of imperative programming languages which provide both sequential and concurrent composition; and it illustrates the way in which the laws are consistent with the other three semantic presentations of the same language. The exposition combines simplicity with generality by postponing consideration of the possibly more complex basic commands of particular programming languages. The proofs are given only as hints, but they are easily reconstructed, even with the aid of a machine.

Essay in celebration of Samson Abramsky's sixtieth birthday.

1 Introduction

Well-known methods for presenting semantics of a programming language are: denotational [1], deductive [2, 3], operational [4, 5] and algebraic [6, 7]. Each presentation is useful as a formal specification of a different Software Engineering tool.

1. The denotational semantics defines a program in terms of all its legitimate behaviours, when executed on any occasion, and in any possible external environment (including other programs). It provides a theoretical foundation for implementation and use of program test environments, which assist in location, diagnosis and correction of unintended effects in the execution of a program.
2. The deductive semantics (originally called axiomatic), provides a set of proof rules, capable of verifying general properties of all possible executions of a particular program. It is the theoretical foundation for program analysis tools (extended static checkers), and also for semi-automatic verifiers, that assist in finding and checking proofs of program correctness.
3. The operational semantics is a set of rules for running a particular program to produce just one of its possible executions. It is the theoretical foundation of any implementation of the language, by a combination of interpreters, compilers and run-time libraries.

B. Coecke, L. Ong, and P. Panangaden (Eds.): Abramsky Festschrift, LNCS 7860, pp. 139–149, 2013.

4. The algebraic semantics (which is more directly axiomatic) has the simplest and most elegant presentation. It helps directly in efficient reasoning about a program, and in optimising its implementation. An additional role of algebra is to help establish relevant aspects of the mutual consistency of the other forms of semantics. In application, the algebra could contribute to the definition of consistent interfaces between the major components of a Design Automation toolset for Concurrent Software Engineering.

The unification of the four semantic presentations proceeds in four steps. (1) The denotational model is shown to satisfy each law of the algebra. (2) A selection of the laws of the algebra is given an equivalent presentation as a proof rule, or as a pair of rules. (3) The basic triple of Hoare logic is given an algebraic definition, which translates (in both directions) between each structural proof rule of Hoare logic and a rule from (2). (4) The basic triple (transition) of Milner [4, 5] is similarly defined, and shown to translate between each rule of an operational semantics and another of the rules from (2). Thus the selected laws of the algebra are equivalent to the conjunction of the rules of the other two semantics. The proofs are highly modular, and they are presented separately for each operator.

There are many simple and useful, algebraic laws which are valid for the denotational model, but which have no direct counterpart in the deductive or the operational semantics. This suggests that the algebraic method will have much to contribute to the exploration of the principles of programming, and the formalisation of its discoveries for application at the interfaces between software engineering tools.

2   Denotations

Let Act be a set, whose elements are interpreted as individual occurrences of basic atomic actions of a program. It includes actions occurring both inside and in the environment of a computer system that is executing the program. Let Dep be a relation between elements of Act. The statement that x Dep y is interpreted as saying that x is necessary to enable y , in the sense that action y depends on (prior) occurrence of all the actions that it depends on. In game semantics, Dep might serve as a justification relation. A dependency is often drawn as an arrow between two actions, where the actions are drawn as nodes in a graphical diagram of program execution. Examples of such a diagrams include: (1) message sequence charts, where the vertical arrows represent control dependency in a process or thread, and horizontal arrows represent communications or calls between threads; (2) a Petri occurrence net, where the actions are drawn as transitions, and there is an implicit place for token storage on each arrow; or (3)a hardware waveform diagram, where the actions are rising or falling edges of voltage level on a wire, and arrows between the level changes represent dependencies enforced elsewhere in the circuit. All these examples show actions as the points, and the arrows as the line segments, of a discrete non-metric geometry of interaction.

The purpose of the Act and Dep parameters is to allow formalisation of the meaning of the basic commands of a programming language. For example, the following axioms can be postulated to apply to objects, variables, and communication channels: the 0th action of any object is its allocation, and the last action is its disposal. When the nth action is not a disposal:

- the nth action of an object enables the $(n+1)^{st}$ action;
- the nth action of an output port enables the nth action of the input port of that channel;
- on a single-buffered channel, the nth input enables the $(n+1)^{st}$ output;
- the nth assignment to a variable enables all the reads of the nth assignment;
- the $(n+1)^{st}$ assignment depends on all reads of nth assignment.

The last clause merely says that every read of a variable reads the value most recently assigned to it. This axiom applies to familiar strong memory models. Its violation is characteristic of weaker memory models, where fences have to be inserted to achieve a similar effect.

Let Tra be the powerset of Act. An element of Tra (denoted $p, q, r, \ldots$) is interpreted as a complete and successful trace of the execution of a particular program on a particular occasion, whether in the past, the present or the future. Let Prog be the powerset of Tra. An element of Prog (denoted $P, Q, R, \ldots$) is interpreted as a complete description of all possible and successful traces of the execution of a program, in all possible environments of use. If no trace of a program can be successfully completed, the program is represented by the empty set of traces. This is an error like a syntax error: ideally, a compiler should be able to detect it, and consequently ensure that the program is never executed. Such non-execution must be clearly distinguished from the empty trace, which contains no actions, and is easy to execute rather than impossible.

The user specification of a program is its most general description, describing only those traces which will be acceptable to the end users. The program itself is the most specific description: it will describe only those traces which record a possible complete behaviour of the program when executed. Correctness is inclusion ($\subseteq$) of the latter in the former. Even a single assertion, describing a set of possible states of the machine before or after execution of a program, can be interpreted as a set of traces, namely those which end (alternatively, which begin) in one of the states described by the assertion. A single state is described by an assertion which only that state satisfies. We exploit these interpretations to obtain a simple homogeneous algebra, with just a single sort.

Of course, there is good reason why distinct sorts, with different notations, are often used for these different kinds of description. For example, programs need to be expressed in some notation (a computable programming language), for which there exists an implementation of adequate efficiency and stability on the hardware available to execute the program. Specifications, on the other hand, are normally allowed to exploit the full expressive power of mathematics, including scientific concepts relevant to the real world environment of a particular application. A single state is often expressed as a tuple, describing the structure of the state of an executing machine. Assertions are often restricted to Boolean terms that can be evaluated in the current state of the machine at run time. The simpler distinct notations generally used for each of these special cases are shorter than descriptions of general traces; they are more useful, more comprehensible and easier to reason with. But distinct notations tend to obscure or even accentuate differences between languages and theories. Disregard of syntactic distinctions is an essential preliminary to unification of the underlying semantics.

A denotational semantics is formalised as a collection of definitions of the basic commands of a programming language, and of the operators by which they are composed into programs. Each action occurrence in a trace is the execution of a basic command. There is also a basic command Id, interpreted as a program that has no action, because it does nothing. There are three binary operators: semicolon (;) standing for sequential composition, star (∗) standing for concurrent composition, and ∨ standing for disjunction or choice. These form the signature of the algebra. In many cases, there are several definitions that will satisfy the same algebra, and some interesting alternatives will occasionally be indicated in the text. The main thread of development presents a model that is (where necessary) a compromise between simplicity of exposition and authenticity to application.

2.1   Basic Commands

$$\mathsf{Id} = \{\{\}\}$$

This is the command that performs no action.

Each of the other basic commands of the programming language is also defined as a set of traces. Each trace is a unit set, containing just a single occurrence of the action of executing the command. We will assume that there is an infinite set of possible executions of the command, which can occur in different programs, in different contexts and on different occasions. As a result, it is trivial to model resource allocation and disposal: each allocated resource is distinct, because its allocation was distinct from all allocations of all other resources.

2.2   Sequential Composition

$$P; Q = \{p \cup q \mid p \in P \text{ and } q \in Q \text{ and } p \times q \subseteq \mathsf{Seq}\}$$

where $\mathsf{Seq} = (\neg(\mathsf{Dep}^*))^\cup$, and $p \times q$ is the Cartesian product, Dep^* is the reflexive transitive closure of Dep and $(\cdot)^\cup$ denotes relational converse.

This definition states that a trace of $P; Q$ is the union of all the actions of some trace p of P with all the actions of another trace q of Q. Furthermore, there is no dependency (direct or indirect) of any action occurrence in p on any action occurrence in q. Such a dependency would certainly prevent the completion of p before the execution of q starts; and this should surely be an allowed method of implementation. But our definition also allows many other implementations, in which actions of q can occur concurrently with (or before) those of p , subject only to the given dependency constraint. This freedom of implementation is widely exploited by the optimisations performed by the main compilers for today's programming languages. The strongest reasonable definition of sequential composition would replace the above definition of Seq by simply Dep*. This requires that all actions of p precede all actions of q.

2.3   Concurrent Composition

$$P * Q = \{p \cup q \mid p \in P \text{ and } q \in Q \text{ and } p \times q \subseteq \text{Par}\}$$

where $Par = \neg(\text{Dep}^*) \cup (\neg(\text{Dep}^*))^{\cup}$. Again, this is the weakest reasonable definition of concurrent composition. The condition on $p \times q$ rules out a class of impossible traces, where an event in p depends on an event in q, and vice-versa; such a dependency cycle would in practice end in deadlock, which would prevent the successful completion of the trace.

2.4   Choice

$$P \vee Q = P \cup Q$$

This is simplest possible definition of choice: $P \vee Q$ is executed either by executing P or by executing Q. The criterion of selection is left indeterminate. Other definitions of choice can be implemented by an operator (e.g., a conditional) that controls the choice by specifying when one of the operands will have no traces. The details are omitted here.

2.5   Galois Inverses

Galois inverses (of functions that distribute through big unions) are defined in the usual way for a complete lattice of sets.

1. $Q \leftarrowtail R = \bigcup(P \mid P; Q \subseteq R)$
2. $P \rightarrowtail R = \bigcup(Q \mid P; Q \subseteq R)$
3. $P \longrightarrow\!\!* R = \bigcup(\{Q \mid P * Q \subseteq R\})$

The first of these inverses is a generalisation of Dijkstra's [8] weakest precondition $wp(Q, R)$. It is a description of the most general program P whose execution before Q will satisfy the overall specification R. The second is a version of the Back/Morgan specification statement [9, 10], the most general description of the program Q whose execution after P will satisfy the specification R. The third is very similar, except that P and Q are executed concurrently rather than sequentially. It is called "magic wand" in separation logic.

2.6   Iteration

$$P^* = \bigcup\{X \mid \text{Id} \cup P \cup (X*; X*) \subseteq X\}.$$

This is Pratt's definition [11], using the Knaster-Tarski fixed-point theorem. The same technique can be used to define the more general concept of recursion, under the condition of monotonicity of the function involved.

3   Algebra and Logic

This section explains the algebraic properties of the listed operators, and gives hints why they are satisfied by the denotational definitions of the previous sections. The properties are mostly expressed as the familiar laws of associativity, commutativity, and distribution. The less familiar laws are those applicable to concurrency. In this section, the elements of the algebra are all sets; and it is convenient to denote them by lower case letters $p, q, r, \ldots$.

This section also relates the algebra to the familiar rules of a deductive and an operational semantics. It selects a subset of the equational and inequational algebraic laws, and expresses them in the form of proof rules, which can be derived from them, and from which the laws can themselves be derived. It gives algebraic definitions of the basic judgements of a deductive and of an operational semantics. It then shows how the selected laws can be derived from the semantic rules, and vice-versa. This is the same method that is used to show that natural deduction is just a logical form of presentation for the laws of Boolean algebra.

The Hoare triple $p\{q\}r$ says that if q is executed after p, then the overall effect will satisfy the specification r. It is therefore defined as the algebraic inequation $p; q \subseteq r$. The logical implication $p \Rightarrow p'$ between assertions is defined by the inequation $p; \mathsf{Id} \subseteq r$. Similarly, the Milner transition $r \xrightarrow{p} q$ means that one of the ways of executing r is to execute p first and then q. This is simply defined as exactly the same inequation $p; q \subseteq r$! The silent action τ is defined as Id. As a result, the basic operational rule of CCS ($p; q \xrightarrow{p} q$) follows just from the reflexivity of $\subseteq$. From these definitions, it is easy to show that the main structural rules of Hoare and Milner calculi are the same as rules of deduction, which are interderivable with a subset of the axioms in the algebra. Note that our rules for operational semantics are based on "big steps", and in general they differ from those used by Milner in his definition of CCS [5].

Our definitions also ignore the restrictions that are normally placed on the judgements of the two rule-based semantics. Hoare logic usually restricts p and r to be assertions, and Milner transitions (in a small-step semantics) usually restrict q to be a basic action. Furthermore, p and r are usually machine states, often represented by displaying the structure of the program that remains to be executed in the future (the continuation). These restrictions are fully justified by their contribution to simpler reasoning about programs and to greater efficiency of their implementation. However, the denotational model shows that the restrictions are semantically unnecessary, and we shall ignore them.

In summary, a significant part of the algebraic semantics, including the novel laws for concurrency, can be derived from the rules of the two rule-based semantics. Additional evidence is thereby given of the realism and applicability of the algebraic laws, and of their conformity to an already widely shared understanding of the fundamental concepts of programming.

3.1   Monotonicity

Theorem 1. *Sequential composition is monotonic with respect to set inclusion* $\subseteq$.

This is a simple consequence of the implicit existential quantifier in the definition of this operator (and of others).

Monotonicity of a binary operator is normally expressed as two proof rules

$$(a) \quad \frac{p \subseteq p'}{p; q \subseteq p'; q} \qquad (b) \quad \frac{q \subseteq q'}{p; q \subseteq p; q'}$$

Using the properties of partial ordering, these rules are interderivable with the single rule

$$(c) \quad \frac{p \subseteq p' \quad p'; q \subseteq r' \quad r' \subseteq r}{p; q \subseteq r}$$

When translated to Hoare triples, (a) and (b) give the two clauses of the familiar Rule of Consequence. When translated to Milner transitions, (c) gives a stronger version of the structural equivalence rule of process algebra. The strengthening consists in replacement of $=$ by $\subseteq$.

3.2   Sequential Composition

Theorem 2. ; *is associative and has unit* Id.

Proof of associativity does not depend on the particular definition of Seq, which can be an arbitrary relation between actions. It depends only on the fact that Cartesian product distributes through set union.

Associativity can be expressed in two complementary axioms

$$p; (q; r) \subseteq (p; q); r \qquad (p; q); r \subseteq p; (q; r).$$

Using monotonicity of ; and antisymmetry of $\subseteq$, the first of these can be expressed as a proof rule

$$(a) \quad \frac{p; q \subseteq s \quad s; r \subseteq r'}{p; (q; r) \subseteq r'}$$

Similarly, the second axiom is expressible as

$$(b) \quad \frac{p; s \subseteq r' \quad q; r \subseteq s}{(p; q); r \subseteq r'}$$

When translated to Hoare triples, (a) is the familiar rule of sequential composition. When translated to transitions, (b) gives a (less familiar, large-step) rule for sequential composition.

3.3   Concurrent Composition

Theorem 3. $*$ *is associative and commutative and has unit* Id. *Furthermore, it is related to sequential composition by the laws*

(a1) $p; q \subseteq p * q$
(a2) $q; p \subseteq p * q$
(b1) $p; (q * r) \subseteq (p; q) * r$
(b2) $(p * q); r \subseteq p * (q; r)$
 (c) $(p * q); (p' * q') \subseteq (p; p') * (q; q')$

The proof of these four laws depends only on the fact that the Seq relation is included in Par, and that Par is commutative. When $*$ is commutative, $(a1)$ and $(a2)$ are equivalent. When ; and $*$ share the same unit, all the laws follow from (c). They are listed separately, to cater for possible alternative models.

These laws are known as exchange laws, by analogy with the similar interchange law of two-categories. They permit the interchange of ; and $*$ as major and minor connectives of a term. In category theory, the law is a weak equality, and holds only when both sides are defined. In our case, the law is a strong inequality, and the right hand side always includes the left.

The exchange laws formalise the principle of sequential consistency. They allow any formula containing only basic actions, connected by sequential and concurrent composition, to be reduced to a set of stronger forms, in which all concurrent compositions have been eliminated. Furthermore, any pair of basic commands, which appear directly or indirectly separated by ; in the original formula, appear in the same order in all the stronger interleavings. Of course many of the interleavings could turn out to be empty, because they violate dependency ordering; for example, the left hand side of $(a1)$ is empty if any action of p depends (indirectly, perhaps) on any action of q. The full strength of the principle of sequential consistency would require another axiom: that every formula is equal to the union of all the stronger and more interleaved forms derived from it. This would unfortunately be an infinite axiom set.

$(b2)$ is interderivable with the principle of local reasoning, the fundamental contribution of separation logic [3]. This is called the frame rule; it serves the same role as the rule of adaptation in Hoare logic; but it is more powerful and much simpler.

$$\frac{p; q \subseteq r}{(p * f); q \subseteq r * f.}$$

$(b1)$ is interderivable with one of the rules given in the operational semantics of CCS [5].

$$\frac{r \xrightarrow{p} q}{r * f \xrightarrow{p} q * f}$$

This rule is interpreted as follows. Suppose r is a process that can first do p and then behave as the continuation q. Then when r is executed concurrently with a process f , the combination can also do p first, and then behave like the continuation q running concurrently with the whole of f.

(c) is interderivable with the main concurrency rule of concurrent separation logic (which is usually expressed with the operator $\|$ in place of $*$ between q and q'):

$$\frac{p;q \subseteq r \quad p';q' \subseteq r'}{(p \| p');(q * q') \subseteq r * r'}.$$

This law expresses a principle of modular reasoning. A concurrent composition can be proved correct by proving properties of its operands separately.

When translated to transitions, (c) is the main concurrency rule of a process algebra like CCS. In a small-step semantics like that of CCS, $q * q'$ is defined as a basic action iff q and q' are an input and an output on the same channel; and it is then equal to Id (which we have identified with τ).

3.4   Units

Theorem 4. *Id is the unit of both sequential and parallel composition.*

From this, two weaker properties are selected for translation into rules.

(a) $p;Id \subseteq p$
(b) $Id;p \subseteq p$.

The rule derived from (a) is the Hoare rule for Id, and (b) is an operational rule for Id, which is not accepted as a rule of a small-step semantics.

3.5   Choice

Theorem 5. $\vee$ *is associative, commutative and idempotent. It is monotonic and increasing in both arguments. It also admits distribution in both directions by concurrent and by sequential composition. This last property can be expressed*

(a) $p;(q \vee q') \subseteq p;q \vee p;q'$
(b) $(p \vee p');q \subseteq p;q \vee p';q$.

As in previous examples, these properties are interderivable with standard rules. The rule derived from (a) gives the standard rule in Hoare logic for non-deterministic choice. (b) gives a very similar Milner rule, expressed in terms of big-step transitions.

3.6   Galois Adjoints

The algebraic properties of Galois inverses are well-known. For example, they are monotonic, and give an approximate inverse to an operator :

$$(q \twoheadleftarrow r);q \subseteq r \qquad p \subseteq q \twoheadleftarrow (p;q)$$

The equations that Dijkstra [8] gives as definitions of the operators of a programming language can all be derived as theorems. For example: the definition of sequential composition is

$$(p; q) \leftarrow r = p \leftarrow (q \leftarrow r).$$

However, there seems to be no exact finite equational characterisation of concurrent composition in terms of its adjoint.

3.7   Iteration

Pratt [11] has given a complete axiomatisation of iteration by just three elegant algebraic equations. (1) is the familiar fixed point property. (2) is monotonicity. And (3) is $(p \leftrightarrow p)^* = p \leftrightarrow p$.

An obvious conclusion from this section is that an algebraic semantics of a programming language can be more powerful than a combination of both its deductive and its operational presentations, and simpler, by objective criteria than each of them separately. It is more powerful in the expression of more laws, and in their applicability to an unrestricted class of operands. To supply the missing laws, a rule-based semantics usually defines a concept of by equivalence, for example, in terms of contextual congruence or bisimulation. The equivalence theorems are often proved by induction over the terms of the language, sometimes jointly with induction over the length of a computation. The inductions are often simple and satisfying. The disadvantage of inductive proofs in general is that any extension to the language (or to its axioms) has to be validated by adding new clauses to every theorem previously proved by induction. This reduces the modularity of the proofs, and makes extension of the programming language more difficult than it is by the direct addition of new algebraic axioms. Of course, in an algebraic presentation, it is still highly desirable to prove consistency of the new axioms with the original model. Alternatively, a whole new model, may be required, and a new proof of all the original axioms. To avoid this, a general parameterised model may be helpful.

4   Conclusion

As well as enabling greater modularity, extensibility and reusability of semantic reasoning, the algebraic laws seem simpler (by objective criteria) than the rules of a deductive semantics, and also simpler than an operational semantics. The obvious conclusion is that algebra could play an expanded role in the exploration of the principles of programming.

I hope that this message will appeal to the hearts and stimulate the minds of Samson Abramsky and his many colleagues and admirers. They have made earlier and far deeper contributions to the unification of the semantics of programming than those reported here. The best outcome of this essay would be to make their results more widely accessible and more widely applicable to the practical problems of software engineering.

Acknowledgements. This essay reports the results of research conducted with many collaborators. Many of these results have been previously published [12–18].

References

1. Stoy, J.E.: Denotational Semantics: The Scott-Strachey Approach to Programming Language Theory. MIT Press (1977)
2. Hoare, C.A.R.: An axiomatic basis for computer programming. Communications of the ACM 12(10), 576–580 (1969)
3. O'Hearn, P.W.: Resources, concurrency and local reasoning. In: Gardner, P., Yoshida, N. (eds.) CONCUR 2004. LNCS, vol. 3170, pp. 49–67. Springer, Heidelberg (2004)
4. Plotkin, G.D.: A structural approach to operational semantics. Technical Report DAIMI FN-19, Aarhus University (1981)
5. Milner, R.: A Calculus of Communication Systems. LNCS, vol. 92. Springer, Heidelberg (1980)
6. Hennessy, M.: Algebraic Theory of Processes. MIT Press (1988)
7. Baeten, J., Basten, T., Reniers, M.A.: Process Algebra: Equational Theories of Communicating Processes. Cambridge Tracts in Theoretical Computer Science, vol. 50. Cambridge University Press (2009)
8. Dijkstra, E.W.: A Discipline of Programming. Prentice Hall, Englewood Cliffs (1976)
9. Back, R.J., Wright, J.: Refinement calculus: a systematic introduction. Springer (1998)
10. Morgan, C.: Programming from specifications. Prentice-Hall, Inc. (1990)
11. Pratt, V.R.: Action logic and pure induction. In: van Eijck, J. (ed.) JELIA 1990. LNCS, vol. 478, pp. 97–120. Springer, Heidelberg (1991)
12. Hoare, C.A.R., Hayes, I.J., He, J., Morgan, C., Roscoe, A.W., Sanders, J.W., Sørensen, I.H., Spivey, J.M., Sufrin, B.: Laws of programming. Commun. ACM 30(8), 672–686 (1987)
13. Hoare, C.A.R., Jifeng, H.: Unifying Theories of Programming. Prentice Hall (1998)
14. Wehrman, I., Hoare, C.A.R., O'Hearn, P.W.: Graphical models of separation logic. Inf. Process. Lett. 109(17), 1001–1004 (2009)
15. Hoare, T., Wickerson, J.: Unifying models of data flow. In: Software and Systems Safety - Specification and Verification, pp. 211–230 (2011)
16. Hoare, C.A.R., Hussain, A., Möller, B., O'Hearn, P.W., Petersen, R.L., Struth, G.: On locality and the exchange law for concurrent processes. In: Katoen, J.-P., König, B. (eds.) CONCUR 2011. LNCS, vol. 6901, pp. 250–264. Springer, Heidelberg (2011)
17. Hoare, T., Möller, B., Struth, G., Wehrman, I.: Concurrent Kleene algebra and its foundations. J. Log. Algebr. Program. 80(6), 266–296 (2011)
18. Hoare, T., van Staden, S.: The laws of programming unify process calculi. In: Gibbons, J., Nogueira, P. (eds.) MPC 2012. LNCS, vol. 7342, pp. 7–22. Springer, Heidelberg (2012)

Unfixing the Fixpoint:
The Theories of the λY-Calculus

Furio Honsell and Marina Lenisa

Dipartimento di Matematica e Informatica, Università di Udine, Italy
furio.honsell@comune.udine.it, marina.lenisa@uniud.it

Dedicated to Samson Abramsky
on the occasion of his 60th birthday

Abstract. We investigate the theories of the λY-*calculus*, *i.e.* simply typed λ-calculus with *fixpoint* combinators. Non-terminating λY-terms exhibit a rich behavior, and one can reflect in λY many results of untyped λ-calculus concerning theories. All theories can be characterized as *contextual theories* à la Morris, w.r.t. a suitable set of *observables*. We focus on theories arising from natural classes of observables, where Y can be approximated, albeit not always initially. In particular, we present the standard theory, induced by *terminating terms*, which features a canonical interpretation of Y as "minimal fixpoint", and another theory, induced by *pure* λ-terms, which features a non-canonical interpretation of Y. The interest of these two theories is that the term model of the λY-calculus w.r.t. the first theory gives a *fully complete model* of the maximal theory of the simply typed λ-calculus, while the term model of the latter theory provides a *fully complete model* for the observational equivalence in unary PCF. Throughout the paper we raise open questions and conjectures.

Introduction

Y, the *fixpoint combinator* lies at the heart of computation, and quite naturally PCF has been a paradigm language for many decades. However, λY-calculus, the purely functional core of PCF, *i.e.* simply typed λ-calculus extended with fixpoint combinators, has not been often studied *per se*. In this paper, we outline a general investigation of the theories of λY, inspired by what has been done in the untyped λ-calculus, see *e.g.* [Bar84, HP09].

From this investigation, we expect to achieve a better understanding of how theories of the λY, and hence of PCF, relate to *e.g. iteration* theories [BE93, PS00], what are the constraints on possible *non initial* interpretations of Y, and which properties of λY-terms can be naturally encoded by non-terminating λ-processes. We think that this research can be quite rewarding given the remarkable results obtained in the semantics of simply typed λ-calculus using games, and other categories, since the fundamental work of Samson Abramsky on full abstraction of PCF, see [AJM00].

B. Coecke, L. Ong, and P. Panangaden (Eds.): Abramsky Festschrift, LNCS 7860, pp. 150–165, 2013.
© Springer-Verlag Berlin Heidelberg 2013

Ultimately, we would be like to answer general questions on the flexibility of notions such as games or continuous functions in modeling adequately the rich computational behavior of syntactical combinators. *E.g.*: "Are all λY-theories modeled by game models? If not, which are they?" Abramsky and Luke Ong [AO93], and one of the authors [HR92], were among the first to realize the constraints imposed by Scott-domains on the semantics of the untyped λ-calculus. Since then a vast literature arose in this area, see *e.g.* [DFII99, CG09, IIP09] for the untyped λ-calculus. This paper addresses the above issues for the typed λY-calculus. In particular, we follow a journey around λY-theories analogue to that for the untyped λ-calculus. We start by defining theories contextually, given a set of *observables*. This amounts to reasoning on *term models*, *i.e.* on a model-independent semantics. A straightforward *transfer* result allows us to reflect on the λY-calculus essentially all the complexities of the theories of untyped λ-calculus. But "sometimes less is more" and many more issues arise in the typed setting than one would have expected at the outset. A wealth of intriguing connections appear. For example, interpretations of Y in naturally defined, non standard, theories behave as *sequential* composition in unary PCF, or *if then else* in binary PCF.

Summary. In Section 1, we present the syntax of the λY-calculus. In Section 2, we study general λY-theories and preorders, and we prove a *Transfer Theorem*, providing a correspondence between theories of the untyped λ-calculus and λY-theories. In Section 3, we focus on two special λY-theories related to the maximal theory on typed λ-calculus and to the observational equivalence on unary PCF, respectively. Final remarks, conjectures and open problems appear in Section 4.

1   The λY-Calculus

The λY-calculus is a simply typed lambda-calculus with two base constants $\bot, \top$, and fixpoint combinators Y_σ at each type. The following definitions are standard.

Definition 1 (Syntax).
Types:
$$\sigma ::= o \mid \sigma \to \sigma$$

Raw terms:
$$M ::= x \mid \bot \mid \top \mid MM \mid \lambda x : \sigma.M \mid Y_\sigma ,$$

where $\bot, \top$ *are constants and* $x \in Var$.

Definition 2 (Well-Typed Terms). *The* proof system *for typing terms derives judgements* $\Gamma \vdash M : \sigma$, *where* Γ *is a* type environment, *i.e. a finite set of assumptions* $\{x_1 : \sigma_1, \ldots, x_n : \sigma_n\}$. *The rules of the proof system are the following:*

$$\frac{}{\Gamma \vdash \bot : o} \qquad \frac{}{\Gamma \vdash \top : o} \qquad \frac{}{\Gamma \vdash Y_\sigma : (\sigma \to \sigma) \to \sigma} \qquad \frac{}{\Gamma, x : \sigma \vdash x : \sigma}$$

$$\frac{\Gamma, x : \sigma \vdash M : \tau}{\Gamma \vdash \lambda x{:}\sigma.M : \sigma \to \tau} \qquad \frac{\Gamma \vdash M : \sigma \to \tau \quad \Gamma \vdash N : \sigma}{\Gamma \vdash MN : \tau}$$

We denote by Λ_Y (Λ_Y^0) the set of well-typed (closed) λY-terms.
Term contexts are defined as usual. In the sequel, we will denote by $C[\ ] : \sigma \to \tau$
a closed context expecting a term of type σ, and producing a term of type τ.

Definition 3 (Reduction/Conversion). *The* reduction *relation between well-typed terms is the least relation generated by the following rules together with the rules for transitive and congruence closure (which we omit):*
(β) $\Gamma \vdash (\lambda x{:}\sigma.M)N \Rightarrow M[N/x]$: τ, where $\Gamma, x : \sigma \vdash M : \tau$, and $\Gamma \vdash N : \sigma$
(η) $\Gamma \vdash \lambda x{:}\sigma.Mx \Rightarrow M$: $\sigma \to \tau$, provided $x \notin M$
(Y) $\Gamma \vdash Y_\sigma M \Rightarrow M(Y_\sigma M)$: σ, where $\Gamma \vdash M$: $\sigma \to \sigma$.
Conversion, *denoted by* =, *is the symmetric and transitive closure of reduction.*

In the following, we will often omit the environment Γ and/or the type, when they are clear from the context.

2 λY-Theories

We focus on the theories of the λY-calculus, *i.e.* congruence relations on (closed) well-typed terms, which are closed under the conversion relation. We show that all λY-theories admit a contextual characterization. Moreover, we prove a *Transfer Theorem*, giving a correspondence between λ-theories and λY-theories.

2.1   Contextual Characterization of λY-Theories

It is well-known that all theories on the untyped λ-calculus are *contextual, i.e.* they admit a contextual characterization à la Morris, see [HR92]. An analogous result holds for λY-theories.

Definition 4 (Contextual λY-Theory). *A λY-theory $\sim$ is* contextual *if there exists a set of terms $\mathcal{Q} \subseteq \Lambda_Y^0$ closed under conversion such that, for all σ and all $M, N \in \Lambda_Y^0$ of type σ,*

$$M \sim N : \sigma \iff \forall C[\ ] : \sigma \to \tau.\ (C[M] \in \mathcal{Q} \Leftrightarrow C[N] \in \mathcal{Q})\ .$$

The terms in $\mathcal{Q}$ are called convergent *or* observable *terms.*

The following result holds:

Theorem 1.
(i) If $\emptyset \neq \mathcal{Q} \subsetneq \Lambda_Y^0$ and $\mathcal{Q}$ is closed under conversion, then the contextual theory $\sim_\mathcal{Q}$ is non-trivial.
(ii) Every λY-theory is contextual.

Proof.
(i) The proof is standard.
(ii) Let $\sim$ be a λY-theory, define

$$\mathcal{Q} = \{M \mid \exists A, B. \ (A \sim B : \sigma \ \wedge \ M \sim \lambda x : \sigma \to \sigma \to \sigma.xAB)\} \ ,$$

where x does not occur in A or B. Let us denote by $\sim_\mathcal{Q}$ the contextual theory induced by $\mathcal{Q}$. If $M \sim N$, it is immediate to show that also $M \sim_\mathcal{Q} N$. Vice versa, if $M \nsim N$, then also $M \nsim_\mathcal{Q} N$, since for $C[\,] \equiv \lambda x : \sigma \to \sigma \to \sigma.xM[\,]$ we have $C[M] \in \mathcal{Q}$, while $C[N] \notin \mathcal{Q}$. $\qquad\square$

It is useful to introduce also the notion of *contextual preorder* defined by:

Definition 5 (Contextual Preorder). *A preorder $\lesssim$ on closed λ-terms is contextual if there exists a set of terms $\mathcal{Q}$ closed under conversion such that, for all σ and all $M, N \in \Lambda_Y^0$ of type σ,*

$$M \lesssim N : \sigma \iff \forall C[\,] : \sigma \to \tau. \ (C[M] \in \mathcal{Q} \Rightarrow C[N] \in \mathcal{Q}) \ .$$

Any preorder $\lesssim$ induces a corresponding theory $\sim = \lesssim \cap (\lesssim)^{-1}$.

Interesting contextual preorders (theories) are those that admit a characterization as *logical relations*, *i.e.* the (pre)equivalence of terms at higher types is determined by the (pre)equivalence at the base type as follows:

Definition 6 (Logical Preorder/Theory). *Let $\lesssim_\mathcal{Q}$ ($\sim_\mathcal{Q}$) be a contextual preorder (theory) with observables in $\mathcal{Q}$. We say that*
(i) the preorder $\lesssim_\mathcal{Q}$ is a logical relation if, for all $M, N \in \Lambda_Y^0$,
$$M \lesssim_\mathcal{Q} N : o \iff \forall C[\,] : \sigma \to \tau. \ (C[M] \in \mathcal{Q} \ \Rightarrow \ C[N] \in \mathcal{Q})$$
$$M \lesssim_\mathcal{Q} N : \sigma \to \tau \iff \forall P \lesssim_\mathcal{Q} Q. \ MP \lesssim_\mathcal{Q} NQ : \tau.$$
(ii) the theory $\sim_\mathcal{Q}$ is a logical relation if, for all $M, N \in \Lambda_Y^0$,
$$M \sim_\mathcal{Q} N : o \iff \forall C[\,] : \sigma \to \tau. \ (C[M] \in \mathcal{Q} \ \Leftrightarrow \ C[N] \in \mathcal{Q})$$
$$M \sim_\mathcal{Q} N : \sigma \to \tau \iff \forall P \sim_\mathcal{Q} Q. \ MP \sim_\mathcal{Q} NQ : \tau.$$

A natural question to ask is when a preorder (theory) is a logical relation. A sufficient condition is the following:

Definition 7. *Let $\lesssim_\mathcal{Q}$ ($\sim_\mathcal{Q}$) be a contextual preorder (theory) with observables in $\mathcal{Q}$. Then*
(i) the preorder $\lesssim_\mathcal{Q}$ is well-behaved if, for all $M, N \in \Lambda_Y^0$ of type σ,

$$M \in \mathcal{Q} \ \wedge \ N \notin \mathcal{Q} \ \Longrightarrow \ \exists C[\,] : \sigma \to o. \ (C[M] \nlesssim_\mathcal{Q} C[N] : o) \ .$$

(ii) the theory $\sim_\mathcal{Q}$ is well-behaved if, for all $M, N \in \Lambda_Y^0$ of type σ,

$$M \in \mathcal{Q} \ \wedge \ N \notin \mathcal{Q} \ \Longrightarrow \ \exists C[\,] : \sigma \to o. \ (C[M] \nsim_\mathcal{Q} C[N] : o) \ .$$

Proposition 1.
(i) Any well-behaved contextual preorder on the λY-calculus is a logical relation.
(ii) Any well-behaved contextual theory on the λY-calculus is a logical relation.

Proof.

(i) Let $\lesssim_Q$ be a well-behaved contextual preorder, and let $\lesssim'_Q$ be the preorder defined by:

$M \lesssim'_Q N : o$ iff $\forall C[\ ] : \sigma \to \tau. \ (C[M] \in Q \Rightarrow C[N] \in Q)$

$M \lesssim'_Q N : \sigma \to \tau$ iff $\forall P \lesssim'_Q Q. \ MP \lesssim'_Q NQ : \tau.$

We prove that $M \lesssim_Q N \iff M \lesssim'_Q N$.

In order to prove that $M \lesssim'_Q N : \sigma \implies M \lesssim_Q N : \sigma$ (*), we first show that:

(a) $M \lesssim'_Q N : \sigma \implies \forall C[\ ] : \sigma \to \tau. \ (C[M] \lesssim'_Q C[N] : \tau).$

(b) $M \lesssim'_Q N : \sigma \implies (M \in Q \Rightarrow N \in Q).$

To prove item (a) one proceeds by extending the preorder $\lesssim'_Q$ to open terms by substitution with $\lesssim'_Q$-related closed terms as follows. Let M, N open terms with free variables $\boldsymbol{x}$ we define: $M \lesssim'_Q N$ iff $\forall \boldsymbol{P} \lesssim'_Q \boldsymbol{Q}. \ M[\boldsymbol{P}/\boldsymbol{x}] \lesssim'_Q N[\boldsymbol{Q}/\boldsymbol{x}].$ Then we prove the thesis for all possibly open terms, by induction on contexts.

The proof of item (b) requires the hypothesis that the preorder is well-behaved. Namely, assume by contradiction $M \lesssim'_Q N : \sigma$, $M \in Q$, but $N \notin Q$. Then, since the preorder is well-behaved, there exists $C[\ ] : \sigma \to o$ such that $C[M] \not\lesssim_Q C[N] : o$. But, by item (a), $C[M] \lesssim'_Q C[N] : o$. Contradiction.

Now we are in the position of proving (*). Assume $M \lesssim'_Q N : \sigma$. Then by (a), for any context $C[\ ] : \sigma \to \tau$, $C[M] \lesssim'_Q C[N] : \tau$, and, by item (b), $C[M] \in Q \Rightarrow C[N] \in Q$.

In order to prove the converse, *i.e.* $M \lesssim_Q N : \sigma \implies M \lesssim'_Q N : \sigma$, we proceed by induction on the type σ. For $\sigma = o$ the thesis is trivial, by definition of $\lesssim_Q$ and $\lesssim'_Q$. For $\sigma = \sigma_1 \to \sigma_2$, let $M \lesssim_Q N : \sigma_1 \to \sigma_2$, if $P \lesssim'_Q N : \sigma_1$, then, by (*), $P \lesssim_Q N : \sigma_1$. Therefore $MP \lesssim_Q NP \lesssim_Q NQ : \sigma_2$, hence by induction hypothesis $MP \lesssim'_Q NP : \sigma_2$, thus $M \lesssim'_Q N : \sigma_1 \to \sigma_2$.

(ii) Similarly to item (i) above.   □

2.2 λ-Theories and λY-Theories

The class of λY-theories is rich. Consider, for example, the *unsolvable* λY terms of order 0. As for the untyped λ-calculus, there are no constraints on the equational behavior of such "easy" terms, [Bar84]. At any type τ there are infinitely many non convertible such terms, *e.g.* $Y_{\sigma \to \tau} I M$ for any M, where I denotes the identity of type $(\sigma \to \tau) \to (\sigma \to \tau)$.

The richness of λY-theories is witnessed by the *Transfer Theorem* below, which provides a correspondence between λ-theories, *i.e.* theories on the untyped λ-calculus, and λY-theories. The gist of this translation is an encoding of untyped λ-terms into well-typed λY-terms, whereby untyped terms are transformed into well-typed ones, by suitably inserting terms of the form $Y_\sigma I$ of appropriate types σ, where I denotes the identity of type $\sigma \to \sigma$. A consequence of the Transfer Theorem is that there are $2^{\aleph_0}$ λY-theories.

Definition 8 (Encoding λ-terms into λY-terms). *Let* $in_\sigma : (\sigma \to \sigma) \to \sigma$ *and* $out_\sigma : \sigma \to (\sigma \to \sigma)$ *be the λY-terms defined by:*

$$in_\sigma = Y_{(\sigma \to \sigma) \to \sigma} I \quad and \quad out_\sigma = Y_{\sigma \to (\sigma \to \sigma)} I \ .$$

Then we define the encoding $\mathcal{E}_\sigma : \Lambda \to \Lambda_Y$, *which, given an untyped term, yields a λY-term of type σ, as follows:*

$$\mathcal{E}_\sigma(M) = \begin{cases} x : \sigma & \text{if } M \equiv x \\ in_\sigma(\lambda x : \sigma.\mathcal{E}_\sigma(M_1)) : \sigma & \text{if } M \equiv \lambda x.M_1 \\ out_\sigma(\mathcal{E}_\sigma(M_1))\mathcal{E}_\sigma(M_2) : \sigma & \text{if } M \equiv M_1 M_2 \end{cases}$$

Notice that the encoding $\mathcal{E}_\sigma$ is parametric w.r.t. σ.

Theorem 2 (Theory Correspondence). *Let $\sim_\lambda$ be a λ-theory, and σ any type. Then there exists a λY-theory $\sim_{\lambda Y}$ such that, for all $M, N \in \Lambda^0$,*

$$M \sim_\lambda N \iff \mathcal{E}_\sigma(M) \sim_{\lambda Y} \mathcal{E}_\sigma(N) .$$

Proof. (Sketch) Let $\sim_\lambda$ be a λ-theory, take $\sim_{\lambda Y}$ to be the λY-theory induced by the conversion and contextual closure of $\{(\mathcal{E}_\sigma(M), \mathcal{E}_\sigma(N)) \mid M \sim_\lambda N\}$. The argument lies in the fact that $Y_{(\sigma \to \sigma) \to \sigma}I$ and $Y_{\sigma \to (\sigma \to \sigma)}I$ have a completely inactive rôle computationally, see comment in the proof of Theorem 3 below. □

The type σ in the above theorem is generic. This result, albeit extremely simple, indicates that the computational complexity of untyped λ-calculus is immediately captured by the Y combinator. This result should be compared also to the results in [Lai03] for FPC.

As a corollary of Theorem 2 above, given the results in *e.g.* [Bar84], we have that:

Corollary 1. *There are $2^{\aleph_0}$ λY-theories.*

However, all the theories deriving from Theorem 2 are included in the theory which equates all non-normalizable constant-free terms. A different argument based on the "easy" nature of unsolvables of order 0 is necessary in order to show that:

Theorem 3. *There are $2^{\aleph_0}$ maximal λY-theories.*

Proof. $Y_{(o \to o) \to (o \to o)}I$ plays the rôle of $(\lambda x.xx)(\lambda x.xx)$ in untyped λ-calculus. Because of its computationally inactive rôle, it can be "anything it should not be", [BB79]. For example, $Y_{(o \to o) \to (o \to o)}I$ can encode the characteristic function of any subset of Church numerals. Any theory extending two such theories would therefore equate $\lambda xy.x$ and $\lambda xy.y$, and hence it would be inconsistent. □

2.3 Approximable Theories

The traditional understanding of Y is that of an *initial* or *least* fixed point. The pragmatics underpinning this concept is to explain away the Y combinator, by approximating its action with an *iterated* application of M on a *kick off* term N_0. Canonically, the kick-off term is $\perp$.

But this is only the "tip of the iceberg". We call this "iceberg" *approximable theories*. These are the theories of λY which support a form of generalized initiality.

Definition 9 (Approximable Theory). *A contextual* λY*-theory* $\sim_{\mathcal{Q}}$*, with* $\mathcal{Q}$ *the set of convergent terms, is* approximable *if for all* σ *there exists* $N_\sigma \in \Lambda_Y^0$ *such that*

$$\forall M : \sigma. \ \forall C[\ ] : \sigma \to \tau. \ \exists n. \ C[Y_\sigma M] \sim_{\mathcal{Q}} C[M^n(N_0)]$$

It goes without saying that approximable theories feature an Approximation Theorem. It should be interesting to study this in the context of *iteration* theories [BE93, PS00].

The standard argument, often used in connection with finite models of PCF, that the Y combinator can be dropped, is clearly due to the fact that the theories are uniformly approximable.

3   Canonical and Non-canonical Interpretations of Fixpoint Combinators

Canonical theories of the λY-calculus arise from the interpretation of Y_σ combinators as minimal fixpoint combinators, as in the standard Scott model. Different interpretations of the fixpoint combinators give rise to different (non-canonical) theories.

In this section, we focus on a canonical theory, $\sim_{YC}$, and on a non-canonical one, $\sim_{YN}$. The interest of these two theories lies in the fact that the first is connected to the maximal theory of the simply typed λ-calculus, and it provides a *fully-complete* interpretation of it, while the latter gives a *fully complete* interpretation of the observational equivalence on unary PCF.

3.1   A Canonical λY-Theory

The canonical λY-theory $\sim_{YC}$ on which we focus on can be defined as the contextual theory obtained by taking as convergent those terms that are convertible to a normal form without $\bot$. This is the paramount example of an approximable theory.

Definition 10 (Canonical λY-Theory).
(i) Let $\lesssim_{YC}$ *be the preorder defined by, for all* $M, N \in \Lambda_Y^0$,

$$M \lesssim_{YC} N : \sigma \text{ iff } \forall C[\ ] : \sigma \to \tau. \ (C[M] \in \mathcal{Q}_{YC} \Rightarrow C[N] \in \mathcal{Q}_{YC}) ,$$

where $\mathcal{Q}_{YC} = \{M \in \Lambda_Y^0 \mid \exists M' \text{ normal form. } (\bot \notin M' \wedge M = M')\}$.
(ii) Let $\sim_{YC}$ *be the theory induced by* $\lesssim_{YC}$*, i.e.* $\sim_{YC} = \lesssim_{YC} \cap (\lesssim_{YC})^{-1}$.

Canonical preorder and theory are logical relations, which admit a very simple characterization at the base type:

Proposition 2.
(i) $M \lesssim_{YC} N : o \iff (M \in \mathcal{Q}_{YC} \Rightarrow N \in \mathcal{Q}_{YC})$
    $M \lesssim_{YC} N : o \iff \forall P \lesssim_{YC} Q. \ (MP \lesssim_{YC} NQ)$.
(ii) $M \sim_{YC} N : o \iff (M \in \mathcal{Q}_{YC} \Leftrightarrow N \in \mathcal{Q}_{YC})$
    $M \sim_{YC} N : o \iff \forall P \sim_{YC} Q. \ (MP \sim_{YC} NQ)$.

Proof.
(i) First one can easily show that $M \lesssim_{YC} N : o \iff (M \in \mathcal{Q}_{YC} \Rightarrow N \in \mathcal{Q}_{YC})$. Then the thesis follows from the fact that $\lesssim_{YC}$ is well-behaved. Namely, let M, N be terms of type σ such that $M \in \mathcal{Q}_{YC}$ but $N \notin \mathcal{Q}_{YC}$. Then, if $\sigma = o$, the discriminating context is $(\lambda x : o.x)[\ ]$, otherwise, for $\sigma = \sigma_1 \to \ldots \to \sigma_n \to o$, $C[\ ]$ is $[\ ]\Pi_1 \ldots \Pi_n$, where $\Pi_1, \ldots, \Pi_n$ are suitable projections "extracting" the discriminating subterms.
(ii) Analogous to the above proof. $\hfill\square$

The following properties are satisfied by the preorder $\lesssim_{YC}$ and the corresponding theory $\sim_{YC}$:

Lemma 1.
(i) $\bot \lesssim_{YC} \top : o$.
(ii) At any type there are only finitely many equivalence classes w.r.t. $\sim_{YC}$.
(iii) For any type σ and any term $M : \sigma \to \sigma$,

$$Y_\sigma M \sim_{YC} M^{p(\sigma)} \bot_\sigma \ ,$$

where

- *$\bot_\sigma$, for $\sigma = \sigma_1 \to \ldots \to \sigma_n \to o$, denotes $\lambda x : \sigma.\bot$,*
- *$p(\sigma)$ is any number greater than the number of $\sim_{YC}$-equivalence classes at type σ, e.g. $p(o) = 2$ and $p(\sigma \to \tau) = p(\tau)^{p(\sigma)}$.*

Proof.
(i) Immediate form Proposition 2.
(ii) Clearly, at type o there are only two equivalence classes, $[\bot]_{\sim_{YC}}$ and $[\top]_{\sim_{YC}}$. Hence, by the characterization of $\sim_{YC}$ given in Proposition 4, there are only finitely many equivalence classes at any type $\sigma \to \tau$.
(iii) Since $\bot \lesssim_{YC} Y_\sigma M : \sigma$, then $M^{p(\sigma)}\bot_\sigma \lesssim_{YC} M^{p(\sigma)}(Y_\sigma M) = Y_\sigma M$, hence $M^{p(\sigma)}\bot_\sigma \lesssim_{YC} Y_\sigma M$. In order to prove the converse, *i.e.* $Y_\sigma M \lesssim_{YC} M^{p(\sigma)}\bot_\sigma$, one proceeds by showing that if there exists a context $C[\ ]$ such that $C[Y_\sigma M] \Rightarrow^* P$, for some P normal and $\bot$-free, and the number of reductions of $Y_\sigma M$ in the chain are less than n, then there exists P' such that both $C[M^n(Y_\sigma M)] \Rightarrow^* P'$, for some P' normal and such that $\bot \notin P'$, without any reductions of $Y_\sigma M$. Hence we have also that $C[M^n(\bot_\sigma)] \Rightarrow^* P'$ and we can replace $M^n(\bot_\sigma)$ for $Y_\sigma M$ in $C[\ ]$. Because of item (i) n can be chosen uniformly for all terms of type σ. $\hfill\square$

As a consequence of item (iii) of the above lemma, we have:

Theorem 4. *The λY-theory $\sim_{YC}$ is approximable.*

The term model determined by the theory $\sim_{YC}$ on the λY-calculus is *sequential*, in the sense that each equivalence class at type $\sigma \to \tau$ behaves either as a constant function in all arguments or it is strict in at least one argument, *i.e.* when this argument is $\bot$, the result of the application is $\bot$.

Theorem 5. *The term model of the λY-calculus induced by the theory $\sim_{YC}$ is sequential.*

Proof. First of all, notice that:
(a) $Y_\sigma I \sim_{YC} \perp_\sigma$, for all σ.
(b) Normal forms are strict in the head variable.
(c) Since the theory is approximable, every term $Y_\sigma M$ can be replaced by $M^k(Y_{(\sigma \to \sigma) \to \sigma} IM)$ for some k, getting a $\sim_{YN}$-equivalent term.
Given (a)–(c), the thesis follows easily by induction on terms.   □

Relating the Canonical Theory to the Simply Typed λ-Calculus. The λY-theory $\sim_{YC}$ is related to the maximal theory of the simply typed λ-calculus with constants $\perp, \top$ at the base type o, defined by:

$$M \sim_\lambda N : \sigma \text{ iff } \forall C[\,] : \sigma \to \tau. \ (C[M] \in \mathcal{Q}_\lambda \Leftrightarrow C[N] \in \mathcal{Q}_\lambda) \,,$$

where $\mathcal{Q}_\lambda = \{M \in \Lambda^0 \mid M \text{ of type } \sigma \wedge M \neq \perp_\sigma\}$.
  In the following, we show that the term model of the λY-calculus w.r.t. $\sim_{YC}$ is fully complete for the theory $\sim_\lambda$ of the simply typed λ-calculus.
  Cleary, any term of the simply typed λ-calculus can be viewed as a term of the λY-calculus via a trivial emdedding $\mathcal{I}$. Vice versa, one can define a mapping $\mathcal{L} : \Lambda_Y \to \Lambda$, by encoding Y_σ combinators as follows:

$$\mathcal{L}(Y_\sigma) = \lambda x : \sigma \to \sigma.x^{p(\sigma)}(\perp_\sigma) \,.$$

The above is justified by item (iii) of Lemma 1.
  Then, it is easy to check that:

Proposition 3.
(i) $M \sim_\lambda N \iff \mathcal{L}(M) \sim_{YC} \mathcal{L}(N)$.
(ii) $M \sim_{YC} N \iff \mathcal{I}(M) \sim_\lambda \mathcal{I}(N)$.

Hence, we have:

Theorem 6. *The term model of the λY-calculus w.r.t. $\sim_{YC}$ is fully complete w.r.t. the maximal theory $\sim_\lambda$ of the simply typed λ-calculus.*

3.2   A Non-canonical λY-Theory

In this section we focus on a non-canonical λY-theory $\sim_{NY}$, which exhibits a number of intriguing connections with many results in the literature on models of unary PCF. It can be defined as the contextual theory obtained by taking as convergent terms those that are convertible to a term in which $\perp$ does not appear. Its counterpart in the context of the untyped λ-calculus is the theory discussed in [HR92].

Definition 11 (Non-canonical λY-theory).
(i) Let $\lesssim_{YN}$ be the preorder defined by, for all $M, N \in \Lambda_Y^0$,

$$M \lesssim_{YN} N : \sigma \quad \text{iff} \quad \forall C[\;] : \sigma \to \tau.(C[M] \in \mathcal{Q}_{YN} \Rightarrow C[N] \in \mathcal{Q}_{YN}) \;,$$

where $\mathcal{Q}_{YN} = \{M \in \Lambda_Y^0 \mid \exists M'. (\bot \notin M' \land M = M')\}$.
(ii) Let $\sim_{YN}$ be the theory induced by $\lesssim_{YN}$, i.e. $\sim_{YN} = \lesssim_{YN} \cap (\lesssim_{YN})^{-1}$.

Non canonical preorder and theory are logical relations, admitting the following characterization:

Proposition 4.
(i) $M \lesssim_{YN} N : o \iff (M \in \mathcal{Q}_{YN} \Rightarrow N \in \mathcal{Q}_{YN})$
$\quad M \lesssim_{YN} N : o \iff \forall P \lesssim_{YN} Q. (MP \lesssim_{YN} NQ)$.
(ii) $M \sim_{YN} N : o \iff (M \in \mathcal{Q}_{YN} \Leftrightarrow N \in \mathcal{Q}_{YN})$
$\quad M \sim_{YN} N : o \iff \forall P \sim_{YN} Q. (MP \sim_{YN} NQ)$.

Proof.
(i) First one can easily show that $M \lesssim_{YN} N : o \iff (M \in \mathcal{Q}_{YN} \Rightarrow N \in \mathcal{Q}_{YN})$. Then the thesis follows from the fact that $\lesssim_{YN}$ is well-behaved. Namely, let M, N be terms of type σ such that $M \in \mathcal{Q}_{YN}$ but $N \notin \mathcal{Q}_{YN}$. Then, if $\sigma = o$, the discriminating context is $(\lambda x : o.x)[\;]$, otherwise, for $\sigma = \sigma_1 \to \ldots \to \sigma_n \to o$, $C[\;]$ is $[\;](Y_{\sigma_1} I) \ldots (Y_{\sigma_n} I)$.
(ii) Analogous to the above proof. $\qquad\qquad\square$

The following properties are satisfied by the preorder and the theory $\sim_{YN}$:

Lemma 2.
(i) $\bot \lesssim_{YN} \top : o$ and $Y_o I \sim_{YN} \top : o$.
(ii) At any type there are only finitely many equivalence classes w.r.t. $\sim_{YN}$.
(iii) For any type $\sigma \to \tau$ and any term $N : \sigma$,

$$(Y_{\sigma \to \tau} I)N \sim_{YN} \begin{cases} Y_\tau I : \tau & \text{if } Y_\sigma I \lesssim_{YN} N \\ \bot : \tau & \text{otherwise} \; . \end{cases}$$

(iv) For any type σ and any term $M : \sigma \to \sigma$,

$$Y_{(\sigma \to \sigma) \to \sigma} IM \lesssim_{YN} Y_\sigma M \; .$$

(v) For any type σ and any term $M : \sigma \to \sigma$,

$$Y_\sigma M \sim_{YI} M^{p(\sigma)} M_0 \; ,$$

where

- $M_0 \equiv Y_{(\sigma \to \sigma) \to \sigma} IM : \sigma$,
- $p(\sigma)$ *is any number greater than the number of $\sim_{YI}$-equivalence classes at type σ.*

Proof.

(i) Immediate, from Proposition 4.

(ii) Clearly, at type o there are only two equivalence classes, $[\bot]_{\sim_{YN}}$ and $[\top]_{\sim_{YN}}$. Hence, using the characterization of $\sim_{YN}$ given in Proposition 4, there are only finitely many equivalence classes at any type $\sigma \to \tau$.

(iii) First one shows that for all σ, τ, $\quad Y_{\sigma \to \tau} I(Y_\sigma I) \sim_{YN} Y_\tau I \quad (*)$. This is immediate, observing that, for any context $C[\ ]$, both terms are "inactive", *i.e.* either they reduce via the fixpoint reduction rule without involving the context, or if they appear in a redex involving the context, then they play a "passive" role as argument. Hence $\bot \in^* C[Y_{\sigma \to \tau} I(Y_\sigma I)]$ iff $\bot \in^* C[Y_\tau I]$, where by $\bot \in^* M$ we denote the fact that for all M' such that $M = M'$, $\bot \in M'$.

Now assume $Y_\sigma I \lesssim_{YN} M$, *i.e.* $\forall C[\ ].\ \bot \in^* C[M] \Rightarrow \bot \in^* C[Y_\sigma I]$.

We prove that $\forall C[\ ].\ \bot \in^* C[Y_{\sigma \to \tau} IM] \Leftrightarrow \bot \in^* C[Y_\tau I]$.

($\Rightarrow$) Assume $\bot \in^* C[Y_{\sigma \to \tau} IM]$. Then $\bot \in^* C'[Y_\sigma I]$, where $C'[\ ] = C[Y_{\sigma \to \tau} I[\ ]]$. Then, by $(*)$, $\bot \in^* C[Y_\tau I]$.

($\Leftarrow$) If $\bot \in^* C[Y_\tau I]$, then since $Y_\tau I$ and $Y_{\sigma \to \tau} IM$ are both inactive, then also $\bot \in^* C[Y_{\sigma \to \tau} IM]$.

Now assume $Y_\sigma I \not\lesssim_{YN} M$, *i.e.* there exists $C[\ ]$ such that $\bot \notin^* C[Y_\sigma I]$ but $\bot \in^* C[M]$. Then we show that $\bot \in^* C[Y_{\sigma \to \tau} IM]$. Namely, $Y_\sigma I$ is inactive, and hence there exists $C'[\ ]$ such that $C[\ ] = C'[\ ]$, $\bot \notin C'[\ ]$, but $\bot \in^* C'[M]$. Hence $\bot \in M$, and $\bot \in^* C'[Y_{\sigma \to \tau} IM]$.

(iv) The proof follows by an argument similar to the ones used above.

(v) By item (iv), for all k, $M^k \bot \lesssim_{YN} Y_\sigma M$. Hence $M^{p(\sigma)} \bot \lesssim_{YN} Y_\sigma M$. In order to prove the converse, *i.e.* $Y_\sigma M \lesssim_{YN} M^{p(\sigma)} \bot$, one proceeds by showing that if there exists a context $C[\ ]$ such that $C[Y_\sigma M] \Rightarrow^* P$, $\bot \notin P$, and the number of reductions of $Y_\sigma M$ in the chain are less than n, then there exists P' such that $C[M^n(Y_\sigma IM)] \Rightarrow^* P'$, $\bot \notin P'$, without any reduction of $Y_\sigma M$, and hence also $C[M^n(Y_{(\sigma \to \sigma) \to \sigma} IM)] \Rightarrow^* P'$. Hence we can replace $M^n(Y_{(\sigma \to \sigma) \to \sigma} IM)$ for $Y_\sigma M$ in $C[\ ]$. Because of item (i) n can be chosen uniformly for all terms of type σ. □

As a consequence of item (v) of the above lemma, we have that:

Theorem 7. *The λY-theory $\sim_{YN}$ is approximable.*

Moreover, we have:

Theorem 8. *The term model of the λY-calculus induced by the theory $\sim_{YN}$ is sequential.*

Proof. First of all, notice that:

(a) The terms $Y_\sigma I$ are strict in all arguments, namely:

$$Y_{\sigma_1 \to \ldots \to \sigma_n \to o} IM_1 \ldots M_n = \begin{cases} \top & \text{if } \forall i.\ Y_{\sigma_i} I \leq_{YN} M_i \\ \bot & \text{otherwise .} \end{cases}$$

(b) Normal forms are strict in the head variable.

(c) Finally, since the theory is approximable, every term $Y_\sigma M$ can be replaced by $M^k(Y_{(\sigma \to \sigma) \to \sigma} IM)$ for some k, getting a $\sim_{YN}$-equivalent term.
Given (a)–(c), the thesis follows easily by induction on terms.   □

Relating the Non-canonical Theory to Unary PCF. Interestingly, one can show that the λY-theory $\sim_{YN}$ captures exactly the behavioral equivalence of unary PCF, providing a fully complete model for it.

More precisely, we can define a mapping from unary PCF terms into λY-terms and vice versa, preserving the correspondence between theories.

We recall that unary PCF is a simply typed λ-calculus over a single base type o, containing two constants $\bot, \top$, and with a "sequential composition" operation $\wedge$ of type $o \to (o \to o)$. The conversion relation of unary PCF is generated by the $\beta\eta$-conversion together with the equations $\bot \wedge M = M \wedge \bot = M$ and $\top \wedge M = M \wedge \top = M$. We denote by Λ_{UP} (Λ^0_{UP}) the set of well-typed (closed) terms of unary PCF. The *behavioral equivalence* on unary PCF is the contextual theory induced by the set $\mathcal{Q}_{UP} = \{M \in \Lambda^0_{UP} \mid M \text{ of type } \tau \Rightarrow M = \bot_\tau\}$, i.e.:

$$M \sim_{UP} N : \sigma \text{ iff } \forall C[\,] : \sigma \to \tau. \ (C[M] = \bot_\tau \Leftrightarrow C[N] = \bot_\tau) .$$

Alternatively,
$$M \sim_{UP} N : o \iff (M = \bot \Leftrightarrow N = \bot)$$
$$M \sim_{UP} N : \sigma \to \tau \iff \forall P \sim_{UP} Q : \sigma. \ (MP \sim_{UP} NQ).$$
Correspondingly, one can define a preorder $\lesssim_{UP}$.

The observational equivalence $\sim_{UP}$ over unary PCF corresponds to the theory $\sim_{YN}$ on the λY-calculus, in the sense that one can define a bijective correspondence between equivalence classes of PCF terms w.r.t. $\sim_{UP}$ and equivalence classes of λY-terms w.r.t. $\sim_{YN}$.

Definition 12.
(i) Let $\mathcal{T} : \Lambda_{UP} \to \Lambda_Y$ be the (type-respecting) mapping inductively defined by:
$\mathcal{T}(M) = M$ *if* $M \in Var$ *or* $M \in \{\bot, \top\}$
$\mathcal{T}(\lambda x : \sigma.M) = \lambda x : \sigma.\mathcal{T}(M)$
$\mathcal{T}(\wedge) = Y_{o \to (o \to o)} I$
$\mathcal{T}(MN) = \mathcal{T}(M)\mathcal{T}(N).$
(ii) Let $\mathcal{S} : \Lambda_Y \to \Lambda_{UP}$ be the (type-respecting) mapping inductively defined by:
$\mathcal{S}(M) = M$ *if* $M \in Var$ *or* $M \in \{\bot, \top\}$
$\mathcal{S}(\lambda x : \sigma.M) = \lambda x : \sigma.\mathcal{S}(M)$

$$\mathcal{S}(Y_\sigma I) = \begin{cases} \top & \text{if } \sigma \equiv o \\ \lambda x : \sigma'.\lambda z : \tau.(x\mathcal{S}(Y_{\sigma_1} I) \dots \mathcal{S}(Y_{\sigma_n} I) \wedge \mathcal{S}(Y_\tau I)z) & \text{if } \sigma = \sigma' \to \tau \end{cases}$$

where $\sigma' = \sigma_1 \to \dots \to \sigma_n \to o$ *and* $\tau = \tau_1 \to \dots \to \tau_m \to o$.
$\mathcal{S}(Y_\sigma) = \lambda x : \sigma \to \sigma.x^{p(\sigma)}\mathcal{S}(Y_{(\sigma \to \sigma) \to \sigma} Ix)$
where $p(\sigma)$ is greater than the number of $\sim_{YI}$-equivalence classes at type σ,

$$\mathcal{S}(MN) = \begin{cases} \mathcal{S}(Y_\sigma I)\mathcal{S}(P_1) \dots \mathcal{S}(P_n) & \text{if } MN \equiv Y_\sigma IP_1 \dots P_n \\ \mathcal{S}(M)\mathcal{S}(N) & \text{otherwise} . \end{cases}$$

Then we have:

Proposition 5.
(i) For any PCF-term M of type σ, $M \sim_{UP} \mathcal{S}(\mathcal{T}(M)) : \sigma$.
(ii) For any λY-term M of type σ, $M \sim_{YN} \mathcal{T}(\mathcal{S}(M)) : \sigma$.
(iii) For all PCF-terms M, N of type σ,

$$M \sim_{UP} N : \sigma \iff \mathcal{T}(M) \sim_{YI} \mathcal{T}(N) : \sigma .$$

(iv) For all λY-terms M, N of type σ,

$$M \sim_{YN} N : \sigma \iff \mathcal{S}(M) \sim_{UP} \mathcal{S}(N) : \sigma .$$

Proof.
(i) First of all, we extend the equivalence $\sim_{UP}$ to open terms as follows. Let M, N be terms of type $\sigma \to \tau$ with free variables $x_1, \ldots, x_n$ of type $\sigma_1, \ldots, \sigma_n$, respectively. Then we define

$$M \sim_{UP} N \text{ iff } \forall \boldsymbol{P} \sim_{UP} \boldsymbol{Q} : \boldsymbol{\sigma}.\ M[\boldsymbol{P}/\boldsymbol{x}] \sim_{UP} N[\boldsymbol{P}/\boldsymbol{x}] : \tau .$$

Then the proof of item (i) proceeds by induction on the (possibly) open term M.
(ii) The proof is similar to the proof of the above item, using the extension of $\sim_{YN}$ to open terms.
(iii) The proof follows from the fact that $\forall M \in \Lambda_{UP}.\ (M = \bot : \tau \Leftrightarrow \bot \in^* \mathcal{T}(M))$. This latter fact is proved by induction on M.
(iv) The proof follows from the fact that $\forall M \in \Lambda_Y.\ \bot \in^* M \Leftrightarrow \bot \in^* \mathcal{S}(M) = \bot : \tau$. This latter fact is proved by induction on M. $\square$

A consequence of Proposition 5 is the following:

Theorem 9. *The term model of the λY-calculus w.r.t. $\sim_{YN}$ is fully complete for the observational equivalence on unary PCF.*

4   Final Remarks, Conjectures, Open Problems

Infinitary Böhm Trees. Coalgebraic versions of λ-calculus and infinitary Böhm trees are closely related to λY. More results are needed here, involving the λY analogue of the *lazy* λ-calculus [AO93] equating all unsolvable λY terms of order n, for each n.

Categorical Formalization. It would be interesting to cast the results in this paper in a categorical setting.

More Non-standard Approximable Theories. Clearly, given a model of finitary PCF we are quite freed in interpreting the Y combinator. For instance, one can start iterations from the *maximal* element, if it exists. Or simply fix the fixpoint combinator to yield, on any given combinator, an appropriate value, chosen at will. A case in point would be to take YI always to be I. For each such choice the "game" is to find the contextual characterization which uses the most insightful observables.

Binary PCF. A very intriguing example derives from the universal model of binary PCF, because it yields a novel perspective on the *if then else* combinator. The construction generalizes the steps we followed for the unary PCF, the role of the sequential composition being replaced by that of *if then else*. The main surprise lies in the natural contextual theory capturing this choice of the fixed point. The set of observable terms amounts to the set of terms which can be reduced to a term of the λIY-calculus, *i.e.* terms where all abstracted variables *do* occur. We assume at least three constants of type o: $\bot, \text{tt}, \text{ff}$.

Conjecture 1.

(i) $\bot_o \lesssim_{YI} \text{tt}, \text{ff} : o$ and $Y_o I \sim_{YI} \text{tt}$.

(ii) At any type there are only finitely many equivalence classes w.r.t. $\sim_{YI}$.

(iii) For any type $\sigma \to \tau$ and any term $N : \sigma$,

$$(Y_{\sigma \to \tau} I)N \sim_{YI} \begin{cases} Y_\tau I & \text{if } Y_\sigma I \lesssim_{YI} N \\ \lambda x_1 : \tau_1 \ldots x_n : \tau_n.\text{ff} & \text{if } \lambda x_1 : \sigma_1 \ldots x_n : \sigma_n.\text{ff} \lesssim_{YI} N \\ \lambda x_1 : \tau_1 \ldots x_n : \tau_n.\bot & \text{otherwise} . \end{cases}$$

(v) For any type σ there exists a natural number $p(\sigma)$ such that, for any term $M : \sigma \to \sigma$,

$$Y_\sigma M \sim_{YI} M^{p(\sigma)}(Y_{(\sigma \to \sigma) \to \sigma} IM) .$$

Models of λY-Theories. By Proposition 3, each model of the maximal theory $\sim_\lambda$ on the simply typed λ-calculus is a model of the theory $\sim_{YC}$ of the λY-calculus, and vice versa. As a consequence, the PER model of [AL01] provides a fully complete model of the λY-theory $\sim_{YC}$.

Similarly, by Proposition 5, each model of the theory $\sim_{UP}$ on unary PCF is a model of the λY-theory $\sim_{NC}$. Models of unary PCF have been studied *e.g.* in [Lai03, BLP03]. In particular, in [Lai03] it is shown that any *standard order-extensional model* of unary PCF is fully complete either for unary PCF or for unary PCF extended with *parallel or*. More precisely, any standard order-extensional model of unary PCF, which is *sequential*, is fully complete for unary PCF, while non-sequential models are fully complete for the extended language. *E.g.* the standard Scott model is fully complete for unary PCF with parallel or, while the bidomain model of [Lai03] is fully complete for unary PCF.

It is interesting to notice that, in the context of games, we can recover both kinds of models.

Namely, the game model of unary PCF built over the Sierpinski game, being sequential, is fully complete. On the other hand, one can build a non-sequential game model by changing the definition of tensor product, as in [HL13]. In the standard notion of tensor product of games, see *e.g.* [AJM00], on the game $A \otimes B$, at each step, the player who has the turn can move exactly in one of the two components, A or B. In [HL13], an alternative notion of tensor product, *i.e.* $A \vee B$, has been considered, where at each step the player who has the turn can either move in A, or in B, or in *both* components. A form of parallelism is then recovered in the game model. This construction is based on Conway's *selective sum*, while tensor of traditional game semantics resembles of Conway's *disjunctive* sum, [Con01].

In [HL13], it has been shown that the game $A \vee B$, together with a non-standard definition of strategy composition, gives rise to a tensor product in a category of *coalgebraic games*. This category turns out to be linear, *i.e.* symmetric monoidal closed together with a symmetric monoidal comonad. An analogous construction can be carried out *e.g.* in the category of [AJM00]-games. Working in this category, one could build a non-sequential model of unary PCF over the Sierpinski game $\mathcal{O}$. Parallel or $\vee : o \to (o \to o)$ can then be interpreted by the strategy on $!\mathcal{O} \vee !\mathcal{O} \longrightarrow \mathcal{O}$, where Opponent opens in the right-hand $\mathcal{O}$-component, and Player answers with a *pair* of moves asking *both* arguments; then if Opponent answers in at least one argument (*i.e.* at least one argument is different from $\bot$), Player provides the final answer in the right-hand component. In this way, the theory of standard Scott model is recovered in the context of games.

Open Questions. We conclude with a few open questions:

- Which λY-theories are approximable?
- Are bidomain models complete w.r.t. λY?
- Are game models *complete* w.r.t. λY?

Fixing an answer to such questions would help also to fix ideas on unfixing fixpoints.

References

[AJM00] Abramsky, S., Jagadeesan, R., Malacaria, P.: Full abstraction for PCF. Information and Computation 163, 404–470 (2000)

[AO93] Abramsky, S., Ong, C.-H.L.: Full Abstraction in the Lazy lambda-calculus. Information and Computation 105(2), 159–268 (1993)

[AL01] Abramsky, S., Lenisa, M.: Fully Complete Minimal PER Models for the Simply Typed λ-calculus. In: Fribourg, L. (ed.) CSL 2001. LNCS, vol. 2142, pp. 443–457. Springer, Heidelberg (2001)

[BB79] Baeten, J., Boerboom, B.: Omega can be anything it should not be. Proc. of Koninklijke Netherlandse Akademie van Wetenschappen, Serie A, Indag. Matematicae 41 (1979)

[Bar84] Barendregt, H.: The Lambda Calculus: Its Syntax and Semantics. North-Holland, Amsterdam (1984)

[BE93] Bloom, S., Esik, Z.: Iteration Theories. EATCS Monographs on Theoretical Computer Science. Springer (1993)

[BLP03] Bucciarelli, A., Leperchey, B., Padovani, V.: Relative Definability and Models of Unary PCF. In: Hofmann, M.O. (ed.) TLCA 2003. LNCS, vol. 2701, pp. 75–89. Springer, Heidelberg (2003)

[CS09] Carraro, A., Salibra, A.: Reflexive domains are not complete for the extensional lambda calculus. In: Proc. of LICS 2009, pp. 91–100. IEEE Computer Society Publications (2009)

[Con01]   Conway, J.H.: On Numbers and Games, 2nd edn. A K Peters Ltd. (2001);
          1st edn. Academic Press (1976)

[DFH99]   Di Gianantonio, P., Franco, G., Honsell, F.: Game semantics for un-
          typed $\lambda\beta\eta$-calculus. In: Girard, J.-Y. (ed.) TLCA 1999. LNCS, vol. 1581,
          pp. 114–128. Springer, Heidelberg (1999)

[HL13]   Honsell, F., Lenisa, M.: Categories of Coalgebraic Games with Selective
          Sum, http://sole.dimi.uniud.it/~marina.lenisa/
          Papers/Soft-copy-pdf/sel.pdf (submitted)

[HP09]   Honsell, F., Plotkin, G.: On the completeness of order-theoretic models of
          the λ-calculus. Information and Computation 207(5), 583–594 (2009)

[HR92]   Honsell, F., Ronchi Della Rocca, S.: An Approximation Theorem for Topo-
          logical Lambda Models and the Topological Incompleteness of Lambda Cal-
          culus. Journal of Computer and System Sciences 45(1) (1992)

[Lai03]   Laird, J.: A Fully Abstract Bidomain Model of Unary FPC. In: Hofmann,
          M.O. (ed.) TLCA 2003. LNCS, vol. 2701, pp. 211–225. Springer, Heidelberg
          (2003)

[PS00]   Plotkin, G., Simpson, A.: Complete Axioms for Categorical Fixed-point Op-
          erators. In: Proc. of LICS 2000, pp. 30–41. Computer Society Press of the
          IEEE (2000)

Continuous Domain Theory in Logical Form

Achim Jung

School of Computer Science, University of Birmingham
Birmingham, B15 2TT, United Kingdom

Dedicated to Samson Abramsky
on the occasion of his 60th birthday

Abstract. In 1987 Samson Abramsky presented *Domain Theory in Logical Form* in the *Logic in Computer Science* conference. His contribution to the conference proceedings was honoured with the *Test-of-Time* award 20 years later. In this note I trace a particular line of research that arose from this landmark paper, one that was triggered by my collaboration with Samson on the article *Domain Theory* which was published as a chapter in the *Handbook of Logic in Computer Science* in 1994.

1 Personal Recollections

Without Samson, I would not be where I am today. In fact, I might not have chosen a career in computer science at all. Coming from a mathematics background I was introduced to continuous lattices by Klaus Keimel, and with their combination of order theory, topology and categorical structure, they seemed very interesting objects to study. It was only during my period as a post-doc working for Samson at Imperial College in 1989/90 that I became aware of their use in semantics. Ever since I have been fascinated by the interplay between mathematics and computer science, and how one subject enriches the other.

The time at Imperial was hugely educating for me and it had this quality primarily because of the productive and purposeful research atmosphere that Samson created. I believe in those days we went to the Senior Common Room for tea three times a day: in the morning, after lunch, and again in the afternoon. Usually, a large section of the Theory and Formal Methods group came along and it was our chance to talk about research problems that were on our mind. Samson was there most times and was happy to engage with any question that we brought up, and typically he would be able to point us to a relevant paper or result. We were forever astounded by his overview of the subject and his ability to quote to us not only theorems but also proofs.

In June 1992 Samson and I lectured at a summer school in Prague, organised by Jiří Adámek and Věra Trnková. My course was on domain theory, his on λ-calculus. One evening we had dinner together in one of this city's many charming restaurants and it was on that occasion that he invited me to become a co-author on a survey article on domain theory that was meant to form a chapter of the

B. Coecke, L. Ong, and P. Panangaden (Eds.): Abramsky Festschrift, LNCS 7860, pp. 166–177, 2013.

Handbook of Logic in Computer Science, edited jointly by him, Dov Gabbay and Tom Maibaum. I accepted but admittedly had little idea of what was involved; although I thought I knew a fair bit about the subject, it turned out that my knowledge was patchy and disorganised. I spent most of the year 1993 on this project, drafting chapter after chapter, sending them to Samson and receiving feedback, advice, criticism and encouragement back from him.

The article appeared in 1994 as [AJ94] and it has been pleasing to us how popular it has has been with researchers ever since.

2   The Handbook Article

Up to that point, domains were mostly conceived of as certain *algebraic directed-complete partial orders*, the most influential reference being Gordon Plotkin's *Pisa Lecture Notes*, [Plo81], which circulated widely in copied and re-copied form among researchers. The definition of an algebraic domain was first given by Dana Scott in 1969, [Sco69], in a note that also remained unpublished for many years, [Sco93], but Dana had moved quickly to the more "mathematically respectable" setting of complete lattices. Furthermore, he discovered that the notion of *algebraicity* could be replaced with a more general one, that of *continuity*. His *continuous lattices*, [Sco72], turned out to have many connections with mathematics and a period of fruitful collaboration between him and a group of mathematicians soon followed, culminating in the writing of the *Compendium of Continuous Lattices*, [GHK+80].

When asked about the difference between "algebraic" and "continuous" structures in semantics, Dana's answer was that the latter were closed under an additional construction, that of forming retracts. In his view, this *ought to be* an advantage in setting up a denotational model. By 1993, this intuition was confirmed through the work on modelling probabilistic processes, [SD80, JP89], although continuous structures made their entrance through the real numbers, not through the need for general retractions.

Samson and I agreed that we would approach the subject of domains from the more general *continuous* angle. This suited me well because of my background in topology and functional analysis, and it seemed to offer a fresh perspective in the light of Gordon Plotkin's well-known treatment of the subject. It also forced us to engage with the "infinitary" dcpo structure of domains more deeply whereas many aspects of algebraic domains can be captured satisfactorily by the *poset* of compact elements.

The project went well, I think, and it was pleasing and sometimes surprising how easily and elegantly concepts known from the algebraic world could be generalised to the continuous setting. Early on I found that continuous domains could be generated from a more finitistic structure, which I dubbed *abstract bases*, but Samson pointed out that these had appeared in Mike Smyth's work before, [Smy77], under the name "R-structures". In any case, abstract bases were crucial for showing that it is possible to add operations (in the sense of universal algebra) in a free manner to continuous domains, and this established that the view of powerdomains as free constructions, first expounded in [HP79], worked here as well.

The final chapter of the article was devoted to Stone duality and Samson's *Domain Theory in Logical Form*, [Abr91b], which I will abbreviate to "DTLF" in this note. The general duality part was easy to do as we were able to import all our results from the *Compendium*, among them the beautiful characterisation of continuous domains given by Jimmie Lawson, [Law79], which says that they are precisely the Stone duals of completely distributive lattices.

Adapting Samson's work to the continuous setting, however, proved much more difficult. We didn't try for very long, as we ran out of time, so the version included in the Handbook chapter is for algebraic domains and the only "improvement" over [Abr91b] is that I renamed his "P predicate" to "C predicate." I was intrigued, however, and have spent a good part of my research time since then trying to extend Domain Theory in Logical Form to the continuous setting. Here I describe what I, together with collaborators, have found.

3 Domain Theory in Logical Form

At the heart of Samson's *Domain Theory in Logical Form* is the duality between *bounded distributive lattices* and *spectral spaces* discovered by Marshall Stone in the late 30s, [Sto37].[1] Three observations are key to its use in DTLF:

1. Most algebraic domains, when equipped with the Scott topology, are spectral spaces. In particular, this is true for Scott domains and the more encompassing class of bifinite domains.
2. Bounded distributive lattices are the Lindenbaum-Tarski algebras of negation-free propositional theories.
3. Constructions on algebraic domains have logical counterparts as free distributive lattice presentations.

To give an example of the last item, assume that the domain D is the dual of the lattice L. Then the dual of the Plotkin powerdomain of D can be presented as follows:

generators $\{\Box a \mid a \in L\} \cup \{\Diamond a \mid a \in L\}$
relations $\Box(\bigwedge_{i \in I} a_i) = \bigwedge_{i \in I} \Box a_i$ $\Box 0 = 0$
$\Diamond(\bigvee_{i \in I} a_i) = \bigvee_{i \in I} \Diamond a_i$ $\Diamond 1 = 1$
$\Box(a \vee b) \leq \Box a \vee \Diamond b$ $\Box a \wedge \Diamond b \leq \Diamond(a \wedge b)$

and the logical significance of the Plotkin powerdomain construction becomes immediately apparent.

---

[1] The paper remained far less well-known than his earlier [Sto36], possibly because mathematicians had no natural examples for spectral spaces and also, because the morphisms between them, now called *perfect maps*, seemed unnaturally restricted. Hilary Priestley's version of the duality, [Pri70], was much more successful.

The general setup of DTLF can be summarised in the following diagram:

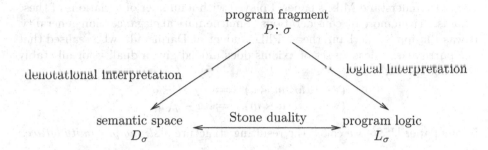

program fragment
$P\colon \sigma$

denotational interpretation   logical interpretation

semantic space   Stone duality   program logic
D_σ L_σ

In this note, "semantic space" stands for algebraic or continuous domain but it could in fact be any type of structure employed to give a denotational meaning to programs. The "program logic" is typically propositional, and often enhanced with modal operators. Judgements are of the form $P\colon \sigma \models \phi$, where σ is a type, P is a program (fragment) of type σ, and ϕ is a formula in L_σ. Alternatively, the formulas in L_σ can be used in "Hoare triples" $\{\phi\}\ P\ \{\psi\}$ with the usual interpretation. The fundamental idea of DTLF is that denotational and logical interpretation should determine each other *completely* via Stone duality.

As I said before, at the object level this works well for algebraic domains as long as one restricts to the bifinite ones. However, the topological maps that correspond to lattice homomorphisms are the *perfect* ones, i.e., those that are not only continuous but also reflect compact saturated sets.[2] Scott-continuous functions, the inevitable choice in domain theory, don't have that extra property.

Samson's solution to this puzzle was to distinguish between the "structural" category of domains, where the morphisms are embedding-projection pairs, and the Scott-continuous function space as a "type constructor." The fact is that the former *do* have nice counterparts under Stone duality, namely, lattice embeddings (injective lattice homomorphisms). One pay-off of this is that the somewhat technical *bilimit* construction of domains can dually be represented simply by a directed union of logical theories.

Extending this work to continuous domains requires a Stone duality that works for these spaces. At the time, the obvious choice was to move from lattices to *frames* which are known to be capable of representing all (sober) topological spaces, and to take advantage of the fact that continuous domains are indeed always sober in their Scott topology. The price to pay is that one is then working with an infinitary operation,[3] corresponding to the arbitrary union of open sets. There seemed to be no hope that this could be avoided as duals of ordinary (i.e., finite arity) algebraic structures always exhibit a zero-dimensional nature, and continuous spaces such as the real numbers just don't have that property. There was, however, Mike Smyth's then newly published work on a duality for stably compact spaces, [Smy92], which employed *proximity lattices* on the logical

---

[2] A set is *saturated* if it is upwards closed with respect to the specialisation order.

[3] More precisely, an operation of unbounded arity.

side. The difference to distributive lattices is that an idempotent relation $\prec$ is added to the algebraic structure, plus a number of axioms that link the two. In trying to understand Mike's paper, I played with a number of variations of these axioms, driven more by considerations of mathematical elegance than generality. It was Philipp Sünderhauf, then a PhD student at Darmstadt, who realised that one particularly pleasing set of axioms does indeed give a duality for all stably compact spaces:[4]

$$(\forall m \in M.\, m \prec a) \iff \bigvee M \prec a$$
$$(\forall m \in M.\, a \prec m) \iff a \prec \bigwedge M$$

In our paper [JS96] we called the resulting structure a *strong proximity lattice*.

Theorem 1. *The set* $\mathsf{spec}(L)$ *of round prime filters of a strong proximity lattice L forms a stably compact space when equipped with the usual spectral topology generated by the sets* $\Phi(a) = \{F \in \mathsf{spec}(L) \mid a \in L\}$. *Conversely, given a stably compact space X, the sets (U, K) with U open, K compact saturated, and $U \subseteq K$ form a strong proximity lattice, where are the lattice operations are the componentwise set-theoretic ones and the approximation relation is given by* $(U, K) \prec (U', K') \iff K \subseteq U'$.

Every distributive lattice carries a trivial proximity, namely the lattice order and so one sees that this theorem is a direct generalisation of that of Stone. However, many concepts from the classical case appear in a new light in the more general setting. Of particular importance to the story to be told here is the following: The unit map Φ of Stone duality maps a lattice element a to the compact-open set $\Phi(a) = \{F \in \mathsf{spec}(L) \mid a \in F\}$. In Samson's setting this means that every set $\Phi(a)$ is of the form $\uparrow M$ with M a finite set of compact elements. This is the link between domain logic and the concrete representation of algebraic domains as ideal completions of posets. On the other hand, the unit map of the generalised duality of Theorem 1 returns *pairs* (U, K) where U is an open set and K compact saturated. If we view the elements of a strong proximity lattice as (equivalence classes of) propositional formulas, then this says that every formula a has an *open* reading $[\![a]\!]^o$ and a *compact* reading $[\![a]\!]^c$ where furthermore $[\![a]\!]^o \subseteq [\![a]\!]^c$. The maps $[\![-]\!]^o$ and $[\![-]\!]^c$ are very well-behaved; they are lattice homomorphisms from L to the frame of opens of $\mathsf{spec}L$ and the lattice $\mathcal{K}L$ of compact saturated sets, respectively. In fact, this is what sets the duality of strong proximity lattices apart from the one in [Smy92].

As in Samson's case, identifying the correct morphisms is not easy, and it has to be admitted that the paper [JS96] turns a blind eye to this problem. What we did provide was to define a Stone dual for continuous functions between stably compact spaces in the form of certain relations, modelled on Scott's *approximable mappings*.

---

[4] The definition of *stably compact space* is a bit involved and the interested reader is referred to [Jun04] or [GHK⁺03] for a precise definition. As a first approximation, in a stably compact space the compact saturated sets behave exactly as compact sets do in Hausdorff spaces.

It was at this point that M. Andrew Moshier joined the effort, and he boldly changed our approximable mappings into relations between strong proximity lattices that resemble the internal approximation structure $\prec$. Furthermore, he realised that the axioms of strong proximity lattices look a lot more respectable when they are formulated as derivation rules for *sequents*, in the style of Gentzen's sequent calculus:

$$\frac{}{\bot \vdash}\,(L\bot) \qquad\qquad \frac{\Gamma \vdash \Delta}{\Gamma \vdash \Delta, \bot}\,(R\bot)$$

$$\frac{\Gamma \vdash \Delta}{\top, \Gamma \vdash \Delta}\,(L\top) \qquad\qquad \frac{}{\vdash \top}\,(R\top)$$

$$\frac{\phi, \psi, \Gamma \vdash \Delta}{\phi \wedge \psi, \Gamma \vdash \Delta}\,(L\wedge) \qquad \frac{\Gamma \vdash \Delta, \phi \quad \Gamma \vdash \Delta, \psi}{\Gamma \vdash \Delta, \phi \wedge \psi}\,(R\wedge)$$

$$\frac{\phi, \Gamma \vdash \Delta \quad \psi, \Gamma \vdash \Delta}{\phi \vee \psi, \Gamma \vdash \Delta}\,(L\vee) \qquad \frac{\Gamma \vdash \Delta, \phi, \psi}{\Gamma \vdash \Delta, \phi \vee \psi}\,(R\vee)$$

$$\frac{\Gamma \vdash \Delta}{\Gamma', \Gamma \vdash \Delta, \Delta'}\,(\text{weakening})$$

(The comma between formulas on the left is meant to be read as a conjunction, and on the right as a disjunction. Double lines indicate that a rule can be read in both directions.)

The "forcing relation" $\vdash$ in these rules can be read alternatively as representing internal approximation $\prec$ or as a morphism between strong proximity lattices. A version of the cut-rule acts as composition. Importantly, the existence of an inverse to the cut-rule must be postulated to take account of the fact that $\prec$ is interpolative. We get the duality theorem:

Theorem 2. *The category of continuous sequent calculi and compatible consequence relations is dually equivalent to the category of stably compact spaces and closed relations.*

Without spelling out precisely the definitions of all the terms appearing in this theorem, perhaps the general flavour of the result can be appreciated: The duality is between a *logical* category of theories on the one hand, and a topological category with relations (rather than continuous maps), on the other.

Much of Samson's Domain Theory in Logical Form can be extended to this setting, and this was worked out by Mathias Kegelmann, [Keg99]. In particular, domain constructions can be given a "logical form". Mathias does this for product, coproduct, powerdomains, and the relation space; the bilimit construction is studied in [JKM01], and the example which originally motivated the move to continuous domains, the probabilistic powerdomain construction, is dealt with in [MJ02].

So far so good, but (at least) three questions remained:

1. How to capture the domain theoretic function space construction?
2. What are the "natural" morphisms of strong proximity lattices?
3. What is the role of the compact saturated interpretation $[\![-]\!]^c$ of propositions?

3.1   The Continuous Function Space Construction

Despite spending quite some time on this question, from the point of view of DTLF I consider it an open problem. We may take some consolation from the fact that the analogous problem in the algebraic setting caused Samson considerable difficulties, too. This is due to two facts. First, the category of algebraic domains is not closed under the continuous function space construction. As Smyth showed in his celebrated 1983 paper, [Smy83a], one has to restrict (at least) to *bifinite domains* if one wants to be certain that the function space between two domains is again algebraic. For Samson this meant that he had to impose additional axioms on his lattices to make sure that the Stone dual was indeed bifinite. Luckily, though, these additional axioms don't get much in the way in DTLF since one can always rely on the fact that, semantically, all constructions of interest return bifinite domains when applied to such structures.

Second, and more annoying, is the fact that a complete logical characterisation of the function space requires one to adopt the axiom

$$(a \to \bigvee_{i \in I} a_i') = \bigvee_{i \in I} (a \to a_i')$$

for all those formulas a whose semantics is a *coprime* element in the lattice of open sets.[5] As a consequence, throughout DTLF one needs to keep track whether an element generated in one of the constructions has this property or not. Luckily, this can be done and the whole setup, though more complicated now, remains inductively definable.

Trying to transfer Samson's solution to the continuous world, there is good news and there is bad. The good news is that we know when we can expect a function space to be a continuous domain again; it happens when the inputs are *FS-domains*, [Jun90]. However, defining an analogue to Samson's coprimality predicate has so far exceeded this author's patience or ability. While it is clear that a coprime compact saturated set is one that is generated as an upper set by a single point, the condition for the corresponding open set would be that it is downward directed; in other words, it should be an open filter. Whether or not these two conditions can be tracked through all domain constructions, and especially the probabilistic powerdomain, I don't know.

Another problem makes its entrance at this point. Even if we knew how to formalise the Stone duals of FS-domains, we would not then be able to rely on the

---

[5] An element a of a lattice is called *coprime* if it is contained in a finite union $\bigcup M$ of opens precisely if it is already contained in one of the $m \in M$, which is exactly what the axiom expresses.

fact that all our constructions preserve these conditions, contrary to the situation in classical DTLF. The issue is the probabilistic powerdomain construction for which it is not known whether it is closed on the class of FS-domains (nor on any other cartesian closed category of continuous domains), [JT98].

It turns out that an answer to the second question can be found by studying the third one, so this is how I will proceed now.

3.2   The Role of Compactness — First Interpretation

The interpretation of open sets in computation was expounded most clearly by Mike Smyth in his landmark paper [Smy83b]: They are exactly those properties which are *finitely observable*. This was a very fruitful view and in some ways DTLF is the logical extension of this insight. Compactness, on the other hand, while one of the basic notions of topology, is not that easy to interpret though by the time Samson and I wrote the Handbook chapter there were already a number of hints that it was a useful descriptional device: Gordon Plotkin had shown that the elements of his powerdomain could be characterised as convex compact[6] subsets of the given domain, and similar descriptions are available for the other two classical powerdomain constructions as well. He also formulated the intriguing "2/3 SFP Theorem" which says that two of the three conditions that characterise bifinite domains can be expressed by a compactness condition, namely, that the domain in question be stably compact in its Scott topology. Related to this is the role of compactness in the identification of maximal cartesian closed categories of continuous domains, [Jun90].

Since then Martín Escardó has shown [Esc04] that compactness is related to quantifiability, in the following sense: For X some topological space one asks whether it is possible to establish whether a predicate, given as a continuous map from X to $\mathbf{2}$ (Sierpiński space), holds for all elements of X. The answer is that this can be answered "continuously", that is, as a continuous map $\forall_X$ from $\mathbf{2}^X$ to $\mathbf{2}$ if and only if X is compact. This is not just a theorem of topology but in fact a program can be written for $\forall_X$ provided X is effectively given and the predicate to be tested is likewise given as a subroutine.

Another approach to compactness is to extend Steve Vickers's idea of a *topological system*, [Vic89], where elements of a "space" are related to elements of a frame by a relation $\Vdash$. The statement $x \Vdash a$ can then be read as "x is an element of the open set a", or as "x satisfies the observable property a", or as "x is a model of the proposition a." In the given context one is tempted to replace "element" by "compact subset" and let $\prec$ play the role of $\Vdash$. The purely mathematical import of this has been explored by Olaf Klinke under the name *interaction algebra* in [Kli12].

All of the above, however, do not yet combine to produce a convincing story of why there is a compact interpretation of domain logic, nor what this compact interpretation represents, nor how it can be usefully employed in semantics. Indeed, what is missing is a serious case study of this approach in the same vein as

---

[6] With respect to the Lawson topology.

Samson's [Abr90, Abr91a]. An obvious candidate is to attempt a DTLF reconstruction of the striking result of Joseé Desharnais, Abbas Edalat and Prakash Panangaden, [DEP98, DEP02], about the completeness of a small and elegant Hennessy-Milner type logic for probabilistic processes.

3.3   The Role of Compactness — Second Interpretation

From the angle of Stone duality, some progress in extending and interpreting Theorem 1 has been made. The key insight is that on a stably compact space the complements of compact saturated sets form a topology, called the *co-compact topology*. In other words, stably compact spaces are *bitopological* structures and it is only because the two topologies in fact determine each other that this fact is not usually highlighted. Furthermore, a perfect map between such spaces is precisely one which is bicontinuous.

These observations motivate an alternative reading of the pairs (U, K) in Theorem 1: The second component should be $X \setminus K$ and the condition $U \subseteq K$ should be read as $U \cap (X \setminus K) = \emptyset$. So the pair (U, K) can be interpreted as a *partial predicate* in the sense of three-valued logic: it is (observably) true on U, (observably) false on $X \setminus K$ and undecided (or undecidable) everywhere else.

This turned out to be a fruitful starting point and in [JM06] Drew Moshier and I developed a duality theory for bitopological spaces analogous to the one for frames and topological spaces. More precisely, we define:

Definition 1. *A* d-frame *consists of two frames* L_+ *and* L_-, *together with two relations* con, tot $\subseteq L_+ \times L_-$. *Morphisms between d-frames are pairs* h_+, h_- *of frame homomorphisms which preserve* con *and* tot.

The following is now fairly straightforward:

Theorem 3. *There is a dual adjunction between the category of d-frames and the category of bitopological spaces.*

As is shown in [JM06], the duality of strong proximity lattices can be seen as a special case of Theorem 3, and the same is true for Stone's original dualities for Boolean algebras and distributive lattices, respectively. A particularly pleasing aspect is the fact that there is no doubt about the notion of a *d-frame homomorphism*; specialising them to the strong proximity lattice case one obtains what could rightly be called their natural morphisms. The fact that concretely they manifest themselves as pairs of relations perhaps explains why we were unable to identify them in [JS96].

With regards to DTLF, however, the bitopological or bilogical reading is yet to be fully justified. As we said before, the open interpretation of a proposition gives rise to the idea of observability or more precisely, semidecidability. An open that corresponds to the complement of the compact interpretation typically doesn't have that property and in some cases is very much *non-observable*. Why these complements form a topology, therefore, remains somewhat of a mystery — at least to this author.

4 Conclusions

It is probably fair to say that extending Samson's *Domain Theory in Logical Form* from algebraic domains to continuous ones has been a much harder task than we imagined in 1993, and it has forced us to examine very closely its various ingredients. While one could claim with some justification that the *multi-lingual sequent calculus* of Theorem 2 is the correct generalisation, some key questions remain open. What is more, making progress on these appears to depend on solving the long-standing problem of the behaviour of the probabilistic powerdomain construction on cartesian closed categories.

Let me end by expressing the hope that this summary of results and open problems will help to encourage researchers to study this fascinating and deep theory which Samson's work has opened up for us.

References

[Abr90]   Abramsky, S.: The lazy lambda calculus. In: Turner, D. (ed.) Research Topics in Functional Programming, pp. 65–117. Addison Wesley (1990)

[Abr91a]   Abramsky, S.: A domain equation for bisimulation. Information and Computation 92, 161–218 (1991)

[Abr91b]   Abramsky, S.: Domain theory in logical form. Annals of Pure and Applied Logic 51, 1–77 (1991)

[AJ94]   Abramsky, S., Jung, A.: Domain theory. In: Abramsky, S., Gabbay, D.M., Maibaum, T.S.E. (eds.) Semantic Structures. Handbook of Logic in Computer Science, vol. 3, pp. 1–168. Clarendon Press (1994)

[DEP98]   Desharnais, J., Edalat, A., Panangaden, P.: A logical characterization of bisimulation for labeled Markov processes. In: 13th IEEE Symposium on Logic in Computer Science, Indianapolis 1998, pp. 478–489 (1998)

[DEP02]   Desharnais, J., Edalat, A., Panangaden, P.: Bisimulation for labelled Markov processes. Information and Computation 179, 163–193 (2002)

[Esc04]   Escardó, M.H.: Synthetic topology of data types and classical spaces. In: Desharnais, J., Panangaden, P. (eds.) Domain-theoretic Methods in Probabilistic Processes. Electronic Notes in Theoretical Computer Science, vol. 87, pp. 21–156. Elsevier Science Publishers B.V. (2004)

[GHK+80]   Gierz, G., Hofmann, K.H., Keimel, K., Lawson, J.D., Mislove, M., Scott, D.S.: A Compendium of Continuous Lattices. Springer (1980)

[GHK+03]   Gierz, G., Hofmann, K.H., Keimel, K., Lawson, J.D., Mislove, M., Scott, D.S.: Continuous Lattices and Domains. Encyclopedia of Mathematics and its Applications, vol. 93. Cambridge University Press (2003)

[HP79]   Hennessy, M.C.B., Plotkin, G.D.: Full abstraction for a simple parallel programming language. In: Bečvář, J. (ed.) MFCS 1979. LNCS, vol. 74, pp. 108–120. Springer, Heidelberg (1979)

[JKM01]   Jung, A., Kegelmann, M., Moshier, M.A.: Stably compact spaces and closed relations. In: Brookes, S., Mislove, M. (eds.) 17th Conference on Mathematical Foundations of Programming Semantics. Electronic Notes in Theoretical Computer Science, vol. 45, 24 pages. Elsevier Science Publishers B.V. (2001)

[JM06]   Jung, A., Moshier, M.A.: On the bitopological nature of Stone duality. Technical Report CSR-06-13, School of Computer Science, The University of Birmingham, 110 pages (2006)

[JP89]   Jones, C., Plotkin, G.: A probabilistic powerdomain of evaluations. In: Proceedings of the 4th Annual Symposium on Logic in Computer Science, pp. 186–195. IEEE Computer Society Press (1989)

[JS96]   Jung, A., Sünderhauf, P.: On the duality of compact vs. open. In: Andima, S., Flagg, R.C., Itzkowitz, G., Misra, P., Kong, Y., Kopperman, R. (eds.) Papers on General Topology and Applications: Eleventh Summer Conference at the University of Southern Maine. Annals of the New York Academy of Sciences, vol. 806, pp. 214–230 (1996)

[JT98]   Jung, A., Tix, R.: The troublesome probabilistic powerdomain. In: Edalat, A., Jung, A., Keimel, K., Kwiatkowska, M. (eds.) Proceedings of the Third Workshop on Computation and Approximation. Electronic Notes in Theoretical Computer Science, vol. 13, 23 pages. Elsevier Science Publishers B.V. (1998)

[Jun90]   Jung, A.: The classification of continuous domains. In: Proceedings of the Fifth Annual IEEE Symposium on Logic in Computer Science, pp. 35–40. IEEE Computer Society Press (1990)

[Jun04]   Jung, A.: Stably compact spaces and the probabilistic powerspace construction. In: Desharnais, J., Panangaden, P. (eds.) Domain-Theoretic Methods in Probabilistic Processes. Electronic Notes in Theoretical Computer Science, vol. 87, pp. 5–20. Elsevier Science Publishers B.V. (2004)

[Keg99]   Kegelmann, M.: Continuous domains in logical form. PhD thesis, School of Computer Science, The University of Birmingham (1999)

[Kli12]   Klinke, O.: A bitopological point-free approach to compactifications. PhD thesis, School of Computer Science, The University of Birmingham (2012)

[Law79]   Lawson, J.D.: The duality of continuous posets. Houston Journal of Mathematics 5, 357–394 (1979)

[MJ02]   Moshier, M.A., Jung, A.: A logic for probabilities in semantics. In: Bradfield, J.C. (ed.) CSL 2002. LNCS, vol. 2471, pp. 216–231. Springer, Heidelberg (2002)

[Plo81]   Plotkin, G.D.: Post-graduate lecture notes in advanced domain theory (incorporating the "Pisa Notes"). Dept. of Computer Science, Univ. of Edinburgh (1981)

[Pri70]   Priestley, H.A.: Representation of distributive lattices by means of ordered Stone spaces. Bulletin of the London Mathematical Society 2, 186–190 (1970)

[Sco69]   Scott, D.S.: A type theoretic alternative to ISWIM, CUCH, OWHY. University of Oxford (1969) (manuscript)

[Sco72]   Scott, D.S.: Continuous lattices. In: Lawvere, E. (ed.) Toposes, Algebraic Geometry and Logic. Lecture Notes in Mathematics, vol. 274, pp. 97–136. Springer (1972)

[Sco93]   Scott, D.S.: A type-theoretical alternative to ISWIM, CUCH, OWHY. Theoretical Computer Science 121, 411–440 (1993); Reprint of a manuscript written in 1969

[SD80]   Saheb-Djahromi, N.: CPO's of measures for nondeterminism. Theoretical Computer Science 12, 19–37 (1980)

[Smy77]   Smyth, M.B.: Effectively given domains. Theoretical Computer Science 5, 257–274 (1977)

[Smy83a]   Smyth, M.B.: The largest cartesian closed category of domains. Theoretical
            Computer Science 27, 109–119 (1983)
[Smy83b]   Smyth, M.B.: Power domains and predicate transformers: a topological
            view. In: Díaz, J. (ed.) ICALP 1983. LNCS, vol. 154, pp. 662–675. Springer,
            Heidelberg (1983)
[Smy92]   Smyth, M.B.: Stable compactification I. Journal of the London Mathemat-
            ical Society 45, 321–340 (1992)
[Sto36]   Stone, M.H.: The theory of representations for Boolean algebras. Trans.
            American Math. Soc. 40, 37–111 (1936)
[Sto37]   Stone, M.H.: Topological representation of distributive lattices. Časopsis
            pro Pěstování Matematiky a Fysiky 67, 1–25 (1937)
[Vic89]   Vickers, S.J.: Topology Via Logic. Cambridge Tracts in Theoretical Com-
            puter Science, vol. 5. Cambridge University Press (1989)

Presheaf Models of Quantum Computation: An Outline

Dedicated to Samson Abramsky on His 60th Birthday

Octavio Malherbe[1], Philip Scott[2], and Peter Selinger[3]

[1] IMERL-FING, Universidad de la República, Montevideo, Uruguay
malherbe@fing.edu.uy
[2] Dept. of Mathematics and Statistics, University of Ottawa, Canada
phil@site.uottawa.ca
[3] Dept. of Mathematics and Statistics, Dalhousie University, Halifax, Canada
selinger@mathstat.dal.ca

Abstract. This paper outlines the construction of categorical models of higher-order quantum computation. We construct a concrete denotational semantics of Selinger and Valiron's quantum lambda calculus, which was previously an open problem. We do this by considering presheaves over appropriate base categories arising from first-order quantum computation. The main technical ingredients are Day's convolution theory and Kelly and Freyd's notion of continuity of functors. We first give an abstract description of the properties required of the base categories for the model construction to work. We then exhibit a specific example of base categories satisfying these properties.

1 Introduction

Quantum computing is based on the laws of quantum physics. While no actual general-purpose quantum computer has yet been built, research in the last two decades indicates that quantum computers would be vastly more powerful than classical computers. For instance, Shor [34] proved in 1994 that the integer factoring problem can be solved in polynomial time on a quantum computer, while no efficient classical algorithm is known.

Logic has played a key role in the development of classical computation theory, starting with the foundations of the subject in the 1930's by Church, Gödel, Turing, and Kleene. For example, the pure untyped lambda calculus, one of the first models of computation invented by Church, can be simultaneously regarded as a prototypical functional programming language as well as a formalism for denoting proofs. This is the so-called *proofs-as-programs* paradigm. Indeed, since the 1960's, various systems of typed and untyped lambda calculi have been developed, which on the one hand yield proofs in various systems of constructive and/or higher-order logic, while on the other hand denoting functional programs. Modern programming languages such as ML, Haskell, and Coq are often viewed in this light.

Recent research by Selinger, Valiron, and others [30,33] in developing "quantum lambda calculi" has shown that Girard's *linear logic* [12] is a logical system

B. Coecke, L. Ong, and P. Panangaden (Eds.): Abramsky Festschrift, LNCS 7860, pp. 178–194, 2013.
© Springer-Verlag Berlin Heidelberg 2013

that corresponds closely to the demands of quantum computation. Linear logic, a resource sensitive logic, turns out to formalize one of the central principles of quantum physics, the so-called *no-cloning property*, which asserts that a given unknown quantum state cannot be replicated. This property is reflected on the logical side by the requirement that a given logical assumption (or "resource") can only be used once. However, until now, the correspondence between linear logic and quantum computation has mainly been explored at the syntactic level.

In this paper we construct mathematical (semantic) models of higher-order quantum computation. The basic idea is to start from existing low level models, such as the category of superoperators, and to use a Yoneda type presheaf construction to adapt and extend these models to a higher order quantum setting. To implement the latter, we use Day's theory of monoidal structure in presheaf categories, as well as the Freyd-Kelly theory of continuous functors, to lift the required quantum structure [6,11]. Finally, to handle the probabilistic aspects of quantum computation, we employ Moggi's computational monads [24].

Our model construction depends on a sequence of categories and functors $\mathcal{B} \to \mathcal{C} \to \mathcal{D}$, as well as a collection Γ of cones in $\mathcal{D}$. We use this data to obtain a pair of adjunctions

$$[\mathcal{B}^{op}, \mathbf{Set}] \underset{\Phi^*}{\overset{L}{\rightleftarrows}} [\mathcal{C}^{op}, \mathbf{Set}] \underset{G}{\overset{F}{\rightleftarrows}} [\mathcal{D}^{op}, \mathbf{Set}]_\Gamma$$

in which the left-hand adjunction gives an appropriate categorical model of the underlying linear logic, and the right-hand adjunction gives a Moggi monad for probabilistic effects. We then give sufficient conditions on $\mathcal{B} \to \mathcal{C} \to \mathcal{D}$ and Γ so that the resulting structure is a model of the quantum lambda calculus. One can describe various classes of concrete models by appropriate choices of diagrams $\mathcal{B} \to \mathcal{C} \to \mathcal{D}$ and cones Γ.

In this paper, we focus on the categorical aspects of the model construction. Thus, we will not review the syntax of the quantum lambda calculus itself (see [30] and [33] for a quick review). Instead, we take as our starting point Selinger and Valiron's definition of a *categorical model of the quantum lambda calculus* [33]. It was proven in [33] that the quantum lambda calculus forms an internal language for the class of such models. This is similar to the well-known interplay between typed lambda calculus and cartesian closed categories [19]. What was left open in [33] was the construction of a concrete such model (other than the one given by the syntax itself). This is the question whose answer we sketch here. Further details can be found in the first author's PhD thesis [22].

2 Categories of Completely Positive Maps and Superoperators

We first recall various categories of finite dimensional Hilbert spaces that we use in our study. Let V be a finite dimensional Hilbert space, i.e., a finite dimensional complex inner product space. We write $\mathcal{L}(V)$ for the space of linear functions $\rho : V \longrightarrow V$.

Definition 2.1. Let V, W be finite dimensional Hilbert spaces. A linear function $F : \mathcal{L}(V) \longrightarrow \mathcal{L}(W)$ is said to be *completely positive* if it can be written in the form $F(\rho) = \sum_{i=1}^{m} F_i \rho F_i^\dagger$, where $F_i : V \longrightarrow W$ is a linear function and $F_i^\dagger$ denotes the linear adjoint of F_i for $i = 1, \ldots, m$.

Definition 2.2. The category $\mathbf{CPM}_s$ of *simple completely positive maps* has finite dimensional Hilbert spaces as objects, and the morphisms $F : V \longrightarrow W$ are completely positive maps $F : \mathcal{L}(V) \longrightarrow \mathcal{L}(W)$.

Definition 2.3. The category $\mathbf{CPM}$ of *completely positive maps* is defined as $\mathbf{CPM} = \mathbf{CPM}_s^\oplus$, the biproduct completion of $\mathbf{CPM}_s$. Specifically, the objects of $\mathbf{CPM}$ are finite sequences $(V_1, \ldots, V_n)$ of finite-dimensional Hilbert spaces, and a morphism $F : (V_1, \ldots, V_n) \longrightarrow (W_1, \ldots, W_m)$ is a matrix (F_{ij}), where each $F_{ij} : V_j \longrightarrow W_i$ is a completely positive map. Composition is defined by matrix multiplication.

Remark 2.4. The category $\mathbf{CPM}$ is the same (up to equivalence) as the category $\mathbf{W}$ of [28] and the category $\mathbf{CPM}(\mathbf{FdHilb})^\oplus$ of [29].

Note that for any two finite dimensional Hilbert spaces V and W, there is a canonical isomorphism $\varphi_{V,W} : \mathcal{L}(V \otimes W) \longrightarrow \mathcal{L}(V) \otimes \mathcal{L}(W)$.

Remark 2.5. The categories $\mathbf{CPM}_s$ and $\mathbf{CPM}$ are symmetric monoidal. For $\mathbf{CPM}_s$, the tensor product is given on objects by the tensor product of Hilbert spaces $V \bar{\otimes} W = V \otimes W$, and on morphisms by the following induced map
$$f \bar{\otimes} g := \mathcal{L}(V \otimes W) \xrightarrow{\varphi_{V,W}} \mathcal{L}(V) \otimes \mathcal{L}(W) \xrightarrow{f \otimes g} \mathcal{L}(X) \otimes \mathcal{L}(Y) \xrightarrow{\varphi_{X,Y}^{-1}} \mathcal{L}(X \otimes Y).$$
The remaining structure (units, associativity, symmetry maps) is inherited from Hilbert spaces. Similarly, for the symmetric monoidal structure on $\mathbf{CPM}$, define $(V_i)_{i \in I} \otimes (W_j)_{j \in J} = (V_i \otimes W_j)_{i \in I, j \in J}$. This extends to morphisms in an obvious way. For details, see [28].

Definition 2.6. We say that a linear map $F : \mathcal{L}(V) \to \mathcal{L}(W)$ is *trace preserving* when it satisfies $\mathrm{tr}_W(F(\rho)) = \mathrm{tr}_V(\rho)$ for all positive $\rho \in \mathcal{L}(V)$. F is called *trace non-increasing* when it satisfies $\mathrm{tr}_W(F(\rho)) \leqslant \mathrm{tr}_V(\rho)$ for all positive $\rho \in \mathcal{L}(V)$.

Definition 2.7. A linear map $F : \mathcal{L}(V) \to \mathcal{L}(W)$ is called a *trace preserving superoperator* if it is completely positive and trace preserving, and it is a *trace non-increasing superoperator* if it is completely positive and trace non-increasing.

Definition 2.8. A completely positive map $F : (V_1, \ldots, V_n) \longrightarrow (W_1, \ldots, W_m)$ in the category $\mathbf{CPM}$ is called a *trace preserving superoperator* if for all j and all positive $\rho \in \mathcal{L}(V_j)$, $\sum_i \mathrm{tr}(F_{ij}(\rho)) = \mathrm{tr}(\rho)$, and a *trace non-increasing superoperator* if for all j and all positive $\rho \in \mathcal{L}(V_j)$, $\sum_i \mathrm{tr}(F_{ij}(\rho)) \leqslant \mathrm{tr}(\rho)$.

We now define four symmetric monoidal categories of superoperators. All of them are symmetric monoidal subcategories of $\mathbf{CPM}$.

Definition 2.9.

- $\mathbf{Q}_s$ and $\mathbf{Q}'_s$ have the same objects as $\mathbf{CPM}_s$, and $\mathbf{Q}$ and $\mathbf{Q}'$ have the same objects as $\mathbf{CPM}$.
- The morphisms of $\mathbf{Q}_s$ and $\mathbf{Q}$ are trace non-increasing superoperators, and the morphisms of $\mathbf{Q}'_s$ and $\mathbf{Q}'$ are trace preserving superoperators.

Remark 2.10. The categories $\mathbf{Q}_s$, $\mathbf{Q}$, $\mathbf{Q}'_s$, and $\mathbf{Q}'$ are all symmetric monoidal. The symmetric monoidal structure is inherited from $\mathbf{CPM}_s$ and $\mathbf{CPM}$, respectively, and it is easy to check that all the structural maps are trace preserving.

Lemma 2.11. $\mathbf{Q}$ *and* $\mathbf{Q}'$ *have finite coproducts.*

Proof. The injection/copairing maps are as in $\mathbf{CPM}$ and are trace preserving.

3   Presheaf Models of a Quantum Lambda Calculus

Selinger defined an elementary quantum flow chart language in [28], and gave a denotational model in terms of superoperators. This axiomatic framework captures the behaviour and interconnection between the basic concepts of quantum computation (for example, the manipulation of quantum bits under the basic operations of measurement and unitary transformation) in a lower-level language. In particular, the semantics of this framework is very well understood: each program corresponds to a concrete superoperator.

Higher-order functions are functions that can input or output other functions. In order to deal with such functions, Selinger and Valiron introduced, in a series of papers [31,32,33], a typed lambda calculus for quantum computation and investigated several aspects of its semantics. In this context, they combined two well-established areas: the intuitionistic fragment of Girard's linear logic [12] and Moggi's computational monads [24].

The type system of Selinger and Valiron's quantum lambda calculus is based on intuitionistic linear logic. As is usual in linear logic, the logical rules of weakening and contraction are introduced in a controlled way by an operator "!" called "of course" or "exponential". This operator creates a bridge between two different kinds of computation. More precisely, a value of a general type A can only be used once, whereas a value of type $!A$ can be copied and used multiple times. As mentioned in the introduction, the impossibility of copying quantum information is one of the fundamental differences between quantum information and classical information, and is known as the *no-cloning property*. From a logical perspective, this is related to the failure of the contraction rule; thus it seems natural to use linear logic in discussing quantum computation. It is also well known that categorically, the operator "!" satisfies the properties of a *comonad* (see [23]).

Since the quantum lambda calculus has higher-order functions, as well as probabilistic operations (namely measurements), it must be equipped with an evaluation strategy in order to be consistent. Selinger and Valiron addressed this by choosing the *call-by-value* evaluation strategy. This introduces a distinction between *values* and *computations*. At the semantic level, Moggi [24] proposed using the notion of monad as an appropriate tool for interpreting computational behaviour. In our case, this will be a strong monad.

So let us now describe Selinger and Valiron's notion of a *categorical model of the quantum lambda calculus* [33].

3.1   Categorical Models of the Quantum Lambda Calculus

In what follows, let $(\mathcal{C}, \otimes, I, \alpha, \rho, \lambda, \sigma)$ be a symmetric monoidal category [21].

Definition 3.1. A *symmetric monoidal comonad* $(!, \delta, \varepsilon, m_{A,B}, m_I)$ is a comonad $(!, \delta, \varepsilon)$ where the functor ! is a monoidal functor $(!, m_{A,B}, m_I)$, i.e., with natural transformations $m_{A,B} : \, !A \otimes !B \longrightarrow !(A \otimes B)$ and $m_I : I \longrightarrow !I$, satisfying appropriate coherence axioms [16] such that δ and ε are symmetric monoidal natural transformations.

Definition 3.2. A *linear exponential comonad* is a symmetric monoidal comonad $(!, \delta, \varepsilon, m_{A,B}, m_I)$ such that for every $A \in \mathcal{C}$, there exists a commutative comonoid (A, d_A, e_A) satisfying some technical requirements (see [4,33]).

Definition 3.3. Let (T, η, μ) be a strong monad on $\mathcal{C}$. We say that $\mathcal{C}$ has *Kleisli exponentials* if there exists a functor $[-,-]_k : \mathcal{C}^{op} \times \mathcal{C} \to \mathcal{C}$ and a natural isomorphism: $\mathcal{C}(A \otimes B, TC) \cong \mathcal{C}(A, [B, C]_k)$.

Definition 3.4 (Selinger and Valiron [33]). A *linear category for duplication* consists of a symmetric monoidal category $(\mathcal{C}, \otimes, I)$ with the following structure:

- an idempotent, strongly monoidal, linear exponential comonad $(!, \delta, \varepsilon, d, e)$,
- a strong monad (T, μ, η, t) such that $\mathcal{C}$ has Kleisli exponentials.

Further, if the unit I is a terminal object we shall speak of an *affine linear category for duplication*.

Remark 3.5. Perhaps surprisingly, following the work of Benton, a linear category for duplication can be obtained from a structure that is much easier to describe, namely, a pair of monoidal adjunctions [2,23,17]

$$(\mathcal{B}, \times, 1) \underset{(I,i)}{\overset{(L,l)}{\rightleftarrows}} (\mathcal{C}, \otimes, I) \underset{(G,n)}{\overset{(F,m)}{\rightleftarrows}} (\mathcal{D}, \otimes, I),$$

where the category $\mathcal{B}$ has finite products and $\mathcal{C}$ and $\mathcal{D}$ are symmetric monoidal closed. The monoidal adjoint pair of functors on the left represents a linear-non-linear model of linear logic in the sense of Benton [2], in which we obtain a monoidal comonad by setting $! = L \circ I$. The monoidal adjoint pair on the right gives rise to a strong monad $T = G \circ F$ in the sense of Kock [16,17], which is also a computational monad in the sense of Moggi [24].

We now state the main definition of a model of the quantum lambda calculus.

Definition 3.6 (Models of the Quantum Lambda Calculus [33]). An *abstract model of the quantum lambda calculus* is an affine linear category for duplication $\mathcal{C}$ with finite coproducts, preserved by the comonad !. A *concrete model of the quantum lambda calculus* is an abstract model such that there exists a full and faithful embedding $\mathbf{Q} \hookrightarrow \mathcal{C}_T$, preserving tensor $\otimes$ and coproduct $\oplus$ up to isomorphism, from the category $\mathbf{Q}$ of norm non-increasing superoperators (see Definition 2.9) into the Kleisli category of the monad T.

Remark 3.7. To make the connection to quantum lambda calculus: the category $\mathcal{C}$, the Kleisli category $\mathcal{C}_T$, and the co-Kleisli category $\mathcal{C}_!$ all have the same objects, which correspond to *types* of the quantum lambda calculus. The morphisms $f : A \longrightarrow B$ of $\mathcal{C}$ correspond to *values* of type B (parameterized by variables of type A). A morphism $f : A \longrightarrow B$ in $\mathcal{C}_T$, which is really a morphism $f : A \longrightarrow TB$ in $\mathcal{C}$, corresponds to a *computation* of type B (roughly, a probability distribution of values). Finally, a morphism $f : A \longrightarrow B$ in $\mathcal{C}_!$, which is really a morphism $f : !A \longrightarrow B$ in $\mathcal{C}$, corresponds to a *classical value* of type B, i.e., one that only depends on classical variables. The idempotence of "!" implies that morphisms $!A \longrightarrow B$ are in one-to-one correspondence with morphisms $!A \longrightarrow !B$, i.e., classical values are duplicable. For details, see [33].

3.2 Outline of the Procedure for Obtaining a Concrete Model

We construct the model in two stages. The first (more elaborate) stage constructs *abstract* models by applying certain general presheaf constructions to diagrams of functors $\mathcal{B} \to \mathcal{C} \to \mathcal{D}$. In Section 3.8 we find the precise conditions required on diagrams $\mathcal{B} \to \mathcal{C} \to \mathcal{D}$ to obtain a valid abstract model. In the second stage, we construct a *concrete* model of the quantum lambda calculus by identifying particular base categories so that the remaining conditions of Definition 3.6 are satisfied. This is the content of Sections 3.9 and 3.10.

We divide the two stages of construction into eight main steps.

1. The basic idea of the construction is to lift a sequence of functors $\mathcal{B} \xrightarrow{\Phi} \mathcal{C} \xrightarrow{\Psi} \mathcal{D}$ into a pair of adjunctions between presheaf categories

$$[\mathcal{B}^{op}, \mathbf{Set}] \underset{\Phi^*}{\overset{L}{\rightleftarrows}} [\mathcal{C}^{op}, \mathbf{Set}] \underset{\Psi^*}{\overset{F_1}{\rightleftarrows}} [\mathcal{D}^{op}, \mathbf{Set}].$$

   Here, Φ^* and Ψ^* are the precomposition functors, and L and F_1 are their left Kan extensions. By Remark 3.5, such a pair of adjunctions potentially yields a linear category for duplication, and thus, with additional conditions, an abstract model of quantum computation. Our goal is to identify the particular conditions on $\mathcal{B}$, $\mathcal{C}$, $\mathcal{D}$, Φ, and Ψ that make this construction work.

2. By Day's convolution construction (see [6]), the requirement that $[\mathcal{C}^{op}, \mathbf{Set}]$ and $[\mathcal{D}^{op}, \mathbf{Set}]$ are monoidal closed can be achieved by requiring $\mathcal{C}$ and $\mathcal{D}$ to be monoidal. The requirement that the adjunctions $L \dashv \Phi^*$ and $F_1 \dashv \Psi^*$ are monoidal is directly related to the fact that the functors Ψ and Φ are

strong monoidal. More precisely, this implies that the left Kan extension is a strong monoidal functor [10] which in turn determines the enrichment of the adjunction [14]. We also note that the category $\mathcal{B}$ must be cartesian.

3. One important complication with the model, as discussed so far, is the following. The Yoneda embedding $Y : \mathcal{D} \to [\mathcal{D}^{op}, \mathbf{Set}]$ is full and faithful, and by Day's result, also preserves the monoidal structure $\otimes$. Therefore, if one takes $\mathcal{D} = \mathbf{Q}$, all but one of the conditions of a concrete model (from Definition 3.6) are automatically satisfied. Unfortunately, however, the Yoneda embedding does not preserve coproducts, and therefore the remaining condition of Definition 3.6 fails. For this reason, we modify the construction and use a modified presheaf category with a coproduct preserving Yoneda embedding. More specifically, we choose a set Γ of cones in $\mathcal{D}$, and use the theory of continuous functors by Lambek [18] and Freyd and Kelly [11] to construct a reflective subcategory $[\mathbf{Q}^{op}, \mathbf{Set}]_\Gamma$ of $[\mathbf{Q}^{op}, \mathbf{Set}]$, such that the modified Yoneda embedding $\mathbf{Q} \longrightarrow [\mathbf{Q}^{op}, \mathbf{Set}]_\Gamma$ is coproduct preserving. Our adjunctions, and the associated Yoneda embeddings, now look like this:

$$
\begin{array}{ccccc}
[\mathcal{B}^{op}, \mathbf{Set}] & \xrightarrow{\ L \dashv \Phi^* \ } & [\mathcal{C}^{op}, \mathbf{Set}] & \xrightarrow{\ F \dashv G \ } & [\mathcal{D}^{op}, \mathbf{Set}]_\Gamma \\
Y \uparrow & & Y \uparrow & & Y_\Gamma \uparrow \\
\mathcal{B} & \xrightarrow{\ \Phi \ } & \mathcal{C} & \xrightarrow{\ \Psi \ } & \mathcal{D}
\end{array}
$$

The second pair of adjoint functors $F \dashv G$ is itself generated by the composition of two adjunctions:

$$
[\mathcal{C}^{op}, \mathbf{Set}] \underset{\Psi^*}{\overset{F_1}{\rightleftarrows}} [\mathcal{D}^{op}, \mathbf{Set}] \underset{G_2}{\overset{F_2}{\rightleftarrows}} [\mathcal{D}^{op}, \mathbf{Set}]_\Gamma
$$

Here $\mathcal{D} = \mathbf{Q}$ and the pair of functors $F_2 \dashv G_2$ arises from the reflection of $[\mathbf{Q}^{op}, \mathbf{Set}]_\Gamma$ in $[\mathbf{Q}^{op}, \mathbf{Set}]$. The structure of the modified Yoneda embedding $\mathbf{Q} \longrightarrow [\mathbf{Q}^{op}, \mathbf{Set}]_\Gamma$ depends crucially on general properties of functor categories [18,11]. Full details are given in [22].

To ensure that the reflection functor remains strongly monoidal, we will use Day's reflection theorem [7], which yields necessary conditions for the reflection to be strong monoidal, by inducing a monoidal structure from the category $[\mathbf{Q}^{op}, \mathbf{Set}]$ into its subcategory $[\mathbf{Q}^{op}, \mathbf{Set}]_\Gamma$. In particular, this induces a constraint on the choice of Γ: all the cones considered in Γ must be preserved by the opposite functor of the tensor functor in $\mathcal{D}$.

4. Notice that the above adjunctions are examples of what in topos theory are called *essential geometric* morphisms, in which both functors are left adjoint to some other two functors: $L \dashv \Phi^* \dashv \Phi_*$. Therefore, this shows that the comonad "!" obtained will preserve finite coproducts.

5. The condition for the comonad "!" to be idempotent turns out to depend on the fact that the functor Φ is full and faithful; see Section 3.4.

6. In addition to requiring that "!" preserves coproducts, we also need "!" to preserve the tensor, i.e., to be strongly monoidal, as required in Definition 3.6. This property is unusual for models of intuitionistic linear logic and

restricts the possible choices for the category $\mathcal{C}$. In brief, since the left Kan extension along Φ is a strong monoidal functor, we find a concrete condition on the category $\mathcal{C}$ that is necessary to ensure that the property holds when we lift the functor Φ to the category of presheaves; see Section 3.5.

7. Our next task is to translate these categorical properties to the Kleisli category. We use the comparison Kleisli functor to pass from the framework we have already established to the Kleisli monoidal adjoint pair of functors. Also, at the same time, we shall find it convenient to characterize the functor $H : \mathcal{D} \to [\mathcal{C}^{op}, \mathbf{Set}]_T$ as a strong monoidal functor. The above steps yield an abstract model of quantum computation, parameterized by $\mathcal{B} \to \mathcal{C} \to \mathcal{D}$ and Γ.

8. Finally, in Section 3.9, we will identify specific categories $\mathcal{B}$, $\mathcal{C}$, and $\mathcal{D}$ that yield a concrete model of quantum computation. We let $\mathcal{D} = \mathbf{Q}$, the category of superoperators. We let $\mathcal{B}$ be the category of finite sets. Alas, identifying a suitable candidate for $\mathcal{C}$ is difficult. For example, two requirements are that $\mathcal{C}$ must be affine monoidal and must satisfy the condition of equation (1) in Section 3.5 below. We construct such a $\mathcal{C} = \mathbf{Q}''$ related to the category $\mathbf{Q}$ of superoperators with the help of some universal constructions.

The above base category $\mathbf{Q}''$ plays a central role in our construction. While the higher-order structural properties of the quantum lambda calculus hold at the pure functor category level, the interpretation of concrete quantum operations takes place mostly at this base level.

Let us now discuss some details of the construction.

3.3   Categorical Models of Linear Logic on Presheaf Categories

The first categorical models of linear logic were given by Seely [27]. The survey by Melliès is an excellent introduction [23]. Current state-of-the-art definitions are Bierman's definition of a linear category [4], simplified yet more by Benton's definition of a linear-non-linear category ([2], cf. Remark 3.5 above). Benton proved the equivalence of these two notions [2,23].

Definition 3.8 (Benton [2]). A *linear-non-linear category* consists of:

(1) a symmetric monoidal closed category $(\mathcal{C}, \otimes, I, \multimap)$,
(2) a category $(\mathcal{B}, \times, 1)$ with finite products,
(3) a symmetric monoidal adjunction: $(\mathcal{B}, \times, 1) \underset{(G,n)}{\overset{(F,m)}{\rightleftarrows}} (\mathcal{C}, \otimes, I)$.

Remark 3.9. We use Kelly's characterization of monoidal adjunctions to simplify condition (3) in Definition 3.8 above to:

(3') an adjunction: $(\mathcal{B}, \times, 1) \underset{G}{\overset{F}{\rightleftarrows}} (\mathcal{C}, \otimes, I)$, and there exist isomorphisms

$m_{A,B} : FA \otimes FB \to F(A \times B)$ and $m_I : I \to F(1)$, making $(F, m_{A,B}, m_I) : (\mathcal{B}, \times, 1) \to (\mathcal{C}, \otimes, I)$ a strong symmetric monoidal functor.

Details of this characterization can found in [23].

We can characterize Benton's linear-non-linear models (Definition 3.8) on presheaf categories using Day's monoidal structure [6]. This is an application of monoidal enrichment of the Kan extension, see [10]. We use the following:

Proposition 3.10 (Day-Street[10]). *Suppose we have a strong monoidal functor $\Phi : (\mathcal{A}, \otimes, 1) \to (\mathcal{B}, \otimes, I)$ between two monoidal categories, i.e., we have natural isomorphisms $\Phi(a) \otimes \Phi(b) \cong \Phi(a \otimes b)$ and $I \cong \Phi(I)$. Consider the left Kan extension along Φ in the functor category $[\mathcal{B}^{op}, \mathbf{Set}]$, where the copower is the cartesian product on sets: $Lan_\Phi(F) = \int^a \mathcal{B}(-, \Phi(a)) \times F(a)$. Then Lan_Φ is strong monoidal.*

Remark 3.11. If $\mathcal{A}$ is cartesian then the Day tensor (convolution) $[\mathcal{A}^{op}, \mathbf{Set}] \times [\mathcal{A}^{op}, \mathbf{Set}] \xrightarrow{\otimes_D} [\mathcal{A}^{op}, \mathbf{Set}]$ is a pointwise product of functors. Also if the unit of a monoidal category $\mathcal{C}$ is a terminal object then the unit of $\otimes_D$ is also terminal.

3.4   Idempotent Comonad in the Functor Category

A comonad $(!, \epsilon, \delta)$ is said to be *idempotent* if $\delta : \, ! \Rightarrow \, !!$ is an isomorphism.

Let $(!, \epsilon, \delta)$ be the comonad generated by an adjunction $(\mathfrak{B}, \times, 1) \underset{G}{\overset{F}{\rightleftarrows}} (\mathfrak{C}, \otimes, I)$.

Then $\delta = F\eta_G$ with $\eta : I \to GF$. Thus if η is an isomorphism then δ is also an isomorphism. In the context of our model construction, how can we guarantee that η is an isomorphism? Consider the unit $\eta_B : B \Rightarrow \Phi^*(Lan_\Phi(B))$ of the adjunction generated by the Kan extension:

$$[\mathcal{B}^{op}, \mathbf{Set}] \underset{\Phi^*}{\overset{Lan_\Phi}{\rightleftarrows}} [\mathcal{C}^{op}, \mathbf{Set}].$$

Proposition 3.12 ([5]). *If Φ is full and faithful then $\eta_B : B \Rightarrow \Phi^*(Lan_\Phi(B))$ is an isomorphism.*

3.5   A Strong Comonad

In this section we study conditions that force the idempotent comonad above to be a strong monoidal functor. This property is part of the model we are building and is one of the main differences with previous models of intuitionistic linear logic [23].

To achieve this, consider a fully faithful functor $\Phi : \mathcal{B} \longrightarrow \mathcal{C}$, as in Section 3.2. Let $[\mathcal{C}^{op}, \mathbf{Set}] \xrightarrow{\Phi^*} [\mathcal{B}^{op}, \mathbf{Set}]$ be the precomposition functor, i.e., the right adjoint of the left Kan extension.

Lemma 3.13 ([9]). *If there exists a natural isomorphism*

$$\mathcal{C}(\Phi(b), c) \times \mathcal{C}(\Phi(b), c') \cong \mathcal{C}(\Phi(b), c \otimes c'), \tag{1}$$

where $b \in \mathcal{B}$ and $c, c' \in \mathcal{C}$ and Φ is a fully faithful functor satisfying $\Phi(1) = I$, then Φ^* is a strong monoidal functor.

In Section 3.9 we shall build a category satisfying this specific requirement among others. More precisely, from our viewpoint, this will depend on the construction of a certain category that we will name $\mathbf{Q}''$, which is a modification of the category $\mathbf{Q}$ of superoperators. Also, we will consider a fully faithful strong monoidal functor $\Phi : (\mathbf{FinSet}, \times, 1) \to (\mathcal{C}, \otimes_{\mathcal{C}}, I)$ that generates the first adjunction in Section 3.2, where $\mathcal{C} = \mathbf{Q}''$.

3.6   The Functor $H : \mathcal{D} \to \hat{\mathcal{C}}_T$

Let $\mathcal{C}$ and $\mathcal{D}$ be categories. Consider an adjoint pair of functors $[\mathcal{C}^{op}, \mathbf{Set}] \underset{G}{\overset{F}{\rightleftarrows}} [\mathcal{D}^{op}, \mathbf{Set}]_\Gamma$, as mentioned in Section 3.2, item 3. Let $T = G \circ F$ and $\hat{\mathcal{C}} = [\mathcal{C}^{op}, \mathbf{Set}]$. In this section we consider the construction of a coproduct preserving and tensor preserving functor $H : \mathcal{D} \to \hat{\mathcal{C}}_T$ with properties similar to the Yoneda embedding, for a general category $\mathcal{D}$.

Let $F_1 \dashv G_1$ and $F_2 \dashv G_2$ be two monoidal adjoint pairs with associated natural transformations (F_1, m_1), (G_1, n_1) and (F_2, m_2), (G_2, n_2). We shall use the following notation: $F = F_2 \circ F_1$, $G = G_1 \circ G_2$, and $T = G \circ F$. We now describe a typical situation of this kind generated by a functor $\Psi : \mathcal{C} \to \mathcal{D}$.

Let us consider $F_1 = Lan_\Psi$ and $G_1 = \Psi^*$. With some co-completeness condition assumed, we can express $F_1(A) = \int^c \mathcal{D}(-, \Psi(c)) \otimes A(c)$ and $G_1 = \Psi^*$.

On the other hand we consider $F_2 = Lan_Y(Y_\Gamma) : [\mathcal{D}^{op}, \mathbf{Set}] \to [\mathcal{D}^{op}, \mathbf{Set}]_\Gamma$, where $Y_\Gamma : \mathcal{D} \to [\mathcal{D}^{op}, \mathbf{Set}]_\Gamma$ is the co-restriction of the Yoneda functor given by $Y_\Gamma(d) = \mathcal{D}(-, d)$. Thus we have $F_2(D) = \int^d D(d) \otimes Y_\Gamma(d)$. Assuming that $[\mathcal{D}^{op}, \mathbf{Set}]_\Gamma$ is co-complete and contains the representable presheaves, then the right adjoint G_2 is isomorphic to the inclusion functor.

Definition of H.

We want to study the following situation:

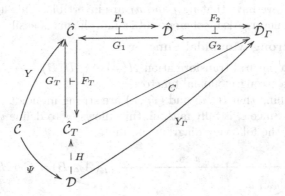

The goal is to determine a full and faithful functor, denoted H in this diagram, that preserves tensor and coproduct.

First, notice that the perimeter of this diagram commutes on objects: $F_1(\mathcal{C}(-, c)) = \int^{c'} \mathcal{D}(-, \Psi(c')) \otimes \mathcal{C}(c', c) = \mathcal{D}(-, \Psi(c))$ and when we evaluate again, using F_2, we obtain:

$$F_2(\mathcal{D}(-, \Psi(c))) = \int^{d'} \mathcal{D}(d', \Psi(c)) \otimes Y_\Gamma(d') = Y_\Gamma(\Psi(c)) = \mathcal{D}(-, \Psi(c)).$$

Summing up, we have that $F(\mathcal{C}(-, c)) = \mathcal{D}(-, \Psi(c))$ up to isomorphism.

Suppose now that Ψ is essentially onto on objects and we have that:

$$\mathcal{D}(-, d) \cong \mathcal{D}(-, \Psi(c))$$

for some $c \in \mathcal{C}$, i.e., we can make a choice, for every $d \in |\mathcal{D}|$, of some $c \in |\mathcal{C}|$ such that $\Psi(c) \cong d$. Let us call this choice a "choice of preimages". We can therefore define a map $H : |\mathcal{D}| \to |\hat{\mathcal{C}}_T|$ by $H(d) = \mathcal{C}(-, c)$ on objects.

Then we can define a functor $H : \mathcal{D} \to \hat{\mathcal{C}}_T$ in the following way: let $d \xrightarrow{f} d'$ be an arrow in the category $\mathcal{D}$. We apply Y_Γ obtaining $\mathcal{D}(-, d) \xrightarrow{Y_\Gamma(f)} \mathcal{D}(-, d')$. This arrow is equal to $\mathcal{D}(-, \Psi(c)) \xrightarrow{Y_\Gamma(f)} \mathcal{D}(-, \Psi(c'))$ for some $c, c' \in \mathcal{C}$, and for the reason stipulated above is equal to $F(\mathcal{C}(-, c)) \xrightarrow{Y_\Gamma(f)} F(\mathcal{C}(-, c'))$. Now we use the fact that the comparison functor $C : \hat{\mathcal{C}}_T \to \hat{\mathcal{D}}_\Gamma$, i.e.,

$$C : \hat{\mathcal{C}}_T(\mathcal{C}(-, c), \mathcal{C}(-, c')) \to \hat{\mathcal{D}}_\Gamma(F(\mathcal{C}(-, c)), F(\mathcal{C}(-, c'))),$$

is full and faithful. Thus there is a unique $\gamma : \mathcal{C}(-, c) \to \mathcal{C}(-, c')$ such that $C(\gamma) = Y_\Gamma(f)$. Then we can define $H(f) = \gamma$ on morphisms and (as mentioned above) $H(d) = \mathcal{C}(-, c)$ on objects, where c is given by our choice of preimages.

$C : \hat{\mathcal{C}}_T \to \hat{\mathcal{D}}_\Gamma$ is a Strong Monoidal Functor

We define $C(A) \otimes_{\hat{\mathcal{D}}_\Gamma} C(B) \xrightarrow{u_{AB}} C(A \otimes_{\mathcal{C}_T} B)$ as $F(A) \otimes_{\hat{\mathcal{D}}_\Gamma} F(B) \xrightarrow{m_{AB}} F(A \otimes B)$. It is easy to check naturality. Also define $I \xrightarrow{u_I = m_I} C(I) = F(I)$. Since m_{AB} and m_I are invertible in $\hat{\mathcal{D}}_\Gamma$, we have that u_{AB} and u_I are invertible. This implies that (C, m) is a strong functor. Also, coherence of isomorphisms is easily checked.

$H : \mathcal{D} \to \hat{\mathcal{C}}_T$ is a Strong Monoidal Functor

We want to define a natural transformation $H(A) \otimes_{\hat{\mathcal{C}}_T} H(B) \xrightarrow{\psi_{A,B}} H(A \otimes_{\mathcal{D}} B)$ that makes H into a strong monoidal functor.

We begin by recalling that (C, u) and (Y_Γ, y) are strong monoidal, i.e., u and y are isomorphisms. Since C is fully faithful, this allows us to define $\psi_{A,B}$ as the unique map making the following diagram commute:

$$Y_\Gamma(A) \otimes Y_\Gamma(B) \xrightarrow{\quad\quad\quad y_{A,B} \quad\quad\quad} Y_\Gamma(A \otimes B) = C \circ H(A \otimes B).$$

with $u_{HA, HB}$ and $C(\psi_{A,B})$ going to $C(H(A) \otimes H(B))$.

We define ψ_I similarly. Furthermore, ψ is a natural transformation and satisfies all the axioms of a monoidal structure. We refer to [22] for the details.

H Preserves Coproducts

Here we focus on the specific problem of the preservation of finite coproducts by the functor H defined in Section 3.6. First, note that the category $[\mathcal{C}^{op}, \mathbf{Set}]$ has finite coproducts, computed pointwise. Moreover, the Kleisli category $\mathcal{C}_T$ inherits the coproduct structure from $\hat{\mathcal{C}}$ since:

Proposition 3.14. *If $\mathcal{C}$ has finite coproducts, then so does $\mathcal{C}_T$.*

Therefore, $[\mathcal{C}^{op}, \mathbf{Set}]_T$ has finite coproducts. Recall that the comparison functor $C : [\mathcal{C}^{op}, \mathbf{Set}]_T \to [\mathcal{D}^{op}, \mathbf{Set}]_\Gamma$ is fully faithful. Also, by a well known property of representable functors (see [18]), we have that $H : \mathcal{D} \to [\mathcal{C}^{op}, \mathbf{Set}]_T$ preserves coproducts iff $[\mathcal{C}^{op}, \mathbf{Set}]_T(H-, A) : \mathcal{D}^{op} \to \mathbf{Set}$ preserves products for every $A \in [\mathcal{C}^{op}, \mathbf{Set}]_T$. Using these two facts we prove the following:

Proposition 3.15. *If the class Γ contains all the finite product cones, then H preserves finite coproducts.*

We refer to [22] for the details. From this, we impose that Γ contains all the finite product cones. This is another requirement to obtain a model.

3.7 $F_T \dashv G_T$ Is a Monoidal Adjunction

We recall how a monoidal adjoint pair $(F, m) \dashv (G, n)$ induces a monoidal structure for the adjunction $F_T \dashv G_T$ associated with the Kleisli construction.

Lemma 3.16. *Let $F \dashv G$ be a monoidal adjunction, let $T = GF$, and consider the Kleisli adjunction $C \underset{G_T}{\overset{F_T}{\rightleftarrows}} \mathcal{C}_T$ generated by this adjunction. Then $\mathcal{C}_T$ is a monoidal category and $F_T \dashv G_T$ is a monoidal adjunction.*

Proof. Since $F \dashv G$ is a monoidal adjunction, it follows that $T = GF$ is a monoidal monad. The result then follows by general properties of monoidal monads and monoidal adjunctions.

3.8   Abstract Model of the Quantum Lambda Calculus

Summing up the parts from previous sections, we have the following theorem.

Theorem 3.17. *Given categories $\mathcal{B}$, $\mathcal{C}$ and $\mathcal{D}$, and functors $\mathcal{B} \xrightarrow{\Phi} \mathcal{C} \xrightarrow{\Psi} \mathcal{D}$, satisfying*

- *$\mathcal{B}$ has finite products, $\mathcal{C}$ and $\mathcal{D}$ are symmetric monoidal,*
- *$\mathcal{B}$, $\mathcal{C}$, and $\mathcal{D}$ have coproducts, which are distributive w.r.t. tensor,*
- *$\mathcal{C}$ is affine,*
- *Φ and Ψ are strong monoidal,*

- Φ and Ψ preserve coproducts,
- Φ is full and faithful,
- Ψ is essentially surjective on objects,
- for every $b \in \mathcal{B}$, $c, c' \in \mathcal{C}$ we have $\mathcal{C}(\Phi(b), c) \times \mathcal{C}(\Phi(b), c') \cong \mathcal{C}(\Phi(b), c \otimes c')$.

Let Γ be any class of cones preserved by the opposite tensor functor, including all the finite product cones. Let Lan_Φ, Φ^*, F and G be defined as in Section 3.2 and subsequent sections. Then

$$[\mathcal{B}^{op}, \mathbf{Set}] \xrightarrow[\Phi^*]{\overset{Lan_\Phi}{\underset{\perp}{\longrightarrow}}} [\mathcal{C}^{op}, \mathbf{Set}] \xrightarrow[G]{\overset{F}{\underset{\perp}{\longrightarrow}}} [\mathcal{D}^{op}, \mathbf{Set}]_\Gamma$$

forms an abstract model of the quantum lambda calculus.

Proof. Relevant propositions from previous sections.

3.9   Towards a Concrete Model: Constructing $\mathbf{FinSet} \xrightarrow{\Phi} \mathbf{Q}'' \xrightarrow{\Psi} \mathbf{Q}$

The category $\mathbf{Q}$ of superoperators was defined in Section 2. Here, we discuss a category $\mathbf{Q}''$ related to $\mathbf{Q}$, together with functors $\mathbf{FinSet} \xrightarrow{\Phi} \mathbf{Q}'' \xrightarrow{\Psi} \mathbf{Q}$. The goal is to choose $\mathbf{Q}''$ and the functors Φ and Ψ carefully so as to satisfy the requirements of Theorem 3.17.

Recall the definition of the free affine monoidal category $(\mathcal{F}wm(\mathcal{K}), \otimes, I)$:

- Objects are finite sequences of objects of $\mathcal{K}$: $\{V_i\}_{i \in [n]} = \{V_1, \dots, V_n\}$.
- Maps $(\varphi, \{f_i\}_{i \in [m]}) : \{V_i\}_{i \in [n]} \longrightarrow \{W_i\}_{i \in [m]}$ are determined by:

   (i) an injective function $\varphi : [m] \to [n]$,
   (ii) a family of morphisms $f_i : V_{\varphi(i)} \to W_i$ in the category $\mathcal{K}$.

- Tensor $\otimes$ is given by concatenation, with unit I given by the empty sequence.

Proposition 3.18. *There is a canonical inclusion* $Inc : \mathcal{K} \to \mathcal{F}wm(\mathcal{K})$ *satisfying: for any symmetric monoidal category $\mathcal{A}$ whose tensor unit is terminal and any functor $F : \mathcal{K} \to \mathcal{A}$, there is a unique strong monoidal functor* $G : \mathcal{F}wm(\mathcal{K}) \to \mathcal{A}$, *up to isomorphism, such that $G \circ Inc = F$.*

We apply this universal construction to the situation where $\mathcal{K}$ is a discrete category. For later convenience, we let $\mathcal{K}$ be the discrete category with finite dimensional Hilbert spaces as objects. Then $\mathcal{F}wm(\mathcal{K})$ has sequences of Hilbert spaces as objects and dualized, compatible, injective functions as arrows.

Now consider the identity-on-objects inclusion functor $F : \mathcal{K} \to \mathbf{Q}'_s$, where $\mathbf{Q}'_s$ is the category of simple trace-preserving superoperators defined in Section 2. Since $\mathbf{Q}'_s$ is affine, by Proposition 3.18 there exists a unique (up to natural isomorphism) strong monoidal functor $\hat{F}$ such that:

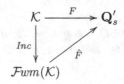

Remark 3.19. This reveals the purpose of using equality instead of $\leqslant$ in the definition of a trace-preserving superoperator (Definition 2.9). When the codomain is the unit, there is only one map $f(\rho) = \mathrm{tr}(\rho)$, and therefore $\mathbf{Q}'_s$ is affine.

Now we remind the reader about the general properties of the free finite coproduct completion $\mathcal{C}^+$ of a category $\mathcal{C}$. The category $\mathcal{C}^+$ has as its objects finite families of objects of $\mathcal{C}$, say $V - \{V_a\}_{a \in A}$, with A a finite set. A morphism from $V = \{V_a\}_{a \in A}$ to $W = \{W_b\}_{b \in B}$ consists of the following:

- a function $\varphi : A \to B$,
- a family $f = \{f_a\}_{a \in A}$ of morphisms of $\mathcal{C}$, where $f_a : V_a \to W_{\varphi(a)}$.

The coproduct in $\mathcal{C}^+$ is just concatenation of families of objects of $\mathcal{C}$.

Proposition 3.20. *Given any category $\mathcal{A}$ with finite coproducts and any functor $F : \mathcal{C} \to \mathcal{A}$, there is a unique finite coproduct preserving functor $G : \mathcal{C}^+ \to \mathcal{A}$, up to natural isomorphism, such that $G \circ Inc = F$.*

If $\mathcal{C}$ is a symmetric monoidal category then $\mathcal{C}^+$ is also symmetric monoidal. In addition, if we assume that the categories $\mathcal{C}$ and $\mathcal{A}$ are symmetric monoidal, then Inc is a symmetric monoidal functor. If F is a symmetric monoidal functor and tensor distributes over coproducts in $\mathcal{A}$, then G is a symmetric monoidal functor. Moreover, if F is strong monoidal then so is G.

In the sequel we want to apply Proposition 3.20 to a concrete category, but first:

Remark 3.21. By definition, $\mathbf{Q}_s$ is a full subcategory of $\mathbf{Q}$, and the inclusion functor $In : \mathbf{Q}_s \to \mathbf{Q}$ is strong monoidal. Also, since every trace preserving superoperator is trace non-increasing, $\mathbf{Q}'_s$ is a subcategory of $\mathbf{Q}_s$, and the inclusion functor $E : \mathbf{Q}'_s \to \mathbf{Q}_s$ is strong monoidal as well.

We apply the machinery of Proposition 3.20 to the composite functor

$$\mathcal{F}wm(\mathcal{K}) \xrightarrow{\hat{F}} \mathbf{Q}'_s \xrightarrow{E} \mathbf{Q}_s \xrightarrow{In} \mathbf{Q},$$

where In and E are as defined in Remark 3.21.

Definition 3.22. Let $\mathbf{Q}'' = (\mathcal{F}wm(\mathcal{K}))^+$ and let Ψ be the unique finite coproduct preserving functor making the following diagram commute:

$$\mathcal{F}wm(\mathcal{K}) \xrightarrow{\hat{F}} \mathbf{Q}'_s \xrightarrow{E} \mathbf{Q}_s \xrightarrow{In} \mathbf{Q}. \qquad (2)$$

with Inc downward to $(\mathcal{F}wm(\mathcal{K}))^+$ and Ψ.

Note that such a functor exists by Proposition 3.20, and it is strong monoidal.

Remark 3.23. Since $\Psi\{\{V_i^a\}_{i\in[n_a]}\}_{a\in A} = \coprod_{a\in A}\{(V_1^a\otimes\ldots\otimes V_{n_a}^a)_*\}_{*\in 1}$, the functor Ψ is essentially onto objects. Specifically, given any object $\{V_a\}_{a\in A} \in |\mathbf{Q}|$, we can choose a preimage (up to isomorphism) as follows:

$$\Psi\{\{V_i^a\}_{i\in[1]}\}_{a\in A} = \coprod_{a\in A}\{(V_1^a)_*\}_{*\in 1} \cong \{V_a\}_{a\in A}. \tag{3}$$

Lemma 3.24. *Let $\mathcal{C}$ be an affine category. Then there is a fully faithful strong monoidal functor $\Phi : (\mathbf{FinSet}, \times, 1) \to (\mathcal{C}^+, \otimes_{\mathcal{C}+}, I)$ that preserves coproducts.*

Definition 3.25. Recall that $\mathcal{F}wm(\mathcal{K})$ is an affine category and $\mathbf{Q}'' = \mathcal{F}wm(\mathcal{K})^+$. Let $\Phi : \mathbf{FinSet} \to \mathbf{Q}''$ be the functor defined by Lemma 3.24.

Remark 3.26. With the above choice of $\Phi : \mathbf{FinSet} \to \mathbf{Q}''$, equation (1) in Lemma 3.13 is just the characterization of cartesian products in $\mathbf{FinSet}$ using representable functors.

Theorem 3.27. *The choice $\mathcal{B} = \mathbf{FinSet}$, $\mathcal{C} = \mathbf{Q}''$, $\mathcal{D} = \mathbf{Q}$, with the functors Φ as in Definition 3.25 and Ψ as in Definition 3.22, and with Γ the class of all finite product cones in $\mathcal{D}^{op}$, satisfies all the properties required by Theorem 3.17.*

3.10 A Concrete Model

Theorem 3.28. *Let $\mathbf{Q}$, $\mathbf{Q}''$, Φ, Ψ, and Γ be defined as in Sections 2 and 3.9. Then*

$$[\mathbf{FinSet}^{op}, \mathbf{Set}] \xrightleftharpoons[\Phi^*]{\overset{Lan_\Phi}{\perp}} [(\mathbf{Q}'')^{op}, \mathbf{Set}] \xrightleftharpoons[G]{\overset{F}{\perp}} [\mathbf{Q}^{op}, \mathbf{Set}]_\Gamma$$

forms a concrete model of the quantum lambda calculus.

Proof. This follows from Theorems 3.17 and 3.27.

4 Conclusions and Future Work

We have constructed mathematical (semantic) models of higher-order quantum computation, specifically for the quantum lambda calculus of Selinger and Valiron. The central idea of our model construction was to apply the presheaf construction to a sequence of three categories and two functors, and to find a set of sufficient conditions for the resulting structure to be a valid model. The construction depends crucially on properties of presheaf categories, using Day's convolution theory and the Kelly-Freyd notion of continuity of functors.

We then identified specific base categories and functors that satisfy these abstract conditions, based on the category of superoperators. Thus, our choice of base categories ensures that the resulting model has the "correct" morphisms at base types, whereas the presheaf construction ensures that it has the "correct" structure at higher-order types.

Our work has concentrated solely on the existence of such a model. One question that we have not yet addressed is specific properties of the interpretation of quantum lambda calculus in this model. It would be interesting, in future work, to analyze whether this particular interpretation yields new insights into the nature of higher-order quantum computation, or to use this model to compute properties of programs.

Acknowledgements. This research was supported by the Natural Sciences and Engineering Research Council of Canada (NSERC) and by the Program for the Development of Basic Sciences, Uruguay (PEDECIBA).

References

1. Abramsky, S., Coecke, B.: A categorical semantics of quantum protocols. In: Proc. 19th Annual IEEE Symp. on Logic in Computer Science (LICS 2004), pp. 415–425. IEEE Computer Soc. Press (2004)
2. Benton, N.: A mixed linear and non-linear logic: proofs, terms and models (extended abstract). In: Pacholski, L., Tiuryn, J. (eds.) CSL 1994. LNCS, vol. 933, pp. 121–135. Springer, Heidelberg (1995)
3. Bierman, G.: On intuitionistic linear logic. Ph.D. thesis, Computer Science department, Cambridge University (1993)
4. Bierman, G.: What is a categorical model of intuitionistic linear logic? In: Dezani-Ciancaglini, M., Plotkin, G. (eds.) TLCA 1995. LNCS, vol. 902, pp. 78–93. Springer, Heidelberg (1995)
5. Borceux, F.: Handbook of Categorical Algebra 1. Cambridge University Press (1994)
6. Day, B.: On closed categories of functors. Lecture Notes in Math., vol. 137, pp. 1–38. Springer (1970)
7. Day, B.: A reflection theorem for closed categories. J. Pure Appl. Algebra 2, 1–11 (1972)
8. Day, B.: Note on monoidal localisation. Bull. Austral. Math. Soc. 8, 1–16 (1973)
9. Day, B.: Monoidal functor categories and graphic Fourier transforms, ArXiv:math/0612496 (2006)
10. Day, B., Street, R.: Kan extensions along promonoidal functors. Theory and Applications of Categories 1(4), 72–78 (1995)
11. Freyd, P., Kelly, G.M.: Categories of continuous functors I. J. Pure and Appl. Algebra 2, 169–191 (1972)
12. Girard, J.-Y.: Linear logic. Theoretical Computer Science 50(1), 1–101 (1987)
13. Im, G.B., Kelly, G.M.: A universal property of the convolution monoidal structure. J. Pure and Appl. Algebra 43, 75–88 (1986)
14. Kelly, G.M.: Doctrinal adjunction. Lecture Notes in Math., vol. 420, pp. 257–280. Springer (1974)
15. Kelly, G.M.: Basic Concepts of Enriched Category Theory. LMS Lecture Notes, vol. 64. Cambridge University Press (1982)
16. Kock, A.: Monads on symmetric monoidal closed categories. Arch. Math. 21, 1–10 (1970)
17. Kock, A.: Strong functors and monoidal monads. Archiv der Mathematik 23 (1972)
18. Lambek, J.: Completions of Categories. Lecture Notes in Math., vol. 24. Springer (1966)

19. Lambek, J., Scott, P.J.: Introduction to Higher Order Categorical Logic. Cambridge University Press (1986)
20. Laplaza, M.L.: Coherence for distributivity. Lecture Notes in Math., vol. 281, pp. 29–65. Springer (1972)
21. Mac Lane, S.: Categories for the Working Mathematician, 2nd edn. Springer (1998)
22. Malherbe, O.: Categorical models of computation: partially traced categories and presheaf models of quantum computation. Ph.D. thesis, University of Ottawa (2010), Available from arXiv:1301.5087
23. Melliès, P.-A.: Categorical models of linear logic revisited (2002) (Preprint), Appeared as: Categorical semantics of linear logic. In: Curien, P.-L., Herbelin, H., Krivine, J.-L., Melliès, P.-A. (eds.) Interactive Models of Computation and Program Behaviour. Panoramas et Synthèses, vol. 27. Société Mathématique de France (2009)
24. Moggi, E.: Computational lambda-calculus and monads. Technical Report ECS-LFCS-88-66, Lab. for Foundations of Computer Science, U. Edinburgh (1988)
25. Moggi, E.: Notions of computation and monads. Information and Computation 93(1), 55–92 (1991)
26. Nielsen, A., Chuang, I.L.: Quantum Computation and Quantum Information. Cambridge University Press (2000)
27. Seely, R.: Linear logic, *-autonomous categories and cofree coalgebras. In: Gray, J.W., Scedrov, A. (eds.) Categories in Computer Science and Logic. Contemporary Mathematics, vol. 92, pp. 371–382. Amer. Math. Soc. (1989)
28. Selinger, P.: Towards a quantum programming language. Math. Structures in Comp. Sci. 14(4), 527–586 (2004)
29. Selinger, P.: Dagger compact closed categories and completely positive maps. In: Selinger, P. (ed.) Proceedings of the Third International Workshop on Quantum Programming Languages (QPL 2005), Chicago. ENTCS, vol. 170, pp. 139–163 (2007)
30. Selinger, P., Valiron, B.: A lambda calculus for quantum computation with classical control. Mathematical Structures in Computer Science 16, 527–552 (2006)
31. Selinger, P., Valiron, B.: On a fully abstract model for a quantum functional language. In: Proceedings of the Fourth International Workshop on Quantum Programming Languages. ENTCS, vol. 210, pp. 123–137. Springer (2008)
32. Selinger, P., Valiron, B.: A linear-non-linear model for a computational call-by-value lambda calculus (Extended abstract). In: Amadio, R. (ed.) FOSSACS 2008. LNCS, vol. 4962, pp. 81–96. Springer, Heidelberg (2008)
33. Selinger, P., Valiron, B.: Quantum lambda calculus. In: Gay, S., Mackie, I. (eds.) Semantic Techniques in Quantum Computation, pp. 135–172. Cambridge University Press (2009)
34. Shor, P.W.: Algorithms for quantum computation: discrete logarithms and factoring. In: Goldwasser, S. (ed.) Proc. 35th Annual Symposium on Foundations of Computer Science, pp. 124–134. IEEE Computer Society Press (1994)
35. Valiron, B.: Semantics for a higher order functional programming language for quantum computation. Ph.D. thesis, University of Ottawa (2008)

Nothing Can Be Fixed

Keye Martin

Naval Research Laboratory
Washington, DC 20375
keye.martin@nrl.navy.mil

Abstract. We establish the existence of zero elements in certain partially ordered monoids and use them to prove the existence of least fixed points in domain theory. This algebraic stance is the magic underlying Pataraia's constructive proof of the fixed point theorem.

To Samson, on the 30th Anniversary of His 30th Birthday

In the Michaelmas Term of 2000, Samson gave a seminar on Pataraia's constructive proof of the fixed point theorem. Because of his remarkable lucidity that day, every detail of the presentation has stayed with me for over twelve years, and as a result, I now have something new to report: there are times when algebraic zeroes can yield fixed points, hence our title. Alternate interpretations, such as "nothing can stay the same" (like one's age) or "things are broken and cannot be repaired," are probably coincidental.

Definition 1. A *partially ordered monoid* is a monoid $(M, \cdot, 1)$ with a partial order $\leq$ such that

$$a \leq b \ \& \ x \leq y \Longrightarrow ax \leq by$$

for all $a, b, x, y \in M$. It is *directed complete* when all of its directed sets have suprema and is said to have a *zero* when there is an element e with $e = ex = xe$ for all x. Zero elements are unique when they exist.

Theorem 1. *If M is a directed complete monoid with $1 \leq x$ for all $x \in M$, then M has a zero.*

Proof. Let $x, y \in M$. Using $1 \leq x$ and $1 \leq y$, multiply the first on the right by y and the second on the left by x to get $x, y \leq xy$. Then M is a directed set. Let $e = \bigsqcup M$. We then have $e \leq ex, xe$ but also $ex, xe \leq e$ since e is above every element of M. Then $e = ex = xe$ is the zero element of M. $\qquad\square$

The last result enables an algebraic proof of the fixed point theorem in domain theory:

B. Coecke, L. Ong, and P. Panangaden (Eds.): Abramsky Festschrift, LNCS 7860, pp. 195–196, 2013.
© Springer-Verlag Berlin Heidelberg 2013

Theorem 2. *A monotone map $f : D \to D$ on a dcpo D with least element $\perp$ has a least fixed point.*

Proof. Let $S = \{x \in D : x \sqsubseteq f(x)\}$. Notice that $S \neq \emptyset$ since $\perp \in S$ and is a dcpo by the monotonicity of f. Let $P(S)$ denote the set of monotone maps above the identity which take S into S. Then $P(S)$ is a directed complete monoid under composition with least element 1. By Theorem 1, it has a zero e. Since $f \in P(S)$, we then have $f \circ e = e$, which implies that $f(e(x)) = e(x)$ for all $x \in S$ and thus that f has a fixed point.

To prove f has a least fixed point, let M denote the set of $A \subseteq D$ closed under directed suprema in D with $\perp \in A$ and $f(A) \subseteq A$. Under the operation of intersection and order of reverse inclusion, M is a directed complete monoid with identity D. By Theorem 1, it has a zero e, and as seen above, f has a fixed point fix$(f) \in e$. Given any $x = f(x) \in D$, the set $\{a : a \sqsubseteq x\} \in M$ and thus contains e. Then fix$(f) \sqsubseteq x$.   □

We applied Theorem 1 twice in the proof of Theorem 2 only to make the point that both the existence of the fixed point as well as its leastness can be handled with Theorem 1. Alternatively, the same effect can be achieved by taking S in the first part of Theorem 2 to be $e \in M$.

References

1. Escardo, M.H.: Joins in the frame of nuclei. Applied Categorical Structures 11, 117–124 (2003)
2. Pataraia, D.: A constructive proof of Tarski's fixed-point theorem for dcpo's. Presented in the 65th Peripatetic Seminar on Sheaves and Logic, Aarhus, Denmark (November 1997)

Dialogue Categories and Frobenius Monoids

Paul-André Melliès*

Abstract. About ten years ago, Brian Day and Ross Street discovered a beautiful and unexpected connection between the notion of ∗-autonomous category in proof theory and the notion of Frobenius algebra in mathematical physics. The purpose of the present paper is to clarify the logical content of this connection by formulating a two-sided presentation of Frobenius algebras. The presentation is inspired by the idea that every logical dispute has two sides consisting of a Prover and of a Denier. This dialogical point of view leads us to a correspondence between dialogue categories and Frobenius pseudomonoids. The correspondence with dialogue categories refines Day and Street's correspondence with ∗-autonomous categories in the same way as tensorial logic refines linear logic.

Forewords

A few weeks before writing this paper, I learned that my dear friend Kohei Honda passed away in London. This sudden accident was a tremendous shock, and his disparition haunts me. Vivid memories come back of the wonderful three years we spent together in Edinburgh. Kohei and I met for the first time in early 1996. Samson Abramsky had just moved from Imperial College to the Laboratory for the Foundations of Computer Science — taking there the position of Robin Milner who had just left Edinburgh to join the University of Cambridge. Samson wanted to create a new group there and he was looking for two Research Assistants. He decided to hire Kohei and me. This was really a bold choice Samson made on that occasion because Kohei and I were coming from territories quite alien to semantics. Kohei was already recognized for his discovery of the asynchronous π-calculus with Mario Tokoro, independently and at about the same time as Gérard Boudol, see [9] for details. Kohei was absolutely fanatic about the π-calculus and he would openly declare that game semantics was only a small fragment of π — I like to think that the future will tell him right in some interesting and unexpected way. I should say that I was just as stubborn myself about rewriting theory. Back in France, Pierre-Louis Curien had advised me to join Samson's group if I wanted to learn semantics — but I was so much hooked on rewriting theory when I arrived at the LFCS that it took me two long years before really working on linear logic and game semantics.

During the three years we spent together in Edinburgh, Kohei and I very soon became this slightly eccentric pair of French and Japanese researchers sharing an office on the ground floor of the JCMB building. The office was dark and cold, with two narrow window panes facing a few bushes and an anonymous alley... but I spent there among

---

* CNRS, Laboratoire PPS, UMR 7126, Université Paris Diderot, Sorbonne Paris Cité, F-75205 Paris, France.

B. Coecke, L. Ong, and P. Panangaden (Eds.): Abramsky Festschrift, LNCS 7860, pp. 197–224, 2013.
© Springer-Verlag Berlin Heidelberg 2013

the most luminous hours of my life, and I am sure that Kohei was just as enthusiastic developing his own stream of ideas.

Samson was an exquisite leader and nothing of the effervescence of the *interaction group* — this is the way we decided to call ourselves — would have been possible without his sharp understanding of logic and of semantics combined with a frenetic curiosity for the surrounding fields. Any topic could be freely discussed in the group and there was absolutely no feeling of intellectual property among us. As a matter of fact, many ideas which I have worked out in Paris in the past fifteen years were already germinating at the time. I distinctively remember Kohei and Nobuko Yoshida explaining how call-by-value programs should be interpreted by letting Player start the game rather than Opponent[1]. I also remember Samson explaining how higher-order states could be interpreted by relaxing the visibility condition on strategies[2]. And I remember Martin Wehr developping a narcotic interest in n-dimensional categories and trying to convince all of us that n-dimensional syntax would become the foundation of logic and of programming languages[3]. These are only a few illustrations coming to my mind so numerous were the ideas floating around in this small group of dedicated people.

This short period of my life in Edinburgh defines a lot about who I am today, and I am happy to dedicate the present work to Samson as a testimony of friendship and gratitude. My primary purpose here is to entertain him with a connection between two of his favorite topics of interest: game semantics and logic on the one hand, Frobenius algebras and the categorical approach to physics on the other hand.

1   Frobenius Algebras and 2-Dimensional Cobordism

Let $n > 0$ be a positive integer. The basic idea of topological field theory is to construct a symmetric monoidal functor

$$\text{Cob}(n) \quad \longrightarrow \quad Vect$$

from the category of n-dimensional cobordism to the category *Vect* of vector spaces on a given field k. The category $\text{Cob}(n)$ is defined as follows:

- its objects are the closed oriented $(n-1)$-dimensional manifolds,
- its morphisms $M \to N$ are the bordisms from M to N, that is, the oriented n-dimensional manifold B equipped with an orientation-preserving diffeomorphism $\partial B \cong (-M) \cup N$. Here $-M$ denotes the manifold M equipped with the opposite orientation. Two bordisms $B, B' : M \to N$ are considered equal in $\text{Cob}(n)$ if there is an orientation-preserving diffeomorphism which extends the diffeomorphism $\partial B \cong (-M) \cup N \cong \partial B'$.

---

[1] A paper developing this idea was presented by Kohei and Nobuko at the ICALP 1997 conference, see [10] for details.

[2] A paper developing this idea was presented by Samson, Kohei and Guy McCusker at the LICS 1998 conference, see [1] for details.

[3] Martin presented some of his ideas on higher dimensional syntax in the CTCS 1999 conference, see [21] for details.

- For any object M in Cob(n), the identity map id_M is represented by the product bordism $B = M \times [0, 1]$,
- Composition of morphisms in Cob(n) is defined by gluing bordisms together. The operation of gluing is not canonical but the point is that it defines a unique class of manifolds modulo diffeomorphism.

The category Cob(n) can be endowed with the structure of a symmetric monoidal category, whose tensor product $\otimes$ is given by taking the disjoint sum of two $(n-1)$-dimensional manifolds, and whose unit I is given by the empty manifold. A natural question is to understand what information is contained in a topological field theory of a given dimension n. The answer is very well known in the case of dimension $n = 2$. In that case, a topological field theory is the same thing as a commutative and cocommutative Frobenius algebra in the category *Vect*. This observation justifies the notion of *Frobenius monoid* in any monoidal category $\mathcal{V}$. A Frobenius algebra is then the same thing as a Frobenius monoid in the category *Vect*.

Definition 1 (Frobenius Monoid). *A bimonoid A in a monoidal category $\mathcal{V}$ is an object equipped a monoid structure (A, m, e) and a comonoid structure (A, d, u). In other words, it is an object A equipped with a binary operation m and a binary co-operation d*

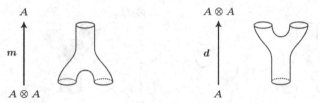

both of them associative, and equipped with a unit e and a co-unit u

A Frobenius monoid *is defined as a bimonoid A satisfying the two equalities below:*

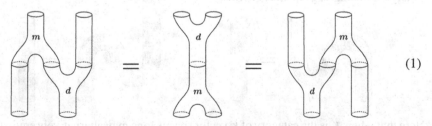

$$(1)$$

A Frobenius monoid in a symmetric monoidal category $\mathcal{V}$ is called commutative (resp. cocommutative) when its underlying monoid (resp. comonoid) is commutative (resp. cocommutative).

Note that the characterization of topological field theories of dimension 2 extends to every symmetric monoidal category $\mathcal{V}$.

Proposition 1. *A symmetric monoidal functor* $\mathrm{Cob}(2) \to \mathcal{V}$ *into a symmetric monoidal category* $\mathcal{V}$ *is the same thing as a commutative and cocommutative Frobenius monoid in* $\mathcal{V}$.

2 Frobenius Pairs

Once the notion of Frobenius algebra has been extracted from the definition of topological field theory, it makes sense to study it independently of its topological origins. In this paper, we will do something quite counterintuitive from the topological point of view, but which makes a lot of sense from the logical point of view. In the same way as a logical dispute involves a Prover and a Denier, we will decouple the monoid side (A, m, e) from the comonoid side (B, d, u) in the definition of a Frobenius monoid. Each side A and B is meant to describe an aspect of the «split personality» of the Frobenius monoid. The operations of the monoid (A, m, e) are depicted in light blue whereas the co-operations of the comonoid (B, d, u) are depicted in dark red:

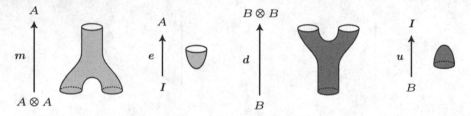

Once the notion of Frobenius monoid in a monoidal category $\mathcal{V}$ has been split in two, an interesting question is to understand how its two sides A and B are coupled inside a Frobenius monoid. The first thing to ask is that the two objects A and B are involved in an *exact pairing* $A \dashv B$ defined as a pair of morphisms

$$\eta \ : \ I \ \longrightarrow \ B \otimes A \qquad\qquad \varepsilon \ : \ A \otimes B \ \longrightarrow \ I$$

satisfying the zig-zag equalities below:

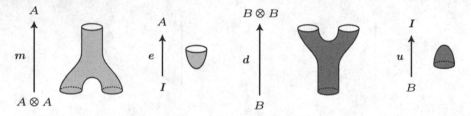

Note that when $\mathcal{V}$ is the category of k-vector spaces, one may alternatively equip the two spaces A and B with a non-degenerate binary form $\varepsilon : A \otimes B \to k$. This exact pairing $A \dashv B$

should be moreover compatible with the monoid and comonoid structures of A and B in the following sense. We define a monoid-comonoid pairing

$$(A,m,e) \quad \dashv \quad (B,d,u) \tag{2}$$

between a monoid and a comonoid as an exact pairing $A \dashv B$ between the underlying objects satisfying the two equalities:

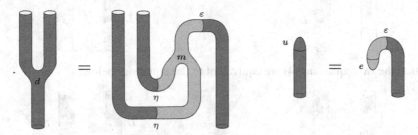

These equations mean that the comonoid structure (B,d,u) on the object B may be recovered from the monoid structure (A,m,e) on the object A, and conversely, that the monoid structure (A,m,e) on the object A may be recovered from the comonoid structure (B,d,u) on the object B. In a symmetric way, one requires the existence of a comonoid-monoid pairing

$$(B,d,u) \quad \dashv \quad (A,m,e) \tag{3}$$

defined as an exact pairing $B \dashv A$ between the underlying objects:

$$\eta' : I \longrightarrow B \otimes A \qquad \varepsilon' : A \otimes B \longrightarrow I$$

which moreover satisfies the two equations below:

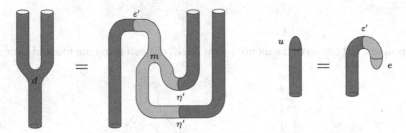

In the same way as before, the two equalities say that that the comonoid structure (B,d,u) on the object B may be recovered from the monoid structure (A,m,e) on the object A, and conversely. This leads to our definition of Frobenius pair.

Definition 2 (Frobenius Pairs). *A Frobenius pair in a monoidal category $\mathcal{V}$ consists of a monoid-comonoid pairing (2) and a comonoid-monoid pairing (3) between a monoid (A,m,e) and a comonoid (B,d,u) together with an isomorphim $L : A \to B$*

between the underlying objects A and B. One also requires that the equalities below are satisfied:

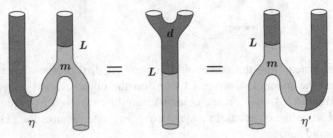

$$\tag{4}$$

Note that the two equations (4) are equivalent to the equations below:

These equalities may be understood in the following way. The monoid-comonoid pairing $(A,m,e) \dashv (B,d,u)$ induces a left action of the monoid (A,m,e) on the object B, defined as

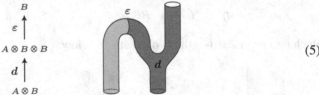

$$\tag{5}$$

There is also a left action of the monoid A on itself, defined using the monoid structure:

Equation (4) means that the morphism L transports the left action of the monoid A on itself into the action (5) on the object B. In a symmetric way, the exact pairing $B \dashv A$ induces a right action of the monoid A on B, and the second equation (4) amounts to ask that the morphism L transports the canonical right action of the monoid A on itself in the right action of the monoid A on the object B. The ultimate justification for the notion of Frobenius pair is the following correspondence with Frobenius monoids:

Proposition 2. *A Frobenius pair (A,B) in a monoidal category $\mathcal{V}$ is the same thing as a Frobenius monoid A equipped with an exact pairing $A \dashv B$.*

Proof. Given a Frobenius monoid A together with an exact pairing $A \dashv B$ with unit η and counit ε, one defines the unit η' and counit ε' of the exact pairing $B \dashv A$ and the isomorphism L as follows:

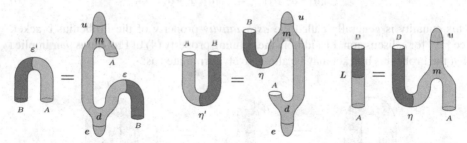

The object B inherits its comonoid structure (B, d, u) from the monoid structure (A, m, e) of the object A and the exact pairing $A \dashv B$. One checks that the resulting structure coincides with the comonoid structure on B induced from the exact pairing $B \dashv A$. This already ensures that the pair (A, m, e) and (B, d, u) satisfy the equalities (2) and (3). Finally, one easily checks that the two equalities (4) are satisfied, and that the pair (A, B) thus defines a Frobenius pair. Conversely, every Frobenius pair (A, B) defines a Frobenius monoid with monoid structure (A, m, e) and comonoid structure (A, d', u') induced from the isomorphism L with (B, d, u). A careful inspection shows that the relationship between Frobenius pairs (A, B) and Frobenius monoid A equipped with a duality $A \dashv B$ is one-to-one.

Remark. The idea of presenting Frobenius algebras as a pair consisting of a monoid A and of its canonical right dual $B = A^*$ is essentially folklore, and appears already in [5]. So, the only novelty here is that we do not ask that the object B coincides with the canonical right dual A^*. More on that specific point will be said when we move to ribbon categories in §5.

3   The Frobenius Bracket

Given a Frobenius pair in a monoidal category, the following morphism

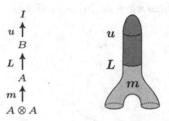

defines a bilinear form

$$\{\!|-,-|\!\} \quad : \quad A \otimes A \quad \longrightarrow \quad I$$

called the *Frobenius bracket*. The definition of Frobenius bracket together with the associativity af the product $a_1 \bullet a_2 = m(a_1, a_2)$ ensures that the following equality is satisfied:

$$\{\!| a_1 \bullet a_2, a_3 |\!\} \quad = \quad \{\!| a_1, a_2 \bullet a_3 |\!\} \tag{6}$$

This equality is generally called the *associativity* property of the Frobenius bracket, see [19] for a discussion. In addition, the defining property (4) of Frobenius pair implies that the Frobenius bracket may be alternatively formulated as:

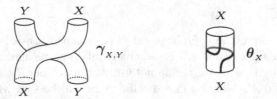

4   Helical Frobenius Pairs

We suppose from now on that we work in a balanced monoidal category in the sense of [11,12,13] typically given by the category $\mathcal{V} = Mod(H)$ of representations of a quantum group H. The braiding γ and the twist θ of the category $\mathcal{V}$ are represented as follows:

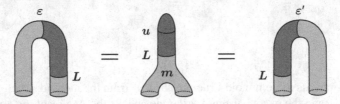

Note that the twist θ_X should be understood as the operation of applying a rotation of angle 2π on the border X of the 2-dimensional manifold. This extra structure on the category $\mathcal{V}$ enables us to formulate the following definition of *helical* Frobenius monoid.

Definition 3 (Helical Frobenius Monoids). *A Frobenius monoid A in a balanced monoidal category is called helical when the two equalities below are satified:*

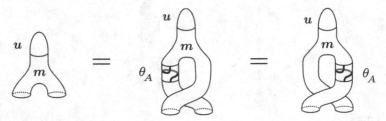

We proceed as in §2 and immediately introduce the corresponding two-sided notion of helical Frobenius pair:

Definition 4 (Helical Frobenius Pairs). *A Frobenius pair in a balanced monoidal category is called helical when the two equalities below are satisfied:*

Since the morphism L is reversible in the definition of a Frobenius pair, one may replace this helicality condition by the equivalent one:

$$(7)$$

We will see that this formulation of helicality is more natural than the original one when we move one dimension up to the 2-categorical notion of Frobenius amphimonoid. It should be noted that this latter condition (7) is equivalent to asking that the Frobenius bracket is commutative in the sense that the two equalities below are satisfied:

The equivalence follows from the fact that the twist is a natural isomorphism from the identity functor into itself, and thus satisfies the equality:

The equation (7) should be understood as a commutativity property of the Frobenius bracket:

$$\{\!|\, a_1, a_2 \,|\!\} \;=\; \{\!|\, a_2, a_1 \,|\!\}. \tag{8}$$

Together with the associativity (6) the commutativity of the Frobenius bracket implies the following cyclicity property:

$$\{\!\{a_1 \bullet a_2, a_3\}\!\} \quad = \quad \{\!\{a_3 \bullet a_1, a_2\}\!\} \quad = \quad \{\!\{a_2 \bullet a_3, a_1\}\!\} \tag{9}$$

where $a_1 \bullet a_2$ is a notation for the product $m(a_1, a_2)$ of the two elements a_1 and a_2. It is worth recalling here that a symmetric monoidal category is the same thing as a balanced monoidal category whose twist θ_X is equal to the identity id_X for every object X. A helical Frobenius algebra in a symmetric monoidal category is called *symmetric*. A typical illustration is provided by matrix algebras $A \otimes A^*$ where the cyclicity equations (8–9) reflect the cyclicity of the trace functional. As expected, one needs to modulate the two equations (8–9) by a twist θ when one works in a general balanced monoidal category.

At this stage, Proposition 2 may be refined into the following correspondence between helical Frobenius monoids and helical Frobenius pairs:

Proposition 3. *A helical Frobenius pair (A, B) in a balanced monoidal category $\mathscr{V}$ is the same thing as a helical Frobenius monoid A equipped with an exact pairing $A \dashv B$.*

5 Frobenius Pairs in Ribbon Categories

The two-sided formulation of a Frobenius monoid as a pair (A, B) relies on the existence of an exact pairing $A \dashv B$ between the two sides A and B of the Frobenius pair. It is thus interesting to see what happens when one embeds the notion of Frobenius pair in a monoidal category $\mathscr{V}$ which is *already* equipped with an exact pairing $A \dashv A^\dagger$ for every object A. This is precisely what happens in the case of a ribbon category like the category $\mathscr{V} = Mod_f(H)$ of *finite dimensional* representations of a quantum group H. Recall that a ribbon category[4] is defined as a balanced monoidal category $\mathscr{V}$ where every object A comes equipped with an exact pairing $A \dashv A^\dagger$ whose counit $\varepsilon_A : A \otimes A^\dagger \to I$ satisfies the equality below:

$$\tag{10}$$

A nice consequence of the definition of ribbon category is that the right dual $A^\dagger$ is also a left dual of the object A, with counit ε'_A of the exact pairing $A^\dagger \dashv A$ defined as:

---

[4] The notion of ribbon category is also called tortile category in [11,18].

$$= \qquad (11)$$

Another nice property is that every Frobenius pair (A,B) in a ribbon category $\mathcal{V}$ satisfies the equality [5] below:

$$= \qquad (12)$$

It is worth observing that the opposite category $\mathcal{V}^{op(0,1)}$ of a balanced monoidal category $\mathcal{V}$ is also balanced, with the same braiding and twist combinators as the original category. By $\mathcal{V}^{op(0,1)}$, we mean the monoidal category $\mathcal{V}$ where the orientation of the tensor product (of dimension 0) and of the morphisms (of dimension 1) has been reversed. The transformation $\mathcal{V} \mapsto \mathcal{V}^{op(0,1)}$ thus consists in applying a central symmetry on the string diagrams. The family of exact pairings $A \dashv A^{\dagger}$ induces a monoidal functor

$$\dagger \;:\; \mathcal{V} \;\longrightarrow\; \mathcal{V}^{op(0,1)}$$

which transports the ribbon structure of $\mathcal{V}$ to the ribbon structure of $\mathcal{V}^{op(0,1)}$ in the obvious sense. Note that one would obtain the very same functor $\dagger$ by starting from the family of exact pairings $A^{\dagger} \dashv A$ defined in (11). Now, every exact pairing $A \dashv A^{\dagger}$ in $\mathcal{V}$ induces an exact pairing $A \dashv A^{\dagger}$ in the opposite category $\mathcal{V}^{op(0,1)}$ with unit defined as the image $\varepsilon_A^{\dagger} : I \to A^{\dagger} \otimes^{op} A$ of the counit $\varepsilon_A : A \otimes A^{\dagger} \to I$ of the original exact pairing. From this follows that every ribbon structure on $\mathcal{V}$ induces a ribbon structure on $\mathcal{V}^{op(0,1)}$.

Now, suppose given a Frobenius pair (A,B) in such a ribbon category $\mathcal{V}$. The monoidal structure of the functor $\dagger$ ensures that the comonoid structure of the object B is transported to a monoid structure on the object $B^{\dagger}$. The resulting monoid structure $(B^{\dagger}, d^{\dagger}, u^{\dagger})$ may be constructed either from the exact pairing $B^{\dagger} \dashv B$ or from the exact pairing $(B^{\dagger}, d^{\dagger}, u^{\dagger})$. From this follows that the monoid $(B^{\dagger}, d^{\dagger}, u^{\dagger})$ is involved in two exact pairings with the comonoid (B, d, u), either as a left dual or as a right dual:

$$(B^{\dagger}, d^{\dagger}, u^{\dagger}) \;\dashv\; (B, d, u) \qquad\qquad (B, d, u) \;\dashv\; (B^{\dagger}, d^{\dagger}, u^{\dagger})$$

---

[5] The equality is in fact satisfied by any bilinear form $A \otimes B \to I$ in a ribbon category.

with unit η'_B and counit ε'_B in the first case, and with unit η_B and counit ε_B in the second case. These exact pairings should be compared with the exact pairings between (A, m, e) and (B, d, u) involved in the definition of the Frobenius pair:

$$(A, m, e) \dashv (B, d, u) \qquad\qquad (B, d, u) \dashv (A, m, e)$$

with unit η and counit ε in the first case and with unit η' and counit ε' in the second case. Each comparison induces a monoid isomorphism between the monoid (A, m, e) and the monoid $(B^\dagger, d^\dagger, u^\dagger)$. The two isomorphisms are respectively defined as:

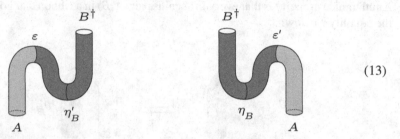

$$(13)$$

The notion of helical Frobenius pair plays an important role at this stage, and this is precisely the reason why we introduced it in §4. The point is that the two isomorphisms $A \to B^\dagger$ coincide precisely when the Frobenius pair is helical. We leave the reader check this statement starting from the observation that the equality (10) holds in any ribbon category. So, in the case of a helical Frobenius pair, one obtains an isomorphism of monoids

$$(A, m, e) \underset{^*(-)}{\overset{(-)^*}{\rightleftarrows}} (B^\dagger, d^\dagger, u^\dagger)$$

isomorphism of monoid

where the isomorphisms $(-)^* : A \to B^\dagger$ and $^*(-) : B \to A^\dagger$ are defined as:

From these definitions, one deduces the following equations:

These equations lead to an alternative but equivalent formulation of helical Frobenius pairs (A,B) living in a ribbon category:

Proposition 4. *A helical Frobenius pair (A,B) in a ribbon category is the same thing as a monoid (A,m,e) and a comonoid (B,d,u) equipped with a monoid isomorphism*

$$(-)^* \quad : \quad (A,m,e) \quad \longrightarrow \quad (B^\dagger, d^\dagger, u^\dagger)$$

and an isomorphism $L : A \to B$ between the underlying objects satisfying the equalities:

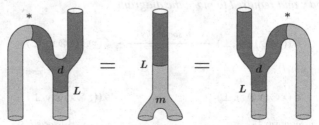

Here, we use the $*$ notation for the two evaluation brackets between A and B defined as follows:

$$
\quad = \quad \qquad = \qquad \tag{14}
$$

We let the reader check the statement. Starting from the alternative formulation of Proposition 4, the two evaluation brackets $\varepsilon : A \otimes B \to I$ and $\varepsilon' : B \otimes A \to I$ of the Frobenius pair (A,B) are recovered as the two operations $*$ depicted in (14).

6   Dialogue Categories and Chiralities

At this point, it is time to introduce the notion of dialogue category, which underlies tensorial logic in the same way as the notion of $*$-autonomous category underlies linear logic, see [4,8] for details. Tensorial logic is a primitive logic of tensor and negation whose purpose is to circumscribe the primary ingredients of logic. Our main ambition here is to extend to dialogue categories the correspondence between $*$-autonomous categories and Frobenius algebras originally discovered by Day and Street [6][19] and then independently rediscovered a few years later by Egger [7].

Definition 5 (Dialogue Categories). *A dialogue category is a monoidal category $(\mathscr{C},\otimes,e)$ equipped with an object $\bot$ together with a family of bijections*

$$\varphi_{x,y} \quad : \quad \mathscr{C}(x \otimes y, \bot) \quad \cong \quad \mathscr{C}(y, x \multimap \bot)$$

natural in y for all objects x of the category $\mathscr{C}$, and a family of bijections

$$\psi_{x,y} \quad : \quad \mathscr{C}(x \otimes y, \bot) \quad \cong \quad \mathscr{C}(x, y \multimap \bot)$$

natural in x for all objects y of the category $\mathscr{C}$.

We will be more specifically interested in the notion of *helical dialogue category* introduced in [16,17].

Definition 6 (Helical Dialogue Category). *A helical dialogue category is a dialogue category $\mathscr{C}$ equipped with a family of bijections*

$$wheel_{x,y} \quad : \quad \mathscr{C}(x \otimes y, \bot) \longrightarrow \mathscr{C}(y \otimes x, \bot)$$

natural in x and y and required to make the diagram

$$
\begin{array}{ccc}
\mathscr{C}((y \otimes z) \otimes x, \bot) & \xrightarrow{\ associativity\ } & \mathscr{C}(y \otimes (z \otimes x), \bot) \\
{\scriptstyle wheel_{x,y \otimes z}} \uparrow & & \downarrow {\scriptstyle wheel_{y,z \otimes x}} \\
\mathscr{C}(x \otimes (y \otimes z), \bot) & & \mathscr{C}((z \otimes x) \otimes y, \bot) \\
{\scriptstyle associativity} \downarrow & & \uparrow {\scriptstyle associativity} \\
\mathscr{C}((x \otimes y) \otimes z, \bot) & \xrightarrow[\ wheel_{x \otimes y, z}\ ]{} & \mathscr{C}(z \otimes (x \otimes y), \bot)
\end{array}
\qquad (15)
$$

commute for all objects x, y, z of the category $\mathscr{C}$.

A useful graphical mnemonics for the *wheel* combinator is to draw it in the following way:

$$wheel_{x,y} \quad : \qquad \qquad \longmapsto \qquad \qquad \qquad (16)$$

In that graphical formulation, the coherence diagram expresses that the diagram below commutes:

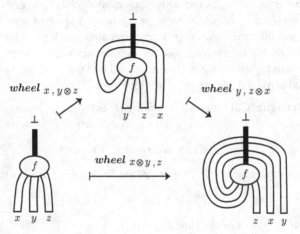

The bare notion of dialogue category is fundamental but one may argue that it does not properly reflect the symmetries of logic, and more specifically the two-sided nature of logical disputes. The equivalent notion of *dialogue chirality* was introduced for that reason, see [15] for details. We recall below the two-sided notion of helical dialogue chirality corresponding to the one-sided notion of helical dialogue category. The formal correspondence between them[6] is established in [16].

Definition 7 (Helical Chirality). *A helical chirality is a pair of monoidal categories*

$$(\mathscr{A}, \oslash, true) \qquad\qquad (\mathscr{B}, \oslash, false)$$

equipped with a monoidal equivalence and an adjunction

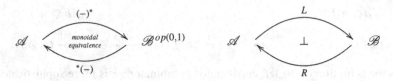

and with two families of bijections

$$\chi^L_{m,a,b} \; : \; \langle m \oslash a | b \rangle \; \longrightarrow \; \langle a | m^* \oslash b \rangle$$

$$\chi^R_{m,a,b} \; : \; \langle a \oslash m | b \rangle \; \longrightarrow \; \langle a | b \oslash m^* \rangle$$

natural in a, b and m, where the evaluation bracket is defined as

$$\langle - | - \rangle \; := \; \mathscr{A}(-, R(-)) \; : \; \mathscr{A}^{op} \times \mathscr{B} \; \longrightarrow \; Set$$

The currification combinators χ^L and χ^R are moreover required to make the three diagrams commute:

$$
\begin{array}{ccc}
\langle (m \oslash n) \oslash a | b \rangle & \xrightarrow{\;\;\chi^L_{m \oslash n}\;\;} & \langle a | (m \oslash n)^* \oslash b \rangle \\
\Big\downarrow {\scriptstyle associativity} & & \Big\uparrow {\scriptstyle associativity \atop monoidality\, of\, negation} \\
\langle m \oslash (n \oslash a) | b \rangle \xrightarrow{\;\chi^L_m\;} \langle n \oslash a | m^* \oslash b \rangle & \xrightarrow{\;\chi^L_n\;} & \langle a | n^* \oslash (m^* \oslash b) \rangle
\end{array}
\qquad (17)
$$

$$
\begin{array}{ccc}
\langle a \oslash (m \oslash n) | b \rangle & \xrightarrow{\;\;\chi^R_{m \oslash n}\;\;} & \langle a | b \oslash (m \oslash n)^* \rangle \\
\Big\downarrow {\scriptstyle associativity} & & \Big\uparrow {\scriptstyle associativity \atop monoidality\, of\, negation} \\
\langle (a \oslash m) \oslash n | b \rangle \xrightarrow{\;\chi^R_n\;} \langle a \oslash m | b \oslash n^* \rangle & \xrightarrow{\;\chi^R_m\;} & \langle a | (b \oslash n^*) \oslash m^* \rangle
\end{array}
\qquad (18)
$$

---

[6] The notion of helical chirality described here is called "ambidextrous" in [16]. We keep the terminology "helical" here in order to stress the correspondence with helical dialogue categories.

$$\langle (m \otimes a) \otimes n \,|\, b\rangle \xrightarrow{\;\chi_n^R\;} \langle m \otimes a \,|\, b \otimes n^*\rangle \xrightarrow{\;\chi_m^L\;} \langle a \,|\, m^* \otimes (b \otimes n^*)\rangle$$

$$\downarrow \text{associativity} \qquad\qquad\qquad\qquad\qquad\qquad\qquad \downarrow \text{associativity} \qquad (19)$$

$$\langle m \otimes (a \otimes n) \,|\, b\rangle \xrightarrow{\;\chi_m^L\;} \langle a \otimes n \,|\, m^* \otimes b\rangle \xrightarrow{\;\chi_n^R\;} \langle a \,|\, (m^* \otimes b) \otimes n^*\rangle$$

for all objects a, m, n of the category $\mathscr{A}$ and all objects b of the category $\mathscr{B}$.

Every helical dialogue category $\mathscr{C}$ defines a helical dialogue chirality by taking $\mathscr{A} = \mathscr{C}$, $\mathscr{B} = \mathscr{C}^{op(0,1)}$, $La = a \multimap \bot$ and $Rb = \bot \circ\!\!- b$. The right currification combinator χ^R is simply defined using the dialogue structure of the category $\mathscr{C}$:

$$\langle a \otimes m \,|\, b\rangle \qquad\qquad\qquad\qquad\qquad\qquad \langle a \,|\, b \otimes m^*\rangle$$
$$\|\qquad\qquad\qquad\qquad\qquad\qquad\qquad\qquad\qquad\qquad \|$$
$$\mathscr{C}(a \otimes m, \bot \circ\!\!- b) \xrightarrow{\;\psi_{a \otimes m, b}^{-1}\;} \mathscr{C}(a \otimes m \otimes b, \bot) \xrightarrow{\;\psi_{a, m \otimes b}\;} \mathscr{C}(a, \bot \circ\!\!- (m \otimes b))$$

whereas the definition of the left currification combinator χ^L is more sophisticated and requires the helical structure:

$$\langle m \otimes a \,|\, b\rangle \qquad\qquad\qquad\qquad\qquad\qquad \langle a \,|\, m^* \otimes b\rangle$$
$$\|\qquad\qquad\qquad\qquad\qquad\qquad\qquad\qquad\qquad\qquad \|$$
$$\mathscr{C}(m \otimes a, \bot \circ\!\!- b) \xrightarrow{\;\psi_{m \otimes a, b}^{-1}\;} \mathscr{C}(m \otimes a \otimes b, \bot) \xrightarrow{\;wheel_{m, a \otimes b}\;} \mathscr{C}(a \otimes b \otimes m, \bot) \xrightarrow{\;\psi_{m \otimes b, a}\;} \mathscr{C}(a, \bot \circ\!\!- (b \otimes m))$$

7 Categorical Bimodules

In order to understand the connection between *-autonomous categories and Frobenius algebras noticed by Day and Street — and then to extend it to dialogue categories — one needs to work in a suitable bicategory of categorical bimodules or distributors (following Bénabou's original terminology). Given two categories $\mathscr{A}$ and $\mathscr{B}$, an $\mathscr{A}\mathscr{B}$-bimodule M is defined as a functor

$$M \quad : \quad \mathscr{A}^{op} \times \mathscr{B} \quad \longrightarrow \quad Set.$$

The notion of bimodule considered here is set-theoretic, but it may be easily adapted to enriched settings, where the category Set is typically replaced by the category $Vect$ of vector spaces, see [20] for details. The bicategory (or weak 2-category) of bimodules has

- small categories as objects,
- $\mathscr{A}\mathscr{B}$-bimodules M as 1-dimensional cells $M : \mathscr{A} \to \mathscr{B}$,
- natural transformations

$$\theta \quad : \quad N \Rightarrow M \quad : \quad \mathscr{A}^{op} \times \mathscr{B} \longrightarrow Set$$

as 2-dimensional cells

$$\theta \quad : \quad M \Rightarrow N \quad : \quad \mathscr{A} \longrightarrow \mathscr{B}$$

in the weak 2-category.

Note the reverse direction of the natural transformations. This specific orientation enables to define a monoidal 2-functor:

$$Cat \quad \to \quad BiMod$$

which transports every functor $F : \mathscr{A} \to \mathscr{B}$ to the bimodule

$$F_{\bullet} \quad : \quad (a,b) \quad \mapsto \quad \mathscr{A}(Fa,b) \quad : \quad \mathscr{A}^{op} \times \mathscr{B} \quad \longrightarrow \quad Set.$$

It is possible to see **BiMod** as a 2-dimensional Kleisli construction on the small limit completion $\mathscr{C} \mapsto [\mathscr{C}, Set]^{op}$ of categories. One recovers the more familiar convention corresponding to the small colimit completion $\mathscr{C} \mapsto [\mathscr{C}^{op}, Set]$ of categories by taking the weak 2-category $\textbf{BiMod}^{op(1,2)}$ obtained from **BiMod** by reversing the orientation of the 1- and 2-dimensional cells. As a matter of fact, there also exists a monoidal 2-functor

$$Cat \quad \to \quad BiMod^{op(1,2)}$$

defined in the following way. First of all, it is good to remember that the operation $op :$ $\mathscr{C} \mapsto \mathscr{C}^{op}$ which transforms a category into its opposite category defines a 2-functor

$$op \quad : \quad Cat \quad \longrightarrow \quad Cat^{op(2)}.$$

The weak 2-category **BiMod** is symmetric monoidal with tensor product defined as product of categories. The underlying monoidal category is also autonomous, which simply means that it is a ribbon category with a trivial twist θ. From this follows that there exists a functor (and in fact a monoidal 2-functor)

$$\dagger \quad : \quad BiMod \quad \longrightarrow \quad BiMod^{op(0,1)}$$

which transports every category $\mathscr{A}$ to its dual $\mathscr{A}^{\dagger}$ in **BiMod**. By a miracle of mathematics, this dual $\mathscr{A}^{\dagger}$ happens to coincide with the opposite category $\mathscr{A}^{op}$. Putting all this together, one obtains the monoidal 2-functor

$$Cat \quad \xrightarrow{op} \quad Cat^{op(2)} \quad \longrightarrow \quad BiMod^{op(2)} \quad \xrightarrow{\dagger} \quad BiMod^{op(0,1,2)}$$

which transports every category $\mathscr{A}$ to itself and every functor $F : \mathscr{A} \to \mathscr{B}$ to the bimodule

$$F^{\bullet} \quad : \quad (a,b) \quad \mapsto \quad \mathscr{A}(a,Fb) \quad : \quad \mathscr{A}^{op} \times \mathscr{B} \quad \longrightarrow \quad Set.$$

Another miracle of categorical bimodules is that for every functor $F : \mathscr{A} \to \mathscr{B}$, the bimodule $F^{\bullet} : \mathscr{B} \to \mathscr{A}$ is left adjoint to the bimodule $F_{\bullet} : \mathscr{A} \to \mathscr{B}$ in the weak 2-category **BiMod**.

8   Frobenius Pseudomonoids

Here, we introduce the notion of Frobenius pseudomonoid whose main purpose is to reflect the properties of a dialogue category $\mathscr{A}$ transported from **Cat** to the monoidal bicategory **BiMod**. A preliminary step in the definition of Frobenius pseudomonoid is to adapt the notion of exact pairing to the 2-categorical setting.

Definition 8 (Lax Pairing). *A lax pairing $\mathscr{A} \dashv \mathscr{B}$ in a monoidal bicategory is a pair of 1-dimensional cells*

$$\eta_{[1]} : \mathscr{A} \otimes \mathscr{B} \longrightarrow I \qquad\qquad \varepsilon_{[1]} : I \longrightarrow \mathscr{B} \otimes \mathscr{A}$$

together with a pair of 2-dimensional cells

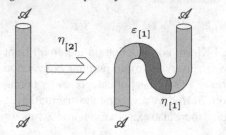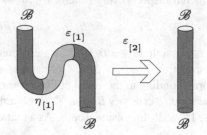

such that the composite 2-dimensional cell

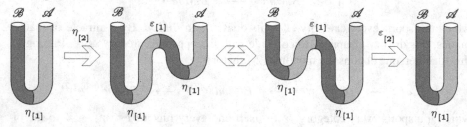

coincides with the identity on the 1-dimensional cell $\varepsilon_{[1]}$ and symmetrically, such that the composite 2-dimensional cell

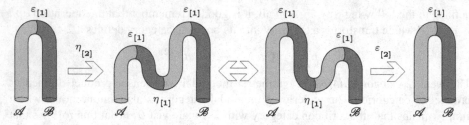

coincides with the identity on the 1-dimensional cell $\eta_{[1]}$.

At this stage, we are ready to refine the notion of *form* also introduced by Day and Street [6] in a monoidal bicategory.

Definition 9 (Frobenius Form). *A Frobenius form on a pseudomonoid $\mathscr{A}$ in a monoidal bicategory is a lax pairing $\mathscr{A} \dashv \mathscr{A}$ equipped with a 2-dimensional cell*

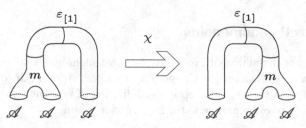

called the associativity law *of the Frobenius form, and required to make the following variation of MacLane's pentagonal diagram commute:*

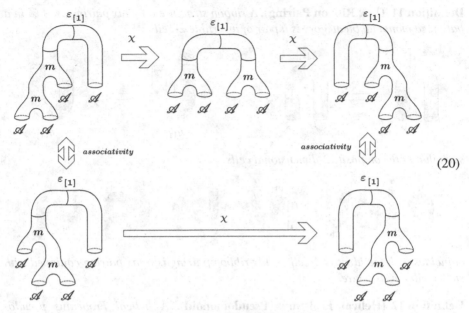

(20)

This leads us to our definition of Frobenius pseudomonoid. Note that our definition departs from the definition given by Street in [19], see the end of §9 for a comparison.

Definition 10 (Frobenius Pseudomonoid).

A Frobenius pseudomonoid is a pseudomonoid $\mathscr{A}$ equipped with a Frobenius form.

Observe that once transported in the bicategory **BiMod**, every dialogue category $\mathscr{A}$ defines such a Frobenius pseudomonoid with Frobenius form defined as

$$\varepsilon_{[1]} \; : \; (a_1, a_2) \mapsto \mathscr{A}(a_1 \otimes a_2, \bot) \qquad \eta_{[1]} \; : \; (a_1, a_2) \mapsto \mathscr{A}(\bot \multimap a_1, a_2)$$

and χ simply defined as the associativity law of the monoidal category $\mathscr{A}$. On the other hand, note that the notion of *Frobenius pseudomonoid* introduced above does not coincide with the notion of *Frobenius monoid* in the particular case when the underlying monoidal 2-category $\mathscr{W}$ is a monoidal category — seen as a 2-category with trivial 2-dimensional cells. The point is that nothing ensures in Definition 10 that the two comonoid structures on $\mathscr{A}$ induced from the exact pairing $\mathscr{A} \dashv \mathscr{A}$ coincide, although we require this property in our definition of Frobenius monoid. Depending on the taste of the reader, this unpleasant situation may be seen as a result of the maximalist nature of Definition 1 or as a result of the minimalist nature of Definition 10. This justifies in any case to resolve the matter by formulating a 2-categorical version of helicality. To that purpose, we need to work in a balanced monoidal bicategory, defined as a monoidal bicategory $\mathscr{W}$ equipped with a braiding and a twist compatible with the 2-dimensional structure.

Definition 11 (Lax Ribbon Pairing). *A ribbon structure on a lax pairing $\mathscr{A} \dashv \mathscr{B}$ in a balanced monoidal bicategory is a pair of invertible 2-cells:*

such that both composite 2-dimensional cells

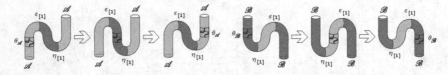

coincides with the identity 2-cell[7] A lax ribbon pairing is a lax pairing equipped with such a ribbon structure.

Definition 12 (Helical Frobenius Pseudomonoid). *A helical Frobenius pseudo-monoid in a balanced monoidal bicategory is a Frobenius pseudomonoid whose lax pairing is equipped with a ribbon structure, and which is moreover equipped with an invertible 2-dimensional cell*

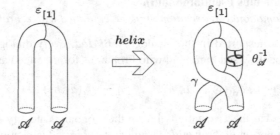

The 2-dimensional cell helix may be understood as a 2-dimensional cell $\{\!| a_2, a_1 |\!\} \Rightarrow \{\!| a_1, a_2 |\!\}$. The helical structure is required to make the diagram commute:

$$\{\!| a_1 \bullet a_2, a_3 |\!\} \xrightarrow{\;\chi\;} \{\!| a_1, a_2 \bullet a_3 |\!\} \xrightarrow{\;helix\;} \{\!| a_2 \bullet a_3, a_1 |\!\}$$

$$\Big\downarrow {\scriptstyle helix} \qquad\qquad\qquad\qquad\qquad\qquad\qquad \Big\downarrow {\scriptstyle \chi} \qquad\qquad (21)$$

$$\{\!| a_3, a_1 \bullet a_2 |\!\} \xleftarrow{\;\chi\;} \{\!| a_3 \bullet a_1, a_2 |\!\} \xleftarrow{\;helix\;} \{\!| a_2, a_3 \bullet a_1 |\!\}$$

---

[7] The composite 2-cell is required to coincide with the 2-dimensional coercion of θ when one defines the twist of a balanced monoidal bicategory as a pseudonatural (rather than natural) transformation, which we do not do here.

Every helical dialogue category $\mathscr{A}$ induces a helical Frobenius pseudomonoid in **BiMod** with *helix* simply defined as the natural transformation

$$wheel^{-1}_{a_1,a_2} \quad : \quad \mathscr{A}(a_2 \otimes a_1, \bot) \quad \Rightarrow \quad \mathscr{A}(a_1 \otimes a_2, \bot).$$

which goes in the reverse direction in the bicategory *BiMod*. We will see in the next section that a helical dialogue category is the same thing as a helical Frobenius pseudomonoid in **BiMod** whose bimodules $\varepsilon_{[1]}$ and $\eta_{[1]}$ are represented by functors L and R in the appropriate sense. We could establish the statement directly, but we find clarifying to reformulate first the notion of helical Frobenius pseudomonoid in a two-sided fashion. This is precisely the way the correspondence between helical dialogue categories and helical Frobenius pseumonoids originally emerged in our work.

9   Frobenius Amphimonoids

Here, we reformulate in a two-sided fashion the notion of lax helical Frobenius monoid... in just the same way as we did in §2 for Frobenius monoids. To that purpose, we start by relaxing the notion of *monoid-comonoid pairing* between a monoid and a comonoid, and introduce the corresponding 2-dimensional notion of *amphimonoid*.

Definition 13 (Biexact Pairing). *A biexact pairing $\mathscr{A} \dashv \mathscr{B}$ is a lax pairing whose 2-dimensional cells $\eta_{[2]}$ and $\varepsilon_{[2]}$ are reversible. A biexact ribbon pairing is a biexact pairing equipped with a ribbon structure.*

Definition 14 (Amphimonoid). *An amphimonoid $(\mathscr{A}, \mathscr{B})$ in a balanced monoidal bicategory $\mathscr{W}$ is defined as a pseudomonoid $(\mathscr{A}, \oslash, true)$ and a pseudocomonoid $(\mathscr{B}, \oslash, false)$ equipped with a biexact ribbon pairing $\mathscr{A} \dashv \mathscr{B}$ (noted $*$ in the picture) and with a pair of invertible 2-dimensional cells*

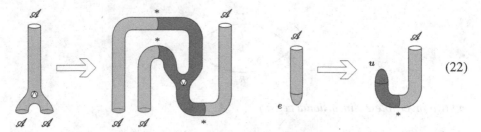

defining a pseudomonoid equivalence between $(\mathscr{A}, \oslash, true)$ and the pseudomonoid structure on $\mathscr{B}$ deduced from the biexact pairing.

An important point about the definition is that every amphimonoid induces a biexact ribbon pairing $\mathscr{B} \dashv \mathscr{A}$ defined as follows:

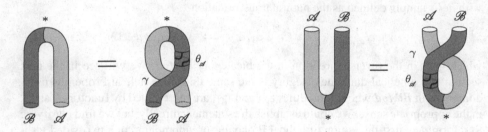

together with a pair of invertible 2-dimensional cells

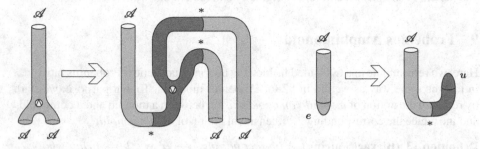

defining a pseudomonoid equivalence between $(\mathscr{A}, \oslash, true)$ and the pseudomonoid structure on $\mathscr{B}$ deduced from the biexact pairing applied in the opposite direction. We are ready now to introduce our two-sided notion of Frobenius pseudomonoid:

Definition 15 (Frobenius Amphimonoid). *A Frobenius amphimonoid* $(\mathscr{A}, \mathscr{B}, L, R)$ *consists of an amphimonoid* $(\mathscr{A}, \mathscr{B})$ *equipped with an adjunction*

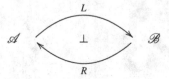

and two invertible 2-dimensional cells:

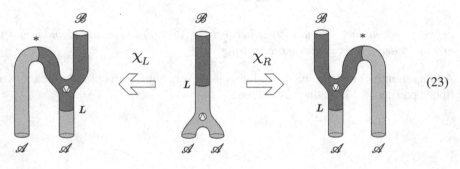

(23)

The 1-dimensional cell $L : \mathscr{A} \to \mathscr{B}$ may be understood as defining a bracket $\langle a|b \rangle$ between the objects $\mathscr{A}$ and $\mathscr{B}$ of the bicategory $\mathscr{V}$. Each side of Equation (23) may be thus seen as implementing a currification *step:*

$$\chi_L : \langle a_1 \otimes a_2 | b \rangle \Rightarrow \langle a_2 | a_1^* \otimes b \rangle \qquad\qquad \chi_R : \langle a_1 \otimes a_2 | b \rangle \Rightarrow \langle a_1 | b \otimes a_2^* \rangle$$

In the definition of a Frobenius amphimonoid, we require that the two combinators χ_L and χ_R make the three coherence diagrams of Equations (17), (18) and (19) commute. We leave the reader depict each coherence diagram as the relevant string diagram.

Every helical dialogue category defines a Frobenius amphimonoid in **BiMod**, by taking $La = a \multimap \bot$ and $Rb = \bot \multimapinv b$.

Proposition 5. *Given an amphimonoid $(\mathscr{A}, \mathscr{B})$ in a balanced monoidal bicategory $\mathscr{W}$, there is a back-and-forth translation between the two following data:*

- *the helical Frobenius structures on the pseudomonoid $(\mathscr{A}, \oslash, true)$,*
- *the Frobenius structures (L, R, χ_L, χ_R) on the amphimonoid $(\mathscr{A}, \mathscr{B})$.*

Proof. The correspondence between the two Frobenius structures works as follows. Given an amphimonoid $(\mathscr{A}, \mathscr{B})$ whose $\mathscr{A}$-side is a Frobenius pseudomonoid $(\mathscr{A}, \oslash, true)$ with Frobenius form noted $\{|-,-|\}$, one defines the 1-dimensional cells L and R of the Frobenius amphimonoid $(\mathscr{A}, \mathscr{B})$ in the following way:

$$(24)$$

The definition of a lax pairing ensures that $L \dashv R$ defines an adjunction in the bicategory $\mathscr{W}$. The 2-dimensional cell χ_R is defined as

$$\{|a_1 \otimes m, a_2|\} \xrightarrow{\ \chi\ } \{|a_1, m \otimes a_2|\}$$

while the 2-dimensional cell χ_L is defined as the composite

$$\{|m \otimes a_1, a_2|\} \xrightarrow{\ helix\ } \{|a_2, m \otimes a_1|\} \xrightarrow{\ \chi^{-1}\ } \{|a_2 \otimes m, a_1|\} \xrightarrow{\ helix^{-1}\ } \{|a_1, a_2 \otimes m|\}$$

each of them appropriately composed with the coercion (22) and the 2-dimensional structure of the biexact pairing $\mathscr{A} \dashv \mathscr{B}$ in order to obtain the expected currification diagrams (23). A careful check establishes that the two combinators χ_L and χ_R just constructed make the three coherence diagrams of Equations (17), (18) and (19) commute. This establishes that $(\mathscr{A}, \mathscr{B})$ together with the adjunction $L \dashv R$ defines a Frobenius amphimonoid in the balanced monoidal bicategory $\mathscr{W}$.

Conversely, given a Frobenius amphimonoid $(\mathscr{A}, \mathscr{B}, L, R)$ in a balanced monoidal bicategory $\mathscr{W}$, one defines a Frobenius form on the pseudomonoid $\mathscr{A}$ in the following way:

The associativity law χ of the Frobenius form is defined using χ_R together with the coercion (22) and the 2-dimensional structure of the biexact pairing $\mathscr{A} \dashv \mathscr{B}$. One obtains in this way a Frobenius pseudomonoid $(\mathscr{A}, \oslash, true)$ whose helical structure is then defined using the currification combinators χ_L and χ_R:

One needs then to check carefully that the helical structure makes the coherence diagram (21) does indeed commute. This establishes that $(\mathscr{A}, \oslash, true)$ equipped with the structure above defines a helical Frobenius pseudomonoid. This concludes the proof.

We like to think of the two-sided notion of Frobenius amphimonoid as *logical* since it is based on the currification combinators χ_L and χ_R whereas the original one-sided formulation of helical Frobenius pseudomonoid would be rather *algebraic* or *topological*. Although the correspondence exhibited in Proposition 5 does not define a one-to-one relationship, it conveys the idea that the notions of helical Frobenius pseudomonoid and of Frobenius amphimonoid should be considered as morally equivalent. This statement is informal but it could be made rigorous by constructing a 2-dimensional equivalence between bicategories corresponding to each notions, in the same way as was done for dialogue categories and chiralities, see [15] for details.

At this point, we are ready to apply Proposition 5 to the specific monoidal bicategory *BiMod*. Every category $\mathscr{A}$ comes equipped with a biexact pairing $\mathscr{A} \dashv \mathscr{A}^{op}$ whose unit and counit are defined as the bimodule:

$$\text{hom} \quad : \quad (a_1, a_2) \mapsto \mathscr{A}(a_1, a_2) \quad : \quad \mathscr{A}^{op} \times \mathscr{A} \longrightarrow Set$$

This leads us to the two main results of the paper:

Theorem (First Correspondence Theorem). *A helical chirality is the same thing as a Frobenius amphimonoid in the bicategory* **BiMod** *whose 1-dimensional cells*

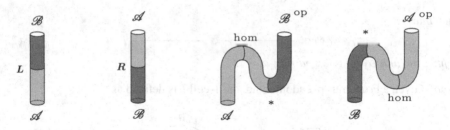

are representable, that is, images of functors along the 2-dimensional functor $(-)_\bullet$: *Cat → BiMod.*

The proof is based on a direct comparison between the definition of helical chirality (Definition 7) and the definition of Frobenius amphimonoid (Definition 15). The second main result of the paper follows then from this result and Proposition 5.

Theorem (Second Correspondence Theorem). *A helical dialogue category is the same thing as a helical Frobenius pseudomonoid in the bicategory* **BiMod** *whose 1-dimensional cells*

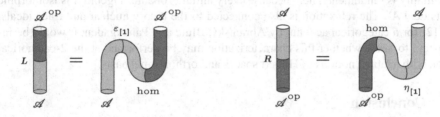

are representable, that is, images of functors along the 2-dimensional functor $(-)_\bullet$: *Cat → BiMod.*

10 Epilogue: A Comparison with Day and Street

One may recover here the correspondence between ∗-autonomous categories and Frobenius pseudomonoids drawn by Day and Street in [6,19].

Definition 16 (∗-autonomous Pseudomonoid). *A* ∗-*autonomous pseudomonoid is a Frobenius pseudomonoid whose Frobenius form is based on a biexact pairing* $\mathscr{A} \dashv \mathscr{A}$.

The definition coincides with the original definition of ∗-autonomous pseudomonoid given by Street in [19] except that we add the requirement that the coherence diagram (20) commutes. In particular, we may establish the following property, which adapts to our notion of Frobenius pseudomonoid the Proposition 3.2 stated by Ross Street in [19] for ∗-autonomous pseudomonoids.

Proposition 6. *A pseudomonoid* $(\mathscr{A}, m, e)$ *is Frobenius if and only if it is equipped with a 1-dimensional cell*

$$\ell \;:\; \mathscr{A} \;\longrightarrow\; I$$

such that

$$\mathscr{A} \otimes \mathscr{A} \xrightarrow{\quad m \quad} \mathscr{A} \xrightarrow{\quad \ell \quad} I \tag{25}$$

defines the unit $\varepsilon_{[1]}$ *of a lax pairing* $\mathscr{A} \dashv \mathscr{A}$.

Proof. Given a Frobenius pseudomonoid, the 1-cell ℓ is defined as

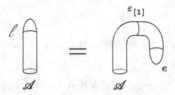

Conversely, given a pseudomonoid equipped with such a 1-dimensional cell ℓ, one defines the Frobenius form as in Equation (25) with coercion $\chi : \{\!| a_1 \bullet a_2, a_3 |\!\} \longrightarrow \{\!| a_1, a_2 \bullet a_3 |\!\}$ induced from the associativity law of the binary product m. Note that Abramsky and Heunen recently characterized the orthonormal basis on a Hilbert space A as a possibly nonunital Frobenius algebra structure on the space A, see [3] for details. The relaxation of unitality is fundamental here because every unital Frobenius algebra A is isomorphic to its dual A^*. The relaxation is also connected to the theory nuclear and trace ideals, see [2] for a categorical account by Abramsky, Blute and Panangaden. It would be interesting to know whether this characterization may be performed at the 2-categorical level, with adapted notions of Hilbert spaces and orthonormal basis.

11 Conclusion

The mathematical style of the paper should not distract the reader from the main idea conveyed here, which is that the primitive mechanisms of reasoning are of a purely topological nature — with encouraging and somewhat surprising affinities to cobordism.

This geometric conception of logic is likely to appear awkward and even disturbing to the unprepared reader. The reason is that we logicians (and non-logicians) are traditionally reluctant to think of language as a *material phenomenon* embedded in space and time. Even worse, we have learned along the years to treat reasoning as a purely desincarnated and formal activity living in the ether of symbolic logic. However, this formalist inclination of the field is probably temporary... and we like to think that the destiny of logic is to become a « geometry of mind » in the same way as physics has become a « geometry of nature ». The purpose of this geometry will not be to explain the « mind » as a whole — the idea would be ridiculous — but rather to shed light on some of its most elementary and fundamental mechanisms, in the same way as physics does with « nature ». And then to investigate in a reflexive (and somewhat ethnographic) turn how these micrological mechanisms interact with the macrological (or foundational) program originally attributed to logic at the beginning of the 20th century.

The dream of « geometrizing logic » is far from accomplished today, but the novelty is that it does not seem entirely inaccessible anymore. In particular, the recent advances of contemporary mathematics — at the crossroad of algebra, topology and physics — provide us with a series of very nice conceptual tools for trying the adventure. By analogy with physics, a tentative starting point in the exploration of this evanescent « geometry of logic » is offered by the study of the configuration space of n logical players (or computer programs) conversing in time on a specific formula. The present paper is a very preliminary attempt to substantiate these geometric intuitions in the specific case $n = 2$ where one benefits from the perfect adequation between tensorial logic and dialogue games.

For lack of space, we have only scratched the surface of the connection between tensorial logic and 2-dimensional cobordism. In particular, we did not include any description of the interplay between the topological flow of negation defining the proofs of tensorial logic (and thus the innocent strategies in dialogue games, see [14] for details) and the lax 2-dimensional cobordism describing the formulas of the logic (and thus the dialogue games themselves). An interesting issue for the connection between logic and physics is probably to understand whether the lax and two-sided account of cobordism developed here in dimension 2 still makes sense in higher dimensions, and whether it is supported by any appropriate physical (or at least geometric) intuition.

References

1. Abramsky, S., Honda, K., McCusker, G.: A fully abstract game semantics for general references. In: Proceedings of the Thirteenth Annual IEEE Symposium on Logic in Computer Science. IEEE Computer Society Press (1998)
2. Abramsky, S., Blute, R., Panangaden, P.: Nuclear and trace ideals in tensored *-categories. Journal of Pure and Applied Algebra 143, 3–47 (1999)
3. Abramsky, S., Heunen, C.: H^*-algebras and nonunital Frobenius algebras. Clifford Lectures, AMS Proceedings of Symposia in Applied Mathematics (2010) (to appear)
4. Barr, M.: *-autonomous categories. Lectures Notes in Mathematics, vol. 752. Springer (1979)
5. Curtis, C., Reiner, I.: Representation Theory of Finite Groups and Associative Algebras. Pure and Applied Mathematics, vol. XI. Interscience Publishers, New York-London (1962)
6. Day, B., Street, R.: Quantum categories, star autonomy, and quantum groupoids. In: Galois Theory, Hopf Algebras, and Semiabelian Categories. Fields Institute Communications, vol. 43, pp. 193–231. American Math. Soc. (2004)
7. Egger, J.: The Frobenius relations meet linear distributivity. Theory and Applications of Categories 24(2), 25–38 (2010)
8. Girard, J.-Y.: Linear logic. Theoretical Computer Science, 50–102 (1987)
9. Honda, K., Tokoro, M.: An Object Calculus for Asynchronous Communication. In: America, P. (ed.) ECOOP 1991. LNCS, vol. 512, pp. 133–147. Springer, Heidelberg (1991)
10. Honda, K., Yoshida, N.: Game Theoretic Analysis of Call-by-Value Computation. In: Degano, P., Gorrieri, R., Marchetti-Spaccamela, A. (eds.) ICALP 1997. LNCS, vol. 1256, pp. 225–236. Springer, Heidelberg (1997)
11. Joyal, A., Street, R.: An introduction to Tannaka duality and quantum groups. In: Carboni, A., Pedicchio, M.C., Rosolini, G. (eds.) Proceedings of the Category Theory, Como 1990. Lecture Notes in Math., vol. 1488. Springer, Heidelberg (1991)
12. Joyal, A., Street, R.: Braided tensor categories. Adv. Math. 102, 20–78 (1993)

13. Kassel, C.: Quantum Groups. Graduate Texts in Mathematics, vol. 155. Springer (1995)
14. Melliès, P.-A.: Game semantics in string diagrams. In: Proceedings of the Annual ACM/IEEE Symposium on Logic in Computer Science (2012)
15. Melliès, P.-A.: Dialogue categories and chiralities (submitted, manuscript available on the author's web page)
16. Melliès, P.-A.: A micrological study of helix negation (submitted, manuscript available on the author's web page)
17. Melliès, P.-A.: Braided notions of dialogue categories (submitted, manuscript available on the author's web page)
18. Shum, M.C.: Tortile tensor categories. Journal of Pure and Applied Algebra 93, 57–110 (1994)
19. Street, R.: Frobenius monads and pseudomonoids. J. Math. Phys. 45, 3930 (2004)
20. Street, R.: Quantum Groups: A Path to Current Algebra. Australian Mathematical Society Lecture Series. Cambridge University Press (2007)
21. Wehr, M.: Higher Dimensional Syntax. In: The Proceedings of the Category Theory in Computer Science (CTCS) Conference (1999)

Anatomy of a Domain
of Continuous Random Variables II

Michael Mislove

Department of Computer Science
Tulane University
New Orleans, LA 70118
mislove@tulane.edu

Abstract. In this paper we conclude a two-part analysis of recent work of Jean Goubault-Larrecq and Daniele Varacca, who devised a model of continuous random variables over bounded complete domains. Their presentation leaves out many details, and also misses some motivations for their construction. In this and a related paper we attempt to fill in some of these details, and in the process, we discover a flaw in the model they built.

Our earlier paper showed how to construct $\Theta\mathsf{Prob}(A^\infty)$, the bounded complete algebraic domain of *thin probability measures* over A^∞, the monoid of finite and infinite words over a finite alphabet A. In this second paper, we apply our earlier results to construct $\Theta RV_{A^\infty}(D)$, the bounded complete domain of continuous random variables defined on supports of thin probability measures on A^∞ with values in a bounded complete domain D, and we show $D \mapsto \Theta RV_{A^\infty}(D)$ is the object map of a monad. In the case $A = \{0, 1\}$, our construction yields the domain of continuous random variables over bounded complete domains devised by Goubault-Larrecq and Varacca. However, we also show that the Kleisli extension $h^\dagger \colon \Theta RV_{A^\infty}(D) \to \Theta RV(E)$ of a Scott-continuous map $h \colon D \to E$ is not Scott continuous, so the construction does not yield a monad on BCD, the category of bounded complete domains and Scott-continuous maps. We leave the question of whether the construction can be rescued as an open problem.

Keywords: Random variable, bounded complete domain, Cartesian closed category.

1 Introduction

Domain theory is fundamental for building computational models. Its use dates to Dana Scott's first models of the untyped lambda calculus, and the applications of domains have now spread well beyond the early focus on programming semantics. One of the seminal advances of the work in semantics was Abramsky's use of Stone Duality [1] to tailor a logic to fit precisely any domain constructed using basic components and adhering to Moggi's monadic approach to building models [21].

B. Coecke, L. Ong, and P. Panangaden (Eds.): Abramsky Festschrift, LNCS 7860, pp. 225–245, 2013.

While there is a broad range of computational effects that fall under this approach, one monad that has caused continuing problems is the *probabilistic power domain*. First explored by Saheb-Djarhomi [23], the Borel probability measures on an underlying domain can be ordered pointwise as valuation maps from the Scott-open sets to the reals. This forms the object level of a free construction over the category DCPO of directed complete partial orders, but it suffers from two flaws: (i) The probabilistic power domain does not satisfy a distributive law with respect to any of the three nondeterminism monads over domains, so Beck's Theorem [3] implies the composition of the probabilistic power domain and any of the nondeterminism domains is not a monad. Second, there there is no Cartesian closed category of domains – dcpos that satisfy the usual approximation assumption – that is known to be invariant under this construct. The best that is known is that the category of *coherent domains* is invariant under the probabilistic choice monad [15], but this category is not Cartesian closed.

To address the first flaw, Varacca and Winskel [25,26] explored weakening the laws of probabilistic choice, and discovered three monads for probabilistic choice based on weakened laws: (i) $p \leq p +_r p$; (ii) $p \geq p +_r p$; and finally (iii) no relation assumed between p and $p +_r p$ (where $p +_r q$ denotes choosing p with probability r and choosing q with probability $1 - r$, for $0 \leq r \leq 1$). They called these constructions *indexed valuation monads*, and each of them enjoys a distributive law with respect to the monads for nondeterminism.

This author took this work a bit further, showing in [18] that one could use one of the indexed valuation models to define a monad of finite random variables over either the domain RB or the domain FS, the latter of which is a maximal CCC of domains, and both of which are closed under all three nondeterminism monads. More recently, Goubault-Larrecq and Varacca attempted to extend this line of work to show that there is a monad of *continuous* random variables over the CCC of bounded complete domains [10]. The category BCD of *bounded complete domains* is more general than Scott domains, the objects used by Dana Scott in devising the first model of the untyped lambda calculus [24]. While BCD is a CCC, it is not closed under the convex power domain monad, and it is not a maximal CCC. The work of Goubault-Larrecq and Varacca inspired the work in this paper and in the earlier one on this subject [20].

1.1   The Model of Goubault-Larrecq and Varacca

The model of continuous random variables devised by Goubault-Larrecq and Varacca [10] restricts probability measures to one particular domain $\mathcal{C}$, which we call the *Cantor fan*, and models probabilistic choice on an arbitrary domain D as the family of (Scott) continuous maps $f \colon \operatorname{supp} \mu \to D$, where $\mu \in \operatorname{Prob}(\mathcal{C})$. To start, the Cantor fan is the ideal completion $\mathcal{C}$ of the rooted full binary tree, where the latter admits the partial order in which the root is the least element, and node m is below node n iff the path from the root to n passes through m. This makes $\mathcal{C}$ a Scott domain whose space of maximal elements is homeomorphic to the middle-third Cantor subset of the unit interval. In addition to its usual convex structure, the domain $\operatorname{Prob}(\mathcal{C})$ of probability measures over $\mathcal{C}$ admits a binary probabilistic choice operator in the spirit of Varacca's *Hoare indexed valuations*, so that $p \leq p +_r p$ holds for each $p \in C$. The definition of $+_r$ relies on the concatenation operator on C, regarding C as the family of finite and infinite words over $\{0, 1\}$. Since concatenation $\cdot : C \times C \to C$ is not monotone, let alone Scott continuous, Goubault-Larrecq and Varacca restrict their model to contain only those measures $\mu \in \mathsf{Prob}(C)$ whose support (in the Lawson topology) is an antichain, since such measures have the property that concatenation defines a Scott continuous operation on the sets on which they are concentrated. So the model is the family

$$\Theta RV(D) = \{(\mu, f) \in \mathsf{Prob}(C) \times [\text{supp}\,\mu \to D] \mid \text{supp}\,\mu \text{ is an antichain}\}.$$

(Here Θ stands for "thin", a term adopted by Goubault-Larrecq and Varacca.) They claim that $\Theta RV(D)$ forms a monad over BCD; the monad laws are displayed explicitly in [10], but the definition of the lift of a Scott-continuous map $\phi \colon D \to RV(E)$ to $\phi^\# \colon RV(D) \to RV(E)$ leaves a lot to the reader to unravel. In fact, we have identified a flaw in that claim that can be traced to the concatenation operator.

1.2 Our Contribution

In this and a preceding paper [20], we clarify the construction devised by Goubault-Larrecq and Varacca. We use an example from probabilistic automata to motivate the order used by Goubault-Larrecq and Varacca. The paper [20] is devoted to understanding the construction of the thin measures over C; this requires a completely different presentation from the one given in [10]. Goubault-Larrecq and Varacca impose the restriction that the only simple measures – affine combinations of finitely many point masses – in $\Theta RV(D)$ are those supported on antichains, and then define $\Theta RV(D)$ to be the least subset of $\mathsf{Prob}(C) \times [\text{supp}\,\mu \to D]$ containing these measures in the first component, and closed under directed suprema; in effect, they are giving a basis for the allowable measures, and capturing the rest by taking directed suprema. The alternative approach in [20] shows their definition is the same thing as defining thin measures in the model to be those that are supported on Lawson-closed antichains, using Stone duality to prove this result. Our results allow one to account for all measures in the model as having the form $\pi_A(\mu)$ where $A \subseteq C$ is a Lawson-closed subset and μ is a probability measure that is supported on a Lawson-closed subset of $\text{Max}(C)$, the Cantor set of maximal elements of C. We completed this analysis by showing the order arises naturally on probabilistic automata. Our results in this paper and in [20] also are broader than those of [10], since they hold for A^∞ for an arbitrary finite alphabet A, whereas Goubault-Larrecq and Varacca restrict themselves to the case $A = \{0, 1\}$.

In this paper we complete our reconstruction and analysis of the continuous random variable model of Goubault-Larrecq and Varacca. Using the results from [20], we define the model of continuous random variables in a fashion similar to that in [10], but we present the complete structure, rather than having to appeal to a completion within a larger domain. This approach also allows us to examine the construction of constituents of the monad, and in particular, the Kleisli extension, in a more accessible way than is given in [10]. We verify that the monad laws hold, but we also show that the Kleisli extension of a Scott-continuous map is not Scott-continuous – in fact, it's not even monotone. This means that the construction yields a monad, but one that does not leave any category of domains and Scott-continuous maps invariant. We leave open the question whether this approach can be rescued to obtain a monad on BCD or any other category of domains.

1.3   The Plan of the Paper

In the next section, we review some background material from domain theory and the other areas we need. The latter includes a version of Stone duality, a result about the probability measure monad on the category of compact Hausdorff spaces and continuous maps, as well as some results from [20] on Lawson-closed antichains in A^∞ for a finite alphabet A. Section 3 summarizes the main results from [20], starting with the motivating example that informs the order we use to define our model of thin probability measures. The next section constitutes the main part of the paper, where we develop the family of continuous random variables over thin probability measures on A^∞, for any finite alphabet A. We show this family is a bounded complete domain. We also show our construct defines the object map of a monad, but, as commented above, the Kleisli extension of a Scott-continuous map is not Scott continuous, so it is unclear exactly what the right category for this monad is. Finally, we show that our results are the same as those of Goubault-Larrecq and Varacca in case $A = \{0, 1\}$, which implies the flaw we have detected applies equally to their construction. In Section 5 we summarize our results and pose some questions for future research.

2   Background

In this section we present the background material we need for our main results.

2.1   Domains

The basis for our results rely fundamentally on domain theory. Most of the results that we quote below can be found in [2] or [7]; we give specific references for those that are not found there.

To start, a *poset* is a partially ordered set. Antichains play a major role in our development: a subset $A \subseteq P$ of a poset is an *antichain* if any two distinct elements in A are incomparable in the order.

A poset is *directed complete* if each of its directed subsets has a least upper bound; here a subset S is *directed* if each finite subset of S has an upper bound in S. A directed complete partial order is called a *dcpo*. The relevant maps between dcpos are the monotone maps that also preserve suprema of directed sets; these maps are usually called *Scott continuous*.

These notions can be presented from a purely topological perspective: a subset $U \subseteq P$ of a poset is *Scott open* if (i) $U = {\uparrow}U \equiv \{x \in P \mid (\exists u \in U)\, u \leq x\}$ is an upper set, and (ii) if $\sup S \in U$ implies $S \cap U \neq \emptyset$ for each directed subset $S \subseteq P$. It is routine to show that the family of Scott-open sets forms a topology on any poset; this topology satisfies ${\downarrow}x \equiv \{y \in P \mid y \leq x\} = \overline{\{x\}}$ is the closure of a point, so the Scott topology is always T_0, but it is T_1 iff P is a flat poset. A mapping between dcpos is Scott continuous in the order-theoretic sense iff it is a monotone map that is continuous with respect to the Scott topologies on its domain and range. We let DCPO denote the category of dcpos and Scott-continuous maps; DCPO is a Cartesian closed category.

If P is a dcpo, and $x, y \in P$, then x *approximates* y iff for every directed set $S \subseteq P$, if $y \leq \sup S$, then there is some $s \in S$ with $x \leq s$. In this case, we write $x \ll y$ and we let ${\downarrow}y = \{x \in P \mid x \ll y\}$. A *basis* for a poset P is a family $B \subseteq P$ satisfying ${\downarrow}y \cap B$ is directed and $y = \sup({\downarrow}y \cap B)$ for each $y \in P$. A *continuous poset* is one that has a basis, and a dcpo P is a *domain* if P is a continuous dcpo. An element $k \in P$ is *compact* if $x \ll x$, and P is *algebraic* if $KP = \{k \in P \mid k \ll k\}$ forms a basis. Domains are sober spaces in the Scott topology.

We let DOM denote that category of domains and Scott continuous maps; this is a full subcategory of DCPO, but it is not Cartesian closed. Nevertheless, DOM has several Cartesian closed full subcategories. Two of particular interest to us are the full subcategory SDOM of Scott domains, and BCD its continuous analog. Precisely, a domain is *bounded complete* if every non-empty subset has a greatest lower bound. An equivalent statement to the last condition is that every subset with an upper bound has a least upper bound. Bounded complete domains generalize *Scott domains*, which are algebraic domains for which KP is countable and that also satisfy the property that every non-empty subset has a greatest lower bound. We let BCD denote the category of bounded complete domains and Scott-continuous maps.

Example 1. A prototypical example of a Scott domain is the free monoid $A^\infty = A^* \cup A^\omega$ of finite and infinite words over a finite alphabet A, where we use the prefix order on words: $s \leq t \in A^\infty$ iff $(\exists w \in A^\infty)\, sw = t$. Two words compare iff one is a prefix of the other, and the infimum of any set of words is their longest common prefix. As a domain, $KA^\infty = A^*$, which is countable since A is finite.

Note that this same reasoning applies to any *Scott-closed* subset of A^∞ – examples here are the language of a finite state automaton, where the "alphabet" is the product $S \times Act$ of the set of states and the set of actions.

Domains also have a Hausdorff refinement of the Scott topology which will play a role in our work. The *weak lower topology* on P has the sets of the form if $O = P \setminus {\uparrow}F$ as a basis, where $F \subset P$ is a finite subset. The *Lawson topology* on a domain P is the common refinement of the Scott- and weak lower topologies on P. This topology has the family

$$\{U \setminus \uparrow F \mid U \text{ Scott open } \& \ F \subseteq P \text{ finite}\}$$

as a basis. The Lawson topology on a domain is always Hausdorff.

A domain is *coherent* if its Lawson topology is compact. We denote the closure of a subset $X \subseteq P$ of a coherent domain in the Lawson topology by $\overline{X}^\Lambda$.

Example 2. Bounded complete domains are coherent. A basic example of a bounded complete domain is the unit interval; here $x \ll y$ iff $x = 0$ or $x < y$. The Scott topology on the $[0,1]$ has open sets $[0,1]$ together with $\uparrow x = (x,1]$ for $x \in (0,1]$. Since BCD has finite products, $[0,1]^n$ is a domain in the product order, where $x \ll y$ iff $x_i \ll y_i$ for each i; a basis of Scott-open sets is formed by the sets $\uparrow x$ for $x \in [0,1]^n$ (this last is true in any domain).

The Lawson topology on $[0,1]$ has basic open sets $(x,1] \setminus [y,1]$ for $x < y$ – i.e., sets of the form (x,y) for $x < y$, which is the usual topology. Then, the Lawson topology on $[0,1]^n$ is the product topology from the usual topology on $[0,1]$.

Since $[0,1]$ has a least element, the same results apply for any power of $[0,1]$, where $x \ll y$ in $[0,1]^J$ iff $x_j = 0$ for almost all $j \in J$, and $x_j \ll y_j$ for all $j \in J$. Thus, every power of $[0,1]$ is a bounded complete domain.

A more interesting example of a coherent domain is $\mathsf{Prob}(D)$, the family of probability measures on a coherent domain D, where $\mu \leq \nu$ iff $\mu(U) \leq \nu(U)$ for every Scott-open subset $U \subseteq D$. For example, $\mathsf{Prob}([0,1])$ is a coherent domain. In fact, the category COH of coherent domains and Scott continuous maps is closed under the application of the functor Prob [15].

While coherent domains having least elements are closed under arbitrary products, the category COH of coherent domains and Scott continuous maps is not Cartesian closed. There is an inclusion of the category of coherent domains and Lawson continuous monotone maps into the category of compact ordered spaces and continuous monotone maps that is obtained by equipping coherent domains with the Lawson topology. This is right adjoint to the functor that associates to a compact ordered space its family of closed order-convex subsets ordered by reverse inclusion, where $C \ll D$ iff $D \subseteq C^\circ$. In this case, the Lawson topology is the topology the family inherits from the Vietoris topology on the family of compact subsets of the underlying space.

Finally, we need some results related to power domains, the convex power domain in particular. Details for the following can be found in [19]. For a coherent domain D, the *convex power domain* consists of the family

$$\mathcal{P}_C(D) = \{X \subseteq D \mid X = \downarrow X \cap \uparrow X \text{ is Lawson closed}\}$$

under the *Egli-Milner order*:

$$X \leq Y \quad \text{iff} \quad X \subseteq \downarrow Y \ \& \ Y \subseteq \uparrow X.$$

$\mathcal{P}_C(D)$ is a coherent domain if D is one, where

$$X \ll Y \quad \text{iff} \quad Y \subseteq (\uparrow X)^\circ \ \& \ (\forall x \in X)(\exists y \in Y)\, x \ll y. \tag{1}$$

3   On Lawson-Compact Antichains and Thin Probability Measures over A^∞

3.1   Lawson-Compact Antichains in A^∞

The following results are from Section 2.2 of [20]. They present some results about Lawson-closed sets and Lawson-closed antichains in $AC(A^\infty)$ that we need in developing the model of continuous random variables over the next two sections.

Lemma 1. *If $X \subseteq A^\infty$ is a Lawson compact subset of a coherent domain, then $\downarrow X$ is a Scott-closed subset of A^∞. Moreover there is a canonical map $\pi_{\downarrow X} : A^\infty \to \downarrow X$ that is both Scott- and Lawson continuous.*

Corollary 1. *If $X \subseteq A^\infty$ is a Lawson-compact antichain, then there is a Lawson compact subset $Y \subseteq A^\omega$ (which is necessarily an antichain) for which $\pi_{\downarrow X}(Y) = X$.*

Proposition 1. *Let A be a finite alphabet. Then $X \subseteq A^\infty$ is Scott closed iff $Max\, X$ is Lawson closed and $X = \downarrow(Max\, X)$.*

Theorem 1. *Let A be a finite alphabet and consider the domain A^∞ in the prefix order. Let*

$$AC(A^\infty) = \{X \subseteq A^\infty \mid X = \overline{X}^\Lambda \text{ is an antichain}\}.$$

Then $AC(A^\infty)$ is a Scott domain that is a subdomain of $\mathcal{P}_C(A^\infty)$. In particular,

1. *If $X, Y \in AC(A^\infty)$, then $X \leq Y$ iff $\pi_{\downarrow X}(Y) = X$.*
2. *the supremum of two antichains $X, Y \in AC(A^\infty)$ with an upper bound is given by $X \vee Y = Max(X \cup Y)$, the set of maximal elements of their union.*

Proof. The proof that $AC(A^\infty)$ is a sub-dcpo of $\mathcal{P}_C(A^\infty)$ and that $X \vee Y = Max(X \cup Y)$ is contained in [20], so only the proof of 1) above is lacking.

If $X \leq Y \in AC(A^\infty)$, then $X \subseteq \downarrow Y$ and $Y \subseteq \uparrow X$. This means that every $x \in X$ is below some $y \in Y$, and vice versa, every $y \in Y$ is above some $x \in X$. Since X is an antichain. if $x \leq y \in Y$, then $\pi_{\downarrow X}(y) = x$, which shows $X \subseteq \pi_{\downarrow X}(Y)$. Conversely, if $y \in Y$, then there is some $x \in X$ with $x \leq y$, so again $\pi_{\downarrow X}(y) = x \in X$. Thus $\pi_{\downarrow X}(Y) = X$.

For the converse, if $\pi_{\downarrow X}(Y) = X$, then $x \in X$ implies $x = \pi_{\downarrow X}(y)$ for some $y \in Y$, so $X \subseteq \downarrow Y$. On the other hand, if $y \in Y$, then $\pi_{\downarrow X}(y) \in X$ and $y \in \uparrow \pi_{\downarrow X}(y)$. Hence $Y \subseteq \uparrow X$. $\square$

Proposition 4.47 of [19] implies that the Lawson topology on $\mathcal{P}_C(A^\infty)$ is the same as the topology $\mathcal{P}_C(A^\infty)$ inherits from the Vietoris topology on the family of compact subsets of A^∞, when A^∞ is a coherent domain endowed with the Lawson topology. This implies that the convergence of a directed family of Lawson compact antichains from A^∞ is the same as their convergence in the Vietoris topology. The relevance of this to our work is summarized in the following result.

Theorem 2. *Let A be a finite set, and for each n, let $\pi_n\colon A^\infty \to A^{\leq n} \equiv \{s \in A^* \mid |s| \leq n\}$ be the projection onto the set of words of length at most n. Then π_n is continuous for each n, where we endow A^∞ and $A^{\leq n}$ with either the Scott- or Lawson topologies. Moreover,*

1. *Each Lawson-compact antichain $X \subseteq A^\infty$ satisfies $\{\pi_n(X)\}_n$ is a directed family of finite antichains satisfying $\sup_n \pi_n(X) = X$.*
2. *Conversely, each directed family of finite antichains $F_n \subseteq A^{\leq n}$ satisfies $\sup_n F_n = X$ is a Lawson compact antichain in A^∞ satisfying $\pi_n(X) = F_n$ for each n.*

Some Further Results. We need some additional results about Lawson-compact antichains in A^∞ which are not in [20].

Proposition 2. *Let $X \in AC(A^\infty)$ be a Lawson-compact antichain in A^∞. Then:*

1. *$\downarrow X$ is a bounded complete domain.*
2. *The relative Lawson- and Scott topologies on X from $\downarrow X$ are the same.*

Proof. For 1, Proposition 1 implies $\downarrow X$ is a Scott-closed subset of A^∞, and Scott-closed subset of a bounded complete domain is another such: if $s \in \downarrow X$, then $\downarrow s \subseteq \downarrow X$, so $\downarrow X$ is continuous, and if $\emptyset \neq S \subseteq \downarrow X$, then $\inf_{A^\infty} S \in \downarrow X$.

For 2, the Lawson topology refines the Scott topology, so we only need to show that each relatively-open subset of X in the Lawson topology is relatively Scott open. A basic open subset of X in the relative Lawson topology has the form $X \cap (U \setminus \uparrow F)$, where $U \subseteq \downarrow X$ is Scott open, and $F \subseteq \downarrow X$ is finite. In fact, we may assume $U = \uparrow s$ for some finite word $s \in A^*$, since A^∞ is algebraic. Then, for each $t \in F$, if t and s have an upper bound, then they must compare, and assuming $\uparrow s \setminus \uparrow F \neq \emptyset$, we conclude that $s < t$. If $x \in X \cap \uparrow s \setminus \uparrow F$, then $s < x$ and $t \not\leq x$ for all $t \in F$. But then we can find $s' \in A^*$ with $s < s' \leq x$ and $s' \not\leq t$ for all $t \in F$ since F is finite. Then $x \in X \cap \uparrow s' \subseteq \uparrow s \setminus \uparrow F$, and $X \cap \uparrow s'$ is relatively Scott open. □

Remark 1. Let $X \in AC(A^\infty)$ and let D be a bounded complete domain. Then

1. Part 1 implies $[\downarrow X \to D]$ is a bounded complete domain, since BCD is Cartesian closed.
2. Part 2 implies $f\colon X \to D$ is continuous from the relative Scott topology on X to the Scott topology on D iff f is continuous from the Lawson topology on X to the Scott topology on D. We denote the family of these maps by $[X \to D]$.
3. If $X \in AC(A^*)$ is a finite antichain and D is bounded complete, then $[X \to D] \simeq D^{|X|}$ is a bounded complete domain, since BCD is closed under products.

Proposition 3. *Let D be a bounded complete domain, and let $X \in AC(A^\infty)$, where A is a finite alphabet. Then $X \leq Y \in AC(A^\infty)$ implies there is an embedding-projection pair*

$$f \mapsto f \circ \pi_X \colon [X \to D] \hookrightarrow [Y \to D]; \quad g \mapsto \widehat{g} \colon [Y \to D] \twoheadrightarrow [X \to D],$$

where $\pi_X \colon Y \to X$ is the projection mapping and $\widehat{g}(x) = \inf g(Y \cap \uparrow x)$.

Proof. Given $f \colon X \to D$, $f \circ \pi_X \colon Y \to D$ is well-defined because $X \leq Y$, and it is continuous because it is a composition of continuous maps.

On the other hand, given $g \colon Y \to D$, we first recall $\mathcal{P}_U(D) = (\{C \subseteq D \mid \emptyset \neq C \text{ Scott compact}\}, \supseteq)$ denotes the upper power domain over D, and that D bounded complete implies $\inf \colon \mathcal{P}_U(D) \to D$ is a Soctt-continuous retraction (cf. [19]). Then we define $\overline{g} \colon \downarrow Y \to \mathcal{P}_U(D)$ by $\overline{g}(s) = \uparrow_D g(\uparrow s \cap Y)$. This is well-defined since $s \in \downarrow Y$ implies $\uparrow s \cap Y \neq \emptyset$ is Lawson, hence Scott compact, and the Scott continuity of g implies $g(\uparrow s \cap Y)$ is Scott compact as well.

If $s \leq t$, then obviously $g(\uparrow s \cap Y) \supseteq g(\uparrow t \cap Y)$, so $\overline{g}$ is monotone. For continuity, suppose that $S \subseteq \downarrow Y$ is directed, and let $t = \sup S$ in $\downarrow Y$. Then $\overline{g}(s) \supseteq \overline{g}(t)$ by monotonicity. Conversely, suppose $x \in \overline{g}(s)$ for each $s \in S$. Then for each $s \in S$, there is some $y_s \in \uparrow s \cap Y$ with $g(y_s) \leq x$. Since Y is compact, $\{y_s\}_{s \in S}$ has a limit point $y \in Y$, and since $\{\uparrow s \cap Y \mid s \in S\}$ is a filter base of compact sets, it follows that $y \in \uparrow s \cap Y$ for each $s \in S$. Thus $y \in \uparrow t \cap Y$, and then $g(t) \leq x$. It follows that $\overline{g}(t) = \sup_{s \in S} \overline{g}(s)$, so $\overline{g} \colon \downarrow Y \to \mathcal{P}_U(D)$ by $\overline{g}(s) = \uparrow_D g(\uparrow s \cap Y)$ is Scott continuous.

Now, $\inf \colon \mathcal{P}_U(D) \to D$ is Scott continuous, and $X \leq Y$ implies $X \subseteq \downarrow Y$, so $\widehat{g} \colon X \to D$ by $\widehat{g}(x) = \inf \overline{g}(x)$ is Scott continuous.

Now, given $f \colon X \to D$,

$$\widehat{f \circ \pi_X}(x) = \inf f(Y \cap \uparrow x) = \inf f(x) = f(x)$$

since $X \leq Y$ and X an antichain imply $\pi_X(Y \cap \uparrow x) = x$.

Conversely, if $g \colon Y \to D$ and $y \in Y$, then

$$\widehat{g} \circ \pi_X(y) = \inf g(Y \cap \uparrow \pi_X(y)) \leq g(y). \qquad \square$$

Notation:

- In the following, we let $\bigoplus_{X \in AC(A^\infty)} [X \to D]$ denote the disjoint sum of the domains $[X \to D]$, as X ranges over $AC(A^\infty)$.
- Given $f \in \bigoplus_{X \in AC(A^\infty)} [X \to D]$, we let $X_f = \mathrm{dom}(f)$. Then $f \in [X \to D]$ iff $X = X_f$.
- We order $\bigoplus_{X \in AC(A^\infty)} [X \to D]$ by

$$f \leq g \quad \text{iff} \quad X_f \leq X_g \text{ and } f \circ \pi_{X_f} \leq g.$$

Theorem 3. *Let A be a finite alphabet and let D be a bounded complete domain.*

1. If $X \in AC(A^\infty)$, then $[X \to D]$ is a bounded complete domain.

2. $\bigoplus_{X \in AC(A^\infty)}[X \to D]$ *is a bounded complete domain.*

Proof. We use Theorems 1 and 2 to prove the results. For 1, Theorem 2 implies $\pi_n(X) \in AC(A^{\leq n})$ is a finite antichain for each $n \geq 1$, and so $[\pi_n(X) \to D] \simeq D^{|\pi_n(X)|}$ is bounded complete, since BCD has products. Moreover, the family $\{[\pi_n(X) \to D], f \mapsto \pi_n^m \circ f, g \mapsto \widehat{g}\}_{m \leq n}$ is a family of bounded complete domains and embeddiing-projection pairs, so it has a bilimit, which is also a bounded complete domain. To complete the proof, we show that $[X \to D]$ is that bilimit. This is proved if we show that $\sup_n \widehat{f} \circ \pi_n = f$ for each $f \in [X \to D]$. If $x \in X$, then

$$\sup_n \widehat{f} \circ \pi_n(x) = \sup_n \inf f(X \cap {\uparrow}\pi_n(x)) = \inf f(X \cap {\uparrow}x) = f(x),$$

the second equality following from part 1) of Theorem 2, and the last from the fact that $x \in X \in AC(A^\infty)$.

For part 2), we first show that

$$f \leq g \quad \text{iff} \quad X_f \leq X_g \text{ and } f \circ \pi_{X_f} \leq g$$

is a partial order on $\bigoplus_{X \in AC(A^\infty)}[X \to D]$: indeed, it's clearly reflexive and transitive. If $f \leq g \leq f$, then $X_f \leq X_g \leq X_f$, and so $X_f = X_g$ because $AC(A^\infty)$ is partially ordered. Then $\pi_{X_f}|_{X_g} = \mathrm{id}_{X_f}$. Thus $f = f \circ \pi_{X_f} \leq g = g \circ \pi_{X_g} \leq f$, and they're equal.

Next, let $\mathcal{S} \subseteq \bigoplus_{X \in AC(A^\infty)}[X \to D]$ be a a directed set. Then $\mathcal{S}_0 = \{X_f \mid f \in \mathcal{S}\}$ is a directed family in $AC(A^\infty)$, so it has a least upper bound, $X_0 = \sup_{\mathcal{S}_0} X$. Then $\{[X_f \to D] \mid f \in \mathcal{S}\}$ together with $[X_0 \to D]$ is a cone in $\bigoplus_{X \in AC(A^\infty)}[X \to D]$, using the embedding-projection pairs between $[X_f \to D]$ and $[X_g \to D]$ if $f \leq g \in \mathcal{S}$, and between $[X_f \to D]$ and $[X_0 \to D]$ for each $X_f \in \mathcal{S}_0$. An argument similar to the one in the first part of the proof shows that $\sup_{X \in \mathcal{S}_0} \widehat{f} \circ \pi_X = f$ for each $f \in [X_0 \to D]$, which implies this is a limit cone. This implies that $[X_0 \to D] = \lim_{f \in \mathcal{S}}[X_f \to D]$. Then $(f)_{f \in \mathcal{S}} \in \Pi_{f \in \mathcal{S}}[X_f \to D]$ determines a unique point $h \in \lim_{f \in \mathcal{S}}[X_f \to D] = [X_0 \to D]$. Thus, $\pi_{X_f}(h) = f$ for each $f \in \mathcal{S}$, so $f \leq h$ for each $f \in \mathcal{S}$. Likewise, if $f \leq g$ for each $f \in \mathcal{S}$, then $\pi_{X_f}(g) = f$ for each $f \in \mathcal{S}$, and so $\pi_{X_0}(g) = h$ by the definition of the limit. Hence $h = \sup \mathcal{S}$. So, $\bigoplus_{X \in AC(A^\infty)}[X \to D]$ is a dcpo.

Since $[X \to D]$ is a domain for each $X \in AC(A^\infty)$, the same is true of $\bigoplus_{X \in AC(A^\infty)}[X \to D]$ – a basis is the family $\bigoplus_{X \in AC(A^*)}[X \to \mathcal{B}(D)]$, where $\mathcal{B}(D)$ is any basis for D. And since $[X \to D]$ is bounded complete for each $X \in AC(A^\infty)$ and since $AC(A^\infty)$ itself is bounded complete, the same holds for $\bigoplus_{X \in AC(A^\infty)}[X \to D]$. $\square$

Notation. For a bounded complete domain D, we use $\Theta[A^\infty \to D] \equiv \bigoplus_{X \in AC(A^\infty)}[X \to D]$ to denote the family of Lawson continuous maps from some Lawson-compact antichain $X \in AC(A^\infty)$ to D.

Stone Duality. In modern parlance, Marshall Stone's seminal result states that the category of Stone spaces – compact Hausdorff totally disconnected spaces – and continuous maps is dually equivalent to the category of Boolean algebras and Boolean algebra maps. The dual equivalence sends a Stone space to the Boolean algebra of its compact-open subsets; dually, a Boolean algebra is sent to the set of prime ideals, endowed with the hull-kernel topology. This dual equivalence was used to great effect by Abramsky [1] where he showed how to extract a logic from a domain constructed using Moggi's monadic approach, so that the logic was tailor made for the domain used to build it.

Our approach to Stone duality is somewhat unconventional, but one that also has been utilized in recent work by Gehrke [8,9]. The idea is to realize a Stone space as a projective limit of finite spaces, a result which follows from Stone duality, as we now demonstrate.

Theorem 4 (Stone Duality). *Each Stone space X can be represented as a projective limit $X \simeq \varprojlim_{\alpha \in A} X_\alpha$, where X_α is a finite space. In fact, each X_α is a partition of X into a finite cover by clopen subsets, and the projection $X \twoheadrightarrow X_\alpha$ maps each point of X to the element of X_α containing it.*

We note that a corollary of this result says that it is enough to have a basis for the family of finite Boolean subalgebras of $\mathcal{B}(X)$ in order to realize X as a projective limit of finite spaces, where by a *basis*, we mean a directed family whose union generates all of $\mathcal{B}(X)$. The following example illustrates this point.

Example 3. Let C denote the middle third Cantor set from the unit interval. This is Stone space, and so it can be realized as a projective limit of finite spaces $C \simeq \varprojlim_{\alpha \in A} C_\alpha$. But since C is second countable, we can define a countable family of finite spaces C_n for which $C \simeq \varprojlim_n C_n$. Indeed, we can use the construction of C from $[0,1]$ to define these finite spaces:

- $C_0 = [0,1]$ is the entire space.
- $C_1 = \{[0, \frac{1}{3}], [\frac{2}{3}, 1]\}$ is the result of deleting the middle third from $[0,1]$.
$$\vdots$$
- $C_n = \{[0, \frac{1}{3^n}], \dots, [\frac{3^n - 1}{3^n}, 1]\}$.
$$\vdots$$

Note that C_n has 2^n elements – this is the "top down" approach to building C, as opposed the "bottom up" approach obtained by viewing C as the set of maximal elements of the Cantor fan. In categorical parlance, the approach via Stone duality realizes C as an F-algebra, whereas the Cantor fan realizes C as a (final) F-coalgebra, where F is the functor that sends a space X to $X \cup X$, the disjoint sum of two copies of X.

The Prob Monad on Comp. It is well known that the family of probability measures on a compact Hausdorff space is the object level of a functor which defines a monad on Comp, the category of compact Hausdorff spaces and continuous maps. As outlined in [11], this monad gives rise to several related monads:

- On Comp, it associates to a compact Hausdorff space X the free *barycentric algebra* over X, the name deriving from the counit $\epsilon\colon \mathsf{Prob}(S) \to S$ which assigns to each measure μ on a probabilistic algebra S its barycenter $\epsilon(\mu)$.
- On the category CompMon of compact monoids and continuous monoid homomorphisms, Prob gives rise to a monad that assigns to a compact monoid S the free compact affine monoid over S.
- On the category CompGrp of compact groups and continuous homomorphisms, Prob assigns to a compact group G the free compact affine monoid over G; in this case the right adjoint sends a compact affine monoid to its group of units, as opposed to the inclusion functor, which is the right adjoint in the first two cases.

If we let $\mathsf{SProb}(X)$ denote the family of subprobability measures on a compact Hausdorff space X, then it's routine to show that SProb defines monads in each of the cases just described, where the only change is that the objects now have a 0 (i.e., they are affine structures with 0-element, allowing one to define scalar multiples $r \cdot x$ for $r \in [0,1]$ and $x \in \mathsf{SProb}(X)$, as well as affine combinations).

There is a further result we need about Prob which relates to its role as an endofunctor on Comp and its subcategories. The following result is due to Fedorchuk:

Theorem 5 (Fedorchuk [5]). *The functor* Prob: Comp $\to$ Comp *is normal; in particular,* Prob *preserves inverse limits.*

Remark 2. If we combine this result with the results at the end of Subsection 2.1, then we see that the family of probability measures supported on a Lawson-compact antichain X in A^∞ can be written as the inverse limit of the measures supported on finite subsets $\pi_n(X)$; this follows from our having shown that $X = \sup_n \pi_n(X)$ and the fact (quoted from [19]) that the Lawson topology on the family of antichains is the same as the Vietoris topology, which coincides with the topology used to form the inverse limit.

3.2   A Motivating Example

The following example is from Section 3 of [20].

Definition 1. *A probabilistic automaton is a tuple* (S, A, q_0, D) *where S is a finite set of states, A a finite set of actions, $q_0 \in S$ a start state, and $D \subseteq S \times \mathsf{Prob}(A \times S)$ a transition relation that assigns to each state s_0 a probability distribution* $\sum_{A \times S} r_{(s_0,(a,s))} \delta_{(a,s)}$ *on $A \times S$.*

If we start such an automaton in its start state – which amounts to assigning it the starting distribution δ_{q_0}, and then follow the automaton as it evolves, then we see a sequence of *global trace distributions* that describe the step-by-step evolution of the automaton:

1. δ_{q_0},
2. $\sum_{(a_1,s_1) \in A \times S} r_{(q_0,(a_1,s_1))} \delta_{q_0 a_1 s_1}$,

3. $\sum_{(a_1,s_1)\in A\times S} r_{(q_0,(a_1,s_1))}(\sum_{(a_2,s_2)\in A\times S} r_{(s_1,(a_2,s_2))}\delta_{q_0a_1s_1a_2s_2})$,

$\vdots$

If we strip away the probabilities, we have a nondeterministic finite state automaton (albeit one without final states), and the resulting automaton generates a language that is a subset of $(S \times A)^\infty$. This automaton generates the sequence

$$\{q_0\}, \{(q_0s_1a_1 \mid r_{(q_0,(s_1,a_1))} \neq 0\}, \{q_0s_1a_1s_2a_2 \mid r_{(q_0,(s_1,a_1))}, r_{(s_1,(a_2,s_2))} \neq 0\}, \ldots.$$

Note that the sequence of sets of states this automaton generates is a family of finite antichains, which we showed in Section 2 is a Scott subdomain of $\mathcal{P}_C((S \times A)^\infty)$ under the Egli-Milner order. Moreover, the projections $\pi_{mn}\colon (S \times A)^{\leq n} \to (S \times A)^{\leq m}$ for $m \leq n$ map the antichain of possible states at the nth stage to those at the mth stage, by truncation.

Since Prob is a monad on Comp, the mappings π_{mn} lift to mappings $\mathsf{Prob}(\pi_{mn})\colon \mathsf{Prob}((S \times A)^{\leq n}) \to \mathsf{Prob}((S \times A)^{\leq m})$. Using the mappings π_{mm+1}, we see that each succeeding distribution is projected onto the previous distribution. For example, the second distribution $\sum_{(a_1,s_1)\in A\times S} r_{(q_0,(a_1,s_1))}\delta_{q_0a_1s_1}$ collapses to δ_{q_0}, and the third distribution $\sum_{(a_1,s_1)\in A\times S} r_{(q_0,(a_1,s_1))}(\sum_{(a_2,s_2)\in A\times S} r_{(s_1,(a_2,s_2))}\delta_{q_0a_1s_1a_2s_2})$ collapses to the second. Thus, Prob lifts the order on $AC((S\times A)^\infty)$ to $\mathsf{Prob}(AC((S\times A)^\infty))$, and it is this order we will use in defining the order on the family of thin probability measures, and eventually on the domain of continuous random variables over a bounded complete domain. We now make this observation precise.

3.3   A Bounded Complete Domain of Thin Measures

The following form the main results from [20]; they appear in Sections 4 and 5.

Definition 2. *If Y is a compact Hausdorff space and $X \subseteq Y$ is a compact subspace of Y, then for $\mu \in \mathsf{Prob}(Y)$, then we say μ has* full support *on X if $\operatorname{supp}\mu = X$. We denote by $\mathsf{Prob}^\dagger(X)$ the family of $\mu \in \mathsf{Prob}(Y)$ having full support on X.*

Definition 3. *For a finite alphabet A, we define $\ominus\mathsf{Prob}(A^\infty) \equiv \bigoplus_{X\in AC(A^\infty)} \mathsf{Prob}^\dagger(X)$ to be the* direct sum *of the family of probability measures in $\mathsf{Prob}^\dagger(X)$ as X ranges over $AC(A^\infty)$. These are the* thin probability measures *on A^∞, those that are fully supported on Lawson-compact antichains in A^∞. We order $\ominus\mathsf{Prob}(A^\infty)$ by $\mu \leq \nu$ iff $\pi_{\downarrow(\operatorname{supp}\mu)}(\nu) = \mu$.*

The result summarizes a series of results from [20] about the structure of $\ominus\mathsf{Prob}(A^*)$.

Proposition 4. *Let A be a finite alphabet and let $AC(A^\infty)$ be the family of Lawson-compact antichains in A^∞. Then:*

1. *If $f\colon X \to Y$ is a continuous map between compacta, then $f(\mu) = \nu$ implies $f(\operatorname{supp}\mu) = \operatorname{supp}\nu$.*

2. *The family* $(\Theta Prob(A^\infty), \leq)$ *is a dcpo.*
3. *The mapping* $\mathrm{supp}\colon \Theta Prob(A^\infty) \to AC(A^\infty)$ *sending each measure* μ *to its support in the Lawson topology is Scott continuous.*
4. *If* $\mu \in \Theta Prob(A^\infty)$ *and* $F \subseteq A^*$ *is finite with* $\pi_F(\mathrm{supp}\,\mu) = F$, *then* $\pi_F(\mu) \ll \mu$ *in* $Prob^\dagger(X)$.

Theorem 6. *If A is a finite alphabet, then $\Theta Prob(A^\infty)$ is a bounded complete algebraic domain.*

n-Ary Probabilistic Choice Algebras. In [10], the authors define *coin algebras* as domains P that have a continuous operation $+\colon [0,1] \times P \times P \to P$ satisfying $x \leq x +_p x$ and $x +_1 y$ and $x +_0 y$ are independent of their second and first arguments, respectively. They also show that their family of continuous random variables over a domain X are free coin algebras. We now define a similar class of algebras and prove a similar freeness result.

Definition 4. *For $n > 0$, let $\Delta_n = \{(r_1, \ldots, r_n) \in [0,1]^n \mid \sum_i r_i = 1\}$. An n-ary probabilistic algebra is a domain P that supports an operation $+_n\colon \Delta_n \times P^n \to P$ satisfying the properties:*

1. *$+_n((r_1, \ldots, r_n), (p_1, \ldots, p_n)) \equiv \sum_{i \leq n} r_i p_i\colon \Delta_n \times P^n \to P$ is Scott continuous, and*
2. *For each $i \leq n$, if $(r_1, \ldots, r_n) \in \Delta_n$ and $r_i = 0$, then $(p_1, \ldots, p_n) \mapsto \sum_{j \leq n} r_j p_j$ is independent of its ith input.*

For $A = \{a_1, \ldots, a_n\}$, define $+_n$ on $\Delta_n \times \bigoplus_{X \in AC(A^*)} Prob^\dagger(X)$ as follows:

- Given $\mu_1, \ldots, \mu_n \in \bigoplus_{X \in AC(A^*)} Prob^\dagger(X)$, let $S = \mathrm{Max}(\bigcup_{i \leq n} \mathrm{supp}\,\mu_i)$, and for $x \in \mathrm{supp}\,\mu_i$, let $S(x) = \uparrow x \cap S$.
- If $\mu_i = \sum_{x \in \mathrm{supp}\,\mu_i} r_x \delta_x$, then define $\phi_{a_i}^S(\mu_i) = \sum_{x \in \mathrm{supp}\,\mu_i} \frac{r_x}{|S(x)|} \sum_{y \in S(x)} \delta_{ya_i}$.
- Then define

$$+_n\colon \Delta_n \times \bigoplus_{X \in AC(A^*)} Prob^\dagger(X) \to \bigoplus_{X \in AC(A^*)} Prob^\dagger(X) \quad \text{by}$$

$$+_n((r_1, \ldots, r_n), (\mu_1, \ldots, \mu_n)) = \sum_{i \leq n} r_i \phi_{a_i}^S(\mu_i).$$

Proposition 5. *If $A = \{a, \ldots, a_n\}$ is a finite alphabet, then $\Theta Prob(A^\infty)$ is an n-ary probabilistic algebra under the continuous extension of the operation given above to all of $\Theta Prob(A^\infty)$.*

Theorem 7. *If P is an n-ary probabilistic algebra and A is a finite alphabet with $|A| = n$, then given any monotone map $f\colon A^\infty \to P$, there is a unique continuous map $F\colon \Theta Prob(A^\infty) \to P$ satisfying $F(\sum_{i \leq n} r_i \mu_i) = \sum_{i \leq n} r_i f(\mu_i)$.*

4   Continuous Random Variables

Recall that a *random variable* is a measurable function $f: (X, \Sigma_X) \to (Y, \Sigma_Y)$, where Σ_X and Σ_Y are σ-algebras on X and Y, respectively, where f is measurable iff $f^{-1}(A) \in \Sigma_X$ for each $A \in \Sigma_Y$. If X and Y have topologies that are used to generate Σ_X and Σ_Y, then these algebras are called *Borel σ-algebras*. We are interested in the case that X and Y arise from coherent domains, and the Σ_X and Σ_Y are the Borel algebras generated by the Scott topologies. We note that these are the same as the Borel algebras generated by the Lawson topologies.

If $f: X \to Y$ is continuous with respect to topologies on X and Y, respectively, and if the σ-algebras Σ_X and Σ_Y are the Borel algebras for these topologies, then f is measurable. In our setting, the topologies will either be the Scott- or Lawson topologies X and Y inherit from their ambient domains, but the σ-algebras they generate are the same.

Definition 5. *Let A be a finite alphabet, and let $X \in AC(A^\infty)$ be a Lawson-compact antichain. If D is a bounded complete domain, we let $[X \to D] = \{f: X \to D \mid f \text{ Lawson continuous}\}$, where we endow X with the Lawson topology inherited from A^∞ and D with its Scott topology. We let*

$$\Theta RV_{A^\infty}(D) = \bigoplus_{X \in AC(A^\infty)} Prob^\dagger(X) \times [X \to D]$$

endowed with the partial order

$$(\mu, f) \leq (\nu, g) \quad iff \quad \pi_X(\nu) = \mu \ \& \ f \circ \pi_X|_{\mathrm{supp}\,\nu} \leq g.$$

Theorem 8. *If A is a finite alphabet and D is a bounded complete domain, then $\Theta RV_{A^\infty}(D)$ is a bounded complete domain where*

$$(\mu, f) \ll (\nu, g) \quad iff \quad \mu \leq \nu, \mathrm{supp}\,\mu \subseteq A^* \text{ finite, and}$$
$$f \circ \pi_{\mathrm{supp}\,\mu}(x) \ll g(x) \ (\forall x \in \mathrm{supp}\,\nu).$$

Proof. (Sketch) We know from Theorem 6 that $\Theta Prob(A^*)$ is a bounded complete algebraic domain in the indicated order, and Proposition 4 shows that $\mu \ll \nu$ iff $\pi_F(\mu) \ll \mu$ for each $\mu \in Prob^\dagger(X)$, for each $X \in AC(A^\infty)$. Further, Theorerm 3 implies $\Theta[A^\infty \to D]$ is bounded complete with $[X \to D] \leq [Y \to D]$ iff $X \leq Y \in AC(A^\infty)$. Then the product $\Theta Prob(A^*) \times \Theta[A^\infty \to D]$ is bounded complete. Thus, a directed set $\mathcal{S} \subseteq \Theta RV_{A^\infty}(D)$ has a supremum in $\Theta Prob(A^*) \times \Theta[A^\infty \to D]$ of the form (μ, f) where $\mathrm{supp}\,\mu = X$ and $f \in [X \to D]$ by the proof of Theorem 3, so $(\mu, f) \in \Theta RV_{A^\infty}(D)$, showing $\Theta RV_{A^\infty}(D)$ is directed complete. The facts that $\Theta Prob(A^*) \times \Theta[A^\infty \to D]$, as well as each of its factors are bounded complete domains imply the same is true of the family $\Theta RV_{A^\infty}(D)$. □

4.1   Adding Structure to $\Theta RV_{A^\infty}(D)$

We want to show that $\Theta RV_{A^\infty}(D)$ is the object level of a monad, but to do that, we need some algebraic structure on this family. We start by noting that, for a finite alphabet A, the concatenation operation $\cdot\colon A^\infty \times A^\infty \to A^\infty$ is continuous with respect to the Lawson topology; in fact, $(A^\infty, \cdot)$ is the free compact monoid over A with this topology (this is an easy exercise, beginning with the observation that $\{s\}$ is open in the Lawson topology for any finite word s, since A is finite, and using the fact that concatenation is monotone in the second argument). But concatenation is not monotone: $s \leq t$ does not imply $s \cdot w \leq t \cdot w$. A way around this is to avoid words that compare – this is the reason we have been focusing on measures supported on Lawson-compact antichains, since concatenation is monotone on such subsets.

Next, we can apply the probability monad $\mathsf{Prob}\colon \mathsf{CompMon} \to \mathsf{CompMon}$ on compact Hausdorff monoids, and concatenation lifts to *convolution of measures*: $(\mu, \nu) \mapsto \mu * \nu\colon \varTheta\mathsf{Prob}(A^\infty) \times \varTheta\mathsf{Prob}(A^\infty) \to \varTheta\mathsf{Prob}(A^\infty)$ which makes $(\varTheta\mathsf{Prob}(A^\infty), *)$ a compact monoid (the identity is $\delta_{\langle\rangle}$, point mass over the empty word):

Proposition 6. *Let A be a finite alphabet, then convolution* $*\colon \varTheta\mathsf{Prob}(A^\infty) \times \varTheta\mathsf{Prob}(A^\infty) \to \varTheta\mathsf{Prob}(A^\infty)$ *is Lawson continuous.*

Proof. Since the support of each measure is an antichain, and since convolution is Lawson continuous, it also is monotone. Thus, the only issue is whether $\mu * \nu$ is supported on a Lawson-compact antichain if μ and ν are. But from [11], we know that $\operatorname{supp}\mu * \nu = \operatorname{supp}\mu \cdot \operatorname{supp}\nu$, where we are extending the concatenation operation to subsets of A^∞. On any compact monoid, this is a well-defined, continuous operation, and if $\operatorname{supp}\mu$ and $\operatorname{supp}\nu$ are antichains, then so is $\operatorname{supp}\mu \cdot \operatorname{supp}\nu$: if $x, x' \in \operatorname{supp}\mu$ and $y, y' \in \operatorname{supp}\nu$, then x and x' are incomparable, and so are y and y'. But then $x \cdot y$ is incomparable with $x' \cdot y'$: if $x \cdot y \leq x' \cdot y'$, then $x \leq x' \cdot y'$. Since $x \not\leq x'$, this means there is some w with $x' \cdot w = x$, which implies $x' \leq x$, a contradiction. $\qquad\square$

Example 4. Since convolution is Lawson continuous, it might be tempting to assume that it is also monotone, and hence Scott continuous when restricted to antichains. This is not the case. For example, if $s, t \in A^*$ satisfy $s < t$, and if we choose $u \in A^*$ with $su \not\leq tu$, then we have an example where concatenation $\cdot\colon A^\infty \times A^\infty \to A^\infty$ is not monotone – namely, at $(s, u) \leq (t, u) \in A^\infty \times A^\infty$. This example lifts to $*\colon \varTheta\mathsf{Prob}(A^\infty) \times \varTheta\mathsf{Prob}(A^\infty) \to \varTheta\mathsf{Prob}(A^\infty)$ via $*(\delta_s, \delta_u) = \delta_{su}$ and $*(\delta_t, \delta_u) = \delta_{tu}$.

We will revisit this example when examine the nature of the monad structure on $\varTheta RV_{A^\infty}(D)$ for a bounded complete domain D in Example 5.

For the next result, we recall the notation used in Proposition 5. If $\mu_1, \ldots, \mu_n \in \varTheta\mathsf{Prob}(A^*)$, then

- $S = \operatorname{Max}(\bigcup_{i \leq n} \operatorname{supp}\mu_i)$, let $S_i = {\uparrow}\operatorname{supp}\mu_i \cap S$, and for $x \in \operatorname{supp}\mu_i$, let $S(x) = {\uparrow}x \cap S$.
- $\phi^S_{a_i}(\mu_i) = \sum_{x \in \operatorname{supp}\mu_i} \frac{\mu_i(x)}{|S(x)|} \sum_{y \in S(x)} \delta_{ya_i}$.

Theorem 9. *Let $A = \{a_1, \cdots, a_n\}$ be a finite alphabet, and let D be a bounded complete domain. Then $\Theta RV_{A^\infty}(D)$ is an n-ary probabilistic algebra where*

$$\sum_{i \leq n} r_i(\mu_i, f_i) = \left(\sum_i r_i \phi^S_{a_i}(\mu_i), \bigcup_{i \leq n} f_i \circ \pi_{\mathrm{supp}\,\mu_i}|_{S_i} \right).$$

Proof. From Proposition 5 we know $\Theta\mathrm{Prob}(A^*)$ is an n-ary probabilistic algebra using the definition above for the first component. The proof of Proposition 6 shows that the concatenation of antichains is an antichain. In particular, if $X_1, \ldots, X_n \in AC(A^\infty)$, then $\phi^S_{a_1}(X_1), \ldots, \phi^S_{a_n}(X_n)$ is a family of pairwise disjoint antichains by construction. This implies the function $\bigcup_i f_i \circ \pi_{\mathrm{supp}\,\mu_i}|_{S_i} \colon \bigcup_i \phi_i(X_i) \to D$ is well-defined and it's continuous because the f_i's and the $\pi_{\mathrm{supp}\,\mu_i}|_{S_i}$'s are. The proof of the rest is routine. $\square$

4.2   Towards a Monad

Following the development in [10], the results we have established allow us to show that $\Theta RV_{A^\infty}(D)$ is the object map of a monad.

Theorem 10. *If A is a finite alphabet, the $D \mapsto \Theta RV_{A^\infty}(D)$ is the object map of a monad.*

Proof. We define the unit of the monad by $\eta_D \colon D \to \Theta RV_{A^\infty}(D)$ by $\eta_D(x) = (\delta_{\langle\rangle}, \chi_x)$, where $\chi_x(\langle\rangle) = x$, and $\langle\rangle$ denotes the empty word.

For $h \colon D \to \Theta RV_{A^\infty}(E)$ with E a bounded complete domain, the definition of $h^\dagger \colon \Theta RV_{A^\infty}(D) \to \Theta RV_{A^\infty}(E)$ is more complicated. We define $h^\dagger$ on the basis $(\sum_{i \leq n} r_i \delta_{s_i}, f)$, where $\{s_i \mid i \leq n\} \subseteq A^*$ is a finite antichain and $f \colon \{s_i \mid i \leq n\} \to \mathcal{B}(D)$, a basis for D, and then extend by continuity.

We begin by noting that $h \colon D \to \Theta RV_{A^\infty}(E)$ means $h(x) = (\mu_x, f_x)$, so using π_1 and π_2 to denote the obvious projections to $\bigoplus_{X \in AC(A^\infty)}(X)$ and to $[X \to E]$, respectively, we can write $h(x) = (\pi_1 \circ h(x), \pi_2 \circ h(x))$. Then we can define the mapping $h^\dagger \colon \Theta RV_{A^*}(D) \to \Theta RV_{A^\infty}(E)$ by

$$h^\dagger(\mu, f) = h^\dagger\left(\sum_{x \in \mathrm{supp}\,\mu} r_x \delta_x, f \right) = \left(\sum_{x \in \mathrm{supp}\,\mu} r_x \left(\delta_x * (\pi_1 \circ h \circ f)(x) \right), g \right),$$

where $*$ denotes convolution and $g \colon \bigcup_{x \in \mathrm{supp}\,\mu} x \cdot \mathrm{supp}(\pi_1 \circ h \circ f)(x) \to E$ is $g(x \cdot y) = (\pi_2 \circ h \circ f)(x)(y)$; this makes sense because $x \in \mathrm{supp}\,\mu$ implies $f(x) \in D$, which in turn implies $(\pi_2 \circ h \circ f)(x) \in [\mathrm{supp}(\pi_1 \circ h \circ f)(x) \to E]$, and $y \in \mathrm{supp}(\pi_1 \circ h \circ f)(x)$.

Note that $(\pi_1 \circ h \circ f)(x)$ is a thin probability measure on A^∞, so its support is an antichain. It follows from Proposition 6 that $\mathrm{supp}\,\delta_x * (\pi_1 \circ h \circ f)(x)$ is an antichain for each $x \in \mathrm{supp}\,\mu$, and since $\mathrm{supp}\,\mu$ is an antichain, it follows that $\sum_{x \in \mathrm{supp}\,\mu} r_x (\delta_x * (\pi_1 \circ h \circ f)(x))$ is one as well. Hence $\pi_1(h^\dagger(\mu, f))$ is a thin probability measure on A^∞.

By definition $(\pi_2 \circ h \circ f)(x) \in [\text{supp}(\pi_1 \circ h \circ f)(x) \to E]$ is continuous, and since $\bigcup_{x \in \text{supp}\,\mu} x \cdot \text{supp}(\pi_1 \circ h \circ f)(x)$ is a union of pairwise disjoint compact antichains in A^∞, it follows that $\pi_2(h^\dagger(\mu, f)) = g \colon \bigcup_{x \in \text{supp}\,\mu} x \cdot \text{supp}(\pi_1 \circ h \circ f)(x) \to E$ is continuous.

We now prove $h \mapsto h^\dagger$ satisfies the monad laws:

$\eta_D^\dagger = \text{id}_{\Theta RV_{A^\infty}(D)}$:

$$\eta_D^\dagger(\mu, f) = \Big(\sum_{x \in \text{supp}\,\mu} r_x(\delta_x * (\pi_1 \circ \eta_D \circ f)), (\pi_2 \circ \eta_D \circ f) \Big)$$

$$= \Big(\sum_{x \in \text{supp}\,\mu} r_x(\delta_x * (\delta\langle\rangle)), \chi_{f(x)} \Big) = (\mu, f).$$

$h^\dagger \circ \eta_D = h$:

$$h^\dagger \circ \eta_D(x) = h^\dagger(\delta_{\langle\rangle}, \chi_x) = (\delta_{\langle\rangle} * (\pi_1 \circ h \circ \chi_x), \pi_2 \circ \chi_x)$$

$$= ((\pi_1 \circ h)(x), (\pi_2 \circ h)(x)) = h(x)$$

$k^\dagger \circ h^\dagger = (k^\dagger \circ h)^\dagger$: We assume $k \colon E \to \Theta RV_{A^\infty}(F)$. Then

$$k^\dagger \circ h^\dagger(\mu, f) = k^\dagger \Big(\sum_{x \in \text{supp}\,\mu} r_x \left(\delta_x * (\pi_1 \circ h \circ f)(x) \right), (\pi_2 \circ h \circ f)(x) \Big)$$

$$= k^\dagger \Big(\sum_{x \in \text{supp}\,\mu} r_x(\delta_x * (\mu_{h \circ f)(x)}), g_{(h \circ f)(x)} \Big)$$

Assuming $\mu_{(h \circ f)(x)} = \sum_{y \in \text{supp}\,\mu_{(h \circ f)(x)}} s_y \delta_y$, we can rewrite this as

$$k^\dagger \circ h^\dagger(\mu, f) = k^\dagger \Big(\sum_{x \in \text{supp}\,\mu} r_x(\delta_x * (\sum_{y \in \text{supp}\,\mu_{h \circ f)(x)}} s_y \delta_y)), g_{(h \circ f)(x)} \Big)$$

$$= \Big(\sum_{x \in \text{supp}\,\mu} \sum_{y \in \text{supp}\,\mu_{(h \circ f)(x)}} r_x s_y \delta_x * \delta_y * (\pi_1 \circ k \circ g_{(h \circ f)(x)}(y)),$$

$$\pi_2 \circ k \circ g_{(h \circ f)(x)}(y)) \qquad (2)$$

where throughout we rewrite $\pi_1 \circ k \circ g_{(h \circ f)(x)} = \mu_{k \circ g_{(h \circ f)(x)}}$ and $\pi_2 \circ k \circ g_{(h \circ f)(x)} = g_{k \circ g_{(h \circ f)(x)}}$.

Starting on the other end, we find

$$(k^\dagger \circ h)^\dagger(\mu, f) = \Big(\sum_{x \in \text{supp}\,\mu} r_x(\delta_x * (\pi_1 \circ k^\dagger \circ h \circ f)(x)), (\pi_2 \circ k^\dagger \circ h \circ f)(x) \Big)$$

$$= \Big(\sum_{x \in \text{supp}\,\mu} r_x(\delta_x * \mu_{k^\dagger((h \circ f)(x))}), g_{k^\dagger((h \circ f)(x))} \Big). \qquad (3)$$

Now,

$$k^\dagger((h \circ f)(x)) = k^\dagger(\mu_{(h \circ f)(x)}, g_{(h \circ f)(x)}) = k^\dagger \Big(\sum_{y \in \text{supp}\,\mu_{(h \circ f)(x)}} s_y \delta_y, g_{(h \circ f)(x)} \Big)$$

$$= \Big(\sum_{y \in \text{supp}\,\mu_{(h \circ f)(x)}} s_y \delta_y * (\pi_1 \circ k \circ g_{(h \circ f)(x)}(y)), \pi_2 \circ k \circ g_{(h \circ f)(x)}(y) \Big)$$

Substituting this last in Equation 2 then yields Equation 3, which proves the result.   □

Example 5. The observant reader will have noticed two things: first, we haven't said on what category the construction $D \mapsto \Theta RV_{A^\infty}(D)$ forms a monad, and second, we haven't shown that the Kleisli extension $h^\dagger$ is Scott continuous. The fact is that the second is not true, as we now demonstrate, and this implies that the construction is not a monad on any category of domains and Scott continuous maps.

Consider two elements $s, t \in A^*$ from Example 4 with $s < t$ and the element $u \in A^*$ with $su \not\leq tu$. Then $\delta_s < \delta_t \in \Theta\mathrm{Prob}(A^\infty)$. We take $D = A^\infty$, and let $h \colon A^\infty \to \Theta RV_{A^\infty}(A^\infty)$ by $h(w) = (\delta_w, \iota_w)$, where $\iota_x \colon \{x\} \to A^\infty$ is the inclusion of $x \in A^\infty$ into A^∞. Finally, let $f \colon \{s\} \to A^\infty$ and $g \colon \{t\} \to A^\infty$ satisfy $f(s) = g(t) = u$. Then, $(\delta_s, f) \leq (\delta_t, g) \in \Theta RV_{A^\infty}(A^\infty)$ and our definition of $h^\dagger$ implies

$$\pi_1 \circ h^\dagger(\delta_s, f) = \delta_{su} \quad \text{and} \quad \pi_1 \circ h^\dagger(\delta_t, g) = \delta_{tu}.$$

But $s < t$ and our choice of u imply $su \not\leq tu$, which in turn implies

$$\pi_1 \circ h^\dagger(\delta_s, f) = \delta_{su} \not\leq \delta_{tu} = \pi_1 \circ h^\dagger(\delta_t, g),$$

from which it follows that $h^\dagger(\delta_s, f) \not\leq h^\dagger(\delta_t, g)$, so $h^\dagger \colon \Theta RV_{A^\infty}(A^\infty) \to \Theta RV_{A^\infty}(A^\infty)$ is not monotone, hence not Scott continuous.

4.3   Relation to the Results of Goubault-Larrecq and Varacca

This paper and [20] were inspired by the work of Goubault-Larrecq and Varacca in [10]. Our goal has been to understand their approach in terms of domain-theoretic constructions, and to reveal in more detail what is taking place. While their presentation is necessarily sparse (given the limitations of a conference submission), we have taken more time to develop the approach in detail. We also have chosen a more general setting — instead of focusing on the case of the Cantor fan, we have developed our results assuming we are working over an arbitrary finite alphabet. Nevertheless, our results subsume theirs for $A = \{0, 1\}$, which is to say our construction yields their construction in the case $A = \{0, 1\}$. The proof of this relies on checking that our constructions agree with theirs in the case of the bases for $\Theta\mathrm{Prob}(\{0, 1\}^*)$ and of $\bigoplus_{X \in AC(\{0,1\}^\infty)}[X \to D]$, for D a bounded complete domain. This is a routine check to carry out. Of course, the main consequence is that there is a flaw in their work. Our example above applies equally in their setting, so their construction is not a monad over BCD.

5   Summary and Future Work

In this paper and in [20] we have presented a reconstruction of the model of continuous random variables over bounded complete domains first devised by Goubault-Larrecq and Varraca in [10]. We also have extended the results to apply to an arbitrary finite alphabet, instead of limiting the focus to the case $A = \{0, 1\}$. Our motivation is a more general development that would be directly applicable to settings such as process calculi over finite alphabets, where one wants to add probabilistic choice to an existing model. Our main contributions are the clarification that the structure of the model relies fundamentally on the family of Lawson-compact antichains in the domain A^∞. We have also shown that the monad construction does not lie within BCD – or any category of domains and Scott-continuous maps. We leave as an open problem how to repair this problem – we believe a new idea is needed, since the internal monoid structure on A^∞ using concatenation is not a monotone operation, and so the convolution operation it induces on $\mathsf{Prob}(A^\infty)$ is not monotone either.

Nevertheless, the proof that the monad laws hold – a proof essentially taken from [10] – is valid, so there is a monad. The question is what category it is on. We believe the right category here is one involving monoids and their probability measures, and continuous maps into (bounded complete) domains. But how to make sense of this for computational applications is not clear to us. We also remain intrigued by the construction of the monad, which uses convolution in a way we have not seen before – the second component in the convolved product is parameterized by the first; we'd like to understand this better. This is one reason we believe the probability monad Prob on monoids is at play here, but we do not understand exactly how.

Another problem we are interested in exploring is the relation between automata with discrete state spaces and those with continuous state spaces, e.g., the unit interval. We believe there is a role for the models described here in understanding such systems. As pointed out by one of the anonymous referees, this idea is potentially related to the approximation of labelled Markov processes over continuous state spaces by ones with finite state space, as explored in [6].

Acknowledgements. The author thanks Tyler Barker for several very useful and stimulating discussions, and for pointing out the problem with the montonicity of the Kleisli extension for the monad construction.. The author also thanks the anonymous referees for their helpful suggestions. Finally, the author gratefully acknowledges the support of the US NSF during the preparation of this paper.

References

1. Abramsky, S.: Domain theory in logical form. Annals of Pure and Applied Logic 51, 1–77 (1991)
2. Abramsky, S., Jung, A.: Domain Theory. In: Handbook of Logic in Computer Science, pp. 1–168. Clarendon Press (1994)
3. Beck, J.: Distributive laws, Seminar on Triples and Categorical Homology Theory. Lecture Notes in Mathematics, vol. 80, pp. 119–140 (1969)
4. Brookes, S.D., Hoare, C.A.R., Roscoe, A.W.: A theory of communicating sequential processes. Journal of the ACM 31, 560–599 (1984)

5. Fedorchuk, V.: Probability measures in topology. Russ. Math. Surv. 46, 45–93 (1991)
6. Chaput, P., Danos, V., Panangaden, P., Plotkin, G.: Approximating Markov Processes by Averaging. In: Albers, S., Marchetti-Spaccamela, A., Matias, Y., Nikoletseas, S., Thomas, W. (eds.) ICALP 2009, Part II. LNCS, vol. 5556, pp. 127–138. Springer, Heidelberg (2009)
7. Gierz, G., Hofmann, K.H., Lawson, J.D., Mislove, M., Scott, D.: Continuous Lattices and Domains. Cambridge University Press (2003)
8. Gehrke, M., Grigorieff, S., Pin, J.-É.: Duality and equational theory of regular languages. In: Aceto, L., Damgård, I., Goldberg, L.A., Halldórsson, M.M., Ingólfsdóttir, A., Walukiewicz, I. (eds.) ICALP 2008, Part II. LNCS, vol. 5126, pp. 246–257. Springer, Heidelberg (2008)
9. Gehrke, M.: Stone duality and the recognisable languages over an algebra. In: Kurz, A., Lenisa, M., Tarlecki, A. (eds.) CALCO 2009. LNCS, vol. 5728, pp. 236–250. Springer, Heidelberg (2009)
10. Goubault-Larrecq, J., Varacca, D.: Continuous random variables. In: LICS 2011, pp. 97–106. IEEE Press (2011)
11. Hofmann, K.H., Mislove, M.: Compact affine monoids, harmonic analysis and information theory. In: Mathematical Foundations of Information Flow, AMS Proceedings of Symposia on Applied Mathematics, vol. 71, pp. 125–182 (2012)
12. Hyland, M., Plotkin, G.D., Power, J.: Combining computational effects: commutativity and sum. In: IFIP TCS 2002, pp. 474–484 (2002)
13. Jones, C.: Probabilistic Nondeterminism. PhD Thesis, University of Edinburgh (1988)
14. Jung, A.: The classification of continuous domains (Extended Abstract). In: LICS 1990, pp. 35–40. IEEE Press (1990)
15. Jung, A., Tix, R.: The troublesome probabilistic powerdomain. ENTCS 13, 70–91 (1998)
16. Keimel, K., Plotkin, G.D., Tix, R.: Semantic domains for combining probability and non-Determinism. ENTCS 222, 2–99 (2009)
17. Mislove, M.: Nondeterminism and probabilistic choice: obeying the laws. In: Palamidessi, C. (ed.) CONCUR 2000. LNCS, vol. 1877, pp. 350–374. Springer, Heidelberg (2000)
18. Mislove, M.: Discrete random variables over domains. Theoretical Computer Science 380, 181–198 (2007)
19. Mislove, M.: Topology domain theory and theoretical computer science. Topology and Its Applications 89, 3–59 (1998)
20. Mislove, M.: Anatomy of a domain of continuous random variables I. Submitted to TCS, 19 p.
21. Moggi, E.: Computational Lambda-calculus and monads. In: LICS 1989, pp. 14–23. IEEE Press (1989)
22. Plotkin, G., Power, J.: Notions of computation determine monads. In: Nielsen, M., Engberg, U. (eds.) Fossacs 2002. LNCS, vol. 2303, pp. 342–356. Springer, Heidelberg (2002)
23. Saheb-Djarhomi, N.: CPOs of measures for nondeterminism. Theoretical Computer Science 12, 19–37 (1980)
24. Scott, D.S.: Data types as lattices. SIAM J. Comput. 5, 522–587 (1976)
25. Varacca, D.: Two Denotational Models for Probabilistic Computation. PhD Thesis, Aarhus University (2003)
26. Varacca, D., Winskel, G.: Distributing probability over nondeterminism. Mathematical Structures in Computer Science 16 (2006)

Towards Nominal Abramsky

Andrzej S. Murawski[1] and Nikos Tzevelekos[2],[*]

[1] University of Warwick
[2] Queen Mary, University of London

Abstract. Since the discovery of fully abstract models of PCF in the early 1990s, game semantics has expanded to a wide range of programming paradigms, covering effects like state, control, general references, non-determinism, probability and concurrency. Those models revealed an interesting phenomenon referred to as *Abramsky's cube*: starting from the PCF model and relaxing each of its combinatorial conditions, one was led to capture a corresponding impure effect. In this paper we initiate the construction of an analogous cube for nominal games, a strand of game semantics developed in the last ten years that incorporates *names* as semantic atoms and captures generative effects without using "bad-object" constructors. In particular, we examine the stateful axis of the cube: starting from games for higher-order references we move to full ground references, where strategies respect visibility, and from there to purely functional behaviour and innocent strategies.

Authors' Note

Both authors met Samson at Oxford. Samson arrived there just in time to grill the first of us as a D.Phil. examiner and a little later started supervising the second on his MFoCS course.

Our life paths were closely intertwined afterwards. Andrzej joined the *Algorithmic Game Semantics* team, while Nikos started his D.Phil. with Samson, to be followed by a stint on the *Logic of Interaction and Information Flow* project.

Since Andrzej was supervised by Luke Ong, himself one of Samson's students, we belong to different generations of scientific offspring that can be traced back to Samson. Still, Nikos does not quite like when Andrzej calls him "uncle".

We are truly grateful to Samson for sound, reliable and insightful advice at various stages of our academic lives.

Happy Birthday, Samson!

1 Introduction

Game semantics emerged as a new semantic theory in the 1990s through the quest for a fully abstract model of PCF [AJM00,HO00]. In particular, models proposed by Hyland and Ong [HO00], and Nickau [Nic94] have brought to the fore a number of technical constraints on how games should be designed, such as innocence, bracketing and

---

[*] Supported by a Royal Academy of Engineering research fellowship.

B. Coecke, L. Ong, and P. Panangaden (Eds.): Abramsky Festschrift, LNCS 7860, pp. 246–263, 2013.
© Springer-Verlag Berlin Heidelberg 2013

visibility. Abramsky suggested that relaxations of the constraints can lead to a whole hierarchy of models capturing a variety of impure computational features, a paradigm that came to be known as *Abramsky's cube*. The most immediate illustrations of this methodology were subsequent papers about state [AM97], control [Lai97] and general references [AHM98], in which violations of the above-mentioned three constraints were related precisely to three different programming features. The three directions could be viewed as three axes of a "cube", which has ever since grown to embrace, among others, polymorphism, non-determinism, probability and concurrency.

A related advance in the 2000s was the development of nominal game semantics [AGM+04,Lai04,Tze09], which aimed to provide a more accurate account of generative effects such as references and, specifically, to target the bad-variable problem in game semantics. The problem stemmed from the fact that references were modelled as pairs of reading and writing methods, thus giving rise to objects of reference type whose behaviour need not be compatible with that of genuine reference cells. Nominal game models rely on collections of names that can be used throughout the play as part of a move. Operationally, they correspond to reference names in the implementation.

In this paper we follow the paradigm of Abramsky's cube in the nominal setting and uncover constraints corresponding respectively to the expressive power of general references (references to values of any type can be created), ground-type storage (only references to ground-type values, such as numbers or names, are allowed) and pure functional computation (no references can be created).

Our point of departure is our nominal model of RefML [MT11], which accounts for computation with general references. To study restrictions on the creation of references, we consider two sublanguages, called GrML and FunML respectively, which embody respectively ground-type storage and pure functional computation. The model from [MT11] provides a basic notion of a strategy and we set out to find restrictions corresponding to GrML and FunML. In non-nominal modelling, the borderline between general and ground-type storage could be captured by the visibility condition [AHM98]. Although this condition can be easily reintroduced in the nominal setting, it is not preserved by composition. To regain compositionality, we also need to eliminate the use of higher-order local state, that is, the generation of names of higher-order reference cells by programs. This results in a restriction that we call *groundness*, which provides a semantic match for GrML. To pass from ground-type storage to pure functional computation, we introduce a condition inspired by innocence. In order to make the course of play totally dependent on view, we forbid the creation of any names by programs and stipulate that copycat behaviour is followed whenever the environment requests the value of a reference whose name cannot be found in the current P-view.

The conditions of groundness and innocence are accompanied by factorisation results, as in the original case of the cube, but they are a little more involved due to complications that arise in the nominal setting. An elegant feature of the original cube was the fact that the essence of the passage from functional computation could be attributed to single representative strategies, corresponding respectively to a single integer-valued memory cell and a single higher-order cell. In the nominal setting, in addition to these strategies, one has to use families of name generators. Moreover, in order to pass to

$$\frac{}{u, \Gamma \vdash () : \text{unit}} \qquad \frac{i \in \mathbb{Z}}{u, \Gamma \vdash i : \text{int}} \qquad \frac{a \in (u \cap \mathbb{A}_\theta)}{u, \Gamma \vdash a : \text{ref } \theta} \qquad \frac{(x : \theta) \in \Gamma}{u, \Gamma \vdash x : \theta}$$

$$\frac{u, \Gamma \vdash M_1 : \text{int} \quad u, \Gamma \vdash M_2 : \text{int}}{u, \Gamma \vdash M_1 \oplus M_2 : \text{int}} \qquad \frac{u, \Gamma \vdash M : \text{int} \quad u, \Gamma \vdash N_0 : \theta \quad u, \Gamma \vdash N_1 : \theta}{u, \Gamma \vdash \text{if } M \text{ then } N_1 \text{ else } N_0 : \theta}$$

$$\frac{u, \Gamma \vdash M : \text{ref } \theta \quad u, \Gamma \vdash N : \theta}{u, \Gamma \vdash M := N : \text{unit}} \qquad \frac{u, \Gamma \vdash M : \text{ref } \theta}{u, \Gamma \vdash \,!M : \theta} \qquad \frac{u, \Gamma \vdash M : \text{ref } \theta \quad u, \Gamma \vdash N : \text{ref } \theta}{u, \Gamma \vdash M = N : \text{int}}$$

$$\frac{u, \Gamma \vdash M : \theta}{u, \Gamma \vdash \text{ref}_\theta(M) : \text{ref } \theta} \qquad \frac{u, \Gamma \vdash M : \theta \to \theta' \quad u, \Gamma \vdash N : \theta}{u, \Gamma \vdash MN : \theta'} \qquad \frac{u, \Gamma \cup \{x : \theta\} \vdash M : \theta'}{u, \Gamma \vdash \lambda x^\theta . M : \theta \to \theta'}$$

Fig. 1. Syntax of RefML. $\oplus$ stands for binary integer functions, e.g. $+, -, *, =$.

innocence, it is necessary to provide a facility for storing an unbounded collection of names.

2   RefML

We start off by introducing the programming language RefML [MT11], which we shall work with throughout the paper. Its types are defined by the grammar below.

$$\theta, \theta' \; ::= \; \text{unit} \; \mid \; \text{int} \; \mid \; \text{ref } \theta \; \mid \; \theta \to \theta'$$

RefML is best described as the call-by-value λ-calculus over the ground types unit, int, and ref θ, augmented with basic commands (termination), primitives for integer arithmetic (constants, zero-test, binary integer functions) and higher-order reference manipulation (reference names, dereferencing, assignment, memory allocation, reference equality testing). The typing rules are given in Figure 1, where $\mathbb{A} = \biguplus_\theta \mathbb{A}_\theta$ stands for a countable set of *reference names* (one such set for each type θ), or just *names*, and u refers to a finite subset of $\mathbb{A}$.

Following standard conventions, we write $M; N$ for the term $(\lambda z^\theta . N) M$, where z does not occur in N and θ matches the type of M. let $x = M$ in N will stand for $(\lambda x^\theta . N) M$ in general. The *values* of the language are given by the syntax:

$$V ::= () \mid i \mid a \mid x \mid \lambda x^\theta . M.$$

To define the operational semantics of RefML, we introduce a syntactic notion of store. A *syntactic store* (or just *store*) will simply be a function from a finite set of names to values such that the type of each name matches the type of its assigned value. We write $S[a \mapsto V]$ for the store obtained by updating S so that a is mapped to V (this may extend the domain of S). Given a store S and a term M we say that the pair (S, M) is *compatible* if all names occurring in M are from the domain of S.

The small-step reduction rules are given as judgments of the shape $(S, M) \to (S', M')$, where (S, M), (S', M') are compatible and $\text{dom}(S) \subseteq \text{dom}(S')$. We present them in Figure 2, where we let a, b range over names. Evaluation contexts are given by

$$(S, \text{if } 0 \text{ then } N_1 \text{ else } N_0) \rightarrow (S, N_0) \qquad (S, a = b) \rightarrow (S, 0)$$
$$(S, \text{if } i \text{ then } N_1 \text{ else } N_0) \rightarrow (S, N_1) \qquad (S, a = a) \rightarrow (S, 1)$$
$$(S, (\lambda x.M)V) \rightarrow (S, M[V/x]) \qquad (S, \text{ref}_\theta(V)) \rightarrow (S[a' \mapsto V], a')$$
$$(S, !a) \rightarrow (S, S(a)) \qquad \dfrac{(S, M) \rightarrow (S', M')}{(S, E[M]) \rightarrow (S', E[M'])}$$
$$(S, a := V) \rightarrow (S[a \mapsto V], ())$$

Fig. 2. Small-step operational semantics of RefML (side-conditions: $i \neq 0, a \neq b, a' \notin \text{dom}(S)$)

$$E ::= (\lambda x.N)_- \mid \_N \mid \_\oplus N \mid i \oplus \_ \mid \_ = N \mid a = \_$$
$$\mid !\_ \mid \_ := N \mid a := \_ \mid \text{ref}_\theta(\_) \mid \text{if } \_ \text{ then } N_1 \text{ else } N_0.$$

We say that (S, M) *evaluates* to (S', V) if $(S, M) \twoheadrightarrow (S', V)$, with V a value. For $\vdash M : \text{unit}$ we say that M *converges*, written $M \Downarrow$, if $(\emptyset, M)$ evaluates to some $(S', ())$.

Example 1. It is well known that higher-order references are sufficiently powerful to enable one to define fixed-point combinators [AHM98] and, consequently, divergent terms Ω_θ at any type. Also, for any type θ, we define the terms new_θ by:

$$\text{new}_{\text{unit}} = \text{ref}_{\text{unit}}() \qquad \text{new}_{\theta \to \theta'} = \text{ref}_{\theta \to \theta'}(\lambda x^\theta.\Omega_{\theta'})$$
$$\text{new}_{\text{int}} = \text{ref}_{\text{int}}(0) \qquad \text{new}_{\text{ref}^i \theta''} = \text{ref}(\text{ref}(\cdots \text{ref}(\text{new}_{\theta''})))$$

where θ'' is one of unit, int or a function type. These terms create new names and initialise them with default values.

Definition 2. *The term-in-context* $\Gamma \vdash M_1 : \theta$ **approximates** $\Gamma \vdash M_2 : \theta$ *(written* $\Gamma \vdash M_1 \lesssim M_2$*) if* $C[M_1] \Downarrow$ *implies* $C[M_2] \Downarrow$ *for any context* $C[-]$ *such that* $\vdash C[M_1], C[M_2] : \text{unit}$. *Two terms-in-context are* **equivalent** *if they approximate each other (written* $\Gamma \vdash M_1 \cong M_2$*).*

In the remainder of the paper we shall also discuss two specific fragments of RefML.

- GrML will comprise all RefML-terms in which all occurrences of $\text{ref}_\theta(M)$ are restricted to non-functional types, i.e. θ cannot have the shape $\theta_1 \to \theta_2$. Thus, GrML is the sublanguage of RefML allowing for local storage of ground values only.
- FunML will consist of all RefML-terms that do not have any occurrences of $\text{ref}_\theta(M)$. Thus, FunML is also a subset of GrML. FunML can be viewed as a purely functional fragment of RefML, since terms cannot create reference cells.

3   Game Model

Here we review the game model of RefML first presented in [MT11]. Its distinctive feature is the presence of stores in moves and the possibility of justifying a move with a higher-order reference cell in addition to the standard option of justifying a move with another.

$$M_{A\otimes B} = (I_A \times I_B) \uplus \bar{I}_A \uplus \bar{I}_B \qquad\qquad M_{A\Rightarrow B} = \{\star\} \uplus M_A \uplus M_B$$

$$I_{A\otimes B} = I_A \times I_B \qquad\qquad\qquad\qquad I_{A\Rightarrow B} = \{\star\}$$

$$\lambda_{A\otimes B} = [(\mathrm{i}_A,\mathrm{i}_B) \mapsto PA, \lambda_A \upharpoonright \bar{I}_A, \lambda_B \upharpoonright \bar{I}_B] \qquad \lambda_{A\Rightarrow B} = [\star \mapsto PA, \bar{\lambda}_A[\mathrm{i}_A \mapsto OQ], \lambda_B]$$

$$\vdash_{A\otimes B} = \{((\mathrm{i}_A,\mathrm{i}_B), m) \mid \mathrm{i}_A \vdash_A m \vee \mathrm{i}_B \vdash_B m\} \qquad \vdash_{A\Rightarrow B} = \{(\star,\mathrm{i}_A)\} \cup \{(\mathrm{i}_A,\mathrm{i}_B)\} \cup \vdash_A \cup \vdash_B$$

$$\cup (\vdash_A \upharpoonright \bar{I}_A{}^2) \cup (\vdash_B \upharpoonright \bar{I}_B{}^2)$$

Fig. 3. Arena constructions. We write $\bar{I}_A = M_A \setminus I_A$.

Formally, the model is constructed using mathematical objects (moves, plays, strategies) that feature names drawn from the set

$$\mathbb{A} = \biguplus_\theta \mathbb{A}_\theta .$$

Although names underpin various elements of our model, we do not want to delve into the precise nature of the sets containing them. Hence, all of our definitions preserve name-invariance, i.e. our objects are (strong) *nominal sets* [GP02,Tze09]. Note that we do not need the full power of the theory but mainly the basic notion of name-permutation. Here permutations are bijections $\pi : \mathbb{A} \to \mathbb{A}$ with finite support which respect the indexing of name-sets. For an element x belonging to a (nominal) set X we write $\nu(x)$ for its name-support, which is the set of names occurring in x. Moreover, for any $x, y \in X$, we write $x \sim y$ if there is a permutation π such that $x = \pi \cdot y$.

Our model is couched in the Honda-Yoshida style of modelling call-by-value computation [HY99]. Before we define what it means to play, we introduce the auxiliary concept of an arena.

Definition 3. *An arena* $A = \langle M_A, I_A, \lambda_A, \vdash_A \rangle$ *is given by:*

- *a set of moves* M_A *and a subset* $I_A \subseteq M_A$ *of initial ones,*
- *a labelling function* $\lambda_A : M_A \to \{O, P\} \times \{Q, A\}$,
- *a justification relation* $\vdash_A \subseteq M_A \times (M_A \setminus I_A)$;

satisfying, for each $m, m' \in M_A$, *the conditions (π_i is the ith projection function):*

- $m \in I_A \implies \lambda_A(m) = (P, A)$,
- $m \vdash_A m' \wedge \pi_2(\lambda_A(m)) = A \implies \pi_2(\lambda_A(m')) = Q$,
- $m \vdash_A m' \implies \pi_1(\lambda_A(m)) \neq \pi_1(\lambda_A(m'))$.

We range over moves by m, n and use i, o, p to refer to initial moves, O-moves and P-moves respectively. We let $\bar{\lambda}_A$ be the OP-complement of λ_A. Using the $\otimes$ and $\Rightarrow$ constructions on arenas (Fig. 3), for each type θ we define the corresponding arena $[\![\theta]\!]$, starting from the following definitions.

$$[\![\mathsf{unit}]\!] = \langle \{\star\}, \{\star\}, \emptyset, \emptyset \rangle \qquad\qquad [\![\mathsf{int}]\!] = \langle \mathbb{Z}, \mathbb{Z}, \emptyset, \emptyset \rangle$$

$$[\![\mathsf{ref}\ \theta]\!] = \langle \mathbb{A}_\theta, \mathbb{A}_\theta, \emptyset, \emptyset \rangle \qquad\qquad [\![\theta \to \theta']\!] = [\![\theta]\!] \Rightarrow [\![\theta']\!]$$

We write 1 for $[\![\mathsf{unit}]\!]$, $\mathbb{Z}$ for $[\![\mathsf{int}]\!]$, and $\mathbb{A}_\theta$ for $[\![\mathsf{ref}\ \theta]\!]$; and set $M_\phi = \biguplus_{\theta,\theta'} M_{[\![\theta \to \theta']\!]}$.

Although types are interpreted by arenas, the actual games will be played in *preare-nas*, which are defined in the same way as arenas with the exception that initial moves are O-questions. Given arenas A, B we define the prearena $A \to B$ as follows.

$$M_{A \to B} = M_A \uplus M_B \qquad\qquad \lambda_{A \to B} = [\overline{\lambda}_A [i_A \mapsto OQ], \lambda_B]$$
$$I_{A \to B} = I_A \qquad\qquad\qquad \vdash_{A \to B} = \{(i_A, i_B)\} \cup \vdash_A \cup \vdash_B$$

Our plays shall feature moves attached with stores, where the names appearing in a play take values. We let the set Val_θ of semantic values of type θ be $I_{[\![\theta]\!]}$ (so $\mathsf{Val}_{\mathsf{unit}} = \mathsf{Val}_{\theta \to \theta'} = \{\star\}$, $\mathsf{Val}_{\mathsf{int}} = \mathbb{Z}$, $\mathsf{Val}_{\mathsf{ref}\,\theta} = \mathbb{A}_\theta$), and let $\mathsf{Val} = \uplus_\theta \mathsf{Val}_\theta$. A *store* Σ is a type-preserving finite partial function from $\mathbb{A}$ to Val, and Sto is the set of all stores:

$$\mathsf{Sto} = \{\, \Sigma : \mathbb{A} \rightharpoonup \mathsf{Val} \mid |\Sigma| \text{ finite} \wedge (a \in \mathsf{dom}(\Sigma) \cap \mathbb{A}_\theta \implies \Sigma(a) \in \mathsf{Val}_\theta) \,\}.$$

A move-with-store on a (pre)arena A is a pair m^Σ with $m \in M_A$ and $\Sigma \in \mathsf{Sto}$.

Definition 4. *A justified sequence on a prearena A is a sequence of moves-with-store from $M_A \uplus M_\phi$ such that, apart from the first move which must be of the form i^Σ with $i \in I_A$, every move in s is equipped with a pointer to an earlier move, or to a name inside the store of an earlier move. These pointers are called* justification pointers *and are subject to the following constraints.*

- *If n^T points to m^Σ then either $m, n \in M_A$ and $m \vdash_A n$, or $m, n \in M_{\theta \to \theta'}$ for some θ, θ' and $m \vdash_{[\![\theta \to \theta']\!]} n$. We say that m^Σ justifies n^T.*
- *If n^T points to $a \in \mathsf{dom}(\Sigma)$ of m^Σ then $a \in \mathbb{A}_{\theta \to \theta'}$ for some θ, θ', and n must be an initial question in $M_{[\![\theta \to \theta']\!]}$. We say that m^Σ a-justifies n^T.*

An intuitive way to comprehend pointers to a name $a \in \mathsf{dom}(\Sigma) \cap \mathbb{A}_{\theta \to \theta'}$ is to think of them as pointing to the value $\star$ of a stored in Σ. Since the value of a is of function type, its structure is not revealed at once, but it can be explored by players by invoking the function, that is, by playing in $[\![\theta \to \theta']\!]$ from that initial $\star$.

Note that a justified sequence on A contains moves from M_A, called A-*moves*, and moves from M_ϕ, which hereditarily point inside stores of other moves. The latter are called ϕ-*moves*. We shall say that m^Σ is an *ancestor* of n^T (or that n^T is a descendant of m^Σ) if there is a chain of pointers from n^T to m, possibly passing through stores on the way. Similarly, we say that m^Σ is an a-*ancestor* of n^T (or that n^T is an a-descendant of m^Σ) if there is a chain of pointers from n^T to a in Σ (the chain may also be visiting other stores). Note that each ϕ-move has a unique a-ancestor from M_A.

For each $S \subseteq \mathbb{A}$ and Σ we define the closure of S under Σ as $\Sigma^*(S) = \bigcup_i \Sigma^i(S)$, where $\Sigma^0(S) = S$ and $\Sigma^{i+1}(S) = \Sigma(\Sigma^i(S)) \cap \mathbb{A}$. The set of *available names* of a justified sequence is defined inductively by $\mathsf{Av}(\epsilon) = \emptyset$ and

$$\mathsf{Av}(sn^T) = \begin{cases} \mathsf{Av}(s) & \text{there is an } a\text{-ancestor } m^\Sigma \text{ of } n^T \text{ and } a \notin \mathsf{Av}(s_{\leq m^\Sigma}) \\ \Sigma^*(\mathsf{Av}(s) \cup \nu(n)) & \text{otherwise} \end{cases}$$

where $s_{\leq m^\Sigma}$ is the subsequence of s up to m^Σ. We shall be writing $s \sqsubseteq s'$ to mean that s is a subsequence of s'.

Definition 5. *Let A be a prearena. A justified sequence s on A is called a* **legal sequence***, written $s \in L_A$, if it satisfies the conditions below.*

- *No adjacent moves belong to the same player, and no move points to a move (or the store of a move) of the same player (*Alternation*).*
- *The justifier of each answer is the most recent unanswered question (*Bracketing*).*

We call s a **play** *if it additionally satisfies:*

- *For any $s'm^\Sigma \sqsubseteq s$, $\mathrm{dom}(\Sigma) = \mathsf{Av}(s'm^\Sigma)$ (*Frugality*).*

We write P_A for the set of plays on A.

Example 6. Here are two plays on $\mathbb{A}_{\mathsf{int} \to \mathsf{int}} \to \mathbb{Z} \Rightarrow \mathbb{Z}$ (for the sake of clarity, we omit pointers that would just point at preceding moves). We use double-line pointers to highlight the justification pointers pointing at stores.

$$a^{(a,\star)} \, \star^{(a,\star)} \, 1^{(a,\star)} \, 1^{(a,\star)} \, 3^{(a,\star)} \, 3^{(a,\star)} \qquad a^{(a,\star)} \, \star^{(a,\star)} \, 1^{(a,\star)} \, 1^{(a,\star)} \, 3^{(a,\star)} \, 3^{(a,\star)}$$

The plays will be among those used to interpret the respective terms:

$$x : \mathsf{ref}\,(\mathsf{int} \to \mathsf{int}) \vdash \,!x : \mathsf{int} \to \mathsf{int} \qquad x : \mathsf{ref}\,(\mathsf{int} \to \mathsf{int}) \vdash \lambda h^{\mathsf{int}}.(!x)h : \mathsf{int} \to \mathsf{int}$$

Each name appearing in a legal sequence s, i.e. such that $a \in \nu(s)$, is called a *P-name* of s, written $a \in P(s)$, if it is first introduced in s by a P-move, that is, there is even-length $s'm^\Sigma \sqsubseteq s$ such that $a \in \nu(m^\Sigma) \setminus \nu(s')$. The set of *O-names* of s, $O(s)$, is defined dually. Clearly, $\nu(s) = O(s) \uplus P(s)$. Moreover, let us define γ to be the canonical function on justified sequences which imposes frugality by deleting unavailable names from store-domains and all ϕ-moves that they hereditarily justify. Concretely, $\gamma(\epsilon) = \epsilon$ and:

$$\gamma(sn^T) = \begin{cases} \gamma(s) & \text{if there is an } a\text{-ancestor } m^\Sigma \text{ of } n^T \text{ and } a \notin \mathsf{Av}(s_{\leq m^\Sigma}); \\ \gamma(s) \; n^{T\restriction \mathsf{Av}(sn^T)} & \text{otherwise.} \end{cases}$$

Definition 7. *A* **strategy** *σ on a prearena A, written $\sigma : A$, is a set of even-length plays of A satisfying:*

- *If $so^\Sigma p^{\Sigma'} \in \sigma$ then $s \in \sigma$ (*Even-prefix closure*).*
- *If $s \in \sigma$ and $s \sim t$ then $t \in \sigma$ (*Equivariance*).*
- *If $s_1 p_1^{\Sigma_1}, s_2 p_2^{\Sigma_2} \in \sigma$ and $s_1 \sim s_2$ then $s_1 p_1^{\Sigma_1} \sim s_2 p_2^{\Sigma_2}$ (*Nominal determinacy*).*

Example 8. For each arena A there is an *identity strategy*, $\mathrm{id}_A : A \to A$, defined by

$$\mathrm{id}_A = \{\, s \in P_{A \to A}^{even} \mid \forall s' \sqsubseteq^{even} s. \; s' \restriction A_l = s' \restriction A_r \,\},$$

where the indices l, r distinguish the two copies of A, and $s' \restriction A_x$ is the subsequence of s' containing only moves from the x-copy, along with all ϕ-moves having a-ancestors from the x-copy (for some a).

The behaviour of id_A is called *copycat*. More generally, we say that moves $n^T n'^{T'}$ in a play s are a *copycat pair* if they are consecutive in s, $n^T = n'^{T'}$, and if n^T is justified by $m'^{\Sigma'}$ (or by some $a \in \mathrm{dom}(\Sigma')$) then $n'^{T'}$ is justified by m^Σ (resp. by $a \in \mathrm{dom}(\Sigma)$) where $m^\Sigma m'^{\Sigma'}$ are consecutive in s. It will be useful to spot copycat behaviours occurring in plays exclusively between ϕ-moves with consecutive a-ancestors.

Definition 9. *Let s be an alternating justified sequence in A, $s' \sqsubseteq s$ be ending in $m^\Sigma m'^{\Sigma'}$ and let $a \in \mathrm{dom}(\Sigma) \cap \mathrm{dom}(\Sigma') \cap \mathbb{A}_\phi$ such that $m'^{\Sigma'}$ is not a-justified by m^Σ. We say that (s, s', a) is a **copycat triple** if, for all ϕ-moves n^T in s which have m^Σ or $m'^{\Sigma'}$ as an a-ancestor,*

- *if n has the same polarity as m then there is $n'^{T'}$ such that $n^T n'^{T'}$ are a copycat pair,*
- *if n has the same polarity as m' then there is $n'^{T'}$ such that $n'^{T'} n^T$ are a copycat pair.*

Example 10. We will be economical when writing stores and, in particular, components of the form $(a, \star)$ will often be written simply as a. Also, we will omit mentioning the empty play from strategies. Copycat behaviour is exemplified in the strategy $\sigma : \mathbb{A}_{\mathsf{unit} \to \mathsf{unit}} \to 1 = \{a^a \star^a s\}$ where each $(a^a \star^a s, a^a \star^a, a)$ is a copycat triple. For example, the play

$$a^a \ \underset{O}{\star^a} \ \overset{\frown}{\underset{P}{\star^a}} \ \overset{\frown}{\underset{O}{\star^a}} \ \underset{P}{\star^a} \ \underset{O}{\star^a} \ \underset{P}{\star^a}$$

is in σ. The copycat behaviour means that, when P plays its first move $\star^a$ (underlined), he does not change the value of a in the store. Thus, subsequent questions by O pointing to a in $\star^a$ are responded to by copycat. The strategy turns out to be the denotation of $x : \mathsf{ref}\,(\mathsf{unit} \to \mathsf{unit}) \vdash () : \mathsf{unit}$.

We now turn to defining a suitable notion of interaction between plays. Given arenas A, B, C, we define the prearena $A \to B \to C$ by:

$$M_{A \to B \to C} = M_{A \to B} \uplus M_C \qquad \lambda_{A \to B \to C} = [\lambda_{A \to B}[i_B \mapsto PQ], \bar{\lambda}_C]$$
$$I_{A \to B \to C} = I_A \qquad \vdash_{A \to B \to C} = \vdash_{A \to B} \cup \{(i_B, i_C)\} \cup \vdash_C$$

Let u be a justified sequence on $A \to B \to C$. We define $u \upharpoonright AB$ to be u in which all C-moves are suppressed, along with associated pointers and all ϕ-moves which are a-descendants of C-moves. $u \upharpoonright BC$ is defined analogously. $u \upharpoonright AC$ is defined similarly with the caveat that, if there was a pointer from a C-move to a B-move which in turn had a pointer to an A-move, we add a pointer from the C-move to the A-move. Let us write $u \upharpoonright_\gamma X$ for $\gamma(u \upharpoonright X)$ with $X \in \{AB, BC, AC\}$. Below we shall often say that a move is an O- or a P-move in X meaning ownership in the associated prearena.

Definition 11. *A justified sequence u on $A \to B \to C$ is an **interaction sequence** on A, B, C if it satisfies bracketing and frugality and, for all $X \in \{AB, BC, AC\}$, we have $(u \upharpoonright X) \in L_X$ and the following conditions hold.*

- *$P(u \upharpoonright_\gamma AB) \cap P(u \upharpoonright_\gamma BC) = \emptyset$;*
- *$O(u \upharpoonright_\gamma AC) \cap (P(u \upharpoonright_\gamma AB) \cup P(u \upharpoonright_\gamma BC)) = \emptyset$;*
- *For each $u' \sqsubseteq u$ ending in $m^\Sigma m'^{\Sigma'}$ and $a \in \mathrm{dom}(\Sigma')$ if*

- m' is a P-move in AB and $a \notin \mathsf{Av}(u' \upharpoonright AB)$,
- or m' is a P-move in BC and $a \notin \mathsf{Av}(u' \upharpoonright BC)$,
- or m' is an O-move in AC and $a \notin \mathsf{Av}(u' \upharpoonright AC)$,

then $\Sigma(a) = \Sigma'(a)$ and, moreover, if $a \in \mathbb{A}_\phi$ then $(u \upharpoonright X, u' \upharpoonright X, a)$ are a copycat triple, where X is the respective element of $\{AB, BC, AC\}$.

We write $Int(A, B, C)$ for the set of interaction sequences on A, B, C, and $\sigma \| \tau$ for the set of interactions between strategies $\sigma : A \to B$ and $\tau : B \to C$:

$$\sigma \| \tau = \{\, u \in Int(A, B, C) \mid (u \upharpoonright_\gamma AB) \in \sigma \wedge (u \upharpoonright_\gamma BC) \in \tau \,\}.$$

We shall be referring to the last condition in the definition as the *copycat condition*. According to it, during an interaction the players cannot change the parts of the store which regard names that are not available to them. Moreover, in the case that these names are of functional type, the players are obliged to copycat as far as a-descendants of these names are concerned.

Example 12. Consider strategies $\sigma : \mathbb{A}_{\mathsf{unit} \to \mathsf{int}} \to 1 \Rightarrow \mathbb{Z}$ and $\tau : 1 \Rightarrow \mathbb{Z} \to \mathbb{Z}$ given by the set of all even prefixes of plays of the form shown on the left below (for all $i \in \mathbb{Z}$).

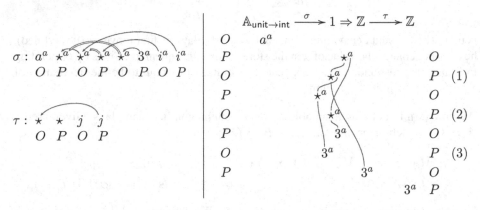

Their interaction is on the right above. We mark polarities for σ on the left of the diagram, and for τ on the right. Consider point (1) in the interaction. In τ, P plays $\star^a$ but a is not available at that point, hence P must copycat from that point on at a-descendants of (that occurrence of) $\star^a$. This is precisely what happens in points (2) and (3).

Definition 13. *Given strategies $\sigma : A \to B$ and $\tau : B \to C$ we define the composite strategy $\sigma; \tau : A \to C$ to be $\{\, s \in P_{A \to C} \mid \exists u \in \sigma \| \tau.\ s = u \upharpoonright_\gamma AC \,\}$.*

Strategy composition is well-defined and associative.

Definition 14. $\mathcal{G}$ *is the category of arenas and strategies, in which strategies in the prearena $A \to B$ are morphisms between A and B.*

In [MT11] we have shown how to interpret RefML in $\mathcal{G}$ so as to obtain a full abstraction result. We refer to this interpretation by writing $[\![\Gamma \vdash M]\!]$.

Example 15. Terms new_θ from Example 1 are interpreted by the strategies $\text{nu}_\theta : 1 \to \mathbb{A}_\theta$, which create a fresh name of type θ and initialise it accordingly.

$$\text{nu}_\theta = \{\, \star a^{(a,v)} \mid a \in \mathbb{A}_\theta \land v \in \{0,\star\} \,\}$$

In the remainder of the paper we identify subclasses of strategies that correspond to denotations of GrML and FunML-terms respectively.

4 Groundness

This section is devoted to finding a class of strategies that characterise ground storage, as embodied in GrML. The work predating nominal game semantics [AHM98] has established *visibility* as the condition characterising the absence of higher-order references. Visibility relies on the concept of a P-view [HO00], which can be adapted easily to our setting.

Definition 16. *The P-view $\ulcorner s \urcorner$ of a play s is inductively defined by:*

$$\ulcorner \epsilon \urcorner = \epsilon, \quad \ulcorner m^\Sigma \urcorner = m^\Sigma, \quad \ulcorner s\, p^\Sigma \urcorner = \ulcorner s \urcorner p^\Sigma, \quad \ulcorner s\, \overparen{x\, s'\, o}^T \urcorner = \ulcorner s \urcorner \overparen{x\, o}^T,$$

*where x is some m^Σ, and o^T points either to x or to a name in its store. A play s is visible if, for any even-length prefix $s'p^\Sigma$ of s, the justifier of p^Σ occurs in $\ulcorner s' \urcorner$. A strategy is **visible** if it contains only visible plays.*

Remark 17. Note that if a play satisfies visibility then its P-view is a justified sequence. Nonetheless, it may fail to be a play because of violating frugality. For example, the following odd-length play on the prearena $1 \to (\mathbb{A}_{\text{unit}} \Rightarrow 1)$

$$\star \quad \overparen{\star \quad \overparen{a^a \quad \star^a}} \quad b^{a,b}$$
$$O \quad P \quad O \quad P \quad O$$

has P-view $\star \star b^{a,b}$, which breaks frugality in its last move.

In this section we first make the perhaps surprising observation that visible strategies fail to compose in the game model introduced in the previous section. We repair the failure by insisting on an additional nominal constraint.

Example 18. Consider the strategy $\sigma : 1 \to ((\mathbb{Z} \Rightarrow \mathbb{Z}) \Rightarrow 1)$ specified by the play on the left below, which breaks visibility in its last move. We label the moves of the prearena as shown on the right.

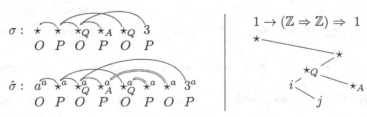

We can see that $\sigma = \mathrm{nu}_{\mathsf{unit}\to\mathsf{unit}}; \hat{\sigma}$, where $\hat{\sigma} : \mathbb{A}_{\mathsf{unit}\to\mathsf{unit}} \to ((\mathbb{Z} \Rightarrow \mathbb{Z}) \Rightarrow 1)$ is specified by the play on the left above (labelling of moves follows the same pattern). Interestingly, both $\mathrm{nu}_{\mathsf{unit}\to\mathsf{unit}}$ and $\hat{\sigma}$ satisfy visibility. After composition, though, the two a-justified moves of $\hat{\sigma}$ will be deleted, since a is no longer an available name. Observe that, thanks to these two a-justified moves, the justifier of the last P-move appears in the view. With a hidden, the last move breaks visibility.

Note that the failure of compositionality stems from the special way in which P-names of higher-order reference cells are treated. This leads us to consider strategies in which such names do not occur. Below we write $\mathbb{A}_\phi = \biguplus_{\theta,\theta'} \mathbb{A}_{\theta\to\theta'}$.

Definition 19. *A strategy σ is **ground** if it is visible and $P(s) \cap \mathbb{A}_\phi = \emptyset$ for any $s \in \sigma$.*

Intuitively, the definition corresponds to removing the capability to generate higher-order reference names.

Lemma 20. *Ground strategies compose. Consequently, for any GrML-term $\Gamma \vdash M$, $[\![\Gamma \vdash M]\!]$ is ground.*

We will also have a converse of the above in the form of a definability result for finite strategies (Corollary 32). The first steps to its proof will be two factorisation arguments that remove violations of groundness.

Lemma 21. *Let $\sigma : A_1 \to A_2$. There exists a visible strategy $\overline{\sigma} : \mathbb{A}_{\mathsf{unit}\to\mathsf{unit}} \otimes A_1 \to A_2$ such that $\langle !_{A_1}; \mathrm{nu}_{\mathsf{unit}\to\mathsf{unit}}, \mathrm{id}_{A_1} \rangle; \overline{\sigma} = \sigma$. Moreover, if $P(s) \cap \mathbb{A}_\phi = \emptyset$ for any $s \in \sigma$ then $P(s) \cap \mathbb{A}_\phi = \emptyset$ for any $s \in \overline{\sigma}$.*

Proof. We are going to augment plays from σ using moves pointing to the higher-order reference represented by $\mathbb{A}_{\mathsf{unit}\to\mathsf{unit}}$ in such a way that visibility will hold. At the same time the added moves will be consistent with the copycat behaviour required during composition.

Formally, the extension $\overline{s}$ of a play $s \in \sigma$ is defined as follows. Given a store Σ, we write Σ^a for $\Sigma \cup \{(a, \star)\}$.

- $\overline{\epsilon} = \epsilon$, $\overline{so^\Sigma} = \overline{s}o^{\Sigma^a}$ (o a question), $\overline{sp^\Sigma} = \overline{s}p^{\Sigma^a}$ (p an answer).
- $\overline{sp^\Sigma} = \overline{s}\underbrace{\star^{\Sigma_1^a} \cdots \star^{\Sigma_1^a}}_{k}p^{\Sigma^a}$ (p a question), where $\overline{s} = \cdots o^{\Sigma^a}o\, m_k^{\Sigma_k^a} \cdots m_2^{\Sigma_2^a} m_1^{\Sigma_1^a}$ and

  $o^\Sigma o$ (or a name in its store) justifies p^Σ in sp^Σ. Moreover, we require that the ith (counting from left to right) occurrence of $\star^{\Sigma_i^a}$ in $\star^{\Sigma_1^a} \cdots \star^{\Sigma_1^a}$ be justified by $(a, \star)$ from Σ_i^a. We depict the definition below, where the dashed line is a justification pointer to a move or to a store.

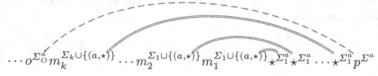

$$\cdots o^{\Sigma_o^a} m_k^{\Sigma_k \cup \{(a,\star)\}} \cdots m_2^{\Sigma_1 \cup \{(a,\star)\}} m_1^{\Sigma_1 \cup \{(a,\star)\}} \star^{\Sigma_1^a} \star^{\Sigma_1^a} \cdots \star^{\Sigma_1^a} p^{\Sigma^a}$$

- $\overline{so^\Sigma} = \overline{s}o^{\Sigma^a}\underbrace{\star^{\Sigma^a} \cdots \star^{\Sigma^a}}_{k}$ (o an answer), where the sequence $\star^{\Sigma^a} \cdots \star^{\Sigma^a}$ answers all

  the a-justified questions (labelled $\star^{\Sigma_1^a}$ above) in $\overline{s}$ that occur after the justifier of o^{Σ^a}.

One can then take $\bar{\sigma}$ to be the least strategy containing all plays $\bar{s}$, where s ranges over σ. It is easy to see that no new P-names are introduced by the construction (a is an O-name).   □

The second result delegates the creation of higher-order reference names and thus rids a strategy of P-names from $\mathbb{A}_\phi$. In order to overapproximate the types of names that can be used as P-names in a prearena A, we define the associated *reference set* $R(A)$. First, for each type θ, we define $R(\theta)$ by

$$R(\text{unit}) = R(\text{int}) = \emptyset, \;\; R(\text{ref } \theta) = \{\theta\} \cup R(\theta), \;\; R(\theta_1 \to \theta_2) = R(\theta_1) \cup R(\theta_2).$$

This is extended to prearenas as follows. For each prearena A,

$$R(A) = \bigcup_{m \in M_A} \left\{ \{\theta\} \cup R(\theta) \mid \nu(m) \cap \mathbb{A}_\theta \neq \emptyset \right\}.$$

To isolate the higher-order types in $R(A)$, we write $\text{HON}(A)$ for the subset of $R(A)$ consisting of function types.

Lemma 22. *Let* $\sigma : A_1 \to A_2$ *and* $A = \bigotimes_{\theta \in \text{HON}(A_1 \to A_2)} (\llbracket \theta \rrbracket \Rightarrow \mathbb{A}_\theta)$. *Let also* $\text{gen}_\theta = \llbracket \vdash \lambda x^\theta.\text{ref}_\theta(x) \rrbracket : 1 \to (\llbracket \theta \rrbracket \Rightarrow \mathbb{A}_\theta)$. *There exists a strategy* $\bar{\sigma} : A \otimes A_1 \to A_2$ *such that* $\langle !_{A_1} ; \langle \text{gen}_\theta \rangle_{\theta \in \text{HON}(A_1 \to A_2)}, \text{id}_{A_1} \rangle ; \bar{\sigma} = \sigma$. *Moreover, if* σ *is visible, so is* $\bar{\sigma}$.

Proof. The main idea is to delegate the creation of new P-names to the additional A component by inserting extra moves from A in front of P-moves. More precisely, given $s \in \sigma$, we define an enriched play $\bar{s}$ as follows, where each v_i is a question to the appropriate $\llbracket \theta \rrbracket \Rightarrow \mathbb{A}_\theta$.

- $\overline{so^\Sigma p^T} = \bar{s} \, o^\Sigma v_1^\Sigma a_1^{\Sigma_1} \cdots v_{k-1}^{\Sigma_{k-1}} v_k p^{\Sigma_k}$, where $\text{dom}(T) \setminus \text{dom}(\Sigma) = \{a_1, \cdots, a_k\}$, $v_i = T(a_i)$, and $\Sigma_i = T \upharpoonright \text{dom}(\Sigma) \cup \{a_1, \cdots, a_i\}$.

In addition, $\bar{\epsilon} = \epsilon$.   □

Corollary 23. *Let* $\sigma : A_1 \to A_2$. *There exists a ground strategy*

$$\bar{\sigma} : \mathbb{A}_{(\text{unit} \to \text{unit})} \otimes \left(\bigotimes_{\theta \in \text{HON}(A_1 \to A_2)} (\llbracket \theta \rrbracket \Rightarrow \mathbb{A}_\theta) \right) \otimes A_1 \to A_2$$

such that $\langle !_{A_1} ; \langle \text{nu}_{\text{unit} \to \text{unit}}, \langle \text{gen}_\theta \rangle_{\theta \in \text{HON}(A_1 \to A_2)} \rangle, \text{id}_{A_1} \rangle ; \bar{\sigma} = \sigma$.   □

Thanks to the corollary the definability problem for finite strategies can be reduced to the same problem for ground strategies.

5 Innocence

Here we would like to find a semantic match for FunML by a notion of innocence [HO00]. FunML embodies purely functional computation in presence of reference types: although terms may receive, update and read the value of references, they cannot create new ones. The notion of innocence defined below extends the standard notion appropriately to deal with moves that carry higher-order store. Traditionally, the notion of innocence stipulates that each P-move of a strategy be determined by the P-view up to the point just before the move is played. In our case, the notion needs to be customised so as to take into account the names, and the corresponding parts of the store, which become unavailable in the P-view. The last two conditions below stipulate that P cannot play any names which do not appear in his view, and neither can he change their values.

Definition 24. *A ground strategy* $\sigma : A$ *is* **innocent** *if it satisfies the following conditions.*

- *If* $sp^\Sigma \in \sigma$ *then* $\nu(p^\Sigma) \subseteq \nu(s)$ (strong determinacy).
- *If* $sp^\Sigma, s' \in \sigma$ *and* $s'o^T \in P_A$ *with* $\gamma(\ulcorner s \urcorner) = \gamma(\ulcorner s'o^T \urcorner)$ *then there exists* $s'o^T p'^{\Sigma'} \in \sigma$ *such that* $\gamma(\ulcorner sp^\Sigma \urcorner) \sim \gamma(\ulcorner s'o^T p'^{\Sigma'} \urcorner)$ (innocence).
- *If* $sp^\Sigma \in \sigma$ *and* $\gamma(\ulcorner sp^\Sigma \urcorner) = s'p^{\Sigma'}$ *then* $\nu(p^{\Sigma'}) \cap \nu(s) \subseteq \nu(s')$ (innocent P-availability).
- *If* $s' \sqsubseteq s \in \sigma$ *ends in* $o^\Sigma p^T$ *and* $a \in \mathrm{dom}(T) \setminus \nu(\gamma(\ulcorner s' \urcorner))$ *then* $T(a) = \Sigma(a)$ *and, moreover, if* $a \in \mathbb{A}_\phi$ *then* (s, s', a) *are a copycat triple* (innocent P-storage).

Remark 25. Note that the first and third conditions above can be equivalently expressed, modulo the other conditions, as a single one:

- *If* $sp^\Sigma \in \sigma$ *and* $\gamma(\ulcorner sp^\Sigma \urcorner) = s'p^{\Sigma'}$ *then* $\nu(p^{\Sigma'}) \subseteq \nu(s')$.

Moreover, given the above condition, innocence can be equivalently stated as:

- *If* $sp^\Sigma, s' \in \sigma$ *and* $s'o^T \in P_A$ *with* $\gamma(\ulcorner s \urcorner) = \gamma(\ulcorner s'o^T \urcorner)$ *then there exists* $s'o^T p'^{\Sigma'} \in \sigma$ *such that* $\gamma(\ulcorner sp^\Sigma \urcorner) = \gamma(\ulcorner s'o^T p'^{\Sigma'} \urcorner)$.

Due to innocent P-availability and innocent P-storage, innocent strategies are uniquely determined by their behaviour on available names, that is, names appearing in the P-view after application of γ. For instance, the behaviour of an innocent strategy on an O-question asking the value of an unavailable name is a trivial copycat. Combined with the innocence condition, our observation allows us to characterise innocent strategies by their *view-functions*, defined as follows.

$$\mathsf{vf}(\sigma) = \{\gamma(\ulcorner s \urcorner) \mid s \in \sigma\}$$

Lemma 26. *Innocent strategies compose. Consequently, for any* FunML-*term* $\Gamma \vdash M$, $[\![\Gamma \vdash M]\!]$ *is an innocent strategy.*

Next we show a factorisation result for ground strategies involving innocent ones. Our first step will be to factor out violations of strong determinacy, namely, fresh-name creation, in exactly the same way as in Lemma 22. We set $\mathsf{GRN}(A) = R(A) \setminus \mathsf{HON}(A)$.

Lemma 27. *Let* $\sigma : A_1 \to A_2$ *be a ground strategy,* $A = \bigotimes_{\theta \in \mathsf{GRN}(A_1 \to A_2)} ([\![\theta]\!] \to \mathbb{A}_\theta)$ *and* $\mathsf{gen}_\theta = [\![\vdash \lambda x^\theta.\mathrm{ref}_\theta(x)]\!] : 1 \to ([\![\theta]\!] \Rightarrow \mathbb{A}_\theta)$. *There exists a strongly deterministic ground strategy* $\overline{\sigma} : A \otimes A_1 \to A_2$ *such that* $\langle !_{A_1}; \langle \mathsf{gen}_\theta \rangle_{\theta \in \mathsf{GRN}(A_1 \to A_2)}, \mathrm{id}_{A_1} \rangle; \overline{\sigma} = \sigma$.

In the setting without names, a factorisation to innocence would just use an integer reference, which would serve for storing the history of the play [AM97]. If one tries to apply the same rationale in the nominal setting, one soon realises that names constitute a basic obstacle because they cannot be obviously mapped into integers. In order to bridge the gap, we are going to use integers that correspond to the order in which names appear in a play, and external 'oracles' which will maintain a list of names and be able to add to it (enlisting) as well as access names at a given position (look-up).

We first fix an encoding function from plays to integers. Given a play s, the function produces a code $\#(s)$. The function first translates each name $a \in \mathbb{A}_\theta$ into a pair (i, θ), if a is the ith name of type θ appearing in s, and subsequently performs some standard encoding from nested strings of integers (with pointers) into integers. Therefore, the function is not injective, but orbit injective: $s \sim s' \iff \#(s) = \#(s')$. We also fix an ordering of names appearing inside plays such that names introduced earlier (i.e. closer to the beginning of the play) appear earlier in the ordering.[1]

We next describe the family of strategies oracle_θ which we shall use. The strategy $\text{oracle}_\theta : 1 \to (\mathbb{A}_\theta \Rightarrow 1) \otimes (\mathbb{Z} \Rightarrow \mathbb{A}_\theta)$ responds to the initial question with the answer $(\star_e, \star_1)$. After that, the answer to any question a posed at $\star_e$ will be $\star$, which should be viewed as confirmation that a has been added to the list. The strategy implements the look-up function by responding to any question i, posed at $\star_1$ and such that the ith question posed at $\star_e$ from the beginning of the play is a, with a.

Any strongly deterministic ground strategy $\sigma : A$ shall be converted to an innocent one which uses an external oracle for each type $\theta \in R(A)$, and a reference of type int. Inside that reference, the strategy shall keep an encoding of the whole play so far (using the function $\#(\_)$). Whenever O makes a move, say the last move in the play so^Σ, P can consult the int-reference in order to obtain a version of s where names are represented by integers. Then, P queries the external oracles (via their look-up functionality) with each integer representation in $\#(s)$, and receives the corresponding actual names as answers. At this point, P has completely reconstructed s in an innocent manner. P next updates the oracles with all the names newly introduced by o^Σ (using the enlisting functionality), and then plays his move as dictated by σ.

Lemma 28. *Let* $A = \bigotimes_{\theta \in R(A_1 \to A_2)} ((\mathbb{A}_\theta \Rightarrow 1) \otimes (\mathbb{Z} \Rightarrow \mathbb{A}_\theta))$ *and* $\sigma : A_1 \to A_2$ *be a strongly deterministic ground strategy. There exists an innocent strategy* $\overline{\sigma} : A \otimes \mathbb{A}_{\text{int}} \otimes A_1 \to A_2$ *such that* $\langle !_{A_1}; \langle\langle \text{oracle}_\theta \rangle_{\theta \in R(A_1 \to A_2)}, \text{new}_{\text{int}}\rangle, \text{id}_{A_1}\rangle; \overline{\sigma} = \sigma$.

Proof. We define $\overline{\sigma}$ to be the least innocent strategy extending $\sigma' = \bigcup\{\overline{s} \mid s \in \sigma\}$, where $\overline{s}$ is a set of plays defined below by induction on the length of the play. For the base case we set $\overline{\epsilon} = \{\epsilon\}$.

Now suppose $s = i^{\Sigma_i} s' o^\Sigma p^T$. We let $\overline{s}$ contain all plays of the form

$$(\langle (\star_e, \star_1)_\theta \rangle_{\theta \in R(A_1 \to A_2)}, \hat{a}, i)^{\hat{\Sigma}_i} s'' o^{\hat{\Sigma}} s_1 s_2 p^{\hat{T}}$$

[1] Note here that names may first appear inside stores, which are not ordered. In such a case, though, and because of the availability condition, they are reachable through the store through previously introduced names, the ordering of which can be used to order the new names. E.g. in the play $a^{(a,b),(b,0)} c^{(a,b'),(c,d),(b,0),(b',0),(d,0)}$ we can order our names as a, b, c, b', d.

where $\hat{a} \in \mathbb{A}_{\mathsf{int}}$ a fresh name, $\hat{\Sigma}_{\mathsf{i}} = \Sigma_{\mathsf{i}}[\hat{a} \mapsto 0]$, $\hat{\Sigma} = \Sigma[\hat{a} \mapsto \#(\mathsf{i}^{\Sigma_{\mathsf{i}}} s')]$ and $s'' \in \hat{s}'$ is given by the induction hypothesis. Let $a_1, \cdots, a_n, b_1, \cdots, b_m$ be the names in $\nu(\mathsf{i}^{\Sigma_{\mathsf{i}}} s' o^{\Sigma})$ ordered according to the canonical ordering, so that $a_1, \cdots, a_n$ are the elements of $\nu(\mathsf{i}^{\Sigma_{\mathsf{i}}} s')$ and $b_1, \cdots, b_m$ those of $\nu(o^{\Sigma}) \setminus \nu(\mathsf{i}^{\Sigma_{\mathsf{i}}} s')$. We set s_1 to be the sequence $i_1^{\hat{\Sigma}} a_1^{\hat{\Sigma}} i_2^{\hat{\Sigma}} a_2^{\hat{\Sigma}} \cdots i_n^{\hat{\Sigma}} a_n^{\hat{\Sigma}}$, such that $a_j \in \mathbb{A}_{\theta}$ (some θ) is the i_jth name of type θ in $a_1, \cdots, a_n$ and $i_j^{\hat{\Sigma}}$ is justified by $\star_{1\theta}$. Moreover, s_2 is the sequence $b_1^{\hat{\Sigma}} \star^{\hat{\Sigma}} \cdots b_m^{\hat{\Sigma}} \star^{\hat{\Sigma}}$, where each $b_j^{\hat{\Sigma}}$ is justified by the according initial $\star_{\mathsf{e}\,\theta}$. Finally, $\hat{T} = T[\hat{a} \mapsto \#(s)]$.

First, in order to show that there exists an innocent extension $\bar{\sigma}$ of σ', it suffices to show that σ' is in fact a strongly deterministic ground strategy satisfying the innocent P-availability and innocent P-storage conditions, and in addition:

- for all $s_1 p_1^{\Sigma_1}, s_2 p_2^{\Sigma_2} \in \sigma'$, if $\gamma(\ulcorner s_1 \urcorner) = \gamma(\ulcorner s_2 \urcorner)$ then $\gamma(\ulcorner s_1 p_1^{\Sigma_1} \urcorner) = \gamma(\ulcorner s_2 p_2^{\Sigma_2} \urcorner)$.

By construction, σ' is obviously strongly deterministic and ground, and depends solely on moves and names that are available in the P-view. We can therefore show that it satisfies the above conditions. Moreover, since $\bar{\sigma}$ contains extended versions of all plays from σ, we have that $\langle !_{A_1}; \langle\langle \mathsf{oracle}_{\theta} \rangle_{\theta \in R(A_1 \to A_2)}, \mathsf{new}_{\mathsf{int}} \rangle, \mathsf{id}_{A_1} \rangle; \bar{\sigma} = \sigma$. $\square$

Corollary 29. *Let* $\sigma : A_1 \to A_2$ *be a ground strategy,* $\Theta_1 = \mathsf{GRN}(A_1 \to A_2)$ *and* $\Theta_2 = R(A_1 \to A_2)$. *There exists an innocent strategy*

$$\bar{\sigma} : \left(\bigotimes_{\theta \in \Theta_1} (\llbracket \theta \rrbracket \Rightarrow \mathbb{A}_{\theta}) \right) \otimes \mathbb{A}_{\mathsf{int}} \otimes \left(\bigotimes_{\theta \in \Theta_2} (\mathbb{A}_{\theta} \Rightarrow 1) \otimes (\mathbb{Z} \Rightarrow \mathbb{A}_{\theta}) \right) \otimes A_1 \to A_2$$

such that $\langle !_{A_1}; \langle\langle \mathsf{gen}_{\theta} \rangle_{\theta \in \mathsf{GRN}(A_1 \to A_2)}, \mathsf{nu}_{\mathsf{int}}, \langle \mathsf{oracle}_{\theta} \rangle_{\theta \in R(A_1 \to A_2)} \rangle, \mathsf{id}_{A_1} \rangle; \bar{\sigma} = \sigma$. $\square$

Remark 30 (Factoring the oracle). It is interesting to note that each strategy oracle_{θ} can be decomposed into an innocent strategy and three reference cells, of types int, ref θ and unit $\to$ unit respectively. That is, $\mathsf{oracle}_{\theta} = \langle \mathsf{nu}_{\mathsf{int}}, \mathsf{nu}_{\mathsf{ref}\,\theta}, \mathsf{nu}_{\mathsf{unit}\to\mathsf{unit}} \rangle; \overline{\mathsf{oracle}}_{\theta}$, where $\overline{\mathsf{oracle}}_{\theta} : \mathbb{A}_{\mathsf{int}} \otimes \mathbb{A}_{\mathsf{ref}\,\theta} \otimes \mathbb{A}_{\mathsf{unit}\to\mathsf{unit}} \to (\mathbb{A}_{\theta} \Rightarrow 1) \otimes (\mathbb{Z} \Rightarrow \mathbb{A}_{\theta})$ is an innocent strategy which behaves as follows:[2]

- when O provides a new name a to be enlisted, the strategy responds with $\star^{\Sigma}$, where Σ records that the ith name played by O is a (this uses the references of types int and ref θ);
- when, on the other hand, O asks what is the ith name that has been enlisted then the strategy uses the reference of type unit $\to$ unit in order to go back in the play (in the same fashion as in Lemma 22), until it finds a P-move $\star^{\Sigma}$ which includes a pair of values (i, a), at which point it carries back that a as an answer to i.

---

[2] Formally, $\overline{\mathsf{oracle}}_{\theta}$ is the least innocent strategy which contains all plays of the form $(a_1, a_2, a_3)^{\Sigma_{\mathsf{i}}} (\star_{\mathsf{e}}, \star_1)^{\Sigma_{\mathsf{i}}[a_1 \mapsto 0]}$ and, in addition, if $(a_1, a_2, a_3)^{\Sigma_{\mathsf{i}}} (\star_{\mathsf{e}}, \star_1)^{\Sigma_{\mathsf{i}}} s \in \overline{\mathsf{oracle}}_{\theta}$ then:

- $(a_1, a_2, a_3)^{\Sigma_{\mathsf{i}}} (\star_{\mathsf{e}}, \star_1)^{\Sigma_{\mathsf{i}}'} s\, a^{\Sigma}_{\star} \Sigma[a_1 \mapsto \Sigma(a_1)+1][a_2 \mapsto a] \in \overline{\mathsf{oracle}}_{\theta}$.
- $(a_1, a_2, a_3)^{\Sigma_{\mathsf{i}}} (\star_{\mathsf{e}}, \star_1)^{\Sigma_{\mathsf{i}}'} s\, i^{\Sigma} s_1 s_2\, a^{\Sigma} \in \overline{\mathsf{oracle}}_{\theta}$, where s_1 is a copycat sequence of questions $\star^{\Sigma[a_1 \mapsto i]}$ pointing to a_3 in preceding stores (starting from the store of i^{Σ}), and such that its last element points to a P-move $\star^{\Sigma'}$ with $\Sigma'(a_1) = i$. The sequence s_2 comprises of a series of answers $\star^{\Sigma'}$ to the questions of s_1, and $a = \Sigma'(a_2)$.

Although factorisation results typically deconstruct a strategy σ of a category of games $\mathcal{G}_1$ into a characteristic strategy from $\mathcal{G}_1$ and a strategy from $\mathcal{G}_2$, where $\mathcal{G}_2$ a subcategory of $\mathcal{G}_1$, the factorisation above does not follow this pattern, since the ground strategy oracle$_\theta$ is deconstructed into a strategy containing nu$_{\text{unit}\to\text{unit}}$ (which is not ground). Note, though, that if the initial σ of Lemma 28 were finite (up to name permutations) then there would not be a need for such oracles, as σ would only contain plays with boundedly many names, which could be stored in a bounded set of external references.

Finally, we call an innocent strategy σ *compact* if $\mathsf{vf}(\sigma)$ is finite up to name-permutations, that is, if the set
$$\{\{\pi \cdot s \mid \pi \in \text{PERM}\} \mid s \in \mathsf{vf}(\sigma)\} \text{ is finite.}$$

Lemma 31. *Let $\Gamma \vdash \theta$ be a typing context. For each compact innocent strategy $\sigma :$ $\llbracket \Gamma \vdash \theta \rrbracket$ there is an FunML-term $\Gamma \vdash M : \theta$ such that $\sigma = \llbracket \Gamma \vdash M \rrbracket$.*

Corollary 32. *Let $\Gamma \vdash \theta$ be a typing context and $\sigma : \llbracket \Gamma \vdash \theta \rrbracket$ a strategy that is finite up to name-permutations. There is a RefML-term $\Gamma \vdash M : \theta$ such that $\sigma = \llbracket \Gamma \vdash M \rrbracket$. If σ is ground then there is a GrML-term $\Gamma \vdash M : \theta$ such that $\sigma = \llbracket \Gamma \vdash M \rrbracket$.*

6 Conclusion

We have considered three languages embodying respectively general store, ground store and pure functional computation. These have been related to three families of strategies in a nominal game model as shown below.

RefML	GrML	FunML
strategy	ground strategy	innocent strategy

In particular, our notions of groundness and innocence are nominal generalizations of the standard notions of visibility and innocence.

Another theme in research on game semantics was universality, i.e. the fact that all recursively presentable strategies were definable. We believe that, in the nominal setup, universality is bound to fail for ground and innocent strategies (wrt GrML and FunML respectively), because of the inability of these languages to store unbounded collections of names. RefML does not seem to suffer from the same limitation, as lists of names of type θ can be maintained through the type, say, ref (int $\to$ ref (θ)).

Our results illustrate that, with some extra effort, the methodology of the semantic cube can also bear fruit in the nominal setting, though the results that are emerging are perhaps not as elegant as in the original case.

References

AGM$^+$04. Abramsky, S., Ghica, D.R., Murawski, A.S., Ong, C.-H.L., Stark, I.D.B.: Nominal games and full abstraction for the nu-calculus. In: Proceedings of LICS, pp. 150–159. IEEE Computer Society Press (2004)

262   A.S. Murawski and N. Tzevelekos

AHM98.   Abramsky, S., Honda, K., McCusker, G.: Fully abstract game semantics for general references. In: Proceedings of IEEE Symposium on Logic in Computer Science, pp. 334–344. Computer Society Press (1998)

AJM00.   Abramsky, S., Jagadeesan, R., Malacaria, P.: Full abstraction for PCF. Information and Computation 163, 409–470 (2000)

AM97.   Abramsky, S., McCusker, G.: Call-by-value games. In: Nielsen, M. (ed.) CSL 1997. LNCS, vol. 1414, pp. 1–17. Springer, Heidelberg (1998)

GP02.   Gabbay, M.J., Pitts, A.M.: A new approach to abstract syntax with variable binding. Formal Aspects of Computing 13, 341–363 (2002)

HO00.   Hyland, J.M.E., Ong, C.-H.L.: On Full Abstraction for PCF: I. Models, observables and the full abstraction problem, II. Dialogue games and innocent strategies, III. A fully abstract and universal game model. Information and Computation 163(2), 285–408 (2000)

HY99.   Honda, K., Yoshida, N.: Game-theoretic analysis of call-by-value computation. Theoretical Computer Science 221(1-2), 393–456 (1999)

Lai97.   Laird, J.: Full abstraction for functional languages with control. In: Proceedings of 12th IEEE Symposium on Logic in Computer Science, pp. 58–67 (1997)

Lai04.   Laird, J.: A game semantics of local names and good variables. In: Walukiewicz, I. (ed.) FOSSACS 2004. LNCS, vol. 2987, pp. 289–303. Springer, Heidelberg (2004)

MT11.   Murawski, A.S., Tzevelekos, N.: Game semantics for good general references. In: Proceedings of LICS, pp. 75–84. IEEE Computer Society Press (2011)

Nic94.   Nickau, H.: Hereditarily sequential functionals. In: Matiyasevich, Y.V., Nerode, A. (eds.) LFCS 1994. LNCS, vol. 813, pp. 253–264. Springer, Heidelberg (1994)

Tze09.   Tzevelekos, N.: Full abstraction for nominal general references. Logical Methods in Computer Science 5(3) (2009)

A   Appendix

In this section we present some more advanced strategy examples.

Example 33. Let us consider the following strategy $\sigma : 1 \to ((\mathbb{Z} \Rightarrow \mathbb{Z}) \Rightarrow (\mathbb{Z} \Rightarrow \mathbb{Z}))$. The strategy is specified by plays of the form shown on the left below, where sum $= j_1 + \cdots + j_k$, and we have labelled the moves of the prearena as on the right below.

Thus, the strategy answers the initial $\star$ with the higher-order move $\star$. From that point on, at each O-question $\star_Q$ to $\star$, the strategy replies with an answer $\star_A$. When O queries the value of the returned $\star_A$, by playing some O-question i to it, the strategy propagates the question to all preceding $\star_Q$'s, and returns as an answer the sum of all the answers to those questions. This behaviour can be matched by the semantics of the following term (the last line below implicitly uses recursion).

let $i = \text{ref}_{\text{int}}(0)$, $F = \text{ref}_{\text{int}\to\text{int}\to\text{int}}(\lambda x^{\text{int}}.\lambda y^{\text{int}}.0)$ in

$$\lambda f^{\text{int}\to\text{int}}. \; i\text{++}; \text{ let } g = \; !F \text{ in } F := \lambda x^{\text{int}}. \text{if } (x - !i) \text{ then } f \text{ else } gx;$$

$$\lambda y^{\text{int}}. \, (!F)(!i)y + (!F)(!i-1)y + \cdots + (!F)1y$$

The term implements the informal description of the strategy described above: it uses an internal higher-order reference F where it stores all input functions f (the ith such function is stored in $F(i)$), and returns a function which, on input y, returns the sum of applying all previous f's to y.

Example 34. Let us revisit the strategy σ from Example 33 under the light of the factorisation in Lemma 21. In particular, σ can be factorised as $\mathsf{nu}_{\text{unit}\to\text{unit}}; \hat{\sigma}$, where $\hat{\sigma} : \mathbb{A}_{\text{unit}\to\text{unit}} \to ((\mathbb{Z}\Rightarrow\mathbb{Z})\Rightarrow(\mathbb{Z}\Rightarrow\mathbb{Z}))$ is a ground strategy specified by plays of the form:

with $\text{sum} = j_1 + \cdots + j_k$. In fact, the strategy $\hat{\sigma}$ defined above is a simplified version of the one obtained via the factorisation theorem, but it follows the same rationale of using the reference of type unit $\to$ unit for breaking inside the P-view in a visible way. The strategy corresponds to the term below,

let $i = \text{ref}_{\text{int}}(0)$, inp $= \text{ref}_{\text{int}}(0)$, sum $= \text{ref}_{\text{int}}(0)$ in

$\quad\quad \lambda f^{\text{int}\to\text{int}}.$ let $g = (\text{if }!i\text{ then }!F\text{ else }\lambda x^{\text{unit}}.x)$ in

$\quad\quad\quad\quad i\mathord{+}\mathord{+};\ F := \lambda x^{\text{unit}}.\,(\text{sum} := !\text{sum} + f(!\text{inp});\ g());$

$\quad\quad\quad\quad \lambda y^{\text{int}}.\,\text{sum} := !\text{sum} + fy;\ \text{inp} := y;\ g();\ !\text{sum}$

where F a free variable of type ref (unit $\to$ unit).

Techniques for Formal Modelling and Analysis
of
Quantum Systems

Simon J. Gay[1] and Rajagopal Nagarajan[2,*]

[1] School of Computing Science, University of Glasgow, UK
Simon.Gay@glasgow.ac.uk
[2] Department of Computer Science, School of Science and Technology,
Middlesex University, London, UK
R.Nagarajan@mdx.ac.uk

Abstract. Quantum communication and cryptographic protocols are well on the way to becoming an important practical technology. Although a large amount of successful research has been done on proving their correctness, most of this work does not make use of familiar techniques from formal methods such as formal logics for specification, formal modelling languages, separation of levels of abstraction, and compositional analysis. We argue that these techniques will be necessary for the analysis of large-scale systems that combine quantum and classical components. We summarize the results of our investigation using different approaches: behavioural equivalence in process calculus, model-checking and equivalence checking. Quantum teleportation is used as an example to illustrate our techniques.

Prologue

We were both PhD students of Samson Abramsky, in the Theory and Formal Methods group, which he led, in the Department of Computing at Imperial College London. During our time at Imperial in the early 1990s, the group provided a superbly stimulating and well-resourced environment and established many lasting friendships. Samson's involvement in the "CONFER" project enabled us to go to a number of workshops around Europe, meeting other researchers and PhD students who remain colleagues to this day.

Samson's big ideas during that time were game semantics and interaction categories, both of which made use of structures drawn from the development of linear logic. Game semantics led to the definition of fully abstract models of functional programming languages, while interaction categories [2,3] aimed to provide a Curry-Howard-style logical basis for typed concurrent programming. Both of us worked on interaction categories; indeed, we worked closely together

---

* Partially supported by "Process Algebra Approach to Distributed Quantum Computation and Secure Quantum Communication", Australian Research Council Discovery Project DP110103473.

B. Coecke, L. Ong, and P. Panangaden (Eds.): Abramsky Festschrift, LNCS 7860, pp. 264–276, 2013.

during the overlapping period of our PhDs. After he had provided the basic theory of interaction categories (and there was a lot of it!), Samson gave us the freedom to explore its consequences and develop applications and examples.

In 1995 Samson moved to Edinburgh, and Simon moved to Royal Holloway to take up a lectureship. Game semantics became a large, active and successful research area, which occupied Samson for several more years. Simon's attention switched to π-calculus, which had been a sideline during his PhD, and especially to the topic of session types. Raja remained at Imperial for a few more years, working as a researcher on a joint project led by Chris Hankin and Samson.

In 2000, all of us relocated: Samson moved to Oxford, Simon to Glasgow and Raja took up a lectureship at Warwick. Around this time, both Raja and Samson independently became interested in quantum computing. Raja's interest was in the use of formal methods, successfully developed in classical computing, to analyse and verify quantum protocols. He recruited Simon to collaborate on an early application [27] of process calculus and model-checking to quantum systems. Simon's attention had also been caught by Peter Selinger's paper [29] on the denotational semantics of a quantum programming language, and there seemed to be exciting opportunities for new applications of familiar techniques from theoretical computer science. Samson, with Bob Coecke, developed the programme of categorical quantum mechanics [4], based on various elaborations of compact closed categories—a connection, at least formally, with interaction categories.

Thus we again found ourselves working in the same area as Samson, and enjoyed being involved in the development of these new angles on quantum information processing, drawing on techniques and tools from semantics. Ian Mackie and Simon organised the EPSRC-funded QNET network, with strong involvement and support from Samson's group in Oxford, which led to several successful workshops and the book *Semantic Techniques in Quantum Computation* [16], and has been followed by the Computer Science and Physics network run by Samson, Bob Coecke, Andreas Döring and Jamie Vicary.

The present paper, which we are delighted to be able to contribute to Samson's Festschrift volume, combines an introduction to the field of quantum information, and an overview of our own work in this area.

1 Introduction

Quantum computing and quantum communication (more generally, *quantum information processing*) appear in the media from time to time, usually with misleading statements about the principles of quantum mechanics, the nature of quantum information processing, and the power of quantum algorithms. In this article, we begin by clarifying the fundamental concepts of quantum information and discussing what quantum computing systems are and are not capable of. We then outline several reasons for being interested in quantum information processing. Moving on to the main theme, we first motivate the application of formal methods to quantum information processing. We then describe the different techniques we have used in specification and verification of quantum protocols, illustrating them with an example.

There are several reasons to be interested in quantum information processing. First, the subject is really about understanding the information-processing power permitted by the laws of physics, and this is a fundamental scientific question. Second, quantum algorithms might help to solve certain classes of problem more efficiently; if, however, NP-complete problems cannot be solved efficiently even by a quantum computer, then understanding why not is also a question of fundamental interest. Third, quantum cryptography provides a neat answer, in advance, to any threat that quantum computing might pose to classical cryptography. Fourth, as integrated circuit components become smaller, quantum effects become more difficult to avoid. Quantum computing might be necessary in order to continue the historical trend of miniaturization, even if it offers no complexity-theoretic improvement. Finally, Feynman [15] suggested that quantum computers could be used to simulate complex (quantum) physical systems whose behaviour is hard to analyze classically.

Will QIP become practically significant? Some aspects are already practical: there are companies selling Quantum Key Distribution systems today. Whether or not there is a real demand for quantum cryptography remains to be seen, but it seems likely that the promise of absolute security will attract organizations that feel they cannot take any chances. Quantum computing seems to be feasible in principle, although there are still formidable scientific and engineering challenges. But many experimental groups are working hard, and physicists and engineers are very clever. Remember that in 1949 the statement "In the future, computers may weigh no more than 1.5 tonnes" was a speculative prediction.

The remainder of this paper is organised as follows. In Section 2 we give a brief introduction to the main ideas of quantum information processing. In Section 3 we motivate the development of formal methods for quantum systems, and introduce the three strands that we have been working on. In Sections 4, 5 and 6 we explain, in turn, the use of process calculus, model-checking, and equivalence-checking, using quantum teleportation as an example in each case. Finally, Section 7 concludes.

2   Quantum Information Processing

The idea of quantum information processing (QIP) is to represent information by means of physical systems whose behaviour *must* be described by the laws of quantum physics. Typically this means very small systems, such as a single atom (in which the spin state, up or down, gives the basic binary distinction necessary for digital information representation) or a single photon (in which polarization directions are used). Information is then processed by means of operations that arise from quantum physics. Quantum mechanics leads to several fundamental properties of quantum information, which between them lead to various counter-intuitive effects and the possiblity of behaviour that cannot occur in classical systems.

2.1 Superposition

The state of a classical bit is either 0 or 1. The state of a quantum bit (qubit) is $\alpha|0\rangle + \beta|1\rangle$, where the states $|0\rangle$ and $|1\rangle$ are the *basis states* (in the *standard* or *computational* basis). In general, α and β are complex numbers and $|\alpha|^2 + |\beta|^2 = 1$. If both α and β are non-zero, then the state is a *superposition* of the basis states, for example $\frac{1}{\sqrt{2}}|0\rangle - \frac{1}{\sqrt{2}}|1\rangle$. It is not correct to say, as often stated in the media, that a qubit can be in two states at once. It is in one state, but that state may be a superposition of the basis states. Note that any two orthogonal states may form a basis. For example, the pair $\{\frac{1}{\sqrt{2}}|0\rangle + \frac{1}{\sqrt{2}}|1\rangle, \frac{1}{\sqrt{2}}|0\rangle - \frac{1}{\sqrt{2}}|1\rangle\}$, sometimes written $\{|+\rangle, |-\rangle\}$, forms the *Hadamard* basis. Although we often work with the standard basis, it does not have a privileged status; indeed, whether or not a particular quantum state is regarded as a superposition depends on the choice of basis. The state $|+\rangle$ is in a superposition with respect to the standard basis, but not with respect to the Hadamard basis.

2.2 Measurement

It is not possible to inspect the contents of a quantum state. The most we can do is a measurement. Measuring a qubit that is in state $\alpha|0\rangle + \beta|1\rangle$, in the standard basis, has a random result: with probability $|\alpha|^2$ the result is $|0\rangle$, and with probability $|\beta|^2$ the result is $|1\rangle$. After the measurement, the qubit is in the basis state corresponding to the result.

2.3 Operations on a Superposition

An operation acts on every basis state in a superposition. For example, starting with the three-qubit state $\frac{1}{2}|000\rangle + \frac{1}{2}|010\rangle - \frac{1}{2}|110\rangle - \frac{1}{2}|111\rangle$ and applying the operation "invert the second bit" produces the state $\frac{1}{2}|010\rangle + \frac{1}{2}|000\rangle - \frac{1}{2}|100\rangle - \frac{1}{2}|101\rangle$. This is sometimes known as *quantum parallelism* and in the media it is often described as carrying out an operation simultaneously on a large number of values. However, it is not possible to discover the results of these simultaneous operations. A measurement would produce just one of the basis states. This is absolutely not a straightforward route to "parallelism for free".

2.4 No Cloning

It is not possible to define an operation that reliably makes a perfect copy of an unknown quantum state. This is known as the *no cloning theorem*. It contrasts sharply with the classical situation, where the existence of uniform copying procedures is one of the main advantages of digital information. Every word in the statement of the no cloning theorem is significant. For example, with the knowledge that a given qubit is either $|0\rangle$ or $|1\rangle$, it is possible to discover its state (by means of a simple measurement) and then set another qubit to the same state, thus creating a copy. It is also possible in general to create approximate copies, or to copy with a certain probability of perfect success but a certain probability of complete failure. It is possible to transfer an unknown quantum state from one physical carrier to another, but the process destroys the original state. This is known as *quantum teleportation*, and we will return to it later.

2.5   Entanglement

The states of two or more qubits can be correlated in a way that is stronger than any possible classical correlation. An example is the two-qubit state $\frac{1}{\sqrt{2}}|00\rangle + \frac{1}{\sqrt{2}}|11\rangle$. Measuring either qubit produces, with equal probability, the state $|00\rangle$ or $|11\rangle$. Measuring the other qubit is then guaranteed to produce the same result as the first measurement. This correlation is preserved by quantum operations on the state, in a way that cannot be reproduced classically. This phenomenon is called *entanglement* and it is a key resource for quantum algorithms and communication protocols.

3   Formal Methods for QIP

The correctness of quantum algorithms and protocols can be analyzed mathematically. Simple protocols such as teleportation can be checked with a few lines of algebra, Shor's [30] and Grover's [23] algorithms have been extensively studied, and Mayers [26] and others have proved the security of quantum key distribution. But what about *systems*, which are constructed from separate components and combine quantum and classical computation and communication? Experience in classical computing science has shown that correctness of a complete implemented system is a very different question from correctness of the idealized mathematical protocol that it claims to implement. This is the *raison d'être* of the field of formal methods.

Our 2002 paper [27] suggested applying formal methods to quantum systems, with the same motivation as for classical systems:

- *formal modelling languages*, for unambiguous definitions;
- analysis of *systems*, rather than idealized situations;
- *systematic verification methodologies*, rather than *ad hoc* reasoning;
- the possibility of *tool support*.

We have been working on three strands: (1) the quantum process calculus CQP [17,19], partly in collaboration with Davidson [11]; (2) quantum model-checking based on temporal logic, in collaboration with Papanikolaou [20,21,28]; (3) quantum equivalence-checking, in collaboration with Ardeshir-Larijani [5]. Our work on process calculus has focussed on the development of basic theory, leading up to the definition of behavioural equivalence. This approach has also been studied by Ying *et al.*, who have developed qCCS [32]. Our work on model-checking uses a different style of specification language, more closely related to Promela. Some further work [10] makes connections between these two themes. Related work on model-checking include [7,14]. Our most recent work addresses the question of equivalence of sequential quantum programs, expressed in a language based on Selinger's QPL [29].

4 Quantum Teleportation in CQP

Teleportation [8] is a protocol for transferring an unknown qubit state from one participant, Alice, to another, Bob. The protocol uses classical communication — in fact, communication of just two classical bits — to achieve the transfer of a quantum state which is specified by two complex numbers. The trick is that there must be some pre-existing entanglement, shared by Alice and Bob.

Let x and y refer to two qubits that, together, are in the entangled state $\frac{1}{\sqrt{2}}|00\rangle + \frac{1}{\sqrt{2}}|11\rangle$. Let u be a qubit in an unknown state, that is given to Alice. The protocol consists of the following steps.

1. Alice applies the *controlled not* (CNot) operator to u and x. This is a two-qubit operator whose effect on each basis state is to invert the second bit if and only if the first bit is 1.
2. Alice applies the *Hadamard* (H) operator to x. This operator is a change of basis from $\{|0\rangle, |1\rangle\}$ to $\{\frac{1}{\sqrt{2}}(|0\rangle + |1\rangle), \frac{1}{\sqrt{2}}(|0\rangle - |1\rangle)\}$.
3. Alice measures u and x, obtaining a two-bit classical result.
4. Alice sends this two-bit classical value to Bob.
5. Bob uses this classical value to determine which of four so-called *Pauli* operators I, X, Y or Z should be applied to y. In the definition below, we use the notation $\sigma_0 = I, \sigma_1 = X, \sigma_2 = Z, \sigma_3 = Y$. (This is non-standard but convenient for this example; usually σ_2 and σ_3 are exchanged). The operators are defined as follows:

$$
\begin{array}{ll}
I: & \text{identity} \\
\mathsf{X}: & |0\rangle \mapsto |1\rangle \quad |1\rangle \mapsto |0\rangle \\
\mathsf{Y}: & |0\rangle \mapsto i|1\rangle \quad |1\rangle \mapsto -i|0\rangle \\
\mathsf{Z}: & |0\rangle \mapsto |0\rangle \quad |1\rangle \mapsto -|1\rangle
\end{array}
$$

6. The state of y is now the original state of u (and u has lost its original state and is in a basis state).

Although the measurement in step 3 has a probabilistic result, the use of the classical value to determine a compensating operation in step 5 means that the complete protocol is deterministic in its effect on the state of Bob's qubit.

The teleportation protocol is often described by the circuit diagram in Figure 1.

The following definitions in the process calculus CQP (Communicating Quantum Processes) [17,19] model the teleportation protocol. *Alice, Bob* and *Teleport* are processes; q is a formal parameter representing a qubit; *in*, *out*, a and b are formal parameters representing channels; c is a private channel; x, y are local names for freshly allocated qubits, which will be instantiated with the names of actual qubits during execution. The language is based on pi-calculus and most of the syntax should be familiar.

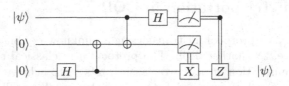

Fig. 1. Quantum teleportation as a circuit diagram

$Alice(q, in, out) = in?[u] . \{u, q *= \mathsf{CNot}\} . \{u *= \mathsf{H}\} . out![\text{measure } u, q] . \mathbf{0}$
$Bob(q, in, out) \;= in?[r] . \{y *= \sigma_r\} . out![y] . \mathbf{0}$
$Teleport(a, b) \;\;= (\mathsf{qbit}\ x, y)(\{x *= \mathsf{H}\} . \{x, y *= \mathsf{CNot}\} .$
$\qquad\qquad\qquad (\mathsf{new}\ c)(Alice(x, a, c) \mid Bob(y, c, b))$

In *Teleport*, the actions before (new c) put the qubits x and y into the necessary entangled state. In order to help with writing a specification, *Alice* is given the qubit to be teleported as a message on channel *in*, and at the end of the protocol, *Bob* outputs the final qubit on *out*.

CQP has an operational semantics defined by labelled transition rules; it also has a type system in which the no cloning theorem is represented by linear typing. The example above, for simplicity, does not include type declarations.

The desired behaviour of teleportation is that a qubit (quantum state) is received on a and the same quantum state is sent on b; the protocol should behave like an identity operation:

$$Identity(a, b) = a?[x] . b![x] . \mathbf{0}$$

We can now write a specification of teleportation:

$$Teleport(a, b) \cong Identity(a, b)$$

where $\cong$ is a behavioural equivalence. Equivalent processes cannot be distinguished by any observer: they output the same values in the same circumstances, they produce the same probability distributions of measurement results, and in general interact in the same way with their environment.

As usual, we would like behavioural equivalence to be a congruence:

$$\forall P, Q, C. \quad P \cong Q \Rightarrow C[P] \cong C[Q]$$

where C is a process context. Congruence supports equational reasoning, and the universal composability properties defined by Canetti [9] in a different setting. Developing a congruence for a quantum process calculus was an open problem for several years [24], but very recently we have defined a congruence for CQP [11] and Feng *et al.* have independently defined one for qCCS [13]. Our equivalence is a form of probabilistic branching bisimulation [31], with appropriate extensions to deal with the quantum state. We have proved that the specification of teleportation is satisfied. The work on bisimulation and congruence for CQP is joint with Tim Davidson.

5   Model-Checking for Quantum Protocols

In this section we introduce the Quantum Model Checker (QMC) and its application to the verification of quantum protocols. QMC, which we have implemented together with Nick Papanikolaou, is a software tool. It automatically explores all possible behaviours arising from a protocol model, and enables logic properties expressed with Quantum Computation Tree Logic (QCTL) [6] to be checked over the resulting structure.

In QMC, the quantum state $|\psi\rangle$ is represented internally in an implicit way: rather than storing the so-called *state vector representation* of $|\psi\rangle$ (which grows exponentially in length as a function of the total number of qubits in $|\psi\rangle$), we use the *stabilizer array representation* [1], which is a binary representation of the set of Pauli operators that fix (or stabilize) $|\psi\rangle$. Using the stabilizer array representation, we gain significant computational benefits in terms of both space and time when simulating a given protocol, given that simulation of stabilizer circuits is performed using a polynomial time algorithm and the representation of the state grows polynomially with the total number of qubits.

5.1   Quantum Teleportation in QMC

We have designed an imperative-style concurrent specification language for the needs of the quantum model-checking tool QMC. For the purpose of this paper, we will demonstrate the syntax of this language by example. In this language the teleportation protocol (assuming we are trying to teleport the state $|\psi\rangle = |0\rangle$) may be expressed by the program in Figure 2. Working within the stabilizer formalism, we can teleport any of the one-qubit stabilizer states: $|0\rangle$, $|1\rangle$, $\frac{1}{\sqrt{2}}(|0\rangle \pm |1\rangle)$, $\frac{1}{\sqrt{2}}(|0\rangle \pm i|1\rangle)$.

In our setting, we allow for global variables (such as e1, e2), typed communication channels (such as ch) which are always global, and local (private) variables for each process (such as a,b,c,d,q). Communication is asynchronous, with executability rules restricting the way in which process interleaving is performed. For instance, the process Bob cannot start unless channel ch is filled with a value.

A protocol model will always consist of definitions of one or more processes; the commands performed by each of these processes must be interleaved (so as to emulate concurrent execution), and non–determinism (which occurs explicitly in selection structures (if :: a -> ...:: b -> ...fi) and implicitly when measurements are performed) must be resolved, producing an execution tree for the modelled system.

5.2   Specifying Properties

The properties of quantum protocols which we are interested in reasoning about are properties of the quantum state (e.g. which qubits are 'active' in a given state, which qubits are entangled with the rest of the system) over time. We are also interested in the outcomes of measurements, and the way in which the values

```
program Teleport;
var e1,e2:qubit; ch:channel of integer;
process Alice;
var q:qubit; a,b:integer;
begin
 q := newqubit;
 e1 := newqubit; e2 := newqubit;
 had e1; cnot e1 e2;
 cnot q e1; had q;
 a := meas q;
 b := meas e1;
 ch!a; ch!b;
end;
process Bob;
var c,d: integer;
begin
 ch?c; ch?d;
 if
 :: ((c=1) and (d=0)) -> X q; break;
 :: ((c=0) and (d=1)) -> Z q; break;
 :: ((c=1) and (d=1)) -> X q; Z q; break;
 :: ((c=0) and (d=0)) -> break;
 fi
end;
endprogram.
```

Fig. 2. QMC source program for quantum teleportation

of classical variables evolve. We use quantum computation tree logic (QCTL) [6] for this purpose.

QCTL adds the usual temporal connectives (AX, EF, EU) of computational tree logic [12] to the propositional logic EQPL [25]. The meaning of formulae in EQPL is expressed in terms of valuations, which are truth-value assignments for the symbols $qb_0, qb_1, \ldots, qb_n$ corresponding to each qubit in the system. For instance, the quantum state $\frac{1}{\sqrt{2}}(|00\rangle + |11\rangle)$ is understood as a pair of valuations (v_1, v_2) for a 2-qubit system such that $v_1(qb_0) = 0$, $v_1(qb_1) = 0$, $v_2(qb_0) = 1$, $v_2(qb_1) = 1$.

The formulae accepted by the QMC tool for verification allow the user to reason about the state of individual qubits, and involve usual logical connectives such as negation and implication. There are two levels of formulae: classical formulae, which hold only if all valuations in a state satisfy them, and quantum formulae, which are essentially logical combinations of classical formulae. For instance, the quantum conjunction in the formula $\phi_1 \curlywedge \phi_2$ is only satisfied if both the classical formulae ϕ_1 and ϕ_2 are satisfied in the current state. A particularly distinctive type of quantum formula is of the form $[Q]$, where Q is a list of qubit variables $qb_i, qb_j, \ldots$; this type of formula is satisfied only if the qubits listed are disentangled from all other qubits in the system.

Example of Property for Verification. The requirement for the teleportation protocol is that, at the end of the protocol, no matter what the measurement outcomes, the third qubit will be in the same state as the first qubit was to begin with, and this qubit will be disentangled from the rest of the system. We can express this requirement, for the case where the input is the quantum state $|0\rangle$, in the input language of QMC using the specification

```
finalstateproperty ([q2]) #/\ (!q2);
```

which corresponds to the EQPL formula $[q_2] \curlywedge (\neg q_2)$. The first part of the formula asserts that the last qubit ($q2$) is disentangled from the rest of the quantum state, while the second part asserts that the current valuation assigns to this qubit a value of 0. The entire formula is true if both parts are true, indicated by the connective of quantum conjunction (we represent $\curlywedge$ in ASCII form by #/\).

Alternatively, it is also possible in QMC to specify that the final state of a chosen qubit is the same as the initial state of a chosen qubit, again with the requirement (which is checked) that the chosen qubits are not entangled with the rest of the state. With this approach, we can define a model which non-deterministically chooses a state to teleport, and specify that the state is teleported, independently of its particular value; exhaustive model-checking then verifies that all stabilizer states are correctly teleported.

6 Beyond Stabilizer States: Checking Equivalence

Our work on quantum model-checking is based on the stabilizer formalism, because according to the Gottesman-Knill Theorem [22], that is what we can efficiently simulate with classical algorithms. This has two effects on the results we can obtain: (1) we can only analyse quantum systems whose operations are restricted to the Clifford group (which consists of all the operators we have seen so far along with a *phase* operator); (2) when exhaustively analysing the behaviour of a system on all possible quantum inputs, we can only consider inputs that are stabilizer states. Note, however, that the stabilizer formalism, although efficiently classically simulatable, contains many entangled states and supports a range of interesting quantum protocols.

We can avoid the second of the above limitations by taking advantage of linearity, if we focus our attention on systems that compute functions, mapping a quantum input to a quantum output. Protocols such as teleportation and error-correction can be formulated in this way. Furthermore, correctness of such a protocol can be expressed as equivalence with a particular specification protocol which is taken to be obviously correct. For example, the specification of teleportation is that a quantum state is transferred from input to output. If the teleportation protocol is formulated as a function, then its specification is that it should be equivalent to the identity function.

```
program Teleportation_Specification
input   q0:qbit
output q0:qbit
```

```
program Teleportation_Implementation
input q0:qbit
// Preparing an entangled pair.
newqbit q1;
newqbit q2;
q1 *= H;
q1,q2 *= CNot;
//Entangling the input qubit.
q0,q1 *= CNot;
q0 *= H;
// Measurement and corrections.
measure q0 then q2*=Z else q2*=I end;
measure q1 then q2*=X else q2*=I end
// The quantum state is now on q2
output q2:qbit
```

Fig. 3. Teleportation: Specification and Implementation

The appropriate way to view a quantum protocol as a function is to consider its action as a superoperator, i.e. a linear operator on the space of density matrices. In this way, both measurements and unitary operators are taken into account. By linearity, to check that superoperators f and g are equivalent, it is sufficient to choose a basis for the space of density matrices and check that for each basis element v, $f(v) = g(v)$. It turns out that it is possible to choose a basis consisting only of stabilizer states [18], and this brings equivalence-checking into the realm of automated analysis in the stabilizer formalism.

With Ebrahim Ardeshir-Larijani, we have implemented a tool [5] which takes as input two programs and checks whether or not they are equivalent, by evaluating them on all elements of a stabilizer basis. The language is based on Selinger's QPL [29]. For example, verification of a teleportation protocol consists of checking equivalence of the two programs in Figure 3. In comparison with the discussion of teleportation in Section 4, this model does not define Alice and Bob separately, and removes the communication; the protocol has been converted into a sequential program.

Compared with the verification of teleportation by the QMC system, we have a stronger conclusion: that *all* quantum states are successfully teleported, not just stablizer states. Retrospectively, we can now intepret the QMC verification as a guarantee that all states are correctly teleported, assuming that it is reasonable to view a QMC program as a superoperator, because QMC checked all stabilizer states and therefore included a basis. Equivalence checking requires less computation than QMC, because a stabilizer basis is smaller than the set of all stabilizer states (for n qubits there are approximately $2^{(n^2)/2}$ stabilizer states but a basis for the space of density matrices has only 2^{2n} elements).

7 Conclusion

We have outlined the principles of quantum information processing, and argued that formal methods will be necessary in order to guarantee the correctness of practical quantum systems. We have illustrated three particular approaches: behavioural equivalence in process calculus, model-checking and equivalence checking. We used quantum teleportation as a running example.

Future work will include the development of equational axiomatizations of behavioural equivalence in CQP, improving the efficiency of QMC and extending equivalence checking to include concurrent programs. On the more practical side, we intend to work on more substantial examples including cryptographic systems.

References

1. Aaronson, S., Gottesman, D.: Improved simulation of stabilizer circuits. Physical Review A 70, 052328 (2004)
2. Abramsky, S., Gay, S.J., Nagarajan, R.: Interaction categories and the foundations of typed concurrent programming. In: Broy, M. (ed.) Deductive Program Design: Proceedings of the 1994 Marktoberdorf International Summer School. NATO ASI Series F: Computer and Systems Sciences. Springer (1995)
3. Abramsky, S.: Interaction Categories (Extended Abstract). In: Burn, G.L., Gay, S.J., Ryan, M.D. (eds.) Theory and Formal Methods 1993: Proceedings of the First Imperial College Department of Computing Workshop on Theory and Formal Methods. Workshops in Computer Science, pp. 57–70. Springer (1993)
4. Abramsky, S., Coecke, B.: A categorical semantics of quantum protocols. In: Proceedings of the 19th Annual IEEE Symposium on Logic in Computer Science (LICS 2004), pp. 415–425. IEEE Computer Society (2004); Also arXiv:quant-ph/0402130
5. Ardeshir-Larijani, E., Gay, S.J., Nagarajan, R.: Equivalence checking of quantum protocols. In: Piterman, N., Smolka, S.A. (eds.) TACAS 2013 (ETAPS 2013). LNCS, vol. 7795, pp. 478–492. Springer, Heidelberg (2013)
6. Baltazar, P., Chadha, R., Mateus, P.: Quantum computation tree logic – model checking and complete calculus. International Journal of Quantum Information 6(2), 219–236 (2008)
7. Baltazar, P., Chadha, R., Mateus, P., Sernadas, A.: Towards model-checking quantum security protocols. In: First International Conference on Quantum, Nano, and Micro Technologies, ICQNM. IEEE Computer Society (2007)
8. Bennett, C.H., Brassard, G., Crépeau, C., Jozsa, R., Peres, A., Wootters, W.K.: Teleporting an unknown quantum state via dual classical and Einstein-Podolsky-Rosen channels. Physical Review Letters 70, 1895–1899 (1993)
9. Canetti, R.: Universally composable security: A new paradigm for cryptographic protocols. In: 42nd IEEE Symposium on Foundations of Computer Science, FOCS, pp. 136–145. IEEE Computer Society (2001)

10. Davidson, T., Gay, S.J., Mlnařík, H., Nagarajan, R., Papanikolaou, N.: Model checking for Communicating Quantum Processes. International Journal of Unconventional Computing 8(1), 73–98 (2012)
11. Davidson, T.A.S.: Formal Verification Techniques using Quantum Process Calculus. PhD thesis, University of Warwick (2011)
12. Emerson, E.A.: Temporal and modal logic, vol. B: Formal Models and Semantics, pp. 995–1072. MIT Press (1990)
13. Feng, Y., Duan, R., Ying, M.: Bisimulation for quantum processes. In: 38th ACM Symposium on Principles of Programming Languages, POPL. ACM (2011)
14. Feng, Y., Yu, N., Ying, M.: Model checking quantum Markov chains. arXiv:1205.2187 [quant-ph] (2012)
15. Feynman, R.P.: Simulating physics with computers. International Journal of Theoretical Physics 21(6-7), 467–488 (1982)
16. Gay, S.J., Mackie, I.C. (eds.): Semantic Techniques in Quantum Computation. Cambridge University Press (2010)
17. Gay, S.J., Nagarajan, R.: Communicating quantum processes. In: 32nd ACM Symposium on Principles of Programming Languages, POPL, pp. 145–157 (2005); Also arXiv:quant-ph/0409052
18. Gay, S.J.: Stabilizer states as a basis for density matrices. arXiv:1112.2156 (2011)
19. Gay, S.J., Nagarajan, R.: Types and typechecking for Communicating Quantum Processes. Mathematical Structures in Computer Science 16(3), 375–406 (2006)
20. Gay, S.J., Nagarajan, R., Papanikolaou, N.: QMC: A model checker for quantum systems. In: Gupta, A., Malik, S. (eds.) CAV 2008. LNCS, vol. 5123, pp. 543–547. Springer, Heidelberg (2008)
21. Gay, S.J., Papanikolaou, N., Nagarajan, R.: Specification and verification of quantum protocols. In: Semantic Techniques in Quantum Computation. Cambridge University Press (2010)
22. Gottesman, D.: Class of quantum error-correcting codes saturating the quantum Hamming bound. Physical Review A 54, 1862 (1996)
23. Grover, L.: A fast quantum mechanical algorithm for database search. In: 28th ACM Symposium on the Theory of Computation, STOC, pp. 212–219. ACM Press (1996)
24. Lalire, M.: Relations among quantum processes: bisimilarity and congruence. Mathematical Structures in Computer Science 16(3), 407–428 (2006)
25. Mateus, P., Sernadas, A.: Weakly complete axiomatization of exogenous quantum propositional logic. Information and Computation 204(5), 771–794 (2006)
26. Mayers, D.: Unconditional Security in Quantum Cryptography. Journal of the ACM 48(3), 351–406 (2001)
27. Nagarajan, R., Gay, S.J.: Formal verification of quantum protocols. arXiv:quant-ph/0203086 (March 2002)
28. Papanikolaou, N.K.: Model Checking Quantum Protocols. PhD thesis, University of Warwick (2009)
29. Selinger, P.: Towards a quantum programming language. Mathematical Structures in Computer Science 14(4), 527–586 (2004)
30. Shor, P.W.: Algorithms for quantum computation: discrete logarithms and factoring. In: 35th IEEE Symposium on Foundations of Computer Science, FOCS (1994)
31. Trčka, N., Georgievska, S.: Branching bisimulation congruence for probabilistic systems. Electronic Notes in Theoretical Computer Science 220(3), 129–143 (2008)
32. Ying, M., Feng, Y., Duan, R., Ji, Z.: An algebra of quantum processes. ACM Transactions on Computational Logic 10(3), 19 (2009)

Quantum Field Theory for Legspinners

Prakash Panangaden

School of Computer Science
McGill University
Montréal, Québec, Canada
prakash@cs.mcgill.ca

Happy birthday Samson.

Abstract. The notion of a particle in quantum field theory is dependent
on the observer. This fundamental ambiguity in the definition of what
seems a basic "objectively" observable concept is unsettling. In this short
note I will survey the basics of field quantization and then discuss the
Unruh effect which illustrates this phenomenon. I will describe an abstract version of quantum field theory in which a single mathematical
object, a complex structure, captures all the ambiguity in the definition
of a particle. There is nothing original in this paper, however, this particular presentation is not easy to extract from the extant literature and
seems not be be known as widely as it deserves.

1 Introduction

I am delighted to have the chance to help celebrate Samson's 60th birthday. I
first heard of him in 1984 when I was struggling to understand fair merge in
dataflow and saw his marvellously original papers on the subject of semantics
of nondeterminism. I met him for the first time later that year at a workshop in
Carnegie-Mellon university. We discovered that we had both been leg-spinners
in our youth[1] and this, helped cement what has turned out to be an almost 30
year long friendship. Samson seemed to have a remarkably spooky way of being
interested in all the things that I was interested in except that he did them
much better and earlier. The one exception was quantum mechanics where I
had the edge on him having done a PhD in physics in the 1970s. However, he
has overtaken me here too and done beautiful work with Bob Coecke and others
at Oxford and elsewhere. Long ago I promised him notes on "Quantum Field
Theory for Legspinners"; this note is far short of what I promised but it is a
partial repayment of the huge debt that I owe him.

In order to set up quantum field theory it is worth recalling some of the
reasons why quantum field theory differs from quantum mechanics. Quantum
mechanics was intended to be a theory of point particles interacting at relatively
low energies. At higher energies a new phenomenon is observed; the creation and
disappearance of particles. Quantum mechanics had conservation of particles

---

[1] Look it up if you don't know what that means.

B. Coecke, L. Ong, and P. Panangaden (Eds.): Abramsky Festschrift, LNCS 7860, pp. 277–290, 2013.
© Springer-Verlag Berlin Heidelberg 2013

built into it, in quantum field theory one needs entirely new mathematics to describe the creation and annihilation of particles; it has to be a many-particle theory. It turns out that there are fundamental ambiguities in what a particle is which I will emphasize in this article.

2   Geometric Mechanics

The best way to understand classical mechanics is from a geometric perspective. There are several excellent books; I found the textbooks by Woodhouse [1,2] to be excellent as well as unpublished (and hard to find) lecture notes by Robert Geroch [3]. The standard references by Marsden and Ratiu [4] is also excellent.

Geometric mechanics starts from a *configuration space*, taken to be a smooth manifold M. One should think of this as a "snapshot" of the system. Notice that M need not be $\mathbb{R}^n$; one could think of particles constrained to all kinds of configurations, such as pendulums swinging along spheres. Configuration space is not a complete description of a mechanical system, since there are no dynamics at all. In fact, the configuration space just contains information about position. In order to describe the dynamics completely we also need the momenta. If we also take momenta into account, we end up with *phase space*, which mathematically corresponds to the *cotangent bundle* over M.

It turns out that the cotangent bundle T_*M of any manifold M comes equipped with a "canonical" 2-form. This is called a symplectic[2] form; in the physics literature this is called a "Poisson bracket."

The 2-form Ω satisfies the following three properties:

(S1) It is antisymmetric: $\Omega_{\alpha\beta} = -\Omega_{\beta\alpha}$.
(S2) It is invertible, in the sense that there is an $\Omega^{\alpha\beta}$ satisfying $\Omega^{\alpha\gamma}\Omega^{\gamma\beta} = \delta^\alpha_\beta$, where the last symbol is the Kronecker delta.
(S3) $\Delta_{[\alpha}\Omega_{\beta\gamma]} = 0$, where the bracketed indices denote complete antisymmetrization. In general,

$$T_{[abc]} = \sum_{\sigma \in S_n} (-1)^{\mathrm{sgn}(\sigma)} T_{\sigma(a)\sigma(b)\sigma(c)},$$

and the antisymmetrization can be taken over indices of multiple tensors, as above.[3]

Any 2-form satisfying these three properties is called a *symplectic form*.

We can now finally define the arena in which dynamics can happen to be a *symplectic manifold*: a smooth manifold equipped with a symplectic form. It follows that such a manifold is automatically even-dimensional. In fact, a lot of

---

[2] The name "symplectic" has been introduced by Hermann Weyl in 1939 as the Greek adjective corresponding to the word "complex", which for him referred to the linear line complexes introduced by Plücker that satisfied condition (S1) below, because the word "complex" by that time had got strong connotations with complex numbers.

[3] Incidentally, parentheses around indices similarly denote complete symmetrization.

mechanics could alternatively be called the geometry of symplectic manifold. A symplectic manifold is one of the two major pieces out of which Hilbert spaces are constructed.

As phase space is supposed to give the "kinematics", we can trace every point along its tangent curve, thus extrapolating its "future" and "past". Hence the blank canvas of phase space comes "painted with curves", which are called *dynamical trajectories*. The whole picture is also called the *phase portrait*. The dynamical trajectories of different points cannot intersect, because behaviour is presupposed to be deterministic. Together, the dynamical trajectories must fill the whole of space, since every point lies on a tangent curve.

The tangent vectors of the family of curves in the phase portrait form a vector field, called *dynamics*: there is a smooth scalar field on T_*M called the *hamiltonian* H, and there is an associated vector field, called the *hamiltonian vector field*, denoted by H^α, given by

$$H^\alpha = \Omega^{\alpha\beta} \nabla_\beta H.$$

The latter assertion follows from the theory of differential equations, that is lifted from $\mathbb{R}^n$ via local charts. The integral curves of H^α give the phase portrait discussed above. The upshot is that the symplectic form and the Hamiltonian determine the dynamics of a system.

3 Basic Elements of Quantum Mechanics

In quantum mechanics, the state space of a physical system is represented by a Hilbert space $\mathcal{H}$. Two nonzero vectors of $\mathcal{H}$ will represent the same physical state if they are linearly dependent. Thus the state space is really the projective space of $\mathcal{H}$. However, $\mathcal{H}$ is still often called the state space.

The major change with respect to classical mechanics is that observables are now Hermitian operators on the Hilbert space; their algebra is now non-commutative. Why should this be? Why couldn't they have been functions on the state space as in classical physics? The reason is that measuring an observable changes the state so one cannot just describe an observable as a mapping of states to numbers but rather as a mapping of states to states.

3.1 Time Evolution

The time evolution is described by a family of unitary operators $U(t) : \mathcal{H} \rightarrow \mathcal{H}$, so that the state vector at time t, $|\psi(t)\rangle$, is given by

$$|\psi(t)\rangle = U(t) |\psi(0)\rangle.$$

It is a fundamental law of quantum mechanics that

$$U(t) = e^{-iHt/\hbar}$$

for a Hermitian operator H, also called the Hamiltonian, which depends on the physics of the specific system considered. The infinitesimal version of the time-evolution equation then reads

$$i\hbar \frac{\partial}{\partial t} |\psi(t)\rangle = H |\psi(t)\rangle,$$

This is the celebrated Schrödinger equation.

3.2 Quantization

Where does one get the Hamiltonians for various systems? There is a (heuristic) process called quantization which constructs a quantum theory from a given classical theory, in particular, for each classical observable one needs to produce a corresponding quantal observable. A principled account of quantization from a geometric perspective is given by Woodhouse [2].

	Classical		Quantal
State space	Manifold		(Projective) Hilbert space
Observable	Real-valued function	quantization	Hermitian operator
Time evolution	Hamiltonian	$\longrightarrow$	Hamiltonian

In our simple case, we just replace the quantities x and p in the classical Hamiltonian by the quantum mechanical operators $\mathbf{x}$ and $\mathbf{p}$. Thus, for example, from the classical Hamiltonian $H = \frac{p^2}{2m} + V(x)$ for a particle in a potential field, one obtains the quantum mechanical Hamiltonian

$$H = \frac{\mathbf{P}^2}{2m} + V(\mathbf{x}) = -\frac{1}{2m}\frac{d^2}{dx^2}\psi + V(x),$$

which is correct up to setting $\hbar = 1$.

4   The Harmonic Oscillator

In a quadratic potential $V(x) = \frac{1}{2}kx^2$, the Hamiltonian is

$$H = \frac{\mathbf{p}^2}{2m} + \frac{1}{2}k\mathbf{x}^2.$$

The solution of the corresponding classical system is $x = A\sin(\omega t + \phi)$, where $\omega = \sqrt{k/m}$. In anticipation of analogous solutions we write the Hamiltonian as

$$H = \frac{\mathbf{p}^2}{2m} + \frac{1}{2}m\omega^2\mathbf{x}^2.$$

While the eigenvectors of H can be found using Hermite polynomials and other tricks for dealing with the differential equations involved. There is, however, a nicer algebraic way which makes the connection with quantum field theory clearer.

Introduce the operator

$$a = \mathbf{x}\sqrt{\frac{m\omega}{2}} + i\mathbf{p}\sqrt{\frac{1}{2m\omega}}$$

and its adjoint

$$a^\dagger = \mathbf{x}\sqrt{\frac{m\omega}{2}} - i\mathbf{p}\sqrt{\frac{1}{2m\omega}},$$

so that

$$\mathbf{x} = \frac{1}{\sqrt{2m\omega}}[a^\dagger + a],$$

$$\mathbf{p} = i\sqrt{\frac{m\omega}{2}}[a^\dagger - a] \quad \text{and hence}$$

$$H = \omega\left(a^\dagger a + \tfrac{1}{2}\right).$$

Defining $N = a^\dagger a$, we have

$$H = \omega\left(N + \tfrac{1}{2}\right)$$

and hence to find the eigenvalues of H, it is sufficient to find the eigenvalues of N.

Also, it is straightforward to check that, $[a, a^\dagger] = 1$, $[N, a] = -a$ and $[N, a^\dagger] = a^\dagger$.

Let $|n\rangle$ be an eigenvector of N with an eigenvalue n. (Anticipating, but not supposing, that n will be an integer.) $N|n\rangle = n|n\rangle$ implies that

$$N(a^\dagger|n\rangle) = (a^\dagger + a^\dagger N)|n\rangle = (n+1)(a^\dagger|n\rangle),$$

i.e. that $a^\dagger|n\rangle$ is an eigenvector of N with eigenvalue $n+1$, unless it is the zero vector. Similarly observe that

$$N(a|n\rangle) = (-a + aN)|n\rangle = (n-1)(a|n\rangle),$$

i.e. that $a|n\rangle$ is an eigenvector of N with eigenvalue $n-1$, unless it is the zero vector. We call $a^\dagger$ the raising operator and a the lowering operator.

Note that

$$\langle\psi|N|\psi\rangle = \langle\psi|a^\dagger a|\psi\rangle = ||a|\psi\rangle||^2 \geq 0,$$

so the spectrum of N is bounded below by zero.[4]

By repeated application of the lowering operator a to $|n\rangle$, we obtain eigenvectors with lower and lower eigenvalues, or the zero vector. Since the spectrum of N is bounded below, after a finite number (at most $\lfloor n\rfloor + 1$) of applications,

---

[4] This implies that the spectrum of H is bounded below by $\frac{1}{2}\omega$, i.e. the lowest possible energy is positive.

we must have obtained a zero vector. If m is the least integer such that $a^m \left| n \right\rangle$ is nonzero, we get $a(a^m \left| n \right\rangle) = 0$, so also $N(a^m \left| n \right\rangle) = (a^\dagger a)(a^m \left| n \right\rangle) = 0$, which means that $a^m \left| n \right\rangle$ is an eigenvector of N with eigenvalue zero. But we also know that $a^m \left| n \right\rangle$ is an eigenvector of N with eigenvalue $n - m$, therefore $n = m$ is a nonnegative integer.

Furthermore, if $\left\| \left| n \right\rangle \right\| = 1$, then

$$\left\| a^\dagger \left| n \right\rangle \right\|^2 = \left\langle n \left| aa^\dagger \right| n \right\rangle = \left\langle n \left| (1 + a^\dagger a) \right| n \right\rangle = \left\langle n \left| (1 + N) \right| n \right\rangle = (n + 1),$$

so in particular, we never get a zero vector when applying $a^\dagger$ to an eigenvector of N. This means that by repeated application of the raising operator we obtain eigenvalues with arbitrarily large eigenvalues. Therefore, all nonnegative integers are eigenvalues of N.

It is not hard to show that all the eigenspaces are one-dimensional, so up to physically unimportant phase, there is a unique normalized n-eigenvector $\left| n \right\rangle$ for each nonnegative integer n. From this and the calculation above it then follows that

$$a^\dagger \left| n \right\rangle = \sqrt{n + 1} \left| n + 1 \right\rangle$$

and similarly

$$a \left| n \right\rangle = \sqrt{n} \left| n - 1 \right\rangle.$$

We have found all the eigenvalues of N and hence of H.

5   The Klein-Gordon Field Theory

Klein-Gordon field theory is a *free* spinless quantum field theory. It can be viewed as a collection of harmonic oscillators as described in the previous section. The Klein-Gordon equation is:

$$\left[\partial_\mu \phi \, \partial^\mu \phi - m^2 \phi \right] = 0.$$

This is well understood as a classical field theory. We often write it in the short form:

$$(\Box - m^2)\phi = 0$$

where $\Box$ is shorthand for $-\partial^2/\partial t^2 + \partial^2/\partial x^2 + \partial^2/\partial y^2 + \partial^2/\partial z^2$. Since this equation is linear the space of solutions forms a vector space. This space forms the phase space for the classical field theory. The symplectic form is

$$\Omega(\phi_1, \phi_2) = \int_\Sigma (\phi_1 \nabla^a \phi_2 - \phi_2 \nabla^a \phi_1) d\sigma_a$$

where ∇^a is the derivative, Σ is a hypersurface large enough that data about ϕ and its first derivative on Σ determines the subsequent evolution (a Cauchy surface) and $d\sigma_a$ is the volume element on the hypersurface. One thinks of ϕ on a Cauchy surface as being like a "position" and the first derivative normal to the surface as being like a "momentum". The fact that these data can be integrated to give ϕ as a function of position and time means that we can think of the space of 4-dimensional solutions (functions of space and time) as the phase space.

5.1   Quantization of the Klein-Gordon field

This involves two main steps

- make basic observables into operators, obeying canonical commutation relations (CCRs)
- look for Hilbert space representations for these operators.

Now the phase space is the infinite-dimensional space of solutions of the classical equation. In order to tame the infinite-dimensionality we "put the field in a box", that is, we pretend that the space is a torus. This amounts to imposing periodic boundary conditions of size L. The motivation for this is to get a discrete spectrum. Later we can consider $L \to \infty$ and see what happens.

The periodicity allows us to do a Fourier decomposition of ϕ:

$$\phi(t, \mathbf{x}) = L^{-\frac{3}{2}} \sum_{\mathbf{k}} \phi_{\mathbf{k}}(t) e^{i \mathbf{k} \cdot \mathbf{x}}$$

with Fourier coefficients $\phi_{\mathbf{k}}(t)$ for each of the Fourier modes $\mathbf{k} = \frac{2\pi}{L}(n_1, n_2, n_3)$, where the n_i are integers.

Fourier theory tells us that the coefficients $\phi_{\mathbf{k}}(t)$ satisfy

$$\phi_{\mathbf{k}}(t) = L^{-\frac{3}{2}} \int \phi(t, \mathbf{x}) e^{-i \mathbf{k} \cdot \mathbf{x}} d^3 x.$$

Since we are considering ϕ a real valued function we know $\overline{\phi(t, \mathbf{x})} = \phi(t, \mathbf{x})$ and so $\phi_{\mathbf{k}}(t) = \phi_{-\mathbf{k}}(t)$.

We can now rewrite the Lagrangian:

$$\mathcal{L} = \sum_{\mathbf{k}} \left\{ \frac{1}{2} |\dot{\phi}_{\mathbf{k}}|^2 - \frac{1}{2} \omega_{\mathbf{k}}^2 |\phi_{\mathbf{k}}|^2 \right\},$$

where $\omega_{\mathbf{k}} = \sqrt{\mathbf{k}^2 + m^2}$.

Note that each component of this sum looks like an oscillator! On this basis we shall think of the field theory we are describing as a collection of decoupled harmonic oscillators, one at each Fourier mode $\mathbf{k}$.[5] This is a step forward since we know how to quantize oscillators. In the present setting we get "raising" and "lowering" operators called *creation* and *annihilation* operators $a_{\mathbf{k}}^{\dagger}$ and $a_{\mathbf{k}}$ for each Fourier mode $\mathbf{k}$.

Now we have particles! Each creation operator creates a particle of a particular momentum (mode). The corresponding annihilation operators destroy the particles. The *vacuum* is the *unique* state that is killed by *all* the annihilation operators. It is usually written $|0\rangle$; it should not be confused with the zero vector of the Hilbert space.

---

[5] That the oscillators are 'decoupled' in this setting just means that the creation and annihilation operators commute when the Fourier modes are different.

5.2   Bosonic Fock Space

What is the space on which the $a_{\mathbf{k}}$ and $a_{\mathbf{k}}^{\dagger}$ act? The naive answer, just taking the infinite tensor product, will not work as it is "too large". The correct answer is *bosonic* or *symmetric Fock space* [5,6].

Definition 1. *The* symmetrized tensor product $\mathcal{H} \otimes_s \mathcal{H}$ *of a Hilbert space* $\mathcal{H}$ *with itself is defined as the equalizer (or coequalizer) of the identity* $\mathrm{id}_{\mathcal{H} \otimes \mathcal{H}}$ *and 'flip' map* $\tau : \mathcal{H} \otimes \mathcal{H} \to \mathcal{H} \otimes \mathcal{H}; u \otimes v \mapsto v \otimes u$. *That is,*

$$\mathcal{H} \otimes_s \mathcal{H} \overset{e}{\hookrightarrow} \mathcal{H} \otimes \mathcal{H} \rightrightarrows \mathcal{H} \otimes \mathcal{H} \overset{q}{\to} \mathcal{H} \otimes_s \mathcal{H}.$$

The effect of the coequalizer is $q : u \otimes v \mapsto \frac{1}{2}(u \otimes v + v \otimes u)$.

Similarly, the 3-fold symmetrized tensor product is the equalizer (coequalizer) of the six possible permutations $\mathcal{H} \otimes \mathcal{H} \otimes \mathcal{H} \to \mathcal{H} \otimes \mathcal{H} \otimes \mathcal{H}$.

Definition 2. *Given a Hilbert space* $\mathcal{H}$, *its* Bosonic *or* symmetric Fock space $\mathcal{F} = \mathcal{F}_{\mathrm{sym}}(\mathcal{H})$ *is the direct sum of symmetrized tensor products of* $\mathcal{H}$,

$$\mathcal{F}_{\mathrm{sym}}(\mathcal{H}) = \mathbb{C} \oplus \mathcal{H} \oplus (\mathcal{H} \otimes_s \mathcal{H}) \oplus (\mathcal{H} \otimes_s \mathcal{H} \otimes_s \mathcal{H}) \oplus \dots$$

where $\otimes_s$ *is defined as above.*

Heuristically, the Fock space is

$$e^{\mathcal{H}} = \mathbb{C} \oplus \mathcal{H} \oplus \frac{\mathcal{H} \otimes \mathcal{H}}{s_2} \oplus \frac{\mathcal{H}^{\otimes 3}}{s_3} \oplus \dots$$

where each quotient $/s_n$ is by the equalizer/coequalizer of the $n!$ permutations on $\mathcal{H}^{\otimes n}$.

Since for ordinary exponentials we have $e^{x+y} = e^x \cdot e^y$ the analogy implies $\mathcal{F}_{\mathrm{sym}}(\mathcal{H} \oplus \mathcal{K}) \cong \mathcal{F}_{\mathrm{sym}}(\mathcal{H}) \otimes \mathcal{F}_{\mathrm{sym}}(\mathcal{K})$. Indeed, this is the case as can be checked by explicitly constructing the isomorphism.

Given $\Psi \in \mathcal{F}_{\mathrm{sym}}(\mathcal{H})$ we can write it explicitly as

$$\Psi = (\psi_0, \psi_1, \psi_2, \dots, \psi_n, \dots)$$

where each ψ_n is a completely symmetric n-index tensor. The components ψ_n correspond to probability amplitudes for n-particle states. Thus ψ_0 is the probability amplitude of the vacuum, ψ_1 is the probability amplitude of a 1-particle state, and so on.

Now we wish to represent the operation of creating or annihilating a particle σ in or from the field. Given $\sigma \in \mathcal{H}$ we define

$$a^{\dagger}(\sigma)\Psi = \left(0, \psi_0 \sigma, \sqrt{2}(\psi_1 \otimes_s \sigma), \sqrt{3}(\psi_2 \otimes_s \sigma), \dots\right),$$

which corresponds to the creation of a σ particle in the state Ψ.

Similarly the annihilation of a σ particle is given by the operator

$$a(\sigma)\Psi = \left(\langle \psi_1, \sigma \rangle, \sqrt{2}\langle \psi_2, \sigma \rangle, \sqrt{3}\langle \psi_3, \sigma \rangle, \dots\right),$$

where the angled brackets denote the contraction or trace, namely $\langle \psi_2, \sigma \rangle = \psi_2^{ab}\sigma_b$, $\langle \psi_3, \sigma \rangle = \psi_3^{abc}\sigma_c$, and so on.

5.3 Summary

It all seems very canonical but that is misleading. The underlying spacetime is Minkowski spacetime and this has preferred coordinates: preferred because they correspond to the global symmetries of the spacetime. Given this preferred time coordinate it becomes clear what "positive" and "negative" frequency means. The decomposition of the filed $\phi(t, \mathbf{x})$ has a component with time dependence $e^{i\omega t}$: this is a positive frequency piece whereas the Hermitian conjugate piece looks like $e^{-i\omega t}$: it is the negative frequency piece? A very important point to note here is that the positive and negative frequency solutions are *complex* while the original classical field is real. This observation will be important later.

What happens if different time coordinates are used? Then one can obtain a totally different set of creation and annihilation operators.

6 Quantum Field Theory Abstractly

The algebraic approach to quantum field theory is based on looking at the observables. The state space is constructed later as a representation for the abstract algebra. The present abstract framework was developed by I. E. Segal, see, for example [7] and used by Ashtekar and Magnon [8] to develop quantum field theory in curved spacetimes.

The algebra of interest in quantum field theory is a *-algebra which is constructed from the classical quantities. Incidentally the observables by themselves do not form a *-algebra, the observables are a subset of the *-algebra of physical interest. The *-algebra is obtained by taking the free *-algebra generated by the solutions to the KG equation; recall that the solutions of the KG equation form a vector space. To each solution ϕ is associated two elements of the *-algebra, written $F(\phi)$ and $F^*(\phi)$. We impose the equation $F(\phi) = F^*(\phi)$ which makes the basic operators self-adjoint. This does not trivialize the $*$ structure because, for example, $(aF)^* = \bar{a}F$ where a is a complex number and $\bar{a}$ denotes complex conjugation.

Dirac's quantization rule is the following: "when constructing the algebra of quantum operators the quantum analogues of classical operators no longer commute, instead the commutators are given by the classical Poisson brackets." The commutator of two operators $[A, B]$ is defined as $AB - BA$ and measures the failure of A and B to commute. The algebraic condition suggested by Dirac's rule is

$$[F(\phi_1), F(\phi_2)] = i\Omega(\phi_1, \phi_2)I$$

where i is the square root of -1, I is the identity element of the algebra and we have chosen units in which physical constants (like c, the velocity of light and h, Planck's constant) are equal to 1. This equation is imposed on the algebra.

The space of states is chosen to carry a representation of the algebra. Additional input from physics is needed to select a preferred space from the set of possible spaces. We are going to demand that the space of states support the "wave-particle duality" of quantum field theory and carry the structures necessary to describe the creation and annihilation of particles. In short we are going to construct a Fock space. First we demand that the space of states $\mathcal{F}$ contain a Hilbert space $\mathcal{H}$. In order to define $\mathcal{H}$ we proceed as described below. As a real vector space $\mathcal{H}$ is isomorphic to the space, V, of solutions to the classical field equations. Intuitively $\mathcal{H}$ is going to be thought of as the space of one particle states. Second we demand that $\mathcal{F}$ be the Fock space over $\mathcal{H}$; this means that we want the space of states to be the "many-particle" states of the quantum field. Thirdly we demand that every one of the basic operators $F(\phi)$ be represented as the sum of a creation operator and an annihilation operator.

Where does the Hilbert space structure come from? It turns out that one needs to decide which parts of a classical solution correspond to the propagation of positive energy particles and which corresponds to the propagation of negative energy particles. Thus a classical real solution to the KG equation is "decomposed" into complex solutions and this is where the notion of particle comes in. I will therefore interrupt the discussion of the Hilbert space structure and proceed to the heart of the paper.

7   Complex Structures and Polarizations

A choice of negative and positive frequency components amounts to a decomposition of the Hilbert space into two isomorphic pieces. Note that from the discussion of the Klein-Gordon field we saw that the choice of a positive and negative frequency decomposition results in complex vector spaces whereas we started with a real vector space. Thus the process of decomposition seems to be linked with the notion of introducing a complexification into the theory. In this section we make this link explicit [9].

Definition 3. *Given a real vector space V, we define a **complex structure** on V to be a linear map $J : V \rightarrow V$ such that $J^2 = -I$.*

It is easy to see that V has to be even-dimensional or infinite-dimensional.

Consider the complex vector space $V_C = V \oplus iV$ where a complex number $x + iy$ acts on $(u, v) \in V_C$ by $(x + iy)(u, v) = (xu - yv, xv + yu)$; i.e. we can think of (u, v) as $u + iv$. If we have a complex structure defined on V it can be extended to a complex structure J_c on V_c by linearity.

Definition 4. *A **polarization** on a complex vector space is a pair of projection operators $P^{\pm}$ such that*

1. $P^+ + P^- = I$,
2. $\overline{(P^+\phi)} = P^-(\phi)$
3. $\overline{(P^-\phi)} = P^+(\phi)$

It follows immediately from (1) that $P^+P^- = P^-P^+ = 0$.

From a polarization one can define a complex structure J on V_c as follows:

$$J\phi = iP^+(\phi) - iP^-(\phi). \tag{1}$$

From a complex structure one can define a polarization as follows:

$$P^+(\phi) = \frac{1}{2}(\phi - iJ\phi) \tag{2}$$

$$P^-(\phi) = \frac{1}{2}(\phi + iJ\phi). \tag{3}$$

It is easy to see by explicit calculation that the $P^\pm$ defined this way are projection operators and have the other properties required of a polarization. It is also easy to check that J defined this way is a complex structure.

If $\phi \in V_c$ is in the "real part" i.e. is of the form $(u, 0)$ then we have $P^+(u, 0) = (x, y)$ and, from the requirement that $\overline{(P^+\phi)} = P^-(\phi)$ we have that $P^-(u, 0) = (x, -y)$. Then the action of J is $J(u, 0) = i(x, y) - i(x, -y) = (-y, x) + (-y, -x) = (-2y, 0)$ i.e. it is well-defined as a complex structure on V the original real vector space.

Thus the physical question of how one chooses positive and negative frequency decompositions can be reduced to the mathematical question of choosing a complex structure. In ordinary quantum field theory one computes the Fourier transform of ϕ and obtains a canonical decomposition into positive and negative frequency components.

Using the condition that every basic operator be representable as the sum of a creation operator and an annihilation operator and using the explicit formulas for the action of these operators on Fock space as well as the commutation conditions that have been imposed on the basic operators we can show that

$$\langle \phi, \psi \rangle = 1/2[\Omega(\phi, J\psi) + i\Omega(\phi, \psi)].$$

In other words the symplectic structure and the complex structure determine the inner product on $\mathcal{H}$.

7.1 Defining the Vacuum

We have seen that choosing a complex structure defines the positive and negative frequency solutions of a theory. This choice is not unique and one needs some input from the physics to pick out the "right" complex structure. We consider what happens when two observers have different notions of positive and negative energy frequencies. Suppose we have two complete, orthonormal sets of of complex solutions to the Klein-Gordon equation, $\{f_i\}$ and $\{q_j\}$. By orthonormal we mean that the union of the f_i and their complex conjugates satisfy the following equations

$$\langle f_i, f_j \rangle = - \langle f_i^*, f_j^* \rangle = \delta_{ij}.$$

So the Klein-Gordon "inner product" only behaves like an inner product when restricted to positive frequency solutions. By complete we mean that they form a basis in the complex vector space of all solutions.

If $\hat{\phi}(x)$ is our field operator, then the creation and annihilation operators with respect to the f-basis are defined by

$$\hat{\phi}(x) = \sum_i \left(\hat{a}_i f_i + \hat{a}_i^\dagger f_i^* \right),$$

and the vacuum $|0\rangle$ is defined as the unique state that is killed by all the annihilation operators:

$$\hat{a}_i |0\rangle = 0.$$

Since we are dealing with complete sets, we can write the f_i and g_j in terms of each other:

$$g_j = \sum_i \left(\alpha_{ij} f_i + \beta_{ij} f_i^* \right) \quad g_j^* = \sum_i \left(\alpha_{ij}^* f_i^* + \beta_{ij}^* f_i \right)$$
$$f_i = \sum_j \left(\alpha_{ji} g_j + \beta_{ji} g_j^* \right) \quad f_i^* = \sum_j \left(\alpha_{ji}^* g_j^* + \beta_{ji}^* g_j \right).$$

So, for example, $\alpha_{ij} = \langle g_j, f_i \rangle$.

We could equally well expand the field operator in the g-basis. Then we have

$$\hat{\phi}(x) = \sum_j \left(\hat{b}_j g_j + \hat{b}_j^\dagger g_j^* \right),$$

for some other creation and annihilators $\hat{b}_j$ and $\hat{b}_j^\dagger$, and we also have another vacuum defined by $\hat{b}_j |0\rangle' = 0$. The question we are interested in answering is: what does a one vacuum look like in the other basis?

7.2 Bogolioubov Transformations

It is a routine calculation to find that

$$\hat{a}_i = \sum_j \left[\alpha_{ji} \hat{b}_j + \beta_{ji} \hat{b}_j^\dagger \right] \quad \hat{b}_j = \sum_i \left[\alpha_{ij} \hat{b}_i + \beta_{ij} \hat{b}_i^\dagger \right]$$
$$\hat{a}_i^\dagger = \sum_j \left[\alpha_{ji}^* \hat{b}_j^\dagger + \beta_{ji}^* \hat{b}_j \right] \quad \hat{b}_j^\dagger = \sum_i \left[\alpha_{ij}^* \hat{b}_i^\dagger + \beta_{ij}^* \hat{b}_i \right].$$

These are called the *Bogoliubov transformations*. Now we have two number operators:

$$\hat{N}_i = \hat{a}_i^\dagger \hat{a}_i \quad \hat{N}_j' = \hat{b}_j^\dagger \hat{b}_j.$$

So we can take one vacuum and with it calculate the expectation value of the other number operator:

$$\langle 0|' \hat{N}_i |0\rangle' = \sum_j |\beta_{ij}|^2.$$

We see that under the Bogolioubov transformations the annihilation operators pick up a creation part, and the coefficients give rise to the non-zero right-hand side here. It is this mixing of the creation and annihilation operators that is responsible for particle creation. The Bogolioubov transformation formalism was first used in order to describe particle by Leonard Parker [10] in the 1960s.

7.3   Rindler Spacetime

Recall that a vector field is a Killing field if the Lie derivative of the metric along that vector field vanishes. In Minkowski spacetime we have the *boost Killing field*:

$$t\frac{\partial}{\partial z} + z\frac{\partial}{\partial t}.$$

The integral curves of this Killing field are timelike in the right and left Rindler wedges. So in these regions of the spacetime we could use these curves to define a time coordinate. They curves are curves of constant acceleration, so for a uniformly accelerating observer these are the "natural" time coordinates. An accelerating observer will see the diagonals of the figure as horizons. So for such an observer, the Rindler wedge is his "natural" home.

The coordinates of a uniformly accelerated observer are the Rindler coordinates (ρ, η, x, y). These are related to the Minkowski coordinates (t, z, x, y) by the transformations

$$t = \rho\sinh\eta, \ z = \rho\cosh\eta.$$

The line element of the Rindler spacetime is

$$ds^2 = \rho^2 d\eta - d\rho^2 - dx^2 - dy^2.$$

Lines of constant acceleration are lines of constant ρ, and the value of the acceleration is ρ^{-1}. In terms of the scaled coordinates (τ, η, x, y), where the acceleration a is factored out:

$$\rho = a^{-1}e^{a\xi}, \ \eta = a\tau.$$

$\xi = 0$ corresponds to acceleration a. We will use τ to define positive and negative frequency, and thus the vacuum for an accelerating observer. It turns out that, to the accelerated observer, the Minkowski background looks like a thermal bath: this is what's known as the *Unruh effect* [11] or the *Fulling-Davies-Unruh effect* [12,13]. It dramatically illustrates the differences between what one observer perceives as a vacuum and another sees as a "hot" radiation bath. Unruh and Wald [14] carefully analyzed what different observers would see in this situation. An excellent review of the Unruh effect is a Reviews of Modern Physics article [15].

8   Conclusions

The story is well known to physicists but less known among the computer science community. It is my hope that the group around Abramsky and Coecke working on categorical quantum mechanics would be stimulated to investigate a functorial version of quantization. Baez [16] has remarked that this is not possible, nevertheless it seems to me to be worth understanding why not more deeply and perhaps seeing if it is possible from a different perspective.

Acknowledgements. I would like to thank Samson Abramsky for inviting me spend a sabbatical at Oxford during the academic year 2010-11 and suggesting that I give lectures on quantum field theory to the group there. I would like to thank the note takers from those lectures: Chris Heunen, Ray Lal, Shane Mansfield, Nadish de Silva, Jakub Zavodny, Colin Stephen, Julia Evans and Alex Lang. I have greatly enjoyed my discussions on quantum field theory with that group, apart from the note takers this includes Jamie Vicary, Bob Coecke, Aleks Kissinger, Andreas Döring and, of course, Samson himself. I owe a great deal to Abhay Ashtekar, Leonard Parker, Rafael Sorkin, Robert Wald and Robert Geroch from whom I learned most of this material in the 1970s. I gratefully acknowledge the support of an EPSRC grant that allowed me to spend my sabbatical year in Oxford.

References

1. Woodhouse, N.M.J.: Introduction to analytical dynamics. Oxford University Press (1987)
2. Woodhouse, N.M.J.: Geometric Quantization, 2nd edn. Clarendon Press (1997)
3. Geroch, R.: Lectures on geometric quantum mechanics. Mimeographed notes
4. Marsden, J.E., Ratiu, T.: Introduction to Mechanics and Symmetry. Texts in Applied Mathematics, vol. 17. Springer (1994)
5. Geroch, R.: Mathematical Physics. Chicago Lectures in Physics. University of Chicago Press (1985)
6. Geroch, R.: Lectures on quantum field theory. Mimeographed notes (1971)
7. Baez, J., Segal, I.E., Zhou, Z.: Introduction to Algebraic and Constructive Quantum Field Theory. Princeton University Press (1992)
8. Ashtekar, A., Magnon, A.: Quantum fields in curved space-times. Proceedings of the Royal Society of London. A. Mathematical and Physical Sciences 346(1646), 375–394 (1975)
9. Panangaden, P.: Positive and negative frequency decompositions in curved space-times. J. Math. Phys. 20, 2506–2510 (1979)
10. Parker, L.: Particle creation in expanding universes. Phys. Rev. Lett. 21, 562–564 (1968)
11. Unruh, W.G.: Notes on black hole evaporation. Phys. Rev. D 14, 870–892 (1976)
12. Fulling, S.A.: Nonuniqueness of canonical field quantization in riemannian space-time. Phys. Rev. D 7(10), 2850–2862 (1973)
13. Davies, P.C.W.: Scalar particle production in schwarzschild and rindler metrics. J. Phys. A 8(4), 609–616 (1975)
14. Unruh, W.G., Wald, R.M.: What happens when an accelerating observer detects a rindler particle. Phys. Rev. D 29(6), 1047–1056 (1984)
15. Crispino, L., Higuchi, A., Matsas, G.: The unruh effect and its applications. Reviews of Modern Physics 80(3), 787 (2008)
16. Baez, J.: Notes on geometric quantization. Available on Baez' web site

Bicompletions of Distance Matrices

To Samson Abramsky on the occasion of his 60th birthday

Dusko Pavlovic

Royal Holloway, University of London, and University of Twente
dusko.pavlovic@rhul.ac.uk

Abstract. In the practice of information extraction, the input data are usually arranged into *pattern matrices*, and analyzed by the methods of linear algebra and statistics, such as principal component analysis. In some applications, the tacit assumptions of these methods lead to wrong results. The usual reason is that the matrix composition of linear algebra presents information as flowing in waves, whereas it sometimes flows in particles, which seek the shortest paths. This wave-particle duality in computation and information processing has been originally observed by Abramsky. In this paper we pursue a particle view of information, formalized in *distance spaces*, which generalize metric spaces, but are slightly less general than Lawvere's *generalized metric spaces*. In this framework, the task of extracting the 'principal components' from a given matrix of data boils down to a *bicompletion*, in the sense of enriched category theory. We describe the bicompletion construction for distance matrices. The practical goal that motivates this research is to develop a method to estimate the hardness of attack constructions in security.

1 Introduction

Dedication. When Samson Abramsky offered me the position of 'Human Capital Mobility Research Fellow' in his group at Imperial College back in 1993, I was an ex-programmer with postdoctoral experience in category theory. It was a questionable investment. Category theoretical models of computation were, of course, already in use in theoretical computer science; but the emphasis was on the word 'theoretical'. A couple of years later, I left academia to build software using categorical models. While it is clear and well understood that Samson's work and results consolidated and enriched categorical methods of theoretical computer science, their applications in the practice of computation may not be as well known. In the long run, I believe, the impact of the methods and of the approach that we learned from Samson will become increasingly clear, as the abstract structures that we use, including the fully abstract ones, are becoming more concrete, more practical, and more often indispensable.

In the present paper, I venture into an extended exercise in enriched category theory, directly motivated by concrete problems of security [17,16] and of data analysis [18]. Although the story is not directly related to Samson's own work, I hope that it is appropriate for the occasion, since he is the originator of the general spirit of categorical variations on computational themes, even if I can never hope to approach his balance and style.

B. Coecke, L. Ong, and P. Panangaden (Eds.): Abramsky Festschrift, LNCS 7860, pp. 291–310, 2013.
© Springer-Verlag Berlin Heidelberg 2013

Motivation: Distances between Algorithms

Suppose that you are given an algorithm a, and you need to construct another algorithm b, such that some predicate $P(a, b)$ is satisfied. Or more concretely, suppose that a is a software system, and b should be an attack on a, contradicting a's security claim by realizing a property $P(a, b)$. Since reverse engineering is easy [2,5], we can assume that the code of a is readily available, and your task is thus to code the attack b. Note that a is in principle an algorithmic pattern, that can be implemented in many ways, and may have many versions and instances. So your attack b should also be an algorithmic pattern, related to a by some polymorphic transformation. The derivation of b from a should thus be polymorphic, i.e. a uniform construction: it should be a program p that inputs a description of a and outputs a corresponding description $p(a) = b$. How hard is it to find p? An approach to answering such questions is suggested in algorithmic information theory [25,13]. The notion of *Kolmogorov complexity* is that the distance from an algorithm a to an algorithm b can be measured by the length of the shortest programs that construct b from a, i.e.

$$d(a, b) = \bigwedge_{p(a)=b} |p| \qquad (1)$$

where $|p|$ denotes the length of the program p. It is easy to see that the above formula yields the triangle law $d(a, b) + d(b, c) \overset{+}{\geq} d(a, c)$, where the superscript '+' means that the uniform order relation $\geq$ is taken up to a constant, which is in this case the length of the program composition operation, needed to get a program to construct c from a by composing a program that constructs c from b with a program that constructs b from a. Algorithmic information theory always works with such order relations [13,4]. The equation $d(a, a) \overset{+}{=} 0$ holds in the same sense, up to the constant length of the shortest identity program, that just inputs and outputs identical data. This distance of algorithms, in the style of Kolmogorov complexity, was proposed in [16] as a tool to measure how hard it is to construct an attack on a given system. The point was that a system could be effectively secure even when some attacks on it exist, provided that these attacks are provably hard to construct. The goal of the present note is to spell out some general results about distance that turn out to be needed for this particular application.

But why do we need general results about distances to answer the concrete question about the hardness of constructing attack programs from system programs? The reason is that the task of finding an attack algorithm not too far from a system algorithm naturally leads to the task of construcing a *completion* of the space around the system algorithm. The attacker sees the system, and may be familiar with some other algorithms in its neighborhood; but it is not known whether an attack exists, and how far it is. The task of discovering the attack is the task of completing the space around the system. And the construction of a completion is easier in general, than in some concrete cases.

How does a real attacker search for an algorithm p to derive an attack b from the system a? He is not trying to guess the construction in isolation, but in the context of his algorithmic knowledge. This knowledge has at least two components. On one hand, there is some algorithmic knowledge A about the software systems $a_0, a_1, a_2 \ldots$, and a distance measure $A \times A \xrightarrow{d_A} [0, \infty]$ between them, which express how they are related with each other. On the other hand, there is some algorithmic knowledge B about the attacks $b_0, b_1, b_2 \ldots$, and their distances $B \times B \xrightarrow{d_B} [0, \infty]$. Last but not least, there is some knowledge which attacks are related to which systems. This knowledge is expressed as a distance matrix $A \times B \xrightarrow{\Phi} [0, \infty]$, where shorter distances suggest easier attacks. In order to determine whether there are any attacks in the proximity of a given system a, our task is to conjoin the distance space A of systems with the distance space B of attacks consistently with the distance matrix $A \times B \xrightarrow{\Phi} [0, \infty]$ where the observed connections between the systems and attacks are recorded. In this conjoined space, we need to find the unknown attacks close to the target system. We find them by completing the space of the known attacks. But since the completion is in general an infinite object, we first study it abstractly, to determine how to construct just the parts of interest.

Related Work. The completions that we study are based on Lawvere's view of metric spaces as enriched categories [10]. Lawvere's generalized metric spaces were extensively used in denotational semantics of programming languages [22,3,9], and recently in ecology [12], following a renewed mathematical interest in the enriched category approach [11]. In my own work, closely related results arose in the framework of information extraction and concept analysis [18]. That work was, however, not based on distance spaces as categories enriched in the additive monoid $[0, \infty]$, but on *proximity spaces*, or *proxets*, as categories enriched in the multiplicative monoid $[0, 1]$. Proxets are a more natural framework for concept analysis, because they generalize posets, as categories enriched over the multiplicative monoid $\{0, 1\}$, and the existing theory and intuitions are largely based on posets. Distance spaces, on the other hand, appear to be a more convenient framework for relating algorithms.

Outline of the Paper. In Sec. 2 we define distance spaces and describe some examples. In Sec. 3 we spell out the notions of limit in distance spaces, the basic completion constructions, and the adjunctions as they arise from the limit preserving morphisms. In Sec. 4, we introduce distance matrices, and describe their decomposition. In Sec. 5 we put the previously presented components together to construct the bicompletions of distance matrices. Sec. 6 provides a summary of the obtained results and a discussion of future work.

2 Distance Spaces

2.1 Definition and Background

Definition 2.1. *A distance space is a set A with a metric $d_A : A \times A \to [0, \infty]$ which is*

- *reflexive: $d(x, x) = 0$,*
- *transitive: $d(x, y) + d(y, z) \geq d(x, z)$, and*
- *antisymmetric: $d(x, y) = 0 = d(y, x) \implies x = y$*

A contraction between the distance spaces A and B is a function $f : A \to B$ such that for all $x, y \in A$ holds $d_A(x, y) \geq d_B(fx, fy)$. The category of distance spaces and contractions is denoted Dist.

Background. In topology, distance spaces have been studied since the 1930s under the name *quasi-metric spaces* [23,8]. The prefix 'quasi' refers to the fact that the metric symmetry law $d(x, y) = d(y, x)$ is not necessarily satisfied. When the antisymmetry law is not satisfied either, then the topologists speak of *pseudo-quasi-metric spaces* [24]. Lawvere [10] observed that pseudo-quasi-metric spaces, which he called *generalized metric spaces*, could be viewed as enriched categories [7]. They are enriched over the additive monoid $[0, \infty]$, viewed as a monoidal category with a uniqe arrow $x \to y$ if and only if $x \geq y$. The distance $d(x, y) \in [0, \infty]$ is thus viewed as the 'hom-set' in the enriched sense. Lawvere's main result was the characterization of the Cauchy completion of a metric space as an enriched category construction. This view of distances and contractions turned out to provide an alternative to domains for denotational semantics [22], and their categorical completions were elaborated in [3,9]. Distance spaces as defined in 2.1 are a special case of generalized metric spaces, since they are required to satisfy the antisymmetry law. This is mainly a matter of convenience, as the following lemma shows.

Lemma 2.2. *A map $d_A : A \times A \to [0, \infty]$ which is reflexive and transitive in the sense of Def. 2.1 is also antisymmetric if and only if it satisfies either of the following equivalent conditions*

- $(\forall z.\, d\,(z, x) = d\,(z, y)) \Rightarrow x = y$
- $(\forall z.\, d\,(x, z) = d\,(y, z)) \Rightarrow x = y$

Proof. In the presence of transitivity and reflexivity, $d\,(x, y) = 0$ holds if and only if $\forall z.\, d\,(z, x) \geq d\,(z, y)$, or equivalently if and only if $\forall z.\, d\,(x, z) \leq d\,(y, z)$. The result follows.   □

Corollary 2.3. *Distance spaces are just the* skeletal *generalized metric spaces.*

2.2   Examples

The first example of a distance space is, of course, the interval $[0, \infty]$ itself, with the metric

$$d_{[0,\infty]}\,(x, y) \;=\; x \multimap y = \begin{cases} y - x & \text{if } x < y \\ 0 & \text{otherwise} \end{cases} \tag{2}$$

The $\multimap$ notation is convenient because the operation $d_{[0,\infty]} = \multimap : [0, \infty] \times [0, \infty] \to [0, \infty]$ makes $[0, \infty]$ into a closed category

$$x + y \geq z \iff x \geq y \multimap z \tag{3}$$

Any metric space is obviously an example of a distance space. But in distance spaces, the distance $d(a, b)$ from a to b does not have to be the same as the distance $d(b, a)$ from b to a. E.g., a may be on a hill, and b in the valley, and traveling one way may be easier than traveling the other way. For our purposes described in the Introduction, this distinction is quite important, since a program constructing an attack b from a system code a does not have to be related in any obvious way to the program performing the construction the other way.

For a non-metric family of distance spaces, take any poset $(S, \sqsubseteq_S)$ and define a distance space (WS, d_{WS}) by setting $d_{WS}(x, y) = 0$ if $x \sqsubseteq_S y$, otherwise ∞. The other way around, any distance space A induces two posets, ΥA and ΛA, with the same underlying set and

$$x \sqsubseteq_{\Upsilon A} y \iff d_A(x, y) = 0 \qquad\qquad x \sqsubseteq_{\Lambda A} y \iff d_A(x, y) < \infty$$

The constructions W, Υ and Λ form the adjunctions $\Lambda \dashv W \dashv \Upsilon : \mathsf{Dist} \to \mathsf{Pos}$. Since W : $\mathsf{Pos} \hookrightarrow \mathsf{Dist}$ is an embedding, Pos is thus a reflective and correflective subcategory of Dist.

Distance spaces are thus a common generalization of posets and metric spaces. For an example not arising from posets of metric spaces, take any family of sets $X \subseteq \wp X$, and define

$$d(x, y) = |y \setminus x| \tag{4}$$

The distance of x and y is thus the number of elements of y that are not in x. If X is a set of terms, say in a dictionary, and X is a set of documents, each viewed as a set of terms, then the distance between two documents is the number of terms that occur in one document and not in the other. In natural language processing, documents are usually presented as multisets (bags) of terms, and the distance is defined in terms of multiset subtraction, which generalizes the set difference used in (4). In any case, it is clear that the asymmetry of the notion of distance is as essential for such applications as it is for the one described in the Introduction.

2.3   Basic Constructions

Given two distance space A and B, we define:

- *dual A^o*: take the same underlying set and define the dual metric to be $d_{A^o}(x, y) = d_A(y, x)$;
- *product $A \times B$*: take the cartesian product of the underlying sets and set the product metric to be $d_{A \times B}(x, u, y, v) = d_A(x, y) \vee d_B(u, v)$
- the *power B^A*: take the set of contractions $\mathsf{Dist}(A, B)$ to be the underlying set and set the metric to be $d_{B^A}(f, g) = \bigvee_{x \in A} d_B(fx, gx)$.

These constructions induce the natural correspondences

$$\mathsf{Dist}(A, B) \times \mathsf{Dist}(A, C) \cong \mathsf{Dist}(A, B \times C) \quad \text{and} \quad \mathsf{Dist}(A \times B, C) \cong \mathsf{Dist}(A, C^B)$$

Terminology. Contractions $f : A \to B$ are called *covariant*, whereas contractions $f : A^o \to B$ are *contravatiant*.

3 Sequences and Their Limits

3.1 Left and Right Sequences

Intuitively, to complete a metric space means to add enough points so that every suitably convergent sequence has a limit. But usually many different sequences have the same limit. The main problem of the standard theory of completions is to recognize such sequences. The categorical approach overcomes this problem by considering *canonical* sequences. Instead of the sequences $s, t : \mathbb{N} \to A$ such that $\lim_{i \to \infty} s_i = \psi = \lim_{i \to \infty} t_i$, we consider a canonical sequence $\psi : A \to [0, \infty]$ where ψx intuitively denotes the distance from ψ to x.

Definition 3.1. *In a distance space A, a* (canonical) *sequence is defined to be a contraction into $[0, \infty]$. More precisely, we define that*

- *a* left *sequence is a covariant contraction* $\overleftarrow{\lambda} : A \to [0, \infty]$
  - *we write its value at $x \in A$ as $\overleftarrow{\lambda} x$*

- *a* right *sequence is a contravariant contraction* $\overrightarrow{\varrho} : A^o \to [0, \infty]$
  - *we write its value at $x \in A$ as $x \overrightarrow{\varrho}$.*

Each of the sets of sequences

$$\overleftarrow{A} = \left([0, \infty]^A \right)^o \qquad and \qquad \overrightarrow{A} = [0, \infty]^{(A^o)}$$

forms a distance space, with the metrics

$$d_{\overleftarrow{A}}\left(\overleftarrow{\lambda}, \overleftarrow{\theta} \right) = \bigvee_{x \in A} \overleftarrow{\theta} x \multimap \overleftarrow{\lambda} x \qquad and \qquad d_{\overrightarrow{A}}\left(\overrightarrow{\varrho}, \overrightarrow{\mu} \right) = \bigvee_{x \in A} x\overrightarrow{\varrho} \multimap x\overrightarrow{\mu}$$

Remarks. The conditions $d_A(x, y) \geq \overleftarrow{\lambda} x \multimap \overleftarrow{\lambda} y$ and $d_A(x, y) \geq y\overrightarrow{\varrho} \multimap x\overrightarrow{\varrho}$, which say that $\overleftarrow{\lambda}$ and $\overrightarrow{\varrho}$ are left and right contraction respectively, are by (3) respectively equivalent to

$$\overleftarrow{\lambda} x + d(x, y) \geq \overleftarrow{\lambda} y \qquad\qquad d(x, y) + y\overrightarrow{\varrho} \geq x\overrightarrow{\varrho}$$

3.2 Limits

Definition 3.2. *An element u of a distance space A is an* upper bound *of a right sequence $\overrightarrow{\varrho}$ in A if for all $x \in A$ holds*

$$x\overrightarrow{\varrho} \geq d_A(x, u) \tag{5}$$

An element ℓ of a distance space A is a lower bound *of a left sequence $\overleftarrow{\lambda}$ in A if for all $y \in A$ holds*

$$\overleftarrow{\lambda} y \geq d_A(\ell, y) \tag{6}$$

Proposition 3.3. *An element* $u \in A$ *is an upper bound* $\overrightarrow{\varrho}$ *and* $\ell \in A$ *is a lower bound of* $\overleftarrow{\lambda}$ *if and only if the following conditions hold for all* $x, y \in A$

$$d_A(u, y) \geq \bigvee_{x \in A} x\overrightarrow{\varrho} \multimap d_A(x, y) \tag{7}$$

$$d_A(x, \ell) \geq \bigvee_{y \in A} \overleftarrow{\lambda} y \multimap d_A(x, y) \tag{8}$$

Proof. Condition (3) implies that (9) and (10) are respectively equivalent with

$$x\overrightarrow{\varrho} + d_A(u, y) \geq d_A(x, y) \tag{9}$$
$$d_A(x, \ell) + \overleftarrow{\lambda} y \geq d_A(x, y) \tag{10}$$

The claim follows by instantiating y to u in (7) and x to ℓ in (8).   □

Definition 3.4. *The supremum* $\bigsqcup \overrightarrow{\varrho}$ *of the right sequence* $\overrightarrow{\varrho}$ *and the infimum* $\prod \overleftarrow{\lambda}$ *of the left sequence* $\overleftarrow{\lambda}$ *are the elements of A that satisfy for every* $x, y \in A$

$$d_A\left(\bigsqcup \overrightarrow{\varrho}, y\right) = \bigvee_{x \in A} x\overrightarrow{\varrho} \multimap d_A(x, y) \tag{11}$$

$$d_A\left(x, \prod \overleftarrow{\lambda}\right) = \bigvee_{y \in A} \overleftarrow{\lambda} y \multimap d_A(x, y) \tag{12}$$

Suprema and infima constitute the limits *of a distance space.*
 The distance space A is right (resp. left) complete *if every right (resp. left) sequence has a limit. The suprema and the infima thus yield the operations*

$$\bigsqcup : \overrightarrow{A} \to A \qquad and \qquad \prod : \overleftarrow{A} \to A$$

One apparent shortcoming of treating sequences categorically, i.e. saturating them to canonical sequences, is that it is not obvious how to define continuity, i.e. how to distinguish the contractions which preserve suprema or infima. Clearly, a left continuous contraction $f : A \to B$ should map the infimum of a left sequence $\overleftarrow{\lambda}$ in A into the infimum of the f-image of $\overleftarrow{\lambda}$ in B. But what is the f-image of $\overleftarrow{\lambda} : A \to [0, \infty]$ in B? This question calls for a slight generalization of the concept of sequence, and limit.

3.3 Weighted Limits

Limits are a special case of *weighted limits*, which are studied in general enriched categories [7, Ch. 3]. We just sketch theory of weighted limits in distance spaces.

Definition 3.5. *For distance spaces A and K we define*

- left diagrams *as pairs of contractions* $\left\langle k : K \to A, \overleftarrow{\lambda} : K \to [0, \infty]\right\rangle$
- right diagrams *as pairs of contractions* $\left\langle k : K \to A, \overrightarrow{\varrho} : K^o \to [0, \infty]\right\rangle$

Terminology and Notation. The component $k : K \to A$ of a diagram is called its *shape*. Using the angular brackets to denote the functions into cartesian products, we also write

$$- \langle k, \overleftarrow{\lambda} \rangle : K \to A \times [0, \infty] \text{ for } \langle k : K \to A, \overleftarrow{\lambda} : K \to [0, \infty] \rangle$$
$$- \langle k, \overrightarrow{\varrho}^o \rangle : K \to A \times [0, \infty]^o \text{ for } \langle k : K \to A, \overrightarrow{\varrho} : K^o \to [0, \infty] \rangle$$

Definition 3.6. *The weighted supremum* $\coprod_{\overrightarrow{\varrho}} k$ *of the right diagram* $\langle k, \overrightarrow{\varrho}^o \rangle : K \to A \times [0, \infty]^o$ *and the weighted infimum* $\prod_{\overleftarrow{\lambda}} k$ *of the left diagram* $\langle k, \overleftarrow{\lambda} \rangle : K \to A \times [0, \infty]$ *are the elements of A that satisfy for every* $x, y \in A$

$$d_A \left(\coprod_{\overrightarrow{\varrho}} k, y \right) = \bigvee_{x \in K} x\overrightarrow{\varrho} \multimap d_A (kx, y) \tag{13}$$

$$d_A \left(x, \prod_{\overleftarrow{\lambda}} k \right) = \bigvee_{y \in K} \overleftarrow{\lambda} y \multimap d_A (x, ky) \tag{14}$$

Remarks. Limits arise as a special case of weighted limits, by viewing sequences as diagrams of shape $k = \text{id} : A \to A$. A contraction $f : A \to B$ thus maps, say, a left sequence $\langle \text{id}, \overleftarrow{\lambda} \rangle : A \to A \times [0, \infty]$ to the diagram $\langle f, \overleftarrow{\lambda} \rangle : A \to B \times [0, \infty]$ in B. More generally, it maps a left sequence $\langle k, \overleftarrow{\lambda} \rangle : K \to A \times [0, \infty]$ to the diagram $\langle f \circ k, \overleftarrow{\lambda} \rangle : K \to B \times [0, \infty]$ in B. It is thus clear and easy to state what it means that a contraction preserves a weighted limit.

Definition 3.7. *A contraction* $f : A \to B$ *preserves*

- *weighted suprema if* $f \left(\coprod_{\overrightarrow{\varrho}} k \right) = \coprod_{\overrightarrow{\varrho}} (f \circ k)$, *and*
- *weighted infima if* $f \left(\prod_{\overleftarrow{\lambda}} k \right) = \prod_{\overleftarrow{\lambda}} (f \circ k)$.

On the other hand, although convenient to work with, weighted limits of diagrams in distance spaces also boil down to the limits of suitable sequences. We just state this fact, since it simplifies the construction of the completions; but leave the proof for another paper, since the proof construction is not essential for the goal of the present paper.

Proposition 3.8. *A distance space has*

- *the weighted suprema of all right diagrams if and only if it has the suprema of all right sequences;*
- *the weighted infima of all left diagrams if and only if it has the infima of all left sequences.*

3.4 Completions

Every element a of a distance space A induces two *representable* sequences

$$\begin{array}{ll}
\Delta a : A \to [0, \infty] & \nabla a : A^o \to [0, \infty] \\
\quad x \mapsto d_A (a, x) & \quad x \mapsto d_A (x, a)
\end{array}$$

These induced contractions $\Delta : A \to \overleftarrow{A}$ and $\nabla : A \to \overrightarrow{A}$ correspond to the *Yoneda-Cayley embeddings* [15, Sec. III.2]. They make $\overleftarrow{A}$ into the lower completion, and $\overrightarrow{A}$ into the upper completion of the distance space A.

Proposition 3.9. *$\overleftarrow{A}$ is left complete and $\overrightarrow{A}$ is right complete. Each of them is universal among distance spaces with the corresponding completeness properties, in the sense that*

- *any monotone $f : A \to C$ into a complete distance space C induces a unique $\prod$-preserving morphism $f_\# : \overleftarrow{A} \to C$ such that $f = f_\# \circ \Delta$;*
- *any monotone $g : A \to D$ into a cocomplete distance space D induces a unique $\bigsqcup$-preserving morphism $g^\# : \overrightarrow{A} \to D$ such that $g = g^\# \circ \nabla$.*

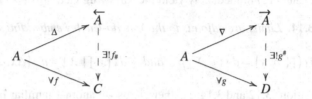

These constructions for have been thoroughly analyzed in [3,9]. Here we just state the basic facts that justify our notations, and substantiate the further developments.

Proposition 3.10. *("The Yoneda Lemma") For every $\overrightarrow{\varrho} \in \overrightarrow{A}$ and $\overleftarrow{\lambda} \in \overleftarrow{A}$ and holds*

$$a\overrightarrow{\varrho} = \bigvee_{x \in A} x(\nabla a) \multimap x\overrightarrow{\varrho} = d_{\overrightarrow{A}}\left(\nabla a, \overrightarrow{\varrho}\right)$$

$$\overleftarrow{\lambda} b = \bigvee_{x \in A} (\Delta b) x \multimap \overleftarrow{\lambda} x = d_{\overleftarrow{A}}\left(\overleftarrow{\lambda}, \Delta b\right)$$

Instantiating in the preceding proposition $\overleftarrow{\lambda}$ to Δa and $\overrightarrow{\varrho}$ to ∇b yields

Corollary 3.11. *The embeddings $\Delta : A \to \overleftarrow{A}$ and $\nabla : A \to \overrightarrow{A}$ are isometries*

$$d_A(a, b) = d_{\overrightarrow{A}}(\nabla a, \nabla b) = d_{\overleftarrow{A}}(\Delta a, \Delta b)$$

3.5 Adjunctions

Notation. In any distance space A, if is often convenient to abbreviate $d_A(x, y) = 0$ to $x \underset{A}{\leadsto} y$. For $f, g : A \to B$, it is easy to see that $f \underset{B^A}{\leadsto} g$ if and only if $fx \underset{B}{\leadsto} gx$ for all $x \in A$.

Proposition 3.12. *For any contraction $f : A \to B$ holds*

$$(a) \iff (b) \iff (c) \quad and \quad (d) \iff (e) \iff (f)$$

where

(a) $f\left(\bigsqcup \vec{\varrho}\right) = \bigsqcup_f \left(\vec{\varrho}\right)$

(b) $\exists f_* : B \to A \ \forall x \in A \ \forall y \in B. \ d_B \left(fx, y\right) = d_A \left(x, f_* y\right)$

(c) $\exists f_* : B \to A. \ \mathrm{id}_A \rightsquigarrow f_* f \wedge f f_* \rightsquigarrow \mathrm{id}_B$

(d) $f\left(\prod \overleftarrow{\lambda}\right) = \prod_f \left(\overleftarrow{\lambda}\right)$

(e) $\exists f^* : B \to A \ \forall x \in A \ \forall y \in B. \ d_B \left(f^* y, x\right) = d_A \left(y, fx\right)$

(f) $\exists f^* : B \to A. \ f^* f \rightsquigarrow \mathrm{id}_A \wedge \mathrm{id}_B \rightsquigarrow f f^*$

Each of the morphisms f^* and f_* is uniquely determined by f, whenever they exist.

Definition 3.13. A right adjoint *is a contraction satisfying (a-c) of Prop. 3.12; a* left adjoint *satisfies (d-f). A (distance) adjunction between the distance spaces A and B is a pair of contractions* $f^* : A \rightleftarrows B : f_*$ *related as in (b-c) and (e-f).*

Equations (11) and (12) immediately yield the following fact.

Proposition 3.14. *Limits are adjoints to the Yoneda-Cayley embeddings:*

$$d_A \left(\bigsqcup \vec{\varrho}, y\right) = d_{\vec{A}} \left(\vec{\varrho}, \nabla y\right) \quad and \quad d_A \left(x, \prod \overleftarrow{\lambda}\right) = d_{\overleftarrow{A}} \left(\Delta x, \overleftarrow{\lambda}\right)$$

Putting Propositions 3.12 and 3.14 together yields yet another familiar fact.

Proposition 3.15. *The sup-completion* $\nabla : A \to \vec{A}$ *preserves any infima that exist in A. The inf-completion* $\Delta : A \to \overleftarrow{A}$ *suprema that exist exist in A.*

3.6 Projectors and Nuclei

Proposition 3.16. *For any adjunction* $f^* : A \rightleftarrows B : f_*$ *holds*

$$(a) \Longleftrightarrow (b) \quad and \quad (c) \Longleftrightarrow (d)$$

where

(a) $\forall xy \in B. \ d_A \left(f_* x, f_* y\right) = d_B \left(x, y\right)$

(b) $f^* f_* = \mathrm{id}_B$

(c) $\forall xy \in A. \ d_B \left(f^* x, f^* y\right) = d_A \left(x, y\right)$

(d) $f_* f^* = \mathrm{id}_A$

Definition 3.17. *A map g from a distance space A to a distance space B is an* embedding *if it preserves the distance, i.e. satisfies* $d_A \left(x, y\right) = d_B \left(gx, gy\right)$ *for all* $x, y \in A$. *An adjoint of an embedding is called a* projection.

An adjunction $p^* : A \rightleftarrows B : e_*$ *of a left projection and right adjoint, as in Prop. 3.16(a-b), is called a* reflection. *An adjunction* $e^* : A \rightleftarrows B : p_*$ *of a left embedding and right projection, as in Prop. 3.16(c-d), is called a* coreflection.

Definition 3.18. *A* nucleus *of the adjunction* $f^* : A \rightleftarrows B : f_*$ *consists of a distance space* $\wr f \wr$ *together with*

– *embeddings* $A \overset{e_*}{\hookrightarrow} \mathcal{U}f\mathcal{S} \overset{e^*}{\hookleftarrow} B$
– *projections* $A \overset{p^*}{\twoheadrightarrow} \mathcal{U}f\mathcal{S} \overset{p_*}{\twoheadleftarrow} B$

such that $f^* = e^*p^*$ *and* $f_* = e_*p_*$.

Proposition 3.19. *Any adjunction factors through its nucleus by reflection followed by a coreflection. The nucleus of the adjunction* $f^* : A \rightleftarrows B : f_*$ *is in the form*

$$\mathcal{U}f\mathcal{S} = \{\langle x, y \rangle \in A \times B \mid f^*x = y \wedge x = f_*y\} \tag{15}$$

and the factoring is

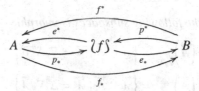

Any right adjoint factors through the nucleus by a right projection followed by a right embedding, and any left adjoint factors through the nucleus by a left projection followed by a left embedding. This factorization is unique up to isomorphism.

Proof. For any adjunction $f^* : A \rightleftarrows B : f_*$, form the distance spaces

$$\mathcal{U}f\mathcal{S}_A = \{x \in A \mid f_*f^*x = x\} \qquad \mathcal{U}f\mathcal{S}_B = \{y \in B \mid f^*f_*y = y\}$$

are easily seen to be isomorphic with the nucleus. The factorisation is thus

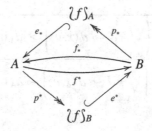

□

3.7 Cones and Cuts

The *cone extensions* are the contractions $\Delta^{\#}$ and $\nabla_{\#}$

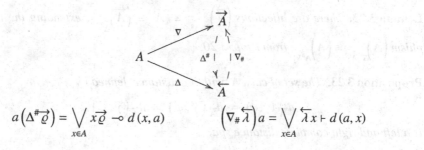

$$a\left(\Delta^{\#}\vec{\varrho}\right) = \bigvee_{x \in A} x\vec{\varrho} \multimap d(x, a) \qquad \left(\nabla_{\#}\overleftarrow{\lambda}\right)a = \bigvee_{x \in A} \overleftarrow{\lambda}x \vdash d(a, x)$$

induced by the universal properties of the Yoneda embeddings ∇ and Δ, as per Prop. 3.9. Since $\Delta^{\#}$ thus preserves suprema, and $\nabla_{\#}$ preserves infima, Prop. 3.12 implies that each of them is an adjoint, and it is not hard to see that they are adjoint to each other, i.e. $\Delta^{\#} : \overrightarrow{A} \rightleftarrows \overleftarrow{A} : \nabla_{\#}$.

Proposition 3.20. *For every* $\overrightarrow{\varrho} \in \overrightarrow{A}$ *every* $\overleftarrow{\lambda} \in \overleftarrow{A}$ *holds*

$$\left(\overrightarrow{\varrho} \rightsquigarrow \nabla_{\#}\Delta^{\#}\overrightarrow{\varrho} \quad and \quad \nabla_{\#}\Delta^{\#}\overrightarrow{\varrho} \rightsquigarrow \overrightarrow{\varrho} \right) \quad \Longleftrightarrow \quad \exists \overleftarrow{\lambda} . \, \overrightarrow{\varrho} = \Delta^{\#}\overleftarrow{\lambda}$$

$$\left(\overleftarrow{\lambda} \rightsquigarrow \Delta^{\#}\nabla_{\#}\overleftarrow{\lambda} \quad and \quad \Delta^{\#}\nabla_{\#}\overleftarrow{\lambda} \rightsquigarrow \overleftarrow{\lambda} \right) \quad \Longleftrightarrow \quad \exists \overrightarrow{\varrho} . \, \overleftarrow{\lambda} = \nabla_{\#}\overrightarrow{\varrho}$$

The transpositions make the following subspaces isomorphic

$$\left(\overrightarrow{A} \right)_{\nabla_{\#}\Delta^{\#}} = \left\{ \overrightarrow{\varrho} \in \overrightarrow{A} \mid \overrightarrow{\varrho} = \nabla_{\#}\Delta^{\#}\overrightarrow{\varrho} \right\}$$

$$\left(\overleftarrow{A} \right)_{\Delta^{\#}\nabla_{\#}} = \left\{ \overleftarrow{\lambda} \in \overleftarrow{A} \mid \overleftarrow{\lambda} = \Delta^{\#}\nabla_{\#}\overleftarrow{\lambda} \right\}$$

Proof. Unfolding the definitions of $\nabla_{\#}$ and $\Delta^{\#}$ gives

$$a\left(\nabla_{\#}\Delta^{\#}\overrightarrow{\varrho} \right) = \bigvee_{u \in A} \left(\bigvee_{x \in A} x\overrightarrow{\varrho} \multimap d(x, u) \right) \multimap d(a, u)$$

which shows that the first claim follows from the fact that for every $u \in A$ holds

$$\frac{\bigvee_{x \in A} x\overrightarrow{\varrho} \multimap d(x, u) \geq a\overrightarrow{\varrho} \multimap d_A(a, u)}{a\overrightarrow{\varrho} + \left(\bigvee_{x \in A} x\overrightarrow{\varrho} \multimap d(x, u) \right) \geq d_A(a, u)}$$

$$a\overrightarrow{\varrho} \geq \left(\bigvee_{x \in A} x\overrightarrow{\varrho} \multimap d(x, u) \right) \multimap d_A(a, u)$$

$\square$

Definition 3.21. *The* cones *in a distance space A are the sequences in* $\left(\overrightarrow{A} \right)_{\nabla_{\#}\Delta^{\#}}$ *and* $\left(\overleftarrow{A} \right)_{\Delta^{\#}\nabla_{\#}}$. *A* cut *in A is a pair of cones $\gamma = \langle \overrightarrow{\gamma}, \overleftarrow{\gamma} \rangle \in \left(\overrightarrow{A} \right)_{\nabla_{\#}\Delta^{\#}} \times \left(\overleftarrow{A} \right)_{\Delta^{\#}\nabla_{\#}}$ such that* $\overrightarrow{\gamma} = \nabla_{\#}\overleftarrow{\gamma}$. *The set of cuts is denoted by* $\overleftrightarrow{A}$.

Lemma 3.22. *There are bijections* $\left(\overrightarrow{A} \right)_{\nabla_{\#}\Delta^{\#}} \cong \overleftrightarrow{A} \cong \left(\overleftarrow{A} \right)_{\Delta^{\#}\nabla_{\#}}$, *extending the isomorphism* $\left(\overrightarrow{A} \right)_{\nabla_{\#}\Delta^{\#}} \cong \left(\overleftarrow{A} \right)_{\Delta^{\#}\nabla_{\#}}$ *from Prop. 3.20.*

Proposition 3.23. *The set of cuts* $\overleftrightarrow{A}$ *with the distance defined by*

$$d_{\overleftrightarrow{A}}(\gamma, \varphi) = d_{\overrightarrow{A}}(\overrightarrow{\gamma}, \overrightarrow{\varphi}) = d_{\overleftarrow{A}}(\overleftarrow{\gamma}, \overleftarrow{\varphi})$$

is a left and right complete distance space.

Notation. We often abuse notation and write

- $\overrightarrow{\varrho}$ for the associated cone $\nabla_{\#}\overrightarrow{\varrho}$, and
- $\overleftarrow{\lambda}$ for the associated cone $\Delta^{\#}\overleftarrow{\lambda}$.

Proof. of Prop. 3.23 The $\overleftrightarrow{A}$-infima are constructed in $\overrightarrow{A}$, the $\overleftrightarrow{A}$-suprema in $\overleftarrow{A}$. To spell this out, consider $\overleftarrow{\lambda} : \overleftrightarrow{A} \to [0, \infty]$ and $\overrightarrow{\varrho} : \overleftrightarrow{A}^{o} \to [0, \infty]$. Extend them along the isomorphisms

$$\left(\overrightarrow{A}\right)_{\nabla_{\#}\Delta^{\#}} \cong \overleftrightarrow{A} \cong \left(\overleftarrow{A}\right)_{\Delta^{\#}\nabla_{\#}} \cong \overleftrightarrow{A}$$

to get $\overleftarrow{\lambda} : \left(\overrightarrow{A}\right)_{\nabla_{\#}\Delta^{\#}} \to [0, \infty]$ and $\overrightarrow{\varrho} : \left(\overleftarrow{A}\right)_{\Delta^{\#}\nabla_{\#}}^{o} \to [0, \infty]$. Then

$$\prod \overleftarrow{\lambda} = \overleftarrow{\lambda} \circ \nabla \in \left(\overrightarrow{A}\right)_{\nabla_{\#}\Delta^{\#}} \qquad \coprod \overrightarrow{\varrho} = \overrightarrow{\varrho} \circ \Delta \in \left(\overleftarrow{A}\right)_{\Delta^{\#}\nabla_{\#}}$$

The claim now boils down to showing that the inclusion $\left(\overrightarrow{A}\right)_{\nabla_{\#}\Delta^{\#}} \hookrightarrow \overrightarrow{A}$ preserves infima, whereas the inclusion $\left(\overleftarrow{A}\right)_{\Delta^{\#}\nabla_{\#}} \hookrightarrow \overleftarrow{A}$ preserves the suprema. But this is immediate from the next Lemma.   □

Lemma 3.24. *The limits of the cut sequences*

$$\overrightarrow{\Upsilon} : \overrightarrow{A}^{o} \to [0, \infty] \qquad\qquad \overleftarrow{\Lambda} : \overrightarrow{A} \to [0, \infty]$$

$$\overrightarrow{K} : \overleftarrow{A}^{o} \to [0, \infty] \qquad\qquad \overleftarrow{\Psi} : \overleftarrow{A} \to [0, \infty]$$

can be computed as follows

$$a\left(\coprod \overrightarrow{\Upsilon}\right) = \bigwedge_{\overrightarrow{\xi} \in A} a\overrightarrow{\xi} + \overrightarrow{\xi}\overrightarrow{\Upsilon} \qquad\qquad \left(\prod \overleftarrow{\Lambda}\right)a = \overleftarrow{\Lambda}(\nabla a)$$

$$a\left(\coprod \overrightarrow{K}\right) = (\Delta a)\overrightarrow{K} \qquad\qquad \left(\prod \overleftarrow{\Psi}\right)a = \bigwedge_{\overleftarrow{\zeta} \in A} \overleftarrow{\Psi}\overleftarrow{\zeta} + \overleftarrow{\zeta}a$$

Corollary 3.25. *A distance space A has all suprema if and only if it has all infima.*

Dedekind-MacNeille Completion Is a Special Case. If A is a poset, viewed as the distance space WA, then $\overleftrightarrow{W}A$ is the Dedekind-MacNeille completion of A. The above construction extends the Dedekind-MacNeille completion of posets [14] to distance spaces, in the sense that it satisfies in the same universal property, spelled out in [1].

4   Distance Matrices

4.1   Definitions

Definition 4.1. *A distance matrix Φ from distance space A to distance space B is a sequence $\Phi : A^{o} \times B \to [0, \infty]$. We denote it by $\Phi : A \nrightarrow B$, and the value of Φ at $x \in A$*

and $y \in B$ is written $x\Phi y$. The matrix composition of $\Phi : A \looparrowright B$ and $\Psi : B \looparrowright C$ is defined

$$x(\Phi\,;\Psi)z = \bigwedge_{y\in B} x\Phi y + y\Psi z$$

With this composition and the identities $\mathrm{Id}_A : A \looparrowright A$ *where* $x(\mathrm{Id}_A)x' = d_A(x, x')$, *distance spaces and distance space matrices form the category* **Matr.**

Remark. Note that the defining condition $d_A(u, x) + d_B(y, v) \geq d(x\Phi y, u\Phi v)$, which says that Φ is a contraction $A^o \times B \to [0, \infty]$, can be equivalently written

$$d_A(u, x) + x\Phi y + d_B(y, v) \geq u\Phi v \tag{16}$$

Definition 4.2. *Transposing the indices yields the* transposed *matrix:*

$$\frac{\Phi \;:\; A \looparrowright B \;:\; x\Phi y}{\Phi^o \;:\; B^o \looparrowright A^o \;:\; y\Phi^o x}$$

The dual $\Phi^{\ddagger} : B \looparrowright A$ *of a matrix* $\Phi : A \looparrowright B$ *has the entries*

$$\frac{\Phi \;:\; A \looparrowright B \;:\; x\Phi y}{\Phi^{\ddagger} \;:\; B \looparrowright A \;:\; y\Phi^{\ddagger}x = \bigvee_{\substack{u\in A \\ v\in B}} u\Phi v \multimap (d_A(u, x) + d_B(y, v))}$$

A matrix $\Phi : A \looparrowright B$ *where* $\Phi^{\ddagger\ddagger} = \Phi$ *is called a* suspension.

Remarks. The transposition is obviously an involutive operation, i.e. $\Phi^{oo} = \Phi$. It is easy to derive from Prop. 3.20 that $d_\Phi(x, y) \geq d_{\Phi^{\ddagger\ddagger}}(x, y)$ holds for all $x \in A$ and $y \in B$, and that $\Phi = \Phi^{\ddagger\ddagger}$ holds if and only if there is some $\Psi : B \looparrowright A$ such that $\Phi = \Psi^{\ddagger}$. Since $\Phi \rightsquigarrow \Psi \Rightarrow \Psi^{\ddagger} \rightsquigarrow \Phi^{\ddagger}$, it follows that $\Phi \rightsquigarrow \Phi^{\ddagger\ddagger}$ implies $\Phi^{\ddagger} = \Phi^{\ddagger\ddagger\ddagger}$.

Proposition 4.3. $\Phi : A \looparrowright B$ *and* $\Phi^{\ddagger} : B \looparrowright A$ *satisfy* $\Phi\,;\Phi^{\ddagger} \rightsquigarrow \mathrm{Id}_A$ *and* $\Phi^{\ddagger}\,;\Phi \rightsquigarrow \mathrm{Id}_B$.

Proof. The condition $\Phi\,;\Phi^{\ddagger} \rightsquigarrow \mathrm{Id}_A$ is proven as follows:

$$\frac{\displaystyle\bigvee_{\substack{u\in A \\ v\in B}} u\Phi v \multimap (d_A(u, x') + d_B(y, v)) \;\geq\; x\Phi y \multimap d_A(x, x')}{\dfrac{x\Phi y + \left(\displaystyle\bigwedge_{\substack{u\in A \\ v\in B}} u\Phi v \multimap (d_A(u, x') + d_B(y, v))\right) \;\geq\; d_A(x, x')}{x\Phi y + y\Phi^{\ddagger}x' \;\geq\; d_A(x, x')}}$$

The second condition is proven analogously.   □

Definition 4.4. *A matrix* $\Phi : A \looparrowright B$ *is* embedding *if* $\Phi ; \Phi^{\ddagger} = \mathrm{Id}_A$; *and a* projection *if* $\Phi^{\ddagger} ; \Phi = \mathrm{Id}_B$.

Definition 4.5. *A* decomposition *of a matrix* $\Phi : A \looparrowright B$ *consists of a distance space D, with*

- *projection matrix* $P : A \looparrowright D$, *i.e.* $d_D (d, d') = \bigwedge_{x \in A} dP^{\ddagger}x + xPd'$,
- *embedding matrix* $E : D \looparrowright B$, *i.e.* $d_D (d, d') = \bigwedge_{y \in B} dEy + yE^{\ddagger}d'$,

such that $\Phi = P ; E$, *i.e.* $x\Phi y = \bigwedge_{d \in D} xPd + dEy$.

Matrices as Adjunctions. A matrix $\Phi : A \looparrowright B$ can be equivalently presented as either of the two contractions $\Phi_{\bullet}$ and $\Phi^{\bullet}$, which extend to Φ_* and Φ^* using Prop. 3.9

$$\frac{A^o \times B \xrightarrow{\Phi} [0, \infty]}{A \xrightarrow{\Phi_{\bullet}} \overleftarrow{B} \qquad B \xrightarrow{\Phi^{\bullet}} \overrightarrow{A}}$$
$$\overrightarrow{A} \xrightarrow{\Phi^*} \overleftarrow{B} \qquad \overleftarrow{B} \xrightarrow{\Phi_*} \overrightarrow{A}$$

$$\left(\Phi^*\overrightarrow{\varrho}\right)b = \bigvee_{x \in A} x\overrightarrow{\varrho} \multimap x\Phi b \qquad \left(\Phi_*\overleftarrow{\lambda}\right)a = \bigvee_{y \in B} \overleftarrow{\lambda}y \multimap a\Phi y \qquad (17)$$

Both extensions, and their nucleus, are summarized in the following diagram

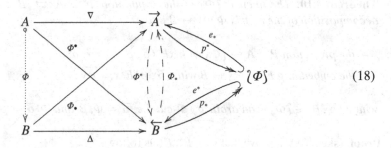

$$(18)$$

The adjunction $\Phi^* : \overrightarrow{A} \rightleftarrows \overleftarrow{B} : \Phi_*$ means that

$$d_{\overleftarrow{B}}\left(\Phi^*\overrightarrow{\varrho}, \overleftarrow{\lambda}\right) = \bigvee_{y \in B} \overleftarrow{\lambda}y \multimap (\Phi^*\overrightarrow{\varrho})y = \bigvee_{x \in A} x\overrightarrow{\varrho} \multimap x(\Phi_*\overleftarrow{\lambda}) = d_{\overrightarrow{A}}\left(\overrightarrow{\varrho}, \Phi_*\overleftarrow{\lambda}\right)$$

holds. The other way around, it can be shown that any adjunction between $\overrightarrow{A}$ and $\overleftarrow{B}$ is completely determined by the induced matrix from A to B.

Proposition 4.6. *The matrices* $\Phi \in \mathrm{Matr}(A, B)$ *are in a bijective correspondence with the adjunctions* $\Phi^* : \overrightarrow{A} \rightleftarrows \overleftarrow{B} : \Phi_*$.

Lemma 4.7. $d_{\overleftarrow{B}}(\Phi^*\nabla x, \Delta y) = x\Phi y = d_{\overrightarrow{A}}(\nabla x, \Phi_*\Delta y)$

4.2 Decomposition through Nucleus

Proposition 4.8. *For every* $\vec{\alpha} \in \vec{A}$ *every* $\overleftarrow{\beta} \in \overleftarrow{B}$ *holds*

$$\vec{\alpha} \rightsquigarrow \Phi_* \Phi^* \vec{\alpha} \qquad and \qquad \Phi_* \Phi^* \vec{\alpha} \rightsquigarrow \vec{\alpha} \iff \exists \overleftarrow{\beta} \in \overleftarrow{B}. \, \vec{\alpha} = \Phi^* \overleftarrow{\beta}$$

$$\overleftarrow{\beta} \rightsquigarrow \Phi^* \Phi_* \overleftarrow{\beta} \qquad and \qquad \Phi^* \Phi_* \overleftarrow{\beta} \rightsquigarrow \overleftarrow{\beta} \iff \exists \vec{\alpha} \in \vec{A}. \, \overleftarrow{\beta} = \Phi_* \vec{\alpha}$$

The adjunction $\Phi^* : A \rightleftarrows B : \Phi_*$ *induces the isomorphisms between the following distance spaces*

$$\langle\Phi\rangle_A = \left\{ \vec{\alpha} \in \vec{A} \mid \vec{\alpha} = \Phi_* \Phi^* \vec{\alpha} \right\}$$

$$\langle\Phi\rangle_B = \left\{ \overleftarrow{\beta} \in \overleftarrow{B} \mid \overleftarrow{\beta} = \Phi^* \Phi_* \overleftarrow{\beta} \right\}$$

$$\langle\Phi\rangle = \left\{ \gamma = \langle \vec{\gamma}, \overleftarrow{\gamma} \rangle \in \vec{A} \times \overleftarrow{B} \mid \vec{\gamma} = \Phi_* \overleftarrow{\gamma} \wedge \Phi^* \vec{\gamma} = \overleftarrow{\gamma} \right\}$$

with the metric

$$d_{\langle\Phi\rangle}(\gamma, \varphi) = d_{\vec{A}}\left(\vec{\gamma}, \vec{\varphi}\right) = d_{\overleftarrow{B}}\left(\overleftarrow{\gamma}, \overleftarrow{\varphi}\right)$$

Definition 4.9. $\langle\Phi\rangle$ *is called the* nucleus *of the matrix* Φ. *Its elements are the* Φ-cuts.

Theorem 4.10. *The nucleus* $\langle\Phi\rangle$ *of the adjunction* $\Phi^* : \vec{A} \rightleftarrows \overleftarrow{B} : \Phi_*$ *induces the decomposition of the matrix* $\Phi : A \leftrightarrow B$ *into*

- *the projection* $P^* : A \leftrightarrow \langle\Phi\rangle$ *with* $xP^*\langle\vec{\alpha}, \overleftarrow{\beta}\rangle = x\vec{\alpha}$, *and*
- *the embedding* $E^* : \langle\Phi\rangle \leftrightarrow B$ *with* $\langle\vec{\alpha}, \overleftarrow{\beta}\rangle E^* y = \overleftarrow{\beta} y$

where $\langle\vec{\alpha}, \overleftarrow{\beta}\rangle \in \langle\Phi\rangle$ *is an arbitrary* Φ-cut, *i.e.* $\vec{\alpha} = \Phi_* \overleftarrow{\beta}$ *and* $\Phi^* \vec{\alpha} = \overleftarrow{\beta}$.

Proof. (sketch) We prove that $\Phi = P^*; E^*$ as follows:

$$x(P^*; E^*)y = \bigwedge_{\vec{\alpha}} xP^*\langle\vec{\alpha}, \Phi^*\vec{\alpha}\rangle + \langle\vec{\alpha}, \Phi^*\vec{\alpha}\rangle Ey$$

$$= \bigwedge_{\vec{\alpha}} x\vec{\alpha} + \left(\Phi^*\vec{\alpha}\right)y$$

$$\leq x\nabla x + (\Phi^*\nabla x)\, y$$

$$= d_A(x, x) + d_{\overleftarrow{B}}(\Phi^*\nabla x, \Delta y)$$

$$= x\Phi y$$

using Lemma 4.7 at the last step. The facts that P^* is a projection and E^* is an embedding matrix are proved using the following lemma, which says that $\langle\Phi\rangle$ is $\coprod$-generated by A and $\prod$-generated by B. □

Lemma 4.11. *The $\wr\Phi\wr$-infima are computed in $\overrightarrow{A}$, whereas its suprema are computed in $\overleftarrow{B}$. To state this precisely, consider $\overleftarrow{\lambda} : \wr\Phi\wr \to [0,\infty]$ and $\overrightarrow{\varrho} : \wr\Phi\wr^o \to [0,\infty]$. Extend them along the isomorphisms $\wr\Phi\wr_A \cong \wr\Phi\wr \cong \wr\Phi\wr_B$ to get $\overleftarrow{\lambda} : \wr\Phi\wr_A \to [0,\infty]$ and $\overrightarrow{\varrho} : \wr\Phi\wr_B^o \to [0,\infty]$. Then*

$$\prod \overleftarrow{\lambda} = \overleftarrow{\lambda} \circ \nabla \in \wr\Phi\wr_A \qquad\qquad \bigsqcup \overrightarrow{\varrho} = \overrightarrow{\varrho} \circ \Delta \in \wr\Phi\wr_B$$

are constructed in $\overrightarrow{A}$ and $\overleftarrow{B}$, because $\wr\Phi\wr_A \hookrightarrow \overrightarrow{A}$ preserves the infima, whereas $\wr\Phi\wr_B \hookrightarrow \overleftarrow{B}$ preserves the suprema.

Corollary 4.12. *The monotone maps $A \xrightarrow{\nabla} \overrightarrow{A} \xrightarrow{p^*} \wr\Phi\wr \xleftarrow{p_*} \overleftarrow{B} \xleftarrow{\Delta} B$*

- *preserve any infima that exist in A, and any suprema that exist in B,*
- *generate $\wr\Phi\wr$ by the suprema from A and by the infima from B, in the sense that for any $\langle \overrightarrow{\alpha}, \overleftarrow{\beta} \rangle \in \wr\Phi\wr$ holds*

$$\bigsqcup_{\overrightarrow{\alpha}} \nabla = \langle \overrightarrow{\alpha}, \overleftarrow{\beta} \rangle = \prod_{\overleftarrow{\beta}} \Delta$$

5   Bicompletion

Any distance space morphism $f : A \to B$ induces two matrices, $\Omega f : A \leftrightarrow B$ and $\mho f : B \leftrightarrow A$ with

$$x\Omega f y = d_B(fx, y) \qquad\qquad y\mho f x = d_B(y, fx)$$

Lemma 5.1. *For every matrix $\Omega f : A \leftrightarrow B$ induced by a distance space morphism $f : A \to B$ holds $\Omega f^\ddagger = \mho f$.*

Proof. Since $y\mho f x = d_B(y, fx)$ by definition, the claim boils down to $y(\Omega f)^o x = d_B(y, fx)$, which can be proved as follows

$$y(\Omega f)^o x = \bigvee_{\substack{u \in A \\ v \in B}} d_B(fu, v) \multimapdotinv (d_B(y, v) + d_A(u, x))$$

$$\geq d_B(fx, fx) \multimapdotinv (d_B(y, fx) + d_A(x, x)) = d_B(y, fx)$$

$\square$

5.1   Nucleus as a Completion

Lemma 5.2. *If the distance space B is complete, then for any matrix $\Phi : A \leftrightarrow B$ there is a distance space morphism $f : A \to B$ such that $\Phi = \Omega f$.*

Corollary 5.3. *If both A and B are complete, then any matrix $\Phi : A \leftrightarrow B$ corresponds to an adjunction $\Phi^* : A \rightleftarrows B : \Phi_*$ such that $\Phi = \Omega\Phi^* = \mho\Phi_*$.*

Definition 5.4. *A distance matrix homomorphism* $h : \Phi \to \Gamma$ *where* $\Phi : A \looparrowright B$ *and* $\Gamma : C \looparrowright D$, *is a pair of contractions* $h = \langle h_0 : A \to C, h_1 : B \to D \rangle$ *such that*

- $\Omega h_0 ; \Gamma = \Phi ; \Omega h_1$,
- h_0 *preserves any suprema that may exist in A,*
- h_1 *preserves any infima that may exist in B.*

Let MMat *denote the category of distance space matrices and matrix morphisms.*

Definition 5.5. *A matrix* $\Phi : A \looparrowright B$ *is* complete *if A has suprema and B infima[1], and* $\Phi : A^o \times B \to [0, \infty]$ *preserves the infima. Let* CMat *denote the category of complete matrices and matrix homomorphisms.*

Proposition 5.6. $\mathrm{Id}_{\wr\Phi\wr} : \wr\Phi\wr \looparrowright \wr\Phi\wr$ *is the completion of* $\Phi : A \looparrowright B$. *In other words, the functor* $\wr{-}\wr : $ MMat $\to$ CMat *is left adjoint to the full inclusion* CMat $\hookrightarrow$ MMat. *The unit of the adjunction* $\eta = \langle \eta_0, \eta_1 \rangle : \Phi \to \wr\Phi\wr$ *consists of*

$$\eta_0 : A \xrightarrow{\nabla} \overrightarrow{A} \xrightarrow{p^*} \wr\Phi\wr \quad and \quad \eta_1 : B \xrightarrow{\Delta} \overleftarrow{B} \xrightarrow{p_*} \wr\Phi\wr$$

6 Summary and Discussion

Given an arbitrary distance matrix $\Phi : A \looparrowright B$, we have constructed the completion $\Phi \xrightarrow{\eta} \wr\Phi\wr$ such that

- $A \xrightarrow{\eta_0} \wr\Phi\wr$ is $\bigsqcup$-generating and $\prod$-preserving,
- $B \xrightarrow{\eta_1} \wr\Phi\wr$ is $\prod$-generating and $\bigsqcup$-preserving.

In terms of the motivating example of program transformations, and of the task of conjoining the algorithmic knowledge about systems and about attacks, every Φ-cut is thus a supremum of the system specifications in A, and an infimum of the attack specifications in B. Moreover, the suprema of Φ-cuts can be computed in $\overleftarrow{B}$, whereas the infima can be computed in $\overrightarrow{A}$. While the suprema[2] capture composite systems validating some composite properties, the infima describe composite attacks where the *in*validated properties add up.

But what has been achieved by providing this very abstract account? It turns out that the actual completions provide fairly concrete information. There is no space to illustrate this, but we sketch a high level view. The prior knowledge, represented by the distance spaces A and B is updated by the empiric data, represented by the matrix $\Phi : A \looparrowright B$. In the completion $\wr\Phi\wr$, the empiric relations of as and bs are expressed as distances. Following [21,13, Ch. 4], the task of *explaining* these empiric links can then be viewed as the task of finding short programs p with $p(a) = b$. After such completions, some distances previously recorded in A and B may increase, since some programs may be closer related *a posteriori* than *a priori*.

---

[1] By Corollary 3.25, both A and B are thus complete.

[2] not unlike colimits of software specifications [20,19].

The obvious task for future work is to refine the concrete applications of the presented construction. This is to some extent covered in the full paper, which is in preparation. The further work on quantifying the hardness of program derivations, and of program transformations, branches in many directions. Distances arise naturally in this framework, as described already in [16, Sec. 4.2]. In a different direction, it seems interesting to study the bicompletions in other categorical frameworks, in particular where the dualities fail in a significant way, as demonstrated a long time ago [6].

References

1. Banaschewski, B., Bruns, G.: Categorical characterization of the MacNeille completion. Archiv der Mathematik 18(4), 369–377 (1967)
2. Barak, B., Goldreich, O., Impagliazzo, R., Rudich, S., Sahai, A., Vadhan, S.P., Yang, K.: On the (Im)possibility of obfuscating programs. In: Kilian, J. (ed.) CRYPTO 2001. LNCS, vol. 2139, pp. 1–18. Springer, Heidelberg (2001)
3. Bonsangue, M.M., van Breugel, F., Rutten, J.J.M.M.: Generalized metric spaces: completion, topology, and power domains via the yoneda embedding. Theor. Comput. Sci. 193(1-2), 1–51 (1998)
4. Downey, R., Hirschfeldt, D.: Algorithmic Randomness and Complexity. Springer-Verlag New York, Inc., Secaucus (2010)
5. Goldwasser, S., Kalai, Y.T.: On the impossibility of obfuscation with auxiliary input. In: Proceedings of the 46th Annual IEEE Symposium on Foundations of Computer Science, FOCS 2005, pp. 553–562. IEEE Computer Society, Washington, DC (2005)
6. Isbell, J.R.: Subobjects, adequacy, completeness and categories of algebras. Rozprawy matematyczne. Państwowe Wydawnictwo Naukowe (1964)
7. Kelly, G.M.: Basic Concepts of Enriched Category Theory. London Mathematical Society Lecture Note Series, vol. 64. Cambridge University Press (1982); Reprinted in Theory and Applications of Categories, vol. 10, pp. 1–136 (2005)
8. Kelly, J.C.: Bitopological spaces. Proc. London Math. Soc. 13, 71–89 (1963)
9. Künzi, H.P., Schellekens, M.P.: On the yoneda completion of a quasi-metric space. Theor. Comput. Sci. 278(1-2), 159–194 (2002)
10. William Lawvere, F.: Metric spaces, generalised logic, and closed categories. Rendiconti del Seminario Matematico e Fisico di Milano 43, 135–166 (1973)
11. Leinster, T.: The magnitude of metric spaces (2010), arxiv.org:1012.5857
12. Leinster, T., Cobbold, C.: Measuring diversity: the importance of species similarity. Ecology (2012) (to appear)
13. Li, M., Vitányi, P.: An introduction to Kolmogorov complexity and its applications, 2nd edn. Graduate texts in computer science. Springer (1997)
14. MacNeille, H.M.: Extensions of partially ordered sets. Proc. Nat. Acad. Sci. 22(1), 45–50 (1936)
15. Lane, S.M.: Categories for the Working Mathematician. Graduate Texts in Mathematics, vol. 5. Springer (1971) (second edition 1997)
16. Pavlovic, D.: Gaming security by obscurity. In: Gates, C., Hearley, C. (eds.) Proceedings of NSPW 2011, pp. 125–140. ACM, New York (2011), arxiv:1109.5542
17. Pavlovic, D.: Quantifying and qualifying trust: Spectral decomposition of trust networks. In: Degano, P., Etalle, S., Guttman, J. (eds.) FAST 2010. LNCS, vol. 6561, pp. 1–17. Springer, Heidelberg (2011)
18. Pavlovic, D.: Quantitative Concept Analysis. In: Domenach, F., Ignatov, D.I., Poelmans, J. (eds.) ICFCA 2012. LNCS, vol. 7278, pp. 260–277. Springer, Heidelberg (2012)

19. Pavlovic, D., Smith, D.R.: Software development by refinement. In: Aichernig, B.K., Maibaum, T. (eds.) Formal Methods at the Crossroads. From Panacea to Foundational Support. LNCS, vol. 2757, pp. 267–286. Springer, Heidelberg (2003)
20. Smith, D.R.: Composition by colimit and formal software development. In: Futatsugi, K., Jouannaud, J.-P., Meseguer, J. (eds.) Algebra, Meaning, and Computation. LNCS, vol. 4060, pp. 317–332. Springer, Heidelberg (2006)
21. Solomonoff, R.J.: A formal theory of inductive inference. Part I., Part II. Information and Control 7, 1–22, 224–254 (1964)
22. Wagner, K.R.: Liminf convergence in omega-categories. Theor. Comput. Sci. 184(1-2), 61–104 (1997)
23. Wilson, W.A.: On quasi-metric spaces. Amer. J. Math. 52(3), 675–684 (1931)
24. Kim, Y.W.: Pseudo quasi metric spaces. Proc. Japan Acad. 10, 1009–10012 (1968)
25. Zvonkin, A.K., Levin, L.A.: The complexity of finite objects and the algorithmic concepts of information and randomness. Russian Math. Surveys 25(6), 83–124 (1970)

Partial Recursive Functions and Finality

Gordon Plotkin

LFCS, School of Informatics, University of Edinburgh

Abstract. We seek universal categorical conditions ensuring the representability of all partial recursive functions. In the category **Pfn** of sets and partial functions, the natural numbers provide both an initial algebra and a final coalgebra for the functor $1 + -$. We recount how finality yields closure of the partial functions on natural numbers under Kleene's μ-recursion scheme. Noting that **Pfn** is not cartesian, we then build on work of Paré and Román, obtaining weak initiality and finality conditions on natural numbers algebras in monoidal categories that ensure the (weak) representability of all partial recursive functions. We further obtain some positive results on strong representability. All these results adapt to Kleisli categories of cartesian categories with natural numbers algebras. However, in general, not all partial recursive functions need be strongly representable.

1 Introduction

It is a great pleasure to write in celebration of Samson Abramsky's 60th birthday. The interaction between category theory and computer science has long been central in Samson's work. Here we touch lightly on several themes of this kind which have been of interest to him: coalgebras, computability, definability, domain equations, linearity, and—even—natural numbers objects [11].

Our interest is in finding universal categorical conditions that ensure the representability of all partial recursive functions. The case of the primitive recursive functions is well understood. In general terms, the existence of a "natural numbers" algebra

$$1 \longrightarrow N \longleftarrow N$$

with sufficient initiality properties ensures the representability of all primitive recursive functions. More precisely, all primitive recursive functions are representable in any cartesian closed category with a weak natural numbers object, i.e., a weakly initial natural numbers algebra [7], and, more generally, in any cartesian category with a so-called weak stable natural numbers object [7,2,10].

Natural numbers algebras can equivalently be written in the form

$$1 + N \longrightarrow N$$

and it is then natural to consider the dual notion of natural numbers coalgebras

$$N \longrightarrow 1 + N$$

B. Coecke, L. Ong, and P. Panangaden (Eds.): Abramsky Festschrift, LNCS 7860, pp. 311–326, 2013.
© Springer-Verlag Berlin Heidelberg 2013

and ask for final ones. As is known, for example from domain theory [5, Example IV-7.15], the natural numbers form a final such coalgebra in the category **Pfn** of sets and partial functions. We verify this directly in Section 2. We further recount there how finality leads to Kleene's μ-recursion scheme.

One may therefore hope that all partial recursive functions are representable in any category possessing a natural numbers algebra with sufficiently strong initiality and finality properties. Such conditions should apply to **Pfn**, and, more broadly, to categories considered in general frameworks for partial functions, such as those of [3] or [4].

Unfortunately, **Pfn** is not cartesian. Rather, cartesian product equips **Pfn** with a symmetric monoidal structure. So the above work on representability in cartesian categories does not immediately apply. Instead, in Section 3, we turn to the work of Paré and Román [12]. They gave a notion of stable left (or right) natural numbers objects in monoidal categories that ensures the representability of all primitive recursive functions. Their proof uses the uniqueness clause of initiality. However we prefer to use only existence, as that is the common assumption used to ensure representability. This can be done using structural functions (such as symmetry) and, following Paré and Román, suitable versions of these can be defined over weak stable natural numbers objects. In [1] Alves et al considered the symmetric monoidal case using similar methods, but working in an informal type-theoretic setting rather than a categorical one.

Putting all this together in Section 4, we finally obtain universality properties that ensure the representability of all partial recursive functions (Theorem 1) and that can be applied to categories of partial functions. The notion of representability that we use is somewhat weak and there is a natural stronger one. We show that all total recursive functions, and, more generally, all partial recursive functions with recursive graphs, are strongly representable, under weak additional assumptions (Theorem 2). If we also assume that all definable partial functions are partial recursive, then all partial recursive functions are strongly representable (Corollary 1). However this fails in general, and we provide a syntactic category which has a stable natural numbers object which is also final but in which no partial recursive function with a non-recursive graph is strongly representable (Theorem 3).

For categorical terminology used below, the reader may refer, for example, to [2].

2   The Category of Sets and Partial Functions

We begin by reviewing some general ideas. Suppose we are in a category with a terminal object and binary sums. Then, as remarked in the introduction, natural numbers algebras $1 \xrightarrow{\text{zero}} N \xleftarrow{\text{succ}} N$ are in 1-1 correspondence with F-algebras $(N, \alpha : F(N) \to N)$ where F is the endofunctor $F(A) =_{\text{def}} 1 + A$. This correspondence sends (zero, succ) to

$$\alpha \;=_{\text{def}}\; 1 + N \xrightarrow{[\text{zero,succ}]} N$$

(Weak) natural numbers objects correspond in this way to (weakly) initial F-algebras.

One can also discuss F-*coalgebras* of given endofunctors F. These are structures of the form $(A, \alpha : A \to F(A))$. In the case where $F = 1 + -$, we call such coalgebras *natural numbers coalgebras*. A *homomorphism* of F-coalgebras $h : (A, \alpha) \to (B, \beta)$ is a morphism $h : A \to B$ such that the following diagram commutes:

$$
\begin{array}{ccc}
A & \xrightarrow{\ \alpha\ } & F(A) \\
{\scriptstyle h}\downarrow & & \downarrow{\scriptstyle F(h)} \\
B & \xrightarrow[\ \beta\ ]{} & F(B)
\end{array}
$$

and one is interested in (weakly) final coalgebras.

A natural place to begin to explore these ideas is the category **Pfn** of sets and partial functions, since partial recursive functions are morphisms there. We know that the natural numbers form an initial algebra $\alpha : F(\mathbb{N}) \cong \mathbb{N}$ in **Set** (the category of sets and total functions) where, as above, $F(X) = \mathbb{1} + X$ and $\alpha(\mathrm{inl}(*)) = 0$ and $\alpha(\mathrm{inr}(n)) = n+1$. As α is an isomorphism (as is, by Lambek's Lemma, the algebra map of the initial algebra of any endofunctor), we obtain a natural numbers coalgebra $\alpha^{-1} : \mathbb{N} \to F(\mathbb{N})$ in **Set**. Concretely one has:

$$
\alpha^{-1}(k) \;=\; \begin{cases} \mathrm{inl}(*) & (k = 0) \\ \mathrm{inr}(k') & (k = k' + 1) \end{cases}
$$

This natural numbers coalgebra is not final in **Set**. However sums in **Set** are also sums in **Pfn**, and so F extends to **Pfn**. As we now check, the coalgebra is final there.

We have to show that for any $\beta : Y \rightharpoonup \mathbb{1} + Y$ there is a unique map $h : Y \rightharpoonup \mathbb{N}$ such that the following diagram commutes in **Pfn**:

$$
\begin{array}{ccc}
Y & \xrightarrow{\ \beta\ } & \mathbb{1} + Y \\
{\scriptstyle h}\downarrow & & \downarrow{\scriptstyle \mathbb{1} + h} \\
\mathbb{N} & \xrightarrow[\ \alpha^{-1}\ ]{} & \mathbb{1} + \mathbb{N}
\end{array}
$$

As α is an isomorphism this is equivalent to asking that the following diagram commutes:

$$
\begin{array}{ccc}
Y & \xrightarrow{\ \beta\ } & \mathbb{1}+Y \\
\Big\downarrow{\scriptstyle h} & & \Big\downarrow{\scriptstyle \mathbb{1}+h} \\
\mathbb{N} & \xleftarrow[\ \alpha\ ]{} & \mathbb{1}+\mathbb{N}
\end{array}
$$

Using Kleene equality we can write this out as an equation:

$$
h(y) \ \simeq\ \begin{cases} 0 & (\beta(y) \simeq \mathrm{inl}(*)) \\ h(y')+1 & (\beta(y) \simeq \mathrm{inr}(y')) \\ \text{undefined} & (\beta(y)\!\uparrow) \end{cases} \tag{1}
$$

where, as usual, we write $e\uparrow$ to assert that an expression e is undefined (and write $e\downarrow$ to assert it is defined).

One can show there is a unique such h. For uniqueness, for any h, h' satisfying the equation one proves by induction on k that, for all y, $h(y) \simeq k$ if, and only if, $h'(y) \simeq k$. For existence, one can set:

$$
h(y) \ \simeq_{\text{def}}\ \mu k \in \mathbb{N}.\ s^k(\beta(y)) \simeq \mathrm{inl}(*)
$$

where $s =_{\text{def}} \beta \circ \mathrm{inr}^{-1}$, and check h satisfies (1). Here, as usual, $\mu k \in \mathbb{N}.\ \varphi(k)$ is the smallest $k \in \mathbb{N}$ such that $\varphi(k)$ holds, if there is one, and is undefined otherwise.

Given this connection with minimisation it may not now be surprising that we can obtain Kleene's μ-recursion scheme from finality. Suppose we have $P: \mathbb{N}^{n+1} \rightharpoonup \mathbb{N}$. Then we apply finality to the coalgebra

$$
\beta : \mathbb{N}^{n+1} \longrightarrow \mathbb{1}+\mathbb{N}^{n+1}
$$

where

$$
\beta(\mathbf{x}, k) \ \simeq\ \begin{cases} \mathrm{inl}(*) & (P(\mathbf{x},k) \simeq 0) \\ \mathrm{inr}(\mathbf{x}, k+1) & (P(\mathbf{x},k)\!\downarrow\ \text{and}\ \not\simeq 0) \\ \text{undefined} & (P(\mathbf{x},k)\!\uparrow) \end{cases}
$$

Substituting into (1), we find that the unique $h : \mathbb{N}^{n+1} \rightharpoonup \mathbb{N}$ whose existence is guaranteed by finality satisfies the following equation:

$$
h(\mathbf{x}, k) \ \simeq\ \begin{cases} 0 & (P(\mathbf{x},k) \simeq 0) \\ h(\mathbf{x}, k+1)+1 & (P(\mathbf{x},k)\!\downarrow\ \text{and}\ \not\simeq 0) \\ \text{undefined} & (P(\mathbf{x},k)\!\uparrow) \end{cases} \tag{2}
$$

We then see that h can be defined by the minimisation

$$h(\mathbf{x}, k) \quad \simeq \quad \mu k'. P(\mathbf{x}, k + k') \simeq 0 \wedge \forall k'' < k'. P(\mathbf{x}, k + k'') \!\downarrow$$

as, with this definition, one checks that h satisfies (2). Specialising, we obtain:

$$h(\mathbf{x}, 0) \quad \simeq \quad \mu k \in \mathbb{N}. P(\mathbf{x}, k) \simeq 0 \wedge \forall k' < k. P(\mathbf{x}, k') \!\downarrow$$

and so $h(-, 0) : \mathbb{N}^n \rightharpoonup \mathbb{N}$ is the partial function obtained by μ-recursion from P, thereby establishing the advertised connection between finality and Kleene's μ-recursion scheme.

3 Primitive Recursive Functions in Monoidal Categories

We assume given a monoidal category $\mathbf{C}$ with the standard structural maps:

$$\mathsf{a}_{A,B,C} : A \otimes (B \otimes C) \cong (A \otimes B) \otimes C \qquad \mathsf{l}_A : \mathrm{I} \otimes A \cong A \qquad \mathsf{r}_A : A \otimes \mathrm{I} \cong A$$

satisfying the usual equations. We need some notation. For any object A define A^n by setting $A^0 = \mathrm{I}$ and $A^{n+1} = A^n \otimes A$. For $n \geq 0$ and $c_i : \mathrm{I} \to A$ $(i = 1, \ldots, n)$, define $\langle c_1, \ldots, c_n \rangle : \mathrm{I} \to A^n$ by: $\langle \rangle = \mathrm{id}_\mathrm{I}$ and $\langle c_1, \ldots, c_n, c_{n+1} \rangle = (\langle c_1, \ldots, c_n \rangle \otimes c_{n+1}) \circ \mathsf{l}_\mathrm{I}^{-1}$.

We next assume given a *natural numbers algebra* in C, by which we now mean a structure

$$\mathrm{I} \xrightarrow{\ \text{zero}\ } \mathrm{N} \xleftarrow{\ \text{succ}\ } \mathrm{N}$$

We define $\underline{k} : \mathrm{I} \to \mathrm{N}$ for $k \in \mathbb{N}$ to be $\text{succ}^k \circ \text{zero}$, and for any $\mathbf{k} = k_1, \ldots, k_n$ we write $\underline{\mathbf{k}}$ for $\langle \underline{k_1}, \ldots, \underline{k_n} \rangle : \mathrm{I} \to \mathrm{N}^n$. We then say that a morphism $f : \mathrm{N}^n \to \mathrm{N}$ *represents* a (total) function $f : \mathbb{N}^n \to \mathbb{N}$ if, for all $k_1, \ldots, k_n \in \mathbb{N}$, we have:

$$\underline{f} \circ \langle \underline{k_1}, \ldots, \underline{k_n} \rangle = \underline{f(k_1, \ldots, k_n)}$$

For example, zero represents the constant 0 and succ represents the successor function.

The natural numbers algebra $\mathrm{I} \xrightarrow{\ \text{zero}\ } \mathrm{N} \xleftarrow{\ \text{succ}\ } \mathrm{N}$ is a *right stable natural numbers object* if, for any structure of the form

$$P \xrightarrow{\ f\ } B \xleftarrow{\ g\ } B$$

there is a unique morphism $h : P \otimes \mathrm{N} \to B$ such that the following diagram commutes:

(and left stable natural numbers objects are defined symmetrically). As usual, one drops uniqueness for the weak notion. A (weak) right (or left) stable natural numbers object is a (weak) natural numbers object, in the evident sense.

From now on we assume our natural numbers algebra is a weak right stable natural numbers object.

Taking $P = N^n$ in the definition of weak right stable natural numbers object we find that the morphism h whose existence is asserted satisfies the following two equations:

$$\begin{aligned} h \circ \langle \underline{k_1}, \ldots, \underline{k_n}, \underline{0} \rangle &= f \circ \langle \underline{k_1}, \ldots, \underline{k_n} \rangle \\ h \circ \langle \underline{k_1}, \ldots, \underline{k_n}, \underline{k+1} \rangle &= g \circ h \circ \langle \underline{k_1}, \ldots, \underline{k_n}, \underline{k} \rangle \end{aligned}$$

So, in particular, taking $B = N$ we find that the representable total functions on natural numbers are closed under the scheme of *pure iteration with n parameters*. This, given $f : N^n \to N$ and $g : N \to N$, yields $h : N^{n+1} \to N$ such that:

$$\begin{aligned} h(k_1, \ldots, k_n, 0) &= f(k_1, \ldots, k_n) \\ h(k_1, \ldots, k_n, k+1) &= g(h(k_1, \ldots, k_n, k)) \end{aligned}$$

As we now show, weak stability can be used to obtain representations of structural maps involving N, viz. terminal maps, projections, symmetries, and diagonals. First, considering $I \xrightarrow{\mathrm{id}_I} I \xleftarrow{\mathrm{id}_I} I$ and applying weak initiality we obtain a morphism $t_N : N \to I$ such that:

$$\begin{aligned} t_N \circ \underline{0} &= \langle \rangle \\ t_N \circ \underline{k+1} &= t_N \circ \underline{k} \end{aligned}$$

By induction on k, we then have $t_N \circ \underline{k} = \langle \rangle$. Using t_N, we obtain a morphism $t_{N^n} : N^n \to I$ such that $t_{N^n} \circ \underline{\mathbf{k}} = \langle \rangle$. Then, using t_N and the t_{N^n}, we see that the projections $\pi_i^n : N^n \to N$ $(i = 1, n)$ are representable. We also define $\pi_1 : A \otimes N \to A$ to be $r_A \circ (A \otimes t_N)$, and define $\pi_2 : N \otimes A \to A$ similarly; for any $k \in \mathbb{N}$ and $c : I \to A$ we have $\pi_1 \circ \langle c, \underline{k} \rangle = \pi_2 \circ \langle \underline{k}, c \rangle = c$.

Regarding symmetry, considering $N \xrightarrow{(\text{zero} \otimes N) \circ l_N^{-1}} N \otimes N \xleftarrow{\text{succ} \otimes N} N \otimes N$ and applying weak stability, we obtain a morphism $\sigma_{N,N} : N \otimes N \to N \otimes N$ such that:

$$\begin{aligned} \sigma_N \circ (\underline{k_1} \otimes \underline{0}) &= \underline{0} \otimes \underline{k_1} \\ \sigma_N \circ (\underline{k_1} \otimes \underline{k+1}) &= (\text{succ} \otimes N) \circ \sigma_N \circ (\underline{k_1} \otimes \underline{k}) \end{aligned}$$

and, by induction on k, we have $\sigma_{N,N} \circ (\underline{k_1} \otimes \underline{k}) = (\underline{k} \otimes \underline{k_1})$. Using $\sigma_{N,N}$, we then obtain morphisms $\sigma_{N^m, N^n} : N^m \otimes N^n \to N^n \otimes N^m$ such that $\sigma_{N^m, N^n} \circ (\underline{\mathbf{k}} \otimes \underline{\mathbf{k}'}) = (\underline{\mathbf{k}'} \otimes \underline{\mathbf{k}})$.

Regarding diagonal maps, considering $I \xrightarrow{(\underline{0} \otimes \underline{0}) \circ l_I^{-1}} N \otimes N \xleftarrow{\text{succ} \otimes \text{succ}} N \otimes N$ and applying weak initiality, we obtain a morphism $\Delta_N : N \to N \otimes N$ such that:

$$\begin{aligned} \Delta_N \circ \underline{0} &= (\underline{0} \otimes \underline{0}) \circ l_I^{-1} \\ \Delta_N \circ \underline{k+1} &= (\text{succ} \otimes \text{succ}) \circ \Delta_N \circ \underline{k} \end{aligned}$$

and then, by induction on k, we have $\Delta_N \circ \underline{k} = (\underline{k} \otimes \underline{k}) \circ l_I^{-1}$. Using t_N and Δ_N we then obtain diagonal morphisms $\Delta_m : N \to N^m$ $(m \geq 0)$, and, in turn using the Δ_m and σ, we further obtain diagonal morphisms $\Delta_{n,m} : N^n \to (N^n)^m$ $(m, n \geq 0)$ such that $\Delta_{n,m} \circ \mathbf{k} = \langle \mathbf{k}, \ldots, \mathbf{k} \rangle$

Finally, using the $\Delta_{n,m}$ and categorical composition, we see that the representable functions are closed under composition, i.e., that if $f : N^m \to N$ is representable, and so are $g_i : N^n \to N$, for $i = 1, \ldots, m$, then $h : N^n \to N$ is representable, where, for $k_1, \ldots, k_n \in N$:

$$h(k_1, \ldots, k_n) =_{\text{def}} f(g_1(k_1, \ldots, k_n), \ldots, g_m(k_1, \ldots, k_n))$$

For suppose that $f : N^m \to N$ is represented by the morphism $\underline{f} : N^m \to N$ and that, for $i = 1, \ldots, m$, $g_i : N^n \to N$ is represented by the morphism $\underline{g_i} : N^n \to N$. Then their composition $h : N^n \to N$ is represented by the morphism $\underline{h} : N^n \to N$, where

$$\underline{h} =_{\text{def}} N^n \xrightarrow{\Delta_{n,m}} (N^n)^m \xrightarrow{(\ldots (I \otimes \underline{g_1}) \otimes \ldots \otimes \underline{g_m})} N^m \xrightarrow{\underline{f}} N$$

By a result of Gladstone [6], all primitive recursive functions can be obtained starting from the base functions (zero, successor, and the projections) and closing under composition and pure iteration (even allowing only one parameter). We therefore have:

Proposition 1. *All primitive recursive functions are representable in any monoidal category with a weak stable right (or left) natural numbers object.*

(The case of a weak stable left natural numbers object follows by symmetry from that of a right one.)

4   Partial Recursive Functions in Monoidal Categories

We assume given a monoidal category C, as in the previous section, which also has binary sums. It would be natural to make a distributivity assumption. For example we might assume that the tensor right-distributes over binary sums, i.e., that the canonical map $B \otimes A + C \otimes A \to (B + C) \otimes A$ is an isomorphism. However, as with other structural maps, this proves unnecessary in the presence of weak stability.

Turning to natural numbers objects, we further assume given a natural numbers algebra

$$I \xrightarrow{\text{zero}} N \xleftarrow{\text{succ}} N$$

which is a weak right stable natural numbers object such that the map

$$I + N \xrightarrow{\alpha} N$$

is an isomorphism, where $\alpha =_{\text{def}} [\text{zero}, \text{succ}]$, and is such that the coalgebra

$$N \xrightarrow{\alpha^{-1}} I + N$$

is weakly final.

The $\underline{k}$ are defined as above, but we need a wider notion of representability. Say that a morphism $g : N^n \to N$ *represents* a partial function $f : N^n \rightharpoonup N$ if, for all $k_1, \ldots, k_n \in N$, if $f(k_1, \ldots, k_n) \simeq k$ then $g \circ \langle \underline{k_1}, \ldots, \underline{k_n} \rangle = \underline{k}$.

We know that all primitive recursive functions are representable, and one sees, much as in the total case, that the representable functions are closed under composition. So it remains to show that the representable functions are closed under Kleene's μ-recursion scheme.

We first need a weak version of right distributivity. Applying weak stability to the structure

$$A + B \xrightarrow{(A \otimes \text{zero}) \text{or}_A^{-1} + (B \otimes \text{zero}) \text{or}_B^{-1}} (A \otimes N) + (B \otimes N) \xrightarrow{(A \otimes \text{succ}) + (B \otimes \text{succ})} (A \otimes N) + (B \otimes N)$$

we obtain a map

$$(A + B) \otimes N \xrightarrow{d_{A,B,N}} (A \otimes N) + (B \otimes N)$$

and, as can be shown by induction on k, for any k and any $a : I \to A$ and $b : I \to B$, we have

$$d_{A,B,N} \circ ((\text{inl} \circ a) \otimes \underline{k}) = \text{inl} \circ (a \otimes \underline{k}) \quad \text{and} \quad d_{A,B,N} \circ ((\text{inr} \circ b) \otimes \underline{k}) = \text{inr} \circ (b \otimes \underline{k})$$

Iterating, for any n we obtain a map:

$$(A + B) \otimes N^n \xrightarrow{d_{A,B,N^n}} (A \otimes N^n) + (B \otimes N^n)$$

such that for any $k_1, \ldots, k_n$ and any $a : I \to A$ and $b : I \to B$, we have

$$d_{A,B,N} \circ ((\text{inl} \circ a) \otimes \langle \underline{k_1}, \ldots, \underline{k_n} \rangle) = \text{inl} \circ (a \otimes \langle \underline{k_1}, \ldots, \underline{k_n} \rangle)$$

and

$$d_{A,B,N} \circ ((\text{inr} \circ b) \otimes \langle \underline{k_1}, \ldots, \underline{k_n} \rangle) = \text{inr} \circ (b \otimes \langle \underline{k_1}, \ldots, \underline{k_n} \rangle)$$

Spelling out weak finality, we have that for any coalgebra $\beta : B \to I + B$ there is a morphism $h : B \to N$ such that (equivalently) either of the following two diagrams commute:

Looking at the second diagram, we obtain two equations, holding for any b, b':
$I \to B$:

$$h \circ b = \text{zero} \qquad (\text{if } \beta \circ b = \text{inl}) \tag{3}$$

$$h \circ b = \text{succ} \circ h \circ b' \qquad (\text{if } \beta \circ b = \text{inr} \circ b') \tag{4}$$

Now, to show closure under μ-recursion, suppose $P: \mathbb{N}^n \times \mathbb{N} \rightharpoonup \mathbb{N}$ is represented by a morphism $\underline{P}: \mathbb{N}^n \otimes \mathbb{N} \to \mathbb{N}$. Then we apply weak finality to the coalgebra

$$\mathbb{N}^{n+1} \xrightarrow{\Delta_{n+1,2}} (\mathbb{N}^{n+1})^2$$
$$\xrightarrow{(\alpha^{-1} \circ \underline{P} \circ 1_{\mathbb{N}^{n+1}}) \otimes \mathbb{N}^{n+1}} (I + \mathbb{N}) \otimes \mathbb{N}^{n+1}$$
$$\xrightarrow{d_{I,\mathbb{N},\mathbb{N}^{n+1}}} (I \otimes \mathbb{N}^{n+1}) + (\mathbb{N} \otimes \mathbb{N}^{n+1})$$
$$\xrightarrow{[\pi_1, (\mathbb{N}^n \otimes \text{succ}) \circ \pi_2]} I + \mathbb{N}^{n+1}$$

and obtain a morphism

$$h: \mathbb{N}^{n+1} \to \mathbb{N}$$

obeying the following two equations:

$h \circ \langle \underline{k_1}, \dots, \underline{k_n}, \underline{k} \rangle = \text{zero}$ $\qquad$ (if $\underline{P} \circ \langle \underline{k_1}, \dots, \underline{k_n}, \underline{k} \rangle = \text{zero}$)
$h \circ \langle \underline{k_1}, \dots, \underline{k_n}, \underline{k} \rangle = \text{succ} \circ h \circ \langle \underline{k_1}, \dots, \underline{k_n}, \underline{k+1} \rangle$ $\qquad$ (if $\underline{P} \circ \langle \underline{k_1}, \dots, \underline{k_n}, \underline{k} \rangle = \text{succ} \circ \underline{k'}$,
$\qquad$ for some k')

One then proves by induction on l that, for all $k_1, \dots, k_n, k$, we have:

$$\mu k'. (P(k_1, \dots, k_n, k+k') \simeq 0 \wedge \forall k'' < k'. P(\mathbf{x}, k+k'') \downarrow) \simeq l \Rightarrow h \circ \langle \underline{k_1}, \dots, \underline{k_n}, \underline{k} \rangle = \underline{l}$$

and so we see that h represents the partial function

$$f(k_1, \dots, k_n, k) \simeq_{\text{def}} \mu k'. P(k_1, \dots, k_n, k+k') \simeq 0 \wedge \forall k'' < k'. P(\mathbf{x}, k+k'') \downarrow$$

We therefore have, as required, that the representable functions are closed under Kleene's μ-recursion scheme, as $h \circ (\mathbb{N}^k \otimes \text{zero}) \circ r_{\mathbb{N}^n}^{-1}$ represents the partial function

$$g(k_1, \dots, k_n) \simeq_{\text{def}} \mu k. P(k_1, \dots, k_n, k) \simeq 0 \wedge \forall k' < k. P(\mathbf{x}, k') \downarrow$$

Our discussion has established:

Theorem 1. *Let* **C** *be a monoidal category with binary sums and a weak left (or right) natural numbers object* $I \xrightarrow{\text{zero}} \mathbb{N} \xleftarrow{\text{succ}} \mathbb{N}$ *such that* $[\text{zero}, \text{succ}]$ *is an isomorphism and* $(\mathbb{N}, [\text{zero}, \text{succ}]^{-1})$ *is a weakly final natural numbers coalgebra. Then all partial recursive functions are representable in* **C**.

There is a natural stronger notion of representability of partial functions over $\mathbb{N}$ which we now investigate. Say that a morphism $g: \mathbb{N}^n \to \mathbb{N}$ *strongly represents* a partial function $f: \mathbb{N}^n \rightharpoonup \mathbb{N}$ if, for all $k_1, \dots, k_n \in \mathbb{N}$, $f(k_1, \dots, k_n) \simeq k$ if, and only if, $g \circ \langle \underline{k_1}, \dots, \underline{k_n} \rangle = \underline{k}$.

Lemma 1. *Let* **C** *be a monoidal category with a weak left (or right) natural numbers object* $I \xrightarrow{\text{zero}} N \xleftarrow{\text{succ}} N$ *such that* $\underline{0} \neq \underline{1}$. *Then all representable total functions are strongly representable.*

Proof. We first remark that if $\underline{k} = \underline{k'}$ then $k = k'$. For if not, as the predecessor function is representable, we get $\underline{0} = \underline{1}$, contradicting our assumption.

Now, suppose that $g : N^n \to N$ represents a total function $f : N^n \to N$, and choose $k_1, \ldots, k_n$. Then $g \circ \langle \underline{k_1}, \ldots, \underline{k_n} \rangle = \underline{f(k_1, \ldots, k_n)}$. So if $g \circ \langle \underline{k_1}, \ldots, \underline{k_n} \rangle = \underline{k}$ then, by the remark, we have, as required, $f(k_1, \ldots, k_n) = k$. □

Theorem 2. *Let* **C** *be a monoidal category with binary sums and a weak left (or right) natural numbers object* $I \xrightarrow{\text{zero}} N \xleftarrow{\text{succ}} N$ *such that* $[\text{zero}, \text{succ}]$ *is an isomorphism and* $(N, [\text{zero}, \text{succ}]^{-1})$ *is a weakly final natural numbers coalgebra. Then:*

1. *If* $\underline{0} \neq \underline{1}$ *then all total recursive functions are strongly representable in* **C**.
2. *If* $\text{succ} \circ c \neq \text{zero}$ *for all* $c : I \to N$, *then all partial recursive functions with recursive graphs are strongly representable in* **C**.

Proof. The first part follows immediately from Theorem 1 and Lemma 1. For the second part, suppose that $g : N^n \to N$ has a recursive graph. Then there is a recursive function $P : N^{n+1} \to N$ such that $P(\mathbf{k}, k')$ holds iff $g(\mathbf{k}) \simeq k'$. Let $\underline{P}$ represent P, and define $h : N^{n+1} \to N$ and $f : N^{n+1} \to N$ as in the above derivation of μ-recursion from weak finality. Then $h \circ (N^k \otimes \text{zero}) \circ r_{N^n}^{-1}$ represents g. To show the representation is strong, it suffices to show that h strongly represents f (we already know it represents f).

To that end, fixing $\mathbf{k}$, we show, by course-of-values induction on l, that, for all k', if $h \circ \langle \underline{\mathbf{k}}, \underline{k'} \rangle = \underline{l}$ then $f(\mathbf{k}, k') \simeq l$. Suppose, first, that $P(\mathbf{k}, k') \simeq 0$. Then we have $f(\mathbf{k}, k') \simeq 0$ and, using (3), that $\underline{l} = h \circ \langle \underline{\mathbf{k}}, \underline{k'} \rangle = \underline{0}$. Then, by the assumption, we have $l = 0$ and this case concludes.

Otherwise we have $P(\mathbf{k}, k') \downarrow$ and $\neq 0$ and then we have $f(\mathbf{k}, k') \simeq f(\mathbf{k}, k' + 1) + 1$ and, using (4), that $\underline{l} = h \circ \langle \underline{\mathbf{k}}, \underline{k'} \rangle = \text{succ} \circ h \circ \langle \underline{\mathbf{k}}, \underline{k' + 1} \rangle$. Hence, by the assumption, we have $l \neq 0$, and we can apply the induction hypothesis, as succ has a left inverse. □

The strong representability of all partial recursive functions can be established under a further, computability, assumption. Assuming that $\underline{0} \neq \underline{1}$ holds in our given category, every morphism $g : N^n \to N$ can be seen as *defining* a partial function $\overline{g} : N^n \to N$, where

$$\overline{g}(k_1, \ldots, k_n) \simeq k \quad \equiv_{\text{def}} \quad g \circ \langle \underline{k_1}, \ldots, \underline{k_n} \rangle \simeq \underline{k}$$

Note that g strongly represents $\overline{g}$. We have:

Corollary 1. *Let* **C** *be a monoidal category with binary sums and a weak left (or right) natural numbers object* $I \xrightarrow{\text{zero}} N \xleftarrow{\text{succ}} N$ *such that* $[\text{zero}, \text{succ}]$ *is an isomorphism and* $(N, [\text{zero}, \text{succ}]^{-1})$ *is a weakly final natural numbers coalgebra.*

Then, if $\underline{0} \neq \underline{1}$ *and if all strongly representable partial functions are partial recursive, all partial recursive functions are strongly representable.*

Proof. A theorem of Visser [14, III.7] states that any class of unary partial recursive functions that (1) contains an upper bound of every partial recursive function and (2) is closed under right composition with all total recursive functions consists of all unary partial recursive functions.

Consider the class of all strongly representable (equivalently definable) unary partial functions. By assumption, these are all partial recursive. By Theorem 1, the first of the two conditions hold. By Theorem 2 every total recursive function is strongly representable and it is easy to see that the class of strongly representable unary partial functions is closed under right composition with strongly representable unary total functions. So the second condition also holds and Visser's theorem applies, showing that all unary partial recursive functions are strongly representable. It follows easily that all n-ary partial recursive functions are strongly representable. $\square$

The corollary applies to various free categories such as the free monoidal category of the kind assumed given in this section.

These results can be applied to Kleisli categories. Suppose we have a cartesian category $\mathbf{C}$ with binary sums and a commutative strong monad T. Then the cartesian structure of $\mathbf{C}$ induces a symmetric monoidal structure on the Kleisli category $\mathbf{C}_T$ [8,13]. Further, $\mathbf{C}_T$ inherits binary sums from $\mathbf{C}$. As we are now in a symmetric situation, there is no need to distinguish between left and right (weak) natural numbers objects; so assume next that $1 \xrightarrow{\text{zero}} N \xleftarrow{\text{succ}} N$ is a (weak) stable natural numbers object in $\mathbf{C}$. One can check that it is also a (weak) stable numbers object in $\mathbf{C}_T$ (more precisely that $1 \xrightarrow{\eta_N \circ \text{zero}} N \xleftarrow{\eta_N \circ \text{succ}} N$ is). So, if we further assume that $[\eta_N \circ \text{zero}, \eta_N \circ \text{succ}]$ is an isomorphism whose inverse provides a weak final natural numbers coalgebra in $\mathbf{C}_T$, then all the above general results apply to $\mathbf{C}_T$.

In [3,4] categories of partial functions are seen as Kleisli categories for so-called "lifting" monads on cartesian categories. As an example, in any distributive category, $- + 1$ is an equational lifting monad in the sense of [3]. As lifting monads are commutative, the discussion of Kleisli categories applies to them.

We know from Theorem 2 that, under a weak condition, all partial recursive functions with recursive graphs are strongly representable. We now see that this need not be the case if the graphs are not recursive. We first show how, given a consistent extension $\mathbf{T}$ of Peano arithmetic, to construct a distributive category $\mathbf{C}$ containing a stably initial natural numbers object which also provides a final coalgebra in the Kleisli category of the lifting monad $- + 1$. The desired counterexample is then obtained by a suitable choice of $\mathbf{T}$.

So let $\mathbf{T}$ be a consistent extension of Peano arithmetic. We allow ourselves to employ symbols for primitive recursive functions and assume their recursive definitions available in $\mathbf{T}$, and make use of evident multifix notation for them.

Fix three distinct variables z, x and y. Given formulas $\varphi(z)$ and $\psi(z)$ whose only possible free variable is z, and a formula $\gamma(x, y)$ whose only possible free variables are x and y, say that γ is a **T**-*relation from φ to ψ* if:

$$\vdash_{\mathbf{T}} \varphi(x) \wedge \gamma(x, y) \Rightarrow \psi(y)$$

that it is **T**-*function from φ to ψ* if, in addition:

$$\vdash_{\mathbf{T}} \varphi(x) \wedge \gamma(x, y) \wedge \gamma(x, y') \Rightarrow y = y'$$

and that it is *a total **T**-function from φ to ψ* if, further:

$$\vdash_{\mathbf{T}} \varphi(x) \Rightarrow \exists y . \gamma(x, y)$$

Define an equivalence relation on **T**-relations from φ to ψ by:

$$\gamma \sim \gamma' \equiv \vdash_{\mathbf{T}} \varphi(x) \Rightarrow (\gamma(x, y) \Leftrightarrow \gamma'(x, y))$$

Note that if $\gamma \sim \gamma'$ then γ is a (total) **T**-function from φ to ψ if, and only if γ' is.

The objects of **pC** are the formulas φ whose only possible free variable is z and the morphisms $[\gamma] : \varphi \to \psi$ of **pC** are the $\sim$-equivalence classes of **T**-functions γ from φ to ψ. Identities and composition are given by:

$$\varphi \xrightarrow{\mathrm{id}_\varphi} \varphi = [y = x]$$

and

$$[\delta] \circ [\gamma] = [\exists w . \gamma(x, w) \wedge \delta(w, y)]$$

where $[\gamma] : \varphi \to \psi$ and $\delta : \psi \to \chi$.

The total **T**-functions form a subcategory **C** of **pC** which we now investigate. It is distributive. The final object is $z = 0$ with $\varphi \xrightarrow{t} 1 = [y = 0]$. Binary products are given by $\varphi \times \psi = \varphi(\pi_1(z)) \wedge \psi(\pi_2(z))$, with projections $\pi_i = [y = \pi_i(x)]$ $(i = 1, 2)$ and with $\langle \gamma, \delta \rangle = [\gamma(x, \pi_1(z)) \wedge \delta(x, \pi_2(z))]$, for $[\gamma] : \chi \to \varphi, [\delta] : \chi \to \psi$ (we make use of a surjective pairing function).

The initial object is $\perp$ with $0 \xrightarrow{i} \varphi = [\perp]$. Binary sums are given by

$$\varphi + \psi = (\exists w . z = 2w \wedge \varphi(w)) \vee (\exists w . z = 2w + 1 \wedge \psi(w))$$

with coprojections $\mathrm{inl} = [y = 2x]$ and $\mathrm{inr} = [y = 2x + 1]$ and with

$$[[\gamma], [\delta]] = [(\exists w . x = 2w \wedge \gamma(w, y)) \vee (\exists w . x = 2w + 1 \wedge \delta(w, y))]$$

for $[\gamma] : \varphi \to \chi, [\delta] : \psi \to \chi$. It is not hard to see that products distribute over sums.

Next, we have a natural numbers algebra

$$1 \xrightarrow{\mathrm{zero}} \mathrm{N} \xleftarrow{\mathrm{succ}} \mathrm{N}$$

where $N = \top$, zero $=_{\text{def}} [y = 0]$, and succ $=_{\text{def}} [y = \text{s}(x)]$. Considered as an algebra $\alpha: 1 + N \to N$, we have:

$$\alpha = [(x = 0 \land y = 0) \lor (\exists w.\, x = 2w + 1 \land y = \text{succ}(w))]$$

Note that $\underline{k} = [y = \text{s}^k(0)]$. Also, succ $\circ\, c \neq$ zero, for all $c: 1 \to N$, as $\mathbf{T}$ is a consistent extension of Peano arithmetic.

We next check that our natural numbers algebra is a stable natural numbers object. As $\mathbf{C}$ is cartesian, it is enough to show that for any structure of the form

$$\varphi \xrightarrow{\;[\gamma]\;} \psi \xleftarrow{\;[\delta]\;} \psi$$

there is a unique $[\theta]: \varphi \times N \to \psi$ such that the following diagram commutes:

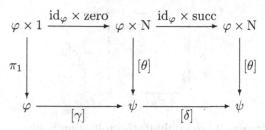

The diagram commutes if, and only if both

$$\vdash_{\mathbf{T}} \varphi(x_1) \Rightarrow (\theta(\langle x_1, 0\rangle, y) \leftrightarrow \gamma(x_1, y))$$

and

$$\vdash_{\mathbf{T}} \varphi(x_1) \Rightarrow (\theta(\langle x_1, \text{s}(x_2)\rangle, y) \Leftrightarrow \exists w.\, \theta(\langle x_1, x_2\rangle, w) \land \delta(w, y))$$

hold. For uniqueness, given θ and θ' satisfying these two conditions, one shows that

$$\vdash_{\mathbf{T}} \varphi(x_1) \Rightarrow (\theta(\langle x_1, x_2\rangle, y) \Leftrightarrow \theta'(\langle x_1, x_2\rangle, y))$$

holds, using induction on x_2. For existence, one defines θ using codes for sequences, following the standard method used to show that the primitive recursive functions are representable in Peano arithmetic.

We next interest ourselves in the Kleisli category $\mathbf{C}_L$, where $L =_{\text{def}} - + 1$ is the equational lifting monad available in any distributive category. By a remark made above, $1 \xrightarrow{\text{zero}} N \xleftarrow{\text{succ}} N$ is a stable natural numbers object in $\mathbf{C}_L$ as it is in $\mathbf{C}$. The $\underline{k}$ in $\mathbf{C}_L$ are as in $\mathbf{C}$, but composed with the unit $\eta_N: N \to N + 1$. As η_N has a left inverse, the condition that succ $\circ\, c \neq$ zero for all $c: 1 \to N$ is inherited by $\mathbf{C}_L$ from $\mathbf{C}$.

We wish to check next that $(N, [\eta_N \circ \text{zero}, \eta_N \circ \text{succ}]^{-1})$ is a final $(1 + -)$-coalgebra in the Kleisli category $\mathbf{C}_L$. There is an equivalence of categories

$$F \dashv G: \mathbf{C}_L \cong \mathbf{pC}$$

where both F and G are the identity on objects,

$$F([\gamma]) = [(\exists w.\, \gamma(x,w) \wedge y = 2w) \vee (\neg\exists w.\, \gamma(x,w) \wedge y = 1)]$$

for $[\gamma]: \varphi \to \psi$ in $\mathbf{pC}$ and

$$G([\delta]) = [\delta(x, 2y)]$$

for $[\delta]: \varphi \to \psi$ in $\mathbf{C}_L$. Under this equivalence $(\mathrm{N}, [\eta_{\mathrm{N}} \circ \mathrm{zero}, \eta_{\mathrm{N}} \circ \mathrm{succ}]^{-1})$ is a final $(1 + -)$-coalgebra in $\mathbf{C}_L$ if, and only if, $(\mathrm{N}, [\mathrm{zero}, \mathrm{succ}]^{-1})$ is in $\mathbf{pC}$.

We therefore now check that the latter is such a coalgebra, guided by the corresponding discussion in Section 2. Noting that, in $\mathbf{pC}$, every object is a retract of N, it is enough to check that for any coalgebra $[\gamma]: \mathrm{N} \to 1 + \mathrm{N}$ there is a unique morphism $[\delta]: \mathrm{N} \to \mathrm{N}$ such that the following diagram commutes:

$$
\begin{array}{ccc}
\mathrm{N} & \xrightarrow{\;[\gamma]\;} & 1 + \mathrm{N} \\[2pt]
{\scriptstyle[\delta]}\Big\downarrow & & \Big\downarrow{\scriptstyle 1 + [\delta]} \\[2pt]
\mathrm{N} & \xleftarrow[\;\alpha\;]{} & 1 + \mathrm{N}
\end{array}
$$

This diagram commutes if, and only if, the following holds:

$$\vdash_{\mathbf{T}} \delta(x,y) \Leftrightarrow \exists v.\, \gamma(x,v) \wedge [(v = 0 \wedge y = 0) \vee (\exists v'.\, v = 2v' + 1 \wedge \exists w.\, \delta(v',w) \wedge y = \mathrm{s}(w))]$$

equivalently if, and only if, both

$$\vdash_{\mathbf{T}} \delta(x,0) \Leftrightarrow \gamma(x,0) \tag{5}$$

and

$$\vdash_{\mathbf{T}} \delta(x,\mathrm{s}(y)) \Leftrightarrow \exists w.\, \gamma(x,\mathrm{s}(w)) \wedge \delta(w,y) \tag{6}$$

hold.

The uniqueness of δ, up to $\sim$, is shown by induction on y. For its existence, we first define $[\theta]: \mathrm{N} \times \mathrm{N} \to \mathrm{N}$ by weak stability so that

$$\vdash_{\mathbf{T}} \theta(\langle x_1, 0 \rangle, y) \Leftrightarrow \gamma(x_1, y) \quad \text{and} \quad \vdash_{\mathbf{T}} \theta(\langle x_1, \mathrm{s}(x_2) \rangle, y) \Leftrightarrow \exists w.\, \theta(\langle x_1, x_2 \rangle, \mathrm{s}(w)) \wedge \gamma(w, y)$$

and then set:

$$\delta(x,y) =_{\mathrm{def}} \theta(\langle x, y \rangle, 0) \wedge \forall y' < y.\, \neg\theta(\langle x, y' \rangle, 0)$$

The formula $\delta(x,y)$ is evidently $\mathbf{T}$-functional and it evidently satisfies (5). To show it satisfies (6), one first shows that

$$\vdash_{\mathbf{T}} \theta(\langle x_1, s(x_2) \rangle, y) \Leftrightarrow \exists w.\, \gamma(x_1, \mathrm{s}(w)) \wedge \theta(\langle w, x_2 \rangle, y) \tag{7}$$

holds, using induction on x_2. Using (7), one then shows that

$$\vdash_{\mathbf{T}} \gamma(x_1, \mathrm{s}(w)) \Rightarrow [(\forall y' < \mathrm{s}(y). \neg\theta(\langle x_1, y'\rangle, 0)) \Leftrightarrow (\forall y' < y. \neg\theta(\langle w, y'\rangle, 0))] \quad (8)$$

holds. Finally, one proves $\delta(x, y)$ satisfies (6) by using its definition and then (7) and (8).

A formula $\chi(x_1, \ldots, x_n)$ *semi-represents* a relation $R \subseteq \mathbb{N}^n$ in an extension $\mathbf{T}$ of Peano arithmetic, if, for all $k_1, \ldots, k_n$, $R(k_1, \ldots, k_n)$ holds if, and only if, $\vdash_{\mathbf{T}} \chi(\underline{k_1}, \ldots, \underline{k_n})$ does.

Theorem 3. *There is a distributive category* $\mathbf{C}$ *with a stable natural numbers object*

$$1 \xrightarrow{\mathrm{zero}} \mathrm{N} \xleftarrow{\mathrm{succ}} \mathrm{N}$$

such that in the Kleisli category $\mathbf{C}_L$, *where* $L = (- + 1)$:

1. $(\mathrm{N}, [\mathrm{zero}, \mathrm{succ}]^{-1})$ *is a final natural numbers coalgebra, and*
2. $\mathrm{succ} \circ c \neq \mathrm{zero}$, *for all* $c : 1 \to \mathrm{N}$, *but*
3. *the only strongly representable partial recursive functions in* $\mathbf{C}_L$ *are those with a recursive graph.*

Proof. By Theorem 3 of [9] (which gives more than we need) there is a consistent complete extension $\mathbf{T}$ of Peano arithmetic in which the only semi-representable relations are either recursive or non-arithmetical. Define $\mathbf{C}$ as above. Then $\mathbf{C}$ has all the required properties except, perhaps, the last. For that, let $f : \mathbb{N}^n \rightharpoonup \mathrm{N}$ be a partial recursive function, and suppose that it is strongly representable in $\mathbf{C}_L$ by $[\gamma] : \mathrm{N}^n \to \mathrm{N}$. Then, for all $k_1, \ldots, k_n$, we have:

$$f(k_1, \ldots, k_n) \simeq k \quad \equiv \quad [\gamma] \circ \langle \underline{k_1}, \ldots, \underline{k_n}\rangle = \underline{k} \quad \equiv \quad \vdash_{\mathbf{T}} \gamma(\langle \underline{k_1}, \ldots, \underline{k_n}\rangle, \underline{k})$$

(making use of an evident primitive recursive n-tupling function). So the graph of f is semi-representable in $\mathbf{T}$ and is therefore recursive. □

Acknowledgements. I thank Jeff Egger, Phil Scott, and Alex Simpson for very helpful discussions.

References

1. Alves, S., Fernández, M., Florido, M., Mackie, I.: Linear recursive functions. In: Comon-Lundh, H., Kirchner, C., Kirchner, H. (eds.) Rewriting, Computation and Proof. LNCS, vol. 4600, pp. 182–195. Springer, Heidelberg (2007)
2. Barr, M., Wells, C.: Category Theory for Computing Science. Prentice Hall (1998); Also available as Reprints in Theory and Applications of Categories, vol. 22, pp. 1–538 (2012), www.tac.mta.ca/tac/reprints/
3. Bucalo, A., Führmann, C., Simpson, A.K.: An equational notion of lifting monad. Theor. Comput. Sci. 294(1/2), 31–60 (2003)
4. Cockett, J.R.B., Lack, S.: Restriction categories II: partial map classification. Theor. Comput. Sci. 294(1/2), 61–102 (2003)

5. Gierz, G., Hofmann, K.H., Keimel, K., Lawson, J.D., Mislove, M., Scott, D.S.: Continuous Lattices and Domains. Encyclopedia of Mathematics and its Applications, vol. 93. CUP (2003)
6. Gladstone, M.: Simplification of the recursion scheme. J. Symb. Logic 36(4), 653–665 (1971)
7. Lambek, J., Scott, P.J.: Introduction to Higher-Order Categorical Logic. Cambridge Studies in Advanced Mathematics, vol. 7. CUP (1988)
8. Jacobs, B.P.F.: Semantics of weakening and contraction. Annals of Pure and Applied Logic 69, 73–106 (1994)
9. Jockusch Jr., C.G., Soare, R.I.: Π_1^0 classes and degrees of theories. Trans. Amer. Math. Soc. 173(2), 33–56 (1972)
10. Johnstone, P.T.: Sketches of an Elephant: a Topos Theory Compendium, vol. 1. OUP (2002)
11. Mackie, I., Román, L., Abramsky, S.: An internal language for autonomous categories. Journal of Applied Categorical Structures 1, 311–343 (1993)
12. Paré, R., Román, L.: Monoidal categories with natural numbers object. Studia Logica 48(3), 361–376 (1989)
13. Power, A.J., Robinson, E.: Premonoidal categories and notions of computation. Mathematical Structures in Computer Science 7(5), 453–468 (1997)
14. Smoryński, C.: Logical Number Theory I. Springer (1991)

Breaking the Atom with Samson

Jouko Väänänen[*]

Department of Mathematics and Statistics
University of Helsinki
and Institute for Logic, Language and Computation
University of Amsterdam

1 Dependence

The dependence atom $=(x, y)$ was introduced[1] in [11]. Here x and y are finite sets of attributes (or variables) and the intuitive meaning of $=(x, y)$ is that the attributes x completely (functionally) determine the attributes y. One may wonder, whether the dependence atom is truly an atom or whether it has further constituents. My very pleasant co-operation with Samson Abramsky led to the breaking of this atom, with hitherto unforeseen consequences. Here is the story.

A reasonable goal in logic is to capture the intuitive meaning of some concept by means of simple axioms. In the case of dependence atoms such simple axioms are the so-called Armstrong's Axioms[2]:

1. Reflexivity: $=(xy, x)$.
2. Augmentation: $=(x, y)$ implies $=(xz, yz)$.
3. Transitivity: If $=(x, y)$ and $=(y, z)$, then $=(x, z)$.

presented in one of the first[3] papers on database theory [3].

Armstrong's Axioms capture the meaning of dependence atoms completely in the sense that an atom $=(x, y)$ follows from a set Σ of other atoms by these rules if and only if every database in which the dependence atoms Σ hold also $=(x, y)$ holds.

A dependence atom holding in a database can be given the same meaning as a formula holding in a first order structure, but only if we make one very important leap. This is the leap from considering truth in one assignment to considering truth in a team, a set of assignments. This innovation is due to Hodges [9].

---

[*] Research partially supported by grant 251557 of the Academy of Finland. I am grateful to Pietro Galliani, Juliette Kennedy, Juha Kontinen and Fan Yang for reading the manuscript and making helpful comments.
[1] It was, however, known as "functional dependence" in database theory since the 70s.
[2] We write xy for the union $x \cup y$ of the sets x and y.
[3] According to R. Fagin in "Armstrong databases", 7th IBM Symposium on Mathematical Foundations of Computer Science, Kanagawa,Japan, May 1982.

B. Coecke, L. Ong, and P. Panangaden (Eds.): Abramsky Festschrift, LNCS 7860, pp. 327–335, 2013.
© Springer-Verlag Berlin Heidelberg 2013

Let $\mathcal{M}$ be a background structure and X a set of assignments of variables into $\mathcal{M}$. We call such sets *teams*. We define what it means for the team X to satisfy a dependence atom $=(x, y)$ in $\mathcal{M}$, denoted $\mathcal{M} \models_X =(x, y)$, as follows:

$$\forall s, s' \in X(s \restriction x = s' \restriction x \text{ implies } s \restriction y = s' \restriction y). \tag{1}$$

This gives exact meaning to $=(x, y)$ in perfect harmony with the idea that the values of x functionally determine the values of y. This is also the meaning of functional dependence as it started to appear in database theory after [3].

2 Constancy

A special case of $=(x, y)$ is the constancy atom $=(y)$ where $x = \emptyset$:

$$\forall s, s' \in X(s \restriction y = s' \restriction y). \tag{2}$$

The intuitive meaning of $=(y)$ is simply that y is constant. In a context like team semantics, where we have variation in the values of the attributes (or variables), it makes a lot of sense to take also into account the possibility of no variation. So in the context of team semantics, where formulas with free variables $x_1, \ldots, x_n$ are considered, the constancy atom

$$=(x_1 \ldots x_n) \tag{3}$$

limits the teams to singleton (or empty[4]) teams. In singleton (and empty) teams all dependence atoms $=(u, v)$ are true, so (3) has the effect of trivializing all dependence atoms.

A complete axiomatization of the logical consequence of a constancy atom from a set of other constancy atoms is almost too trivial to quote: it consists of just the rule

$$\text{Reflexivity: } =(xy) \text{ implies } =(x).$$

3 Dependence Logic

We can extend the definition of the meaning of dependence atoms to the entire first order logic built from identities $x = y$, relational atoms $R(x_1, \ldots, x_n)$ and the dependence atoms $=(x, y)$ as follows:

---

[4] Teams are sets of assignments and also the empty set is a team.

$$\mathcal{M} \models_X x = y \qquad\qquad \Longleftrightarrow \quad \forall s \in X(s(x) = s(y)).$$
$$\mathcal{M} \models_X \neg x = y \qquad\qquad \Longleftrightarrow \quad \forall s \in X(s(x) \neq s(y)).$$
$$\mathcal{M} \models_X R(x_1, \ldots, x_n) \quad \Longleftrightarrow \quad \forall s \in X((s(x_1), \ldots, s(x_n)) \in R^{\mathcal{M}}).$$
$$\mathcal{M} \models_X \neg R(x_1, \ldots, x_n) \quad \Longleftrightarrow \quad \forall s \in X((s(x_1), \ldots, s(x_n)) \notin R^{\mathcal{M}}).$$
$$\mathcal{M} \models_X \phi \wedge \psi \qquad\qquad \Longleftrightarrow \quad \mathcal{M} \models_X \phi \text{ and } \mathcal{M} \models_X \psi.$$
$$\mathcal{M} \models_X \phi \vee \psi \qquad\qquad \Longleftrightarrow \quad \text{There are } X_1 \text{ and } X_2 \text{ such that}$$
$$X = X_1 \cup X_2, \mathcal{M} \models_{X_1} \phi, \text{ and } \mathcal{M} \models_{X_2} \psi.$$
$$\mathcal{M} \models_X \exists x \phi \qquad\qquad \Longleftrightarrow \quad \mathcal{M} \models_{X'} \phi \text{ for some } X' \text{ such that}$$
$$\forall s \in X \, \exists a \in M(s(a/x) \in X')$$
$$\mathcal{M} \models_X \forall x \phi \qquad\qquad \Longleftrightarrow \quad \mathcal{M} \models_{X'} \phi \text{ for some } X' \text{ such that}$$
$$\forall s \in X \, \forall a \in M(s(a/x) \in X')$$

We call the resulting semantically defined logic *Dependence Logic* [11].

Conceivably one could extend (1) to full dependence logic in different ways. An important guideline in making the choices for the above semantics is that for singleton teams $\{s\}$ this agrees with satisfaction in first order logic, that is, if we use the notation $\mathcal{M} \models_s \phi$ for the proposition that the assignment s satisfies the first order formula ϕ in $\mathcal{M}$, then for first order ϕ (i.e. for ϕ not containing dependence atoms):

$$\mathcal{M} \models_{\{s\}} \phi \Longleftrightarrow \mathcal{M} \models_s \phi. \qquad\qquad (4)$$

4   Downward Closure

Another guiding principle is *downward closure*: If $\mathcal{M} \models_X \phi$ and $Y \subseteq X$, then $\mathcal{M} \models_Y \phi$ for any dependence logic formula ϕ. Why do we want downward closure? The idea is that every dependence logic formula specifies a type of dependence. So, in particular, we do not aim at expressing non-dependence. Also, we do not consider dependencies which are manifested in part of the team only, even if the part was a very big part.

Our concept of dependence is thus *logical*, not *probabilistic*. For $=(x, y)$ to hold in X, every pair $\{s, s'\}$ chosen from X has to satisfy (1), not a single exception is allowed. This property is, of course, downward closed. We simply extend this to all formulas and thereby maintain the idea that every formula determines a weak form of this kind of dependence.

In practical applications probabilistic dependences are much more ubiquitous. In particular, in practical applications one can usually overlook a tiny portion of the team as irrelevant noise, possibly resulting from errors in data handling. In our mathematical theory of team semantics a single row can destroy the dependence manifested by millions of other rows.

Let us see how downward closure arises: Conjunction determines the simultaneity of two dependences. Downward closure is preserved. Disjunction says that the team splits into two subteams, both with their own dependence. Downward closure is preserved: a smaller team splits similarly into subteams obtained by intersecting the original subteams with the smaller team. The existential quantifier says that after some rows are updated, a dependence holds. A smaller team inherits the update canonically. Finally, the universal quantifier says that a given dependence holds even if a certain attribute has simultaneously all possible values. In a smaller team we simultaneously give all possible values to the given attribute in the remaining assignments. In each case downward closure is clearly preserved.

5 Axioms

Given that Armstrong's Axioms govern the dependence atom, what are the axioms governing the entire dependence logic? After all, we have just given the semantics. Ideally the semantics would reflect the completeness of the axioms. As it happens,[5] the above semantics does not reflect the completeness of *any* effectively given set of axioms and rules, because the set of Gödel numbers of valid sentences in dependence logic is a complete Π_2-set in the sense of the Levy hierarchy of set theory [12].

What *is* the meaning of the logical operations of dependence logic, if logical consequence cannot be axiomatized? A trivial answer is that the meaning comes from set theory according to the definition of the semantics. This, however, raises the further question, do we really have to understand set theory to understand the meaning of the logical operations $\wedge, \vee, \neg, \exists$ and $\forall$? Shouldn't "logical" mean something simpler than set theory?

Conceivably there is a fragment of dependence logic which is completely axiomatizable but still rich enough to express some interesting dependence properties. A step in this direction is [10], where a complete axiomatization of the logical consequence relation $\Sigma \models \phi$, where ϕ is first order, is given. Some of the rules of this axiomatization are quite involved but still all the rules have a clear intuitive content. Here is an example of the rules of [10]:

$$\frac{\exists \boldsymbol{y}(\bigwedge_{1 \le j \le n} =(\boldsymbol{z}^j, y_j) \wedge C) \vee \exists \boldsymbol{y}'(\bigwedge_{n+1 \le j \le n+m} =(\boldsymbol{z}^j, y_j) \wedge D)}{\exists \boldsymbol{y} \exists \boldsymbol{y}'(\bigwedge_{1 \le j \le n+m} =(\boldsymbol{z}^j, y_j) \wedge (C \vee D))} \tag{5}$$

Work is underway to extend such results to non-first order—real dependence logic—consequences, and Juha Kontinen and his student Miika Hannula have unpublished results in this direction. In the light of this we may argue that there are meaningful and insightful steps between Armstrong's Axioms for atoms and the axiomatically intractable purely semantic theory of dependence.

6 Breaking the Atom

Are the complicated rules of [10], an example of which is (5), and the even more complicated ones needed for non-first order consequences, really the best way to understand the meaning of $=(x,y)$ and first order logic built on top of it? Maybe $=(x,y)$ can be analyzed in a different way, leading to simpler logical rules. Samson Abramsky suggested to look inside the atom $=(x,y)$ and see what

---

[5] This is essentially due to A. Ehrenfeucht, as Henkin reports in [8].

are its constituents. This led to the topic of the title of this paper, and to the paper [2].

To break the atom $=(x, y)$ we can rewrite its semantics as follows:

$$\forall Y \subseteq X(\text{if } x \text{ is constant on } Y, \text{ then } y \text{ is constant on } Y). \tag{6}$$

Using the constancy atoms this amounts to

$$\forall Y \subseteq X(\text{if } Y \text{ satisfies } =(x), \text{ then } Y \text{ satisfies } =(x)). \tag{7}$$

This resembles the semantics of intuitionistic implication in Kripke-semantics

$$w \Vdash \phi \to \psi \iff \forall u \geq w(\text{if } u \Vdash \phi, \text{ then } u \Vdash \psi),$$

so thinking of subsets of X as "extensions" of X we define a new logical operation:

$$\mathcal{M} \models \phi \to \psi \text{ iff } \forall Y \subseteq X(\text{if } \mathcal{M} \models_Y \phi, \text{ then } \mathcal{M} \models_Y \psi). \tag{8}$$

With this new implication we have a simple definition of the dependence atom:

$$=(x, y) \text{ iff } =(x) \to =(y) \tag{9}$$

with exactly the same semantics in team semantics as the original (1).

The idea that subteams are "extensions" of the team is not far-fetched. We can think of teams as uncertain information about an assignment (see [4] for more on this idea) and then a smaller team represents less uncertainty, i.e. more certainty. The ultimate extension in this sense is a singleton, representing total certainty about the assignment.

An obvious potential advantage of $=(x) \to =(y)$ over $=(x, y)$ is that on the one hand $=(y)$ is a much simpler atom than $=(x, y)$ and on the other hand $\to$ is not just an arbitrary new operation, it is the restriction to team semantics of the classical intuitionistic implication going back to Brouwer, Kolmogorov and Heyting, with an extensive literature about it.

Considering that $\phi \to \psi$ is the restriction of intuitionistic implication to the context of dependence logic, it can be hoped that it inherits some its rich meaning in constructive mathematics, and that this inheritance can be taken advantage of. Indeed, if Armstrong's Axioms are combined with (9) and dependence atoms are replaced by arbitrary formulas, Heyting's axioms for intuitionistic implication and conjunction arise:

1. Reflexivity: $(\phi \wedge \psi) \to \phi$.
2. Augmentation: $\phi \to \psi$ implies $(\phi \wedge \theta) \to (\psi \wedge \theta)$.
3. Transitivity: If $\phi \to \psi$ and $\psi \to \theta$, then $\phi \to \theta$.

This can be interpreted by saying that dependence logic has an intuitionistic element. It is not intuitionistic *per se*, but it shares some aspects with intuitionistic logic. Perhaps dependence logic could be developed completely constructively, but this has not been tried yet.

Another remarkable property of the intuitionistic implication in dependence logic is that it is the adjoint of conjunction, just as it should be:

$$\phi \wedge \psi \models \theta \text{ iff } \phi \models \psi \to \theta. \tag{10}$$

Probably the introduction of intuitionistic implication into dependence logic will eventually lead to better proof theory, not least because of the natural Galois connection (10). But alas, intuitionistic implication is not definable[6] in dependence logic! In fact Fan Yang [13] has shown that adding intuitionistic implication to dependence logic leads to full second order logic. So the introduction of the much needed implication to dependence logic leads to an explosion of the expressive power. Remarkably, we can still keep downward closure, so we have not introduced a negation in the classical sense, even though full second order logic is closed under negation. This is one of the peculiarities of team semantics, and its oddness disperses with closer investigation, for which we refer to [13].

7   Independence

Given that we have made some headway in understanding dependence by introducing the dependence atom and investigating its logic, the question naturally arises, what about independence? With this in mind, in [7] the independence atom $x \perp y$ was introduced[7].

Intuitively speaking, $x \perp y$ says that x and y are so independent of each other that knowing one gives no information about the other. This form of independence turns out to be ubiquitous among attributes in science and society, wherever independence is talked about. As it turned out in discussions with Samson, the independence concept of quantum mechanics in [1] is also of the type $x \perp y$. This observation is the subject of further study in co-operation with Samson.

To give independence exact meaning, let $\mathcal{M}$ be a background structure and X a set of assignments of variables into M. We define what it means for the team X to satisfy an independence atom $x \perp y$ in $\mathcal{M}$, denoted $\mathcal{M} \models_X x \perp y$, as follows:

$$\forall s, s' \in X \exists s''(s'' \restriction x = s \restriction x \text{ and } s'' \restriction y = s' \restriction y). \tag{11}$$

In other words, if a value a occurs in some assignment s as a value of x and a value b occurs as a value of y in some other assignment s', then there is a third assignment s'' which has simultaneously a as the value of x and b as the value of

---

[6] Pietro Galliani has a related but different, and very interesting, analysis of the dependence atom in terms of what he calls public announcement operators and the constancy atoms [5]. The public announcement operators have the advantage over $\to$ that they are definable in dependence logic itself.

[7] As with dependence atom, it turned out (this observation was made by Fredrik Engström) that our independence atom was already studied under a different name (embedded multivalued dependence) in database theory.

y. So from x being a we cannot infer what y is (unless it is constant), and from y being b we cannot infer what x is (unless it is constant).

Speaking of being constant, in fact, the constancy atom $=(x)$ implies $x \perp y$ because we can then choose $s'' = s'$ in (11). This is the curious state of affairs uncovered in [7], which shows that independence is not necessarily the opposite of dependence. Since $=(x)$ implies $=(x,y)$, we can have simultaneously $=(x,y)$ and $x \perp y$. Being constant is one form of independence.

The analogue of Armstrong's Axioms is in the case of independence atom the Geiger-Paz-Pearl [6] axioms:

1. Empty set rule: $x \perp \emptyset$.
2. Symmetry Rule: If $x \perp y$, then $y \perp x$.
3. Weakening Rule: If $x \perp yz$, then $x \perp y$.
4. Exchange Rule: If $x \perp y$ and $xy \perp z$, then $x \perp yz$.

These axioms satisfy in team semantics the same kind of Completeness Theorem[8] as Armstrong's Axioms. So we may regard them really as incorporating the essence of independence on the atomic level.

Independence atoms can be added to dependence logic[9] and we get a proper extension, called independence logic, which no longer satisfies the Downward Closure property. This logic is able to express existential second order properties in a particularly strong sense [5]. If we again add intuitionistic implication, we get full second order logic [13].

8 Speculation: Breaking the Independence Atom

Let us then try to break the independence atom into pieces. The reasons for attempting this are the same as in the case of dependence atom: the logic is non-axiomatizable and trying to axiomatize even just first order consequences[10] leads to rather complicated axioms.

Since we are bound to lose downward closure, intuitionistic implication alone is not enough. The following more complicated *compatible conjunction* suggests itself: We add a new logical connective $\phi \odot \psi$ to dependence logic with the following semantics:

$$\mathcal{M} \models_X \phi \odot \psi \iff$$

$$\forall_{\neq \emptyset} Y, Z \subseteq X((\mathcal{M} \models_Y \phi \text{ and } \mathcal{M} \models_Z \psi) \to$$

$$\exists Y', Z' \subseteq X(Y \subseteq Y', Z \subseteq Z', \mathcal{M} \models_{Y'} \phi, \mathcal{M} \models_{Z'} \psi, \text{ and } Y' \cap Z' \neq \emptyset)).$$

---

[8] Proved in [6] in the case of random variables.

[9] By an unpublished result of Pietro Galliani the dependence atom is definable from the independence atom, so if we add the independence atoms to first order logic, we get the dependence atoms free.

[10] Miika Hannula has a complete axiomatization (unpublished).

In words, every non-empty subteam Y satisfying ϕ and every non-empty subteam Z satisfying ψ, can be extended inside X, respectively, to Y' and Z' such that they still satisfy ϕ and, respectively, ψ, but, moreover, they meet. In a finite model this means that non-empty maximal teams satisfying ϕ and ψ meet. In finite models $\mathcal{M} \models_X \phi \odot \phi$ says the non-empty maximal subteams of X satisfying ϕ all meet. In forcing terms this means that below X the formula ϕ defines a set of compatible teams. In forcing terms $\phi \odot \psi$ is satisfied by teams below which ϕ and ψ are compatible. For sentences ϕ and ψ the sentence $\phi \odot \psi$ is always true. For first order $\phi(x)$ and $\psi(x)$:

$$\mathcal{M} \models \forall x(\phi(x) \odot \psi(x)) \iff \mathcal{M} \not\models \exists x \phi(x) \text{ or}$$
$$\mathcal{M} \not\models \exists x \psi(x) \text{ or else}$$
$$\mathcal{M} \models \exists x(\phi(x) \wedge \psi(x)).$$

Having added the new operation we can now break the independence atom into smaller constituents:

$$x \perp y \iff =(x) \odot =(y). \tag{12}$$

To what avail? In what sense is $=(x) \odot =(y)$ simpler than $x \perp y$? At the moment it is not clear whether the equivalence (12) is an insightful analysis of $x \perp y$. Certainly the atoms $=(x)$ represent a simplification from $x \perp y$, but it is more difficult to estimate the connective $\odot$. It is not one of the logical operations known in logic, and no general theory of $\odot$ exists.

References

1. Abramsky, S.: Relational hidden variables and non-locality. Studia Logica, arXiv:1007.2754 (2013), doi: 10.1007/s11225-013-9477-4
2. Abramsky, S., Väänänen, J.: From IF to BI: a tale of dependence and separation. Synthese 167(2, Knowledge, Rationality & Action), 207–230 (2009)
3. Armstrong, W.W.: Dependency structures of data base relationships. In: IFIP Congress, pp. 580–583 (1974)
4. Galliani, P.: The dynamics of imperfect information. Doctoral Thesis, University of Amsterdam (2012)
5. Galliani, P.: Inclusion and exclusion dependencies in team semantics—on some logics of imperfect information. Ann. Pure Appl. Logic 163(1), 68–84 (2012)
6. Geiger, D., Paz, A., Pearl, J.: Axioms and algorithms for inferences involving probabilistic independence. Inform. and Comput. 91(1), 128–141 (1991)
7. Grädel, E., Väänänen, J.: Dependence and independence. Studia Logica, arXiv:1208.5268 (2013), doi: 10.1007/s11225-013-9479-2
8. Henkin, L.: Some remarks on infinitely long formulas. In: Infinitistic Methods (Proc. Sympos. Foundations of Math., Warsaw, 1959), pp. 167–183. Pergamon, Oxford (1961)
9. Hodges, W.: Some strange quantifiers. In: Mycielski, J., Rozenberg, G., Salomaa, A. (eds.) Structures in Logic and Computer Science. LNCS, vol. 1261, pp. 51–65. Springer, Heidelberg (1997)

10. Kontinen, J., Väänänen, J.: Axiomatizing first order consequences in dependence logic. Annals of Pure and Applied Logic (to appear)
11. Väänänen, J.: Dependence logic. London Mathematical Society Student Texts, vol. 70. Cambridge University Press, Cambridge (2007)
12. Väänänen, J.A.: Second-order logic and foundations of mathematics. Bulletin of Symbolic Logic 7(4), 504–520 (2001)
13. Yang, F.: Expressing second-order sentences in intuitionistic dependence logic. Studia Logica, arXiv:1302.2279 (2013), doi: 10.1007/s11225-013-9476-5

Reasoning about Strategies

Johan van Benthem*

University of Amsterdam and Stanford University

Abstract. Samson Abramsky has placed landmarks in the world of logic and games that I have long admired. In this little piece, I discuss one theme in the overlap of our interests, namely, logical systems for reasoning with strategies - in gentle exploratory mode.

1 Reasoning about Strategies: A Priorip Analysis or Rather Logical Fieldwork?

The notion of a strategy as a plan for interactive behavior is of crucial importance at the interface of logic and games. Truth or validity of formulas corresponds to existence of appropriate strategies in systems of game semantics, and in game theory, it is strategies that describe multi-agent behavior interlocked in equilibria. But strategies themselves are often implicit in logical systems, remaining "unsung heroes" in the meta-language (5). To put them at centre stage, two approaches suggest themselves. One is to assimilate strategies with existing objects whose theory we know, such as proofs or programs. This is the main line in my new book (6). However, one can also drop all preconceptions and follow a "quasi-empirical approach". A traditional core business of logic is analyzing a given reasoning practice to find striking patterns, as has happened with great success in constructive mathematics or in formal semantics of natural language. In this piece, I will analyze a few set pieces of strategic reasoning in basic results about games, and just see where they lead. I restrict attention to two-player games (players will be called i, j), and usually, games of winning and losing only. Also, given the limitations of size for this paper, I will just presuppose many standard notions.

2 The Gale-Stewart Theorem and Its Underlying Temporal Logic of Forcing

Two Basic Theorems. Consider determined games, where one of the players has a winning strategy. This is the area where basic mathematical results about games and strategies started:

---

* I thank the two readers of this paper, and also Chanjuan Liu and Prakash Panangaden for their generous practical help.

B. Coecke, L. Ong, and P. Panangaden (Eds.): Abramsky Festschrift, LNCS 7860, pp. 336–347, 2013.

Theorem 1 (Zermelo's Theorem). *Games with finite depth are determined.*

Proof.   The proof is essentially an algorithm computing positions where players have winning strategies, a precursor to the game theoretic method of Backward Induction (16). Its key recursion defines predicates WIN_i ("player i has a winning strategy from now on") at nodes of the game tree in terms of auxiliary predicates *end* ("endpoint"), $turn_i$ ("it is player i's turn to move"), $move_i$ ("the union of all currently available moves for i"), and win_i ("player i wins at this node"):

$$WIN_i \leftrightarrow ((end \wedge win_i) \vee (turn_i \wedge \langle move_i \rangle WIN_i) \vee (turn_j \wedge [move_i] WIN_i))$$

∎

Notice the different existential and universal modalities in the two cases.[1]

Now we move to infinite games. An *open winning condition* is a set X of histories h with $h \in X$ iff some initial segment of h has all its extensions in X. Call a game "open" where at least one of the players has such a winning condition. Here is another classical result:

Theorem 2 (Gale-Stewart Theorem). *Open infinite games are determined.*

Proof.   The proof revolves around this property of all infinite games:

Weak Determinacy: Either player i has a winning strategy, or player j has a strategy ensuring that player i never reaches a position in the game where i has a winning strategy.

If i has no winning strategy, then j has a "nuisance strategy" by Zermelo reasoning. At i's turns, no move for her can guarantee a win, and so j can "wait and see". If j is to move, there must be at least one successor state where i has no winning strategy: otherwise, i has a winning strategy after all. Continuing this way, j produces runs as described.

Next, without loss of generality, let i be the player with the open winning condition. Then the nuisance strategy is winning for j. Consider any history r that it produces. If r were winning for i, some initial segment $r(n)$ would have all its continuations winning. But then "play whatever" would be a winning strategy for i at $r(n)$: quod non.   ∎

A Temporal Logic of Forcing Powers.   Now we introduce some minimal machinery formalizing these arguments. Extensive games may be viewed as branching tree models M for time, with histories as complete branches h, and stages s as points on these histories:

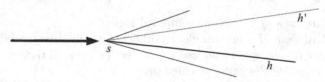

---

[1] A correctness proof for the algorithm is essentially "excluded middle writ-large": either player i has a response to every move by j yielding φ, or player j has a move such that each follow-up by i yields $\neg\varphi$.

The bold-face line is the actual history, only known up to stage s so far. Points can have local properties encoded, while total histories can also have global properties such as Gale-Stewart winning conditions, or the total discounted pay-offs used in evolutionary games.

Such structures, assuming discrete time, interpret a standard branching temporal language ((10) has a survey of flavours), in the format

$$\mathbf{M}, h, s \models \varphi \qquad \text{formula } \varphi \text{ is true at stage } s \text{ on history } h$$

with formulas φ constructed using proposition letters, Boolean connectives, existential and universal temporal operators F, G, H, P, O (future and past on branches, with O for "at the next moment"), as well as existential and universal modalities $\Diamond, \Box$ over all branches at the current stage. Here are the truth conditions for some major operators:

$\mathbf{M}, h, s \models F\varphi$ iff $\mathbf{M}, h, t \models \varphi$ for some point $t \geq s$,

$\mathbf{M}, h, s \models O\varphi$ iff $\mathbf{M}, h, s + 1 \models \varphi$ with $s + 1$ the immediate successor of s on h,

$\mathbf{M}, h, s \models \Diamond\varphi$ iff $\mathbf{M}, h', s \models \varphi$ for some h' equal to h up to stage s.

To this description of the basic structure of the model, we now add a *strategic forcing modality* $\{i\}\varphi$ describing the powers of player i at the current stage of the game:

$\mathbf{M}, h, s \models \{i\}\varphi$ player i has a strategy from s onward playing which ensures that only histories h' result for which, at each stage $t \geq s, \mathbf{M}, h', t \models \varphi$

While this looks local to stages s, φ can also be a global stage-independent property of the histories h'. Note that the condition does not imply that the actual history h satisfies φ: any successful strategy may have to deviate from the current "road to perdition".

As an illustration of the perspicuity of this language, Weak Determinacy becomes the following simple formula:

$$\{i\}\varphi \vee \{j\}\neg\{i\}\varphi$$

Valid Principles. Some obvious laws of reasoning for the resulting *temporal forcing logic* are a combination of some well-known components:

Fact 3. *The following principles are valid in temporal forcing logic:*

(a) *the standard laws of* branching temporal logic,
(b) *the standard logic of a* monotonic neighborhood modality *for* $\{i\}\varphi$, *plus one for its strongly modalized character:* $\{i\}\varphi \rightarrow \Box\{i\}\varphi$,
(c) *three more specifically game-oriented principles:*
   (c_1) $\{i\}\varphi \leftrightarrow ((\mathbf{end} \wedge \varphi) \vee (\mathbf{turn}_i \wedge \Diamond O\{i\}\varphi) \vee (\mathbf{turn}_j \wedge \Box O\{i\}\varphi))$
   (c_2) $\alpha \wedge \Box G((\mathbf{turn}_i \wedge \alpha) \rightarrow \Diamond O\alpha) \wedge ((\mathbf{turn}_j \wedge \alpha) \rightarrow \Box O\alpha))) \rightarrow \{i\}\alpha$
   (c_3) $(\{i\}\varphi \wedge \{j\}\}\varphi) \rightarrow \Diamond(\varphi \wedge \psi)$.

For the list of principles meant under (a), see (10). For those under (b), see (14). The first law of (c) is the fixed-point recursion in the Zermelo argument, and the second an introduction law reminiscent of the axiom for the universal iteration modality in propositional dynamic logic.[2] The third principle is a simple form of independence of strategy choices for the two players that occurs in many logics of simultaneous action.

Proving Our Basic Results Formally. These laws allow us to derive our earlier results. Here are the essential steps in the proof of Weak Determinacy:

- $(\mathbf{turn_i} \wedge \neg\{i\}\varphi) \to \Box O\neg\{i\}\varphi$ \hfill from (c_1)
- $(\mathbf{turn_j} \wedge \neg\{i\}\varphi) \to \Diamond O\neg\{i\}\varphi$ \hfill from (c_1)
- $\neg\{i\}\varphi \to \{j\}\neg\{i\}\varphi)$ \hfill from (c_2)

Now we can also derive the Gale-Stewart Theorem formally. Suppose that φ is an open condition, i.e.:

$$\varphi \to F\Box G\varphi$$

Then it is easy to derive formally that $\{j\}\neg\{i\}\varphi \to \{j\}\neg\varphi$, and combined with Weak Determinacy, this makes the game determined:

$$\{i\}\varphi \vee \{j\}\neg\varphi$$

Zermelo's Theorem follows as well, since "having an endpoint" is an open property of branches, satisfying the implication

$$F\,end \to F\Box GF\,end.$$

Temporal Forcing Logic. Viewed as a system, temporal forcing logic on our tree models has some familiar laws:

Fact 4. *The modal $K4$-axiom $\{i\}\alpha \to \{i\}\{i\}\alpha$ is valid in temporal forcing logic.*

This is not so much the usual "introspection" for knowledge-like modalities, but a sort of "safety": following a winning strategy never takes one outside of the area where one has a winning strategy. But it is also interesting to look at non-validities of the system:

Example 1. Some informative non-validities:
(a) The modal T-axiom $\{i\}\alpha \to \alpha$ fails since the current history need not be the one recommended by i's strategy forcing α. [3] (b) Also invalid is the implication $G\{i\}\alpha \to F\alpha$, that might look plausible as a principle of eventual success. However, it fails anywhere on the infinite $\neg\alpha$ branch in the following model, viewed as a one-person game:

---

[2] Note that the principle stated here is less strong than it may seem: to see this, just apply it to a global winning condition.

[3] But valid again in temporal forcing logic is the special instance $\{i\}\{i\}\alpha \to \{i\}\alpha$.

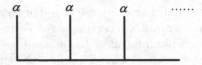

Even though we do not know a complete axiomatization for temporal forcing logic, we do have the wind in our sails:

Fact 5. *Temporal forcing logic is decidable.*

Proof. All temporal modalities, but also the forcing modality, can be defined in monadic second-order logic *MSOL* on trees with successor relations. Histories are maximal linearly ordered sets of nodes, and strategies can be identified with subsets of the tree as well, in a manner shown in (7). Then Rabin's Theorem on decidability of *MSOL* tree logic applies.[4]   ∎

Remark. A short piece like this cannot do justice to links with existing temporal logics for games. Classics such as (2) come to mind as obvious comparisons. (6) explores further connections between our forcing-based logic of strategies with various game-related systems in computational logic.

3   Nondeterminacy, Strategy Stealing, and Temporal Forcing Logics of Special Games

Within our general logic of strategies, further properties come to light in special models. Going beyond the Gale-Stewart Theorem, consider a standard non-determined game.

Example 2. The interval selection game. Take any free ultrafilter U on the natural numbers N. Two players pick successive closed initial segments of N of arbitrary finite lengths, producing a sequence like this:

$$i: [0, n_1], with\ n_1 > 0, \quad j: [n_1 + 1, n_2], with\ n_2 > n_1 + 1, etc.$$

Player i wins if the union of all intervals chosen by her is in U- otherwise, j wins. Winning sets are not open, as sets in U are not determined by finite initial segments. This interval game is not determined, by a so-called "strategy stealing" argument:

Lemma 1. *Player i has no winning strategy.*

Proof. Suppose that player i had a winning strategy, then j could actually use it with a delay of one step to copy i's responses to her own moves, now disguised as j-moves. Both resulting sets of intervals (disjoint up to some finite initial segment) would have their unions in U: which cannot be, since U is free. Player j has no winning strategy for similar reasons.   ∎

---

[4] Many strategy-related modalities on trees are even bisimulation-invariant, so by the main theorem in (15), they are also definable in the modal μ-calculus.

Analyzing this proof in detail reveals interesting logical structure. Let i start, the other case is similar. The strategy σ gives i a first move $\sigma(-)$. Now let j play any move e. i's response is $\sigma(\sigma(-), e)$, after which it is j's turn again. Now crucially, in the interval game, the same sequence of events can be viewed differently, as a move $\sigma(-)$ played by i, followed by a move e; $\sigma(\sigma(-), e)$ played by j, after which it is i's turn. What this presupposes is the following special, but natural property of a game:

Composition Closure: Any player can play any concatenation of available successive moves as one single move. [5]

Now the game tree has the following property. The two stages described here start the same subgames in terms of available moves, but with all turn markings interchanged. Thus, one subgame is a "dual" of the other.[6] The core of j's strategy is now that he uses i's strategy in the other game to produce *identical runs* in both subgames, except for the inverted turn marking. This leads to a contradiction via the following logical *Copy Law*:

Fact 6. *In games with composition closure, the following formula is valid:*

$$\{i\}\varphi \to \Diamond OO\{j\}\varphi_d, \text{ where } \varphi_d \text{ is the formula } \varphi \text{ with all turn occurrences for}$$
$$\text{players } i, j \text{ interchanged.}$$

Many further questions make sense about powers of players in games with special structure, but here, we only conclude that both general and special temporal forcing logics have an interest of their own.[7]

4   Explicit Logics of Strategies as Programs

Forcing modalities profess a general love for strategies without an interest in any specific one. We now go one step further in our logical analysis, introducing *terms that define strategies*, thus enabling us to reason explicitly about strategies themselves. A wide array of motivations for taking this step can be found in (5). Suitable languages can take various forms, but one obvious candidate is *propositional dynamic logic*.

Transition Relations and Programs. Strategies are functions defined on players' turns, with typical instructions like "if she plays this, then I play that". Plans like this may allow more than one "best move", so general relations make

---

[5] One could define this property formally in a modal-temporal action language suitably extending our earlier formalism.

[6] This is not the standard game-theoretic dual, since we do not interchange winning conditions. See (6) for more discussion of different dualizations in games.

[7] Yet further questions would arise if we also introduce "intermediate" forcing modalities $\{\sigma\}^*\varphi$ saying that *partial* strategy σ guarantees reaching a *barrier* of intermediate positions in the game satisfying φ. This would connect with current modal logics of barriers and "cut-sets".

sense as well, providing at least one move per turn. Thus, strategies are additional relations on a game tree that can be defined by programs. Since we need one-step actions only, normally, *flat programs* suffice using only atomic actions, tests, sequence; and choice $\cup$ - often just unions of guarded actions of the form

$$?\varphi; \alpha; ?\psi(9).^8$$

However, consecutive moves become important when we think of forcing outcomes. Using *PDL* programs, we now introduce a new forcing language with a key modality:

$\{\sigma, i\}\varphi$, stating that σ is a strategy for player i forcing the game, against any play of the others, to pass only through states satisfying φ.

While this notion is natural, it still has an explicit definition in more familiar terms, viz. program modalities:

Fact 7. *For any game program expression σ, PDL can define $\{\sigma, i\}\varphi$.*

Proof. The formula $[((?\mathbf{turn}_i; \sigma) \bigcup (?\mathbf{turn}_j; move_j))^*]\varphi$ is the required equivalent, as is easy to see from its truth conditions. [9]   ∎

Still, working with an explicit forcing modality $\{\sigma, i\}\varphi$ provides a natural notation for strategic behavior, and it fits well with actual examples of reasoning about games and interaction.

Remark. *PDL* programs can even do a lot more, since they also model *partial strategies* that can be combined. See (4), (11) for recent work on on propositional dynamic logics of strategy combination, where the key operation is *intersection* of relations. Laws of such systems mix our earlier forcing modalities with program terms, as in the following implication:

$$(\{\sigma\}\varphi \wedge \{\tau\}\psi) \rightarrow \{\sigma \cap \tau\}(\varphi \wedge \psi)$$

Further Benchmarks. Our earlier "quasi-empirical" approach would now compile a repertoire of ubiquitous strategies, and formalize basic reasoning about their properties. We will not do so here. Also, *PDL* programs are geared toward finite termination, whereas we also want to look at natural non-terminating strategies such as "keep moving" – but we omit this extension as well.

5   Zoom, Levels, Invariants, and Definability

Zooming In and Out. It now looks as if we have two competing approaches to logics of strategies, one with existentially quantified forcing modalities, and

---

[8] It is easy to see that, on "expressive" finite game trees (each node is uniquely definable), each strategy is definable by our simplest flat *PDL* programs. But, if definitions are to be uniform across models, fixed-point languages are needed (7).

[9] In the same style, properties of the outcome of running joint strategies σ, τ, too, can be described in *PDL*.

one with explicit program terms that define strategies. But in practice, both options are natural. The fact of the matter is that logic provides different levels of "zoom" on reasoning practices. Sometimes, we want to see underlying details, sometimes we want the broad picture. That is precisely why logical languages come in hierarchies of expressive power.

In the case of games, it may even be useful to *combine* our two formats. It might look as if explicit forcing modalities $\{\sigma, i\}\varphi$ are just more informative than implicit $\{i\}\varphi$. But this is misleading. If we want to say that a player *lacks a strategy* for achieving some purpose, then we need expressions $\neg\{i\}\varphi$, and no natural explicit equivalent will do.

Even so, this combined language of forcing also has some surprises in store. Here is a "triviality result" saying that implicit can always become explicit by means of a strategy "be successful":

$$\sigma_{\varphi,i} = ?\mathbf{turn}_i; move_i, ?\{i\}\varphi$$

Fact 8. *The following equivalence is valid:*

$$\{i\}\varphi \leftrightarrow \{\sigma_{\varphi,i}, i\}\varphi$$

The proof is easy and follows the earlier-mentioned valid recursion principles that govern temporal forcing.

Definitions for Strategies. Here is how we view the preceding observation. Most strategies have bite since they employ *restricted tests* on local assertions about the present or the past of the current node, but not about the *future* (like the above program did with the forward-looking test $?\{i\}\varphi$).

This fine-structure suggests a study of *formats for definability* of strategies in temporal tree models beyond what we have done in the above with our simple *PDL* approach. Key strategies with great power are often defined by finite automata, with Samson's beloved Copy-Cat as a pet example. As a still more special case, *memory-free strategies* have turned out important in game semantics (1), in the field of logics, games and tree automata (13), and interestingly also, in the guise of *Tit-for-Tat*, in evolutionary game theory (16).

Two-Level Views and Invariants. Our view of what is going on here combines levels. Often we want two views together. *Games* have moves and internal properties, such as marking of nodes as turns or wins. But there is also an external *game board* recording observable or other relevant behavior. An example are the ubiquitous "graph games" of computational logic where the graph is the board (19). Usually, there is an obvious *reduction map* ρ sending game states to matching states on the game board satisfying a certain amount of back-and-forth simulation ((6) has many examples). Now, strategies in a game often consist in maintaining some *invariant* at the level of its board. Defining strategies then has to do with defining such invariants. In fact, the forcing modalities in the above triviality result may be seen as, somewhat bleak, invariants.

Excursion. This perspective suggests interesting questions. One of the crucial results about graph games is the Positional Determinacy Theorem (12) saying that graph games with parity winning conditions are determined with positional strategies whose moves depend only on the graph component of the current game state of play. What this suggests is that the set of winning positions projects via the reduction map to a set of board positions that can be definable. A logical explanation of positional determinacy would then be the existence of a *translation* from modal forcing statements in the game to equivalent modal fixed-point assertions about associated graph states.

6   Strategy Logics with Operations on Games

Finally, moving closer to Samson's trademark compositional methodology, we can go yet one step further in our formalizations. So far, we had forcing modalities $\{i\}\varphi$, and when needed, we put in explicit terms for strategies $\{\sigma, i\}\varphi$. But all this still takes place inside the setting of some game that is just given. However, it also makes sense to add *explicit descriptions of games* to the logical language, to obtain a notation, say,

$\{\sigma, i, G\}\varphi$, with a game term G, saying that following the strategy σ forces φ-outcomes only for player i in game G.

Now we can reason about strategies in different games, and how they can be combined. There are in fact several logical systems in the literature that treat relevant operations on games that make sense here– such as choice, sequence, dual, and parallel composition. •

Dynamic Game Logic. One available line is the dynamic logic of games in (17) that extends our forcing modalities with game terms, where the formulas are now interpreted, not inside games, but on their associated game boards. The resulting system is a two-agent *PDL* on neighbourhood models, with typical decomposition axioms such as the one for "choice games":

$$\{G \cup H, i\}\varphi \leftrightarrow \{G, i\}\varphi \vee \{H, i\}\varphi.$$

whose validity can be established by an elementary soundness argument. Other axioms proceed on analogies with *PDL* as well, except that for the game dual.

   Such soundness arguments provide nice material for the logical fieldwork of this paper, since we can tease out something that was left implicit in Parikh's notation: the underlying calculus of strategies.

Example 3.   Strategizing power logic.

Consider the above axiom for choice. Player i starts a game $G \cup H$ by choosing to play either G or H. If i has a strategy σ forcing φ-outcomes in $G \cup H$, its first step describes her choice, *left or right*, and the rest forces φ-outcomes in the chosen game. Vice versa, if she has a strategy σ forcing φ in game G, prefixing it with a move *left* gives her a strategy forcing φ in $G \cup H$.

Under the surface, a general strategy calculus is at work here. Our first argument involved two operations: $head(\sigma)$ gives the first move of strategy σ, and $tail(\sigma)$ the remaining strategy, in a way that validates

$$\sigma = (head(\sigma), tail(\sigma))$$

The second part of the argument prefixed an action a to a given strategy σ, yielding α; σ satisfying obvious laws like

$$head(\alpha; \sigma) = \alpha, tail(\alpha; \sigma) = \sigma.$$

Dynamic game logic encodes a natural notion of game equivalence based on equal powers for players across games, and it has a literature of its own.[10]

Still, it is clear that the strategy calculus we just elicited does not look like our earlier *PDL* programs. The basic operations of *head* and *tail* rather suggests a *co-algebraic* perspective of observing and then looking at the rest of the strategy. This brings us to another line in logics with explicit game terms, namely, the "game semantics" of Samson himself. It would be tedious to explain this extensive research program in a brief paper like this, and so I will just make a few points connecting with the above.

Linear Game Logic. In this case, the logical formulas are just game terms, and systems of linear logic encode game equivalence or inclusion. There is no explicit forcing modality–though one might say that the precise notion of validity associates statements about winning powers with game terms. Still, game semantics takes place in the same temporal models that we have used so far, so it can be analyzed by earlier techniques. In particular, we could add a description language for what goes on inside Samson's games, with forcing modalities and names of specific strategies. I have ideas on how to do such a two-level logic, but these would transcend the boundary of this paper.

A concrete "quasi-empirical" challenge for such systems is similar to what we suggested for dynamic game logic. Begin with the absolute basics, look at the soundness arguments for linear logic in game semantics, and extract the minimum needed to make its reasoning about game constructions work. This reasoning will be more sophisticated than what we have considered before. In particular, parallel games involve "shadow arguments" (say for the soundness of the Cut Rule) about what can take place in subgames, and I am not sure how to represent these minimally.[11,12]

7   Knowledge, Preference, and Game Theory

Many topics in the above are reminiscent of real game theory. Strategy stealing proofs and copy-cat behavior are reminiscent of the central role in game theory

---

[10] The system has been extended to some kinds of parallel games in (8).

[11] More sophisticated arguments about "shadow matches", copying strategies in games, and representing parallel by sequential play, occur in the theory of graph games (19).

[12] But we could also start our fieldwork in this area with minimal logical specification calculi for effects of basic strategies, such as *Copy Cat*.

for simple strategies like *Tit-for-Tat* in infinite evolutionary games (3). I end with mentioning just two points about new structure that should enter if we want to engage with real games.

Knowledge.   In the background of many arguments about strategies is what players *know*. I can hardly "copy" or "steal" a strategy if I do not know what it looks like. Now in many standard arguments for existence of strategies, the talk of knowledge is just didactical wrapping. But it is of interest to take it seriously, merging strategy logics with epistemic logics or other ways of representing information. Next on this road are *imperfect information games*, where players need not know exactly where they are in the game tree. Such games, even when finite, are notoriously non-determined, and analyzing them might throw new light on game logics. Finally, strategies in this case will typically have knowledge-dependent instructions, and what also becomes essential is the informational nature of players: endowed with perfect memory, observation-driven, or yet otherwise. Even their beliefs and policies for belief revision become important in the usual foundations of strategic behavior in game theory. (6) explores this area in detail, but at the end of it all, an overall strategy calculus remains to be found.

Preference.   Another obvious feature of real games is the much more sophisticated dynamics of evaluation that drives behavior and mathematical equilibrium theory. The balance of available moves, beliefs, and *preference* is what drives *rational play* in the usual sense. Players can have any preferences between outcomes of a game (whether endpoints or infinite histories), and again this structure requires extending our logics of strategies. Issues this time include new notions of game equivalence, perhaps dependent on rationality types of players, but also just the analysis of basic game-theoretic arguments about solution methods. In particular, (6) has an extensive study of the typical algorithm of Backward Induction that already poses many challenges to the above. For one, while it does have a natural definition in the first-order fixed-point logic *LFP(FO)*, it does not seem to have an obvious program definition in the above *PDL* terms. For another, the current game-theoretic discussion between Backward Induction, a purely future-looking reasoning style, and "Forward Induction", a way of factoring in the past of the game so far (see (18)), seems to connect with choices in logical modeling at many points.

  I believe that merging the best of computational logics of games and of game theory has a great future, but as will be amply clear, a lot remains to be done.

8   Conclusion

Logical analysis of strategic reasoning is a rich topic that unifies across the study of computation and social interaction. I have looked at a number of ways of pursuing this, in consecutive steps of explicitly defining forcing, strategies, and games. I believe that my interests in doing so are close to Samson's, but there is a caveat. Samson is a type theorist or category theorist at heart, while I am a model theorist. We may be looking at the very same things, and Samson sees a rabbit, while I see a deer. Proof theory versus model theory is a major divide in logic, but it is also a constructive case of complementarity, as has been shown again and again. This mixture of shared interests and different inclinations leads me to a conclusion whose phrasing I borrow from Immanuel Kant: I *can know* that Samson and I are allies, but I *may hope* that we are friends.

References

1. Abramsky, S.: Information, processes and games. In: van Benthem, J., Adriaans, P. (eds.) Handbook of the Philosophy of Information, pp. 483–549. Elsevier Science Publishers, Amsterdam (2008)
2. Alur, R., Henzinger, T.A., Kupferman, O.: Alternating-time temporal logic. J. ACM 49(5), 672–713 (2002)
3. Axelrod, R.: The Evolution of Cooperation. Basic Books, New York (1984)
4. van Benthem, J.: Extensive games as process models. J. of Logic, Lang. and Inf. 11(3), 289–313 (2002)
5. van Benthem, J.: In praise of strategies. In: van Eijck, J., Verbrugge, R. (eds.) Games, Actions and Social Software 2010. LNCS, vol. 7010, pp. 96–116. Springer, Heidelberg (2012)
6. van Benthem, J.: Logic in Games. The MIT Press, Cambridge (2013)
7. van Benthem, J., Gheerbrant, A.: Game solution, epistemic dynamics and fixed-point logics. Fundam. Inf. 100(1-4), 19–41 (2010)
8. van Benthem, J., Ghosh, S., Liu, F.: Modelling simultaneous games in dynamic logic. Synthese 165(2), 247–268 (2008)
9. van Benthem, J., Liu, F.: Dynamic logic of preference upgrade. Journal of Applied Non-Classical Logics 17(2), 157–182 (2007)
10. van Benthem, J., Pacuit, E.: The tree of knowledge in action: Towards a common perspective. In: Advances in Modal Logic, pp. 87–106 (2006)
11. van Eijck, J.: PDL as a multi-agent strategy logic. In: Schipper, B.C. (ed.) Proceedings of the 14th Conference on TARK 2013 – Theoretical Aspects of Reasoning About Knowledge, Chennai, India, pp. 206–215 (2013)
12. Emerson, E.A., Jutla, C.S.: Tree automata, mu-calculus and determinacy. In: Proceedings of the 32nd Annual Symposium on Foundations of Computer Science, pp. 368–377. IEEE Computer Society, Washington, DC (1991)
13. Grädel, E., Thomas, W., Wilke, T. (eds.): Automata, Logics, and Infinite Games. LNCS, vol. 2500. Springer, Heidelberg (2002)
14. Hansen, H.H., Kupke, C., Pacuit, E.: Neighbourhood structures: Bisimilarity and basic model theory. Logical Methods in Computer Science 5(2), 1–38 (2009)
15. Janin, D., Walukiewicz, I.: On the expressive completeness of the propositional mu-calculus with respect to monadic second order logic. In: Sassone, V., Montanari, U. (eds.) CONCUR 1996. LNCS, vol. 1119, pp. 263–277. Springer, Heidelberg (1996)
16. Osborne, M.J., Rubinstein, A.: A Course in Game Theory. MIT Press, Cambridge (1994)
17. Parikh, R.: The logic of games and its applications. In: Annals of Discrete Mathematics. vol. 24, pp. 111–140. Elsevier (1985)
18. Perea, A.: Epistemic Game Theory. Cambridge University Press (2012)
19. Venema, Y.: Lectures on the modal mu-calculus. Tech. rep., Institute for Logic, Language and Computation, University of Amsterdam (2007)

Domain Theory in Topical Form

Steve Vickers

School of Computer Science, University of Birmingham,
Birmingham, B15 2TT, UK
s.j.vickers@cs.bham.ac.uk

In his short story "Pierre Menard Author of the Quixote", Jorge Luis Borges tells the story of a French author who sets out to compose *Don Quixote* – not, you understand, as a mechanical transcription or copy of Cervantes' original, but as a re-creation, word for word and line for line, of fragments of it.

In 1999 I had a similar experience with my paper "Topical Categories of Domains" [3], based on some results from Samson's thesis [1] that also appeared in his "Domain Theory in Logical Form" [2]. My aim was to give a presentation of Samson's results that recreated, as closely as possible, Samson's own presentation.

Needless to say, it was not exactly the same, but why should such a re-creation have been a worthy aim? The answer is one of foundations: I had an idea for refounding the work using toposes, technically by replacing categories of domains by toposes classifying them (or their compact bases). One aim from this was to use the topos theory to give canonical answers to questions of continuity. When solving domain equations $D \cong F(D)$, F needs certain continuity properties that have been formulated in a special purpose way in domain theory. The canonical answer from topos theory would be to require F to be represented by a geometric morphism. As an unexpected bonus, the toposes also recreate the trick of "embedding-projection pairs", introduced in domain theory to deal with the fact that some important constructions F are not functorial with respect to Scott continuous maps. They reappear – in the case of SFP domains – as homomorphisms between the domains as models of a geometric theory.

Topos machinery can be heavy and untransparent, and Samson for one was not persuaded of the benefits. Why would anyone put themselves to the trouble of using toposes? Seeking answers to such objections was the start of my Menardian quest to recreate parts of his thesis: to leave the essential mathematics of his presentation undisturbed, but by logical means have it reinterpreted in terms of the toposes. The measure of success was to be the similarity to what Samson actually wrote.

With regard to the logical means (using geometric logic), I was by then beginning to understand the topos-theoretic techniques better – particularly through some collaboration with Peter Johnstone. However, it still took me a few years to find a narrative form for my paper. As it finally appeared, the Menard part was wrapped in a broad outline of a geometrization programme by which one might seek to apply the techniques quite generally in mathematics. It involved topologizing everything, either as point-free spaces or more generally as toposes,

B. Coecke, L. Ong, and P. Panangaden (Eds.): Abramsky Festschrift, LNCS 7860, pp. 348–349, 2013.
© Springer-Verlag Berlin Heidelberg 2013

and using geometric logic to deal with them in terms of their points. It included bundle ideas to deal with particular families of spaces (for example, SFP domains as a bundle over a topos that classifies their compact bases), and also included a proposal to avoid formal problems arising from the infinitary joins in geometric logic by replacing toposes with Joyal's "arithmetic universes".

In fact, this single paper explicitly sets out the essence of much of my work since. But it is inconceivable that it could have been written without Samson, and I want to mention some of the various ways in which I owe him some gratitude.

The first is obvious from the Menardian nature of my paper. It could no more have been written without Samson than Menard's Quixote could have been written without Cervantes. Without Samson's thesis I would not have had a model to refound.

The second is gratitude to Samson as teacher. My mathematical background was not domain theory, and Samson patiently taught me huge amounts about its different aspects, semantic, logical and topological. I particularly remember a time when I expressed some doubts regarding the importance of powerdomains. No, said Samson, they are the single most successful part of domain theory. He was right. In their localic form (which, of course, is also present in Samson's thesis) of powerlocales, I have since repeatedly found them to be a deep and vital part of geometric reasoning.

The third is gratitude to Samson as employer. After the failure of my computer company (Jupiter Cantab Ltd) in Cambridge, I wanted to return to mathematics and my former director of studies Ken Moody put me in touch with Samson. Samson quickly found me a research post on his project "Formal Semantics for Declarative Languages". I'm not sure I ever really found any worthwhile results in the topic of the project, being at heart a pure mathematician. Yet I was allowed to pursue my real interest, point-free topology and toposes. Its successor project, "Foundational Structures in Computer Science", was in fact typical of the style of serious mathematical research in a context of computer science that Samson did so much to foster in Britain.

So, thank you Samson!

References

1. Abramsky, S.: Domain Theory and the Logic of Observable Properties. Ph.D. thesis, Queen Mary College, University of London (1987)
2. Abramsky, S.: Domain theory in logical form. Annals of Pure and Applied Logic 51, 1–77 (1991)
3. Vickers, S.: Topical categories of domains. Mathematical Structures in Computer Science 9, 569–616 (1999)

Kolmogorov Complexity of Categories[*]

Noson S. Yanofsky[1,2]

[1] Department of Computer and Information Science, Brooklyn College, CUNY,
Brooklyn, N.Y. 11210
[2] The Computer Science Department of the Graduate Center, CUNY,
New York, N.Y. 10016
`noson@sci.brooklyn.cuny.edu`

Abstract. Kolmogorov complexity theory is used to tell what the algorithmic informational content of a string is. It is defined as the length of the shortest program that describes the string. We present a programming language that can be used to describe categories, functors, and natural transformations. With this in hand, we define the informational content of these categorical structures as the shortest program that describes such structures. Some basic consequences of our definition are presented including the fact that equivalent categories have equal Kolmogorov complexity. We also prove different theorems about what can and cannot be described by our programming language.

Keywords: Kolmogorov Complexity, Algorithmic Information, Categories, Functors, Natural Transformations.

Dedicated to Samson Abramsky in honor of his 60th Birthday

1 Introduction

Kolmogorov complexity is a part of theoretical computer science that was pioneered in the early 1960's by Andrey Kolmogorov, Ray Solomonoff, and Gregory Chaitin. For reasons ranging from probability theory, to machine learning, and computational complexity theory, these three researchers gave a universal definition of what it means for a string of symbols to be simple or complex.

Consider the following three strings:

1. 00000000000000000000000000000000000000000000000
2. 11011101111110111111101111111111111011111111111110
3. 01010010110110101011011101111001100000111111010

---

[*] A while back, I showed some of these ideas to Samson Abramsky and he was, as always, full of encouragement and great ideas. I am very grateful to him for all his help over the years. I would like to acknowledge the help and advice of Michael Barr, Marta Bunge, James Cox, Joey Hirsh, Florian Lengyel, Dustin Mulcahey, Philip Rothmaler, and Louis Thral. I want to thank Shayna Leah Hershfeld for many enlightening conversations about polymorphism and type theory. Support for this project was provided by a PSC-CUNY Award, jointly funded by The Professional Staff Congress and The City University of New York.

B. Coecke, L. Ong, and P. Panangaden (Eds.): Abramsky Festschrift, LNCS 7860, pp. 350–362, 2013.

All three consists of 0s and 1s and are of length 45. It should be noticed that if you flipped a coin 45 times the chances of getting any of these three sequences are equal. That is, the chances for each of the strings occurring is $1/2^{45}$. In effect, this shows a failure of classical probability theory in measuring the contents of a string. Whereas you would not be shocked to see a sequence of coins produce string 3, the other two strings would be surprising. The difference between these strings can be seen by looking at short programs that can describe them:

1. `Print 45 0's.`
2. `Print the first 6 primes.`
3. `Print '010100101101101010110111011111001100000111111010'.`

The shorter the program, the less informational content of the string. In contrast, if only a long program can describe the string, then the string has more content. If no short program can describe a string, then it is "incompressible" or "random."

In classical Kolmogorov complexity, rather than talking about programs, one talks about Turing machines. For a string s, the the Kolmogorov complexity, $K(s)$, is defined as the size of the smallest Turing machine that starts with an empty tape and outputs s. Formally, let U be a universal Turing machine, then $K(s) = min\{|p| : U(p, \lambda) = s\}$. We will also need *relative* Kolmogorov complexity: let s and t be two strings, then $K(s|t)$ is the size of the smallest Turing machine that starts with t on the tape and outputs s. Formally, $K(s|t) = min\{|p| : U(p, t) = s\}$. If $K(s) > |s|$ then s is "incompressible" or "random".

This notion of Kolmogorov complexity is used in many different areas of theoretical computer science. It gives an objective measure of how complicated strings are. It is our goal to extend these ideas to many other areas of mathematics, computer science and physics by formulating a notion of Kolmogorov complexity for category theory which is used in all these diverse areas. In order to measure how complicated categories, functors, and natural transformations are, we need a programming language that will describe these categorical structures. In honor of Sammy Eilenberg, one of the founders of category theory who also had a deep interest in computer science, we call this programming language "Sammy." This language will have variables that can hold categories, functors and natural transformations. The operations of the language will perform common constructs that people use to formulate different structures. Each line of the program could have a label that will be used with "If-Then" statements to control the execution of the program.

Notice that numbers, strings, trees, graphs, arrays, and other typical data types are not mentioned in our programming language. This was done on purpose. The other data types can be derived from the categorical structures. Categories and algorithms are more "primitive" than numbers, strings, etc.

This is not the first time a programing language has been formulated to describe categorical structure. An important example is in *Computational Category Theory* by Rydeheard and Burstall [3]. Tatsuya Hagino's thesis [2] is another example. These languages are, however, different from Sammy. Their programming languages are made to be implemented and to get computers to actually calculate with categories. In contrast, there is no intention of implementing Sammy. Our goal is simply to compare different structures by comparing the length of their descriptions. In fact, we will not even write many formal Sammy programs. This is similar to the fact that no one actually ever formally writes the instructions for a Turing machine.

With Sammy, we will talk about the Kolmogorov complexity of categorical structures. We discuss when one structure is more complicated than another. We will also talk about compressibility and randomness. Along these lines, here is a simple example of the type of ideas we will meet. Consider $\mathbb{N}$, the totally ordered category of natural numbers $0 \longrightarrow 1 \longrightarrow 2 \longrightarrow \cdots$, and $\overline{\mathbf{2}}$, the category with two objects and a single isomorphism between them $0 \overset{\sim}{\longrightarrow} 1$. A functor $F : \mathbb{N} \longrightarrow \overline{\mathbf{2}}$ corresponds to an infinite sequence of zeros and ones. The category of all such functors $\overline{\mathbf{2}}^{\mathbb{N}}$ is essentially to the real numbers and has uncountably many elements. How many of these functors can be mathematically described? There are only countably many computer programs that describe such functors. This means that the vast majority of functors $\mathbb{N} \longrightarrow \overline{\mathbf{2}}$ cannot be described by any program and are essentially random.

Not every categorical structure can be described with our programing language. Categorical structures that can be described by Sammy will be called "constructible." For example, I do not know how to start from nothing and make the category of smooth manifolds. However it is probably possible to start from the category of topological spaces and get the category of smooth manifolds. This brings us to the notion of relative Kolmogorov complexity. We will be interested in how long does a program have to be in order to construct a categorical structure *given some categorical structures*.

The fact that certain structures are not constructable with Sammy brings in the whole area of computability theory. There are limitations to what Sammy can perform. Usual self-referential limitations are based on variations of the liar paradox ("This statement is false") such as Gödel ("This statement is unprovable") or Turing ("This program will output the wrong answer when asked if it will halt or go into an infinite loop") (see [5] for a comprehensive survey of such limitations.) In contrast, the limitations of Kolmogorov complexity are based on the Berry Paradox: consider the number described by "The least number that needs more than fifteen words to describe it." This sentence has twelve words. That is, there is a description of a number that is shorter than it is supposed to be. One such limitation within classical Kolmogorov complexity[4] is:

Theorem 1. $K : Strings \longrightarrow \mathbb{N}$ *is not a computable function.*

We will show that there are similar limitations for our Kolmogorov complexity theory.

Section 2 introduces Sammy. That section also describes several "library functions" or "macros" in Sammy which will be helpful in the rest of the paper. Section 3 is the heart of the paper where we define and prove many of the central theorems about our complexity measure. Section 4 is a discussion of computability and non-computability with the Sammy language. The paper concludes with some possible ways this work will progress in the future.

2   A Programing Language for Categories

In order to describe categorical structures, we need a programing language. This language will be called "Sammy". The language will consist of typical operations that are used to describe/create different categories, functors and natural transformations. Programs will be lists of statements that set variables to different values. The variables could be categories, functors, or natural transformations. Since categories are special types of functors, and functors are special types of natural transformations (that is, natural transformations are the deepest type), we might state everything in terms of natural transformations. But that would make the programs needlessly complex. Rather, for the sake of simplicity, we will be ambiguous about the types of our statements (that is, our operations/functions will be polymorphic.) As we have absolutely no intention of implementing Sammy, we can be vague about certain issues.

We begin with constants. There is $\mathbf{0}$, the empty category, $\mathbf{1}$, the category with one object and one morphism, and $\mathbf{2}$, the category $0 \longrightarrow 1$ with two objects and one nontrivial morphism. We will also need the constant category $\mathtt{Cat}$ which corresponds to the category of all small categories. There are also several constant functors: $s : \mathbf{1} \longrightarrow \mathbf{2}$ and $t : \mathbf{1} \longrightarrow \mathbf{2}$ that picks out the source and target of the nontrivial morphism in $\mathbf{2}$. There are the unique morphisms $! : \mathbf{0} \longrightarrow \mathbf{1}$, $! : \mathbf{0} \longrightarrow \mathbf{2}$, $! : \mathbf{0} \longrightarrow \mathtt{Cat}$, $! : \mathtt{Cat} \longrightarrow \mathbf{1}$, and $! : \mathbf{2} \longrightarrow \mathbf{1}$. There are also identity functors and natural transformations.

There are several operations that take a single input. For a functor $F : \mathbb{A} \longrightarrow \mathbb{B}$ if we set $\mathbb{C} = \mathtt{Source}(F : \mathbb{A} \longrightarrow \mathbb{B})$ then $\mathbb{C} = \mathbb{A}$. That is, $\mathtt{Source}$ takes a functor and outputs the category that is the source of the functor. There is a similar operation $\mathbb{C} = \mathtt{Target}(F : \mathbb{A} \longrightarrow \mathbb{B})$. For a given category $\mathbb{A}$, the operation $F = \mathtt{Ident}(\mathbb{A})$ makes $F = Id_{\mathbb{A}}$. For a category $\mathbb{A}$, if we let $\mathbb{C} = \mathtt{Op}(\mathbb{A})$ then $\mathbb{C} = \mathbb{A}^{op}$. The $\mathtt{Op}$ operation also acts on functors.

We will at times have to talk about an actual object and morphism in the category. So for example, a functor $F : \mathbf{1} \longrightarrow \mathbb{C}$ "picks" an object c in $\mathbb{C}$ and a functor $F : \mathbf{2} \longrightarrow \mathbb{C}$ "picks" a morphism $f : c \longrightarrow c'$. Going the other way, an object c in $\mathbb{C}$ "determines" a functor $F_c : \mathbf{1} \longrightarrow \mathbb{C}$ and similarly for a morphism in $\mathbb{C}$. We write this in Sammy as $c = \mathtt{Pick}(F : \mathbf{1} \longrightarrow \mathbb{C})$ and $F_c = \mathtt{Determine}(c)$.

For natural transformations of the appropriate source and target there is a horizontal composition and vertical composition written as $\alpha = \mathtt{Hcomp}(\beta, \gamma)$ and $\alpha = \mathtt{Vcomp}(\beta, \gamma)$. Regular composition of functors is simply a special case of horizontal composition. For categories $\mathbb{A}$ and $\mathbb{B}$, we will have $\mathbb{C} = \mathtt{Pow}(\mathbb{A}, \mathbb{B})$ be the category of all functors and natural transformations from $\mathbb{A}$ to $\mathbb{B}$.

Probably the most important operations are the Kan extensions. For functors $G : \mathbb{A} \longrightarrow \mathbb{B}$ and $F : \mathbb{A} \longrightarrow \mathbb{C}$, a right Kan extension of F along G is a pair $(R, \alpha) = \mathtt{KanEx}(G, F)$ where $R : \mathbb{B} \longrightarrow \mathbb{C}$ and $\alpha : R \circ G \longrightarrow F$. A Kan extension induces another functor that is unique. For every $H : \mathbb{B} \longrightarrow \mathbb{C}$ and $\beta : H \circ G \longrightarrow F$ there is a unique $\gamma = \mathtt{KanInd}(F, G; H, \beta)$ where $\gamma : H \longrightarrow R$ and satisfies $\alpha \cdot \gamma_G = \beta$. Using Kan extensions one can derive, products, coproducts, pushouts, pullbacks, equalizers, coequalizers, (and constructible) limits, colimits, ends, coends, etc. It is a well-known fact that if $G : \mathbb{A} \longrightarrow \mathbb{B}$ is a right adjoint (left adjoint, equivalence, isomorphism), then its left adjoint (right adjoint, quasi-inverse, inverse) $G^* : \mathbb{B} \longrightarrow \mathbb{A}$ can be found as a simple Kan extension of the identity $Id_{\mathbb{A}}$ along G, that it, $G^* = \mathtt{KanEx}(G, Id_{\mathbb{A}})$.

For "bootstrapping" purposes we will need an operation that takes two categories and gives their coproduct and their induced maps. This will help us create categories like $\mathbf{1} \sqcup \mathbf{1}$ which will be needed for our Kan extensions to describe products and coproducts; and $\mathbf{2} \sqcup \mathbf{2}$ which will be needed to describe equalizers and coequalizers.

There is a dual notion of a Kan Lifting. For functors $F : \mathbb{A} \longrightarrow \mathbb{B}$ and $G : \mathbb{C} \longrightarrow \mathbb{B}$ a Kan lifting of F along G is a pair $(R, \alpha) = \mathtt{KanLif}(G, F)$ where $R : \mathbb{A} \longrightarrow \mathbb{C}$ that satisfies a universal property which can easily be written down.

Since Kan extensions and Kan liftings are only defined up to a unique isomorphism, we might ask what is the output of the function $\mathtt{KanEx}(G, F)$? We do not care. The computer decides which of the many possible outputs it will output. It is irrelevant from the categorical perspective. This is similar to a real programing language when we do not know how something is stored or how a function is calculated. The user is ambivalent as to how the computer does certain actions. We are also well-aware that the Kan extensions and Kan liftings might not exist. In that case, the program will not go on.

There is one more operation that needs to be discussed. Let $\mathbb{C}$ be a category. $\mathbb{C}^2$ and $\mathbb{C}^1$ are the categories of arrows and objects of $\mathbb{C}$. The maps $s : \mathbf{1} \longrightarrow \mathbf{2}$ and $t : \mathbf{1} \longrightarrow \mathbf{2}$ induce (using the $\mathtt{Pow}$ operation on functors) maps $\mathbb{C}^s : \mathbb{C}^2 \longrightarrow \mathbb{C}^1$ and $\mathbb{C}^t : \mathbb{C}^2 \longrightarrow \mathbb{C}^1$. The pullback of these two maps, $\mathbb{C}^2 \times_{\mathbb{C}^1} \mathbb{C}^2$ is the composable arrows in the category. The important part of the information about the category is the composability map $\circ : (\mathbb{C}^2 \times_{\mathbb{C}^1} \mathbb{C}^2) \longrightarrow \mathbb{C}^2$. This map will help us get into the nitty-gritty of how a category is defined. So we have the following operation: for a category $\mathbb{C}$, the operation $F = \mathtt{Composable}(\mathbb{C})$ gives us the $\circ$ map.

We would like some control of how the Sammy program will execute. We do this with a conditional branch statement: If $\alpha_1 == \alpha_2$ $\mathtt{Goto}$ L where α_1 and α_2 are natural transformations and L is a label of some program line. With such a conditional branch, we can get all the usual logical operations: AND, NOT, etc. We can also get the unconditional branch $\mathtt{Goto}$ L.

There are a number of remarks that need to be made about Sammy:

This might not be the best language for our purposes. Certain operations can be derived from other operations and hence a smaller more compact language is possible. For example, the $\mathtt{Target}$ operation can be derived from the $\mathtt{Source}$ and $\mathtt{Op}$ operations. Bear in mind that our goal is to count the number of operations up to a coefficient. So we need not be exact. If one operation can be replaced by a constant number of other operations, nothing is lost.

This language can not describe all constructions. (We shall see later.) What can be done with this language will be called "constructible." It is interesting to look at what type of categories can be described by this programming language with no other input.

There is a need for a Church-Turing type thesis. The classic Church-Turing thesis says that whatever can be computed, can be computed by a Turing machine. We need such a thesis that says that whatever can be constructed by categorical means, can be constructed using the Sammy programing language. Alas, this is a thesis and not a theorem because we cannot characterize what can be constructed by categorical means. We will see that there are certain constructions that cannot be performed by Sammy. However, we believe that no programming language can make those constructions.

With classical Kolmogorov complexity, there is much discussion about "self-delimiting" programs. This will not be an issue here. We can easily tell when a Sammy program begins and when it ends.

With Sammy in hand, we introduce some library functions or macros that will be used in the future:

The coequalizer $1 \underset{s}{\overset{s}{\rightrightarrows}} 2 \sqcup 2$ gives the category $* \longleftarrow * \longrightarrow *$ which

can be put in a Kan extension and give us pushouts and pullbacks. We can make many similar constructions.

For functors $L : \mathbb{A} \longrightarrow \mathbb{C}$ and $R : \mathbb{B} \longrightarrow \mathbb{C}$ we can construct the comma categories as the following pullbacks:

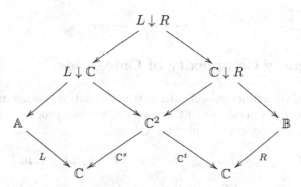

Special instances of comma categories are slice categories and coslice categories.

The coequalizer $1 \underset{t}{\overset{s}{\rightrightarrows}} 2 \overset{\rho}{\longrightarrow} \omega$ gives the (infinite) natural numbers as

a monoid. $\mathbb{N} = \omega^2$ gives the totally ordered category of natural numbers. The successor function is defined as follows:

$$r : \omega \overset{\sim}{\longrightarrow} \omega \times 1 \overset{Id \times s}{\longrightarrow} \omega \times 2 \overset{Id \times \rho}{\longrightarrow} \omega \times \omega \overset{\circ}{\longrightarrow} \omega.$$

That is, take any $n \in \omega$ and associate it with the nontrivial morphism in 2. This becomes the $+1$ member of ω. Then compose n with $+1$. Now take this map r and look at $s = r^2 : \mathbb{N} = \omega^2 \longrightarrow \omega^2 = \mathbb{N}$. This is the successor map.

We construct the category with two objects and a unique isomorphism between them. First make a category with two distinct copies of **2**. By keeping track of the inclusion maps, we have an induced F and G

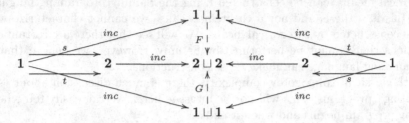

Now use these induced maps in a coequalizer to form the desired category. The figure on the right is helpful.

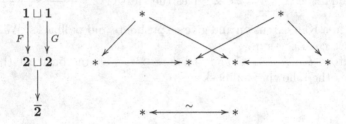

3   Kolmogorov Complexity of Categories

For a category $\mathbb{C}$ (or a functor, or a natural transformation) we define $K_{Sammy}(\mathbb{C})$ to be the number of operations in the smallest Sammy program that describes $\mathbb{C}$. For relative Kolmogorov complexity, letting

$$\Gamma = \{\mathbb{C}_1, \mathbb{C}_2, \ldots, \mathbb{C}_l, F_1, F_2, \ldots, F_m, \mu_1, \mu_2, \ldots, \mu_n\},$$

or Γ as a sub2-category of **Cat** then $K_{Sammy}(\mathbb{C}|\Gamma)$ is the number of operations in the smallest Sammy program that describes $\mathbb{C}$ given Γ as input. We shorten K_{Sammy} to K when no confusion will arise.

If there is a finite number of operations so that one can go from one categorical structure to another and vice versa, we say that the Kolmogorov complexity of these categorical structures are approximately the same. In detail, if there exists a c such that for all appropriate categorical structures, $\mathbb{X}$, one can change $\mathbb{X}$ to $\mathbb{X}'$ and vice versa in c Sammy operations, that is $|K(\mathbb{X}) - K(\mathbb{X}')| \leq c$, then we write $K(\mathbb{X}) \approx K(\mathbb{X}')$. As an example, notice that only one Sammy operation is needed to go from category $\mathbb{A}$ to functor $Id_{\mathbb{A}}$ and vice versa. Hence $K(\mathbb{A}) \approx K(Id_{\mathbb{A}})$.

There is a need for something called an *invariance theorem*. This basically says that the Kolmogorov complexity does not depend on the programing language that is used to describe the objects. Imagine that you do not like the Sammy programing language to describe categorical structures and you decide to invent your own. Perhaps you call it "Saunders" (after the other founder of category theory, Saunders Mac Lane.) Then since presumably both languages can program any constructable categorical structure, they can each program the other's operations. That means there exist compilers that can translate Sammy programs into Saunders programs and there are compilers that can translate Saunders programs into Sammy programs. From this, we can prove the following theorem: There exists a constant c such that for all categorical structures $\mathbf{X}$ we have $|K_{Sammy}(\mathbf{X}) - K_{Saunders}(\mathbf{X})| \leq c$.

Rather than list all the results we have for K, let us examine some paradigmatic theorems:

Theorem 2. *There exists a constant c_{pair} such that for all $\mathbb{C}$ and $\mathbb{D}$ we have* $K(\mathbb{C} \times \mathbb{D}) \leq K(\mathbb{C}) + K(\mathbb{D}|\mathbb{C}) + c_{pair}.$

This essentially says that there is a simple way of taking two categories and forming their product. There is no new information added. But lets look more carefully at what the theorem say. It says that to form $\mathbb{C} \times \mathbb{D}$ one can form $\mathbb{C}$ and then form $\mathbb{D}$ (but you might use some information that you already have since you already formed $\mathbb{C}$) and then do a few lines of Sammy to get their product. The reason for the inequality is because there might be an easier way. For example $\mathbf{0} \times \mathbb{D}$ can be formed in a constant amount of operations: it is $\mathbf{0}$. There is also a similar theorem with $\mathbb{C}$ and $\mathbb{D}$ swapped on the right side of the inequality.

Theorem 3. *There exists a constant c_{double} such that for all $\mathbb{C}$ we have* $K(\mathbb{C} \times \mathbb{C}) \leq K(\mathbb{C}) + c_{double}.$

That is, there is a simple way to double a category and no new information is there.

Theorem 4. *There exists a constant c_{target} such that for all $F : \mathbb{A} \longrightarrow \mathbb{B}$ we have* $K(\mathbb{B}) \leq K(F : \mathbb{A} \longrightarrow \mathbb{B}) + c_{target}.$

This means that one way to describe $\mathbb{B}$ is to first find a program for a functor $F : \mathbb{A} \longrightarrow \mathbb{B}$ and then use the `Target` operation to get $\mathbb{B}$. The inequality comes from the fact that there might be shorter programs to describe $\mathbb{B}$. There are similar such theorems for the source of a functor, for natural transformations, for identity functors, etc.

We state the following theorem about composition in terms of natural transformations for generality.

Theorem 5. *There exists a constant c_{compos} such that for any three natural transformations $\alpha : F \longrightarrow G$, $\beta : F \longrightarrow H$, and $\gamma : G \longrightarrow H$ such that $\beta = \gamma \circ \alpha$ we have*

$$K(\beta) \leq K(\alpha) + K(\gamma|\alpha) + c_{compos}.$$

When γ is the unique natural transformation that satisfies this triangle (e.g. when α is mono) then the inequality in the above theorem becomes an equality. The theorem for Kan extensions is similar.

Theorem 6. *There exists a constant* c_{Kan} *such that for all* $G : \mathbb{A} \longrightarrow \mathbb{B}$ *and* $F : \mathbb{A} \longrightarrow \mathbb{C}$ *if* $(Lan_G(F), \alpha)$ *is the left Kan extension, than*

$$K((Lan_G(F), \alpha)) \leq K(F) + K(G|F) + c_{Kan}$$

or for relative Kolmogorov complexity

$$K((Lan_G(F), \alpha)|\Gamma) \leq K(F|\Gamma) + K(G|\Gamma, F) + c_{Kan}.$$

As a special case, if $G : \mathbb{A} \longrightarrow \mathbb{B}$ is a right adjoint (left adjoint, equivalence, or isomorphism), then the Kan extension along G of the $Id_{\mathbb{A}}$ is the left adjoint (right adjoint, quasi-inverse, inverse) $G^* : \mathbb{B} \longrightarrow \mathbb{A}$. Since it is easy to go from one to the other, we have that $K(G) \approx K(G^*)$. Notice that for an arbitrary adjunction, this does not mean that $K(\mathbb{A}) \approx K(\mathbb{B})$ (we shall see that it is true for an equivalence). Nor does there seem to be any hard-and-fast rule that says something like a left adjoint goes from something with a low Kolmogorov complexity to a high Kolmogorov complexity. It is easy to find counterexamples to such ideas.

If $G : \mathbb{A} \longrightarrow \mathbb{B}$ and $F : \mathbb{A} \longrightarrow \mathbb{C}$ are functors, $R : \mathbb{B} \longrightarrow \mathbb{C}$ is a right Kan extension, $H : \mathbb{B} \longrightarrow \mathbb{C}$, and $\beta : H \circ G \longrightarrow F$ then for the unique induced $\gamma : H \longrightarrow R$, we have that $K(\gamma) \approx K(\beta)$. The reason for this is that you can go from one to the other using composition and the `KanInd` operation. A simple example of this is product:

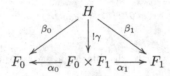

It is easy to see that the information in γ is exactly the information in the βs. It is easy to derive one from the other.

Our work would be in vain if the measure we described was not an invariant of categorical structure. We have the following important theorem.

Theorem 7. *If categories* $\mathbb{A}$ *and* $\mathbb{B}$ *are equivalent, then* $K_{Sammy}(\mathbb{A}) \approx K_{Sammy}(\mathbb{B})$.

Proof. The intuition behind the theorem is that Sammy cannot distinguish categorical structures that are isomorphic. Say the equivalence is given by the functor $G : \mathbb{A} \longrightarrow \mathbb{B}$. From G its easily constructed quasi-inverse is $G^* : \mathbb{B} \longrightarrow \mathbb{A}$. We then have that $K(G) \approx K(G^*)$. We also get that $K(G \circ G^*) \approx K(G^* \circ G)$. If $\alpha : Id_{\mathbb{A}} \longrightarrow GG^*$ is the isomorphic unit of the equivalence given by the Kan extension, then $\alpha^{-1} : GG^* \longrightarrow Id_{\mathbb{A}}$ is easily constructed (we are assuming that Kan extensions work on natural transformations). Since $\alpha^{-1} \circ \alpha = id_{Id}$ we get that $K(\alpha^{-1}) \approx K(Id_{\mathbb{A}})$. We then have

$$K(\mathbb{A}) \approx K(Id_{\mathbb{A}}) \approx K(GG^*) \approx K(G^*G) \approx K(Id_{\mathbb{B}}) \approx K(\mathbb{B}).$$

QED.

There are some important consequences of this theorem. One can easily construct the skeletal category as the coequalizer $\mathbb{C}^2 \underset{t}{\overset{s}{\rightrightarrows}} \mathbb{C} \xrightarrow{\cong} \mathbb{C}_{skeletal}$. This gives us $K(\mathbb{C}) \approx K(\mathbb{C}_{skeletal})$.

In a future paper [6] we will discuss algebraic theories, monads, Morita equivalence and other algebraic notions from the Kolmogorov complexity perspective.

4 Computability and Non-computability with Sammy

There might be a need to deal with finite numbers. We shall let the number n correspond a triple $(\mathbf{n}, P_b, P_e)$ where $\mathbf{n}$ is the totally ordered category with n elements (keep in mind: $0 \longrightarrow 1 \longrightarrow \cdots \longrightarrow n-2 \longrightarrow n-1$), $P_b : \mathbf{1} \longrightarrow \mathbf{n}$ is a functor that points to the beginning of the category (the initial object), and $P_e : \mathbf{1} \longrightarrow \mathbf{n}$ is a functor that points to the end of the category (the terminal object.) Basic operations with such numbers are easy to describe. For example, we can connect $(\mathbf{n}, P_b, P_e)$ and $(\mathbf{m}, P_b', P_e')$ to get $(\mathbf{n} + \mathbf{m} - 1, P_b, P_e')$ with the coequalizer: $\mathbf{1} \underset{P_e}{\overset{P_b'}{\rightrightarrows}} \mathbf{n} \sqcup \mathbf{m} \longrightarrow (\mathbf{n} + \mathbf{m} - 1)$. (In truth, natural numbers can simply be given as functors $\mathbf{1} \longrightarrow \mathbb{N}$. We can manipulate numbers by manipulating such functors. While this is simple and economical, there is a certain appeal to doing it the way we did. Many prefer to think of their numbers as "things" and not just pointers to amounts.)

All the finite totally ordered sets should be considered subcategories of $\mathbb{N}$ and, as such, inherit a partial successor function. Before applying this successor function we must check to make sure that the pointer is not at the P_e position.

A totally ordered category with n elements can be constructed in $O(log_2 n)$ number of Sammy statements. Basically, the idea is that one can look at the binary representation of n and write a program based on that. For example 727 in binary is 1011010111. We can express this number as

$$((((((((((1 \times 2 + 0) \times 2 + 1) \times 2 + 1) \times 2 + 0) \times 2 + 1) \times 2 + 0) \times 2 + 1) \times 2 + 1) \times 2 + 1).$$

Similarly when making our totally ordered category, we can either (a) double the length of the category by connecting one copy of itself to itself, or (b) double itself and add one, depending on the bit at that position. This proves that $K(\mathbf{n}) \leq O(log_2 n)$ which is similar to the classical case.

Notice that the above algorithm did not have any input. In contrast, we can look at a program that loops through input, reads the bit and performs either (a) or (b). This input will be given as a functor from $\mathbf{log_2 n}$ to $\overline{\mathbf{2}}$. The program moves a pointer forward on $\mathbf{log_2 n}$. There will be a conditional branch to see if the pointer is equal to P_e. While this might be a long program, it does not depend on the size of the input. We have thus proved that

$$K(\mathbf{n} \mid (F : \mathbf{log_2 n} \longrightarrow \overline{\mathbf{2}})) = O(1)$$

where F describes n in binary.

Considering numbers as such triples, we have the following theorem:

Theorem 8. *Any partially computable function of natural numbers can be computed with Sammy.*

Proof. We prove that Sammy can perform the initial functions, recursion, composition, and the μ-minimization operator. The zero function is achieved by simply setting $P_e = P_b$. The successor of **n** is achieved by simply composing with **2**. The projection function is simply a Sammy program that accepts n inputs and outputs one of the inputs. Recursion can be done by iteration: we loop through a number until a pointer reaches P_e. Composition is simply composition of Sammy programs. μ-minimization is done by doing a loop along $\mathbb{N}$ the ordered category of *all* natural numbers.   QED.

What about complexity theory? In [6] it is shown that categories and functors can mimic a Turing machine. For every rule of a Turing machine there is a set amount of steps of a Sammy program. Hence our programming language can do whatever a Turing machines can do. The size of the Sammy program is, up to a constant, the same as the number of rules in the Turing machine. That is $K_{Sammy}(F_s) = O(K_{Classical}(s))$ where F_s is a functor that describes a string. In a sense, this says that our Kolmogorov complexity is a generalization of classical Kolmogorov complexity.

We do not see why there should be a theorem that goes the other way. In other words, we do not think that a Turing machine can mimic an arbitrary Sammy program. If, in fact there are some categorical constructions that can be constructed by a Sammy program, but cannot be constructed by a Turing machine, then our Kolmogorov complexity is stronger than classical Kolmogorov complexity theory. Here is an example of a category and a functor that can NOT be constructed by a Turing machine but might be able to be constructed by a Sammy program. Let **Halt** be a the "halting category" whose objects are the natural numbers and whose morphisms are defined below. Similarly there is the "halting functor', H, from $\mathbb{N}$, the totally ordered category of the natural numbers, to $\overline{\mathbf{2}}$, the category with two objects and a unique isomorphism between them, is defined on the right.

$$Hom_{\mathbf{Halt}}(n, n) = \begin{cases} \omega & : \text{ if } \varphi_n(n) \downarrow \\ Id_n & : \text{ if } \varphi_n(n) \uparrow \end{cases} \qquad H(n) = \begin{cases} 1 & : \text{ if } \varphi_n(n) \downarrow \\ 0 & : \text{ if } \varphi_n(n) \uparrow \end{cases}$$

Although, at present time, I do not know how to write a Sammy program to make such constructions, I believe that using infinite limits and colimits one should be able to build a type of infinite-time Turing machine to tell if regular Turing machines will halt or not. (However we are hesitant about making any conjectures. There is an interesting information-theoretic proof of the undecidability of the halting problem given on page 362 of [1]. Much work remains.)

Although we suspect that Sammy can actually program a larger class of functions than a Turing machine, however, there are some categorical constructions that are not programmable by Sammy (or any other language.) It is known that

$K_{Classical} : Strings \longrightarrow \mathbb{N}$ is not a computable function. What about K_{Sammy}? First let us be careful about the definition of K_{Sammy}. It is a function that assigns to every category, functor, and natural transformation a natural number. We might as well assume that it only assigns natural transformations since identity natural transformations are simply functors and identity functors are simply categories. Let us think of $\mathbb{C}at$ as the discrete category of natural transformation. We are going to forget the (two) composition structures on $\mathbb{C}at$ because K_{Sammy} does not behave well in terms of composition. So we have a functor $K_{Sammy} : \mathbb{C}at \longrightarrow \mathbb{N}$. We prove that this functor is not constructible. The proof is a self-reference argument similar to the Berry paradox.

Theorem 9. $K_{Sammy} : \mathbb{C}at \longrightarrow \mathbb{N}$ *is not constructible.*

Proof. Assume (wrongly) that $K = K_{Sammy}$ is, in fact, constructible, then there is a shortest program that describes K. In that case we can ask for the value of $K(K)$ (this is the core of self reference!). Let $K(K) = c$. Also, let n be a natural number and let $P_n : \mathbf{1} \longrightarrow \mathbb{N}$ be a functor such that $P_n(0) = n$. Now use K and and P_n to construct the following pullback:

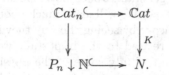

$P_n \downarrow \mathbb{N}$ is the sub-total order of natural numbers that start at n. $\mathbb{C}at_n$ is the discrete set of natural transformations whose shortest program is greater than or equal to n operations. This pullback only needed a few more operations than c. Say that $K(\mathbb{C}at_n|n) = c'$. However we can "hardwire" any n into the program. If we do that, we get $K(\mathbb{C}at_n) = c' + log\ n$. Choose an n such that $n >> c' + log\ n$. Then $\mathbb{C}at_n$ contains objects that require n or more lines of code while we just described $\mathbb{C}at_n$ in $c' + log\ n$ lines of code. This is like a Berry sentence. Contradiction! The only thing assumed is that K was constructible. It is not constructible.   QED.

We see this paper as just the beginning of a larger project to understand the complexity of categorical structures. Our work is far from done. With this notion of Kolmogorov complexity we get different notions of randomness, compressibility, and different notions of information. We would like to find upper bounds on some given categorical structures. We also would like to better clarify what is constructible and what is not. Another goal is to continue finding different categorical versions of the incompleteness theorems. We also would like to study different complexity measures. Rather than asking what is the shortest program that produces a categorical structure, we can ask how much time/space does a program take to create a certain structure. That is, what is the computational complexity of a structure. We can ask how much time does it take for the shortest program to produce that structure (logical depth.) All these measures induce hierarchies and classifications of categorical structures. There are also many other areas that we plan on studying. Here are a few.

There is a relationship between classical Kolmogorov complexity and Shannon's complexity theory. We would like to formulate a notion of Shannon's complexity theory for categories. There should be a definition of entropy of a category which should measure how rigid or flexible categorical structure is. Let $\mathbb{C}$ be a category, then $Aut(\mathbb{C})$ is the group of automorphism functors $F : \mathbb{C} \longrightarrow \mathbb{C}$. Define the "entropy" (or "Hartley entropy") of $\mathbb{C}$ as $H(\mathbb{C}) = Log_2|Aut(\mathbb{C})|$. Just as there is a relationship between these measures for strings, there should be a relationship for categorical structures.

So far we have restricted to classical categories, functors, and natural transformations. What about categories with more structure? For example, what can we say about a category that we know has all limits and colimits? What about enriched categories, higher categories, categories with structure, quasi-categories, etc? These different structures have been applied in almost every area of mathematics, computer science and theoretical physics. What we worked out above is only the first step. Such a study would be extremely interesting to shed some light on coherence theory. In this paper we saw that a pivotal fact of the Kolmogorov complexity of categories is that some categories are defined up to a unique isomorphism. Coherence theory generalizes such notions and is, in a sense, a higher dimensional version of uniqueness We will learn much about categorical information content and coherence theory by seeing the way they interact.

This work should also be related to the important work in quantum information theory. We would like to study some of the physical and mathematical structures that occur in quantum mechanics with the developed Kolmogorov complexity tools.

Another area that we would like to explore is Occams razor [5]. This is usually seen as a criteria in which to judge different physical theories. In short, physicists formulate functors F : "Physical Phenomena" $\longrightarrow$ "Mathematical Structure." Universality of the theory demands that "Physical Phenomena" be as large as possible. In contrast, Occam's razor demands that "Mathematical Structure" have low informational content. We would like to use Kolmogorov complexity on both of these types of categories and the functors that relates them. We feel that with a better understanding of this we would be able to understand the question of why it seems that Occam's razor works so well.

References

1. Calude, C.: Information and Randomness: An Algorithmic Perspective, 2nd edn. Springer, New York (2002)
2. Hagino, T.: A Categorical Programming Language, http://voxoz.com/publications/cat/Category
3. Rydeheard, D.E., Burstall, R.M.: Computational Category Theory, http://www.cs.man.ac.uk/~david/categories/book/book.pdf
4. Li, M., Vitányi, P.M.B.: An Introduction to Kolmogorov Complexity and its Applications, 2nd edn. Springer (1997)
5. Yanofsky, N.S.: The Outer Limits of Reason: What Science, Mathematics, and Logic Cannot Tell Us. MIT Press (2013)
6. Yanofsky, N.S.: Algorithmic Information Theory in Categorical Algebra (work in progress)

Author Index